Exploring Economics

Fourth Canadian Edition

Robert L. Sexton
Pepperdine University

Peter N. Fortura
Algonquin College

Colin C. Kovacs
Algonquin College

Darren Chapman, Contributor
Fanshawe College

NELSON

NELSON

Exploring Economics, Fourth Canadian Edition

by Robert L. Sexton, Peter N. Fortura, and Colin C. Kovacs

COPYRIGHT © 2016, 2013 by Nelson Education Ltd.

Adapted from Exploring Microeconomics, Sixth Edition, and Exploring Macroeconomics, Sixth Edition, by Robert L. Sexton, published by South-Western, Cengage Learning. Copyright ©2013 by South-Western, Cengage Learning.

Printed and bound in Canada
4 5 6   21 20 19 18

For more information contact Nelson Education Ltd., 1120 Birchmount Road, Toronto, Ontario, M1K 5G4. Or you can visit our Internet site at nelson.com

This textbook is a Nelson custom publication. Because your instructor has chosen to produce a custom publication, you pay only for material that you will use in your course.

ISBN-13: 978-0-17-671439-0
ISBN-10: 0-17-671439-1

Cover Credit:
Denkou Images/Cultura/Getty Images

To Cynthia, Laura, and Nicholas

P.N.F.

To Lindsay, Rowan, Seth, and Myles

C.C.K.

To Elizabeth, Katherine, and Tommy

R.L.S.

Brief Contents

Detailed Contents

About the Authors

Robert L. Sexton is Distinguished Professor of Economics at Pepperdine University. Professor Sexton has also been a Visiting Professor at the University of California at Los Angeles in the Anderson Graduate School of Management and the Department of Economics. He also played the role of an assistant coach in the movie *Benchwarmers* (2006).

Professor Sexton's research ranges across many fields of economics: economics education, labour economics, environmental economics, law and economics, and economic history. He has written several books and has published numerous reference articles, many in top economic journals such as the *American Economic Review,* the *Southern Economic Journal,* the *Economics Letters,* the *Journal of Urban Economics,* and the *Journal of Economic Education.* Professor Sexton has also written more than 100 other articles that have appeared in books, magazines, and newspapers.

He received the Pepperdine Professor of the Year Award in 1991 and 1997, was named a Harriet Charles Luckman Teaching Fellow in 1994, and was the recipient of the Howard A. White Award for Teaching Excellence in 2011.

Peter N. Fortura earned his undergraduate degree from Brock University, where he was awarded the Vice-Chancellor's Medal for academic achievement, and his Master of Arts from the University of Western Ontario in London, Ontario. He has taught economics at Algonquin College in Ottawa for over 20 years. Prior to that, he was an economist in the International Department of the Bank of Canada in Ottawa.

He has published articles on Canadian housing prices, Canada's automotive industry, and Canada's international competitiveness. As well, he is the author of the *Study Guide to Accompany Principles of Macroeconomics,* by Mankiw, Kneebone, McKenzie, and Rowe (Nelson Education, 5th edition), and the co-author of the statistics textbook *Contemporary Business Statistics with Canadian Applications* (Pearson, 3rd edition).

He lives in Ottawa with his wife, Cynthia, and their children, Laura and Nicholas.

Colin C. Kovacs received his Master of Arts degree from Queen's University after completing his Bachelor of Arts degree at the University of Western Ontario. He has taught economics, statistics, and finance for nearly 20 years at both the DeVry College of Technology in Toronto and Algonquin College in Ottawa. His research papers have included *Determinants of Labour Force Participation Among Older Males in Canada* and *Minimum Wage—The Past and Future for Ontario.*

He lives in Ottawa with his wife, Lindsay, and their children, Rowan, Seth, and Myles.

Preface

Exploring Economics, Fourth Canadian Edition, offers students a lively, back-to-the-basics approach designed to take the intimidation out of economics. With its short, self-contained learning units and its carefully chosen pedagogy, graphs, and photos, this text helps students master and retain the principles of economics. In addition, the current-events focus and modular format of presenting information makes *Exploring Economics* a very student-accessible and user-friendly text. Driven by more than 60 years of combined experience teaching the economic principles course, the dedication and enthusiasm of Bob Sexton, Peter Fortura, and Colin Kovacs shine through in *Exploring Economics.*

NEW TO THE FOURTH CANADIAN EDITION

Overall Highlights

As with previous editions of *Exploring Economics,* attention has been paid to the structure and layout of each chapter to ensure that the material is presented in as clear and consistent a manner as possible. In addition, special attention has been given to the numerous examples and illustrations presented in each chapter to ensure that they are meaningful and relevant to today's student.

The process of reviewing and expanding the end-of-chapter review questions and problems has continued in this edition. As part of this revision, a new feature has been added to the *For Your Review* section: Blueprint Problems. Designed to provide additional insight into the methodology surrounding key economic concepts, a full and annotated solution accompanies each problem to help students better understand how to successfully complete key questions and problems.

The two features introduced in the previous edition, *Debate* and *Business Connection* boxes, have undergone revision and updating. While their content has been revised, the purpose of each feature remains the same—*Debate* boxes are designed to promote in-class discussion and self-exploration, and the *Business Connection* boxes are designed to highlight the link between economic theory and business principles. New to both features are questions at the end of each box. Designed to make the content more interactive, these questions can be used as the basis for in-class discussion.

Finally, where relevant, additional Canadian content has been added and all statistical information has been updated. For example, the data accompanying the discussion of economic growth in Chapter 15 has been expanded to include a variety of different economies. Most notably, data from emerging economies has been added to the discussion, providing the opportunity for valuable comparison and contrast against more developed economies.

CHAPTER HIGHLIGHTS

Chapter 2: Scarcity, Trade-Offs, and Production Possibilities

This chapter has undergone considerable redesign to provide the reader with a better lead-in to the key topics of demand and supply that follow in Chapters 3 and 4.

Chapter 4: Bringing Supply and Demand Together

The examples provided to illustrate the impact of changes in demand and supply have been completely redesigned. The major reason for this redesign was to ensure that each example was factual, topical, and most importantly, relevant to today's student.

Chapter 6: Consumer Choice and Market Efficiency

The topics of consumer behaviour and consumer choice are partnered with consumer and producer surplus to provide a more in-depth explanation of how consumer decisions are made and how market efficiency is achieved. With this edition, particular attention has been paid to the topic of consumer choice. A complete numerical model illustrating how the consumer equilibrium is achieved now accompanies the topic of consumer choice. In addition, to help support the development of the consumer choice topic, appropriate questions have been added to the end-of-chapter *For Your Review* questions.

Chapter 12: Market Failure and the Environment

The individual discussion of the environment has been expanded to include the topic of market failures. As part of this broader focus, a discussion of public goods is also included.

Chapter 15: Economic Growth in the Global Economy

Greater emphasis and detail is provided on how economic growth has impacted the development of emerging economies. In particular, the group of economies known by the acronym BRICS is discussed. (BRICS stands for five major emerging national economies: Brazil, Russia, India, China, and South Africa.)

Chapter 16: Aggregate Demand and Chapter 17: Aggregate Supply and Macroeconomic Equilibrium

Greater detail has been added to the explanation and illustration of both aggregate demand and aggregate supply shifters.

Finally, where relevant, additional Canadian content, including photos and examples, has been added and all statistical information has been updated.

FEATURES OF THE BOOK

The Section-by-Section Approach

Exploring Economics uses a section-by-section approach in which economic ideas and concepts are presented in short, self-contained units rather than in large blocks of text. Each chapter is composed of approximately six to eight bite-sized sections, typically presented in two to eight pages, that include all of the relevant graphs, tables, applications, boxes, photos, and definitions for the topic at hand. Our enthusiasm for and dedication to this approach stems from studying research on *learning theory*, which indicates that students retain information much better when it is broken down into short, intense, and exciting bursts of "digestible" information. Students prefer information divided into smaller, self-contained sections that are less overwhelming, more manageable, and easier to review before going on to new material. In short, students will be more successful in mastering and retaining economic principles using this approach, which is distinctly more compatible with modern communication styles.

But students aren't the only ones to benefit from this approach. The self-contained sections allow instructors greater flexibility in planning their courses. They can simply select or delete sections of the text as it fits their syllabus.

Highlighted Learning Tools

Key Questions   Each section begins with key questions designed to preview ideas and to pique students' interest in the material to come. These same questions are then used to structure the section material that follows, each question being prominently displayed as a section heading, with additional subheadings provided as needed. In addition to ensuring a clear instructional layout of each section and chapter, these key questions can also be used by students as a review resource. After reading the section material, if students are able to answer the key questions, they can go forward with confidence.

Section Checks   A *Section Check* appears at the end of each section and is designed to summarize the answers to the key questions posed at the beginning of the section. The summaries provided by the *Section Check* give students an opportunity to evaluate their understanding of major ideas before proceeding.

Debate Boxes   *Debate* boxes are designed to provide students with an opportunity to develop and express their opinions about a variety of economic issues. The "For" and "Against" arguments that accompany each debate topic make it easy to use these features to initiate in-class discussions. By engaging in informal debate regarding current economic policy, students will be able to link course content to current events as well as to their own personal lives. Additional questions have been added to encourage critical thinking.

Business Connection Boxes   *Business Connection* boxes are designed to help students see the link between economic theory and business fundamentals. They help students better understand the reasoning behind the empirical validity of economic theory, and they also aid in the grounding of abstract economic theory in more "modern" business principles. Accompanying each *Business Connection* box are questions that can be used to either evaluate student understanding or initiate in-class discussion.

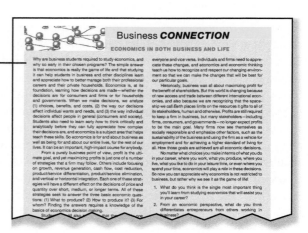

WHY DO WE NEED TO ABSTRACT?

How is economic theory like a GPS? Because of the complexity of human behaviour, economists must abstract to focus on the most important components of a particular problem. This is similar to how a GPS highlights the important information (and does not register many minor details) to help people get from here to there.

Economic theories cannot realistically include every event that has ever occurred. This is true for the same reason that a newspaper or history book does not include every world event that has ever happened. We must abstract. A road map of Canada may not include every creek, ridge, and valley between Vancouver and Halifax—indeed, such an all-inclusive map would be too complicated and confusing to be of much value. However, a GPS programmed to guide the traveller while referencing key details encountered along the way, such as highways and major attractions, will provide enough information to travel by car from Vancouver to Halifax. Likewise, an economic theory provides a broad view, not a detailed examination, of human economic behaviour.

WHAT IS A HYPOTHESIS?

The beginning of any theory is a **hypothesis**, a testable proposition that makes some type of prediction about behaviour in response to certain changes in conditions. In economic theory, a hypothesis is a testable prediction about how people will behave or react to a change in economic circumstances. For example, if the price of iPads increased, we might hypothesize that fewer iPads would be sold, or if the price of iPads fell, we might hypothesize that more iPads would be sold. Once a hypothesis is stated, it is tested by comparing what it predicts will happen to what actually happens.

Photos *Exploring Economics* contains a large number of colourful pictures. These photos are an integral part of the book for both learning and motivation. The photos are carefully placed where they reinforce important concepts, and they are accompanied by captions designed to encourage students to extend their understanding of particular ideas.

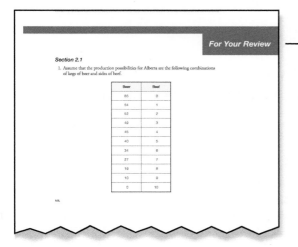

For Your Review

Section 2.1

1. Assume that the production possibilities for Alberta are the following combinations of kegs of beer and sides of beef.

Beer	Beef
55	0
54	1
52	2
49	3
45	4
40	5
34	6
27	7
19	8
10	9
0	10

For Your Review Provided at the end of each chapter, these problems allow students to test their understanding of chapter concepts. The *For Your Review* questions are organized into sections to match the corresponding sections in the text so that students and instructors can easily identify particular topics. To assist in the learning process, solutions to all odd-numbered questions are provided at the back of the text. With a variety of both problems and application-style questions to choose from, this section can also be used by instructors to assign homework questions directly from the text.

b. Given the information above, what is the opportunity cost of the 55th keg of beer in Alberta? Of the 6th side of beef? Of the 9th side of beef?
c. Suppose Alberta is currently producing 4 sides of beef and 45 kegs of beer. What is the opportunity cost of 5 more sides of beef in Alberta?
d. Would the combination of 40 kegs of beer and 4 sides of beef be efficient? Why or why not?
e. Is the combination of 9 kegs of beer and 10 sides of beef possible for Alberta? Why or why not?

Blueprint Problem

Assume that an economy has the following production possibilities.

Wheat (tonnes)	Oil (millions of barrels)
0	20
1	18
2	14
3	8
4	0

a. Construct the production possibilities frontier for this economy.
b. What is the opportunity cost of the 2nd tonne of wheat? Of the 4th tonne of wheat?

Blueprint Problems Integrated into the end-of-chapter *For Your Review* sections, these fully annotated problems and their solutions are intended to provide additional insight into key economic topics and issues. Intentionally designed to mirror the accompanying *For Your Review* problems, each *Blueprint Problem* allows students to "walk through" a completed solution, seeing the essential steps necessary to successfully complete a key economic question.

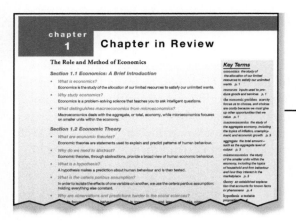

Chapter in Review Cards   Located at the back of the textbook, these detachable *Chapter in Review* cards are designed to give students a summary overview of key chapter concepts at a glance. Each *Chapter in Review* card contains the following information:

- **Chapter Summary:** A point-form summary response to the section's key questions, highlighting the most important concepts of each section, is provided.
- **Key Terms:** A list of key terms allows students to test their mastery of new concepts. Both the definition and page number are included so that students can easily find a key term in a chapter.
- **Key Exhibits/Graphs:** Given the importance and explanatory ability of exhibits and graphical representations in economics, a list of key figures is provided for each chapter.
- **Key Equations:** A list of key equations enables students to quickly refer to important formulas.

SUPPLEMENTARY MATERIALS

About the Nelson Education Teaching Advantage (NETA)

The **Nelson Education Teaching Advantage (NETA)** program delivers research-based instructor resources that promote student engagement and higher-order thinking to enable the success of Canadian students and educators. Be sure to visit Nelson Education's **Inspired Instruction** website at www.nelson.com/inspired to find out more about NETA. Don't miss the testimonials of instructors who have used NETA supplements and watched student engagement increase!

INSTRUCTOR RESOURCES

Downloadable Supplements

All NETA and other key instructor ancillaries can be accessed through http://www.nelson.com/login and http://login.cengage.com, giving instructors the ultimate tools for customizing lectures and presentations.

Instructor's Solutions Manual: Answers to all *For Your Review* questions in the textbook are provided in this manual, now separated from the Instructor's Manual for easier reference. Students can access only the odd-numbered solutions in the Answer Key at the back of the book. The solutions were prepared by the text co-author, Colin Kovacs, and independently checked for accuracy by Nelson Gonzalez.

NETA Test Bank: This resource was prepared by Russell Turner, Fleming College. *Exploring Microeconomics* includes over 1400 multiple-choice questions and *Exploring Macroeconomics* includes over 1775 multiple-choice questions written according to NETA guidelines for effective construction and development of higher-order questions.

Also included in the test banks are more than 570 true/false and more than 230 essay-type questions.

The NETA Test Bank is available in a new, cloud-based platform. **Nelson Testing Powered by Cognero®** is a secure online testing system that allows you to author, edit, and manage test bank content from any place you have Internet access. No special installations or downloads are needed, and the desktop-inspired interface, with its drop-down menus and familiar, intuitive tools, allows you to create and manage tests with ease. You can create multiple test versions in an instant, and import or export content into other systems. Tests can be delivered from your learning management system, your classroom, or wherever you want. Nelson Testing Powered by Cognero can also be accessed through htp://www.nelson.com/login and http://login.cengage.com. Printable versions of the Test Bank in Word and PDF versions are available with the Instructor Resources for the textbook.

NETA PowerPoint: Microsoft® PowerPoint® lecture slides for every chapter have been adapted by Ifeanyichukwu Uzoka of Sheridan College. We offer two separate collections. The Basic PowerPoint collection contains an average of 40 slides per chapter. This collection is a basic outline of the chapter and contains key figures, tables, and photographs from the fourth Canadian edition of *Exploring Economics*. The Expanded PowerPoint collection includes an average of 65 slides per chapter and provides a more complete overview of the chapter. NETA principles of clear design and engaging content have been incorporated throughout, making it simple for instructors to customize the deck for their courses.

Image Library: This resource consists of digital copies of figures, short tables, and photographs used in the book. Instructors may use these images to customize the NETA PowerPoint or create their own PowerPoint presentations.

Instructor's Manuals: The *Instructor's Manuals* to accompany *Exploring Economics,* Fourth Canadian Edition, have been prepared by Phil Ghayad and Michel Mayer of Dawson College. The manuals include teaching tips and active learning exercises. (Answers to all *For Your Review* exercises in the text are now provided in the separate Instructor's Solutions Manual supplement described earlier.)

DayOne: Day One—Prof InClass is a PowerPoint presentation that instructors can customize to orient students to the class and their textbook at the beginning of the course.

MindTap

MindTap for *Exploring Economics* is a personalized teaching experience with relevant assignments that guide students to analyze, apply, and elevate thinking, allowing instructors to measure skills and promote better outcomes with ease. A fully online learning solution, MindTap combines all student learning tools—readings, multimedia, activities, and assessments—into a single Learning Path that guides the student through the curriculum. Instructors personalize the experience by customizing the presentation of these learning tools to their students, even seamlessly introducing their own content into the Learning Path. Instructors can access MindTap for *Exploring Economics* through http://www.nelson.com/login and http://login.cengage.com.

Aplia

Aplia™ is a Cengage Learning online homework system dedicated to improving learning by increasing student effort and engagement. Aplia makes it easy for instructors to assign frequent online homework assignments. Aplia provides students with prompt and detailed feedback to help them learn as they work through the questions, and features interactive tutorials to fully engage them in learning course concepts. Automatic grading and powerful assessment tools give instructors real-time reports of student progress, participation, and performance, and while Aplia's easy-to-use course management features let instructors flexibly administer course announcements and materials online. With Aplia, students will show up to class fully engaged and prepared, and instructors will have more time to do what they do best...teach.

The Aplia course for *Exploring Economics*, Fourth Canadian Edition, was prepared by Norm Smith of Georgian College.

Instructors can access Aplia through http://www.nelson.com/login and http://login.cengage.com.

STUDENT ANCILLARIES

MindTap

MindTap for *Exploring Economics* is a personalized teaching experience with relevant assignments that guide students to analyze, apply, and elevate thinking, allowing instructors to measure skills and promote better outcomes with ease. A fully online learning solution, MindTap combines all student learning tools—readings, multimedia, activities, and assessments—into a single Learning Path that guides the student through the curriculum. Instructors personalize the experience by customizing the presentation of these learning tools to their students, even seamlessly introducing their own content into the Learning Path.

Visit NELSONbrain.com to start using MindTap. Enter the Online Access Code from the card included with your text. If a code card is *not* provided, you can purchase instant access at NELSONbrain.com.

Aplia

Founded in 2000 by economist and Stanford professor Paul Romer, Aplia™ is an educational technology company dedicated to improving learning by increasing student effort and engagement. Currently, Aplia products have been used by more than a million students at over 1300 institutions. Aplia offers a way for you to stay on top of your coursework with regularly scheduled homework assignments that increase your time on task and give you prompt feedback. Interactive tools and additional content are provided to further increase your engagement and understanding.

See http://www.aplia.com for more information. If Aplia isn't bundled with your copy of *Exploring Economics*, you can purchase access separately at NELSONbrain.com. Be better prepared for class with Aplia!

Acknowledgments

Producing the fourth Canadian edition of *Exploring Economics* has truly been a team effort. We would like to thank the editorial, production, and marketing teams at Nelson Education for their hard work and effort. First, our appreciation goes to Anne Williams, vice president, Editorial, Higher Education, who has provided the vision and leadership for the Canadian editions of the text.

We would like to thank Amie Plourde, publisher, at Nelson Education Limited, for her continuing support. Thank you to Elke Price, senior developmental editor, for her helpful advice and constant encouragement. Thanks also to Lila Campbell, production project manager; June Trusty, copy editor; Alexis Hood, marketing manager; and all the marketing and sales representatives at Nelson Education Ltd. Special thanks are extended to Darren Chapman at Fanshawe College for providing the engaging and insightful *Business Connection* and *Debate* boxes. We would also like to thank Susan Kamp for her support and recommendations over the last two editions.

We are grateful to our families for their patience and encouragement.

Finally, we would like to acknowledge the reviewers of the Canadian editions, past and present, for their comments and feedback:

Sarah Arliss, *Seneca College*
Vick Barylak, *Sheridan College*
Aurelia Best, *Centennial College*
Ramesh Bhardwaj, *George Brown College*
Jim Butko, *Niagara College*
Lewis Callahan, *Lethbridge College*
Darren Chapman, *Fanshawe College*
Robert Dale, *Algonquin College*
Carol Derksen, *Red River College*
Bruno Fullone, *George Brown College*
Phillipe Ghayad, *Dawson College*
James Hnatchuk, *Champlain Regional College*
Geraldine Joosse, *Lethbridge College*
Susan Kamp, *University of Alberta*
Michael Leonard, *Kwantlen Polytechnic University*
Margaret Rose Olfert, *University of Saskatchewan*
John Pirrie, *St. Lawrence College*
Geoffrey Prince, *Centennial College*
Sheila J. Ross, *Southern Alberta Institute of Technology*
Judith Skuce, *Georgian College*
Norm Smith, *Georgian College*
Martha Spence, *Confederation College*
Lucia Vojtassak, *Trent University*
Carl Weston, *Mohawk College*

Their thoughtful suggestions were very important to us in providing input and useful examples for the fourth Canadian edition of this book.

P.N.F.
C.C.K.

chapter

1

The Role and Method of Economics

section

1.1

Economics: A Brief Introduction

- What is economics?
- Why study economics?
- What distinguishes macroeconomics from microeconomics?

WHAT IS ECONOMICS?

Some individuals think economics involves the study of the stock market and corporate finance, and it does—in part. Others think that economics is concerned with the wise use of money and other matters of personal finance, and it is—in part. Still others think that economics involves forecasting or predicting what business conditions will be like in the future, and again, it does—in part.

Growing Wants and Scarce Resources

Precisely defined, **economics** is the study of the allocation of our limited resources to satisfy our unlimited wants. **Resources** are inputs—such as land, human effort and skills, and machines and factories—used to produce goods and services. The problem is that our wants exceed our limited resources, a fact that we call *scarcity*. Scarcity forces us to make choices on how to best use our limited resources. This is **the economic problem:** Scarcity forces us to choose, and choices are costly because we must give up other opportunities that we value. This economizing problem is evident in every aspect of our lives. Choosing between a trip to the gym or the coffee shop, or between finishing an assignment or chatting online, can be understood more easily when one has a good handle on the "economic way of thinking."

economics
the study of the allocation of our limited resources to satisfy our unlimited wants

resources
inputs used to produce goods and services

the economic problem
scarcity forces us to choose, and choices are costly because we must give up other opportunities that we value

Articles related to economics— either directly or indirectly— are common in the news media. News headlines might trumpet: Gasoline Prices Soar; Stocks Rise; Stocks Fall; Prime Minister Vows to Increase National Defence Spending; Health-Care Costs Continue to Rise.

Economics Is All Around Us

Although many things that we desire in life are considered to be "noneconomic," economics concerns anything that is considered worthwhile to some human being. For instance, love, sexual activity, and religion have value for most people. Even these have an economic dimension. Consider love and sex, for example. One product of love—the institution of the family—is an important economic decision-making unit. Also, sexual activity results in the birth of children, one of the most important "goods" that many humans want. Economic forces have played a central role in the evolution of the family unit, from the traditional "nuclear family" (Dad, Mom, and two kids) to dual-income families, to dual-income no-kids (DINKS) families. Concerns for spiritual matters have likewise received economists' scrutiny, as they have led to the development of institutions such as churches, mosques, and temples that provide religious and spiritual services. These services are goods that many people want.

Even time has an economic dimension. In fact, perhaps the most precious single resource is time. We all have the same limited amount of time per day, and how we divide our time between work and leisure (including perhaps study, sleep, exercise, etc.) is a distinctly economic matter. If we choose more work, we must sacrifice leisure. If we choose to study, we must sacrifice time with friends, or time spent sleeping or watching TV. Virtually everything we decide to do, then, has an economic dimension.

Living in a world of scarcity means trade-offs. And it is important that we know what these trade-offs are so we can make better choices about the options available to us.

WHY STUDY ECONOMICS?

Among the many good reasons to study economics, perhaps the best reason is that so many of the things of concern in the world around us are at least partly economic in character. A quick look at media headlines reveals the vast range of problems that are related to economics—global warming, health care, education, and social assistance. The study of economics improves your understanding of these concerns. A student of economics becomes aware that, at a basic level, much of economic life involves choosing among alternative possible courses of action—making choices between our conflicting wants and desires in a world of scarcity. Economics provides some clues as to how to intelligently evaluate these options and determine the most appropriate choices in given situations. But economists learn quickly that there are seldom easy, clear-cut solutions to the problems we face: The easy problems were solved long ago!

Many students take introductory postsecondary economics courses because these are part of the core curriculum requirements. But why do the committees that establish these requirements include economics? In part, economics helps develop a disciplined method of thinking about problems as opposed to simply memorizing solutions. The problem-solving tools you will develop by studying economics will prove valuable to you in both your personal and professional life, regardless of your career choice. In short, the study of economics provides a systematic, disciplined way of thinking.

Using This Stuff

The basic tools of economics are valuable to people in all walks of life and in all career paths. Journalists benefit from economics because the problem-solving perspective it teaches trains them to ask intelligent questions whose answers will better inform their readers. Engineers, architects, and contractors usually have alternative ways to build. Architects learn to combine technical expertise and artistry with the limitations imposed by finite resources. That is, they learn how to evaluate their options from an economic perspective. Business owners face similar problems, because costs are a constraint in both creating and marketing a new product. Will the added cost of developing a new and improved product be outweighed by the added sales revenues that are expected to result? Economists can, however, pose these questions and provide criteria that business owners can use in evaluating the appropriateness of one design as compared to another. The point is that the economic way of thinking causes those in many types of fields to ask the right kind of questions.

WHAT DISTINGUISHES MACROECONOMICS FROM MICROECONOMICS?

Like psychology, sociology, anthropology, and political science, economics is considered a social science. Economics, like the other social sciences, is concerned with reaching generalizations about human behaviour. Economics is the study of people. It is the social science that studies the choices people make in a world of limited resources.

Economics and the other social sciences often complement one another. For example, a political scientist might examine the process that led to the adoption of a certain tax policy, whereas an economist might analyze the impact of that tax policy. Or, whereas a psychologist may try to figure out what makes the criminal mind work, an economist might study the factors causing a change in the crime rate. Social scientists, then, may be studying the same issue but from different perspectives.

Conventionally, we distinguish two main branches of economics: macroeconomics and microeconomics. **Macroeconomics** is the study of the **aggregate** or total economy; it looks at economic problems as they influence the whole of society. Topics covered in macroeconomics include discussions of inflation, unemployment, business cycles, and economic growth. **Microeconomics** is the study of the smaller units within the economy. Topics include the decision-making behaviour of firms and households and their interaction in markets for particular goods or services. Microeconomic topics also include discussions of health care, agricultural subsidies, the price of everyday items such as running shoes, the distribution of income, and the impact of labour unions on wages. To put it simply, microeconomics looks at the trees whereas macroeconomics looks at the forest.

macroeconomics
the study of the aggregate economy, including the topics of inflation, unemployment, and economic growth

aggregate
the total amount—such as the aggregate level of output

microeconomics
the study of the smaller units within the economy, including the topics of household and firm behaviour and how they interact in the marketplace

SECTION CHECK

- Economics is the study of the allocation of our limited resources to satisfy our unlimited wants.
- Economics is a problem-solving science that teaches you how to ask intelligent questions.
- Macroeconomics deals with the aggregate, or total, economy, while microeconomics focuses on smaller units within the economy.

1.2 Economic Theory

- What are economic theories?
- Why do we need to abstract?
- What is a hypothesis?
- What is the *ceteris paribus* assumption?
- Why are observations and predictions harder in the social sciences?
- What distinguishes between correlation and causation?
- What are positive analysis and normative analysis?

WHAT ARE ECONOMIC THEORIES?

theory
an established explanation that accounts for known facts or phenomena

hypothesis
a testable proposition

A **theory** is an established explanation that accounts for known facts or phenomena. Specifically, economic theories are statements or propositions about patterns of human behaviour that are expected to take place under certain circumstances. These theories help us to sort out and understand the complexities of economic behaviour. We expect a good theory to explain and predict well. A good economic theory, then, should help us to better understand and, ideally, predict human economic behaviour.

WHY DO WE NEED TO ABSTRACT?

How is economic theory like a GPS? Because of the complexity of human behaviour, economists must abstract to focus on the most important components of a particular problem. This is similar to how a GPS highlights the important information (and does not register many minor details) to help people get from here to there.

Economic theories cannot realistically include every event that has ever occurred. This is true for the same reason that a newspaper or history book does not include every world event that has ever happened. We must abstract. A road map of Canada may not include every creek, ridge, and valley between Vancouver and Halifax—indeed, such an all-inclusive map would be too complicated and confusing to be of much value. However, a GPS programmed to guide the traveller while referencing key details encountered along the way, such as highways and major attractions, will provide enough information to travel by car from Vancouver to Halifax. Likewise, an economic theory provides a broad view, not a detailed examination, of human economic behaviour.

Rafal Olechowski/iStock/Thinkstock

WHAT IS A HYPOTHESIS?

The beginning of any theory is a **hypothesis,** a testable proposition that makes some type of prediction about behaviour in response to certain changes in conditions. In economic theory, a hypothesis is a testable prediction about how people will behave or react to a change in economic circumstances. For example, if the price of iPads increased, we might hypothesize that fewer iPads would be sold, or if the price of iPads fell, we might hypothesize that more iPads would be sold. Once a hypothesis is stated, it is tested by comparing what it predicts will happen to what actually happens.

Using Empirical Analysis

To see if a hypothesis is valid, we must engage in an **empirical analysis.** That is, we must examine the data to see if the hypothesis fits well with the facts. If the hypothesis is consistent with real-world observations, it is accepted; if it does not fit well with the facts, it is "back to the drawing board."

Determining whether a hypothesis is acceptable is more difficult in economics than it is in the natural or physical sciences. Chemists, for example, can observe chemical reactions under laboratory conditions. They can alter the environment to meet the assumptions of the hypothesis and can readily manipulate the variables (chemicals, temperatures, and so on) crucial to the proposed relationship. Such controlled experimentation is seldom possible in economics. The laboratory of economists is usually the real world. Unlike a chemistry lab, economists cannot easily control all the other variables that might influence human behaviour.

empirical analysis
the examination of data to see if the hypothesis fits well with the facts

From Hypothesis to Theory

After gathering their data, economic researchers must then evaluate the results to determine whether the hypothesis is supported or refuted. If supported, the hypothesis can then be tentatively accepted as an economic theory.

Economic theories are always on probation. A hypothesis is constantly being tested against empirical findings. Do the observed findings support the prediction? When a hypothesis survives a number of tests, it is accepted until it no longer predicts well.

WHAT IS THE *CETERIS PARIBUS* ASSUMPTION?

Virtually all economic theories share a condition usually expressed by use of the Latin expression *ceteris paribus.* This roughly means "let everything else be equal" or "holding everything else constant." In trying to assess the effect of one variable on another, we must isolate their relationship from other events that might also influence the situation that the theory tries to explain or predict. To make this clearer, we will illustrate this concept with a couple of examples.

ceteris paribus
holding everything else constant

Suppose you develop your own theory describing the relationship between studying and exam performance: If I study harder, I will perform better on the test. That sounds logical, right? Holding other things constant (*ceteris paribus*), this is likely to be true. However, what if you studied harder but inadvertently overslept the day of the exam? What if you were so sleepy during the test that you could not think clearly? Or what if you studied the wrong material? Although it may look as if additional studying did not improve your performance, the real problem may lie in the impact of other variables, such as sleep deficiency or how you studied.

WHY ARE OBSERVATIONS AND PREDICTIONS HARDER IN THE SOCIAL SCIENCES?

Working from observations, scientists try to make generalizations that will enable them to predict certain events. However, observation and prediction are more difficult in the social sciences than in physical sciences such as chemistry, physics, and astronomy. Why? The major reason for the difference is that the social scientists, including economists, are concerned with *human* behaviour. And human behaviour is more variable and often less readily predictable than the behaviour of experiments observed in a laboratory. However, by looking at the actions of a large group of people, economists can still make many reliable predictions about human behaviour.

Economists Predict on a Group Level

Economists' predictions usually refer to the collective behaviour of large groups rather than to that of specific individuals. Why is this? Looking at the behaviours of a large group allows economists to discern general patterns of actions. For example, consider what would happen if the price of air travel from Canada to Europe was drastically reduced, say from $1500 to $500, because of the invention of a more fuel-efficient jet. What type of predictions could we make about the effect of this price reduction on the buying habits of typical consumers?

Individual Behaviour

Let's look first at the responses of individuals. As a result of the price drop, some people will greatly increase their intercontinental travel, enjoying theatre weekends in London or week-long trips to France to indulge in French food. Some people, however, are terribly afraid to fly, and a price reduction will not influence their behaviour in the slightest. Others might detest Europe and, despite the lowered airfares, prefer to spend a few days in Vancouver instead. A few people might respond to the airfare reduction very negatively: At the lower fare, they might make fewer trips to Europe, because they might believe (rightly or wrongly) that the price drop would be accompanied by a reduction in the quality of service, greater crowding, or reduced safety. In short, we cannot predict with any level of certainty how a given individual will respond to this airfare reduction.

Group Behaviour

Group behaviour is often more predictable than individual behaviour. When the weather gets colder, more firewood is sold. Some individuals may not buy firewood (e.g., if they don't have a fireplace in their home), but we can predict with great accuracy that a group of individuals will establish a pattern of buying more firewood. Similarly, while we cannot say what each individual will do, within a group of persons, we can predict with great accuracy that more flights to Europe from Toronto will be sold at lower prices, holding other things such as income and preferences constant. We cannot predict exactly how many more airline tickets will be sold at $500 than at $1500, but we can predict the direction of the impact and approximate the extent of the impact. By observing the relationship between the price of goods and services and the quantities people purchase in different places and during different time periods, it is possible to make some reliable generalizations about how much people will react to changes in the prices of goods and services. Economists use this larger picture of the group for most of their theoretical analysis.

WHAT DISTINGUISHES BETWEEN CORRELATION AND CAUSATION?

Without a theory of causation, no scientist could sort out and understand the enormous complexity of the real world. But one must always be careful not to confuse correlation with causation. In other words, the fact that two events usually occur together (**correlation**) does not necessarily mean that one caused the other to occur (**causation**). For example, say a groundhog awakes after a long winter of hibernation, climbs out of his hole, sees his shadow, and then six weeks of bad weather ensue. Did the groundhog cause the bad weather? It is highly unlikely.

Perhaps the causality may run in the opposite direction. Although a rooster may always crow before the sun rises, it does not cause the sunrise; rather, the early light from the sunrise causes the rooster to crow.

correlation
two events that usually occur together

causation
when one event causes another event to occur

The Positive Correlation between Ice Cream Sales and Crime

Did you know that when ice cream sales rise, so do crime rates? What do you think causes the two events to occur together? Some might think that a sugar "high" caused by the ice cream causes the higher crime rate. Excess sugar in a snack was actually used in court testimony in a murder case—the so-called "Twinkie defence." However, it is more likely that crime peaks in the summer because of weather, more people on vacation (leaving their homes vacant), teenagers out of school, and so on. It just happens that ice cream sales also peak in those months because of weather. The lesson: One must always be careful not to confuse correlation with causation and to be clear on the direction of the causation.

Steve Estvanik/Shutterstock

People tend to drive slower when the roads are covered with ice. In addition, more traffic accidents occur when the roads are icy. So, does driving slower cause the number of accidents to rise? No, it is the icy roads that lead to both lower speeds and more accidents.

The Fallacy of Composition

One must also be careful with problems associated with aggregation (summing up all the parts), particularly the **fallacy of composition.** This fallacy states that even if something is true for an individual, it is not necessarily true for many individuals as a group. For example, say you are at a concert and you decide to stand up to get a better view of the stage. This works as long as no one else stands up. But what would happen if everyone stood up at the same time? Then, standing up would not let you see better. Hence, what may be true for an individual does not always hold true in the aggregate. The same can be said of arriving to class early to get a better parking place—what if everyone arrived early? Or studying harder to get a better grade in a class that is graded on a curve—what if everyone studied harder? All of these are examples of the fallacy of composition.

fallacy of composition
even if something is true for an individual, it is not necessarily true for a group

WHAT ARE POSITIVE ANALYSIS AND NORMATIVE ANALYSIS?

Positive Analysis

Most economists view themselves as scientists seeking the truth about the way people behave. They make speculations about economic behaviour, and then (ideally) they try to assess the validity of those predictions based on human experience. Their work emphasizes how people *do* behave, rather than how people *should* behave. In the role of scientist, an economist tries to observe, objectively, patterns of behaviour without reference to the appropriateness or inappropriateness of that behaviour. This objective, value-free approach, utilizing the scientific method, is called **positive analysis.** In positive analysis, we want to know the impact of variable A on variable B. We want to be able to test a hypothesis. For example, the following is a positive statement: If rent controls are imposed, vacancy rates will fall. This statement is testable. A positive statement does not have to be a true statement, but it does have to be a testable statement.

positive analysis
an objective, value-free approach, utilizing the scientific method

However, keep in mind that it is doubtful that even the most objective scientist can be totally value-free in his or her analysis. An economist may well emphasize data or evidence that supports his hypothesis, putting less weight on other evidence that might be contradictory. This, alas, is human nature. But a good economist/scientist strives to be as fair and objective as possible in evaluating evidence and in stating conclusions based on the evidence.

Normative Analysis

normative analysis
a subjective, biased approach

Like everyone, economists have opinions and make value judgments. When economists, or anyone else for that matter, express opinions about some economic policy or statement, they are indicating in part how they believe things should be, not just facts as to the way things are. **Normative analysis** is a subjective, biased approach, where one expresses opinions about the desirability of various actions. Normative statements involve judgments about what should be or what ought to happen. For example, one could judge that incomes should be more equally distributed. If there is a change in tax policy that makes incomes more equal, there will be positive economic questions that can be investigated, such as how work behaviour will change. But we cannot say, as scientists, that such a policy is good or bad; rather, we can point to what will likely happen if the policy is adopted.

Positive versus Normative Statements

The distinction between positive and normative analysis is important. It is one thing to say that everyone should have universal health care, a normative statement, and quite another to say that universal health care would lead to greater worker productivity, a testable positive statement. It is important to distinguish between positive and normative analysis because many controversies in economics revolve around policy considerations that contain both. When economists start talking about how the economy should work rather than how it does work, they have entered the normative world of the policymaker.

Why Economists Disagree

Although economists differ frequently on economic policy questions, there is probably less disagreement than the media would have you believe. Disagreement is common in most disciplines: Tech-savy consumers cannot agree which operating system is superior—Windows or Mac; historians can be at odds over the interpretation of historical events; psychologists disagree on proper ways to rear children; and nutritionists debate the merits of large doses of vitamin C.

The majority of disagreements in economics stem from normative issues, as differences in values or policy beliefs result in conflict. As we discussed earlier in this chapter, economists may emphasize specific facts over other facts when trying to develop support for their own hypothesis. As a result, disagreements can arise when one economist gives weight to facts that have been minimized by another, and vice versa.

Freedom versus Fairness

Some economists are concerned about individual freedom and liberty, thinking that any encroachment on individual decision making is, other things equal, bad. People with this philosophic bent are inclined to be skeptical of any increased government involvement in the economy.

On the other hand, some economists are concerned with what they consider an unequal, "unfair," or unfortunate distribution of income, wealth, or power, and view governmental intervention as desirable in righting injustices that they believe exist in a market economy. To these persons, the threat to individual liberty alone is not sufficiently great to reject governmental intervention in the face of perceived economic injustice.

The Validity of an Economic Theory

Aside from philosophic differences, there is a second reason why economists may differ on any given policy question. Specifically, they may disagree as to the validity of a given economic theory for the policy in question. Suppose two economists have identical philosophical views that have led them to the same conclusion: To end injustice and hardship, unemployment should be reduced. To reach the objective, the first economist believes the government should lower taxes and increase spending, whereas the second economist believes increasing the amount of money in public hands by various banking policies will achieve the same results with fewer undesirable consequences. The two economists differ because the empirical evidence for economic theories about the cause of unemployment appears to conflict. Some evidence suggests government taxation and spending policies are effective in reducing unemployment, whereas other evidence suggests that the prime cause of unnecessary unemployment lies with faulty monetary policy. Still other evidence is consistent with the view that, over long periods, neither approach mentioned here is of much value in reducing unemployment, and that unemployment will be part of our existence no matter what macroeconomic policies we follow.

Although you may not believe it after reading the previous discussion, economists don't always disagree. In fact, according to a survey among members of the American Economic Association, most economists agree on a wide range of issues, including rent control, import tariffs, export restrictions, the use of wage and price controls to curb inflation, and the minimum wage.

SECTION CHECK

- Economic theories are statements used to explain and predict patterns of human behaviour.
- Economic theories, through abstraction, provide a broad view of human economic behaviour.
- A hypothesis makes a prediction about human behaviour and is then tested.
- In order to isolate the effects of one variable on another, we use the *ceteris paribus* assumption.
- With its focus on human behaviour, which is more variable and less predictable, observation and prediction are more difficult in the social sciences.
- The fact that two events are related does not mean that one caused the other to occur.
- Positive analysis is objective and value-free, while normative analysis involves value judgments and opinions about the desirability of various actions.

Scarcity

section 1.3

- What is scarcity?
- What are goods and services?

Most of economics is really knowing certain principles well and knowing when and how to apply them. In the following sections, some important tools are presented that will help you understand the economic way of thinking. These few basic ideas will repeatedly occur throughout the text. If you develop a good understanding of these principles and master the problem-solving skills inherent in them, they will serve you well for the rest of your life.

WHAT IS SCARCITY?

scarcity
the situation that exists when human wants exceed available resources

As we have already mentioned, economics is concerned primarily with **scarcity**—the situation that exists when human wants exceed available resources. We may want more "essential" items like food, clothing, schooling, and health care. We may want many other items, like vacations, cars, computers, and concert tickets. We may want more friendship, love, knowledge, and so on. We also may have many goals—perhaps an A in this class, a university education, and a great job. Unfortunately, people are not able to fulfill all of their wants—material desires and nonmaterial desires. And as long as human wants exceed available resources, scarcity will exist.

Scarcity and Resources

The scarce resources used in the production of goods and services can be grouped into four categories: labour, land, capital, and entrepreneurship.

labour
the physical and mental effort used by people in the production of goods and services

Labour is the total of both physical and mental effort used by people in the production of goods and services.

land
the natural resources used in the production of goods and services

Land includes the "gifts of nature" or the natural resources used in the production of goods and services. Trees, animals, water, minerals, and so on are all considered to be "land" for our purposes, along with the physical space normally thought of as land.

capital
the equipment and structures used to produce goods and services

Capital is the equipment and structures used to produce goods and services. Office buildings, tools, machines, and factories are all considered capital goods. When we invest in factories, machines, research and development, or education, we increase the potential to create more goods and services in the future. Capital also includes **human capital,** the productive knowledge and skills people receive from education and on-the-job training.

human capital
the productive knowledge and skill people receive from education and on-the-job training

Entrepreneurship is the process of combining labour, land, and capital together to produce goods and services. Entrepreneurs make the tough and risky decisions about what and how to produce goods and services. Entrepreneurs are always looking for new ways to improve production techniques or to create new products. They are lured by the chance to make a profit. It is this opportunity to make a profit that leads entrepreneurs to take risks.

entrepreneurship
the process of combining labour, land, and capital together to produce goods and services

However, entrepreneurs are not necessarily a Bill Gates (Microsoft), a Wallace McCain (frozen food empire), or a William or Alfred Billes (Canadian Tire). In some sense, we are all entrepreneurs when we try new products or when we find better ways to manage our households or our study time. Rather than money, then, our profits might take the form of greater enjoyment, additional time for recreation, or better grades.

WHAT ARE GOODS AND SERVICES?

goods
items we value or desire

Goods are those items that we value or desire. Goods tend to be tangible—objects that can be seen, held, heard, tasted, or smelled. **Services** are intangible acts for which people are willing to pay, such as legal services, medical services, and dental care. Services are intangible because they are less overtly visible, but they are certainly no less valuable than goods. All goods and services, whether tangible or intangible, are produced from scarce resources and can be subjected to economic analysis. If there are not enough goods and services for all of us, we will have to compete for those scarce goods and services. That is, scarcity ultimately leads to competition for the available goods and services, a subject we will return to often in the text.

service
an intangible act that people want

Bads

bads
items that we do not desire or want

In contrast to goods, **bads** are those items that we do not desire or want. For most people, garbage, pollution, weeds, and crime are bads. People tend to eliminate or minimize bads, so they will often pay to have bads, like garbage, removed. The elimination of the bad—garbage removal, for example—is a good.

Business *CONNECTION*

ECONOMICS IN BOTH BUSINESS AND LIFE

Why are business students required to study economics, and why so early in their chosen programs? The simple answer is that economics is really the game of life and that studying it can help students in business and other disciplines learn and appreciate how to better manage both their professional careers and their private households. Economics is, at its foundation, learning how decisions are made—whether the decisions are for consumers and firms or for households and governments. When we make decisions, we analyze (1) choices, benefits, and costs, (2) the way our decisions affect individual wants and needs, and (3) the way individual decisions affect people in general (consumers and society). Students also need to learn early *how* to think critically and analytically before they can fully appreciate how complex their decisions are, and economics is a subject area that helps teach these skills. So economics is for and about business as well as being for and about our entire lives, for the rest of our lives. It can be an important, high-impact course for anybody.

From a purely business point of view, profit is the ultimate goal, and yet maximizing profits is just one of a number of strategies that a firm may follow. Others include focusing on growth, revenue generation, cash flow, cost reduction, product/service differentiation, product/service elimination, and vertical or horizontal integration. Each one of these strategies will have a different effect on the decisions of price and quantity over short, medium, or longer terms. All of these strategies seek to answer the three basic economic questions: (1) What to produce? (2) How to produce it? (3) For whom? Finding the answers requires a knowledge of the basics of economics decision making.

Students should also recognize that there is only one constant: Time and circumstances change. What worked months or years ago may not work today or in the future, and what's good for individuals is not necessarily good for everyone and vice versa. Individuals and firms need to appreciate these changes, and economics and economic thinking teach us how to recognize and respect our changing environment so that we can make the changes that will be best for our particular goals.

Historically, business was all about maximizing profit for the benefit of shareholders. But this world is changing because of new access and trade between different international economies, and also because we are recognizing that the spaceship we call *Earth* places limits on the resources it gifts to all of its stakeholders, human and otherwise. Profits are still required to keep a firm in business, but many stakeholders—including firms, consumers, and governments—no longer expect profits to be the main goal. Many firms now see themselves as socially responsible and emphasize other factors, such as the sustainability of the business and using the firm as a vehicle for employment and for achieving a higher standard of living for all. How those goals are achieved are all economic decisions.

No matter what choices you make in terms of what you do in your career, where you work, what you produce, where you live, what you like to do in your leisure time, or even where you spend your time, economics will play a role in these decisions. So now you can appreciate why economics is not restricted to business, but rather why we see it as the game of life!

1. What do you think is the single most important thing you'll learn from studying economics that will assist you in your career?

2. From an economic perspective, what do you think differentiates entrepreneurs from others working in business?

3. Do you think entrepreneurs are born, or do you think anyone can learn to be an entrepreneur? What provides the foundation for your opinion?

Everyone Faces Scarcity

We all face scarcity because we cannot have all of the goods and services that we desire. However, because we all have different wants and desires, scarcity affects everyone differently. For example, a child in a developing country may face a scarcity of food and clean drinking water, whereas a rich person may face a scarcity of garage space for his growing antique car collection. Likewise, a harried middle-class working mother may find time for exercise particularly scarce, whereas a pharmaceutical company may be concerned with the scarcity of the natural resources it uses in its production process. Although its effects vary, no one can escape scarcity.

SECTION CHECK

■ Scarcity exists when our wants exceed the available resources of land, labour, capital, and entrepreneurship.
■ Goods and services are things that we value.

Opportunity Cost

- Why do we have to make choices?
- What do we give up when we have to choose?
- Why are "free" lunches not free?

WHY DO WE HAVE TO MAKE CHOICES?

We may want nice homes, two luxury cars in every garage, wholesome and good-tasting food, personal trainers, and therapists, all enjoyed in a pristine environment with zero pollution. If we had unlimited resources, and thus an ability to produce all of the goods and services anyone wanted, we would not have to choose among those desires. If we did not have to make meaningful economic choices, the study of economics would not be necessary. The essence of economics is to understand fully the implications that scarcity has for wise decision making. This suggests another way to define economics: *Economics is the study of the choices we make among our many wants and desires.*

WHAT DO WE GIVE UP WHEN WE HAVE TO CHOOSE?

opportunity cost
the highest or best forgone opportunity resulting from a decision

Drivers who talk on their cellphones or put on make-up while driving are attempting to make better use of their time while in the vehicle. However, the distractions these activities cause can result in a tragic trade-off.

We are all faced with scarcity and, as a consequence, we must make choices. Because none of us can "afford" to buy everything we want, each time we do decide to buy one good or service, we reduce our ability to buy other things we would also like to have. If you buy a new car this year, you may not be able to afford your next best choice—the vacation you've been planning. You must choose. The cost of the car to you is the value of the vacation that must be forgone. The highest or best forgone opportunity resulting from a decision is called the **opportunity cost.** For example, time spent running costs time that could have been spent doing something else that is valuable—perhaps spending time with friends or studying for an upcoming exam. Another way to put this is that "to choose is to lose" or "an opportunity cost is an opportunity lost." To get more of anything that is desirable, you must accept less of something else that you also value.

Minerva Studio/iStock/Thinkstock

One of the reasons why vehicle drivers talk so much on their cellphones is that they have little else to do with their time while driving—a low opportunity cost. However, drivers should not use cellphones while driving because this is a distraction; by not giving full attention to their driving, they are giving up safety. Trade-offs are everywhere. This particular trade-off is why many jurisdictions have made the use of a cellphone while driving illegal.

Bill Gates, Tiger Woods, and Mark Zuckerberg all quit university or college to pursue their dreams. Tiger Woods dropped out of Stanford to join the PGA golf tour. Bill Gates dropped out of Harvard to start a software company. Mark Zuckerberg also dropped out of Harvard to continue working on his social networking site Facebook. Staying in school would have cost each of them millions of dollars. We cannot say it would have been the wrong decision to stay in school, but it would have been costly. For each of them, the opportunity cost of staying in school was high.

Money Prices and Costs

If you go to the store to buy groceries, you have to pay for the items you buy. This amount is called the *money price*. It is an opportunity cost, because you could have used the money to purchase other goods and services. However, additional opportunity costs include the nonprice costs incurred to acquire the groceries—time spent getting to the grocery store, finding a parking space, actually shopping, and waiting in the checkout line. The nonprice costs are measured by assessing the sacrifice involved—the value you place on what you would have done with the time if you had not gone shopping. So the cost of grocery shopping is the price paid for the goods plus the nonprice costs incurred.

Remember that many costs do not involve money but are still costs. Should I major in accounting or human resources? Should I go to college or university? Should I get an M.B.A. now or work and wait a few years to go back to school?

Policymakers are unavoidably faced with opportunity costs too. Consider airline safety. Both money costs and time costs affect airline safety. New airline safety devices cost money (luggage inspection devices, fuel tank safeguards, new radar equipment, and so on), and time costs are quite relevant with the new safety checks. Time waiting in line costs time that could be spent doing something that is valuable. New airline safety requirements could also actually cost lives. If the new safety equipment costs are passed on in the form of higher airline ticket prices, people may choose to travel by car, which is far more dangerous per kilometre than air travel is. Opportunity costs are everywhere!

The Opportunity Cost of Going to School or Having a Child

The average person often does not correctly consider opportunity costs when thinking about costs. For example, the opportunity cost of going to school is not just the direct expense of tuition and books; of course, those expenses do involve an opportunity cost, because the money used for books and tuition could be used for other things that you value. But what about the nonmoney costs? That is, going to school also includes the opportunity cost of your time. Specifically, the time spent going to school is time that could have been spent on a job earning, say, $30 000 a year. And how often do people consider the opportunity cost of raising a child to the age of 18? There are the direct costs: food, visits to the dentist, clothes, piano lessons, and so on. But there are also additional costs incurred in rearing a child. Consider the cost if one parent chooses to give up his or her job to stay at home: Then, the time spent in child-rearing is time that could have been used making money and pursuing a career.

WHY ARE "FREE" LUNCHES NOT FREE?

The expression *there's no such thing as a free lunch* clarifies the relationship between scarcity and opportunity cost. Suppose the school cafeteria is offering "free" lunches today. Although the lunch is free to you, is it really free from society's perspective? The answer is no, because some of society's scarce resources will have been used in the preparation of the lunch. The issue is whether the resources that went into creating that lunch could have been used to produce something else of value. Clearly, the scarce resources that went into the production of the lunch like the labour and materials (food-service workers, lettuce, meat, plows, tractors, fertilizer, and so forth) could have been used in other ways. They had an opportunity cost, and thus were not free. Whenever you hear the word "free"—free libraries, free admission, and so on—an alarm should go off in your head. Very few things are free in the sense that they use none of society's scarce resources. So what does a free lunch really mean? It is, technically speaking, a "subsidized" lunch—a lunch using society's scarce resources, but one for which you personally do not have to pay.

SECTION CHECK

- Scarcity means we all have to make choices.
- When we are forced to choose, we give up the next highest-valued alternative.
- Because the production of any good uses up some of society's resources, there is no such thing as a free lunch.

Marginal Thinking

- What do we mean by *marginal thinking*?
- What is the rule of rational choice?

WHAT DO WE MEAN BY *MARGINAL THINKING*?

Most choices involve how *much* of something to do, rather than whether or not to do something. It is not *whether* you eat, but *how much* you eat. Hopefully, the question is not *whether* to study this semester but instead *how much* to study this semester. For example, "If I studied a little more, I might be able to improve my grade," or "If I had a little better concentration when I was studying, I could improve my grade." This is what economists call **marginal thinking** because the focus is on the additional, or incremental, choices. Marginal choices involve the effects of adding to or subtracting from the current situation. In short, it is the small (or large) incremental changes to a plan of action.

marginal thinking
focusing on the additional, or incremental, choices

Always watch out for the difference between average and marginal costs. Suppose the cost to an airline of flying 250 passengers from Edmonton to Montreal was $100 000. The average cost per seat would be $400 (the total cost divided by the number of seats—$100 000/250). If ten people are on standby and willing to pay $300 for a seat on the flight, should the airline sell them a ticket? Yes! The unoccupied seats earn nothing for the airline. The airline pays the $400 average cost per seat regardless of whether or not someone is sitting in the seat. What the airline needs to focus on are the additional (marginal) costs of a few extra passengers. The marginal costs are minimal—slight wear and tear on the airplane, handling some extra baggage, and ten extra in-flight meals. In this case, thinking at the margin can increase total profits, even if it means selling at less than-average cost of production.

Another good example of marginal thinking is auctions. Prices are bid up marginally as the auctioneer calls out one price after another. When a bidder views the new price (the marginal cost) to be greater than the value she places on the good (the marginal benefit), she withdraws from further bidding.

WHAT IS THE RULE OF RATIONAL CHOICE?

In trying to make themselves better off, individuals will pursue an activity if the expected marginal benefits are greater than the expected marginal costs—this is the **rule of rational choice.** The term *expected* is used with marginal benefits and costs because the world is uncertain in many important respects, so the actual result of changing behaviour may not always make people better off—but on average it will. However, as a matter of rationality, people are assumed to engage only in behaviour that they think ahead of time will make them better off. That is, individuals will pursue an activity only if the expected marginal benefits are greater than the expected marginal costs, or $E(MB) > E(MC)$. This fairly unrestrictive and realistic view of individuals seeking self-betterment can be used to analyze a variety of social phenomena.

Suppose that you have to get up for an 8 A.M. class but have been up very late. When the alarm goes off at 7 A.M., you are weighing the marginal benefits and marginal costs of an extra 15 minutes of sleep. If you perceive the marginal benefits of 15 minutes of sleep to be greater than the marginal costs of those extra minutes, you may choose to hit the snooze button. Or perhaps you may decide to blow off class completely. But it's unlikely you will choose that action if it is the day of the final exam, because it is now likely that the **net benefits**—the difference between the expected marginal benefits and expected marginal costs—of skipping class have changed. When people have opportunities to better themselves, they usually take them. And they will continue to seek those opportunities as long as they expect a net benefit from doing so.

The rule of rational choice is simply the rule of being sensible, and most economists believe that individuals act *as if* they are sensible and apply the rule of rational choice to their daily lives. It is a rule that can help us understand our decision to study, walk, shop, exercise, clean house, cook, and perform just about every other action. It is also a rule that we will continue to use throughout the text because whether we are consumers, producers, or policymakers, we all must compare the expected marginal benefits and the expected marginal costs to determine the best level to consume, produce, or develop policies.

To help illustrate the concepts of marginal thinking and rational choice, consider the number of cakes a small neighbourhood bakery in suburban Vancouver can produce daily. The bakery employs three people. After performing a business analysis, we are able to determine the following daily production schedule: one employee, 25 cakes; two employees, 45 cakes; three employees, 60 cakes. What each employee can individually (or incrementally) produce represents that person's marginal benefit (*MB*)—these values are determined in the following table.

rule of rational choice
individuals will pursue an activity if the expected marginal benefits are greater than the expected marginal costs

net benefits
the difference between the expected marginal benefits and expected marginal costs

What would you be willing to give up to eliminate the rush-hour congestion you face? Think of the number of hours drivers waste each year sitting in traffic in Canada's largest cities. It costs the Canadian economy hundreds of millions of dollars a year in lost wages and wasted fuel.

Employees	Total Production	Marginal Benefit (*MB*)
0	0	
		25
1	25	
		20
2	45	
		15
3	60	

How the bakery pays its employees provides us with another illustration of marginal thinking. If each employee is paid $55 a day, this is the individual (or incremental) cost of each employee—interpreted as the marginal cost (*MC*) of each worker.

We can now use these two illustrations of marginal thinking to help determine whether the bakery has the right number of employees. If a cake sells for $3, the daily *MB* of each employee would be as follows: first employee $75 (25 cakes × $3); second employee $60 (20 cakes × $3); third employee $45 (15 cakes × $3). Based on this information, the first employee represents $20 of positive net benefit [$75(*MB*) − $55(*MC*) = $20 net benefit]; the second employee represents $5 of positive net benefit [$60(*MB*) − $55(*MC*) = $5 net benefit]; while the third employee represents $10 of negative net benefit [$45(*MB*) − $55(*MC*) = −$10 net benefit]. The rule of rational choice would indicate that the bakery should hire the first two employees, but not the third employee.

Zero Pollution Would Be Too Costly

Let's use the concept of marginal thinking to evaluate pollution levels. We all know the benefits of a cleaner environment, but what would we have to give up—that is, what marginal costs would we have to incur—in order to achieve zero pollution? A lot! You could not drive a car, fly in a plane, or even ride a bike, especially if everybody else was riding bikes too (because congestion is a form of pollution). How would you get to school or work, or go to the movies or the grocery store? Everyone would have to grow their own food because transporting, storing, and producing food uses machinery and equipment that pollutes. And even growing your own food would be a problem because many plants emit natural pollutants. We could go on and on. The

DEBATE

SHOULD ALL POLITICIANS HAVE A KNOWLEDGE OF ECONOMICS?

For:

We often hear that politics follows economics, rather than the other way around. In other words, economic problems lie at the root of almost all political decisions. The political decisions are needed because of the economic problems. It's a fact that many policy issues arise because of the scarcity of public funds, with politicians having to make decisions about how those funds are allocated. If we take as an example the rising costs of health care, especially as the population ages, should aging individuals all receive the best care available or only the best care that society can afford? Some would argue that decisions must be made for the greatest good for the most people. Others would argue that not all decisions should be based on what the majority wants. Politicians need to consider both real costs and opportunity costs. Are these not simply economic decisions? If politicians are making these important decisions, shouldn't we expect them all to have at least a basic knowledge of economics so that they can make informed decisions?

Against:

The politicians we elect have a broad range of experience. Suggesting that they should all have economic knowledge is unreasonable, but it would be reasonable for at least some of them to have some economic knowledge. Economic issues are often raised for consideration during public policy arguments. Economists can provide a basic understanding of positive, objective statements, but politicians are saddled with making normative decisions on those statements, which requires only common sense. The theory of common sense is based on the concept that people make rational choices when provided with all of the information, so one does not need to be an economist, just a rational being. Besides, if all of the different choices were considered by society in making decisions, decision making might become impossible or end up costing more than the solutions to the problems. An alternative is to simply get on with it and deal with the consequences if a decision turns out to have been imperfect. For that reason, would you agree that common sense is enough to make important policy decisions?

point is *not* that we shouldn't be concerned about the environment; rather, we have to weigh the expected marginal benefits of a cleaner environment against the expected marginal costs of a cleaner environment. This is not to say the environment should not be cleaner, only that zero pollution levels would be far too costly in terms of what we would have to give up.

Optimal (Best) Levels of Safety

Just as we can have optimal (or best) levels of pollution that are greater than zero, it is also true for crime and safety. Take crime. What would it cost society to have zero crime? It would be prohibitively costly to divert a tremendous amount of our valuable resources toward the total elimination of crime. In fact, it would be impossible to eliminate crime totally. But it would also be costly to reduce crime significantly. Since lower crime rates are costly, society must decide how much it is willing to give up: The additional resources for crime prevention can come only from limited resources, which could be used to produce something else possibly valued even more.

The same is true for safer products. Nobody wants defective tires on their cars, or cars that are unsafe and roll over at low speeds. However, there are optimal amounts of safety that are greater than zero too. The issue is not safe versus unsafe products but rather *how much* safety consumers want. It is not risk versus no risk but rather *how much* risk are we willing to take? Additional safety can come only at higher costs. To make all products perfectly safe would be impossible, so we must weigh the benefits and costs of safer products. In fact, according to one U.S. study by Sam Peltzman, a University of Chicago economist, additional safety features in cars (mandatory safety belts, padded dashboards) in the late 1960s may have had little impact on highway fatalities. Peltzman found that making cars safer led to more reckless driving and more accidents. Although the safety regulations did result in fewer deaths per automobile accident, the total number of deaths remained unchanged because there were more accidents.

Reckless driving has benefits—getting somewhere more quickly—but it also has costs—possibly causing an accident or even a fatality. Rational people will compare the marginal benefits and marginal costs of safer driving and make the choices that they believe will get them to their destination safely. We would expect that even thrill-seekers would slow down if there were higher fines and/or increased law enforcement. It would change the benefit–cost equation for reckless driving (as would bad brakes, bald tires, and poor visibility). On the other hand, compulsory seat belts and air bags might cause motorists to drive more recklessly.

SECTION CHECK

- Economists are usually interested in the effects of additional, or marginal, changes in a given situation.
- The rule of rational choice states that individuals will pursue an activity if they expect the marginal benefits to be greater than the marginal costs, or $E(MB) > E(MC)$.

Incentives Matter

■ Can we predict how people will respond to changes in incentives?
■ What are positive and negative incentives?

CAN WE PREDICT HOW PEOPLE WILL RESPOND TO CHANGES IN INCENTIVES?

In acting rationally, people are responding to incentives. That is, they are reacting to the changes in expected marginal benefits and expected marginal costs. In fact, much of human behaviour can be explained and predicted as a response to incentives. Consider the economic view of crime. Why do criminals engage in their "occupation"? Presumably because the "job," even with its risks, is preferred to alternative forms of employment. For criminals, the benefits of their actions are higher and/or the opportunity costs of them are lower than is the case for noncriminals. In some cases, criminals cannot get a legitimate job at a wage they would find acceptable, so the cost of crime in terms of other income forgone may be quite low. At other times, the likelihood of being caught is small, so the expected cost is negligible. Also, for some, the moral cost of a crime is low, whereas for others it is high. The benefits, in terms of wealth gained, are clear. If the expected gains or benefits from committing a crime outweigh the expected costs, the activity is pursued. For most policy purposes, the primary concern is not what causes the level of crime to be what it is but, rather, what causes the level of crime to change. Changes in the crime rate can be largely explained in terms of such a benefit–cost framework. If the benefits of crime rise, say, in the form of larger real "hauls," and/or if the costs fall due to a reduced likelihood of being caught or of being imprisoned if caught, then economists would expect the amount of crime to rise. Likewise, economists would expect the crime rate to fall in response to increased police enforcement, stiffer punishments, or an increase in the employment rate. Whether this analysis tells the complete story is debatable, but use of the economic framework in thinking about the problem provides valuable insight.

WHAT ARE POSITIVE AND NEGATIVE INCENTIVES?

positive incentives
incentives that either reduce costs or increase benefits, resulting in an increase in the activity or behaviour

negative incentives
incentives that either increase costs or reduce benefits, resulting in a decrease in the activity or behaviour

Almost all of economics can be reduced to incentive [$E(MB)$ versus $E(MC)$] stories, where consumers and producers are driven by incentives that affect expected costs or benefits. Prices, wages, profits, taxes, and subsidies are all examples of economic incentives. Incentives can be classified into two types: positive and negative. **Positive incentives** are those that either increase benefits or reduce costs and thus result in an increased level of the related activity or behaviour. **Negative incentives,** on the other hand, either reduce benefits or increase costs, resulting in a decreased level of the related activity or behaviour. For example, a tax on cars that emit lots of pollution (an increase in costs) would be a negative incentive that would lead to a reduction in emitted pollution. On the other hand, a subsidy (the opposite of a tax) for hybrid cars—part electric, part internal combustion—would be a positive incentive that would encourage greater production and consumption of hybrid cars. Human behaviour is influenced in predictable ways by such changes in economic incentives, and economists use this information to predict what will happen when the benefits and costs of any choice are changed. In short, economists study the incentives and consequences of particular actions.

Darren Brode/Shutterstock.com

A subsidy for hybrid electric vehicles (HEVs) would be a positive incentive that would encourage greater production and consumption of these vehicles. The Toyota Prius *c* is a fuel economy champion, going more than 1000 kilometres on a single tank of gas. The Ford Fusion Hybrid goes about 850 kilometres on a tank of gas.

SECTION CHECK

- People respond to incentives in predictable ways.
- A positive incentive decreases costs or increases benefits, thus encouraging consumption or production, while a negative incentive increases costs or reduces benefits, thus discouraging consumption or production.

Specialization and Trade

- Why do people specialize?
- How do specialization and trade lead to greater wealth and prosperity?

WHY DO PEOPLE SPECIALIZE?

As you look around, you can see that people specialize in what they produce. They tend to dedicate their resources to one primary activity, whether it be child-rearing, driving a bus, or making bagels. Why is this? The answer, short and simple, is opportunity costs. By concentrating on the production of one, or a few, goods, individuals are **specializing.** This allows them to make the best use of (and thus gain the most benefit from) their limited resources. A person, a region, or a country can gain by specializing in the production of the good or service in which they have a comparative advantage. That is, if they can produce a good or service at a lower opportunity cost than others, we say that they have a **comparative advantage** in the production of that good or service.

specializing
concentrating on the production of one, or a few, goods

comparative advantage
occurs when a person or a country can produce a good or service at a lower opportunity cost than others can

For example, should a lawyer who types 100 words per minute hire an administrative assistant to type her legal documents if the assistant can type only 50 words per minute? The answer to this question depends on the particular comparative advantages of the lawyer and the administrative assistant. Consider a job that would take the lawyer five hours and the administrative assistant ten hours to complete. If the lawyer makes $100 an hour, and the administrative assistant earns $10 an hour, who has the comparative advantage?

If the lawyer types her own documents, it will cost $500 ($100 per hour × 5 hours). If she has the administrative assistant type her documents, it will cost $100 ($10 per hour × 10 hours). Clearly, then, the lawyer should hire the administrative assistant to type her documents because the administrative assistant has the comparative advantage (lower opportunity cost) in this case, despite being half as good in absolute terms.

We All Specialize

We all specialize to some extent and rely on others to produce most of the goods and services we want. The work that we choose to do reflects our specialization. For example, we may specialize in selling or fixing automobiles. The wages from that work can then be used to buy goods from a farmer who has chosen to specialize in the production of food. Likewise, the farmer can use the money earned from selling his produce to get his tractor fixed by someone who specializes in that activity.

Specialization is evident not only among individuals but among regions and countries as well. In fact, the story of the economic development of Canada involves specialization. Within Canada, the prairies with their wheat, the Maritime provinces of eastern Canada with their fishing fleets, and British Columbia with its lumber are all examples of regional specialization.

The Advantages of Specialization

In a small business, employees may perform a wide variety of tasks—from hiring to word processing to marketing. As the size of the company increases, each employee can perform a more specialized job, with a consequent increase in output per worker. The primary advantages of specialization are that employees acquire greater skill from repetition, they avoid wasted time in shifting from one task to another, and they do the types of work for which they are best suited. Specialization also promotes the use of specialized equipment for specialized tasks.

The advantages of specialization are seen throughout the workplace. For example, in larger firms, specialists conduct personnel relations and accounting is in the hands of full-time accountants; such jobs are too critical in large firms to be done by someone with half a dozen other tasks to perform. The owner of a small retail store selects the location for the store primarily through guesswork, placing it where she believes sales will be high or where an empty, low-rent building is available. In contrast, larger chains have store sites selected by experts who have experience in analyzing the factors that make different locations relatively more desirable, like traffic patterns, income levels, demographics, and so on.

HOW DO SPECIALIZATION AND TRADE LEAD TO GREATER WEALTH AND PROSPERITY?

Trade, or voluntary exchange, directly increases wealth by making both parties better off (or they wouldn't trade). It is the prospect of wealth-increasing exchange that leads to productive specialization. That is, trade increases wealth by allowing a person, a region, or a nation to specialize in those products that it produces at a lower opportunity cost and to trade for those products that others produce at a lower opportunity cost. That is, we trade with others because it frees up time and resources to do other things that we do better. For example, say Canada is better at producing wheat than Brazil, and Brazil is better at producing coffee than Canada. Canada and Brazil would each benefit if Canada produces wheat and trades some of it to Brazil for coffee. Coffee growers in Canada could grow coffee in expensive greenhouses, but it would result in higher coffee costs and prices, while leaving fewer resources available for employment in more productive jobs, such as wheat production. This is true for individuals, too. Imagine Tom had 10 kilograms of tea and Katherine had 10 kilograms of coffee. However, Tom preferred coffee to tea and Katherine preferred tea to coffee. So if Tom traded his tea to Katherine for her coffee, both parties would be better off. Trade simply reallocates existing goods, and voluntary exchange increases wealth by making both parties better off, or they would not agree to trade.

In short, if we divide the tasks and produce what we do *relatively* best and trade for the rest, we will be better off than if we were self-sufficient—that is, without trade. Imagine life without trade, where you were completely self-sufficient—growing your own food, making your own clothes, working on your own car, building your own house. Do you think you would be better off?

SECTION CHECK

- Specialization is important for individuals, businesses, regions, and nations. It allows them to make the best use of their limited resources.
- Specialization and trade increase wealth by allowing a person, a region, or a nation to specialize in those products that it produces at a lower opportunity cost and to trade for those products that others produce at a lower opportunity cost.

The Three Economic Questions Every Society Faces

- What is to be produced?
- How are the goods and services to be produced?
- Who will get the goods and services?

Collectively, our wants far outstrip what can be produced from nature's scarce resources. So how should we allocate those scarce resources? Some methods of resource allocation might seem bad and counterproductive, like the "survival of the fittest" competition that exists in the jungle. Physical violence has been used since the beginning of time, as people, regions, and countries attack one another to gain control over resources. One might argue that governments should allocate scarce resources on the basis of equal shares or according to need. However, this approach poses problems because of diverse individual preferences, the problem of ascertaining needs, and the negative work and investment incentives involved. In reality, society is made up of many approaches to resource allocation. For now, we will focus on one form of allocating goods and services found in most countries—the market system.

Because of scarcity, certain economic questions must be answered, regardless of the level of affluence of the society or its political structure. We will consider three fundamental questions that inevitably must be faced: (1) What is to be produced? (2) How are the goods and services to be produced? (3) Who will get the goods and services? These questions are unavoidable in a world of scarcity.

WHAT IS TO BE PRODUCED?

How do individuals control production decisions in market-oriented economies? Questions arise such as "Should we produce lots of cars and just a few school buildings, or relatively few cars and more school buildings?" The answer to this and other such questions is called **consumer sovereignty**—how consumers vote on economic affairs with their dollars (or pounds or yen) in a market economy. Consumer sovereignty explains how individual consumers in market economies determine what is to be produced. High-definition televisions, digital cameras, cellphones, digital video recorders (DVRs), iPods, and tablets, for example, became part of our lives because consumers "voted" hundreds of dollars apiece on these goods. As they bought more plasma TVs, consumers "voted" fewer dollars for tube TVs. Similarly, CDs gave way to downloadable music as consumers voted for these items with their dollars. As consumers vote for more fuel-efficient cars and healthier foods, firms that want to remain profitable must listen and respond.

consumer sovereignty
consumers vote on economic affairs with their dollars in a market economy

How Different Types of Economic Systems Answer the Question "What Is to Be Produced?"

Economies are organized in different ways to answer the question of what is to be produced. The dispute over the best way to answer this question has inflamed passions for centuries. Should central planning boards make the decisions, as in China and North Korea? In **command economies,** the government uses central planning to coordinate most economic activities. Under this type of regime, decisions about how many tractors or automobiles to produce are largely determined by a government official or committee associated with the central planning organization. That same group decides on the number and size of school buildings, refrigerators, shoes, and so on. Other countries—including Canada, the United States, much of Europe, and, increasingly, Asia and elsewhere—have largely adopted a decentralized decision-making process in which literally millions of individual producers and consumers of goods and services determine what goods, and how many of them, will be produced. An economy that allocates goods and services through the private decisions of consumers, input suppliers, and firms is often referred to as a **market economy.** Actually, no nation has a pure market economy. Most countries, including Canada, are said to have a **mixed economy.** In such economies, the government and the private sector together determine the allocation of resources.

command economy
the government uses central planning to coordinate most economic activities

market economy
goods and services are allocated based on the private decisions of consumers, input suppliers, and firms

mixed economy
government and the private sector together determine the allocation of resources

HOW ARE THE GOODS AND SERVICES TO BE PRODUCED?

Because of scarcity, all economies, regardless of their political structure, must decide how to produce the goods and services that they want. Goods and services can generally be produced in several ways. For example, a ditch can be dug by many workers using their hands, by a few workers with shovels, or by one person with a backhoe. Someone must decide which method is most appropriate. The larger the quantity of the good and the more elaborate the form of capital, the more labour that is saved and is thus made available for other uses. (Remember, goods like shovels and large earth-moving machines used to produce goods and services are called *capital*.) From this example, you might be tempted to conclude that it is desirable to use the biggest, most elaborate form of capital. But would you really want to plant your spring flowers with huge earth-moving machinery? That is, the most capital-intensive method of production might not always be the best. The best method is the least-cost method.

The Best Form of Production

The best or "optimal" form of production will usually vary from one economy to the next. For example, earth-moving machinery is used to dig large ditches in Canada, the United States, and Europe, whereas in developing countries, such as India, China, or Pakistan, shovels are often used. Similarly, a person in Canada might use a power lawn mower to cut the grass, whereas in a developing country, a hand mower might be used or grass might not be cut at all. Why do these "optimal" forms of production vary so drastically? Compared to capital, labour is relatively cheap and plentiful in developing countries but relatively scarce and expensive in Canada. In contrast, capital (machines and tools, mainly) is comparatively plentiful and cheap in Canada but scarcer and more costly in developing countries. That is, in developing countries, production would tend to be more **labour-intensive**, using a large amount of labour. In Canada, production would tend to be more **capital-intensive**, using a large amount of capital. Each nation tends to use the production processes that conserve its relatively scarce (and thus relatively more expensive) resources and use more of its relatively abundant resources.

labour-intensive
production that uses a large amount of labour

capital-intensive
production that uses a large amount of capital

Sidney Crosby gets paid a lot of money because he controls a scarce resource: his talent and name recognition. As we will see in later chapters, people's talents and other goods and services in limited supply relative to demand will command high prices.

WHO WILL GET THE GOODS AND SERVICES?

In every society, some mechanism must exist to determine how goods and services are to be distributed among the population. Who gets what? Why are some people able to consume or use far more goods and services than others? This question of distribution is so important that wars and revolutions have been fought over it. Both the French and Russian revolutions were concerned fundamentally with the distribution of goods and services. Even in societies where political questions are usually settled peacefully, the question of the distribution of income is an issue that always arouses strong emotional responses. As we will see, in a market economy with private ownership and control of the means of production, the amount of goods and services one is able to obtain depends on one's income, which in turn depends on the quantity and quality of the scarce resources that the individual controls. For example, Sidney Crosby makes a lot of money because he has unique and marketable skills as a hockey player.

To say that this may or may not be "fair" is an opinion at the centre of the *efficiency* versus *equity* dilemma in economics. As an economy, do you focus on getting the most you can from your scarce resources (efficiency) or should the emphasis be on equally distributing the benefits of those resources to all (equity)? Some economists

Bruce Bennett/Getty Images Sport/Thinkstock

believe that individual freedom and choice are central to economic well-being. When limitations are placed on these individual freedoms, these economists believe that economic efficiency will suffer. On the other hand, some economists are concerned with the economic inequalities and unfairness created by production and distribution. For example, to these economists, government intervention is a valuable tool in making society more equitable. Regardless of which side of the debate is chosen, one truth is certain: Decisions regarding the three economic questions raised in this section play a central role in shaping the efficiency and equity of an economy.

SECTION CHECK

- Every economy has to decide what to produce. In a decentralized market economy, millions of buyers and sellers determine what and how much to produce. In a mixed economy, the government and the private sector determine the allocation of resources.
- The best form of production is the one that conserves the relatively scarce (more costly) resources and uses more of the abundant (less costly) resources. When capital is relatively scarce and labour is plentiful, production tends to be labour-intensive. When capital is relatively abundant and labour is relatively scarce, production tends to be capital-intensive.
- In a market economy, the amount of goods and services one is able to obtain depends on one's income. The amount of one's income depends on the quantity and the quality of the scarce resources that the individual controls.

For Your Review

Section 1.1

1. Write your own definition of *economics*. What are the main elements of the definition?

2. Would the following topics be covered in microeconomics or macroeconomics?

   a. the effects of an increase in the supply of lumber on the home-building industry

   b. changes in the national unemployment rate

   c. the effect of interest rates on the machine-tool industry

   d. the effect of interest rates on the demand for investment goods

   e. the way a firm maximizes profits

Section 1.2

3. Are the following statements normative or positive, or do they contain both normative and positive statements?

   a. A higher income tax rate would generate increased tax revenues. Those extra revenues should be used to give more government aid to the poor.

   b. The study of physics is more valuable than the study of sociology, but both should be studied by all postsecondary students.

   c. An increase in the price of wheat will decrease the amount of wheat purchased. However, it will increase the amount of wheat supplied to the market.

   d. A decrease in the price of butter will increase the amount of butter purchased, but that would be bad because it would increase Canadians' cholesterol levels.

   e. The birth rate is reduced as economies urbanize, but that also leads to an increased average age of developing countries' populations.

4. Which of the following economic statements are positive and which are normative?

   a. A tax increase will increase unemployment.

   b. The government should reduce funding for social assistance programs.

   c. Tariffs on imported wine will lead to higher prices for domestic wine.

   d. A decrease in the capital gains tax rate will increase investment.

   e. Goods purchased on the Internet should be subject to provincial sales taxes.

   f. A reduction in interest rates will cause inflation.

5. The following statement represents which fallacy in thinking? Explain why.

   "I earn \$12 per hour. If I am able to earn \$12 per hour, everyone should be able to find work for at least that wage rate."

6. Do any of the following statements involve fallacies? If so, which ones do they involve?

   a. Because sitting in the back of classrooms is correlated with getting lower grades in the class, students should always sit closer to the front of the classroom.

   b. Historically, the stock market rises in years the NFC team wins the Super Bowl and falls when the AFC wins the Super Bowl. I am rooting for the NFC team to win for the sake of my investment portfolio.

   c. When a hockey team spends more to get better players, it is more successful, which proves that all the teams should spend more to get better players.

   d. Gasoline prices were higher last year than in 1970, yet people purchased more gas, which contradicts the law of demand.

   e. An increase in the amount of money I have will make me better off, but an increase in the supply of money in the economy will not make Canadians as a group better off.

Section 1.3

7. Explain the difference between poverty and scarcity.

8. The automotive revolution after World War II reduced the time involved for travel and shipping goods. This innovation allowed the Canadian economy to produce more goods and services since it freed resources involved in transportation for other uses. The transportation revolution also increased wants. Identify two ways in which vehicle manufacturers evoked new wants.

9. Which of the following goods are scarce?

   a. garbage

   b. salt water in the ocean

   c. clothes

   d. clean air in a big city

   e. dirty air in a big city

   f. public libraries

Section 1.4

10. The price of a one-way bus trip from Toronto to Ottawa is $150. Sarah, a school-teacher, pays the same price in February (during the school year) as in July (during her vacation), so the cost is the same in February as in July. Do you agree?

11. You work as a tutor at your school, making $15 per hour. Yesterday, you decided to cancel your two-hour tutoring appointment in order to meet friends for a coffee. The coffee cost you $3.50. What was the opportunity cost of this decision in dollars?

12. Pizza Pizza once ran a promotion that whenever the Ottawa Senators scored six goals or more, Pizza Pizza gave everyone with a ticket to that day's game a free slice of pizza. If holders of ticket stubs have to stand in line for ten minutes, is the slice of pizza really "free"?

13. List the opportunity costs of the following:

    a. going to college or university

    b. missing a lecture

    c. withdrawing and spending $100 from your savings account, which earns 5 percent interest annually

    d. going snowboarding on the weekend before final examinations

Blueprint Problem

Assume that the total benefits (in terms of increased sales) to Paula from hiring additional employees are represented by the following schedule: 1 employee, $40/day; 2 employees, $70/day; 3 employees, $90/day; 4 employees, $100/day.

    a. Calculate the marginal benefit (*MB*) of each employee.

    b. Suppose Paula pays her employees $25/day. How many employees would she be willing to hire?

Blueprint Solution

Number of Employees	Total Daily Benefit
1	$40
2	70
3	90
4	100

This problem is better understood if it is presented in a table.

a.

1 Number of employees	2 Total Daily Benefit	3 Marginal Daily Benefit of Each Employee (*MB*)
0	0	
1	40	40
2	70	30
3	90	20
4	100	10

The above table presents the total benefit of having a certain number of employees. To determine the marginal benefit, calculate the incremental benefit resulting from the addition of each employee. The third column displays the marginal benefit (*MB*) of each employee.

b.

Number of employees	*MB*	*MC*	Net Benefit	Hiring Decision
1	$40	$25	$15	Hire
2	30	25	5	Hire
3	20	25	−5	Do not hire
4	10	25	−5	Do not hire

This question involves using the rule of rational choice. The determination of the Marginal Cost (*MC*) is based on the assumption that Paula pays all of her employees the same daily wage of $25.

Paula will hire only those employees who offer her business positive net benefit, that is $E(MB) > E(MC)$. The determination of net benefit provides the rationale for the hiring decision.

Section 1.5

14. Assume the total benefits to Mark from trips to a local amusement park during the year are given by the following schedule: 1 trip, $60; 2 trips, $115; 3 trips, $165; 4 trips, $200; 5 trips, $225; 6 or more trips, $240.

    a. What is Mark's marginal benefit of the third trip? The fifth trip?

    b. If the admission price to the amusement park was $45 per day, how many times would Mark be willing and able to go in a year? What if the price was $20 per day? Explain.

    c. If the amusement park offered a year-long pass for $200 rather than a per-day admission price, would Mark be willing to buy one? If so, how many times would he go? Explain.

15. Assume the total cost of producing widgets was $4200 for 42 units; $4257 for 43 units; $4332 for 44 units; and $4420 for 45 units.

    a. What is the marginal cost of producing the 43rd unit? The 45th unit?

    b. If the widget producer could sell at $60 per unit however many he could produce, how many would he choose to produce? If he could sell at $80 per unit however many he could produce? Explain.

16. Imagine that you are trying to decide whether to cross a street without using the designated crosswalk at the traffic signal. What are the expected marginal benefits of crossing? What are the expected marginal costs? How would the following conditions change your benefit–cost equation?

    a. The street was busy.

    b. The street was empty and it was 3:00 A.M.

    c. You were in a huge hurry.

    d. There was a police officer 10 metres away.

    e. The closest crosswalk was 1 kilometre away.

    f. The closest crosswalk was 5 metres away.

Section 1.6

17. Which of the following are positive incentives? Negative incentives? Why?

    a. a fine for not cleaning up after your dog defecates in the park

    b. a trip to Hawaii paid for by your parents or significant other for earning an A in your economics course

    c. a higher tax on cigarettes and alcohol

    d. a subsidy for installing solar panels on your house

18. The penalty for drug trafficking in Singapore is death. Do you think there would be more drug traffickers in Singapore if the mandatory sentence was five years, with parole for good behaviour?

19. Under China's family planning laws (commonly referred to as its *one-child policy*), those who follow the policy are offered rewards, loans, and other forms of social assistance, depending on socioeconomic status. People who do not comply with the policy are subject to penalties such as fines and confiscation of personal property. Excess children may also be subject to educational and health sanctions. What behaviour is the Chinese government attempting to promote with these types of incentives? Identify which aspects of the law are negative incentives and which are positive incentives.

Section 1.7

20. Throughout history, many countries have chosen the path of autarky, choosing to not trade with other countries. Explain why this path would make a country poorer.

21. Farmer Fran can grow soybeans and corn. She can grow 1500 kilograms of soybeans or 3000 kilograms of corn on a hectare of her land for the same cost. The price of soybeans is $1.50 per kilogram and the price of corn is $0.60 per kilogram. Show the benefits to Fran of specialization. What should she specialize in?

22. Which region has a comparative advantage in the following goods?

    a. wheat: Colombia or Canada

    b. coffee: Colombia or Canada

    c. lumber: Alberta or British Columbia

    d. oil: Alberta or British Columbia

23. a. Why is it important that the country or region with the lower opportunity cost produce the good?

    b. How would you use the concept of comparative advantage to argue for reducing restrictions on trade between countries?

Section 1.8

24. What are the three basic economic questions? How are decisions made differently in a market economy than in command economies?

25. Recently, the American Film Institute selected *Citizen Kane* as the best movie of all time. *Citizen Kane* is a fictional psychological biography of one of the most powerful newspaper publishers in history, William Randolph Hearst. *Titanic*, an epic romance about the sinking of the *Titanic*, has made the most money of any film in history. Unlike *Titanic*, *Citizen Kane* was not a box office success. Do you think Hollywood will make more movies like *Titanic* or more like *Citizen Kane*? Why?

26. Adam was a university graduate with a double major in economics and art. A few years ago, Adam decided that he wanted to pursue a vocation that utilized both of his talents. In response, he shut himself up in his studio and created a watercolour collection, "Graphs of Famous Recessions." With high hopes, Adam put his collection on display for buyers. After several years of displaying his econ art, however, the only one interested in the collection was his eight-year-old sister, who wanted the picture frames for her room. Recognizing that Adam was having trouble pursuing his chosen occupation, Adam's friend Karl told him that the market had failed. What do you think? Is Karl right?

Appendix

GRAPHS ARE AN IMPORTANT ECONOMIC TOOL

Sometimes the use of visual aids, such as graphs, greatly enhances our understanding of a theory. It is much the same as finding your way to a friend's house with the aid of a map rather than with detailed verbal or written instructions. Graphs are important tools for economists. They allow us to understand better the workings of the economy. To economists, a graph can be worth a thousand words. This text will use graphs throughout to enhance the understanding of important economic relationships. This appendix provides a guide on how to read and create your own graphs.

The most useful graph for our purposes is one that merely connects a vertical line (the **Y-axis**) with a horizontal line (the **X-axis**), as seen in Exhibit 1. The intersection of the two lines occurs at the origin, which is where the value of both variables is equal to zero. In Exhibit 1, the graph has four quadrants or "boxes." In this textbook we will be primarily concerned with the shaded box in the upper right-hand corner. This portion of the graph deals exclusively with positive numbers. Always keep in mind that moving to the right on the horizontal axis and up along the vertical axis each lead to higher values.

Y-axis
the vertical axis on a graph

X-axis
the horizontal axis on a graph

pie chart
a circle subdivided into proportionate slices that represent various quantities that add up to 100 percent

bar graph
represents data using vertical bars rising from the horizontal axis

time-series graph
shows changes in the value of a variable over time

appendix
Exhibit 1   Plotting a Graph

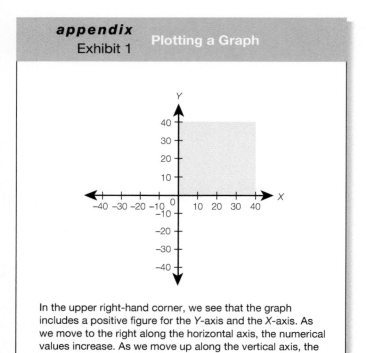

In the upper right-hand corner, we see that the graph includes a positive figure for the Y-axis and the X-axis. As we move to the right along the horizontal axis, the numerical values increase. As we move up along the vertical axis, the numerical values increase.

USING GRAPHS AND CHARTS

Exhibit 2 presents three common types of graphs. A **pie chart** is a circle subdivided into proportionate slices that represent various quantities that add up to 100 percent. The pie chart in Exhibit 2(a) shows what college students earn. That is, each slice in the pie chart represents the percentage of college students in a particular earnings category.

A **bar graph** represents data using vertical bars rising from the horizontal axis. Exhibit 2(b) is a bar graph that shows the sales of wireless phone service by province for a new company that has just entered the Canadian market. The height of the line represents sales in millions of dollars. Bar graphs are used to show a comparison of the sizes of quantities of similar items.

Exhibit 2(c) is a **time-series graph.** This type of graph shows changes in the value of a variable over time. This is a visual tool that allows us to observe important trends over a certain time period. In Exhibit 2(c) we see a graph that shows trends in the stock price of the company Fly-by-Chance for the period January to December. The horizontal axis shows us the passage of time, and the vertical axis shows us the stock price in dollars per share.

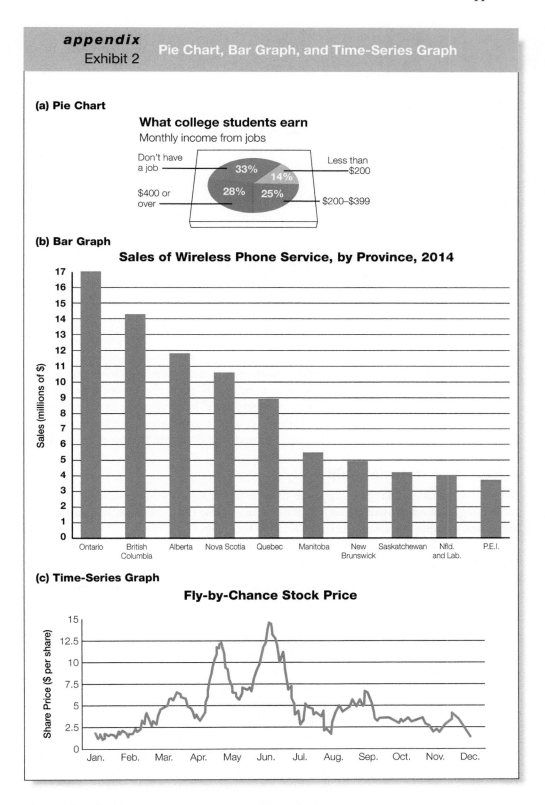

appendix
Exhibit 2   Pie Chart, Bar Graph, and Time-Series Graph

(a) Pie Chart

What college students earn
Monthly income from jobs

Don't have a job — 33%
Less than $200 — 14%
$400 or over — 28%
25% — $200–$399

(b) Bar Graph

Sales of Wireless Phone Service, by Province, 2014

Sales (millions of $)

Ontario, British Columbia, Alberta, Nova Scotia, Quebec, Manitoba, New Brunswick, Saskatchewan, Nfld. and Lab., P.E.I.

(c) Time-Series Graph

Fly-by-Chance Stock Price

Share Price ($ per share)

Jan. Feb. Mar. Apr. May Jun. Jul. Aug. Sep. Oct. Nov. Dec.

USING GRAPHS TO SHOW THE RELATIONSHIP BETWEEN TWO VARIABLES

Although the graphs and chart in Exhibit 2 are important, they do not allow us to show the relationship between two variables (a **variable** is something that is measured by a number, such as your height). To more closely examine the structure and functions of graphs, let us

variable
something that is measured by a number, such as your height

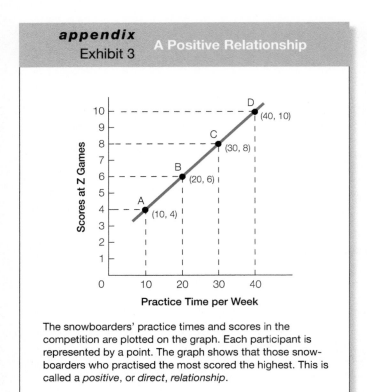

appendix
Exhibit 3   A Positive Relationship

The snowboarders' practice times and scores in the competition are plotted on the graph. Each participant is represented by a point. The graph shows that those snowboarders who practised the most scored the highest. This is called a *positive*, or *direct*, *relationship*.

positive relationship
when two variables change in the same direction

negative relationship
when two variables change in opposite directions

consider the story of Katherine, an avid snowboarder who has aspirations of winning the Z Games next year. To get there, however, she will have to put in many hours of practice. But how many hours? In search of information about the practice habits of other snowboarders, she logged onto the Internet, where she pulled up the results of a study conducted by ESPM 3 that indicated the score of each Z Games competitor and the amount of practice time per week spent by each snowboarder. The results of this study (see Exhibit 3) indicated that snowboarders had to practise 10 hours per week to receive a score of 4.0, 20 hours per week to receive a score of 6.0, 30 hours per week to get a score of 8.0, and 40 hours per week to get a perfect score of 10. What does this information tell Katherine? By using a graph, she can more clearly understand the relationship between practice time and overall score.

A Positive Relationship

The study on scores and practice times revealed what is called a direct relationship, also called a *positive relationship*. A **positive relationship** means that the variables change in the same direction. That is, an increase in one variable (practice time) is accompanied by an increase in the other variable (overall score), or a decrease in one variable (practice time) is accompanied by a decrease in the other variable (overall score). In short, the variables change in the same direction.

A Negative Relationship

When two variables change in opposite directions, we say they are inversely related, or have a **negative relationship.** That is, when one variable rises, the other variable falls, or when one variable decreases, the other variable increases.

Variables That Have a Maximum or a Minimum

Many relationships described in economic models have maximum or minimum values. For example, firms are always looking to make the maximum possible profits; one way they can achieve this is by minimizing their costs. Exhibits 4 and 5 show relationships that have maximum and minimum values.

Exhibit 4 shows the first case—a relationship that begins positive, reaches a maximum, and then ends with a negative relationship. This example of the relationship between tax rates and tax revenue shows what economists refer to as the *Laffer curve*. When the tax rate is zero, the government receives no tax revenue. As the tax rate rises, tax revenue increases because the government receives a larger percentage of people's incomes. In the exhibit, a tax rate of 50 percent generates the maximum tax revenue of $15 million. As the tax rate continues to rise, it may be the case that the incentive to earn more income begins to decline, causing tax revenue to fall. If the tax rate was increased to 100 percent, there would be no incentive to earn income because it would all be taxed away; as a result, no tax revenue would be generated.

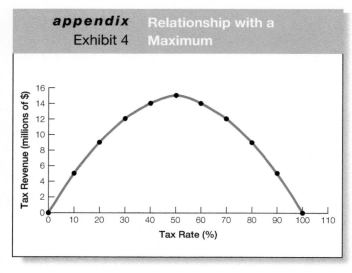

appendix
Exhibit 4   Relationship with a Maximum

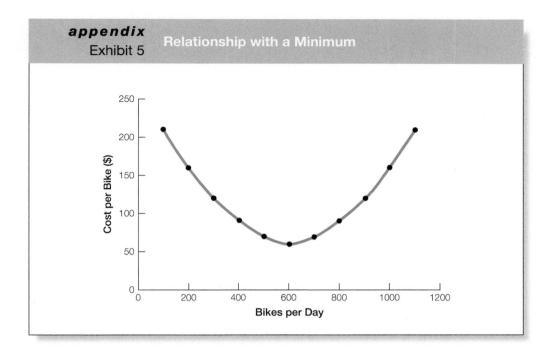

Exhibit 5 illustrates the opposite case—a relationship that begins negative, reaches a minimum, and then returns positive. Most economic costs are seen as following this relationship. As a bicycle manufacturer increases its output, per bike costs of production begin to fall, perhaps as workers develop special skills and the benefits of teamwork emerge. At a level of 600 bikes per day, the cost per bike is minimized at $60 per bike. However, as production is increased beyond 600 bikes per day, the cost per bike begins to rise, perhaps as the bike factory is forced to operate beyond its efficient capacity.

Variables That Are Not Related

There are still other situations in economics in which the change in one variable has no impact on the value of another variable. Exhibit 6 provides a graphical depiction of a curious relationship—a student's grade in economics and the lunar cycle. Since a

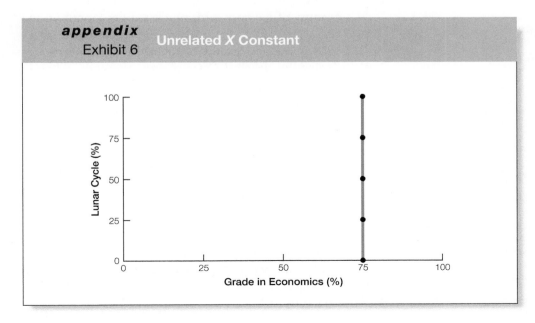

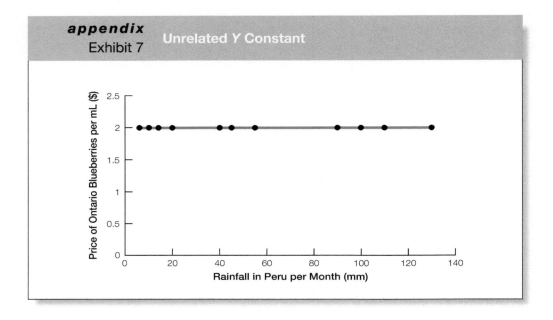

appendix
Exhibit 7   **Unrelated Y Constant**

student's grade in economics is not affected by the lunar cycle, no relationship exists. If a student grade of 75 percent is plotted on the horizontal axis, with the lunar cycle plotted on the vertical axis, the curve is vertical.

Exhibit 7 illustrates another curious relationship—the price of blueberries grown in Ontario and the average rainfall in Peru. Since the price of blueberries grown in Ontario, plotted on the vertical axis, does not vary with the monthly rainfall in Peru, plotted on the horizontal axis, the curve is horizontal.

appendix
Exhibit 8   **A Negative Relationship**

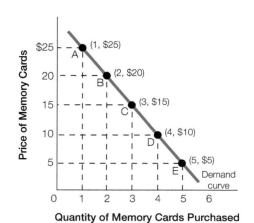

The downward slope of the curve means that price and quantity purchased are inversely, or negatively, related: when one increases, the other decreases. That is, moving down along the demand curve from point A to point E, we see that as price falls, the quantity purchased increases. Moving up along the demand curve from point E to point A, we see that as the price increases, the quantity purchased falls.

THE GRAPH OF A DEMAND CURVE

One of the most important graphs in all of economics is the demand curve. In Exhibit 8, we see Emily's individual demand curve for digital camera memory cards. It shows the price of memory cards on the vertical axis and the quantity of memory cards purchased per month on the horizontal axis. Every point in the space shown represents a price and quantity combination. The downward-sloping line, labelled *Demand curve*, shows the different combinations of price and quantity purchased. Note that the higher you go on the vertical (price) axis, the smaller the quantity purchased on the horizontal (quantity) axis, and the lower the price on the vertical axis, the greater the quantity purchased.

In Exhibit 8, we see that moving up the vertical price axis from the origin, the price of memory cards increases from $5 to $25 in increments of $5. Moving out along the horizontal quantity axis, the quantity purchased increases from zero to five memory cards per month. Point A represents a price of $25 and a quantity of one memory card, point B represents a price of $20 and a quantity of two memory cards, point C, $15 and a quantity of three memory cards, and so on. When we

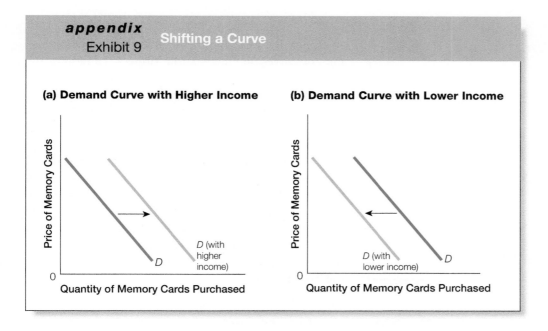

appendix
Exhibit 9   Shifting a Curve

(a) Demand Curve with Higher Income

Price of Memory Cards

D (with higher income)

D

0

Quantity of Memory Cards Purchased

(b) Demand Curve with Lower Income

Price of Memory Cards

D (with lower income)

D

0

Quantity of Memory Cards Purchased

connect all the points, we have what economists call a *curve*. As you can see, curves are sometimes drawn as straight lines for ease of illustration. Moving down along the curve, we see that as the price falls, a greater quantity is demanded; moving up the curve to higher prices, a smaller quantity is demanded. That is, when memory cards become less expensive, Emily buys more memory cards. When memory cards become more expensive, Emily buys fewer memory cards, perhaps choosing to go to the movies or download some music instead.

USING GRAPHS TO SHOW THE RELATIONSHIP AMONG THREE VARIABLES

Although only two variables are shown on the axes, graphs can be used to show the relationship among three variables. For example, say we add a third variable—income—to our earlier example. Our three variables are now income, price, and quantity purchased. If Emily's income rises, say she gets a raise at work, she is now able and willing to buy more memory cards than before at each possible price. As a result, the whole demand curve shifts outward (rightward) compared to the old curve. That is, she uses some of her additional income to buy more memory cards. This is seen in the graph in Exhibit 9(a). On the other hand, if her income falls, say she quits her job to go back to school, she now has less income to buy memory cards. This causes the whole demand curve to shift inward (leftward) compared to the old curve. This is seen in the graph in Exhibit 9(b).

The Difference between a Movement along and a Shift in the Curve

It is important to remember the difference between a movement between one point and another along a curve and a shift in the whole curve. A change in one of the variables on the graph, like price or quantity purchased, will cause a movement along the curve, say from point A to point B, as shown in Exhibit 10. A change in one of the variables not shown (held constant in order to show only the relationship between price and quantity), like income in our example, will cause the whole curve to shift. The change from D_0 to D_1 in Exhibit 10 shows such a shift.

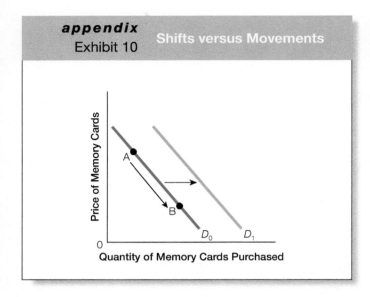

appendix
Exhibit 10   Shifts versus Movements

Quantity of Memory Cards Purchased

SLOPE

In economics, we sometimes refer to the steepness of the lines or curves on graphs as the **slope**—the ratio of the rise over the run. A slope can be either positive (upward sloping) or negative (downward sloping). A curve that is downward sloping represents an inverse, or negative, relationship between the two variables and slants downward from left to right, as seen in Exhibit 11(a). A curve that is upward sloping represents a direct, or positive, relationship between the two variables and slants upward from left to right, as seen in Exhibit 11(b). The numeric value of the slope shows the number of units of change of the Y-axis variable for each unit of change in the X-axis variable. Slope provides the direction (positive or negative) as well as the magnitude of the relationship between the two variables.

slope

the ratio of rise (change in the Y variable) over the run (change in the X variable)

Measuring the Slope of a Linear Curve

A straight-line curve is called a *linear curve*. The slope of a linear curve between two points measures the relative rates of change of two variables. Specifically, the slope of a linear curve can be defined as the ratio of the change in the Y value to the change in the X value. The slope can also be expressed as the ratio of the rise to the run, where the rise is the change in the Y variable (along the vertical axis) and the run is the change in the X variable (along the horizontal axis).

In Exhibit 12, we show two linear curves, one with a positive slope and one with a negative slope. In Exhibit 12(a), the slope of the positively sloped linear curve from point A to point B is 1/2, because the rise is 1 (from 2 to 3) and the run is 2 (from 1 to 3). In Exhibit 12(b), the negatively sloped linear curve has a slope of –4, a rise of –8 (a fall of

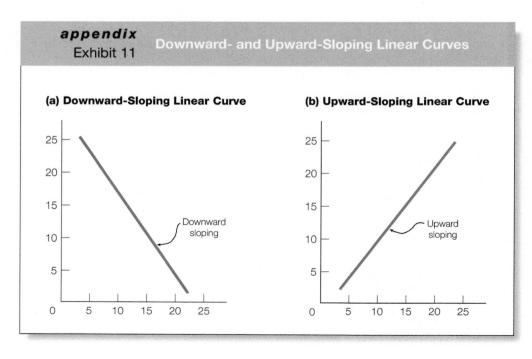

appendix
Exhibit 11   Downward- and Upward-Sloping Linear Curves

(a) Downward-Sloping Linear Curve

Downward sloping

(b) Upward-Sloping Linear Curve

Upward sloping

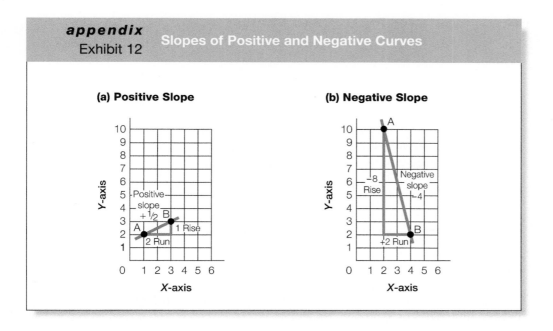

appendix
Exhibit 12 Slopes of Positive and Negative Curves

(a) Positive Slope

(b) Negative Slope

8 from 10 to 2), and a run of 2 (from 2 to 4), which gives us a slope of –4 (–8/2). Note the appropriate signs on the slopes: The negatively sloped line carries a minus sign and the positively sloped line, a plus sign.

Finding the Slope of a Nonlinear Curve

In Exhibit 13, we show the slope of a nonlinear curve. A nonlinear curve is a line that actually curves. Here the slope varies from point to point along the curve. However, we can find the slope of this curve at any given point by drawing a straight-line tangent to that point on the curve. A tangency is when a straight line just touches the curve without actually crossing it. At point A, we see that the positively sloped line that is tangent to the curve has a slope of 1—the line rises one unit and runs one unit. At point B, the line is horizontal, so it has zero slope. At point C, we see a slope of –2 because the negatively sloped line has a rise of –2 units (a fall of two units) for every one unit run.

Remember, many students have problems with economics simply because they fail to understand graphs, so make sure that you understand this material before going on to Chapter 2.

Percentage Change

In economics, the determination of the percentage change in a quantity is a common calculation. The advantage of calculating percentage change (as opposed to simple absolute change) is that percentage change provides a more accurate measure of the magnitude of the change. For example, is an increase in price from $105 to $130 relatively larger or smaller than an increase in price from $50 to $75? In both cases, the difference (absolute increase) is the same at $25, but what about the relative (percentage) change?

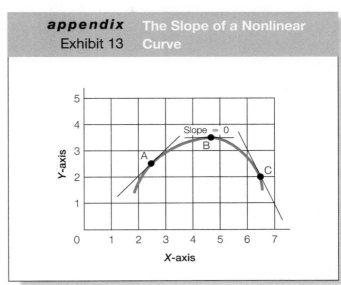

appendix
Exhibit 13 The Slope of a Nonlinear Curve

The Formula for Percentage Change

The percentage change in a value that is originally x_0 and changes to x_1 can be expressed as follows:

$$\%\Delta = \left(\frac{X_1 - X_0}{X_0}\right) \times 100$$

So, is an increase in price from \$105 to \$130 relatively larger or smaller than an increase in price from \$50 to \$75?

The percentage increase in price from \$105 to \$130 is

$$\left(\frac{130 - 105}{105}\right) \times 100 = 23.81\%$$

The percentage increase in price from \$50 to \$75 is

$$\left(\frac{75 - 50}{50}\right) \times 100 = 50\%$$

Therefore, the increase in price from \$50 to \$75 is relatively larger than the increase in price from \$105 to \$130.

For Your Review (Chapter 1 Appendix)

1. What are the coordinates of the points of the following graph?

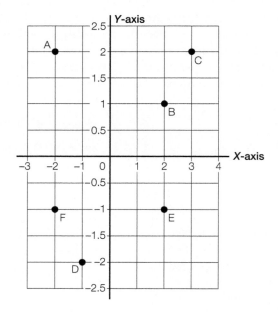

2. Refer to the following pie chart, which shows the percentage of sales by vehicle type in 2013.

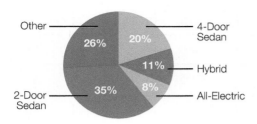

a. What percentage of the cars sold in 2013 were all-electric vehicles?

b. What percentage of the cars sold in 2013 were 4-door sedans?

c. What was the most popular vehicle type for 2013 based on sales?

d. What was the least popular vehicle type for 2013 based on sales?

3. Refer to the following bar graph, which shows the number of boys and girls participating in campus recreational leagues in each of four semesters.

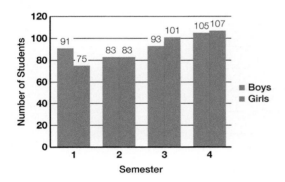

a. In which semesters were more boys than girls registered in campus recreational leagues?

b. In which semesters were more girls than boys registered in campus recreational leagues?

c. In which semesters did the same number of girls and boys register in campus recreational leagues?

d. Looking at all four semesters, what was the total number of boys registered in campus recreational leagues?

4. Plot the relationships described in the following tables on separate graphs (plot the variables in the left-hand columns on the horizontal axis and the variables in the right-hand columns on the vertical axis).

Graph 1		Graph 2		Graph 3	
Temperature (°C)	Ice Cream Sales (cones)	Year	Value of Tom's Car ($)	Shoe size	Grade Point Average (GPA)
20	30	2013	14 000	8	3.5
22	50	2012	15 000	9	3.5
24	70	2011	16 000	10	3.5
26	90	2010	17 000	11	3.5
28	110	2009	18 000	12	3.5

How would you describe the resulting graphs: upward sloping, downward sloping, or unrelated?

5. Refer to the following graph.

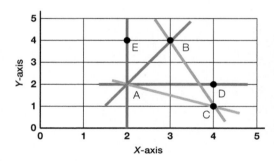

Calculate the slope between the following sets of points.

a.   A to B

b.   B to C

c.   A to C

d.   E to A

e.   A to D

6. Calculate the percentage change in each of the following scenarios.

a.   The temperature increases from 12°C to 18°C.

b.   The price of a laptop computer falls from $800 to $760.

c.   The Consumer Price Index (CPI) increases from 105.3 to 106.1.

d.   The number of emergency calls to campus security decreased from 912 last semester to 862 this semester.

The Production Possibilities Curve

- What is a production possibilities curve?
- What is efficiency?
- How is opportunity cost measured?
- What is the law of increasing opportunity costs?

WHAT IS A PRODUCTION POSSIBILITIES CURVE?

The economic concepts of scarcity, choice, and trade-offs can be shown with a simple graph called a *production possibilities curve*. The **production possibilities curve** represents the potential total output combinations of any two goods for an economy, given the inputs and technology available to the economy. That is, it illustrates an economy's potential for allocating its limited resources in producing various combinations of goods in a given time period.

production possibilities curve
the potential total output combinations of any two goods for an economy, given the inputs and technology available

Because you have only so many hours a week to study, studying more for economics and less for accounting might hurt your grade in accounting, *ceteris paribus*. Life is full of trade-offs.

A Straight-Line Production Possibilities Curve—Grades in Economics and Accounting

What would the production possibilities curve look like if you were "producing" grades in two of your classes—say, economics and accounting? In Exhibit 1, we draw a hypothetical production possibilities curve for your expected grade in economics on the vertical axis and your expected grade in accounting on the horizontal axis. Assume, because of a part-time restaurant job, you choose to study ten hours a week and that you like both courses and are equally adept at studying for both courses.

We see in Exhibit 1 that the production possibilities curve is a straight line. For example, if all ten hours are spent studying

Wavebreak Media/Thinkstock

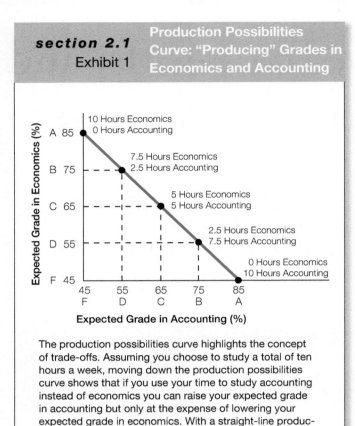

section 2.1
Exhibit 1

Production Possibilities Curve: "Producing" Grades in Economics and Accounting

The production possibilities curve highlights the concept of trade-offs. Assuming you choose to study a total of ten hours a week, moving down the production possibilities curve shows that if you use your time to study accounting instead of economics you can raise your expected grade in accounting but only at the expense of lowering your expected grade in economics. With a straight-line production possibilities curve, the opportunity costs are constant.

economics, the expected grade in economics is 85 percent (an A) and the expected grade in accounting is 45 percent (an F). Moving down the production possibilities curve, we see that as you spend more of your time studying accounting and less on economics, you can raise your expected grade in accounting but only at the expense of lowering your expected grade in economics. Specifically, moving down along the straight-line production possibilities curve, the trade-off is one letter-grade lower in economics for one higher letter-grade in accounting.

Of course, if you increased your study time it would be possible to expect higher grades in both courses. But that would be on a new production possibilities curve; along this production possibilities curve we are assuming that technology and the number of study hours are given. In the next section, the coverage is expanded to cover the more realistic case of a bowed production possibilities curve.

Production Alternatives On the Bowed Production Possibilities Curve

To more clearly illustrate the production possibilities curve, imagine an economy that produces just two goods: food and shelter. The fact that we have many goods in the real world makes actual decision making more complicated, but it does not alter the basic principles being illustrated. Each point on the production possibilities curve shown in Exhibit 2 represents the potential amounts of food and shelter that can be produced in a given time period, given the quantity and quality of resources available in the economy for production.

Note in Exhibit 2 that if we devoted all of our resources to making units of shelter, we could produce 10 units of shelter, but no food (point A). If, on the other hand, we chose to devote all of our resources to food, we could produce 80 units of food, but no shelter (point E).

In reality, nations would rarely opt for production possibility A or E, preferring instead to produce a mixture of goods. For example, the economy in question might produce 9 units of shelter and 20 units of food (point B), or perhaps 7 units of shelter and 40 units of food (point C). Still other combinations along the curve, such as point D, are possible.

Production Alternatives Off the Production Possibilities Curve

The economy cannot operate at point N (not attainable) during the given time period because there are presently not enough resources to produce that level of output. However, it is possible the economy can operate inside the production possibilities curve, at point I (inefficient). If the economy is operating at point I, or at any other point inside the production possibilities curve, it is not at full capacity and is operating inefficiently. In short, the economy is not using all of its scarce resources efficiently; as a result, actual output is less than potential output.

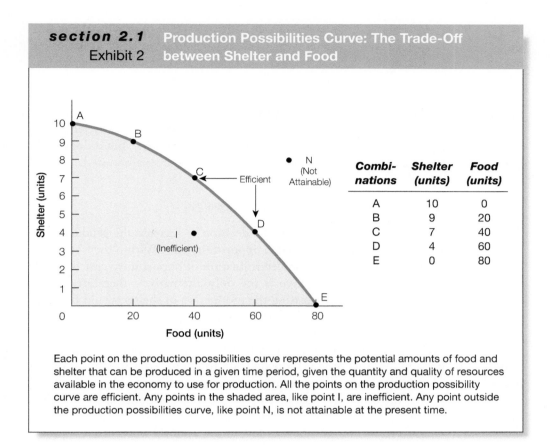

section 2.1   Production Possibilities Curve: The Trade-Off
Exhibit 2   between Shelter and Food

Combi- nations	Shelter (units)	Food (units)
A	10	0
B	9	20
C	7	40
D	4	60
E	0	80

Each point on the production possibilities curve represents the potential amounts of food and shelter that can be produced in a given time period, given the quantity and quality of resources available in the economy to use for production. All the points on the production possibility curve are efficient. Any points in the shaded area, like point I, are inefficient. Any point outside the production possibilities curve, like point N, is not attainable at the present time.

WHAT IS EFFICIENCY?

Most modern economies have resources that are idle, at least for some period of time—like during periods of high unemployment. If those resources were not idle, people would have more scarce goods and services available for their use. Unemployed resources create a serious problem. For example, consider an unemployed construction worker who is unable to find work at a "reasonable" wage, or those unemployed in depressed times when factories are already operating below capacity. Clearly, the resources of these individuals are not being used efficiently.

The fact that factories can operate below capacity suggests that it is not just labour resources that should be most effectively used. Rather, all resources entering into production must be used effectively. However, for several reasons, social concern focuses on labour. First, labour costs are the largest share of production costs. Also, unemployed or underemployed labourers (whose resources are not being used to their full potential) may have mouths to feed at home, whereas an unemployed machine does not (although the owner of the unemployed machine may).

Inefficiency and Efficiency

Suppose for some reason there is widespread unemployment or resources are not being put to their best use. The economy would then be operating at a point, such as I, inside the production possibilities curve where the economy is operating inefficiently. At point I, 4 units of shelter and 40 units of food are being produced. By putting unemployed resources to work or by putting already employed resources to better use, we could expand the output of shelter by 3 units (moving to point C) without giving up any units of food. Alternatively, we could boost food output by 20 units (moving to point D) without reducing shelter output. We could even get more of both food and shelter moving to a point on the curve between C and D. Increasing or improving the utilization of resources, then, can lead to greater output of all goods. An efficient use of our resources means that more of everything we want can be available for our use. Thus, efficiency requires society to use its resources to the fullest extent—getting the most from our scarce resources; that is, there are no wasted resources. If resources are being used efficiently, that is, at some point along a production possibilities curve, then more of one good or service requires the sacrifice of another good or service. Efficiency does not tell us which point along the production possibilities curve is *best*, but it does tell us that points inside the curve cannot be best because some resources are wasted.

HOW IS OPPORTUNITY COST MEASURED?

When an economy is operating efficiently, the decision to increase the production of one good or service will carry with it a related opportunity cost. Within the framework of the production possibility model, the determination of opportunity cost is greatly simplified since the next best alternative is the only alternative—therefore, in our example, the opportunity cost of increasing the production of shelter would be measured in corresponding forgone units of food, and the opportunity cost of expanding food production would be measured in units of forgone shelter.

Note in Exhibit 2 that if the economy is currently operating at point D (producing 4 units of shelter and 60 units of food), the decision to increase the amount of shelter it produces to 7 units will have an opportunity cost of 20 units of food—as this is the amount of food that the economy must give up to gain the additional units of shelter. In the diagram, this gain of shelter and related opportunity cost would involve the movement along the production possibilities curve from point D to point C.

WHAT IS THE LAW OF INCREASING OPPORTUNITY COSTS?

Note that in Exhibits 2 and 3, the production possibilities curve is not a straight line like that in Exhibit 1. It is concave from below (i.e., bowed outward from the origin). Looking at the figures, you can see that at very low food output, an increase in the amount of food produced will lead to only a small reduction in the units of shelter produced. For example, increasing food output from 0 to 20 (moving from point A to point B on the curve) requires the use of resources capable of producing 1 unit of shelter. This means that for the first 20 units of food, 1 unit of shelter must be given up. When food output is higher, however, more units of shelter must be given up when switching additional resources from the production of shelter to food. Moving from point D to point E, for example, an increase in food output of 20 (from 60 to 80) reduces the production of shelter from 4 to 0. At this point, then, the cost of those 20 additional units of food is 4 units of shelter, considerably more than the 1 unit of shelter required in the earlier scenario. This difference shows us that opportunity costs have not remained constant, but have risen, as more units of food and fewer units of shelter are produced.

law of increasing opportunity cost
as more of one item is produced by an economy, the opportunity cost of additional units of that product rises

The **law of increasing opportunity cost** refers to the concept that, as more of one item is produced by an economy, the opportunity cost of additional units of that product rises. It is this increasing opportunity cost, then, that is represented by the bowed production possibilities curve.

The Reason for the Law of Increasing Opportunity Cost

The basic reason for the law of increasing opportunity cost is that some resources and skills cannot be easily adapted from their current uses to alternative uses. For example, at low levels of food output, additional increases in food output can be obtained easily

section 2.1

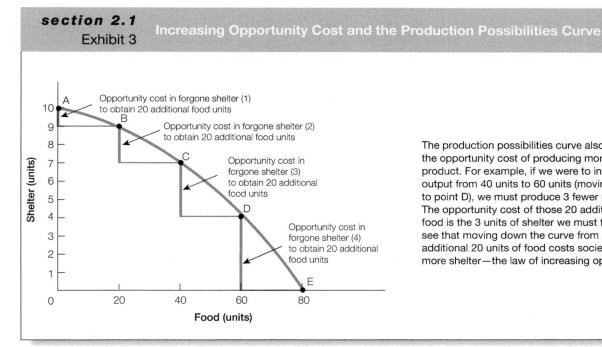

section 2.1
Exhibit 3 Increasing Opportunity Cost and the Production Possibilities Curve

The production possibilities curve also illustrates the opportunity cost of producing more of a given product. For example, if we were to increase food output from 40 units to 60 units (moving from point C to point D), we must produce 3 fewer units of shelter. The opportunity cost of those 20 additional units of food is the 3 units of shelter we must forgo. We can see that moving down the curve from A to E, each additional 20 units of food costs society more and more shelter—the law of increasing opportunity cost.

by switching relatively low-skilled carpenters from making shelter to producing food. However, to get even more food output, workers who are less well suited or appropriate for producing food (i.e., they are better adapted to making shelter) must be released from shelter making in order to increase food output. For example, a skilled carpenter may be an expert at making shelter but a very bad farmer, because he lacks the training and skills necessary in that occupation. So, using the skilled carpenter to farm results in a relatively greater opportunity cost than using the poor carpenter to farm. Hence, the production of additional units of food becomes increasingly costly as progressively even lower-skilled farmers (but good carpenters) convert to farming.

Business *CONNECTION*

WHAT CAN THE PPC OFFER MANAGERS?

The production possibilities curve (PPC) can be extremely helpful to entrepreneurs, especially those in small and medium-sized businesses. The curve represents the potential total output combinations of any two goods for an economy, given the inputs and technology available to the economy. It's not so much that managers will construct their own PPCs, but rather that using the model can help their thinking. The PPC demonstrates a number of economic concepts: growth, choice, opportunity cost, law of diminishing returns, marginal benefits, and inflationary pressures. It can be used in a broad context (e.g., when thinking about investing in consumer goods versus capital goods) or in a narrow perspective (e.g., when deciding on

whether a plant should produce Smooth Joy bars versus Chewy Delight bars).

In general terms, the marketing side of the business is responsible for revenue (as opposed to the operations side, which is responsible for expenses). If managers of the firm feel that demand is growing, they may decide to increase the production of their plant. In terms of the PPC, the firm could presently be operating at three different levels: (1) significantly below capacity, or the PPC curve's boundary, (2) slightly below capacity, or (3) at capacity. If the firm is operating significantly below capacity, it can comfortably increase production without any concern about rising costs of production—it may actually lower

(continued)

average unit prices as it increases production. As the plant approaches full production, it will experience increased costs—for example, managers might have to pay overtime to employees. At capacity, there is no way to increase production without investing in expanding capacity, which can mean investing in capital (equipment) and/or plant size (land).

The PPC also helps the managers to visualize what the level of production should be. Producing at capacity does not allow the plant to look for new accounts, because the increased production increases the company's costs, but producing at levels slightly below capacity allows for a company to increase production both in the short and long term without major cost increases. If the occasional increase turns out to be more permanent, then managers look to expand the business.

It is vital that the marketing and operations side of the business be in sync—the last thing the firm needs is new business if it is at capacity, because that means higher costs and the pressures of meeting delivery times. This situation illustrates one reason why some young businesses fail by growing too fast▢they think all growth is good. In fact, however, only managed growth is good, because taking on more than the firm can deal with can lead it into failure.

The PPC can be helpful to both the marketing and operations sides when they are making decisions on the firm's product mix. For example, the firm can produce product A or product B. On the PPC, this is demonstrated by moving along the curve toward one axis or another. If demand dictates that more of product A should be made, the plant has to decide whether to make less of product B in order to make product A (opportunity cost). But what do managers do when demand for product B remains high and demand for product A increases significantly? Here, the

firm has to decide if it wants to expand. If it can't expand, then the decision could be to meet the increase in demand for product A and decrease production of product B, or the firm could actually increase the price of product A and leave existing production levels where they are. You'll see why this is when you learn about supply and demand in the next few chapters.

Finally, managers should be aware that as they near the plant's capacity, they have to spend considerably more for just a little bit of return. It's the same concept for you as a student—you have to spend a lot more time to move your grade up from 95 percent to 98 percent than you do to raise your grade from 50 to 60 percent. For managers, this means higher costs, and even though they could reach near capacity, would they really want to from a profitability perspective? This demonstrates the mindset of why operation managers might decide to operate at levels slightly below capacity.

Keeping the concepts of the PPC model in mind while making both marketing and operations decisions will be of great benefit to managers. This is more strategic thinking than tactical thinking—areas that successful managers have to be good at all of the time.

1. There are a number of reasons why a firm shouldn't be producing at its capacity. Can you think of some other reasons not discussed here? In each case, in your opinion, why should the firm be operating at less than capacity?

2. It is true that one of the main reasons new firms fail is that they grow too fast. Thinking of the PPC, what are other risks or reasons that could lead to business failure?

3. Why do you think costs increase for a firm the closer it gets to operating at capacity?

SECTION CHECK

- The production possibilities curve represents the potential total output combinations of two goods available to a society, given its resources and existing technology.
- Efficiency requires society to use its resources to the fullest extent—no wasted resources. If the economy is operating within the production possibilities curve, the economy is operating inefficiently.
- The cost of altering production within the production possibilities curve framework, at efficiency, is measured in forgone units of the sole alternative.
- A bowed production possibilities curve means that the opportunity costs of producing additional units of a good rise as society produces more of that good (the law of increasing opportunity costs).

Economic Growth and the Production Possibilities Curve

■ How do we show economic growth on the production possibilities curve?
■ How can we summarize the production possibilities curve?

HOW DO WE SHOW ECONOMIC GROWTH ON THE PRODUCTION POSSIBILITIES CURVE?

How have some nations been able to rapidly expand their output of goods and services over time, whereas others have been unable to increase their standards of living at all?

The economy can grow only with qualitative or quantitative changes in the factors of production—land, labour, capital, and entrepreneurship. Advancement in technology, improvements in labour productivity, or new sources of natural resources (such as previously undiscovered oil) could all lead to outward shifts of the production possibilities curve.

This idea can be clearly illustrated by using the production possibilities curve (Exhibit 1). In terms of the production possibilities curve, economic growth means an outward shift in the possible combinations of goods and services produced. With growth comes the possibility to have more of both goods than were previously available. Suppose we were producing at point C (7 units of shelter, 40 units of food) on our original production possibilities curve. Additional resources and/or new methods of using them (technological progress) can lead to new production possibilities creating the potential for more of all goods (or more of some with no less of others). These increases would shift the production possibilities curve outward. For example, if the government introduces programs that make it easier for workers to get an education and relevant workplace expertise (called *human capital*), such as training workers to make shelter, this increases the productivity of these workers. As a result, they will produce more units of shelter. This means, ultimately, that fewer resources will be used to make shelter, freeing them to be used for farming—resulting in more units of food. Notice that at point F (future) on the new curve, it is possible to produce 9 units of shelter and 70 units of food, more of both goods than was previously produced, at point C. Alternatively, as evidenced by land degradation and depletion of natural resources, resources can be lost over time. This has a negative impact on production, shifting the production possibilities curve inward.

Growth Doesn't Eliminate Scarcity

With all of this discussion of growth, it is important to remember that growth, or increases in a society's output, does not make scarcity disappear. Even when

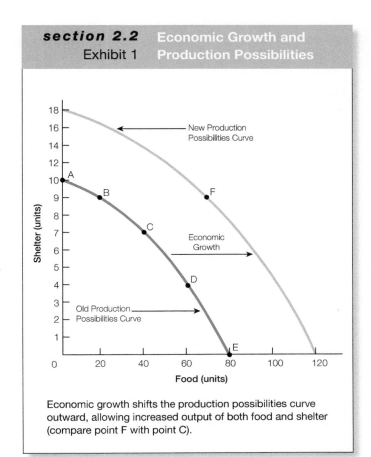

section 2.2 Economic Growth and
Exhibit 1 Production Possibilities

Economic growth shifts the production possibilities curve outward, allowing increased output of both food and shelter (compare point F with point C).

output has grown more rapidly than the population so that people are made better off, they still face trade-offs: At any point along the production possibilities curve, in order to get more of one thing, you must give up something else. There are no free lunches on the production possibilities curve.

Capital Goods versus Consumption Goods

Economies that choose to invest more of their resources for the future will grow faster than those that don't. To generate economic growth, a society must produce fewer consumer goods—like pizza, digital cameras, cellphones, cars, and so on—in the present and produce more capital goods. The society that devotes a larger share of its productive capacity to capital goods (machines, factories, tools, and education), rather than consumption goods (computer games, pizza, and vacations), will experience greater economic growth. It must sacrifice some present consumption of consumer goods and services in order to experience growth in the future. Why? Investing in capital goods, like computers and other new technological equipment, as well as upgrading skills and knowledge, expands the ability to produce in the future. It shifts the economy's production possibilities outward, increasing the future production capacity of the economy. That is, the economy that invests more now (consumes less now) will be able to produce, and therefore consume, more in the future. In Exhibit 2, we see that Economy A invests more in capital goods than Economy B. Consequently, Economy A's production possibilities curve shifts out farther than Economy B's over time.

To better understand the significance of these two production alternatives, it may help to apply the distinction to the Canadian economy. Which type of economy is Canada, Economy A or Economy B? In Canada, consumption expenditure is nearly three times that of investment. As a result, the Canadian economy is best represented by the Economy B illustration. By comparison, China's gross savings amount is more than double that of Canada's. Clearly then, China is best represented by the Economy B illustration.

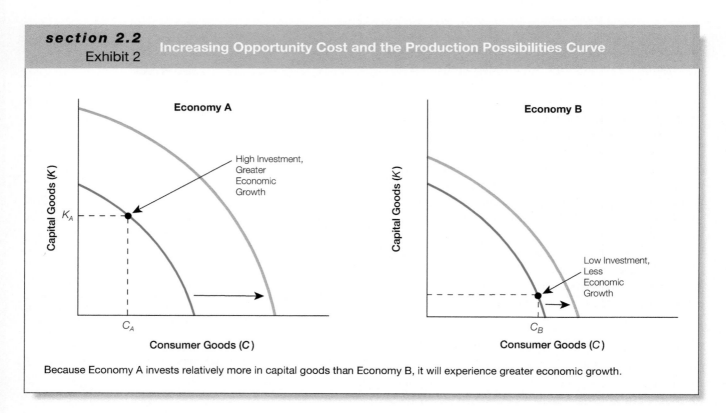

section 2.2
Exhibit 2   **Increasing Opportunity Cost and the Production Possibilities Curve**

Economy A

Capital Goods (*K*)

K_A

High Investment, Greater Economic Growth

C_A

Consumer Goods (*C*)

Economy B

Capital Goods (*K*)

Low Investment, Less Economic Growth

C_B

Consumer Goods (*C*)

Because Economy A invests relatively more in capital goods than Economy B, it will experience greater economic growth.

The Effects of a Technological Change on the Production Possibilities Curve

In Exhibit 3, we see that a technological advance does not have to impact all sectors of the economy equally: There is a technological advance in food production but not in housing production. The technological advance in agriculture causes the production possibilities curve to extend out farther on the horizontal axis, which measures food production. We can move to any point on the new production possibilities curve. For example, the move from point A on the original curve to point B on the new curve would result in 150 more units of food (500 – 350) and the same amount of housing—200 units. Or, we could move from point A to point C, which would allow us to produce more units of both food and housing. How do we produce more housing, when the technological advance occurred in agriculture? The answer is that the technological advance in agriculture allows us to produce more from a given quantity of resources. That is, it allows us to shift some resources out of agriculture into housing. This is actually an ongoing story in Canadian economic history. In colonial days, almost all of the Canadian population made a living in agriculture. Today, it is less than 3 percent.

From the analogue type to touch-screen devices, technological progress has had a dramatic impact on the cellphone industry. At first, cellphones had only one purpose—to allow a person to call someone else while on the move. Today, cellphones can send and receive emails, text message, store music and images, take and send pictures, and even provide television and the Internet.

HOW CAN WE SUMMARIZE THE PRODUCTION POSSIBILITIES CURVE?

The production possibilities curve shown in Exhibit 4 illustrates the choices faced by an economy that makes military goods and consumer goods. How are the economic concepts of scarcity, choice, opportunity costs, efficiency, and economic growth illustrated in this production possibilities curve framework? In Exhibit 4, we can show scarcity because resource combinations outside the initial production possibilities curve, like point D, are unattainable without economic growth. If the economy is operating efficiently, we are somewhere on that production possibilities curve, like point B or point C. However, if the economy is operating inefficiently, we are operating inside

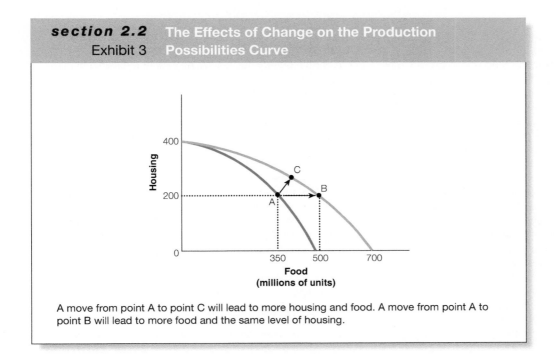

section 2.2   **The Effects of Change on the Production**
Exhibit 3   **Possibilities Curve**

A move from point A to point C will lead to more housing and food. A move from point A to point B will lead to more food and the same level of housing.

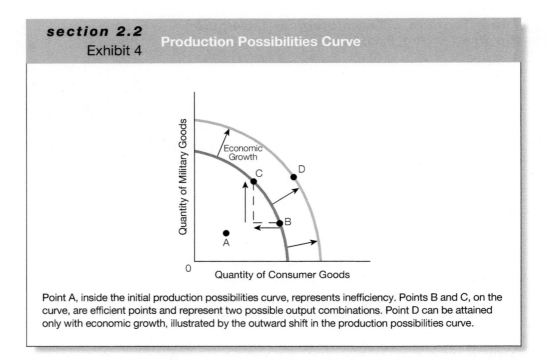

Point A, inside the initial production possibilities curve, represents inefficiency. Points B and C, on the curve, are efficient points and represent two possible output combinations. Point D can be attained only with economic growth, illustrated by the outward shift in the production possibilities curve.

that production possibilities curve, like point A. We can also see in this graph that to get more military goods you must give up consumer goods—that is, there is an opportunity cost. Finally, we see that over time, with economic growth, the whole production possibilities curve can shift outward, making point D now attainable.

DEBATE

WILL CAPITALISM, WHICH RELIES ON GROWTH, BE UNSUSTAINABLE OVER THE LONG TERM?

For:

Resources are the key to long-term economic growth, most notably the factors of production: land, labour, capital, and entrepreneurship. For more than a century, people have largely used the gifts of nature, or resources, to bring about tremendous economic growth. Capitalism, in which ownership and means of production are privately held, with decreasing inventories, has created unparalleled wealth for developed and developing countries, but the wealth has not been distributed fairly across nations. Capitalism undervalues the impact on society of such factors as pollution and clear-cutting, and leaves the private sector to take care of the environment. There is little regard for the environmental impact of waste, excess, and the clean-up costs once the resources have been used. People used to think that the earth would have an endless abundance of resources, but it's now clear that many resources will reach near-critical depletion levels during our lifetime. Can a system in which individuals value their own wealth based on their consumption of "things" be sustained over the coming generations? Will individuals have to reduce their expectations of wealth in order to live comfortable lives in the future?

Against:

The earth's bounty has always been able to sustain human needs and it will continue to do so far into the future. Over time, some species have died away and others have evolved to take their place. As some resources have been used up, people have adjusted by substituting, or by developing technology to replace those that have been used. For example, as fossil fuels become scarcer, we will adapt to alternative fuels such as solar power, which can be stored in batteries. The issue is not availability, but availability at a given price. The scarcer the resource, the more it will cost and the greater the incentive will be to create an alternative at a given price. As for pollution, as we substitute our consumption of fossil fuels (or many other resources for that matter), the less we'll use and therefore the less pollution and waste we'll deposit back into the earth. We have already seen this process happen with the coal-fired plants of the early twentieth century. Humans have always adapted to the changing environment. These are not barriers to economic growth, but opportunities over the long term. Isn't the capitalist system the only way we can solve our insatiable appetite for growth?

section

2.3

Market Prices Coordinate Economic Activity

■ What is a market?

■ What are the roles of buyers and sellers in a market?

■ How does a market system allocate scarce resources?

■ What is a market failure?

WHAT IS A MARKET?

Although we usually think of a market as a place where some sort of exchange occurs, a market is not really a place at all. A **market** is the process of buyers and sellers exchanging goods and services. This means that supermarkets, the Toronto Stock Exchange, drugstores, roadside stands, garage sales, Internet stores, and restaurants are all markets.

Every market is different. That is, the conditions under which the exchange between buyers and sellers takes place can vary. These differences make it difficult to precisely define a market. After all, an incredible variety of exchange arrangements exists in the real world—organized securities markets, wholesale auction markets, foreign exchange markets, real estate markets, labour markets, and so forth.

Goods being priced and traded in various ways at various locations by various kinds of buyers and sellers further compound the problem of defining a market. For some goods, such as housing, markets are numerous but limited to a geographic area. Homes in Niagara Falls, Ontario, for example (about 130 kilometres from downtown Toronto), do not compete directly with homes in Toronto. Why? Because people who work in Toronto will generally look for homes within commuting distance. Even within cities, there are separate markets for homes, differentiated by amenities such as bigger houses, newer houses, larger lots, and better schools.

In a similar manner, markets are numerous but geographically limited for a good such as cement. Because transportation costs are so high relative to the selling price, the good is not shipped any substantial distance and buyers are usually in contact only with local producers. Price and output are thus determined in a number of small markets. In other markets, like those for gold or automobiles, markets are global. The important point is not what a market looks like, but what it does—it facilitates trade.

market
the process of buyers and sellers exchanging goods and services

WHAT ARE THE ROLES OF BUYERS AND SELLERS IN A MARKET?

The roles of buyers and sellers in markets are important. The buyers, as a group, determine the demand-side of the market. Buyers include the consumers who purchase the goods and services and the firms that buy inputs—labour, capital, and raw materials. Sellers, as a group, determine the supply side of the market. Sellers include the firms that produce and sell goods and services, and the resource owners who sell their inputs to firms—workers who "sell" their labour and resource owners who sell raw materials and capital. It is the interaction of buyers and sellers that determines market prices and output—through the forces of supply and demand.

In the next chapter, we focus on how supply and demand work in a competitive market—one in which there are a number of buyers and sellers. Because most markets contain a large degree of competitiveness, the lessons of supply and demand can be applied to many different types of problems.

The supply and demand model is particularly useful in markets like agriculture, finance, labour, construction, services, wholesale, and retail. In short, a model is only as good as it explains and predicts. The model of supply and demand is very good at predicting changes in prices and quantities in many markets, large and small.

HOW DOES A MARKET SYSTEM ALLOCATE SCARCE RESOURCES?

In a world of scarcity, competition is inescapable, and one method of allocating resources among competing uses is the market system. The market system provides a way for millions of producers and consumers to allocate scarce resources. For the most part, markets are efficient. To an economist, **efficiency** is achieved when the economy gets the most out of its scarce resources. In short, efficiency makes the economic pie as large as possible.

efficiency
getting the most from society's scarce resources

Buyers and sellers indicate their wants through their action and inaction in the marketplace, and it is this collective "voice" that determines how resources are allocated. But how is this information communicated? Market prices serve as the language of the market system. By understanding what these market prices mean, you can get a better understanding of the vital function that the market system performs.

Markets may not always conform to your desired tastes and preferences. You may think that markets produce too many fast foods, face-lifts, and Justin Bieber albums. Some markets are illegal—the market for cocaine, the market for stolen body parts, and the market for child pornography. Markets do not come with a moral compass; they simply provide what buyers are willing and able to pay for and what sellers are willing and able to produce.

Market Prices Provide Important Information

Market prices communicate important information to both buyers and sellers. These prices communicate information about the relative availability of products to buyers, and they provide sellers with critical information about the relative value that consumers place on those products. In effect, market prices provide a way for both buyers and sellers to communicate about the relative value of resources. This communication results in a shifting of resources from those uses that are less valued to those that are more valued. We will see how this works beginning in Chapter 3.

The basis of a market economy is the voluntary exchange and the price system that guide people's choices and produce solutions to the questions of what goods to produce and how to produce and distribute them. Take something as simple as the production of a pencil. Where did the wood come from? Perhaps British Columbia or Quebec. The graphite may have come from the mines in northern Ontario, and the rubber maybe from Malaysia. The paint, the glue, the metal piece that holds the eraser—who knows? The point is that market forces coordinated this activity among literally thousands of people, some of whom live in different countries and speak different languages. The market system brought these people together to make a pencil that sells for 25 cents at your bookstore. It all happened because the market system provided the incentive for people to pursue activities that benefit others. This same process produces millions of goods and services around the world, from automobiles and computers to pencils and paper clips. The same is true of the iPod and iPhone.

In countries that do not rely on the market system, there is no clear communication between buyers and sellers. In the former Soviet Union, where quality was virtually nonexistent, there were shortages of quality goods and surpluses of low-quality goods. For example, there were thousands of tractors without spare parts and millions of pairs of shoes that were left on shelves because the sizes did not match those of the population.

Apple employees have learned how to combine almost 500 generic parts to make something of much greater value. The whole is greater than the sum of the parts. There is not one person at Apple or in the world who could put together an iPhone all alone. It takes many people, making many parts, living all over the world.

Property Rights and the Legal System

In a market economy, private individuals and firms own most of the resources. For example, when consumers buy houses, cars, or pizzas, they have purchased the right to use these goods in ways they, not someone else, see fit. These rights are called *property rights*. Property rights are the rules of our economic game. If well defined, property rights give individuals the incentive to maintain, improve, and conserve their property to preserve or increase its value.

The market system can work only if the government enforces the rules. That is, one of the key functions of the government is to provide a legal framework that protects and enforces property rights and contracts. Markets, like baseball games, need umpires. It is the government that plays this role when it defines and protects the rights of people and their property through the legal system and police protection. That is, by providing rules and regulations, government can make markets work more efficiently. Private enforcement is possible, but as economic life becomes more complex, political institutions have become the major instrument for defining and enforcing property rights.

The government defines and protects property rights through the legal system and public policy. The legal system ensures the rights of private ownership, the enforcement of contracts, and the legal status for businesses. The legal system serves as the referee, imposing penalties on violators of our legal rules. Property rights also include intellectual property—the property rights that an owner receives through patents, copyrights, and trademarks. These rights give the owner long-term protection that encourages individuals to write books, music, and software programs and to invent new products. In short, well-defined property rights encourage investment, innovation, exchange, conservation, and economic growth.

WHAT IS A MARKET FAILURE?

The market mechanism is a simple but effective and efficient general means of allocating resources among alternative uses. When the economy fails to allocate resources efficiently on its own, however, it is known as **market failure.** For example, a steel mill

market failure
when the economy fails to allocate resources efficiently on its own

might put soot and other forms of "crud" into the air as a by-product of making steel. When it does this, it imposes costs on others not connected with using or producing steel from the steel mill. The soot may require homeowners to paint their homes more often, entailing a cost. And studies show that respiratory diseases are greater in areas with more severe air pollution, imposing costs and often shortening life itself. In addition, the steel mill might discharge chemicals into a stream, thus killing wildlife and spoiling recreational activities for the local population. In this case, the steel factory emits too much pollution but does not bear the cost of its polluting actions. In other words, by transferring the pollution costs onto society, the firm has lowered its costs of production and is now producing more than the ideal output. This is inefficient because it is an overallocation of resources.

Markets can also produce too little of a good—research, for example. The government might decide to subsidize promising scientific research that may benefit many people, such as cancer research.

Whether the market economy has produced too little (underallocation) or too much (overallocation), the government can improve society's well-being by intervening. The case of market failure will be discussed in more detail in Chapter 12.

In addition, we cannot depend on the market economy to always communicate accurately. Some firms may have market power to distort prices in their favour. For example, the only regional cement company in the area has the ability to charge a higher price and provide a lower-quality product than if the company was in a highly competitive market. In this case, the lack of competition can lead to higher prices and reduced product quality. And without adequate information, unscrupulous producers may be able to misrepresent their products to the disadvantage of unwary consumers.

The Market Distribution of Income

Sometimes a painful trade-off exists between how much an economy can produce efficiently and how that output is distributed—the degree of equality. There is no guarantee that the market economy will provide everyone with adequate amounts of food, shelter, and transportation. That is, not only does the market determine what goods are going to be produced and in what quantities, but it also determines the distribution of output among members of society.

As with other aspects of government intervention, the degree-of-equity argument can generate some sharp disagreements. What is "fair" for one person may seem highly "unfair" to someone else. Although one person may find it terribly unfair for some individuals to earn many times the amount that other individuals who work equally hard earn, another person may find it highly unfair to ask one group, the relatively rich, to pay a much higher proportion of their income in taxes than another group.

SECTION CHECK

- Markets consist of buyers and sellers exchanging goods and services with one another.
- Buyers determine the demand-side of the market and sellers determine the supply side of the market.
- Through voluntary exchange and the price system, the market system provides a way for producers and consumers to allocate scarce resources.
- A market failure occurs when an economy fails to allocate resources efficiently on its own.

The Circular Flow Model

- What are product markets?
- What are factor markets?
- What is the goods and services flow?
- What is the income flow?
- What is the circular flow model?

How do we explain how millions of people in an economy interact when it comes to buying, selling, producing, working, hiring, and so on? In a simple economy, there are two decision makers: the producers of goods and services, which we call *firms*, and households, the buyers of goods and services. Exchanges between these two decision makers take place in product markets and factor markets and involve flows of goods, services, and money.

WHAT ARE PRODUCT MARKETS?

Product markets are the markets for consumer goods and services. In the product market, households are buyers and firms are sellers. Households buy the goods and services that firms produce and sell.

product markets
the markets for consumer goods and services

WHAT ARE FACTOR MARKETS?

Factor, or **input, markets** are the markets where households sell the use of their inputs (capital, land, labour, and entrepreneurship) to firms. In the factor markets, households are the sellers and the firms are the buyers.

factor (input) markets
the market where households sell the use of their inputs (capital, land, labour, and entrepreneurship) to firms

WHAT IS THE GOODS AND SERVICES FLOW?

The **goods and services flow** represents the continuous flow of inputs and outputs in an economy. Households make inputs available to producers through the factor markets. These inputs are then turned into outputs which are then bought by households.

goods and services flow
the continuous flow of inputs and outputs in an economy

WHAT IS THE INCOME FLOW?

The **income flow** represents the continuous flow of income and expenditure in an economy. Households receive money payments from firms as compensation for the labour, land, capital, and entrepreneurship needed to produce goods and services. These payments take the form of wages (salaries), rent, interest payments, and profits, respectively. The payments from households to firms are for the purchase of goods and services.

income flow
the continuous flow of income and expenditure in an economy

WHAT IS THE CIRCULAR FLOW MODEL?

The simple **circular flow model of income and output** is an illustration of the continuous flow of goods, services, inputs, and payments between firms and households. A simple depiction of the model is presented in Exhibit 1. In the top half of the

circular flow model of income and output
an illustration of the continuous flow of goods, services, inputs, and payments between firms and households

exhibit, the product market, households purchase goods and services that firms have produced. In the lower half of the exhibit, the factor (or input) market, households sell the inputs that firms use to produce goods and services. The income flow (going clockwise in Exhibit 1) describes how households receive income—money income—and use that income to buy goods and services—consumption spending. The goods and services flow (going counterclockwise in Exhibit 1) details how households supply inputs—capital, land, labour, and entrepreneurship—to firms that use them in the production of outputs—goods and services.

Let's take a simple example to see how the circular flow model works. Suppose a teacher's supply of labour generates personal income in the form of wages (the factor market), which she can use to buy automobiles, vacations, food, and other goods (the product market). Suppose she buys an automobile (product market); the automobile dealer now has revenue to pay for his inputs (factor market)—wages to workers, purchase of new cars to replenish his inventory, rent for his building, and so on. So we see that in the simple circular flow model, income flows from firms to households (factor markets) and spending flows from households to firms (product markets). The simple circular flow model shows how households and firms interact in product markets and in factor markets and how product markets and factor markets are interrelated.

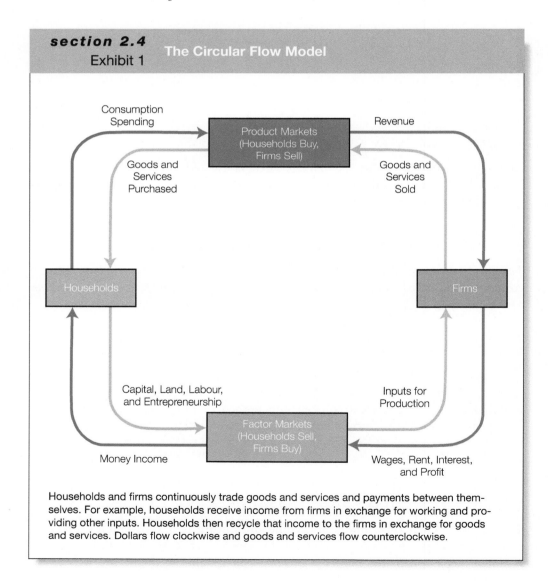

section 2.4
Exhibit 1   The Circular Flow Model

Households and firms continuously trade goods and services and payments between themselves. For example, households receive income from firms in exchange for working and providing other inputs. Households then recycle that income to the firms in exchange for goods and services. Dollars flow clockwise and goods and services flow counterclockwise.

The circular flow model can become much more complex but here it is presented merely to introduce the major markets and players in the economy. For example, the model can be extended to show the role of government, the financial sector, and foreign markets. Our simple model also does not show how firms and households send some of their income to the government for taxes or how households save some of their income for savings. Households are not the only buyers in the economy—firms, government, and foreigners buy some of the goods and services.

SECTION CHECK

- In the product market, households are buyers and firms are sellers.
- In the factor markets, households are the sellers and firms are the buyers.
- The goods and services flow represents the continuous flow of inputs and outputs in an economy.
- The income flow represents the continuous flow of income and expenditure in an economy.
- The circular flow model illustrates the flow of goods, services, and payments among firms and households.

For Your Review

Section 2.1

1. Assume that the production possibilities for Alberta are the following combinations of kegs of beer and sides of beef.

Beer	Beef
55	0
54	1
52	2
49	3
45	4
40	5
34	6
27	7
19	8
10	9
0	10

a. Construct the production possibilities frontier for beer and beef on the grid below.

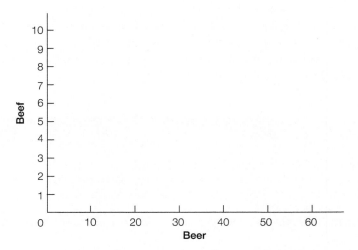

b. Given the information above, what is the opportunity cost of the 55th keg of beer in Alberta? Of the 6th side of beef? Of the 9th side of beef?

c. Suppose Alberta is currently producing 4 sides of beef and 45 kegs of beer. What is the opportunity cost of 5 more sides of beef in Alberta?

d. Would the combination of 40 kegs of beer and 4 sides of beef be efficient? Why or why not?

e. Is the combination of 9 kegs of beer and 10 sides of beef possible for Alberta? Why or why not?

Blueprint Problem

Assume that an economy has the following production possibilities.

Wheat (tonnes)	Oil (millions of barrels)
0	20
1	18
2	14
3	8
4	0

a. Construct the production possibilities frontier for this economy.

b. What is the opportunity cost of the 2nd tonne of wheat? Of the 4th tonne of wheat?

Blueprint Solution

a.

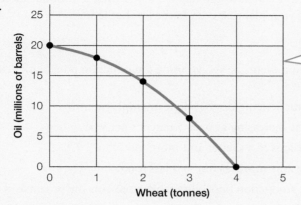

To construct the PPF, plot each output on a separate axis. Since both wheat and oil are dependent variables—dependent on the economy's resources in order to be produced—they can be plotted on either axis.

b. The opportunity cost of the 2nd tonne of wheat is 4 million barrels of oil. The opportunity cost of the 4th tonne of wheat is 8 million barrels of oil.

Wheat (tonnes)		Oil (millions of barrels)	
Total Production	Marginal Production	Total Production	Marginal Production
0		20	
1	1st tonne	18	2 million barrels
2	2nd tonne	14	4 million barrels
3	3rd tonne	8	6 million barrels
4	4th tonne	0	8 million barrels

Calculate the marginal changes in production to help determine these solutions

2. Using the table below, answer the questions that follow it.

Combinations					
	A	B	C	D	E
Pizza	1	2	3	4	5
Robots	20	18	14	8	0

a. What are the assumptions for a given production possibilities curve?

b. What is the opportunity cost of one pizza when moving from point B to point C? When moving from point D to point E?

c. Do these combinations demonstrate constant or increasing opportunity costs?

3. Imagine that you are the sole inhabitant of a small island that produces only two goods: cattle and wheat. About a quarter of the land is not fertile enough for growing wheat, so cattle graze on it. What would happen if you tried to produce more and more wheat, extending your planting even to the less fertile soil?

Sections 2.1 and 2.2

4. How would the following events be shown using a production possibilities curve for shelter and food?

   a. The economy is experiencing double-digit unemployment.

   b. Economic growth is increasing at over 5 percent per year.

   c. Society decides it wants less shelter and more food.

   d. Society decides it wants more shelter and less food.

5. Suppose the following production possibility table represents the province of Quebec.

	A	B	C	D	E	F
Cheese	45	42	36	27	15	0
Tractors	0	10	20	30	40	50

   a. Construct the production possibilities frontier for cheese and tractors.

   b. Does this production possibilities frontier illustrate the law of increasing opportunity cost? Explain.

   c. Suppose a technological advance increases the efficiency of cheese production, leaving tractor production unaffected. What impact would this have on the PPF for the province of Quebec?

   d. Suppose tractors represent *capital goods* and cheese represents *consumption goods*. If the province of Quebec altered its production from combination B to combination E, what impact could this have on the future economic growth of the province?

6. Given the following production possibilities curve, answer the questions that follow it.

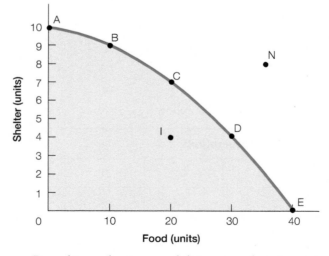

   a. Does this production possibilities curve show increasing opportunity costs? Explain.

   b. What is the opportunity cost of moving from point I to point D? Explain.

   c. What is the opportunity cost of moving from point C to point B?

   d. Which of points A–E is the most efficient? Explain.

e. Which of the identified production alternatives is currently impossible for this economy to achieve? What must happen in order for this production alternative to become attainable?

f. Which of the identified production alternatives is currently attainable but inefficient? What must happen in order for this production alternative to become efficient?

Section 2.2

7. Economy A produces more capital goods and fewer consumer goods than Economy B. Which economy will grow more rapidly? Draw two production possibilities curves, one for Economy A and one for Economy B. Demonstrate graphically how one economy can grow more rapidly than the other.

8. How does a technological advance that increases the efficiency of shoe production affect the production possibilities curve between shoes and pizza? Is it possible to produce more shoes and pizza or just more shoes? Explain.

9. A politician running for prime minister of Canada promises to build new schools and new prisons if elected, without sacrificing any other goods and services. Using the production possibilities curve between schools and prisons, explain under what conditions the politician would be able to keep her promise.

10. Why one nation experiences economic growth and another does not is a question that has intrigued economists since Adam Smith wrote *An Inquiry into the Nature and Causes of the Wealth of Nations* in 1776. Explain why each of the following would limit economic growth.

    a. The politically connected elite secure a large share of a country's output and put the proceeds into foreign banks.

    b. The national philosophy is "Live for the moment and forget about tomorrow."

    c. The government closes all of the schools so more people will be available for work.

    d. The country fears military invasion and spends half of its income on military goods.

Section 2.3

11. Evaluate the validity of the following statement: "Canadians spend millions of dollars every year shopping online, buying everything from investment products to children's toys. However, due to the virtual nature of these transactions (buyers and sellers do not actually meet in person), these exchanges do not occur in what economists would consider markets."

12. What role do buyers and sellers have in a market?

13. Prices communicate information about the relative value of resources. Which of the following would cause the relative value and, hence, the price, of potatoes to rise?

    a. A fungus infestation wipes out half of the Prince Edward Island potato crop.

    b. The price of potato chips rises.

    c. Scientists find that eating potato chips makes you better-looking.

    d. The prices of wheat, rice, and other potato substitutes fall dramatically.

14. People communicate with each other in the market through the effect their decisions to buy or sell have on prices. Indicate how each of the following would affect prices by putting a check in the appropriate space.

    a. People who see an energetic and lovable Jack Russell terrier in a popular TV series want Jack Russell terriers as pets. The price of Jack Russell terriers ____ rises ____ falls.

b. Retirees flock to Tampa, Florida, to live. The price of housing in Tampa ___ rises ___ falls.

c. Weather-related crop failures in Colombia and Costa Rica reduce coffee supplies. The price of coffee ___ rises ___ falls.

d. Wheat fields in Alberta are replaced with oil rigs. The price of wheat ___ rises ___ falls.

e. More and more students graduate from Canadian medical schools. The income of Canadian doctors___ rises ___ falls.

f. Canadians are driving more and they are driving bigger, gas-guzzling cars like sport utility vehicles. The price of gasoline _____ rises _____ falls.

Section 2.4

15. Identify where the appropriate entries go in the circular flow diagram below.

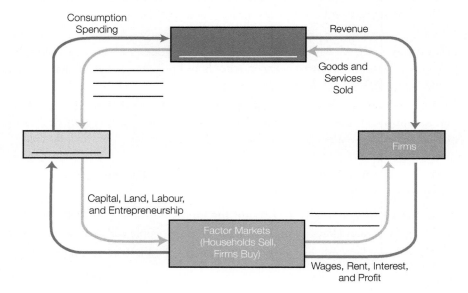

16. Identify whether each of the following transactions takes place in the factor market or the product market.

a. Billy buys a sofa from Home Time Furniture for his new home.

b. Home Time Furniture pays its manager her weekly salary.

c. The manager buys dinner at Billy's Café.

d. After he pays all of his employees their wages and pays his other bills, the owner of Billy's Café takes his profit.

17. Consider the following scenario.

Claire works as a rental agent for Hanson Car Rentals, earning $800 a week. She has set up an automatic $40 withdrawal each week to pay for her gym membership at Fit for Life. Fit for Life pays Markus $70 to teach a weekly kickbox-cardio class. Next week, Markus plans to spend $200 on a rental car from Hanson to visit his aunt in Winnipeg.

a. Which of the events in this scenario occur in the factor market?

b. Which of the events in this scenario occur in the product market?

Demand

- What is the law of demand?
- What is an individual demand schedule and curve?
- What is a market demand curve?

WHAT IS THE LAW OF DEMAND?

Some laws are made to protect us, such as "no speeding" or "no drinking and driving." Other times, observed behaviour is so pervasive it is considered to be a law—like the law of demand. According to the **law of demand,** the quantity of a good or service demanded varies inversely (negatively) with its price, *ceteris paribus.* More directly, the law of demand says that, other things being equal, when the price (P) of a good or service falls, the quantity demanded (Q_D) increases, and conversely, if the price of a good or service rises, the quantity demanded decreases.

$$P \uparrow \Rightarrow Q_D \downarrow \text{ or } P \downarrow \Rightarrow Q_D \uparrow$$

The law of demand puts the concept of basic human "needs," at least as an analytical tool, to rest. Needs are those things that you must have at any price. That is, there are no substitutes. There are usually plenty of substitutes available for any good, some better than others. The law of demand, with its inverse relationship between price and quantity demanded, implies that even so-called needs are more or less urgent depending on the circumstances (opportunity costs). Whenever you hear somebody say, "I need a new car," "I need the latest version of iPhone," or "I need new clothes," always be sure to ask: What does the person really mean? At what price does that person "need" the good?

The Negative Relationship between Price and Quantity Demanded

The law of demand describes a negative (inverse) relationship between price and quantity demanded. When price goes up, the quantity demanded goes down, and vice versa. But why is this so? One reason for the negative relationship is what economists call

law of demand
the quantity of a good or service demanded varies inversely (negatively) with its price, ceteris paribus

Need water? What if the price of water increases significantly? At the new higher price, consumers will still use almost as much water for essentials like drinking and cooking. However, they may no longer "need" to wash their cars as often, water their lawns daily, hose off their sidewalks, run the dishwasher so frequently, take long showers, or flush the toilet as often.

Jetta Productions/Stone/Getty Images

diminishing marginal utility—the concept that in a given time period, an individual will receive less satisfaction from each successive unit of a good consumed. For example, a second ice cream cone will yield less satisfaction than the first, a third will yield less satisfaction than the second, and so on. It follows from diminishing marginal utility that if people derive decreasing amounts of satisfaction from successive units, consumers will buy additional units only if the price is reduced.

Other reasons for this inverse relationship are the substitution and income effects. According to the **substitution effect,** at higher prices, buyers increasingly substitute other goods for the good that now has a higher relative price. For example, if the price of orange juice increases, some consumers may substitute other juices for orange juice, such as apple or tomato juice, or perhaps water, milk, or coffee. According to the **income effect,** higher prices make the buyer feel poorer, causing a lowering of quantity demanded (since they cannot buy the same quantity of goods as they did when prices were lower). For example, when the price of pizza rises, this results in a decrease in the purchasing power of the consumer's income, which will usually lead to the consumer buying less pizza.

substitution effect

at higher prices, buyers increasingly substitute other goods for the good that now has a higher relative price

income effect

at higher prices, buyers feel poorer, causing a lowering of quantity demanded

WHAT IS AN INDIVIDUAL DEMAND SCHEDULE AND CURVE?

The **individual demand schedule** is a table that shows the relationship between the price of the good and the quantity demanded. For example, suppose Elizabeth enjoys eating apples. How many kilograms of apples would Elizabeth be willing and able to buy at various prices during the year? At a price of $3 a kilogram, Elizabeth buys 15 kilograms of apples over the course of a year. If the price is higher, at $4 per kilogram, she might buy only 10 kilograms; if it is lower, say $1 per kilogram, she might buy 25 kilograms of apples during the year. Elizabeth's demand for apples for the year is summarized in the demand schedule in Exhibit 1. Elizabeth might not be consciously aware of the amounts that she would purchase at prices other than the prevailing one, but that does not alter the fact that she has a schedule in the sense that she would have bought various other amounts had other prices prevailed. It must be emphasized that the schedule is a list of alternative possibilities. At any one time, only one of the prices will prevail, so a certain quantity will be purchased.

individual demand schedule

a table that shows the relationship between price and quantity demanded

An Individual Demand Curve

An **individual demand curve** is a graphical representation that shows the inverse relationship between price and quantity demanded. By plotting the different prices and corresponding quantities demanded in Elizabeth's demand schedule in Exhibit 1 and then connecting them, we can create an individual demand curve for Elizabeth (Exhibit 2). From the curve, we can see that when the price is higher, the quantity demanded is lower, and when the price is lower, the quantity demanded is higher. The demand curve shows how the quantity demanded of the good changes as its price varies.

individual demand curve

a graphical representation that shows the inverse relationship between price and quantity demanded

section 3.1	Elizabeth's Demand
Exhibit 1	Schedule for Apples

Price (per kilogram)	Quantity Demanded (kilograms per year)
$5	5
4	10
3	15
2	20
1	25

WHAT IS A MARKET DEMAND CURVE?

Although we introduced this concept in terms of the individual, economists usually speak of the demand curve in terms of large groups of people—a whole nation, a community, or a trading area. As you know, every single individual has his or her demand curve for every product. The horizontal summation of individual demand curves is called the **market demand curve.**

Suppose the consumer group comprises Homer, Marge, and the rest of their small community, Springfield, and that the product is still apples. The effect of price on the quantity of apples demanded by Marge, Homer, and the rest of Springfield is given in the demand schedule and demand curves shown in Exhibit 3. At $4 per kilogram, Homer would be willing and able to buy 20 kilograms of apples per year, Marge would be willing and able to buy 10 kilograms, and the rest of Springfield would be willing and able to buy 2970 kilograms. At $3 per kilogram, Homer would be willing and able to buy 25 kilograms of apples per year, Marge would be willing and able to buy 15 kilograms, and the rest of Springfield would be willing and able to buy 4960 kilograms. The market demand curve is simply the (horizontal) sum of the quantities Homer, Marge, and the rest of Springfield demand at each price. That is, at $4, the quantity demanded in the market would be 3000 kilograms of apples (20 + 10 + 2970 = 3000), and at $3, the quantity demanded in the market would be 5000 kilograms of apples (25 + 15 + 4960 = 5000).

In Exhibit 4, we offer a more complete set of prices and quantities from the market demand for apples during the year. Remember, the market demand curve shows the amounts that all the buyers in the market would be willing and able to buy at various prices. For example, if the price of apples is $2 per kilogram, consumers in the market would collectively be willing and able to buy 8000 kilograms per year. At $1 per kilogram, the amount demanded would be 12 000 kilograms per year.

The market demand curve is the negative (inverse) relationship between price and the total quantity demanded, while holding constant all other factors that affect how much consumers are able and willing to pay, *ceteris paribus*. For the most part, we are interested in how the market works, so we will primarily use the market demand curves.

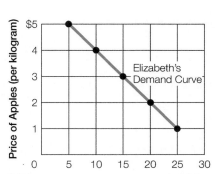

section 3.1 Exhibit 2
Elizabeth's Demand Curve for Apples

The dots represent various quantities of apples that Elizabeth would be willing and able to buy at different prices in a given time period. The demand curve shows how the quantity demanded varies inversely with the price of the good when we hold everything else constant—*ceteris paribus*. Because of this inverse relationship between price and quantity demanded, the demand curve is downward sloping.

market demand curve
the horizontal summation of individual demand curves

Every Boxing Day, eager consumers line up at the break of dawn in front of retailers that are advertising deep discounts and two-for-one deals. Although they didn't want to buy the televisions, game consoles, clothing, and computers at the regular asking prices, many clearly want these goods at a lower price—the law of demand.

Toronto Star via Getty Images

a. Creating a Market Demand Schedule for Apples

Quantity Demanded (kilograms per year)

Price (per kilogram)	Homer	+	Marge	+	Rest of Springfield	=	Market Demand
$4	20	+	10	+	2970	=	3000
$3	25	+	15	+	4960	=	5000

b. Creating a Market Demand Curve for Apples

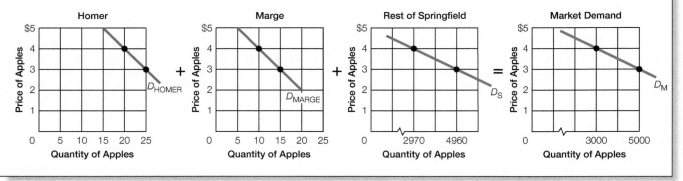

a. Market Demand Schedule for Apples

Price (per kilogram)	Total Quantity Demanded (kilograms per year)
$5	1000
4	3000
3	5000
2	8000
1	12 000

b. Market Demand Curve for Apples

The market demand curve shows the amounts that all buyers in the market would be willing to buy at various prices. If the price of apples is $2 per kilogram, consumers in the market would collectively be willing to buy 8000 kilograms per year. At $1 per kilogram, the amount demanded would be 12 000 kilograms per year.

SECTION CHECK

■ The law of demand states that when the price of a good falls (rises), the quantity demanded rises (falls), *ceteris paribus.*
■ An individual demand curve is a graphical representation of the relationship between the price and the quantity demanded.
■ The market demand curve shows the amount of a good that all the buyers in the market would be willing and able to buy at various prices.

Shifts in the Demand Curve

■ What is the difference between a change in demand and a change in quantity demanded?
■ What are the determinants of demand?
■ Can we review the distinction between changes in demand and changes in quantity demanded?

WHAT IS THE DIFFERENCE BETWEEN A CHANGE IN DEMAND AND A CHANGE IN QUANTITY DEMANDED?

Understanding the relationship between price and quantity demanded is so important that economists make a clear distinction between it and the various other factors that can influence consumer behaviour. A change in a good's price is said to lead to a **change in quantity demanded.** That is, it "moves you along" a given demand curve. The demand curve is drawn under the assumption that all other things are held constant, except the price of the good. However, economists know that price is not the only thing that affects the quantity of a good that people buy. The other factors that influence the demand curve are called *determinants of demand* and a change in these other factors *shifts the entire demand curve.* These determinants of demand are called *demand shifters* and they lead to a **change in demand.**

change in quantity demanded
a change in a good's price leads to a change in quantity demanded, a move along a given demand curve

change in demand
a change in a determinant of demand leads to a change in demand, a shift of the entire demand curve

WHAT ARE THE DETERMINANTS OF DEMAND?

An increase in demand shifts the demand curve to the right; a decrease in demand shifts the demand curve to the left, as seen in Exhibit 1. Changes in demand such as these are the result of demand shifters. Some of the possible demand shifters are the prices of related goods, income, number of buyers, tastes, and expectations. We will now look more closely at each of these variables.

The Prices of Related Goods

In deciding how much of a good or service to buy, consumers are influenced by the price of that good or service, a relationship summarized in the law of demand.

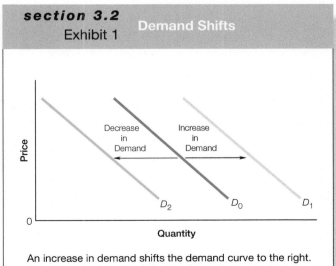

section 3.2
Exhibit 1   **Demand Shifts**

An increase in demand shifts the demand curve to the right. A decrease in demand shifts the demand curve to the left.

However, consumers are also influenced by the prices of *related* goods and services—substitutes and complements.

Substitutes   Substitutes are generally goods for which one could be used in place of the other. To many, substitutes would include butter and margarine, domestic and foreign cars, movie tickets and on-demand TV programs, jackets and sweaters, Petro Canada and Shell gasoline, and Nikes and Adidas.

Suppose you go into a store to buy a couple of six packs of Coca-Cola and you see that Pepsi is on sale for half its usual price. Is it possible that you might decide to buy Pepsi instead of Coca-Cola? Economists argue that this is the case, and empirical tests have confirmed that people are responsive to both the price of the good in question and the prices of related goods. In this example, Pepsi and Coca-Cola are said to be substitutes. Two goods are **substitutes** if an increase (a decrease) in the price of one good causes an increase (a decrease) in the demand for another good, a direct (or positive) relationship. In Exhibit 2(a), we see that as the price of Coca-Cola increased—a movement up along your demand curve for it—you increased your demand for Pepsi, resulting in a shift in the demand for Pepsi (Exhibit 2[b]).

substitute
an increase (a decrease) in the price of one good causes an increase (a decrease) in the demand for another good

Complements   Complements are goods that "go together," often consumed and used simultaneously, such as skis and bindings, peanut butter and jam, hot dogs and buns, digital music players and downloadable music, and printers and ink cartridges. If an increase (a decrease) in the price of one good causes a decrease (an increase) in the demand of another good (an inverse or negative relationship), the two goods are called **complements.** For example, in Exhibit 3(a), we see that as the price of computers increases, the quantity demanded of computers falls (a movement in demand). And with fewer computers being purchased, we would expect people to decrease their demand (a leftward shift) for printers (Exhibit 3[b]).

complement
an increase (a decrease) in the price of one good causes a decrease (an increase) in the demand of another good

Income

Economists have observed that generally the consumption of goods and services is positively related to the income available to consumers. Empirical studies support the notion that as individuals receive more income they tend to increase their purchases

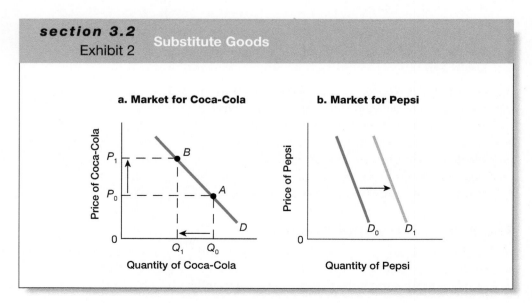

section 3.2
Exhibit 2   Substitute Goods

a. Market for Coca-Cola

b. Market for Pepsi

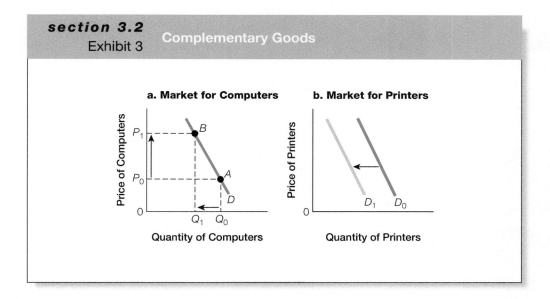

section 3.2

Exhibit 3   **Complementary Goods**

a. Market for Computers

b. Market for Printers

of most goods and services. Other things held equal, rising income usually leads to an increase in the demand for goods (a rightward shift of the demand curve), and decreasing income usually leads to a decrease in the demand for goods (a leftward shift of the demand curve).

Normal and Inferior Goods

If when income increases, the demand for a good increases and decreases when income decreases, the good is called a **normal good.** Most goods are normal goods. Consumers will typically buy more cellphones, clothes, pizzas, and trips to the movies as their incomes rise. However, if when income increases, the demand for a good decreases and increases when income decreases, the good is called an **inferior good.** For example, for most people inferior goods might include inexpensive cuts of meat, used cars, gently-used clothing, and macaroni and cheese. The term *inferior* in this sense does not refer to the quality of the good in question but shows that when income changes, demand changes in the opposite direction (inversely).

    Consider how an increase in income can affect the market for automobiles and the market for public transit. Automobiles are generally considered a normal good, so a rise in income will increase the demand for automobiles (Exhibit 4[a]). However, the

normal good

if income increases, the demand for a good increases; if income decreases, the demand for a good decreases

inferior good

if income increases, the demand for a good decreases; if income decreases, the demand for a good increases

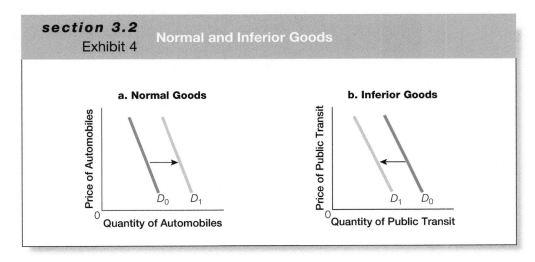

section 3.2

Exhibit 4   **Normal and Inferior Goods**

a. Normal Goods

b. Inferior Goods

Brenda Carson/Shutterstock.com

Body piercing and tattoos have risen in popularity in recent years. As the preference for these types of personal expression increases, the demand for these services is shifted to the right. According to the Pew Research Center, 32 percent of 18- to 29-year-olds acknowledged having at least one tattoo.

demand for public transit may fall, as higher incomes allow consumers to buy automobiles. The demand for public transit would then be an inferior good (Exhibit 4[b]).

For example, if people's incomes rise and they increase their demand for movie tickets, we say that movie tickets are a normal good. But if people's incomes fall and they increase their demand for bus rides, we say bus rides are an inferior good. Whether goods are normal or inferior, the point here is that income influences demand—usually positively, but sometimes negatively.

Number of Buyers

The demand for a good or service will vary with the size of the potential consumer population. The demand for wheat, for example, rises as population increases because the added population wants to consume wheat products, like bread or cereal. Marketing experts, who closely follow the patterns of consumer behaviour with regards to a particular good or service, are usually vitally concerned with the "demographics" of the product—the vital statistics of the potential consumer population, including size, income, and age characteristics. For example, market researchers for baby-food companies keep a close watch on the birth rate.

Tastes

The demand for a good or service may increase or decrease suddenly with changes in fashions or fads. Taste changes may be triggered by advertising or promotion, by a news story, by the behaviour of some popular public figure, and so on. Taste changes are particularly noticeable in apparel. Skirt lengths, coat lapels, shoe styles, and tie sizes change frequently.

Changes in preferences naturally lead to shifts in demand. Much of the predictive power of economic theory, however, stems from the assumption that tastes are relatively stable, at least over a substantial period of time. Tastes *do* change, though. A person may grow tired of one type of recreation or food and try another type. Changes in occupation, number of dependants, state of health, and age also tend to alter preferences. The birth of a baby may cause a family to spend less on recreation and more on food and clothing. Illness increases the demand for medicine and lessens purchases of other goods. A cold winter increases the demand for natural gas. Changes in customs and traditions also affect preferences, and the development of new products draws consumer preferences away from other goods. Digital music files have replaced compact discs, just as flat-screen televisions have replaced traditional tube TVs. A change in information can also impact consumers' demand. For example, an outbreak of *Escherichia coli* or new information about a defective and/or dangerous product, such as a baby crib, can reduce demand.

Expectations

Sometimes the demand for a good or service in a given time period will dramatically increase or decrease because consumers expect the good to change in price or availability at some future date. For example, buyers may expect oil production in Alberta to be lower because of the ongoing delays in getting the Keystone XL pipeline into service. As a result of these expectations of potentially higher future gasoline prices, buyers may increase their current demand for gasoline. That is, the current price for gasoline could shift to the right. Other examples, such as waiting to buy a personal computer because price reductions may be even greater in the future, are also common. Or, if you expect to earn additional income next month, you may be more willing to dip into your current savings to buy something this month.

CAN WE REVIEW THE DISTINCTION BETWEEN CHANGES IN DEMAND AND CHANGES IN QUANTITY DEMANDED?

Economists put particular emphasis on the impact on consumer behaviour of a change in the price of a good. We are interested in distinguishing between consumer behaviour related to the price of a good itself (movement *along* a demand curve) from behaviour related to other factors changing (shifts of the demand curve).

As indicated earlier, if the price of a good changes, we say that this leads to a *"change in quantity demanded."* In Exhibit 5, the movement from A to B is called an *increase in quantity demanded,* and the movement from B to A is called a *decrease in quantity demanded.* Economists use the phrase "increase in quantity demanded" or "decrease in quantity demanded" to describe movements along a given demand curve. If one of the other factors (determinants) influencing consumer behaviour changes, we say there is a *change in demand*. In Exhibit 5, the change from A to C is called an *increase in demand,* and the change from C to A is called a *decrease in demand.* The phrase "increase in demand" or "decrease in demand" is reserved for a shift in the whole curve. So if an individual buys more CDs because the price fell, we say there was an increase in quantity demanded. However, if she buys more CDs even at the current price, say $10, we say there is an increase in demand. The effects of some of the other determinants that cause a change in demand (shifters) are reviewed in Exhibit 6.

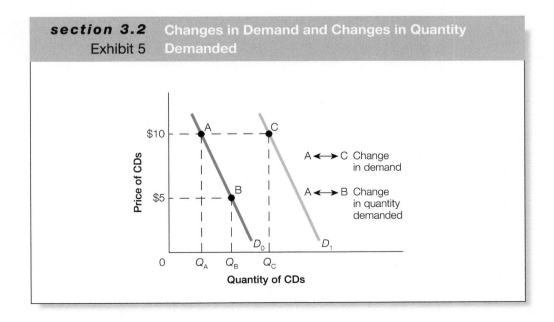

section 3.2   Changes in Demand and Changes in Quantity
     Exhibit 5   Demanded

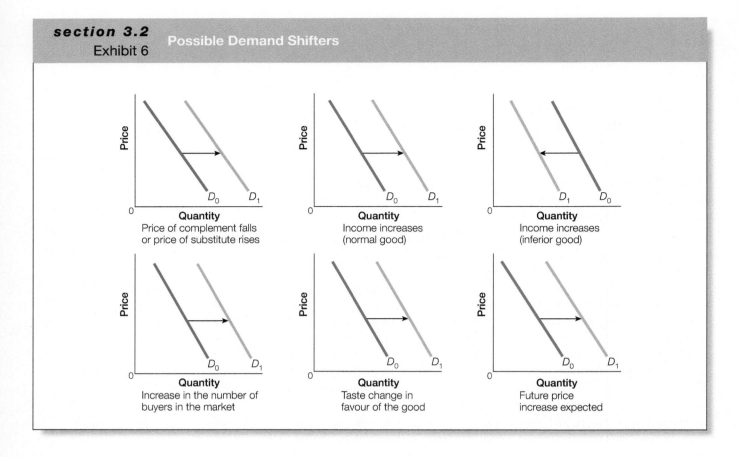

Price of complement falls
or price of substitute rises

Income increases
(normal good)

Income increases
(inferior good)

Increase in the number of
buyers in the market

Taste change in
favour of the good

Future price
increase expected

SECTION CHECK

■ A change in the quantity demanded describes a movement along a given demand curve in response to a change in the price of the good. A change in demand shifts the entire demand curve in response to a change in some determinant of demand.

■ Some possible determinants of demand (demand shifters) are the prices of related goods, income, number of buyers, tastes, and expectations.

Change in Variable and Change in Demand

Variable	Change in Variable	Change in Demand
1. Price of a complement good	↑	

Variable	Change in Variable	Change in Demand
2. Price of a substitute good	↑	
3. Income (normal good)	↑	
4. Income (inferior good)	↑	
5. Number of buyers	↑	
6. Tastes and preferences	↑	
7. Expected future price	↑	

section
3.3

Supply

- What is the law of supply?
- What is an individual supply curve?
- What is a market supply curve?

WHAT IS THE LAW OF SUPPLY?

In a market, the answer to the fundamental question "What do we produce, and in what quantities?" depends on the interaction of both buyers and sellers. Demand is only half the story. The willingness and ability of suppliers to provide goods are equally important factors that must be weighed by decision makers in all societies. As with demand, the price of the good is an important factor. And just as with demand, factors other than the price of the good are also important to suppliers, such as the cost of inputs or advances in technology. Although behaviour will vary among individual suppliers, economists expect, other things being equal, that the quantity supplied will vary directly with the price of the good, a relationship called the **law of supply.** According to the law of supply, the higher the price of the good (P), the greater the quantity supplied (Q_s), and the lower the price of the good, the smaller the quantity supplied, *ceteris paribus.*

In order to get more oil, drillers must sometimes drill deeper or go into unexplored areas, and they still may come up with a dry hole. If it costs more to increase oil production, then oil prices would have to rise in order for producers to increase their output.

law of supply
the higher (lower) the price of the good, the greater (smaller) the quantity supplied, ceteris paribus

$$P\uparrow \Rightarrow Q_s\uparrow \text{ or } P\downarrow \Rightarrow Q_s\downarrow$$

The relationship described by the law of supply is a direct, or positive, relationship, because the variables move in the same direction.

A Positive Relationship between Price and Quantity Supplied

Firms supplying goods and services want to increase their profits, and the higher the price per unit, the greater the profitability generated by supplying more of that good. For example, if you were an apple grower, wouldn't you much rather be paid $5 a kilogram than $1 a kilogram, *ceteris paribus.*

There is another reason that supply curves are upward sloping. In Chapter 2, the law of increasing opportunity costs demonstrated that when we hold technology and input prices constant, producing additional units of a good will require increased opportunity costs. That is, when we produce something, we use the most efficient resources first (those with the lowest opportunity cost) and then draw on less efficient resources (those with a higher opportunity cost) as more of the good is produced. Because costs per unit rise as more are produced, sellers must receive a higher price to increase the quantity supplied, *ceteris paribus.*

WHAT IS AN INDIVIDUAL SUPPLY CURVE?

individual supply curve
a graphical representation that shows the positive relationship between price and quantity supplied

To illustrate the concept of an individual supply curve, consider the amount of apples that an individual supplier, John Macintosh, is willing and able to supply in one year. The law of supply can be illustrated, like the law of demand, by a table or graph. John's supply schedule for apples is shown in Exhibit 1(a). The price–quantity supplied combinations were then plotted and joined to create the individual supply curve shown in Exhibit 1(b). The resulting **individual supply curve** is a graphical representation that

section 3.3
Exhibit 1   An Individual Supply Curve

a. John's Supply Schedule for Apples

Price (per kilogram)	Quantity Supplied (kilograms per year)
$5	80
4	70
3	50
2	30
1	10

b. John's Supply Curve for Apples

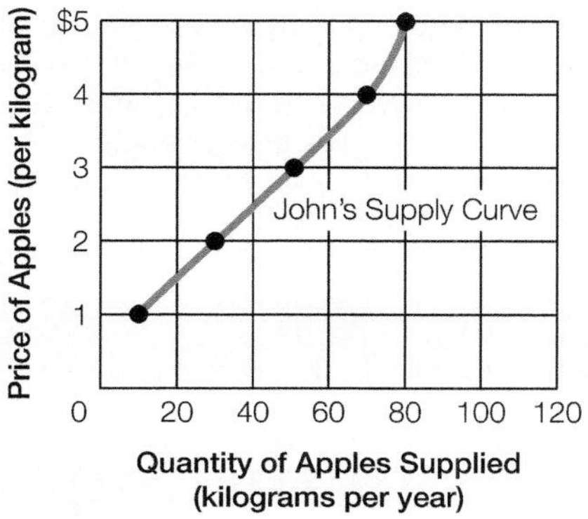

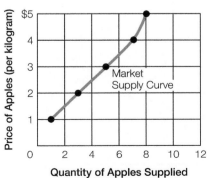

shows the positive relationship between the price and the quantity supplied. Note that the individual supply curve is upward sloping as you move from left to right. At higher prices, it will be more attractive to increase production. Existing firms, or growers, will produce more at higher prices than at lower prices.

WHAT IS A MARKET SUPPLY CURVE?

The **market supply curve** can be thought of as the horizontal summation of individual supply curves. The market supply schedule, which reflects the total quantity supplied at each price by all of the apple producers, is shown in Exhibit 2(a). Exhibit 2(b) illustrates the resulting market supply curve for this group of apple producers.

market supply curve
the horizontal summation of individual supply curves

section 3.3
Exhibit 2   A Market Supply Curve

a. Market Supply Schedule for Apples

		Quantity Supplied (kilograms per year)		
Price	John	+	Other Producers =	Market Supply
$5	80	+	7920 =	8000
4	70	+	6930 =	7000
3	50	+	4950 =	5000
2	30	+	2970 =	3000
1	10	+	990 =	1000

b. Market Supply Curve for Apples

The dots on this graph indicate different quantities of apples that producers would be willing and able to supply at various prices. The line connecting those combinations is the market supply curve.

section 3.4
Shifts in the Supply Curve

■ What is the difference between a change in supply and a change in quantity supplied?

■ What are the determinants of supply?

■ Can we review the distinction between a change in supply and a change in quantity supplied?

WHAT IS THE DIFFERENCE BETWEEN A CHANGE IN SUPPLY AND A CHANGE IN QUANTITY SUPPLIED?

Changes in the price of a good lead to changes in quantity supplied by suppliers, just as changes in the price of a good lead to changes in quantity demanded by buyers. Similarly, a change in supply, whether an increase or a decrease, will occur for reasons other than changes in the price of the product itself, just as changes in demand are due to factors (determinants) other than the price of the good. In other words, a change in the price of the good in question is shown as a movement along a given supply curve, leading to a change in quantity supplied. A change in any other factor that can affect supplier behaviour (input prices, the prices of related products, expectations, number of suppliers, technology, regulation, taxes and subsidies, and weather) results in *a shift in the entire supply curve,* leading to a change in supply.

WHAT ARE THE DETERMINANTS OF SUPPLY?

An increase in supply shifts the supply curve to the right; a decrease in supply shifts the supply curve to the left, as seen in Exhibit 1. We will now look at some of the possible determinants of supply—factors that determine the position of the supply curve—in greater depth.

Input Prices

Suppliers are strongly influenced by the costs of inputs used in the production process, such as steel used for automobiles or microchips used in computers. For

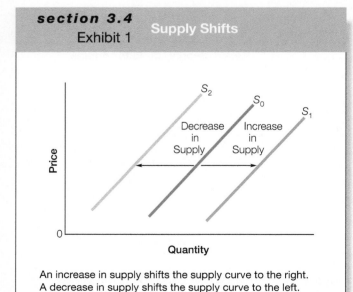

section 3.4
Exhibit 1   Supply Shifts

An increase in supply shifts the supply curve to the right. A decrease in supply shifts the supply curve to the left.

example, higher labour, materials, energy, or other input costs increase the costs of production, causing the supply curve to shift to the left at each and every price. If input prices fall, this will lower the costs of production, causing the supply curve to shift to the right—more will be supplied at each and every price.

The Prices of Related Products

Consider a car manufacturer that produces both electric and natural gas models of its vehicles. If the price of the natural gas vehicles falls, producers will reduce their quantity supplied, as seen in Exhibit 2(a). What effect would this lower price of the natural gas vehicles have on the manufacturer's decision to produce electric models of their cars? Easy question—it would increase the supply of the electric models because electric and natural gas models of car are *substitutes in production* because both goods can be produced using the same resources. You would want to produce relatively fewer of the model that had fallen in price (natural gas) and relatively more of the now more attractive other model (electric).

This example demonstrates why the price of related products is important as a supply shifter as well as a demand shifter. Producers tend to substitute the production of more profitable products for that of less profitable products. This is desirable from society's perspective as well because more profitable products tend to be those considered more valuable by society, whereas less profitable products are usually considered less valuable. Hence, the lower price in the natural gas vehicle market has caused an increase in supply (a rightward shift) in the electric vehicle market, as seen in Exhibit 2(b).

Alternatively, if the price of natural gas vehicles, a substitute in production, increases, then that model becomes more profitable. This leads to an increase in the quantity supplied of natural gas vehicles. Consequently, manufacturers will shift their resources out of the relatively lower priced models (electric); the result is a decrease in supply of electric vehicles.

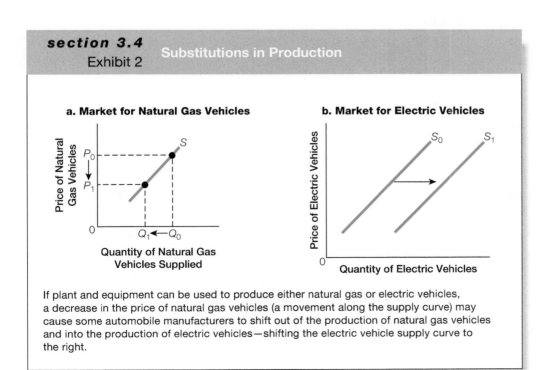

section 3.4
Exhibit 2   **Substitutions in Production**

a. Market for Natural Gas Vehicles

b. Market for Electric Vehicles

If plant and equipment can be used to produce either natural gas or electric vehicles, a decrease in the price of natural gas vehicles (a movement along the supply curve) may cause some automobile manufacturers to shift out of the production of natural gas vehicles and into the production of electric vehicles—shifting the electric vehicle supply curve to the right.

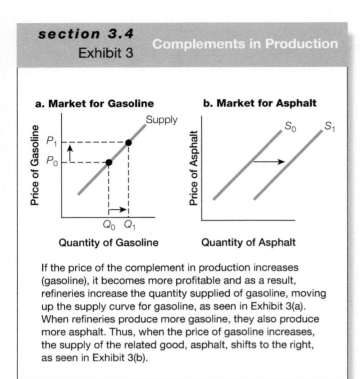

a. Market for Gasoline

b. Market for Asphalt

If the price of the complement in production increases (gasoline), it becomes more profitable and as a result, refineries increase the quantity supplied of gasoline, moving up the supply curve for gasoline, as seen in Exhibit 3(a). When refineries produce more gasoline, they also produce more asphalt. Thus, when the price of gasoline increases, the supply of the related good, asphalt, shifts to the right, as seen in Exhibit 3(b).

Other examples of substitutes in production include farmers who have to decide between producing wheat or corn, or construction companies that have to choose between building single-family houses or commercial buildings.

Some goods are *complements in production.* Producing one good does not prevent the production of the other, but actually enables production of the other. For example, asphalt (which is used in road construction and roof shingles) is a marketable by-product obtained from the process of refining crude oil. Refined crude oil itself has a wide variety of applications, such as gasoline, jet fuel, diesel fuel, and home heating oil. Suppose the price of refined crude oil, say gasoline, rises and as a result, refineries increase the quantity supplied of gasoline, moving up the supply curve for gasoline, as seen in Exhibit 3(a). When refineries produce more gasoline, they automatically produce more asphalt. Thus, when the price of gasoline increases, the supply of the related good, asphalt, shifts to the right, as seen in Exhibit 3(b). Suppose the price of gasoline falls, and as a result, the quantity supplied of gasoline falls; this leads to a decrease (a leftward shift) in the supply of asphalt.

Other examples of complements in production where goods are produced simultaneously from the same resource include a lumber mill that produces lumber and sawdust and an oil refinery that can produce gasoline or heating oil from the same resource—crude oil.

Expectations

Another factor shifting supply is suppliers' expectations. If producers expect a higher price in the future, they will supply less now than they otherwise would have, preferring to wait and sell when their goods will be more valuable. For example, if an oil producer expected the future price of oil to be higher next year, he might decide to store some of his current production of oil for next year when the price would be higher. Similarly, if producers expect now that the price will be lower later, they will supply more now.

Number of Suppliers

We are normally interested in market demands and supplies (because together they determine prices and quantities) rather than in the behaviour of individual consumers and firms. As we discussed earlier, the supply curves of individual suppliers can be summed horizontally to create a market supply curve. An increase in the number of suppliers leads to an increase in supply, denoted by a rightward shift in the supply curve. For example, think of the number of smartphones that have entered the market over the last ten years, shifting the supply curve of smartphones to the right. An exodus of suppliers has the opposite impact, a decrease in supply, which is indicated by a leftward shift in the supply curve.

Business *CONNECTION*

USING DEMAND AND SUPPLY

Just as economics is the game of life, so demand and supply is the game of business. Students sometimes ask whether firms construct their own demand and supply curves, and if so, how. In reality, few firms actually do such analysis and those that do are usually larger firms that have the resources. Most of our economy is built on small and medium-sized enterprises (SMEs) and they simply don't have the time, money, or know-how to build such elaborate models. That triggers another question: Why do we have to learn this anyway if it's not used? The fact is that entrepreneurs and managers use their knowledge of demand and supply every day to make business decisions, even though you won't see evidence of the graphs on their desks.

These decision makers have learned the basics of demand and supply and they know instinctively how certain stimuli will affect their firm. They spend hours trying to understand where their firm's strengths, weaknesses, opportunities, or threats (SWOT) lie, as well as considering how they will respond. Threats generally shift the demand curves leftward, whereas positive responses are opportunities that may shift the curves rightward. A firm building on its strengths will shift demand (and supply) rightward, and ignoring the weaknesses will likely bring leftward shifts of the curves. The process relies less on having to literally illustrate the movements of the curves than it does on understanding that they will move. Managing both internal and external change is what business is all about. Let's investigate a bit more.

Managers constantly face the realities of external changes, and if you've taken basic business courses you will likely be thinking now about political, economic, social, and technological (PEST) factors analysis. A PEST analysis looks at the external issues that entrepreneurs cannot change. All of the PEST factors affect demand for a company's products and how it responds in supplying the product. Managers ignore these factors at their peril.

Once confronted with the external environment, managers do respond. They may want to increase revenues, increasing quantity (Q) or perhaps they leave Q and increase prices (P). Remember that an increase in price will result in a decrease in quantity demanded. Perhaps the managers need

to seek new markets, or compete against substitutions—here they are shifting the demand curve. How do they do that? Remember that managers can't change the PEST factors, they can only use that information. What they can change are the 4Ps (price, product, place, and promotion). Managers can, and do, change Ps to try to meet or change the market demand, shifting the demand curve rightward if they want to grow the market, or shifting it leftward if they are contracting (which they sometimes do).

Once the demand curve has shifted, it's the operations side of the business that responds to meeting the new realities by shifting the supply curve. If the firm doesn't respond and leaves the supply curve static, and the demand has shifted rightward, then it will have produced its own shortage and consumers may turn to competitors to buy the goods they want—which means lost sales, or opportunity costs, to the firm. If on the other hand, the firm ramps up production beyond what consumers want, the firm will have produced its own surplus, which will require lowering prices later or having to accept sunk costs if the firm has to scrap the product. Either way, those are losses to the firm.

Clearly a dance between the theory and the practical application of economics goes on in every firm every day. You don't necessarily have to see evidence of theory to know that it's working—you just have to look at what's happening within the firm daily to see the practical application of demand and supply at work.

1. Which do you think occurs first in the economy: businesses responding to changes in demand or consumers responding to changes in the supply of goods and services? What do you think would happen if the opposite occurred?

2. In your opinion, has the rise of e-commerce and online purchasing increased growth in the economy? In what other ways has e-commerce affected the economy?

3. There is a plethora of "dollar stores" that purchase the oversupply of many manufacturers and sell it at a discount. Do you think this is efficient for the economy? Thinking broadly, do you think consumers and businesses benefit or not? Explain.

Technology

Most of us think of prices as constantly rising, given the existence of inflation, but, in fact, decreases in costs often occur because of technological progress, and such advances can lower prices. Human creativity works to find new ways to produce goods and services using fewer or less costly inputs of labour, natural resources, or capital. In recent years, despite generally rising prices, the prices of electronic equipment such as computers, cellphones, and flat-screen televisions have fallen dramatically. At any given price this year, suppliers are willing to provide many more (of a given quality of) computers than in previous years simply because technology has dramatically reduced the cost of providing them. Graphically, the increase in supply is indicated by a shift to the right in the supply curve.

Regulation

Supply may also change because of changes in the legal and regulatory environment in which firms operate. Government regulations can influence the costs of production to the firm, leading to cost-induced supply changes similar to those just discussed. For example, if new safety or anti-pollution requirements increase labour and capital costs, the increased cost will result, other things equal, in a decrease in supply, shifting the supply curve to the left, or up. An increase in a government-imposed minimum wage may have a similar effect by raising labour costs and decreasing supply in markets that employ many low-wage workers. However, deregulation—the process by which governments reduce or outright eliminate restrictions on individuals or businesses—can shift the supply curve to the right.

Taxes and Subsidies

Certain types of taxes can also increase the costs of production borne by the supplier, causing the supply curve to shift to the left at each price. The opposite of a tax (a subsidy) can lower the firm's costs and shift the supply curve to the right. For example, the government sometimes provides farmers with subsidies to encourage the production of certain agricultural products.

Weather

In addition, weather can certainly affect the supply of certain commodities, particularly agricultural products and transportation services. A drought or freezing temperatures will almost certainly cause the supply curves for many crops to shift to the

DEBATE

IS IT ETHICAL TO GROW CORN FOR FUEL?

For:
Over the past decade, the market has adjusted to rising gas prices by blending ethanol into gasoline. The widespread use of corn-based ethanol has been a boon for farmers, who are free to choose which markets to participate in. Most farmers will choose to grow the crop that provides the greatest return on their investment and at present, corn is an extremely lucrative crop. Note, though, that as there is a rise in the number of hectares devoted to corn, there is a drop in the number of hectares devoted to wheat and soy crops, which increases the price of wheat and soy crops and benefits the farmers who grow those crops. This is the market in action and there is nothing unethical about it. Why has the price of gas at the pumps risen—because of increased consumption (more people driving) or because of an increasing scarcity in the supply of crude oil? Surely you can defend the farmers' decisions.

Against:
In the long term, growing crops for fuel rather than for food will mean higher prices for food around the world and that will hurt the poorest people the most. This is unethical because the market, rather than an act of nature, is causing famine—the poor simply can't afford food. Clearly, the benefits flow to those who can afford fuel, so the poor get relatively little marginal benefit and those who cannot afford the higher costs of basic food staples now pay a much higher marginal cost than they otherwise would. Those who believe the market should consider ethical issues along with prices would likely support a less efficient market. Just because farmers can supply a crop for an alternative use, should they? What do you believe—should we promote growing corn for our transportation needs? Is there a conflict between the wider society's needs and the farmer as an individual?

left, whereas exceptionally good weather can shift a supply curve to the right. For example, record high temperatures coupled with little or no rainfall in central and eastern Canada during the summer of 2012 had a devastating impact on agricultural operations.

CAN WE REVIEW THE DISTINCTION BETWEEN A CHANGE IN SUPPLY AND A CHANGE IN QUANTITY SUPPLIED?

If the price of a good changes, we say this leads to a *change in the quantity supplied.* For example, in Exhibit 4, if the price of wheat rises from P_0 to P_1, the market for wheat experiences a movement from A to B. If one of the other factors influences sellers' behaviour, we say this leads to a *change in supply.* For example, if production costs fall because of a wage decrease or lower fuel costs, other things remaining constant, we would expect an increase in supply—that is, a rightward shift in the supply curve as illustrated by the change from B to C in Exhibit 4. Alternatively, if some variable, like lower input prices, causes the costs of production to fall, the supply curve will shift to the right. Exhibit 5 illustrates the effect of some of the determinants that cause shifts in the supply curve.

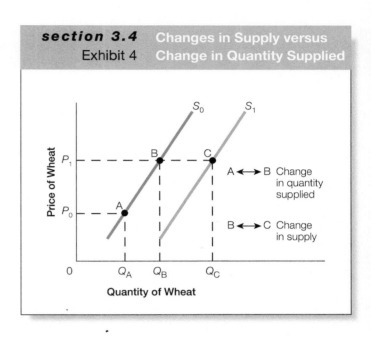

section 3.4 **Changes in Supply versus**
Exhibit 4 **Change in Quantity Supplied**

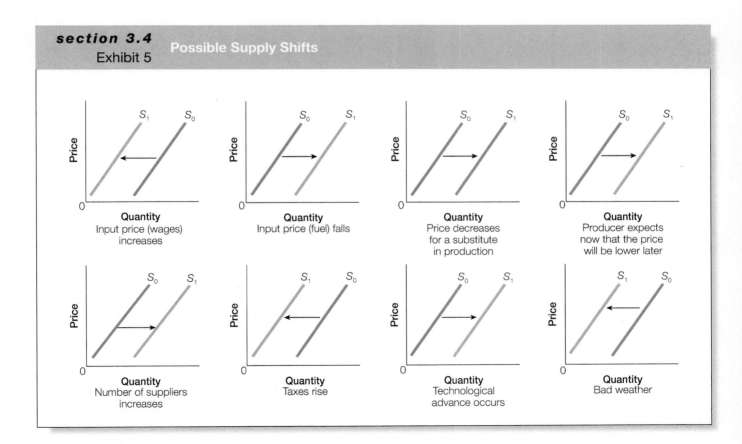

section 3.4 **Possible Supply Shifts**
Exhibit 5

SECTION CHECK

■ A movement along a given supply curve is caused by a change in the price of the good in question. As we move along the supply curve, we say there is a change in the quantity supplied. A shift of the entire supply curve is called a *change in supply.*

■ Input prices, the prices of related products, expectations, the number of suppliers, technology, regulation, taxes and subsidies, and weather can all lead to changes in supply (shifts in supply).

Change in Variable and Change in Supply

Variable	Change in Variable	Change in Supply
1. Input prices	↑	
2. Price of substitute in production	↑	
3. Price of complement in production	↑	
4. Expected future price	↑	

Variable	Change in Variable	Change in Supply
5. Number of suppliers	↑	
6. Government regulation	↑	
7. Taxes	↑	
8. Subsidies	↑	
9. Technology	↑	

For Your Review

Section 3.1

1. Assume the following demand schedule information:

Ben		Boris		Bilal	
P	Q_D	P	Q_D	P	Q_D
$5	1	$5	2	$5	3
4	2	4	4	4	6
3	3	3	6	3	9
2	4	2	8	2	12
1	5	1	10	1	15

a. Complete the market demand schedule if Ben and Bilal are the only demanders and graph the market demand curve.

P	Q_D
$5	
4	
3	
2	
1	

b. Complete the market demand schedule if Boris joins Ben and Bilal in the market and graph the market demand curve.

P	Q_D
$5	
4	
3	
2	
1	

c. Complete the market demand schedule if Ben now leaves the market and only Boris and Bilal remain, and graph the market demand curve.

P	Q_D
$5	
4	
3	
2	
1	

2. Sid moves from downtown Toronto, where he lived in a small condominium, to rural Alberta, where he buys a big house on two hectares of land. Using the law of demand, what do you think is true of land prices in downtown Toronto relative to those in rural Alberta?

3. The following table shows Hillary's demand schedule for Cherry Blossom lotion. Graph Hillary's demand curve.

Price (dollars per mL)	Quantity Demanded (mL per week)
15	5
12	10
9	15
6	20
3	25

4. The following table shows Cherry Blossom lotion demand schedules for Hillary's friends, Marita and Jacquie. If Hillary, Marita, and Jacquie constitute the whole market for Cherry Blossom lotion, complete the market demand schedule and graph the market demand curve.

Price (dollars per mL)	Quantity Demanded (mL per week)			
	Hillary	Marita	Jacquie	Market
15	5	0	15	_____
12	10	5	20	_____
9	15	10	25	_____
6	20	15	30	_____
3	25	20	35	_____

Section 3.2

5. What would be the effects of each of the following on the demand for hamburger in Swift Current, Saskatchewan. In each case, identify the responsible determinant of demand.

   a. The price of chicken falls.

   b. The price of hamburger buns doubles.

   c. Scientists find that eating hamburger prolongs life.

   d. The population of Swift Current doubles.

6. What would be the effect of each of the following on the demand for Chevrolets in Canada? In each case, identify the responsible determinant of demand.

   a. The price of Fords plummets.

   b. Consumers believe that the price of Chevrolets will rise next year.

   c. The incomes of Canadians rise.

   d. The price of gasoline falls dramatically.

7. The following graph shows three market demand curves for cantaloupe. Starting at point A, which point represents

   a. an increase in quantity demanded?

   b. an increase in demand?

   c. a decrease in demand?

   d. a decrease in quantity demanded?

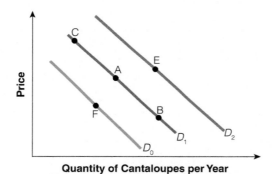

Quantity of Cantaloupes per Year

8. Using the demand curve, show the effect of the following events on the market for beef.

   a. Consumer income increases.

   b. The price of beef increases.

   c. An outbreak of mad cow disease occurs.

   d. The price of chicken (a substitute) increases.

   e. The price of barbecue grills (a complement) increases.

9. Draw the demand curves for the following goods. If the price of the first good listed rises, what will happen to the demand for the second good, and why?

   a. hamburger and ketchup

   b. Coca-Cola and Pepsi

   c. iPhone and an iPhone case

   d. golf clubs and golf balls

   e. a skateboard and a razor scooter

10. If the price of ice cream increased,
    a. what would be the effect on the demand for ice cream?
    b. what would be the effect on the demand for frozen yogurt?

11. Using the graph on the next page, answer the following questions:
    a. What is the shift from D_0 to D_1 called?
    b. What is the movement from (B) to (A) called?
    c. What is the movement from (A) to (B) called?
    d. What is the shift from D_1 to D_0 called?

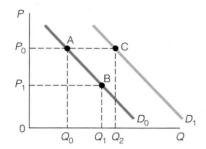

12. Show and describe what would happen to the market demand curve for a good in each of the following cases:
    a. an increase in the price of a substitute and a decrease in the price of a complement
    b. a decrease in the price of a substitute and an increase in the price of a complement
    c. an increase in the number of buyers and an increase in income, for a normal good
    d. a decrease in the number of buyers and an increase in income, for an inferior good
    e. a decrease in expected future prices and a shift in tastes away from the good

Section 3.3

13. Felix is a wheat farmer who has two fields he can use to grow wheat. The first field is right next to his house and the topsoil is rich and thick. The second field is 16 kilometres away in the mountains and the soil is rocky. At current wheat prices, Felix produces only from the field next to his house because the market price for wheat is just high enough to cover his costs of production, including a reasonable profit. What would have to happen to the market price of wheat for Felix to have the incentive to produce from the second field?

14. The following table shows the supply schedule for Rolling Rock Oil Co. Plot Rolling Rock's supply curve on a graph.

Price (dollars per barrel)	Quantity Demanded (barrels per month)
5	10 000
10	15 000
15	20 000
20	25 000
25	30 000

15. The following table shows the supply schedules for Rolling Rock and two other petroleum companies, Armadillo Oil and Pecos Petroleum. Assuming these three companies make up the entire supply side of the oil market, complete the market supply schedule and draw the market supply curve on a graph.

Quantity Supplied (barrels per month)				
Price (dollars per barrel)	Rolling Rock	Armadillo	Pecos	Market
5	10 000	8 000	2 000	_____
10	15 000	10 000	5 000	_____
15	20 000	12 000	8 000	_____
20	25 000	14 000	11 000	_____
25	30 000	16 000	14 000	_____

16. Assume the following supply schedule information.

Sacha		Steve		Sean	
P	Q_s	P	Q_s	P	Q_s
$5	10	$5	15	$5	5
4	8	4	12	4	4
3	6	3	9	3	3
2	4	2	6	2	2
1	2	1	3	1	1

a. Complete the market supply schedule if Sacha and Steve are the only suppliers and graph the market supply curve.

P	Q_s
$5	
4	
3	
2	
1	

b. Complete the market supply schedule if Sean joins Sacha and Steve in the market and graph the market supply curve.

P	Q_s
$5	
4	
3	
2	
1	

c. Complete the market supply schedule if Sacha now leaves the market and only Steve and Sean remain, and graph the market supply curve.

P	Q_s
$5	
4	
3	
2	
1	

Section 3.4

17. Using the graph below, answer the following questions:
    a. What is the shift from S_0 to S_1 called?
    b. What is the movement from (A) to (B) called?
    c. What is the movement from (B) to (A) called?
    d. What is the shift from S_1 to S_0 called?

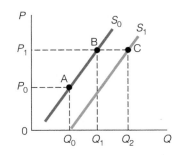

18. Show and describe what would happen to the market supply curve for a good in each of the following cases.
    a. an increase in the number of suppliers and an increase in subsidies
    b. a decrease in the number of suppliers and an increase in taxes
    c. an increase in input prices and increasing costs of regulation
    d. producers expect now that the price will be lower later

19. Many farmers in western Canada have the choice between growing fields of wheat or growing fields of corn, due to the nearly identical resources required to cultivate each crop. If the price of corn increased, what would be the effect on

    a. the supply of corn?

    b. the supply of wheat?

20. What would be the effect of each of the following on the supply of ketchup in Canada? In each case, identify the responsible determinant of supply.

    a. Tomato prices skyrocket (ketchup is made from tomatoes).

    b. Parliament places a 26 percent tax on ketchup.

    c. Entrepreneurs invent a new, faster tomato crusher to make ketchup.

    d. Wayne Gretzky, Justin Bieber, and Jim Carrey each introduce a new brand of ketchup.

21. What would be the effects of each of the following on the supply of coffee worldwide? In each case, identify the responsible determinant of supply.

    a. Freezing temperatures wipe out half of Brazil's coffee crop.

    b. The wages of coffee workers in Latin America rise as unionization efforts succeed.

    c. Indonesia offers big subsidies to its coffee producers.

    d. Genetic engineering produces a super coffee bean that grows faster and needs less care.

    e. Coffee suppliers expect prices to be higher in the future.

22. What would be the effect of each of the following on the supply of automobiles in Canada? In each case, identify the responsible determinant of supply.

    a. North American automobile makers are successful in negotiating wage reductions with their unionized workforce.

    b. Automobile manufacturers in India and China begin to sell their vehicles in Canada.

    c. The Canadian government decides to implement a specific tax on automobiles (the tax is to be paid by the automobile producers).

    d. Technological innovation in computer design and robotic assembly dramatically increase the efficiency of manufacturing automobiles in Canada.

23. The following graph shows three market supply curves for cantaloupe. Compared to point A, which point represents

    a. an increase in quantity supplied?

    b. an increase in supply?

    c. a decrease in quantity supplied?

    d. a decrease in supply?

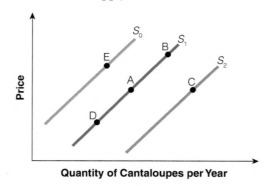

24. Molasses is a marketable by-product of sugar refining. That is, the more product that sugar refineries produce, the more molasses they generate. Molasses itself is used as an additive in livestock feed as well as the principal ingredient in the distillation of rum. If the price of sugar increased, what would be the effect on

    a. the supply of sugar?

    b. the supply of molasses?

Sections 3.2 and 3.4

25. Show the impact of each of the following events on the oil market.

    [*Note:* The 12 countries that comprise the Organization of the Petroleum Exporting Countries (OPEC) exert considerable control of the world market for oil.]

    a. OPEC becomes more effective in limiting the supply of oil.

    b. OPEC becomes less effective in limiting the supply of oil.

    c. The price for natural gas (a substitute for heating oil) rises.

    d. New oil discoveries occur in Alberta.

    e. Electric and hybrid cars become subsidized and their prices fall.

chapter 4

Bringing Supply and Demand Together

4.1 MARKET EQUILIBRIUM PRICE AND QUANTITY (PAGE 92)

4.2 CHANGES IN EQUILIBRIUM PRICE AND QUANTITY (PAGE 95)

4.3 PRICE CONTROLS (PAGE 102)

---

section 4.1

Market Equilibrium Price and Quantity

■ What is the equilibrium price and the equilibrium quantity?

■ What is a shortage and what is a surplus?

In the last chapter, we learned about demand and supply separately. We now bring the market supply and market demand together.

WHAT IS THE EQUILIBRIUM PRICE AND THE EQUILIBRIUM QUANTITY?

market equilibrium
the point at which the market supply and the market demand curves intersect

equilibrium price
the price at the intersection of the market supply and demand curves; at this price, the quantity demanded equals the quantity supplied

equilibrium quantity
the quantity at the intersection of the market supply and demand curves; at this quantity, the quantity demanded equals the quantity supplied

The **market equilibrium** is found at the point at which the market supply and the market demand curves intersect. It is at market equilibrium that two important values are determined: equilibrium price and equilibrium quantity. The **equilibrium price** is the price at the intersection of the market supply and demand curves. At this price, the quantity demanded equals the quantity supplied; that is, the amount that buyers are willing and able to buy is exactly equal to the amount that sellers are willing and able to produce. The **equilibrium quantity** is the quantity at the intersection of the market supply and demand curves. At this quantity, the quantity demanded equals the quantity supplied.

The equilibrium market solution is best understood with the help of a simple graph. Let's return to the apple example we used in our earlier discussions of supply and demand in Chapter 3. Exhibit 1 combines the market demand curve for apples with the market supply curve. At $3 per kilogram, buyers are willing to buy 5000 kilograms of apples and sellers are willing to supply 5000 kilograms of apples. Neither may be "happy" about the price, because the buyers would like a lower price and the sellers would like a higher price. But both buyers and sellers are able to carry out their purchase and sales plans at that $3 price. However, at any other price, either suppliers or demanders would be unable to trade as much as they would like.

section 4.1
Exhibit 1
A Hypothetical Market Supply and Demand Schedule for Apples

Price	Quantity Supplied	Quantity Demanded	Difference	State of Market
$5	8000	1000	7000	Surplus
4	7000	3000	4000	Surplus
3	5000	5000	0	Equilibrium
2	3000	8000	−5000	Shortage
1	1000	12 000	−11 000	Shortage

The equilibrium is $3 per kilogram and 5000 kilograms of apples, where quantity demanded and quantity supplied are equal. At higher prices, quantity supplied exceeds quantity demanded, resulting in a surplus. Below $3, quantity demanded exceeds quantity supplied, leading to a shortage.

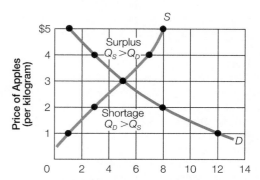

Quantity Demanded and Supplied of Apples
(thousands of kilograms per year)

WHAT IS A SHORTAGE AND WHAT IS A SURPLUS?

What happens when the market price is not equal to the equilibrium price? As you can see in Exhibit 1, at $4 per kilogram, the quantity of apples demanded would be 3000 kilograms, but the quantity supplied would be 7000 kilograms. At that price, a **surplus** would exist, where quantity supplied exceeded quantity demanded. That is, at this price, growers would be willing to sell more apples than demanders would be willing to buy. To cut growing inventories, frustrated suppliers would cut their price and cut back on production. And as price falls, consumers buy more, ultimately eliminating the unsold surplus and returning the market to the equilibrium.

What would happen if the price of apples was cut to $1 per kilogram? The yearly quantity demanded of 12 000 kilograms would be greater than the 1000 kilograms that producers would be willing to supply at that low price. So, at $1 per kilogram, a **shortage** would exist, where quantity demanded exceeded quantity supplied. Because of the apple shortage, frustrated buyers would be forced to compete for the existing supply, bidding up the price. The rising price would have two effects: (1) Producers would be willing

surplus
where quantity supplied exceeds quantity demanded

shortage
where quantity demanded exceeds quantity supplied

An NHL playoff game is a high-demand, limited-supply sporting event. With a number of tickets going to corporate sponsors and individuals affiliated with the two teams playing in the game, in addition to the heightened interest because the home team has made the playoffs, the quantity demanded far exceeds the quantity supplied at the face value of the tickets. Consequently, some fans are willing to pay much more for these tickets from scalpers who buy the tickets at face value and try to resell them at a higher price.

DEBATE

WHERE THERE'S A MARKET, SHOULD PEOPLE BE ALLOWED TO TRADE FREELY, WITHOUT STATE LIMITATIONS OR INTERVENTION?

For:

Just as all humans are said to have a price, so every *thing* has its price. That applies equally to ice cream, school uniforms, bagels, drugs, weapons, sexual favours, and human organs. Trading a product at a price acceptable to at least one buyer satisfies both the consumer and the producer, and so ensures that the market trades at the most efficient level—regardless of legal or moral issues. Both the demand side and the supply side should be free to establish their own trade criteria. After all, trade means satisfying the needs and wants of both the demanders and suppliers, and if both parties agree, who is the state or society to interfere in the transactions? Anyone who advocates for the superiority of a free market system should have no difficulty with moral or ethical issues, because what matters is the superiority of the market, not its particulars. Drug users and sellers should make their own decisions about their actions, for example. The same should be true for weapons and those who sell their bodies. And if individuals make the decision to donate blood or their organs (such as a kidney), why can't they sell those organs to someone who is willing to pay? There are a number of individuals in dire economic situations, especially those in underdeveloped countries, who could benefit from selling one of their kidneys. Don't all markets trade at the most efficient levels, so that people should be allowed to trade freely?

Against:

Not everything has its price. In exploring demand and supply, we find that goods or services trade at levels where both the consumer and supplier are mutually satisfied at an agreed-on price. But not all markets trade at the most efficient levels, and in fact, some markets are unethical or illegal. Some products and services should simply not be offered or sold in a civilized society. While individual choice and need generally take precedence in an open market, we still need to have limitations for the public good. Some people can't make informed decisions—those who are underage, for example, or those who lack the necessary intellectual ability. Even if individuals have the capacity to make informed decisions, do they always have enough information to do so? For example, do individuals in developing countries appreciate the long-term risks associated with donating a kidney, or is the lure of available money unduly influencing their decisions? There are also cases where the public good overrides the individual's benefit, such as in the selling of automatic assault weapons. At some point, individual freedom gives way to society's best interests and safety. What are the moral and ethical grounds to make those decisions and who makes them? Surely society has seen the harm that can come from lack of intervention when these trades take place in the open market, making state limitations and intervention necessary. In fact, aren't there situations where the state should intervene proactively?

to increase the quantity supplied; and (2) the higher price would decrease the quantity demanded. Together, these two effects would ultimately eliminate the shortage, returning the market to the equilibrium.

SECTION CHECK

- ■ The intersection of the supply and demand curve shows the equilibrium price and equilibrium quantity in a market.
- ■ A surplus is where quantity supplied exceeds quantity demanded. A shortage is where quantity demanded exceeds quantity supplied.

Changes in Equilibrium Price and Quantity

- ▪ What happens to equilibrium price and equilibrium quantity when the demand curve shifts?
- ▪ What happens to equilibrium price and equilibrium quantity when the supply curve shifts?
- ▪ What happens when both supply and demand shift in the same time period?

When one of the many determinants of demand or supply (input prices, prices of related products, number of suppliers, expectations, technology, and so on) changes, the demand and supply curves will shift, leading to changes in the equilibrium price and equilibrium quantity. To accomplish an objective and ultimately accurate analysis of a change in demand and supply, it is important that the theoretical concepts first developed in Chapter 3 are correctly applied. One way you can ensure that your demand–supply analysis of a given event is complete is by asking yourself the following three questions:

1. Which side of the market is being affected by the event in question, demand or supply?
2. Is the event in question a "shift" or a "movement"?
3. Is the event in question having an expansionary or contractionary impact on the market?

We first consider a change in demand.

WHAT HAPPENS TO EQUILIBRIUM PRICE AND EQUILIBRIUM QUANTITY WHEN THE DEMAND CURVE SHIFTS?

A shift in the demand curve—caused by a change in the price of a related good (a substitute or a complement), income, the number of buyers, tastes, or expectations—results in a change in both equilibrium price and equilibrium quantity. But how and why does this happen? This result can be best explained through the presentation of a brief case.

Getty Images

The energy drink market in Canada has experienced dramatic growth in recent years. In both 2011 and 2012, sales growth for this sector of the beverage market exceeded 20 percent. The industry leader, Red Bull, with a 42 percent share of the energy drink market, sold an impressive $2.9 billion worth of product in 2012—a 28 percent improvement over the previous year's sales.

With names like Rockstar and Monster, these new beverage products appeal to and are aggressively marketed to the urban fast-paced consumer. How can the record growth in this market segment best be explained? The following are the answers to those three important questions:

1. The case describes how consumer behaviour (fuelled by advertising and lifestyle demands) is impacting market growth; therefore, the event is demand-side.

section 4.2
Exhibit 1   **Growth in the Energy Drink Market**

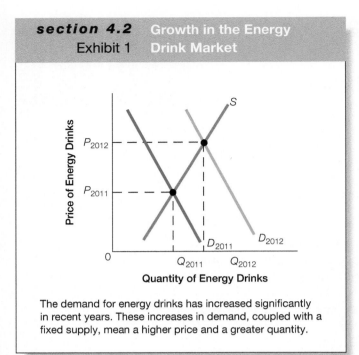

The demand for energy drinks has increased significantly in recent years. These increases in demand, coupled with a fixed supply, mean a higher price and a greater quantity.

2. The case makes no reference to the price of energy drinks changing; therefore, the event will be illustrated as a shift.
3. The case details how the aggressive and targeted advertising of energy drink manufacturers has resonated with busy, time-constrained consumers; therefore, the event is expansionary.

In conclusion, due to the fast-rising demand for energy drinks, this market segment has experienced rapid growth. As shown in Exhibit 1, the rightward shift of the demand curve results in an increase in both equilibrium price and equilibrium quantity.

Let's look at a second case of how changing demand can impact equilibrium price and equilibrium quantity. In 2008–09, measured economic activity in the Canadian economy declined by nearly $20 billion (producing what economists refer to as a *recession*). In response to this recession, while median after-tax family income remained virtually unchanged (for example a family of two or more people consistently received around $65 500), many Canadian families experienced a decline in income due to job loss or reductions in hours worked.

Over this same time period, according to data compiled by the Conference Board of Canada, limited-service restaurants (such as McDonalds and Subway) surpassed full-service restaurants (such as The Keg and Earls) in terms of their overall percentage of sales. From these observations, what conclusions can be drawn about these two segments of the restaurant market? Again, let's answer this using our three questions:

1. The case describes how consumers, in response to a decline in their income, make adjustments to the types of restaurants they visit; therefore, the event is demand-side.
2. The case focuses on the impact of consumer income on demand; therefore, the event will be illustrated as a shift.
3. The case reveals that as consumer incomes declined due to recession pressures, the demand for full-service restaurants declined while the demand for limited-service restaurants increased; therefore, depending on the particular market segment, the event is either expansionary or contractionary.

In conclusion, the case seems to indicate that full-service restaurants fit the definition of a normal good, and limited-service restaurants fit the definition of an inferior good. As shown in Exhibit 2, the restaurant market exhibited two distinct responses. In the full-service segment (panel A), demand declined, shifting the demand curve leftward, causing equilibrium price and quantity to decline. However,

section 4.2
Exhibit 2   **Decline in Consumer Income**

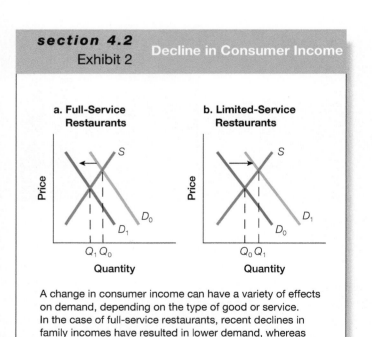

A change in consumer income can have a variety of effects on demand, depending on the type of good or service. In the case of full-service restaurants, recent declines in family incomes have resulted in lower demand, whereas for limited-service restaurants, that same decline in income has produced an increase in demand.

in the limited-service segment (panel B), demand increased, shifting the demand curve rightward, causing equilibrium price and quantity to increase.

WHAT HAPPENS TO EQUILIBRIUM PRICE AND EQUILIBRIUM QUANTITY WHEN THE SUPPLY CURVE SHIFTS?

Like a shift in demand, a shift in the supply curve also influences both equilibrium price and equilibrium quantity, assuming that demand for the product has not changed. Let's look at another case. Between 2000 and 2013, the price of flat-screen televisions declined dramatically. Industry data reveal that in 2000, a 20-inch flat-screen TV would have cost around $1200, whereas by 2013, that same 20-inch TV cost less than $100. Furthermore, an investigation into the technology of manufacturing flat-screen displays reveals that, since 2000, the machines necessary for producing the displays have increased in capacity by 800 percent. Translation: Bigger machines, cheaper TVs. How can this technological development explain the dramatic reduction in the price of flat-screen TVs?

1. The case describes how a technological innovation in production is impacting the ability of electronic manufacturers to produce their product; therefore, the event is supply-side.
2. The case highlights the impact of technology on production; therefore, the event will be illustrated as a shift.
3. The case indicates that as production technology has improved, the ability of manufacturers to make more product available has also increased; therefore, the event is expansionary.

   In conclusion, as shown in Exhibit 3, the lower cost of producing flat-screen TVs— and the subsequent increase in profitability—shifts the supply curve to the right. This increase in supply lowers equilibrium price and increases equilibrium quantity.

Let's look at a second case of how equilibrium price and quantity can be impacted by a change in supply. Tequila, originally associated with Mexican ranchers and cowboys and increasingly the choice of mainstream North American consumers, is an alcoholic beverage produced from the agave plant. With its production carefully regulated and limited to five Mexican states, the recent failure of the agave crop has had a devastating impact on the industry. The price of a bottle of tequila has increased 50 to 60 percent in Canada, translating into about a $10 jump in price at the liquor store. How can demand supply analysis explain the significantly higher price of tequila?

1. The case details how the availability of inputs in a market is a factor in determining market price; therefore the event is supply-side.
2. The case's focus on production inputs as the independent variable means the event will be illustrated as a shift.
3. The case draws a relationship between the failure of the agave crop and the higher price of tequila worldwide (results for Canada provided specifically). As a result, the event is contractionary.

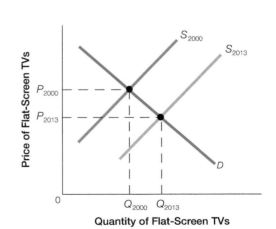

section 4.2   Advances in Production
Exhibit 3   Technology

Advances in the technology of producing flat-screen displays enable manufacturers to produce flat-screen TVs more efficiently and therefore more profitably. This increase in profit encourages more supply, shifting the supply curve rightward. Equilibrium price and quantity increase as a result.

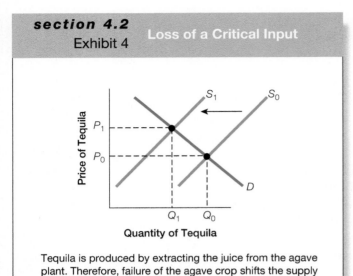

section 4.2
Exhibit 4   Loss of a Critical Input

Price of Tequila

S_1 S_0

P_1

P_0

D

Q_1 Q_0

Quantity of Tequila

Tequila is produced by extracting the juice from the agave plant. Therefore, failure of the agave crop shifts the supply curve for tequila leftward, leading to a higher equilibrium price and lower equilibrium quantity, *ceteris paribus*.

Therefore, the supply of tequila shifts leftward due to the failure of the agave crop, without which tequila cannot be produced. As shown in Exhibit 4, this decline in supply results in the predicted increase in equilibrium price and decrease in equilibrium quantity.

WHAT HAPPENS WHEN BOTH SUPPLY AND DEMAND SHIFT IN THE SAME TIME PERIOD?

We have discussed that as part of the continual adjustment process that occurs in the marketplace, supply and demand can each shift in response to many different factors, with the market then adjusting toward the new equilibrium. We have, so far, considered what happens when just one such change occurs at a time. In these cases, we learned that the results of these adjustments in supply and demand on the equilibrium price and quantity are predictable. However, both supply and demand very often will shift in the same time period. Can we predict what will happen to equilibrium prices and equilibrium quantities in these situations?

As you will see, when supply and demand move at the same time, we can predict the change in one variable (price or quantity), but we are unable to predict the direction of the effect on the other variable with any certainty. This change in the second variable, then, is said to be indeterminate because it cannot be determined without additional information about the size of the relative shifts in supply and demand. This concept will become clearer to you as we work through the following example.

An Increase in Supply and a Decrease in Demand

When considering this scenario, it might help you to break it down into its individual parts. As you learned in the last section, an increase in supply (a rightward shift in the supply curve) results in a decrease in the equilibrium price and an increase in the equilibrium quantity. A decrease in demand (a leftward movement of the demand curve), on the other hand, results in a decrease in both the equilibrium price and the equilibrium quantity. These shifts are shown in Exhibit 5(a). Taken together, then, these changes will clearly result in a decrease in the equilibrium price because both the increase in supply and the decrease in demand work to push this price down. This drop in equilibrium price (from P_0 to P_1) is shown in the movement from E_0 to E_1.

The effect of these changes on equilibrium price is clear, but how does the equilibrium quantity change? The impact on equilibrium quantity is indeterminate because the increase in supply increases the equilibrium quantity and the decrease in demand decreases it. In this scenario, the change in the equilibrium quantity will vary depending on the relative changes in supply and demand. If, as shown in Exhibit 5(a), the decrease in demand is greater than the increase in supply, the equilibrium quantity will decrease. If, however, as shown in Exhibit 5(b), the increase in supply is greater than the decrease in demand, the equilibrium quantity will increase.

section 4.2
Exhibit 5   Shifts in Supply and Demand

a. A Little Increase in Supply and a Big Decrease in Demand

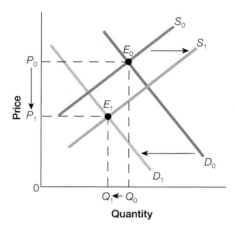

b. A Big Increase in Supply and a Little Decrease in Demand

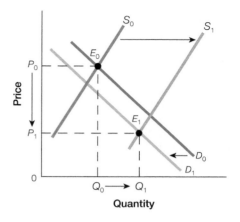

If the decrease in demand (leftward shift) is greater than the increase in supply (rightward shift), the equilibrium price and equilibrium quantity will fall.

If the increase in supply (rightward shift) is greater than the decrease in demand (leftward shift), the equilibrium price will fall and the equilibrium quantity will rise.

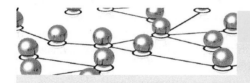

Business *CONNECTION*

EQUILIBRIUM DETERMINES PRICE

Beyond knowing and understanding the equilibrium price and quantity of products in their industry, businesspeople often try to understand what will happen to prices if there is a change in the market. When asked to explain why prices are at a certain level, they quickly reply that present price levels are simply a reflection of market demand and supply. Strictly speaking, they are correct. In the absence of a detailed analysis, which most small and medium-sized enterprises cannot afford, most of these managers or owners might not realize why this is the case. A basic four-step economic analysis would show them what impact a market change might have on their revenues.

In the four-step analysis, the entrepreneur simply responds to a change in the environment by asking these four questions:

1. Which curve is affected? (Is it a demand or supply issue?)

2. Is price the issue, or is it something else? (If it's price, it's a movement *along* the curve; if it's something else, it's a *shift* of the curve. Numerous factors can shift demand and supply—work at finding which factor is affecting the change.)

3. Is the change an increase or a decrease?

4. How much change is involved? (Is the change small or large?)

Managers—and students—can use this scenario with any business problem. The following example illustrates how the analysis plays out. (You're encouraged to walk yourself through any problem to see how useful the analysis steps can be. Read a business article on the Internet for problem ideas. If you can complete the analysis, you're thinking like a manager!)

Scenario: An Apple ad campaign for its new iPhone was successful. At the same time, Apple announced that it's moving some of its iPhone manufacturing back to North America because it can use cheaper automated processes.

Let's deal with each situation separately, using the four-step analysis: (1) Is the ad campaign a demand or supply issue? Clearly, it's a demand issue, so it will affect the demand curve. (2) Is the issue price or something else? It's something else, so it will *shift* the demand curve—what causes the

(continued)

shift is a change in tastes or preferences, which is one of the factors that shift demand. (3) A positive or negative change? The ad campaign is successful, so it will shift the demand curve rightward. (4) How much? Here, you will need to draw a simple demand and supply model, shift the demand curve rightward a little, and then draw a second curve, shifting it rightward a lot.

Now analyze the second issue: (1) Is it a demand or supply issue? It's a supply issue. (2) Is it price, or something else? Something else—in this case, it's a decrease in input (capital) prices. (3) Which direction? Lower input costs will shift the supply curve rightward—Apple can make more units for the same price as before! (4) Finally, by how much? Again, you have to go to your model drawing and shift the supply curve rightward, first a little and then a lot. From the final diagram, you will see that equilibrium quantity will always be more than it was before the changes, but price is indeterminate. To see what happens to price, you look at the intersections of small (or large) changes in demand and large (or small) changes in supply. Depending on your

confidence in which curve will shift more or less to the other side, your answer to a price change will come from there.

To answer these questions, companies often create powerful econometric models to simulate different economic scenarios, often referred to as "what-if" scenarios. This simple yet elegant practical application of economic theory is extremely useful to business managers in forecasting new equilibrium quantities and prices, and even a company's future revenues and profits over time.

1. What tools do you think businesses can use to establish their own demand and supply issues?

2. What role do time and time lags have on a business that is attempting to establish its own market equilibrium? What items would you think would be affected by time lags?

3. In what ways do large businesses have advantages over smaller businesses in establishing their own level of equilibrium? Give some specific examples of how these advantages would affect equilibrium.

The Combinations of Supply and Demand Shifts

The eight possible changes in demand and/or supply are presented in Exhibit 6, along with the resulting changes in equilibrium quantity and equilibrium price. Although you could memorize the impact of the various possible changes in demand and supply, it would be more worthwhile to draw a graph, as shown in Exhibit 7, whenever a situation of changing demand and/or supply arises. Remember that an increase in either demand or supply means a rightward shift in the curve, whereas a decrease in either demand or supply means a leftward shift. Also, when both demand and supply change, one of the two equilibrium values—price or quantity—will change in an indeterminate manner (can increase, decrease, or stay the same) depending on the relative magnitude of the changes in supply and demand.

section 4.2
Exhibit 6 — The Effect of Changing Demand and/or Supply

If Demand	and Supply	Then Equilibrium Quantity	and Equilibrium Price
1. Increases	Stays unchanged	Increases	Increases
2. Decreases	Stays unchanged	Decreases	Decreases
3. Stays unchanged	Increases	Increases	Decreases
4. Stays unchanged	Decreases	Decreases	Increases
5. Increases	Increases	Increases	Indeterminate*
6. Decreases	Decreases	Decreases	Indeterminate*
7. Increases	Decreases	Indeterminate*	Increases
8. Decreases	Increases	Indeterminate*	Decreases

*May increase, decrease, or remain the same, depending on the size of the change in demand relative to the change in supply.

section 4.2
section 4.2
Exhibit 7   The Combinations of Supply and Demand Shifts

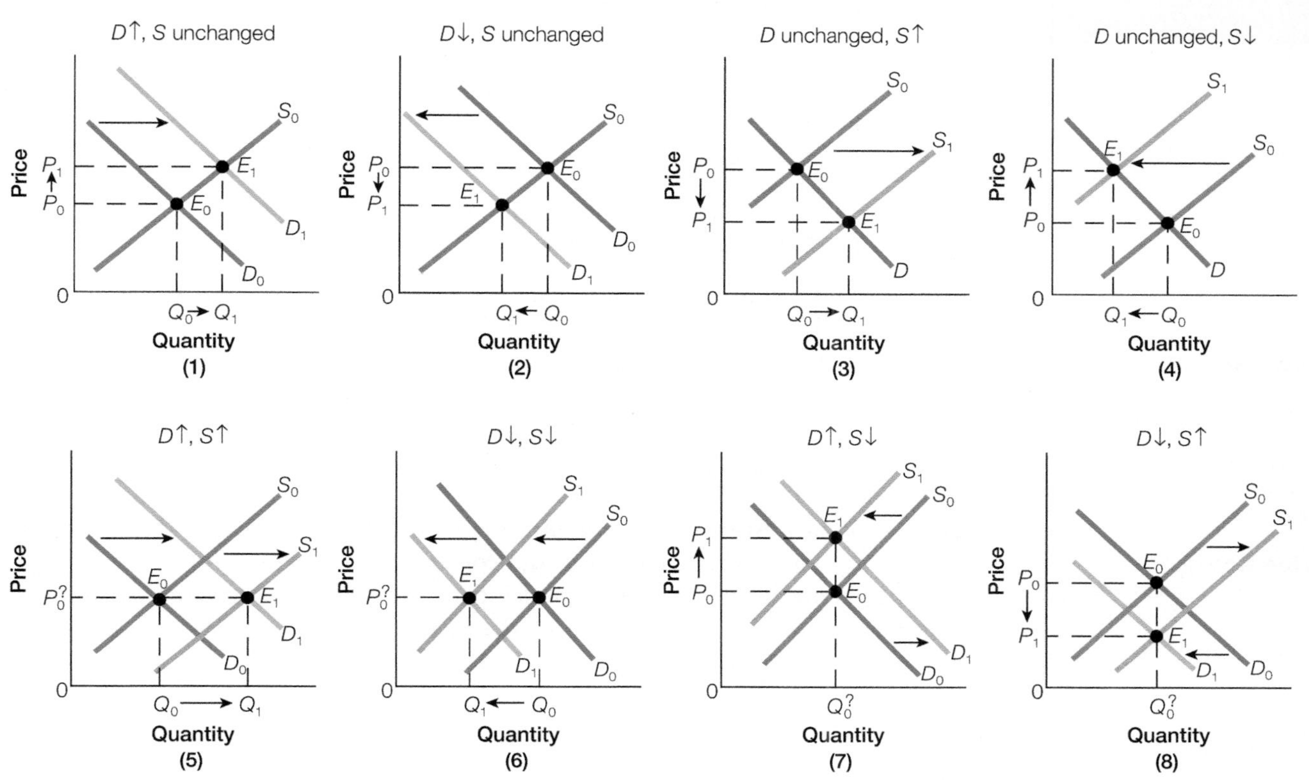

SECTION CHECK

- Changes in demand will cause a change in the equilibrium price and quantity, *ceteris paribus*.
- Changes in supply will cause a change in the equilibrium price and quantity, *ceteris paribus*.
- When there are simultaneous shifts in both supply and demand curves, either the equilibrium price or the equilibrium quantity will be indeterminate without more information.

Price Controls

- What are price controls?
- What are price ceilings?
- What are price floors?

WHAT ARE PRICE CONTROLS?

price controls
government-mandated minimum and maximum prices

price ceiling
a legally established maximum price

price floor
a legally established minimum price

Although nonequilibrium prices can occur naturally, reflecting uncertainty, they seldom last for long. Governments, however, may impose nonequilibrium prices for significant time periods. **Price controls** are government-mandated minimum and maximum prices that sometimes force prices above or below what they would be in equilibrium. The motivations for price controls vary with the market under consideration. For example, a **price ceiling**—a legally established maximum price—is often set for goods deemed important to low-income households, like housing. Or a **price floor**—a legally established minimum price—may be set on wages because wages are the primary source of income for most people.

Price controls are not always implemented by the federal government. Provincial governments can and do impose local price controls. One fairly well-known example of regional price controls is rent controls, which limit how much landlords can charge for rental housing.

WHAT ARE PRICE CEILINGS?

Rent controls have been imposed in Ontario, Quebec, British Columbia, Manitoba, and Prince Edward Island. Although the rules may vary, generally the price (or rent) of an apartment remains fixed over the tenure of an occupant, except for allowable annual increases tied to the cost of living or some other price index. When an occupant moves out, the owners can usually, but not always, raise the rent to a near-market level for the next occupant. The controlled rents for existing occupants, however, are generally well below market rental rates.

Results of Rent Controls

Rent controls distort market signals and lead to shortages. In addition, they often do not even help the intended recipients—low-income households. Most people living in rent-controlled apartments have a good deal, one that they would lose by moving as their family circumstances or income changes. Tenants thus are reluctant to give up their governmentally granted right to a below-market-rent apartment. In addition, because the rents received by landlords are constrained and below market levels, the rate of return (roughly, the profit) on housing investments falls compared to that on other forms of real estate not subject to rent controls, like office rents or mortgage payments on condominiums. Hence, the incentive to construct new housing is reduced. Where rent controls are truly effective, there is generally little new construction going on, resulting in a shortage of apartments that persists and grows over time.

Also, when landlords are limited in what rent they can charge, there is little incentive to improve or upgrade apartments, such as by putting in new kitchen appliances or new carpeting, in order to get more rent. In fact, there is some incentive to avoid routine maintenance, thereby lowering the cost of apartment ownership to a figure approximating the controlled rental price, although the quality of the housing stock will deteriorate over time.

In extreme cases, the repercussions of rent controls can be life-threatening. For example, when four floors of his building caved in, killing three of his neighbours, Uttamchand K. Soiatwala, owner of a successful textile business, refused to leave his two-bedroom, rent-controlled apartment in Mumbai, India. The city then cut off his electricity and water and threatened to arrest his wife, but he still wouldn't leave. In all, 58 tenants refused to leave a rent-controlled apartment building that was considered too dangerous by city officials. Why did these residents take this risk? Cheap rent—$8.50 a month. There is tremendous tension in the market for Mumbai rent-controlled properties between landlords who can't afford to keep up their properties and tenants who will go to extraordinary lengths and even risk their lives to keep their units.

Another impact of rent control is that it promotes housing discrimination. Where rent controls do not exist, a prejudiced landlord might willingly rent to someone he believes is undesirable simply because the undesirable family is the only one willing to pay the requested rent (and the landlord is not willing to lower the rent substantially to get a desirable family, since this could translate into the loss of thousands of dollars in income). With rent controls, many families are likely to want to rent the controlled apartment, some desirable and some undesirable as seen by the landlord, simply because the rent is at a below-equilibrium price. The landlord can indulge in his "taste" for discrimination without any additional financial loss beyond that required by the controls.

Consequently, he will be more likely to choose to rent to a desirable family, perhaps a family without children or pets, rather than an undesirable one, perhaps one with a lower income and so a greater risk of nonpayment.

Exhibit 1 shows the impact of rent control. If the price ceiling is set below the market price, the quantity demanded will increase to Q_D from Q^* and the quantity supplied will fall to Q_S from Q^*. The rent control policy will therefore create a shortage, the difference between Q_D and Q_S.

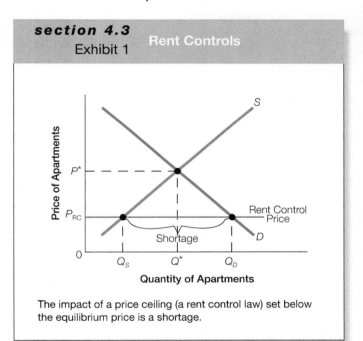

section 4.3
Exhibit 1   **Rent Controls**

The impact of a price ceiling (a rent control law) set below the equilibrium price is a shortage.

WHAT ARE PRICE FLOORS?

The argument for a minimum wage is simple: Existing wages for workers in some types of labour markets do not allow for a very high standard of living, and a minimum wage allows those workers to live better than before. Provincial and territorial government legislation makes it illegal to pay most workers an amount below the current legislated minimum wage.

Let us examine graphically the impact of a minimum wage on low-skilled workers. In Exhibit 2, suppose the government sets the minimum wage, W_{MIN}, above the market equilibrium wage, W_E. In Exhibit 2, we see that the price floor is binding; that is, there is a surplus of low-skilled workers at W_{MIN} because the quantity of labour supplied is greater than the quantity of labour demanded. The reason for the surplus of low-skilled workers (unemployment) at W_{MIN} is that more people are willing to work than employers are willing and able to hire.

If the minimum wage was raised to $30 an hour, one group that could experience a rise in unemployment would be teenagers.

Notice that not everyone loses from a minimum wage. Those workers who continue to hold jobs now have higher incomes (those workers between 0 and Q_D in Exhibit 2). However, many low-skilled workers suffer from a minimum wage—they either lose their jobs or are unable to get them in the first place (those between Q_D and Q_S in Exhibit 2). Although studies disagree somewhat on the precise magnitudes, they largely agree that minimum-wage laws do create some unemployment, and that the unemployment is concentrated among teenagers—the least-experienced and least-skilled members of the labour force.

Exhibit 3 shows the provincial minimum wage rates (including the date on which they became effective) and the 2013 provincial unemployment rates (for both the youth segment of the population and the overall population) from across Canada.

The data in Exhibit 3 reveal two interesting facts regarding minimum wages and youth unemployment: (1) Youth unemployment varies considerably, even between provinces that have similar minimum wage levels, and (2) in all jurisdictions that impose a minimum wage on their labour market, youth unemployment exceeds the rate of unemployment in the overall population.

It is this second conclusion that economists point to when they suggest that effective minimum wages produce unemployment—especially in marginal segments of the labour market, such as the youth segment. Can the entire difference between the overall rate of unemployment and youth unemployment be attributed to the existence of minimum wages? Clearly not, but we must acknowledge it is a contributing factor.

Most Canadian workers are not affected by the minimum wage because in the market for their skills, they earn wages that exceed the minimum wage. For example, a minimum wage will not affect the unemployment rate for accountants. In Exhibit 4, we see the labour market for skilled and experienced workers. In this market the minimum wage (the price floor) is not binding because these workers are earning wages that far exceed the minimum wage—W_E is much higher than W_{MIN}.

The above analysis does not "prove" minimum-wage laws are "bad" and should be abolished. To begin with, there is the empirical question of how much unemployment is caused by minimum wages. Secondly, some might believe that the cost of

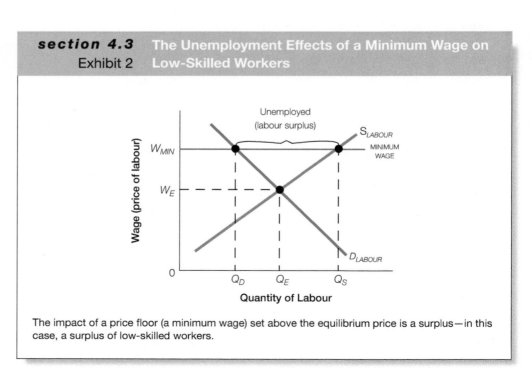

section 4.3   **The Unemployment Effects of a Minimum Wage on**
Exhibit 2   **Low-Skilled Workers**

The impact of a price floor (a minimum wage) set above the equilibrium price is a surplus—in this case, a surplus of low-skilled workers.

section 4.3
Exhibit 3
Provincial Minimum Wages and Unemployment Rates

Province	Minimum Wage ($/hr.)	Effective Date	Unemployment Rate (%) (2013)	
			15–24 Years	15 Years and Over
British Columbia	10.25	May 1, 2012	12.9	6.6
Alberta	10.20	Sep. 1, 2014	8.5	4.6
Saskatchewan	10.20	Oct. 1, 2014	7.8	4.0
Manitoba	10.70	Oct. 1, 2014	10.3	5.3
Ontario	11.00	June 1, 2014	16.1	7.5
Quebec	10.35	May 1, 2014	13.0	7.6
New Brunswick	10.00	Apr. 1, 2012	17.8	10.4
Nova Scotia	10.40	Apr. 1, 2014	18.3	9.0
PEI	10.35	Oct. 1, 2014	18.1	11.5
Newfoundland and Labrador	10.00	July 1, 2010	16.7	11.4
Canada			13.7	7.1

SOURCES: Statistics Canada. Table 109-5324 - Unemployment rate, Canada, provinces, health regions (2013 boundaries) and peer groups, annual (percent), CANSIM (database). And Reference for the minimum wages: information is listed individually on each provinces ministry of labour web site, all the rates are listed in one place here: http://canadaonline.about.com/od/labourstandards/a/minimum-wage-in-canada.htm

unemployment resulting from a minimum wage is a reasonable price to pay for assuring that those with jobs get a "decent" wage. The analysis does point out, however, that there is a cost to having a minimum wage, and the burden of the minimum wage falls not only on low-skilled workers and employers but also on consumers of products made more costly by the minimum wage.

section 4.3
Exhibit 4
The Unemployment Effects of a Minimum Wage on Skilled Workers

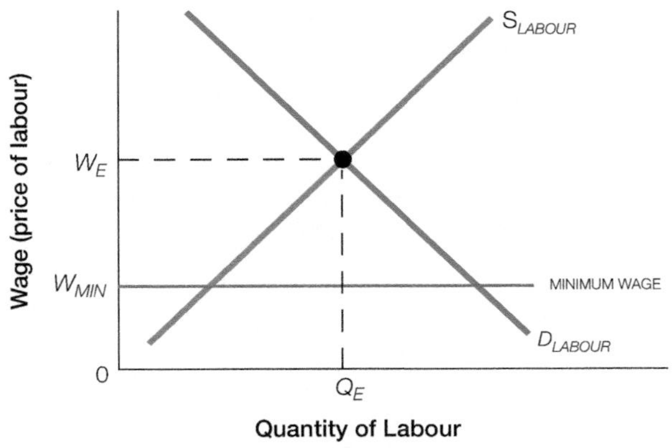

There is no impact of a price floor on the market for skilled and experienced workers. In this market, the price floor (the minimum wage) is not binding.

unintended consequences

the secondary effects of an action that may occur after the initial effects

Unintended Consequences

When markets are altered for policy reasons, it is wise to remember that actions do not always have the results that were initially intended—**unintended consequences** or secondary effects may occur after the initial effects of actions. As economists, we must always look for the secondary effects of an action that may occur along with the initial effects. For example, the government is often well intentioned when it adopts price controls to help low-skilled workers or tenants in search of affordable housing; however, such policies can also cause unintended consequences, which may completely undermine the intended effects. For example, rent controls may have an immediate effect of lowering rents, but secondary effects may well include very low vacancy rates, discrimination against low-income and large families, and deterioration of the quality of rental units. Similarly, a sizable increase in the minimum-wage rate may help many low-skilled workers or apprentices, but will result in higher unemployment and/or a reduction in fringe benefits, such as vacations and discounts to employees. Society has to make tough decisions, and if the government subsidizes some program or group of people in one area, then something must always be given up somewhere else. The "law of scarcity" cannot be repealed!

SECTION CHECK

- Price controls involve government mandates to keep prices above or below the market-determined equilibrium price.
- Price ceilings are government-imposed maximum prices. When price ceilings are set below the equilibrium price, shortages will result.
- Price floors are government-imposed minimum prices. When price floors are set above the equilibrium price, surpluses will result.

For Your Review

Section 4.1

1. If a price is above the equilibrium price, explain the forces that bring the market back to the equilibrium price and quantity. If a price is below the equilibrium price, explain the forces that bring the market back to the equilibrium price and quantity.

2. The following table shows the hypothetical monthly demand and supply schedules for bottles of maple syrup in Winnipeg.

Price	Quantity Demanded (bottles)	Quantity Supplied (bottles)
$6	700	100
7	600	200
8	500	300
9	400	400
10	300	500

a. What is the equilibrium price of a bottle of maple syrup in Winnipeg?

b. At a price of $7 per bottle, is there equilibrium, a surplus, or a shortage? If it is a surplus or shortage, how large is it?

c. At a price of $10, is there equilibrium, a surplus, or a shortage? If it is a surplus or shortage, how large is it?

3. The market for tablet computers is represented by the following demand and supply schedules.

Price ($)	Quantity Demanded (millions of units)	Quantity Supplied (millions of units)
100	8.2	4.7
200	7.6	5.0
300	7.1	5.2
400	6.3	6.3
500	5.9	6.9
600	5.1	7.3
700	4.1	8.1

a. What is the equilibrium price and quantity of tablet computers?

b. Over what range of price would the table computer market exhibit a shortage of computers? How would the market self-regulate a solution to this disequilibrium situation?

c. Over what range of price would the table computer market exhibit a surplus of computers? How would the market self-regulate a solution to this disequilibrium situation?

Sections 4.1 and 4.2

4. Assume the following information for the demand and supply schedules for coffee.

Price ($)	Quantity Demanded (thousands of kg)	Quantity Supplied (thousands of kg)
6	3	9
5	4	7
4	5	5
3	6	3
2	7	1

a. Graph the corresponding demand and supply curves and identify the equilibrium price and quantity of coffee?

b. At the price of $6, would there be a shortage or surplus and how large would it be?

c. At the price of $3, would there be a shortage or surplus and how large would it be?

d. If the demand for coffee decreased by 3000 kg at every price, would there be a shortage or surplus and how much would it be at the price of $4?

e. Using the original amounts of supply and demand, if the supply for coffee increased by 6000 kg at every price, would there be a shortage or surplus and how much would it be at the price of $2?

5. Assume the following information for the demand and supply schedules for Good Z.

Price per Unit	Quantity Demanded	Quantity Supplied
$10	10	55
9	20	50
8	30	45
7	40	40
6	50	35
5	60	30
4	70	25
3	80	20
2	90	15
1	100	10

a. Draw the corresponding supply and demand curves.

b. What is the equilibrium price per unit and quantity traded?

c. If the price was $9, would there be a shortage or a surplus? How large?

d. If the price was $3, would there be a shortage or a surplus? How large?

e. If the demand for Z increased by 15 units at every price, what would be the new equilibrium price and quantity traded?

f. Given the original demand for Z, if the supply of Z was increased by 15 units at every price, what would be the new equilibrium price and quantity traded?

6. The market for baseball tickets at your school's stadium, which seats 2000, is the following:

Price per Unit	Quantity Demanded	Quantity Supplied
$2	4000	2000
4	2000	2000
6	1000	2000
8	500	2000

a. What is the equilibrium price?

b. What is unusual about the supply curve?

c. At what prices would a shortage occur?

d. At what prices would a surplus occur?

e. Suppose that the addition of new students (all big baseball fans) next year will add 1000 to the quantity demanded at each price. What will this increase do to next year's demand curve? What will be the new equilibrium price?

Section 4.2

Blueprint Problem

Using supply and demand curves, show the effect of the following events on the market for traditional laptop PCs.

a. Apple introduces the iPad, a major design departure for personal mobile computing devices.

b. Seeing the success that Apple has had in the tablet market, laptop manufacturers (such as Samsung, Acer, and Sony) introduce their own versions of tablet computers.

Blueprint Solution

a.

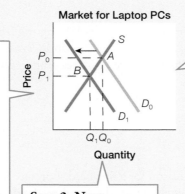

Market for Laptop PCs

Step 2: Event Analysis

Answer the three questions detailed in the chapter:

1. Consumers' preferences are a demand-side variable.

2. Consumer preferences are a shift variable.

3. If consumers prefer the iPad, this comes at the expense of traditional laptop PCs; therefore, theevent is contractionary.

Step 1: The Initial Equilibrium

Using comparative statistics to determine the impact of each event requires starting the analysis from an initial equilibrium—point A.

(Note: You cannot graph the iPad and laptop markets simultaneously—only one market can be graphed at a time.)

Step 3: New Equilibrium

Once the event analysis has been completed, re-establish the market back into equilibrium—point B. Compare the "new" and "initial" equilibriums.

As a result of Apple introducing the iPad, the market for traditional laptop PCs will experience a decrease in demand, causing both the equilibrium price and quantity of laptop PCs to decline.

b.

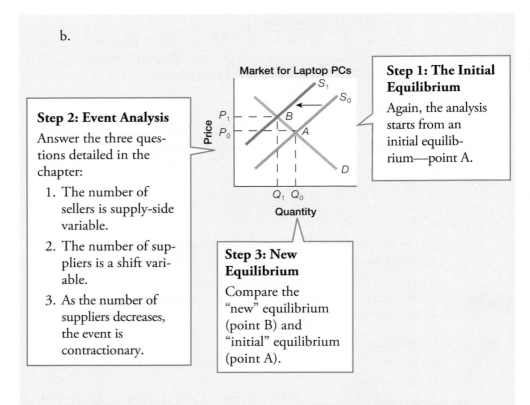

Step 1: The Initial Equilibrium

Again, the analysis starts from an initial equilibrium—point A.

Step 2: Event Analysis

Answer the three questions detailed in the chapter:

1. The number of sellers is supply-side variable.

2. The number of suppliers is a shift variable.

3. As the number of suppliers decreases, the event is contractionary.

Step 3: New Equilibrium

Compare the "new" equilibrium (point B) and "initial" equilibrium (point A).

As a result of other technology producers leaving the laptop PC market in favour of the tablet PC market, the market for laptop PCs will experience a decrease in supply, causing equilibrium price to increase and equilibrium quantity to decline.

7. When asked about the reason for a lifeguard shortage that threatened to keep one-third of the city's beaches closed for the summer, the deputy parks commissioner of Vancouver responded that "Kids seem to want to do work that's more in tune with a career. Maybe they prefer carpal tunnel syndrome to sunburn." What do you think is causing the shortage? What would you advise the deputy parks commissioner to do to alleviate the shortage?

8. Using supply and demand curves, show the effect of each of the following events on the market for wheat.

   a. A major wheat-producing area in Saskatchewan suffers a drought.

   b. The price of corn decreases (assume that many farmers can grow either corn or wheat).

   c. The Prairie provinces have great weather.

   d. The price of fertilizer declines.

   e. More individuals start growing wheat.

9. Beginning from an initial equilibrium, draw the effects of the following changes in terms of the relevant supply and demand curves.

   a. an increase in the price of hot dogs on the hamburger market

   b. a decrease in the number of taxi companies in Halifax on cab trips

   c. the effect of El Niño rainstorms destroying the strawberry crops in Ontario

10. Use supply and demand curves to show the following:

   a. simultaneous increases in supply and demand, with a large increase in supply and a small increase in demand

   b. simultaneous increases in supply and demand, with a small increase in supply and a large increase in demand

   c. simultaneous decreases in supply and demand, with a large decrease in supply and a small decrease in demand

   d. simultaneous decrease in supply and demand, with a small decrease in supply and a large decrease in demand

11. Why do 10 A.M. classes fill up before 8 A.M. classes during class registration? Use supply and demand curves to help explain your answers.

12. What would happen to the equilibrium price and equilibrium quantity in the following cases?

   a. an increase in income for a normal good and a decrease in the price of an input

   b. a technological advance and a decrease in the number of buyers

   c. an increase in the price of a substitute and an increase in the number of suppliers

   d. producers' expectations that prices will soon fall and a reduction in consumer tastes for the good

13. In Canada, why is fresh fruit (apples, strawberries, peaches) less expensive in the summer than in the winter? Use supply and demand curves to help explain your answer.

Section 4.3

14. Refer to the following supply and demand curve diagram.

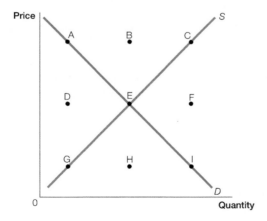

   a. Starting from an initial equilibrium at E, what shift or shifts in supply and/or demand could move the equilibrium price and quantity to each of points A through I?

   b. Starting from an initial equilibrium at E, what would happen if both a decrease in the price of a substitute in production and an increase in income occurred, if it is a normal good?

    c. Starting from an initial equilibrium at E, what would happen if both an increase in the price of an input and an advance in technology occurred?

    d. If a price floor is imposed above the equilibrium price, which of A through I would tend to be the quantity supplied, and which would tend to be the quantity demanded? Which would be the new quantity exchanged?

    e. If a price ceiling is imposed below the equilibrium price, which of A through I would tend to be the quantity supplied, and which would tend to be the quantity demanded? Which would be the new quantity exchanged?

15. Draw a supply and demand curve diagram with a price floor above the equilibrium price, and indicate the quantity supplied and quantity demanded at that price and the resulting surplus.

    a. What happens to the quantity supplied, the quantity demanded, and the surplus if the price floor is raised? If it is lowered?

    b. What happens to the quantity supplied, the quantity demanded, and the surplus if, for a given price floor, the demand curve shifts to the right?

    c. What happens to the quantity supplied, the quantity demanded, and the surplus if, for a given price floor, the supply curve shifts to the right?

16. Draw a supply and demand curve diagram with a price ceiling below the equilibrium price, and indicate the quantity supplied and quantity demanded at that price, and the resulting shortage.

    a. What happens to the quantity supplied, the quantity demanded, and the shortage if the price ceiling is raised? If it is lowered?

    b. What happens to the quantity supplied, the quantity demanded, and the shortage if, for a given price ceiling, the demand curve shifts to the right?

    c. What happens to the quantity supplied, the quantity demanded, and the shortage if, for a given price ceiling, the supply curve shifts to the right?

17. What would be the impact of a rental price ceiling set above the equilibrium rental price for apartments? Below the equilibrium rental price?

18. What would be the impact of a price floor set above the equilibrium price for dairy products? Below the equilibrium price?

19. Giving in to pressure from voters who claim that local theatre owners are gouging their customers with ticket prices as high as $10 per movie, the city council of a local municipality imposes a price ceiling of $2 on all movies. What effect is this likely to have on the market for movies in this particular city? What will happen to the quantity of tickets demanded? What will happen to the quantity supplied? Who gains? Who loses?

chapter

5 Elasticity

Price Elasticity of Demand

- What is price elasticity of demand?
- How do we measure consumers' responses to price changes?
- How do we use the "midpoint method" in calculating price elasticities of demand?
- What determines the price elasticity of demand?

WHAT IS PRICE ELASTICITY OF DEMAND?

In learning and applying the law of demand, we have established the basic fact that quantity demanded changes inversely with changes in price, *ceteris paribus*. But how much does quantity demanded change? The extent to which a change in price impacts quantity demanded may vary considerably from product to product and over the various price ranges for the same product. The **price elasticity of demand** measures the responsiveness of quantity demanded to a change in price. More specifically, price elasticity is defined as the percentage change in quantity demanded divided by the percentage change in price:

$$\text{Price elasticity of demand } (E_D) = \frac{\text{Percentage change in quantity demanded}}{\text{Percentage change in price}}$$

price elasticity of demand
a measure of the responsiveness of quantity demanded to a change in price

Note that, following the law of demand, there is an inverse relationship between price and quantity demanded. For this reason, price elasticity of demand is, in theory, always negative. In practice, however, this quantity is always expressed in absolute value terms, as a non-negative number, for simplicity.

HOW DO WE MEASURE CONSUMERS' RESPONSES TO PRICE CHANGES?

It is important to understand the basic intuition behind elasticities. This can be bestunderstood by initially focusing on the percentage changes in quantity demanded and price.

Think of elasticity as an elastic rubber band. If the quantity demanded is very responsive to even a small change in price, we call it *elastic*. On the other hand, if even a huge change in price results in only a small change in quantity demanded, then the demand is said to be *inelastic*. For example, if a 10 percent increase in the price leads to a 50 percent reduction in the quantity demanded, we say that demand is *elastic* because the quantity demanded is very sensitive to the price change.

$$E_D = \frac{\%\Delta Q_D}{\%\Delta P} = \frac{50\%}{10\%} = 5$$

Demand is elastic in this case because a 10 percent change in price led to a larger (50 percent) change in quantity demanded.

Alternatively, if a 10 percent increase in the price leads to a 1 percent reduction in quantity demanded, we say that demand is *inelastic* because the quantity demanded did not respond much to the price reduction.

$$E_D = \frac{\%\Delta Q_D}{\%\Delta P} = \frac{1\%}{10\%} = 0.10$$

Demand is inelastic in this case because a 10 percent change in price led to a smaller (1 percent) change in quantity demanded.

The Ranges of the Price Elasticity of Demand

Economists refer to a variety of demand curves based on the magnitude of their elasticity. A demand curve or a portion of a demand curve can be elastic, or inelastic, or unit elastic. A demand curve is

Elastic $(E_D > 1)$ if Percentage change in $Q_D >$ Percentage change in P

Inelastic $(E_D < 1)$ if Percentage change in $Q_D <$ Percentage change in P

Unit elastic $(E_D = 1)$ if Percentage change in $Q_D =$ Percentage change in P

Elastic Demand Segments

An **elastic demand segment** is a portion of the demand curve where the percentage change in quantity demanded is greater than the percentage change in price $(E_D > 1)$. In this case, a given percentage increase in price, say 2 percent, leads to a larger percentage change in quantity demanded, say 20 percent, as seen in Exhibit 1(a). If the curve was perfectly elastic, a small percentage increase in price would cause the quantity demanded to fall dramatically to zero. For example, say there were two side-by-side roadside fruit stands selling the same quality of apples. If one stand had lower prices, then the higher-priced fruit stand would soon be selling no apples. In Exhibit 1(b), a perfectly elastic demand curve (horizontal) is illustrated. Economists define the elasticity of demand in this case as infinity, because the quantity demanded is infinitely responsive to even a very small percentage change in price.

elastic demand segment
a portion of the demand curve where the percentage change of quantity demanded is greater than the percentage change in price ($E_D > 1$)

If bus fares increase, will ridership fall a little or a lot? It all depends on the price elasticity of demand. If the price elasticity of demand is elastic, a $0.50 price increase will lead to a relatively large reduction in bus travel as riders find viable substitutes. If the price elasticity of demand is inelastic, a $0.50 price increase will lead to a relatively small reduction in bus ridership as riders are not able to find good alternatives to bus transportation.

© David Wei/Alamy

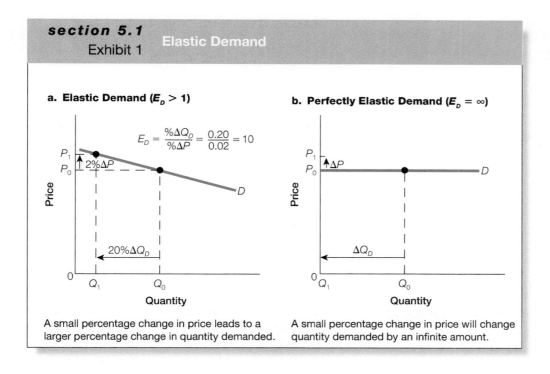

section 5.1
Exhibit 1   Elastic Demand

a. Elastic Demand ($E_D > 1$)

$$E_D = \frac{\%\Delta Q_D}{\%\Delta P} = \frac{0.20}{0.02} = 10$$

2%ΔP

20%ΔQ_D

b. Perfectly Elastic Demand ($E_D = \infty$)

ΔP

ΔQ_D

A small percentage change in price leads to a larger percentage change in quantity demanded.

A small percentage change in price will change quantity demanded by an infinite amount.

Inelastic Demand Segments

An **inelastic demand segment** is a portion of the demand curve where the percentage change in quantity demanded is less than the percentage change in price ($E_D < 1$). In this case, a given percentage (e.g., 10 percent) change in price is accompanied with a smaller (e.g., 5 percent) reduction in quantity demanded, as seen in Exhibit 2(a). If the demand curve is perfectly inelastic, the quantity demanded is the same regardless of the price, as illustrated in Exhibit 2(b).

inelastic demand segment
a portion of the demand curve where the percentage change of quantity demanded is less than the percentage change in price ($E_D < 1$)

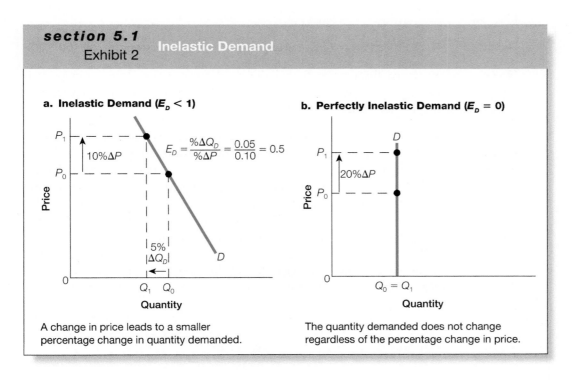

section 5.1
Exhibit 2   Inelastic Demand

a. Inelastic Demand ($E_D < 1$)

10%ΔP

$$E_D = \frac{\%\Delta Q_D}{\%\Delta P} = \frac{0.05}{0.10} = 0.5$$

5% $|\Delta Q_D|$

b. Perfectly Inelastic Demand ($E_D = 0$)

20%ΔP

$Q_0 = Q_1$

A change in price leads to a smaller percentage change in quantity demanded.

The quantity demanded does not change regardless of the percentage change in price.

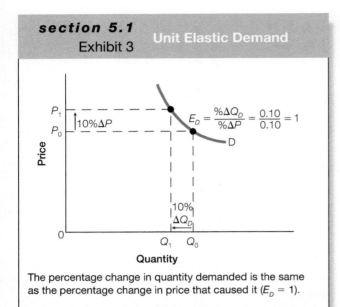

The percentage change in quantity demanded is the same as the percentage change in price that caused it ($E_D = 1$).

unit elastic demand

demand with a price elasticity of 1; the percentage change in quantity demanded is equal to the percentage change in price

Unit Elastic Demand Segments

Goods for which E_D equals one ($E_D = 1$), that is, where the percentage change in quantity demanded is equal to the percentage change in price, are said to have **unit elastic demand.** In this case, the percentage change in quantity demanded is the same as the percentage change in price that caused it. For example, as illustrated in Exhibit 3, a 10 percent increase in price will lead to a 10 percent reduction in quantity demanded.

HOW DO WE USE THE "MIDPOINT METHOD" IN CALCULATING PRICE ELASTICITIES OF DEMAND?

Now that we have looked at the basic theory of elasticities by focusing on the percentage changes in quantity demanded and price, suppose we wanted to perform the same calculation using points from a demand curve. What we would soon realize is that the direction of the calculation has an impact on our answer! To help understand this potential problem, consider the following example:

Point	Price	Quantity
A	$2	100
B	$4	40

When going from point A to point B, the percentage increase in price is 100 percent $\left[\left(\dfrac{\$4-\$2}{\$2}\right) \times 100\right]$ and the percentage decline in quantity is 60 percent $\left[\left(\dfrac{40-100}{100}\right) \times 100\right]$, giving us a price elasticity of demand coefficient of 0.6 (60/100). However, when we go from point B to point A, the percentage decrease in price is 50 percent, and the percentage increase in quantity is 150 percent, giving us a price elasticity of demand coefficient of 3 (150/50).

   The reason for the different answers in the above case was due to the traditional method for calculating percentage. According to the traditional approach, the change in the given values is divided by the initial value in determining percentage change. However, since this initial value can be different depending on whether you are starting from point A or from point B, you can, and often do, get different answers. To solve this problem, a technique known as the *midpoint method* is used in place of the traditional approach. The midpoint method uses a midpoint (or average) of the initial and final values in calculating percentage change, as opposed to an initial value. And since this midpoint value is the same regardless of the direction of the calculation, we always get the same answer. Consider the same example again, now using the midpoint method.

Point	Price	Quantity
A	$2	100
B	$4	40
Midpoint	*$3*	*70*

According to the midpoint method, when going from point A to point B, the percentage increase in price is 67 percent $\left[\left(\dfrac{\$4 - \$2}{\left(\dfrac{\$4 + \$2}{2}\right)}\right) \times 100\right]$ and the percentage

decline in quantity is 86 percent $\left[\left(\dfrac{40 - 100}{\left(\dfrac{40 + 100}{2}\right)}\right) \times 100\right]$, giving us a price elasti-

city of demand coefficient of 1.3 (86/67). Conveniently, when we go from point B to point A, the percentage decrease in price is 67 percent $\left[\left(\dfrac{\$2 - \$4}{\left(\dfrac{\$2 + \$4}{2}\right)}\right) \times 100\right]$ and

the percentage increase in quantity is 86 percent $\left[\left(\dfrac{100 - 40}{\left(\dfrac{100 + 40}{2}\right)}\right) \times 100\right]$, giving

us a price elasticity of demand coefficient of 1.3 (86/67). Problem solved!

Price elasticity of demand between two points, (Q_A, P_A) and (Q_B, P_B), can then be expressed in terms of the midpoint method with the following formula:

$$E_D = \frac{\% \Delta Q_D}{\% \Delta P} = \frac{\dfrac{Q_A - Q_B}{\left(\dfrac{Q_A + Q_B}{2}\right)}}{\dfrac{P_A - P_B}{\left(\dfrac{P_A + P_B}{2}\right)}}$$

WHAT DETERMINES THE PRICE ELASTICITY OF DEMAND?

As you have learned, the elasticity of demand for a specific good refers to movements along its demand curve as its price changes. A lower price will increase quantity demanded, and a higher price will reduce quantity demanded. But what factors will influence the magnitude of the change in quantity demanded in response to a price change? That is, what will make the demand curve relatively more elastic (where Q_D is responsive to price changes), and what will make the demand curve relatively less elastic (where Q_D is less responsive to price changes)?

For the most part, the price elasticity of demand depends on the following factors: (1) the availability of close substitutes, (2) the proportion of income spent on the good, and (3) the amount of time that has elapsed since the price change.

Availability of Close Substitutes

Goods *with* close substitutes tend to have more elastic demands. Why? Because if the price of such a good increases, consumers can easily switch to other, now relatively lower-priced substitutes. There are many examples, such as butter and margarine, one brand of root beer as opposed to another, or different brands of gasoline, where the ease of substitution will make demand quite elastic for most individuals. Goods *without* close substitutes, such as insulin for diabetics, cigarettes for chain smokers, or heroin for addicts, tend to have inelastic demands.

The degree of substitutability may also depend on whether the good is a necessity or a luxury. Goods that are necessities, like food, cannot be easily substituted for and thus tend to have lower elasticities than luxury items, like jewellery.

Narrowly Defined Goods

When the demand for a good is broadly defined, it tends to be less elastic than when it is narrowly defined. For example, the elasticity of demand for food, a very broad category, tends to be inelastic because there are very few substitutes for food. But for a certain type of food, like pizza, a narrowly defined good, it is much easier to find a substitute—perhaps tacos, burgers, or French fries. That is, the demand for a particular type of food is more elastic because there are more and better substitutes than for food as an entire category.

Proportion of Income Spent on the Good

The smaller the proportion of income spent on a good, the lower its elasticity of demand. If the amount spent on a good relative to income is small, then the impact of a change in its price on one's budget will also be small. As a result, consumers will respond less to price changes for these goods than for similar percentage changes in large-ticket items, where a price change could have a potentially large impact on the consumer's budget. For example, a 50 percent increase in the price of salt will have a much smaller impact on consumers' behaviour than a similar percentage increase in the price of a new automobile. Similarly, a 50 percent increase in the cost of university tuition will have a greater impact on students' (and sometimes parents') budgets than a 50 percent increase in beer prices.

Time

For many goods, the more time that people have to adapt to a new price change, the greater the elasticity of demand. Immediately after a price change, consumers may be unable to locate very good alternatives or easily change their consumption patterns. But the more time that passes, the more time consumers have to find or develop suitable substitutes and to plan and implement changes in their patterns of consumption. For example, drivers may not respond immediately to an increase in gas prices, perhaps believing it to be temporary. However, if the price persists over a longer period, we would expect people to drive less, buy more fuel-efficient cars, move closer to work, carpool, take the bus, or even bike to work. Hence, for many goods, especially nondurable goods (goods that do *not* last a long time), the short-run demand curve is generally less elastic than the long-run demand curve, as illustrated by Exhibit 4.

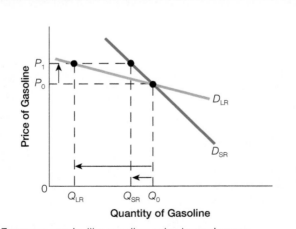

section 5.1
Exhibit 4

Short-Run and Long-Run Demand Curves

For many goods, like gasoline, price is much more elastic in the long run than the short run because buyers take time to change their consumption patterns. In the short run, the increase in price from P_0 to P_1 has only a small effect on the quantity demanded for gasoline. In the long run, the effect of the price increase will be much larger.

Estimated Price Elasticities of Demand

Because of shifts in supply and demand curves, researchers have a difficult task when trying to estimate empirically the price elasticity of demand for a particular good or service. Despite this difficulty, Exhibit 5 presents some estimates for the price elasticity of demand for certain goods. As you would expect, certain goods like air travel, gasoline, and legal services are all relatively price inelastic in the short run because buyers have fewer substitutes. On the other hand, air travel in the long run is much more sensitive to price (elastic) because the available substitutes are much more plentiful. Exhibit 5 shows that the long-run price elasticity of demand for air travel is 2.4, which means that a 1 percent increase in price will lead to a 2.4 percent reduction in quantity demanded. Notice, in each case where the data is available, the estimates of the long-run price elasticities of demand are greater than the short-run price elasticities of demand. In short, the price elasticity of demand is greater when the price change persists over a longer time period.

section 5.1
Exhibit 5   Price Elasticities of Demand for Selected Goods

Good	Short Run	Long Run
Salt	–	0.1
Air travel	0.1	2.4
Gasoline	0.2	0.7
Jewellery and watches	0.4	0.7
Legal services	0.4	–
Alcohol	0.9	3.6
Movies	0.9	3.7
China, glassware	1.5	2.6
Automobiles	1.9	2.2
Chevrolets	–	4.0

SOURCES: Adapted from Robert Archibald and Robert Gillingham, "An Analysis of the Short-Run Consumer Demand for Gasoline Using Household Survey Data," *Review of Economics and Statistics 62* (November 1980), pp. 622–628; Hendrik S. Houthakker and Lester D. Taylor, *Consumer Demand in the United States: Analyses and Projections* (Cambridge, MA: Harvard University Press, 1970), pp. 56–149; and Richard Voith, "The Long-Run of Demand for Consumer Rail Transportation," *Journal of Urban Economics 30* (November 1991), pp. 360–371.

SECTION CHECK

- Price elasticity of demand measures the percentage change in quantity demanded divided by the percentage change in price.
- If the demand for a good is price elastic in the relevant range, quantity demanded is very responsive to a price change. If the demand for a good is relatively price inelastic, quantity demanded is not very responsive to a price change.
- The "midpoint method" for calculating percentage change involves using the average of the changing values, thereby eliminating the direction bias found in the traditional approach.
- The price elasticity of demand depends on (1) the availability of close substitutes, (2) the proportion of income spent on the good, and (3) the amount of time that buyers have to respond to a price change.

section
5.2

Total Revenue and Price Elasticity of Demand

■ How does the price elasticity of demand impact total revenue?
■ How does price elasticity of demand change along a linear demand curve?

HOW DOES THE PRICE ELASTICITY OF DEMAND IMPACT TOTAL REVENUE?

The price elasticity of demand for a good also has implications for total revenue. Total revenue (TR) is simply the price of the good (P) times the quantity of the good sold (Q): $TR = P \times Q$. In Exhibit 1, we see that when the demand is price elastic ($E_D > 1$), total revenues will rise as the price declines because the percentage increase in the quantity demanded is greater than the percentage reduction in price. For example, if the price of a good is cut in half (say from $10 to $5) and the quantity demanded more than doubles (say from 40 to 100), total revenue will rise from $400 ($10 $\times$ 40 = $400) to $500 ($5 $\times$ 100 = $500). Equivalently, if the price rises from $5 to $10 and the quantity demanded falls from 100 to 40 units, then total revenue falls from $500 to $400. As this example illustrates, if the demand curve is relatively elastic, total revenue varies inversely with a price change.

You can see from the following what happens to total revenue when demand is price elastic. (Note: The sizes of the price and quantity arrows represent the sizes of the percentage changes.)

section 5.2   **Elastic Demand and Total**
Exhibit 1   **Revenue**

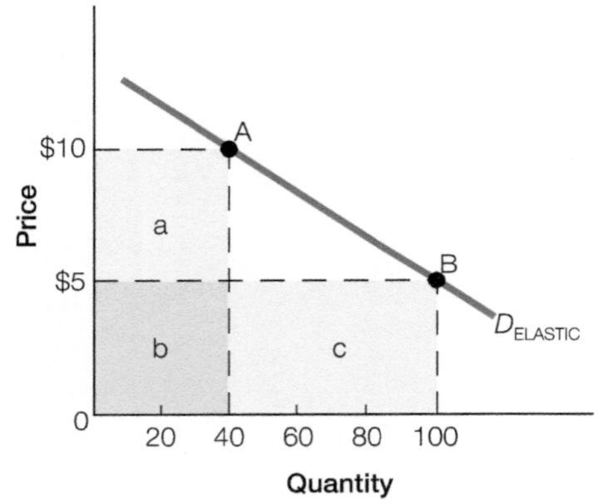

At point A, total revenue is $400 ($10 $\times$ 40), or area (a + b). At point B, the total revenue is $500 ($5 $\times$ 100), or area (b + c). Total revenue has increased by $100. We can also see in the graph that total revenue has increased because the area (b + c) is greater than area (a + b), or c > a.

When Demand Is Price Elastic

$$\downarrow TR = \uparrow P \times Q \downarrow$$

or

$$\uparrow TR = \downarrow P \times Q \uparrow$$

On the other hand, if demand for a good is relatively inelastic ($E_D < 1$), the total revenue will be lower at lower prices than at higher prices because a given price reduction will be accompanied by a proportionately smaller increase in quantity demanded. For example, as seen in Exhibit 2, if the price of a good is cut, say from $10 to $5, and the quantity demanded less than doubles—say it increases from 30 to 40—total revenue will fall from $300 ($10 $\times$ 30 = $300) to $200 ($5 $\times$ 40 = $200). Equivalently, if the price increases from $5 to $10 and the quantity demanded falls from 40 to 30, total revenue will increase from $200 to $300. To summarize, then, if the demand curve is inelastic, total revenue will vary directly with a price change.

When Demand Is Price Inelastic

$$\uparrow TR = \uparrow P \times Q \downarrow$$

or

$$\downarrow TR = \downarrow P \times Q \uparrow$$

In this case, the net effect on total revenue is reversed but easy to see. (Again, the sizes of the price and quantity arrows represent the sizes of the percentage changes.)

An example will help us appreciate the relationship we have just established between price elasticity of demand and total revenue. Is a poor wheat harvest bad for all farmers? Is a great wheat harvest good for all farmers? The answers to these questions may seem obvious at first, but elasticity will reveal to us some interesting solutions.

As shown in Exhibit 3(a), if demand for wheat is inelastic, a reduction in supply without a simultaneous reduction in demand will result in a higher price for wheat and a rise in total revenues for farmers. The increase in price will cause farmers to lose the revenue indicated by area c; however, they will gain the area indicated by area a. The net result will be an overall increase in revenue equal to the area (a − c). Clearly, if some farmers lose their entire crop due to, say, bad weather, they are worse off; however, *collectively* farmers can profit from events that reduce crop size—and they do, because the demand for most agricultural products is inelastic. Interestingly, if all farmers were hurt equally, say, losing one-third of their crop, each farmer would be better off. Of course, consumers would be worse off because the price of agricultural products would be higher.

---

section 5.2
Exhibit 2
Inelastic Demand and Total Revenue

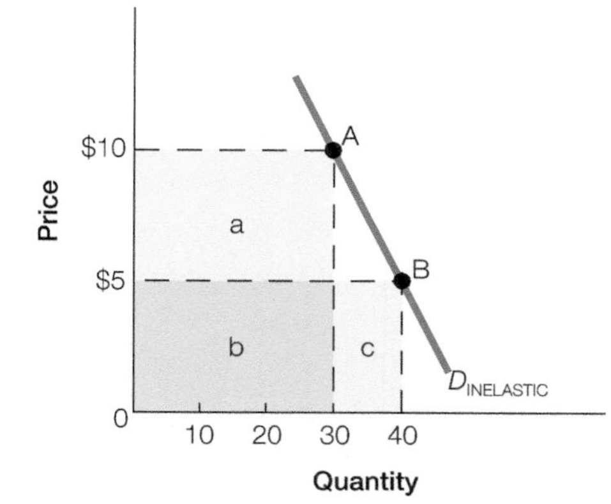

At point A, total revenue is $300 ($10 × 30), or area (a + b). At point B, the total revenue is $200 ($5 × 40), or area (b + c). Total revenue has fallen by $100. We can also see in the graph that total revenue has decreased because area (a + b) is greater than area (b + c), or a > c.

---

section 5.2
Exhibit 3
Elasticities and Total Revenue

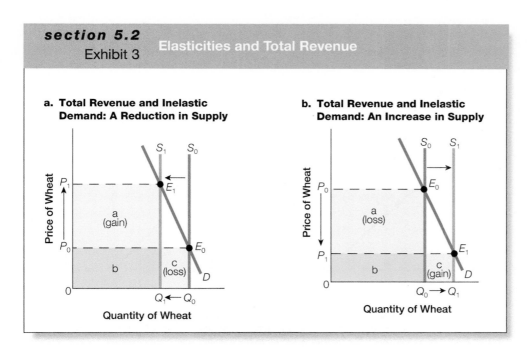

a. Total Revenue and Inelastic Demand: A Reduction in Supply

b. Total Revenue and Inelastic Demand: An Increase in Supply

Alternatively, what if phenomenal weather has led to record wheat harvests or a technological advance has led to more productive wheat farmers? Either event would increase the supply from S_0 to S_1 in Exhibit 3(b). The increase in supply leads to a lower price, from P_0 to P_1. Because the demand for wheat is inelastic, the quantity sold of wheat rises proportionately less than the fall in the price. That is, in percentage terms, the price falls more than the quantity demanded rises. Each farmer is selling a few more bushels of wheat but the price of each bushel has fallen even more, so collectively wheat farmers will experience a decline in total revenue despite the good news.

HOW DOES PRICE ELASTICITY OF DEMAND CHANGE ALONG A LINEAR DEMAND CURVE?

As we showed earlier in the chapter, the slopes of demand curves can be used to estimate their *relative* elasticities of demand: The steeper that one demand curve is relative to another, the more inelastic it is relative to the other. However, beyond the extreme cases of perfectly elastic and perfectly inelastic curves, great care must be taken when trying to estimate the degree of elasticity of one demand curve from its slope. In fact, as we will see, a straight-line demand curve with a constant slope will change elasticity continuously as you move up or down it.

We can easily demonstrate that the elasticity of demand varies along a linear demand curve by using what we already know about the interrelationship between price and total revenue. Exhibit 4 shows a linear (constant slope) demand curve. In Exhibit 4(a), we see that when the price falls on the upper half of the demand curve from P_0 to P_1, and quantity demanded increases from Q_0 to Q_1, total revenue increases. That is, the new area of total revenue (area b + area c) is larger than the old area of total revenue (area a + area b). It is also true that if price increased in this region (from P_1 to P_0), total revenue would fall, because b + c is greater than a + b. In this region of the demand curve, then, there is a negative relationship between price and total revenue. As we discussed earlier, this is a characteristic of an elastic demand curve ($E_D > 1$).

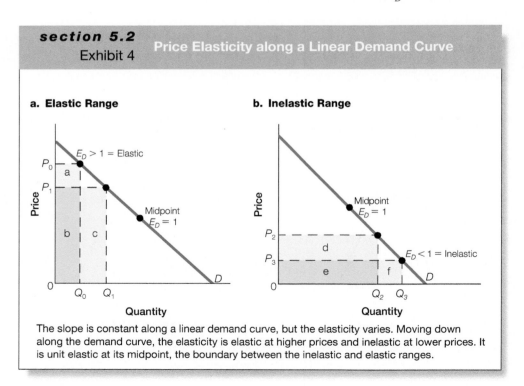

section 5.2
Exhibit 4   **Price Elasticity along a Linear Demand Curve**

a. Elastic Range

$E_D > 1$ = Elastic

b. Inelastic Range

Midpoint
$E_D = 1$

The slope is constant along a linear demand curve, but the elasticity varies. Moving down along the demand curve, the elasticity is elastic at higher prices and inelastic at lower prices. It is unit elastic at its midpoint, the boundary between the inelastic and elastic ranges.

Exhibit 4(b) illustrates what happens to total revenue on the lower half of the same demand curve. When the price falls from P_2 to P_3 and the quantity demanded increases from Q_2 to Q_3, total revenue actually decreases because the new area of total revenue (area e + area f) is less than the old area of total revenue (area d + area e). Likewise, it is clear that an increase in price from P_3 to P_2 would increase total revenue. In this case, there is a positive relationship between price and total revenue, which, as we discussed, is characteristic of an inelastic demand curve ($E_D < 1$). Together, parts (a) and (b) of Exhibit 4 illustrate that, although the slope remains constant, the elasticity of a linear demand curve changes along the length of the curve—from relatively elastic at higher price ranges to relatively inelastic at lower price ranges.

In summary, Exhibit 5 illustrates how total revenue behaves over the entire range of demand. For example, when the price increases from $2 to $3, total revenue increases

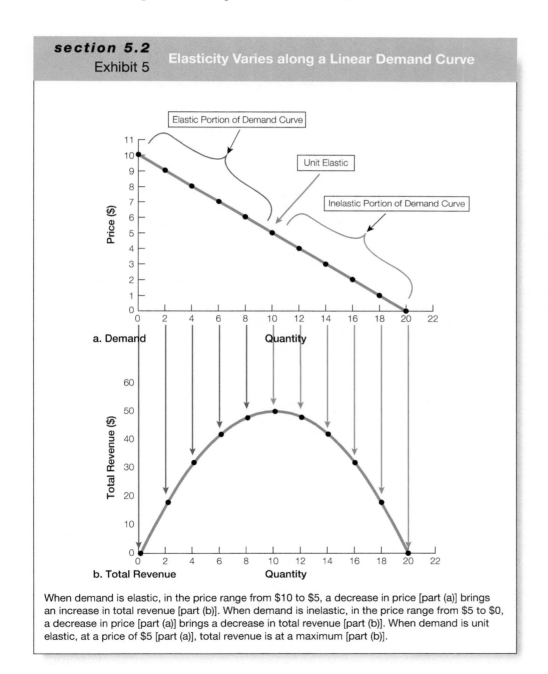

section 5.2
Exhibit 5   **Elasticity Varies along a Linear Demand Curve**

Elastic Portion of Demand Curve

Unit Elastic

Inelastic Portion of Demand Curve

a. Demand

b. Total Revenue

When demand is elastic, in the price range from $10 to $5, a decrease in price [part (a)] brings an increase in total revenue [part (b)]. When demand is inelastic, in the price range from $5 to $0, a decrease in price [part (a)] brings a decrease in total revenue [part (b)]. When demand is unit elastic, at a price of $5 [part (a)], total revenue is at a maximum [part (b)].

from $32 to $42—an increase in price increases total revenue, so demand is inelastic in this portion of the demand curve. But when the price increases from $8 to $9, the total revenue falls from $32 to $18, so demand is elastic in this portion of the demand curve.

Specifically, when the price is high and the quantity demanded is low, this portion of the demand curve is elastic. Why? It is because a $1 reduction in price is a smaller percentage change when the price is high than when it is low. Similarly, an increase in 2 units of output is a larger percentage change when quantity demanded is lower. So we have a relatively small change in price leading to a proportionately greater change in quantity demanded—that is, demand is elastic on this portion of the demand curve.

Of course, the opposite is true when the price is low and the quantity demanded is high. Why? It is because a $1 change in price is a larger percentage change when the price is low and an increase in 2 units of output is a smaller percentage change when the quantity demanded is larger. That is, a relatively larger percentage change in price will lead to a relatively smaller change in quantity demanded—demand is relatively inelastic on this portion of the demand curve.

Business *CONNECTION*

THE IMPORTANCE OF KNOWING WHEN TO COMPETE ON WHAT

Consumers consider many factors when they buy something; among these, price is important but it isn't the only factor. The greater the price (of, say, a home, car, or appliance) as a percentage of income, the greater the role that price plays in the consumer's decision. Lower prices usually mean the consumer benefits at the expense of the producer. In general terms, producers favour lowering prices when they can sell a higher volume of units to make the discount worthwhile. The relationship between a change in price and a change in quantity demanded is a function of elasticity, and that's critical for business managers to understand. In any business, you need to know when to compete on price or on something else. Elasticity of demand helps managers to identify where to compete.

If the demand for the product is elastic, any change in price will affect the quantity demanded. If the producer increases the price, consumers will turn away in large numbers to find lower prices. The seller can expect inventory to take longer to move and total revenue to drop. If the product is perishable, sunk costs will increase as the product spoils. On the other hand, if the producer can lower prices, there will be highly responsive consumers willing to purchase. The margins on these products will likely be razor-thin, but the entrepreneur will be counting on greater sales to offset lower prices.

Because consumers are highly responsive to price changes, we can assume they are less responsive to other marketing factors—such as how the product is packaged, or where to get it, or the amount of promotion that's been invested in it. In a market where the product is elastic, price is paramount. Trying to compete on the other of the 4Ps (product, place, and promotion) will increase costs and lower margins, so when demand is elastic, competing on price is the best option.

If the product has inelastic demand, the seller will want to compete on anything but price. A strategy of positioning the product in the market makes greater sense. This will increase product, promotion, and distribution costs, but those increases will be offset by the higher margins the product should be able to achieve in the market. Such producers know that they won't sell as many products as they would if their product was elastic, so they don't try to compete by being a mass marketer—they will prefer to be in a niche or specialty market, knowing there will be fewer buyers but that those remaining are willing and able to afford their product. These sellers will resist discounting their product at sale prices because they know that would have a limited effect—that would be like leaving dollars on the table. Instead, they will try to change the perception of value in the market while capturing the available dollars.

Either market scenario can be successful, as long as the business stays within the marketing parameters of elasticity in which the product is situated. If a business ventures away from the foundation—an elastic product competing on higher margins, or an inelastic product lowering prices—the total revenue (and costs) will suffer, as will the health of the business.

1. The trend in the economy has been to lower overall prices to consumers, yet there is a large sector of consumers who are very wealthy. Which sector of the economy would you prefer to compete in and why?

2. Large Canadian businesses tend to be resource-based and therefore highly responsive to overall price changes when they occur. What do you think business operators can do to change the effect prices have on their businesses?

3. Think of a product that your company might make that fills a niche market. Using your knowledge of elasticity, how would you price and market this product in order to be successful?

section

5.3

Other Demand Elasticities

■ What is the cross-price elasticity of demand?
■ What is the income elasticity of demand?

WHAT IS THE CROSS-PRICE ELASTICITY OF DEMAND?

Price elasticities of demand are not the only elasticity calculation that economists use to better understand buyer behaviour. Sometimes the quantity of the good demanded is affected by the price of a related good (substitutes and complements). For example, if the price of potato chips falls, what is the impact, if any, on the quantity of soda (a complement) demanded? Or if the price of soda increases, to what degree will iced tea (a substitute) sales be affected? The **cross-price elasticity of demand** is a measure of the impact that a price change of one good will have on the quantity demanded of another good at a given price. Specifically, the cross-price elasticity of demand is defined as the percentage change in the quantity demanded of one good (good A) divided by the percentage change in price of another good (good B), or

$$\text{Cross-price elasticity of demand } (E_{AB}) = \frac{\text{Percentage change in quantity demanded of A}}{\text{Percentage change in the price of B}}$$

cross-price elasticity of demand
a measure of the impact that a price change of one good will have on the quantity demanded of another good at a given price

For many golfers, the right set of clubs is only part of the equation—looking the part is just as important. Canadians spend billions of dollars annually on golf clubs and golf accessories.

The cross-price elasticity of demand indicates not only the degree of the connection between the two variables but also whether the goods in question are substitutes or complements to one another.

Calculating the Cross-Price Elasticity of Demand

Let's calculate the cross-price elasticity of demand between sets of golf clubs and tennis rackets, where a 10 percent increase in the price of a set of golf clubs results in a 20 percent increase in the quantity of tennis rackets demanded. In this case, the cross-price elasticity of demand would be $+2$ ($+20$ percent $\div$ $+10$ percent $= +2$). Consumers responded to the increase in the price of golf clubs by buying fewer sets of golf clubs (moving along the demand curve for golf clubs) and increasing the quantity demanded of tennis rackets at every price (shifting the demand curve for tennis rackets). In general, if the cross-price elasticity is positive, we can conclude that the two goods are substitutes because the price of one good and the demand for the other move in the same direction.

    As another example, let's calculate the cross-price elasticity of demand between sets of golf clubs and sleeves of golf balls, where a 10 percent decrease in the price

of a set of golf clubs results in a 30 percent increase in the quantity of golf balls demanded. In this case, the cross-price elasticity of demand is −3 (+30 percent ÷ −10 percent = −3). The quantity demanded of golf clubs increases as a result of the price decrease, and consumers then purchase additional sleeves of golf balls to use with their new golf clubs. Golf clubs and golf balls, then, are complements. In general, if the cross-price elasticity is negative, we can conclude that the two goods are complements because the price of one good and the demand for the other move in opposite directions.

WHAT IS THE INCOME ELASTICITY OF DEMAND?

income elasticity of demand
a measure of the responsiveness of the quantity demanded of a good to a change in income

Even though the most widely employed demand relationship is that between price and quantity demanded, it is also sometimes useful to relate quantity demanded to income. The **income elasticity of demand** is a measure of the responsiveness of the quantity demanded of a good to a change in income. The income elasticity of demand coefficient not only expresses the degree of the connection between the two variables, but it also indicates whether the good in question is normal or inferior. Specifically, the income elasticity of demand is defined as the percentage change in the quantity demanded at a given price divided by the percentage change in income, or

$$\text{Income elasticity of demand}\,(E_I) = \frac{\text{Percentage change in quantity demanded}}{\text{Percentage change in income}}$$

Calculating the Income Elasticity of Demand

Let's calculate the income elasticity of demand for lobster, where a 10 percent increase in income results in a 15 percent increase in the quantity of lobster demanded at a given price. In this case, the income elasticity of demand is +1.5 (+15 percent ÷ +10 percent = +1.5). Lobster, then, is a normal good because an increase in income results in an increase in demand. In general, if the income elasticity is positive, then the good in question is a normal good because income and demand move in the same direction.

In comparison, let's calculate the income elasticity of demand for beans, where a 10 percent increase in income results in a 15 percent decrease in the demand for beans at each price. In this case, the income elasticity of demand is −1.5 (−15 percent ÷ +10 percent = −1.5). In this example, then, beans are an inferior good because an increase in income results in a decrease in the purchase of beans at a given price. If the income elasticity is negative, then the good in question is an inferior good because the change in income and the change in demand move in opposite directions.

A second interpretation involving the income elasticity of demand coefficient involves the distinction between necessities and luxuries. In the case of a necessity, they are most often associated with an income elasticity of demand coefficient that is $0 < E_I < 1$. This means as income increases, the demand for necessities increases by a smaller proportion than the change in income. Classic examples of this would include the demand for utilities, fresh fruit or vegetables, and shampoo.

Luxuries are most often associated with an income elasticity of demand coefficient that is $E_I > 1$. This means that as income increases, not only does demand increase, it increases by a greater proportion than the increase in income. Common examples of this would include the demand for fine wine, designer clothing, and private education.

SECTION CHECK

- The cross-price elasticity of demand is the percentage change in the quantity demanded of one good divided by the percentage change in the price of another related good (complements and substitutes).
- The income elasticity of demand is the percentage change in quantity demanded divided by the percentage change in income (normal and inferior goods).

Price Elasticity of Supply

- What is the price elasticity of supply?
- What determines the price elasticity of supply?

WHAT IS THE PRICE ELASTICITY OF SUPPLY?

According to the law of supply, there is a positive relationship between price and quantity supplied, *ceteris paribus*. But by how much does quantity supplied change as price changes? It is often helpful to know the degree to which a change in price changes the quantity supplied. The **price elasticity of supply** measures the sensitivity of the quantity supplied to changes in the price of a good. In other words, it measures how responsive the quantity that sellers are willing and able to sell is to changes in the price. Specifically, the price elasticity of supply (E_S) is defined as the percentage change in the quantity supplied divided by the percentage change in price, or

price elasticity of supply
the measure of the sensitivity of the quantity supplied to changes in the price of a good

$$\text{Price elasticity of supply}\,(E_S) = \frac{\text{Percentage change in quantity supplied}}{\text{Percentage change in price}}$$

Calculating the Price Elasticity of Supply

The price elasticity of supply is calculated in much the same manner as the price elasticity of demand. Consider, for example, the case in which it is determined that a 10 percent increase in the price of carrots results in a 25 percent increase in the quantity of carrots supplied after, say, a few harvest seasons. In this case, the price elasticity is +2.5 (+25 percent ÷ +10 percent = +2.5). This coefficient indicates that each 1 percent increase in the price of carrots induces a 2.5 percent increase in the quantity of carrots supplied.

The Ranges of the Price Elasticity of Supply

Economists delineate several ranges of the price elasticity of supply. As with the elasticity of demand, these ranges centre on whether the elasticity coefficient is greater than or less than one. Goods with a supply elasticity that is greater than one ($E_S > 1$) are said to be relatively elastic in supply. With that, a 1 percent change in price will result in a greater than 1 percent change in quantity supplied. In our earlier example, carrots were elastic in supply, because a 1 percent price increase resulted in a 2.5 percent increase in quantity supplied. An example of an elastic supply curve is shown in Exhibit 1(a).

Goods with a supply elasticity that is less than one ($E_S < 1$) are said to be inelastic in supply. This means that a 1 percent change in the price of these goods will induce a proportionately smaller change in the quantity supplied. This situation is shown in the supply curve in Exhibit 1(b).

Finally, there are two extreme cases of price elasticity of supply: perfectly inelastic supply and perfectly elastic supply. In a condition of perfectly inelastic supply, an increase in price will not change the quantity supplied. For example, in a sports arena in the short run (i.e., in a period too brief to adjust the structure), the number of seats available will be almost fixed, say at 20 000 seats. Additional portable seats might be available, but for the most part, even if there is a higher price, there will be only 20 000 seats available. We say that the elasticity of supply is zero, which describes a perfectly inelastic supply curve. Famous paintings, like Leonardo da Vinci's *Mona Lisa*, provide another example; there is only one original in existence and, therefore, only one can be supplied, regardless of price. An example of this condition is shown in Exhibit 1(c).

---

section 5.4
Exhibit 1   The Price Elasticity of Supply

a. Elastic Supply ($E_s > 1$)

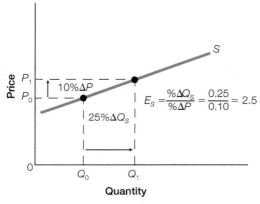

A change in price leads to a larger percentage change in quantity supplied.

b. Inelastic Supply ($E_s < 1$)

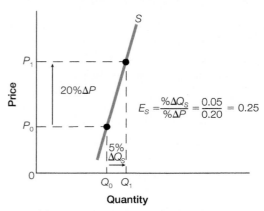

A change in price leads to a smaller percentage change in quantity supplied.

c. Perfectly Inelastic Supply ($E_s = 0$)

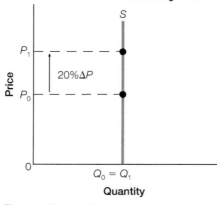

The quantity supplied does not change regardless of the change in price.

d. Perfectly Elastic Supply ($E_s = \infty$)

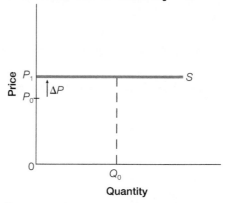

Even a small percentage change in price will change quantity supplied by an infinite amount.

At the other extreme is a perfectly elastic supply curve, where the elasticity equals infinity, as seen in Exhibit 1(d). In a condition of perfectly elastic supply, nothing will be supplied at any price up to a certain level, but at some higher price, sellers would be willing to supply whatever quantity buyers wished to buy. In this case, if the price is below the market price at P_0, the quantity supplied will fall to zero. But at P_1, sellers will sell all that buyers wish to buy. However, most cases fall somewhere between the two extremes of perfectly elastic and perfectly inelastic.

WHAT DETERMINES THE PRICE ELASTICITY OF SUPPLY?

Time is usually critical in supply elasticities (as well as in demand elasticities) because it is more costly for producers to bring forth and release resources in a shorter period of time. For example, the higher wheat prices may cause farmers to grow more wheat, but big changes cannot occur until the next growing season. That is, immediately after harvest season, the supply of wheat is relatively inelastic, but over a longer period that extends over the next growing period, the supply curve becomes much more elastic. Hence, supply tends to be more elastic in the long run than in the short run, as shown in Exhibit 2.

Another example of a good whose supply is highly inelastic in the short run is rental units in most urban areas without rent controls. There is generally only a fixed number of rental units available in the short run. Thus, in the short run, an increase in demand will lead only to higher prices (rents). However, in the long run, these same higher prices (rents) provide an incentive to renovate and build new rental units.

In the short run, firms can increase output by using their existing facilities to a greater capacity, paying workers to work overtime, and hiring additional workers. However, firms will be able to increase output much more in the long run when they can build new factories. In addition, some new firms can enter in the long run. In other words, the quantity supplied will be much more elastic in the long run than in the short run.

Another factor that can influence the price elasticity of supply relates to the level of scarcity and sophistication of the resources and technology used in production. The more complicated the technology or rare the resources needed to produce a particular good or service, the more inelastic the supply. Resources that are very limited in supply—such as technology workers—and very sophisticated technology—such as

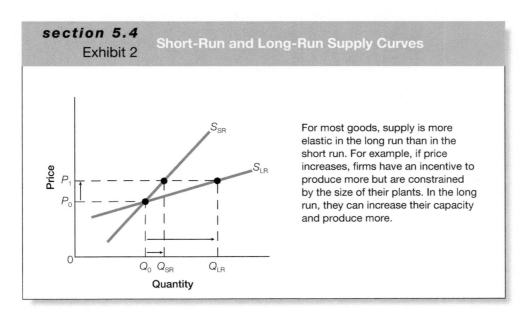

section 5.4
Exhibit 2   **Short-Run and Long-Run Supply Curves**

For most goods, supply is more elastic in the long run than in the short run. For example, if price increases, firms have an incentive to produce more but are constrained by the size of their plants. In the long run, they can increase their capacity and produce more.

computer-assisted design software—take longer for suppliers to acquire and activate in response to a price increase, thereby making price elasticity of supply more inelastic.

Alternatively, when production is associated with resources that are in abundant supply or technology that is simpler, producers are able to both acquire and activate needed resources and technology in a timely fashion, making price elasticity of supply appear to be more elastic.

SECTION CHECK

- The price elasticity of supply measures the relative change in the quantity supplied that results from a change in price.
- Supply tends to be more elastic in the long run than in the short run.

section 5.5 Elasticity and Taxes

- What is tax incidence?
- How does the relative elasticity of supply and demand determine the tax burden?

WHAT IS TAX INCIDENCE?

To varying degrees, all levels of government (federal, provincial/territorial, and municipal) use taxes to generate needed revenue. For example, the harmonized sales tax (HST) that is in effect in some jurisdictions is a consumption-based tax that is calculated as a percentage of the sale price of the product. Although the legislation that accompanies a tax designates who is required to pay the particular tax, the ultimate impact of the tax—also known as the *tax burden*—is less certain. In economics, the term **tax incidence** refers to the analysis of the effect of a particular tax on the distribution of economic welfare. In other words, tax incidence looks at the ultimate burden of a tax.

tax incidence
the analysis of the effect of a particular tax on the distribution of economic welfare

HOW DOES THE RELATIVE ELASTICITY OF SUPPLY AND DEMAND DETERMINE THE TAX BURDEN?

The relative elasticity of supply and demand determines the distribution of the tax burden for a good. As we will see, if demand has a lower elasticity than supply in the relevant tax region, the largest portion of the tax is paid by the consumer. However, if demand is relatively more elastic than supply in the relevant tax region, the largest portion of the tax is paid by the producer.

In Exhibit 1, the pre-tax equilibrium price is $1 and the pre-tax equilibrium quantity is Q_{BT}—the quantity before tax. If the government imposes a $0.50 tax on the seller, the supply curve shifts vertically by the amount of the tax (just as if an input price rose by $0.50).

In the case where demand is relatively less elastic than supply in the relevant region, almost the whole tax is passed on to the consumer, *ceteris paribus*. For example, in

Exhibit 1(a), sellers are very responsive to changes in the price of the good (explaining the relatively flat supply curve), whereas consumers are relatively less responsive (explaining the relatively steep demand curve). In response to the tax, the price paid by consumers rises substantially, indicating that consumers bear most of the burden of the tax. With a post-tax equilibrium price of $1.40, consumers end up paying 40 cents more per unit compared to the per-tax equilibrium price. The price received by producers, however, does not fall by very much, indicating that sellers bear only a small burden of the tax. At 90 cents per unit ($1.40 − $0.50 = $0.90), the producer burden amounts to only 10 cents.

In Exhibit 1(b), demand is relatively more elastic than the supply in the relevant region. Here, we see that the greater burden of the same 50-cent tax falls on the producer, *ceteris paribus*. In response to the tax, the price paid by consumers does not rise very much, but the price received by producers falls substantially. With a post-tax equilibrium price of $1.10, the producer will receive only 60 cents per unit ($1.10 − $0.50 = $0.60), resulting in a 40-cent per-unit tax burden. Consumers, on the other hand, end up paying 10 cents more per unit compared to the pre-tax equilibrium price.

In general, then, the tax burden falls on the side of the market that is less elastic. Note that who actually pays the tax at the time of the purchase has nothing to do with who incurs the ultimate burden of the taxation—that depends on the relative elasticity.

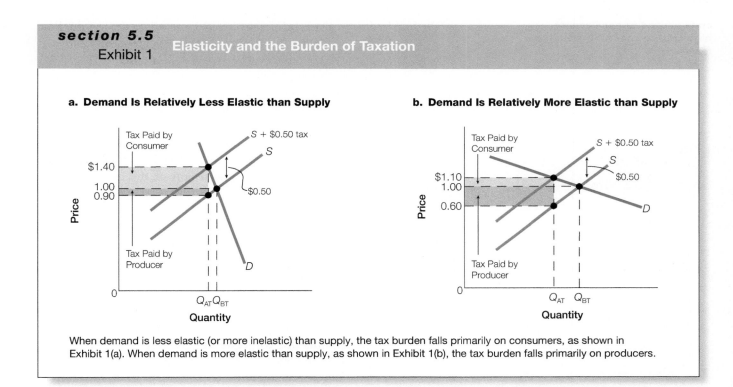

section 5.5

Exhibit 1   **Elasticity and the Burden of Taxation**

a. Demand Is Relatively Less Elastic than Supply

b. Demand Is Relatively More Elastic than Supply

When demand is less elastic (or more inelastic) than supply, the tax burden falls primarily on consumers, as shown in Exhibit 1(a). When demand is more elastic than supply, as shown in Exhibit 1(b), the tax burden falls primarily on producers.

Knowing how the relative elasticity of supply and demand determines the distribution of the tax burden for a good provides us with unique insight into the rationale behind a particular classification of taxes—sin taxes.

A carton of 200 cigarettes in Canada ranges in price from as low as $80 to as much as $113. This variance in price from province to province is due to different rates of provincial and federal taxation. Generally, taxes on a carton of cigarettes represent between 60 and 80 percent of its price. Alcohol and gasoline, two other sin goods, experience similar tax treatment, with nearly 80 percent of the price of a bottle of alcohol being tax

The fact that goods such as alcohol, tobacco, and gasoline are highly inelastic makes them prime candidates for higher taxation. While the government may be accomplishing secondary social objectives through this punitive tax treatment, the ability to effectively generate needed revenue cannot be overlooked as the prime reason.

and 32 percent the price of a litre of gasoline representing various provincial and federal taxes.

Why are these so-called sin goods subjected to such extreme tax treatment? To answer this, we need only to remind ourselves of the primary objective of taxation—revenue generation for the government. The reason why products such as alcohol, cigarettes, and gasoline are taxed so heavily is because they have the greatest ability to generate this much-needed tax revenue. As we discussed earlier in this section, when a tax is imposed on a product, the contractionary impact of the tax shifts the supply curve leftward, forcing price up and quantity sold down (review Section 5.5, Exhibit 1). For sin goods however, due to their highly inelastic demand, prices increase by much more than quantity sold declines (review Section 5.5, Exhibit 1a). The fact that quantity sold falls by a relatively small amount means that the imposition of the tax has only a negligible impact on sales and therefore on the ability of the various levels of government to generate tax revenue.

A second example that will help us appreciate the impact of elasticity on market behaviour involves the methods by which governments enact drug policy. The Canadian government spends hundreds of millions of dollars a year in an effort to stop the flow of illegal drugs into and within Canada. Although these efforts are clearly targeted at suppliers, who really pay the higher enforcement and evasion costs? The government crackdown has increased the probability of apprehension and conviction for drug smugglers. That increase in risk for suppliers increases their cost of doing business—raising the cost of importing and distributing illegal drugs. This would shift the supply curve for illegal drugs to the left, from S_0 to S_1, as seen in Exhibit 2. For most drug users—addicts, in particular—the price of drugs like cocaine and heroin lies in the highly inelastic region of the demand curve. Because the demand for drugs is relatively inelastic in this region, the seller would be able to shift most of this cost onto the consumer (think of this as similar to the tax shift just discussed). The buyer now has to pay a much higher price, P_B, and the seller receives a slightly lower price, P_S. That is, enforcement efforts increase the price of illegal drugs, but only a small reduction in quantity demanded results from this price increase.

Increased enforcement efforts may have unintended consequences due to the fact that buyers bear the majority of the burden of this price increase. Tighter smuggling controls may, in fact, result in higher levels of burglary, muggings, and white-collar crime, as more cash-strapped buyers search for alternative ways of funding their increasingly expensive habit.

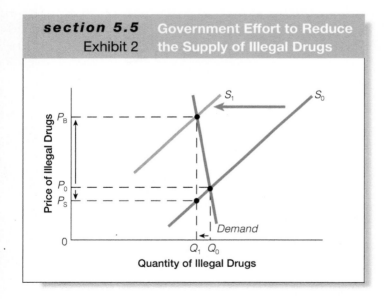

section 5.5
Exhibit 2   **Government Effort to Reduce the Supply of Illegal Drugs**

This is not to say that we should abandon our efforts against illegal drugs. Illegal drugs can impose huge personal and social costs—billions of dollars of lost productivity and immeasurable personal tragedy. However, solely targeting the supply-side can have unintended consequences. Policymakers may get their best results by focusing on a reduction in demand—changing user preferences. For example, if drug education leads to a reduction in the demand for drugs, the demand curve will shift to the left—reducing the price and the quantity of illegal drugs exchanged, as seen in Exhibit 3. The remaining drug users, at Q_1, will now pay a lower price, P_1. This lower price for drugs will lead to fewer drug-related crimes, *ceteris paribus.*

It is also possible that the elasticity of demand for illegal drugs may be more elastic in the long run than the short run. In the short run, as the price rises, the quantity demanded falls less than proportionately because of the addictive nature of illegal drugs (this is also true for goods like tobacco and alcohol, as we have already discussed). However, in the long run, the demand for illegal drugs may be more elastic; that is, the higher price may deter many younger, and poorer, people from experimenting with illegal drugs.

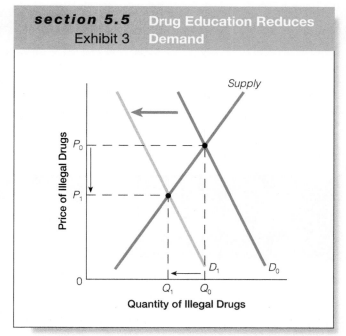

section 5.5   **Drug Education Reduces**
Exhibit 3   **Demand**

DEBATE

ARE EXCISE TAXES ON CIGARETTES THE BEST WAY FOR GOVERNMENTS TO REGULATE SMOKING?

For:

There's no question that smoking is an unhealthy habit with long-term implications for individuals as well as the state. Associated health problems such as emphysema and cancer mean that smoking carries major risks for smokers and results in major costs to health-care systems, which in Canada are publicly funded. The high costs justify taxing smokers and using the taxes as a way of regulating smoking rates: Taxing tobacco helps pay for the social cost of those who choose to smoke. Canadian governments impose excise taxes on various inelastic goods, including gas, alcohol, and tobacco. In 2012–13, the federal and provincial governments raised more than $7.3 billion in taxes on various tobacco products alone.* Governments don't use only the tax system to reduce consumption: Other methods, such as forcing companies to put gross smoke-related photos on cigarette packages, have some effect. But the price of tobacco hits smokers in the pocket and for at least some smokers forces a decrease in smoking, so surely it's the best way for governments to regulate smoking? What are some of the other good reasons why governments use the tax system to regulate smoking rates? Consider the ages of those who smoke and also smokers' abilities to pay.

Against:

Raising taxes on cigarettes has an impact on smoking rates, but there are limits to how much governments can do that and even on how much they are *willing* to do it. Governments may be reluctant to hike tax rates too much because of the risk that the overall amount of revenue coming in may actually start dropping if the rates become too high. If there's a limit to how much governments can raise taxes, they must surely look for other ways to regulate smoking. Raising taxes also has unintended consequences. For example, when one government raises taxes, smokers may simply choose to travel to somewhere that isn't affected and buy cigarettes there. Consider the tobacco products manufactured on First Nations land, where federal and provincial excise taxes are not levied. Surely there are impacts on both smokers and governments in these situations? Some governments have turned to nontax approaches to address tobacco use—the court system, for example. (How have they used the courts to try to curb smoking?) But can you really justify claiming that any one method is better than another in controlling cigarette smoking?

* Physicians for a Smoke-Free Canada, 2013, *Tax Revenues from Tobacco Sales: Provincial and Federal Revenues, 1990–2013.* Accessed at www .smoke-free.ca/pdf_1/totaltax.pdf.

SECTION CHECK

- *Tax incidence* refers to the analysis of the effect of particular taxes of the distribution of economic welfare.
- If demand is more elastic than supply, producers bear the greater burden of the tax; however, if supply is more elastic than demand, consumers bear the greater burden of the tax.

For Your Review

Section 5.1

1. In each case below, indicate which good you think has a relatively *more* price elasticity of demand and identify the most likely reason, in terms of the determinants of the elasticity of demand (more substitutes, greater share of budget, or more time to adjust).

    a. cars or Chevrolets

    b. salt or housing

    c. natural gas this month or over the course of a year

2. How might your elasticity of demand for copying and binding services vary if your work presentation is next week versus in two hours?

3. For each of the following pairs, identify which one of the pair is likely to exhibit more elastic demand:

    a. shampoo; Paul Mitchell Shampoo

    b. air travel prompted by an illness in the family; vacation air travel

    c. paper clips; an apartment rental

    d. prescription heart medication; generic headache remedy

4. Using the midpoint formula for calculating the elasticity of demand, if the price of a good fell from $42 to $38, what would be the elasticity of demand if the quantity demanded changed from

    a. 19 to 21?

    b. 27 to 33?

    c. 195 to 205?

5. Explain why using the midpoint formula for calculating the elasticity of demand gives the same result whether price increases or decreases, but using the initial price and quantity instead of the average does not.

6. Why is a more narrowly defined good (e.g., pizza) likely to have a greater elasticity of demand than a more broadly defined good (e.g., food)?

7. If the elasticity of demand for hamburgers equals −1.5 and the quantity demanded equals 40 000, predict what will happen to the quantity demanded of hamburgers when the price increases by 10 percent. If the price falls by 5 percent, what will happen?

Blueprint Problem

Using the midpoint formula for calculating the elasticity of demand, if the price of a good went from $8 to $6, what is the elasticity of demand if the quantity demanded changed from 15 to 25 units? Interpret your results.

Blueprint Solution

To better visualize this question, consider plotting the data.

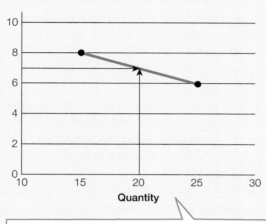

Calculate midpoint values:

$$\frac{25 + 15}{2} = 20$$

$$\frac{\$8 + \$6}{2} = \$7$$

To this visual representation, you can add the midpoints you will need to calculate the percentage change values for price and quantity demanded.

$$\text{Midpoint between two values} = \frac{\text{Sum of values}}{2}$$

Recall the formula for E_D and enter the required values:

$$E_D = \frac{\left(\dfrac{Q_B - Q_A}{Q\,\text{midpoint}}\right)}{\left(\dfrac{P_B - P_A}{P\,\text{midpoint}}\right)} = \frac{\left(\dfrac{25 - 15}{20}\right)}{\left(\dfrac{\$6 - \$8}{\$7}\right)} = \frac{0.5}{-0.29} = |-1.7| = 1.7$$

While the midpoint formula ensures E_D is the same regardless of the direction of the calculation, you still must enter the values consistently. Also, since the sign of the E_D coefficient relates to the inverse relationship between price and quantity demanded (law of demand), it is ignored in interpretation. Therefore, take the absolute value of E_D.

Since the value of E_D is greater than 1 (in this example, 1.7), the interpretation of the response of quantity demanded to the change in price is *elastic*.

Recall the reference value of 1 for interpreting E_D:

$E_D > 1$ elastic

$E_D < 1$ inelastic

$E_D = 1$ unit elastic

8. Good weather produces a bumper crop of apples. As a result, the price falls from $6 to $3 a basket and the quantity demanded increases from 600 to 1100 baskets a week. Over this price range calculate the price elasticity of demand (using the midpoint method).

9. Bad weather spoils the orange crop. As a result, the price rises from $3 to $5 a basket and the quantity demanded decreases from 1500 to 900 baskets a week. Over this price range, calculate the price elasticity of demand (using the midpoint method).

10. Isabella always spends $50 on red roses each month and simply adjusts the quantity she purchases as the price changes. What can you say about Isabella's elasticity of demand for roses?

Section 5.2

11. The Winnipeg Blue Bombers want to boost revenues from ticket sales next season. You are hired as an economic consultant and asked to advise the Blue Bombers whether to raise or lower ticket prices next year. If the elasticity of demand for Blue Bomber game tickets is estimated to be −1.6, what would you advise? If the elasticity of demand equals −0.4?

12. Evaluate the following statement: "Along a downward-sloping linear demand curve, the slope and therefore the elasticity of demand are both 'constant.'"

13. If the midpoint on a straight-line demand curve is at a price of $7, what can we say about the elasticity of demand for a price change from $12 to $10? What about from $6 to $4?

14. If the local bus company raises its price per rider from $2.50 to $2.75 and its total revenues rise, what can we say about its elasticity of demand? What if total revenues fall as a result of the price increase?

15. Assume the following weekly demand schedule for Sunshine DVD Rentals in Moncton.

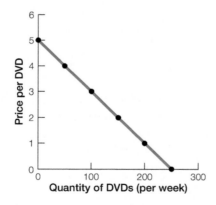

a. When Sunshine DVD Rentals lowers its rental price from $4 to $3, what happens to its total revenue?

b. Between a price of $4 and a price of $3, is the demand for Sunshine DVD rentals elastic or inelastic?

c. Between a price of $2 and a price of $1, is the demand for Sunshine DVD rentals elastic or inelastic?

16. A movie production company faces a linear demand curve for its film, and it seeks to maximize total revenue from the film's distribution. At what level should the price be set? Where is demand elastic, inelastic, or unit elastic? Explain.

Section 5.3

17. If a 10 percent decline in the price of WiFi service increases the quantity of mobile computing devices demanded by 20 percent and increases the quantity of WiFi service demanded by 15 percent, calculate the cross-price elasticity of demand between WiFi service and mobile computing devices.

18. Indicate whether a pair of products are substitutes, complements, or neither based on the following estimates for the cross-price elasticity of demand:

    a. 0.5

    b. −0.5

19. Indicate whether the products are normal, inferior, or neither based on the following estimates for the income elasticity of demand:

    a. 1.7

    b. −1.7

20. If a 10 percent rise in the price of coffee increases the quantity of tea demanded by 25 percent and decreases the quantity of coffee demanded by 20 percent, calculate the cross-elasticity of demand between coffee and tea.

21. Assume you had the following observations on Canadian intercity rail travel: Between 2008 and 2010, rail travel increased from 17.5 passenger kilometres per person to 19 passenger kilometres per person. At the same time, neither per-kilometre railroad price or incomes changed, but the per-kilometre price of intercity airline travel increased by 7.5 percent. Between 2011 and 2013, per capita incomes rose by approximately 13 percent, while the price of travel by rail and plane stayed constant. Intercity rail travel was 20 passenger kilometres per person in 2011 and 19.5 in 2013. Assuming the demand for travel didn't change between these periods:

    a. Calculate the income elasticity of demand for intercity rail travel.

    b. Calculate the cross-price elasticity of demand for intercity rail travel.

    c. Are air travel and rail travel substitutes or complements? Is intercity rail travel a normal or an inferior good?

22. Suppose the demand for Dolce & Gabbana designer jeans increased from 42 000 to 56 000 when per-capita incomes rose from $65 000 to $71 500. Calculate the income elasticity of demand coefficient (remember to use the midpoint method). Are Dolce & Gabbana designer jeans considered a normal or inferior good? Explain why. Are the jeans considered a luxury or necessity? Explain why.

Section 5.4

23. Using the midpoint formula for calculating the elasticity of supply, if the price of a good rose from $95 to $105, what would be the elasticity of supply if the quantity supplied changed from

    a. 38 to 42?

    b. 78 to 82?

    c. 54 to 66?

24. Elasticity of demand in the market for one-bedroom apartments is 2.0, elasticity of supply is 0.5, the current market price is $1000, and the equilibrium number of one-bedroom apartments is 10 000. If the government imposes a price ceiling of $800 on this market, predict the size of the resulting apartment shortage.

25. The price elasticity of supply coefficient for tablet computers is estimated to be equal to 0.6. With current production volumes of 50 million units, what would be the expectation for production volumes in response to a 5 percent increase in the price of tablet computers? What about an 8 percent decline in the price of tablet computers?

Section 5.5

26. Mayor George Henry has a problem. He doesn't want to anger voters by taxing them because he wants to be re-elected, but the town of Gapville needs more revenue for its schools. He has a choice between taxing tickets to professional basketball games or food. If the demand for food is relatively inelastic while the supply is relatively elastic, and if the demand for professional basketball games is relatively elastic while the supply is relatively inelastic, in which case would the tax burden fall primarily on consumers? In which case would the tax burden fall primarily on producers?

27. If both supply curves and demand curves are more elastic in the long run than in the short run, how does the incidence of a tax change from the short run to the long run as a result? What happens to the revenue raised from a given tax over time, *ceteris paribus*?

28. As part of its national "Get-Fit" program, the government instituted a doughnut tax to be paid by doughnut producers. Before the tax, 6000 doughnuts were sold each month at a price of $1.50 per doughnut. After the tax, 5600 doughnuts are being sold every month. Consumers pay $2.00 a doughnut and producers receive $1.40 a doughnut.

    a. In a properly labelled demand/supply diagram, illustrate the impact of this seller tax on the doughnut market.

    b. What is the amount of the tax?

6

Consumer Choice and Market Efficiency

Consumer Behaviour

- What is utility?
- What is diminishing marginal utility?

WHAT IS UTILITY?

To more clearly define the relationship between consumer choice and resource allocation, economists developed a concept of **utility**—a measure of the relative levels of satisfaction that consumers get from the consumption of goods and services. Defining one **util** as equivalent to one unit of satisfaction, economists can indicate relative levels of consumer satisfaction that result from alternative choices. For example, for a java junkie who wouldn't dream of starting the day without a strong dose of caffeine, a cup of coffee might generate 150 utils of satisfaction, while a cup of herb tea might generate only 10 utils.

   Inherently, utility varies from individual to individual depending on specific preferences. For example, Jabari might get 5 utils of satisfaction from eating his first piece of apple pie, while Bara may derive only 4 utils of satisfaction from her first piece of apple pie.

Utility Is a Personal Matter

Economists recognize that it is not really possible to make interpersonal utility comparisons. That is, they know that it is impossible to compare the relative satisfactions of different people. The relative satisfaction gained by various people drinking coffee, for example, simply cannot be measured in comparable terms. Likewise, although we might be tempted to believe that a poorer person would derive greater utility from finding a $100 bill than would a richer person, we should resist the temptation. We simply cannot prove it. The poorer person may be monetarily poor because money and material things are not important to her, and the rich person may have become richer because of his lust for the things money can buy.

utility
a measure of the relative levels of satisfaction that consumers get from consumption of goods and services

util
one unit of satisfaction

Total Utility and Marginal Utility

total utility (TU)

total amount of satisfaction derived from the consumption of a certain number of units of a good or service

marginal utility (MU)

extra satisfaction generated by an additional unit of a good that is consumed in a particular time period

Economists recognize two different dimensions of utility: total utility and marginal utility. **Total utility (TU)** is the total amount of satisfaction derived from the consumption of a certain number of units of a good or service. In comparison, **marginal utility (MU)** is the extra satisfaction generated by an additional unit of a good that is consumed in a particular time period. For example, eating four slices of pizza in an hour might generate a total of 28 utils of satisfaction. The first three slices of pizza might generate a total of 24 utils, while the last slice might generate only 4 utils. In this case, the total utility of eating four slices of pizza is 28 utils and the marginal utility of the fourth slice is 4 utils. Notice in Exhibit 1(a) how total utility increases as consumption increases (we see more total utility after the fourth slice of pizza than after the third). But notice, too, that the increase in total utility from each additional unit (slice) is less than the unit before, which indicates the marginal utility. In Exhibit 1(b), we see how the marginal utility falls as consumption increases.

---

section 6.1
Exhibit 1   **Total and Marginal Utility**

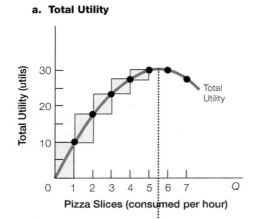

a. Total Utility

b. Marginal Utility

Slices of Pizza (per day)	Total Utility (utils)	Marginal Utility (utils)
0	0	
1	10	10
2	18	8
3	24	6
4	28	4
5	30	2
6	30	0
7	28	−2

As you can see in Exhibit 1(a), the total utility from pizza increases as consumption increases. In Exhibit 1(b) marginal utility decreases as consumption increases. That is, as you eat more pizza, your satisfaction from each additional slice diminishes.

WHAT IS DIMINISHING MARGINAL UTILITY?

Although economists believe that total utility increases with additional consumption, they also argue that the incremental satisfaction—the marginal utility—that results from the consumption of additional units tends to decline as consumption increases. In other words, as an individual consumes more and more of a good, each successive unit generates less and less utility (or satisfaction). This concept is traditionally referred to as the **diminishing marginal utility**. Exhibit 1(b) demonstrates this graphically, where the marginal utility curve has a negative slope.

It follows from the law of diminishing marginal utility that as a person uses more and more units of a good to satisfy a given want, the intensity of the want, and the utility derived from further satisfying that want, diminishes. Think about it: If you are starving, your desire for that first slice of pizza will be great, but as you eat, you gradually become more and more full, reducing your desire for yet another piece.

Why do most individuals take only one newspaper from covered, coin-operated newspaper racks when it would be so easy to take more? Do you think potato chips, candy, or specialty coffees could be sold profitably in the same kind of dispenser? Although ethical considerations keep some people from taking additional papers, the law of diminishing marginal utility is also at work here.

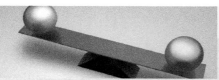

DEBATE

SHOULD CANADA KEEP ON FUNDING PUBLIC-HEALTH CARE AT CURRENT LEVELS?

For:

If we think in terms of utility—a measure of the relative levels of satisfaction that consumers get from consumption of goods or services—it seems foolish to think of cutting back on health care. All Canadians can make use of public-health care when they need to, and they've been doing so for generations. The country's health-care system traces its origins back to the late 1940s in the province of Saskatchewan, and the universal health care as we know it came into existence in 1966. Governments invest in public-health care for a variety of reasons, and most of the positive consequences have justified the higher costs and taxes for citizens over time. There is concern that, with baby boomers retiring and fewer taxpayers in other demographic groups, governments may not be able to continue to fund health care at the present levels without major tax increases. But many would argue that Canadians have bought into the "social contract," where generations coming before and after will help pay for key social benefits such as health, education, and social benefits. Canadians are satisfied with the basic idea of universal health care and with the services it provides. Just because one generation can't meet its own financial obligations doesn't mean that the governments can't fund social programs through debt financing. The positive consequences that come from funding health care far outweigh their cost—when citizens are healthy they're more productive. Surely consumer satisfaction with the concept of health care and with the services provided demands continued funding for health care at present levels?

Against:

Detractors suggest that users should pay for the services they use and should not saddle future generations with the debts of their predecessors. When there was money available in the system, citizens didn't have to choose between health or education or social programs, but now with increasing costs and lower tax revenues, citizens have to make these choices. Some also argue that it's not the state's responsibility to fund health care—that there are private means, such as savings or insurance, that citizens should be using to finance individual needs. The less individuals pay in taxes, the more they can choose to invest or buy insurance for their own health-care needs. Another argument for private health care is that ultimately it provides a greater number of jobs, because with multiple suppliers there is a duplication of services, and therefore a duplication of jobs. That would help the economy. Surely there is no need to continue spending public money that is harder to come by on services that the public could be paying for privately in a market that would offer more consumer choice.

diminishing marginal utility

the concept that, as an individual consumes more and more of a good, each successive unit generates less and less utility (or satisfaction)

section 6.2   Consumer Choice

■ What is the "best" decision for consumers?

■ What is the connection between the law of demand and the law of diminishing marginal utility?

WHAT IS THE "BEST" DECISION FOR CONSUMERS?

We established the fact that marginal utility diminishes as additional units of a good are acquired, but what significance does this fact have for consumers? Remember, consumers try to add to their own total utility, so when the marginal utility generated by the purchase of additional units of one good drops too low, it can become rational for the consumer to purchase other goods rather than purchase more of the first good. In other words, a rational consumer will avoid making purchases of any one good beyond the point at which other goods will yield greater satisfaction for the amount spent—the "bang for the buck."

Marginal utility, then, is an important concept in understanding and predicting consumer behaviour, especially when combined with information about prices. By comparing the marginal utilities generated by the units of the goods that they desire as well as comparing the prices, rational consumers seek the combination of goods that maximizes their satisfaction for a given amount spent. In the next section, we will see how this concept works.

Decisions about what to buy and how much to buy would be easy if we enjoyed everything to the same degree and if we had limitless funds. But that's not reality. In the real world, we like some things more than other things and we are usually forced to stay within a budget. Consumer choice theory shows us how to make optimal decisions.

Consumer Equilibrium

To reach consumer equilibrium, consumers must allocate their incomes in such a way that the marginal utility per dollar's worth of any good is the same for every good. That is, the "bang for the buck" must be equal for all goods at consumer equilibrium. When this goal is realized, one dollar's worth of additional gasoline will yield the same marginal utility as one dollar's worth of additional bread or apples or movie tickets or soap. This concept will become clearer to you as we work through an example illustrating the forces present when consumers are not at equilibrium.

Given a fixed budget, if the marginal utilities per dollar spent on additional units of two goods are not the same, you can increase total satisfaction by buying more of one good and less of the other good. For example, consider the case of Paula, a hard-working college student faced with choosing between hamburgers and milkshakes that are priced at $2 and $1, respectively. She has $11 to spend for the week.

The marginal utility Paula derives from each of the two goods is presented in column B of Exhibit 1. If Paula was solely interested in utility she would choose five hamburgers and five milkshakes because that would maximize her total utility (68 + 34 = 102); that is, adding up all of the marginal utilities for all hamburgers (68 utils) and all milkshakes (34 utils). The only problem with this outcome is that it would cost Paula $15: $10 for the five hamburgers and $5 for the five milkshakes, thus exceeding her $11 per week budget by $4.

So what is the best way for Paula to spend her money? To answer this question, we need to remember that economic decisions are made at the margin. By equalizing the marginal utility per dollar spent for all goods, Paula will be able to ensure she is getting the best bang for her buck. To help Paula optimally allocate her budget, her marginal utility per dollar spent for each hamburger and milkshake is presented in column C of Exhibit 1.

In terms of her first purchase, since the first milkshake gives more marginal utility per dollar spent than the first hamburger (12 utils versus 10 utils), Paula will purchase a milkshake first. For her second purchase, the first hamburger's *MU* per dollar spent (10 utils) is greater than the second milkshakes *MU* per dollar spent (9 utils), so her second purchase will be a hamburger. What about her third purchase? Paula will purchase a second milkshake since its *MU* per dollar spent exceeds the *MU* per dollar spent of the next hamburger (9 utils versus 8 utils). As for the third, fourth, and fifth purchases, these will all be hamburgers, as the *MU* per dollar spent on the second, third, and fourth hamburgers is greater than the *MU* per dollar spent for the third milkshake (8 utils, 7 utils, and 6 utils, respectively, versus 5 utils). Lastly, Paula's final purchase will be a milkshake, since the third milkshake's *MU* per dollar spent is above the *MU* per dollar spent of the fifth hamburger (5 utils versus 4 utils). A summary of the results is presented in Exhibit 2.

section 6.2 Exhibit 1	**Marginal Utility per Dollar Spent**	
A	**B**	**C**
Quantity of Hamburgers Consumed Each Week	**Marginal Utility from Last Hamburger**	$(MU_{hamburger}/P_{hamburger})$
1	20	10
2	16	8
3	14	7
4	12	6
5	8	4
Quantity of Milkshakes Consumed Each Week	**Marginal Utility from Last Milkshake**	$(MU_{milkshake}/P_{hamburger})$
1	12	12
2	9	9
3	5	5
4	4	4
5	3	3

section 6.2   The Path to Consumer Equilibrium: A Summary
    Exhibit 2   of Purchases

Purchase	Item	MU per Dollar Spent	MU	TU	Remaining Income
1st	Milkshake	12	12	12	$11 − $1 = $10
2nd	Hamburger	10	20	32	$10 − $2 = $8
3rd	Milkshake	9	9	41	$8 − $1 = $7
4th	Hamburger	8	16	57	$7 − $2 = $5
5th	Hamburger	7	14	71	$5 − $2 = $3
6th	Hamburger	6	12	83	$3 − $2 = $1
7th	Milkshake	5	5	88	$1 − $1 = 0

consumer equilibrium

allocation of consumer income that balances the ratio of marginal utility to the price of the goods purchased

In conclusion, Paula can accomplish an optimal allocation of her $11 budget by purchasing four hamburgers and three milkshakes. As seen in Exhibit 2, this combination of purchases will generate a total utility of 88 utils, a level of utility greater than any other possible combination of purchases Paula could afford for $11.

What this example shows is that, to achieve maximum satisfaction—**consumer equilibrium**—consumers have to allocate income in a way that balances the ratio of marginal utility to the price of the goods purchased. In other words, in a state of consumer equilibrium,

$$MU_1/P_1 = MU_2/P_2 = MU_3/P_3 = \ldots MU_N/P_N$$

In this situation, each good provides the consumer with the same level of marginal utility per dollar spent.

WHAT IS THE CONNECTION BETWEEN THE LAW OF DEMAND AND THE LAW OF DIMINISHING MARGINAL UTILITY?

The law of demand states that when the price of a good is reduced, the quantity demanded will increase. But why is this the case? By examining the law of diminishing marginal utility in action, we can determine the basis for this relationship between price and quantity demanded. Indeed, the demand curve merely translates marginal utility into dollar terms.

For example, let's say that you are in consumer equilibrium when the price of personal-sized pizza is $4 and the price of a plate of French fries is $1. Further, in equilibrium, the marginal utility on the last pizza consumed is 40 utils, and the marginal utility on the last plate of French fries is 10 utils. So in consumer equilibrium, the *MU/P* ratio for both the pizza and French fries is 10 utils per dollar.

$$\frac{MU_{pizza}}{P_{pizza}} = \frac{40 \text{ utils}}{\$4} = 10 \text{ utils/dollar} = \frac{10 \text{ utils}}{\$1} = \frac{MU_{French\ fries}}{P_{French\ fries}}$$

Now suppose the price of the personal-sized pizza falls to $2, *ceteris paribus*. Instead of the *MU/P* ratio of the pizza being 10 utils per dollar, it is now 20 utils per dollar

(40 utils/$2). This calculation implies, *ceteris paribus,* that you will now buy more pizza at the lower price because you are getting relatively more satisfaction for each dollar that you spend on pizza.

$$\frac{MU_{pizza}}{P_{pizza}} = \frac{40\,\text{utils}}{\$2} = 20\,\text{utils/dollar} > 10\,\text{utils/dollar} = \frac{10\,\text{utils}}{\$1} = \frac{MU_{French\ fries}}{P_{French\ fries}}$$

In other words, because the price of the personal-sized pizza fell, you are now willing to purchase more pizzas. By buying more pizzas, you travel farther out along your marginal utility curve for pizzas, and as a result, the marginal utility for pizza falls. With that change, the ratio of marginal utility per dollar spent for both pizzas and French fries changes in the following way:

$$\frac{MU_{pizza}}{P_{pizza}} = \frac{20\,\text{utils}}{\$2} = 10\,\text{utils/dollar} = \frac{10\,\text{utils}}{\$1} = \frac{MU_{French\ fries}}{P_{French\ fries}}$$

So in consumer equilibrium, the *MU/P* ratio for both pizzas and French fries is again equal.

In other words, as the price of pizzas decreases, consumers will maximize total utility by buying more pizzas, therefore producing a negatively sloped demand curve.

SECTION CHECK

- To maximize consumer satisfaction, income must be allocated so that the ratio of the marginal utility to the price is the same for all goods purchased.
- A fall in a goods price will raise its marginal utility–price (*MU/P*) ratio above that of other good purchased. This relatively greater *MU/P* ratio will lead a rational consumer to purchase more of this good at the expense of other goods.

Consumer and Producer Surplus

- What is consumer surplus?
- What is producer surplus?
- How do we measure the total gains from exchange?

WHAT IS CONSUMER SURPLUS?

In a competitive market, consumers and producers buy and sell at the market equilibrium price. However, what a consumer actually pays for a unit of a good is usually less than the amount she is *willing* to pay. For example, you would be willing and able to pay far more than the market price for a rope ladder to get out of a burning building. You would also be willing to pay more than the market price for a tank of gasoline if you ran out of gas on a desolate highway. **Consumer surplus** is the monetary difference between the price a consumer is willing and able to pay for an additional unit of a good and what the consumer actually pays—the market price. Consumer surplus

consumer surplus
the monetary difference between the price a consumer is willing and able to pay for an additional unit of a good and the price the consumer actually pays; for the entire market, it is the sum of all of the individual consumer surpluses for those consumers who have purchased the good

for the entire market is the sum of all of the individual consumer surpluses for those consumers who have purchased the good.

Marginal Willingness to Pay Falls as More Is Consumed

Suppose it is a very hot day and iced tea is going for $1 per glass but Mark is willing to pay $4 for the first glass, $2 for the second glass, and $0.50 for the third glass, reflecting the law of demand. How much consumer surplus will Mark receive? First, it is important to note the general fact that if the consumer is a buyer of several units of a good, the earlier units will have greater marginal value and therefore create more consumer surplus, because *marginal willingness to pay* falls as greater quantities are consumed in any period. In fact, you can think of the demand curve as a marginal benefit curve—the additional benefit derived from consuming one more unit. Notice in Exhibit 1 that Mark's demand for iced tea has a step-like slope. This is demonstrated by Mark's willingness to pay $4 and $2 successively for the first two glasses of iced tea. Thus, Mark will receive $3 of consumer surplus for the first glass ($4 – $1) and $1 of consumer surplus for the second glass ($2 – $1), for a total of $4, as seen in Exhibit 1. Mark will not be willing to purchase the third glass because it would provide less value than its price warrants ($0.50 versus $1) and reduce consumer surplus as a result.

In Exhibit 2, we can easily measure the consumer surplus in the market by using a market demand curve rather than an individual demand curve. In short, the market consumer surplus is the area under the market demand curve and above the market price (area A in Exhibit 2). The market for chocolate contains millions of potential buyers, so we will get a smooth demand curve. That is, each of the millions of potential buyers has his or her own willingness to pay. Because the demand curve represents the marginal benefits consumers receive from consuming an additional unit, we can conclude that all buyers of chocolate receive at least some consumer surplus in the market, because the marginal benefit is greater than the market price—the shaded area in Exhibit 2.

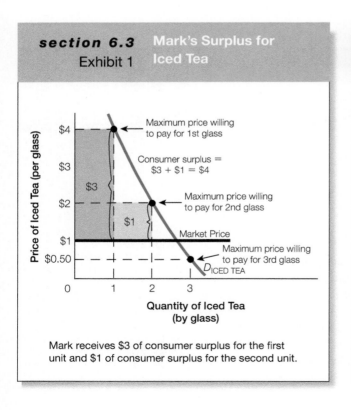

section 6.3
Exhibit 1   Mark's Surplus for Iced Tea

Mark receives $3 of consumer surplus for the first unit and $1 of consumer surplus for the second unit.

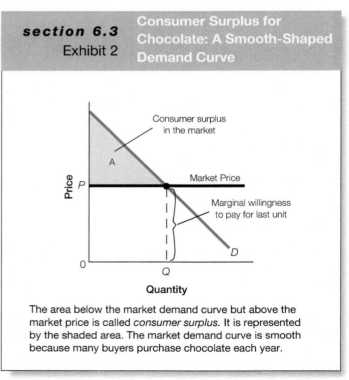

section 6.3
Exhibit 2   Consumer Surplus for Chocolate: A Smooth-Shaped Demand Curve

The area below the market demand curve but above the market price is called *consumer surplus*. It is represented by the shaded area. The market demand curve is smooth because many buyers purchase chocolate each year.

Price Changes and Changes in Consumer Surplus

Imagine that the price of your favourite beverage fell because of an increase in supply. Wouldn't you feel better off? An increase in supply and a lower price will increase your consumer surplus for each of the units you were already consuming, and will also increase consumer surplus from increased purchases at the lower price. Conversely, a decrease in supply will cause an increase in price and will lower the amount of consumer surplus.

Exhibit 3 shows the gain in consumer surplus associated with, say, a technological advance that shifts the supply curve to the right. As a result, equilibrium price falls (from P_0 to P_1) and quantity rises (from Q_0 to Q_1). Consumer surplus then increases from area P_0AB to area P_1AC, or a gain in consumer surplus of P_0BCP_1. The increase in consumer surplus has two parts. First, there is an increase in consumer surplus because Q_0 can now be purchased at a lower price; this amount of additional consumer surplus is illustrated by area P_0BDP_1 in Exhibit 3. Second, the lower price makes it advantageous for buyers to expand their purchases from Q_0 to Q_1. The net benefit to buyers from expanding their consumption from Q_0 to Q_1 is illustrated by the area BCD.

WHAT IS PRODUCER SURPLUS?

As we have just seen, the difference between what a consumer would be willing and able to pay for a quantity of a good and what a consumer actually has to pay is called *consumer surplus*. The parallel concept for producers is called *producer surplus*. **Producer surplus** is the difference between what a producer is paid for a good and the cost of producing that unit of the good. The supply curve shows the minimum amount that sellers must receive to be willing to supply any given quantity.

Imagine it is 30 degrees in the shade. Do you think you would get more consumer surplus from your first glass of iced tea than you would from a fifth glass?

producer surplus
the difference between what a producer is paid for a good and the cost of producing that unit of the good; for the market, it is the sum of all of the individual sellers' producer surpluses—the area above the market supply curve and below the market price

---

section 6.3   The Impact on Consumer Surplus
Exhibit 3   of an Increase in Supply

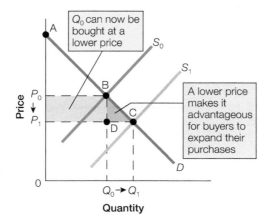

As a result of the increase in supply, the price falls from P_0 to P_1. The initial consumer surplus at P_0 is the area ABP_0. The increase in the consumer surplus from the fall in price is P_0BCP_1.

section 6.3
Exhibit 4   **A Firm's Producer Surplus**

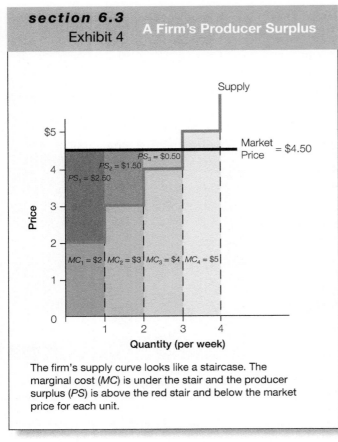

The firm's supply curve looks like a staircase. The marginal cost (*MC*) is under the stair and the producer surplus (*PS*) is above the red stair and below the market price for each unit.

That is, the supply curve reflects that marginal cost curve to sellers, just like the demand curve is the marginal benefit curve to consumers. Because some units can be produced at a cost that is lower than the market price, the seller receives a surplus, or a net benefit, from producing those units.

For each unit produced, the producer surplus is the difference between the market price and the marginal cost of producing that unit. For example, in Exhibit 4, the market price is $4.50. Say the firm's cost is $2 for the first unit, $3 for the second unit, $4 for the third unit, and $5 for the fourth unit. Since producer surplus for a particular unit is the difference between the market price and the seller's cost of producing that unit, producer surplus would be as follows: The first unit would yield $2.50, the second unit would yield $1.50, the third unit would yield $0.50, while the fourth unit would add nothing to producer surplus, because the market price is less than the seller's cost.

Total producer surplus for the market is obtained by summing all of the producer surpluses of all the sellers—the area above the market supply curve and below the market price up to the quantity actually produced—the shaded area in Exhibit 5. Producer surplus is a measurement of how much sellers gain from trading in the market.

Suppose there is an increase in demand and the market price rises, say from P_0 to P_1; the seller now receives a higher price per unit, so additional producer surplus is generated. In Exhibit 6, we see the additions to producer surplus. Part of the added surplus (area P_1DBP_0) is due to a higher price for the quantity

section 6.3
Exhibit 5   **Market Producer Surplus**

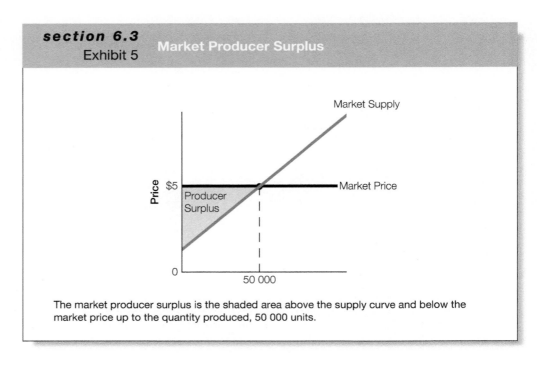

The market producer surplus is the shaded area above the supply curve and below the market price up to the quantity produced, 50 000 units.

section 6.3   The Impact of an Increase
Exhibit 6   in Demand on Producer
Surplus

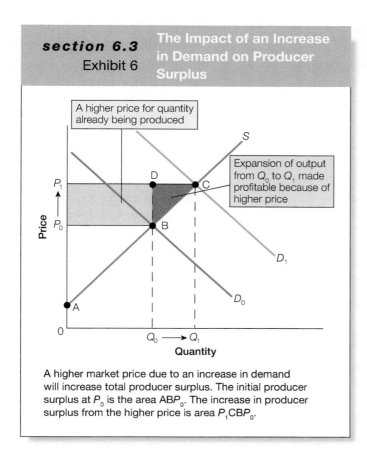

A higher market price due to an increase in demand
will increase total producer surplus. The initial producer
surplus at P_0 is the area ABP_0. The increase in producer
surplus from the higher price is area P_1CBP_0.

section 6.3   Consumer and Producer
Exhibit 7   Surplus

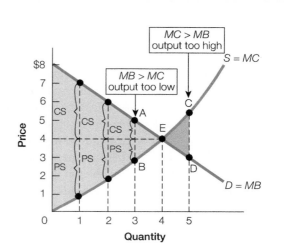

Increasing output beyond the competitive equilibrium
output decreases welfare because the cost of producing
this extra output exceeds the value the buyer places on
it ($MC > MB$). Producing 5 units rather than 4 units leads
to a deadweight loss of area ECD. Reducing output
below the competitive equilibrium output level reduces
total welfare because the buyer values the extra output
by more than it costs to produce that output. Producing
3 units rather than 4 units leads to a deadweight loss of
area EAB ($MC < MB$). At the competitive market equilibrium price and quantity, the net welfare gains to society
are as large as possible ($MC = MB$).

already being produced (up to Q_0) and part (area DCB) is due to the expansion of
output made profitable by the higher price (from Q_0 to Q_1).

HOW DO WE MEASURE THE TOTAL GAINS FROM EXCHANGE?

With the tools of consumer and producer surplus, we can better analyze the total gains
from exchange. The demand curve represents a collection of maximum prices that
consumers are willing and able to pay for additional quantities of a good or service.
It also shows the marginal benefits derived by consumers. The supply curve represents
a collection of minimum prices that suppliers require to be willing and able to supply
each additional unit of a good or service. It also shows the marginal cost of production. Both are shown in Exhibit 7. For example, for the first unit of output, the buyer
is willing to pay up to $7 and the seller would have to receive at least $1 to produce
that unit. However, the equilibrium price is $4, as indicated by the intersection of the
supply and demand curves. It is clear that the two would gain from getting together
and trading that unit because the consumer would receive $3 of consumer surplus
($7 − $4) and the producer would receive $3 of producer surplus ($4 − $1).

Both would also benefit from trading the second and third units of output—in fact,
both would benefit from trading every unit up to the market equilibrium output. That
is, buyers purchase each good, except for the very last unit, for less than the maximum
amount that they would have been willing to pay; sellers receive, except for the very

last unit, more than the minimum price that they would have been willing to accept to supply the good. Once the equilibrium output is reached at the equilibrium price, all of the mutually beneficial trade opportunities between the suppliers and the demanders will have taken place, and the sum of consumer surplus and producer surplus is maximized. This is where the marginal benefit to buyers is equal to the marginal cost to producers. Both buyers and sellers are better off from each of the units traded than they would have been if they had not exchanged them.

total welfare gains
the sum of consumer and producer surplus

It is important to recognize that, in this case, the **total welfare gains** to the economy from trade in this good is the sum of the consumer and producer surplus created. That is, consumers benefit from additional amounts of consumer surplus and producers benefit from additional amounts of producer surplus. Improvements in welfare come from additions to both consumer and producer surplus. In competitive markets, where there are large numbers of buyers and sellers, at the market equilibrium price and quantity, the net gains to society are as large as possible. Not producing the efficient level of output leads to what economists call a **deadweight loss**. A deadweight loss is the net loss of total surplus that results from the misallocation of resources.

deadweight loss
net loss of total surplus that results from the misallocation of resources

Why would it be inefficient to produce only three units? The demand curve in Exhibit 7 indicates that the buyer is willing to pay $5 for the third unit. The supply curve shows that it costs the seller only $3 to produce that unit. That is, as long as the buyer values the extra output by more than it costs to produce that unit, total welfare would increase by expanding output. In fact, if output is expanded from three units to four units, total welfare (the sum of consumer and producer surpluses) will increase by area AEB in Exhibit 7.

What if five units are produced? The demand curve shows that the buyer is willing to pay only $3 for the fifth unit. However, the supply curve shows that it would cost about $5.50 to produce the fifth unit. So, increasing output beyond equilibrium decreases total welfare because the cost of producing this extra output is greater than the value the buyer places on it. If output is reduced from five units to four units, total welfare will increase by the area ECD in Exhibit 7.

Business *CONNECTION*

HOW CLEVER PRICING SQUEEZES CONSUMER SURPLUS

Consumer surplus is the difference between the price at which a consumer values a product and the actual price that the consumer pays. Someone who values a product at $1000 and buys it on sale for $400 realizes a consumer surplus of $600. As a consumer, you've more than likely experienced significant consumer surplus when you've walked out of a store with a great bargain—it's that "Yeah, baby!" feeling. Interestingly, the greater the consumer surplus, the easier it is for the seller to take the consumer's cash. So as a producer, to increase sales you either have to lower prices or increase perceived value for an easier (and faster) sale.

The other concept of note here is producer surplus: The difference between what a product sells for and what it costs. Producer surplus is also known as *gross profit* or *gross margin*. Companies recognize that the simplest way to increase surplus to their customers is to lower prices, but

doing so lowers their own profit. So there is great motivation to raise the perceived value and avoid discounts.

Well-managed businesses are keenly aware of the power of consumer surplus and they use it to increase sales and bring in higher incremental revenues—the profit linked to the number of products manufactured for one production unit. They can use several tactics to achieve this: (1) They can introduce products into the market at high prices that drop over time. Think of those who want to be the first to own new technology—they will happily pay a high price just to be able to own it before anyone else. (2) Another tactic is to add features to the product that increase perceived value at a rate greater than their cost. Your smartphone is a prime example of this tactic—most customers use just an iota of the all of the potential the smartphone offers. (3) Still another tactic is to develop a sense of "cool" through marketing

(continued)

programs that overshadow the basic use of the product. Think in terms of Apple's original iPod commercials with the black silhouette and white ear buds—who wanted a generic MP3 player back then?

Keeping up high perceived value over time is difficult (due to changes in technology or competition) and expensive in terms of marketing costs. So companies know that price discounts are likely inevitable over time, and that if they don't give discounts they may end up with higher inventories and the associated costs that go with that. Smart companies recognize that gradually offering more and more of a discount increases consumer surplus while increasing the seller's revenues—they don't leave potential revenues on the table.

The future of marketing for all companies will be to uncover opportunities using conventional economic theories in ways that haven't been used before. Understanding the potential that economics offers is a powerful tool for businesses and allows them to compete and win—and in the case of consumer surplus, do so by keeping the customer happy and satisfied.

1. How can firms use the externality concept to their advantage in marketing their services or products?

2. Do you think firms should be held accountable for all of the society costs caused by negative externalities? Why or why not?

3. Considering your response to question (2) above, do you think firms should directly benefit from the positive externalities that their firms produce for society? If so, how could society distribute those benefits to the firms?

In a competitive equilibrium, supply equals demand at the equilibrium. This means that the buyers value the last unit of output consumed by exactly the same amount that it cost to produce. If consumers valued the last unit by more than it cost to produce, welfare could be increased by expanding output. If consumers valued the last unit by less than it cost to produce, then welfare could be increased by producing less output.

In sum, *market efficiency* occurs when we have maximized the sum of consumer and producer surplus, when the marginal benefit of the last unit consumed is equal to the marginal cost of productivity, $MB = MC$.

SECTION CHECK

■ The difference between how much a consumer is willing and able to pay and how much a consumer has to pay for a unit of the good is called *consumer surplus*.

■ An increase (decrease) in supply will lead to an increase (decrease) in consumer surplus.

■ Producer surplus is the difference between what a producer is paid for a good and the cost of producing that good. An increase (decrease) in demand will lead to an increase (decrease) in producer surplus.

■ The economy's total welfare gains from exchange can be measured by the sum of consumer and producer surplus.

For Your Review

Section 6.1

1. If someone says, "You'd have to pay me to eat one more bite," what do we know about that person's marginal utility? What do we know about that person's total utility?

2. The following table shows Rene's total utility from eating escargot. Fill in the blanks that show the marginal utility that Rene derives from eating escargot.

Escargot		
Per Day	Total Utility	Marginal Utility
1	10	_____
2	18	_____
3	24	_____
4	28	_____
5	30	_____
6	30	_____

3. At the local ski resort, the rates for a day on the slopes are as follows:

4-hour pass = \$23

Full-day pass (8 hours) = \$33

How does this pricing policy relate to what we know about marginal utility?

4. Using your results from question 2, plot both Rene's total and marginal utility curves on graphs.

5. Where possible, complete the following table by filling in the empty cells.

Number of Smartphone Apps.	Total Utility	Marginal Utility
0		—
1	12	
2	22	
3		7
4		4
5	33	
6		−2

6. Suppose it is "All You Can Eat" night at your favourite restaurant. Once you've paid \$9.95 for your meal, how do you determine how many helpings to consume? Should you continue eating until your food consumption has yielded \$9.95 worth of satisfaction? What happens to the marginal utility from successive helpings as consumption increases?

Section 6.2

7. Brandy spends her entire weekly budget of $20 on soft drinks and pizza. A soft drink and a slice of pizza are priced at $1 and $2, respectively. Brandy's marginal utility from soft drink and pizza consumption is 6 utils and 4 utils, respectively. What advice could you give Brandy to help her increase her overall satisfaction from the consumption of soft drinks and pizza? What will happen to the marginal utility per dollar from soft drink consumption if Brandy follows your advice? What will happen to the marginal utility per dollar from pizza consumption?

8. Suppose you were studying late one night and you were craving a Domino's pizza. How much marginal utility would you receive from the delivered pizza? How much marginal utility would you receive from a pizza that was delivered immediately after you finished a five-course holiday dinner? Where would you be more likely to eat more pizza in a single sitting, at home or at a crowded party (particularly if you're not sure how many pizzas have been ordered)? Use marginal utility analysis to answer the last question.

Blueprint Problem

The utility derived from consuming various quantities of pork and tuna are presented in the following table.

Pork		Tuna	
Kilograms	Total Utility	Kilograms	Total Utility
0	0	0	0
1	16	1	10
2	30	2	16
3	38	3	20
4	42	4	22
5	42	5	24

Suppose the price of pork is $4/kg and the price of tuna is $2/kg. If our consumer has a limited budget of $12, how many kilograms of pork and tuna will that person purchase in an effort to achieve consumer equilibrium?

Blueprint Solution

Pork				Tuna			
Kilograms	*TU*	*MU*	*MU/P*	Kilograms	*TU*	*MU*	*MU/P*
0	0	—	—	0	0	—	—
1	16	16	4	1	10	10	5
2	30	14	3.5	2	16	6	3
3	38	8	2	3	20	4	2
4	42	4	1	4	22	2	1
5	42	0	0	5	24	2	1

Recall the condition that will bring our consumer to consumer equilibrium:

$$\frac{MU_{pork}}{P_{pork}} = \frac{MU_{tuna}}{P_{tuna}}$$

In order to use this condition to bring our consumer to the optimal combination of pork and tuna, the *MU* per dollar spent for each kilogram of both pork and tuna needs to be computed. It is suggested that this be done in a table, such as this one presented above.

To ensure our consumer reaches his or her consumer equilibrium, each purchase needs to be evaluated.

Consider the first purchase; since the first kilogram of tuna offers more *MU* per dollar spent than the first kilogram of pork (5 utils versus 4 utils), the consumer will purchase tuna. As for the second purchase, here the first kilogram of pork offers more *MU* per dollar spent than the second kilogram of tuna (4 utils versus 3 utils); therefore the consumer will purchase their first kilogram of pork.

Notice what is being compared in the second purchase—the first kilogram of pork (that has yet to be bought) against the second kilogram of tuna (given that the first kilogram was bought in the first purchase).

In terms of the third purchase, since the *MU* per dollar spent for the second kilogram of pork exceeds that for the second kilogram of tuna, the consumer will purchase a second kilogram of pork. For the fourth purchase, the second kilogram of tuna produces more *MU* per dollar spent compared to the third kilogram of pork; therefore the consumer will purchase the second kilogram of tuna.

To summarize these purchases and illustrate their impact on the consumer's budget, total utility, and marginal utility enjoyed, a table such as the following could be constructed.

Purchase	Item	Budget Remaining	MU (utils)	TU (utils)
1st	Tuna	$12 − $2 = $10	10	10
2nd	Pork	$10 − $4 = $6	16	26
3rd	Pork	$6 − $4 = $2	14	40
4th	Tuna	$2 − $2 = 0	6	46

Note that the budget is exhausted in equilibrium

Note the total amount of utility:
2 kg of tuna (16 utils of utility) + 2 kg of pork (30 utils of utility) = 46 utils of utility

9. The table below details the amount of utility a typical student derives from consuming cups of coffee and muffins. The price of a cup of coffee is $2, the price of a muffin is $1, and the student has a total of $9 to spend (and spends it all). Based on all this information, how many cups of coffee and muffins will our typical student purchase in consumer equilibrium?

Cups of Coffee		Muffins	
Number of Cups	Total Utility	Number of Muffins	Total Utility
0	0	0	0
1	16	1	6
2	29	2	10
3	40	3	11
4	49	4	11
5	54	5	9

10. Using the data from problem 9, what would happen to our utility-maximizing student's behaviour if the price of a muffin decreased to $0.50 (all other information remains constant)?

11. Complete the following table by filling in the missing cells.

Hockey Games			Football Games		
Number	TU	MU	Number	TU	MU
0	0	—	0		—
1	20		1		18
2	36		2	30	
3		12	3	36	
4		10	4		6
5	66	8	5	45	
6	72		6		0

If the price of a hockey ticket is $16, the price of a football ticket is $12, and local sports fans have a budget of $88, determine how many hockey games and football games they will attend using the utility-maximizing rule.

Section 6.3

12. Refer to the following exhibit.

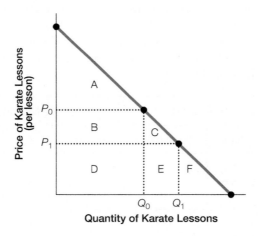

a. If the price of each karate lesson is P_0, the consumer surplus is equal to what area?

b. If the price falls from P_0 to P_1, the change in consumer surplus is equal to what area?

13. Steve loves potato chips. His weekly demand curve is shown in the following exhibit.

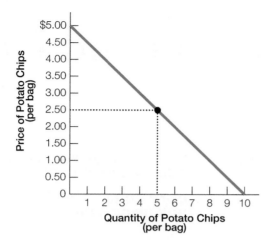

a. How much is Steve willing to pay for one bag of potato chips?

b. How much is Steve willing to pay for a second bag of potato chips?

c. If the actual market price of potato chips is $2.50 and Steve buys five bags as shown, what is the value of his consumer surplus?

d. What is Steve's total willingness to pay for five bags?

14. If a freeze ruined this year's lettuce crop, show what would happen to consumer surplus.

15. If demand for apples increased as a result of a news story that highlighted the health benefits of two apples a day, what would happen to producer surplus?

16. How is total surplus (the sum of consumer and producer surpluses) related to the efficient level of output? Using a supply and demand curve, demonstrate that producing less than the equilibrium output will lead to an inefficient allocation of resources—a deadweight loss.

17. Suppose Phil's supply curve for widgets is as follows: At $20, he will supply 1; at $30, he will supply 2; at $40, he will supply 3; at $50, he will supply 4; and at $60, he will supply 5.

a. If the price of widgets is $40, what is his producer surplus?

b. If the price of widgets rises from $40 to $50, how much will his producer surplus change?

Production and Costs

Profits: Total Revenues Minus Total Costs

- What are explicit and implicit costs?
- What are profits?
- What are sunk costs?

WHAT ARE EXPLICIT AND IMPLICIT COSTS?

As we discussed in Chapter 1, costs exist because resources are scarce and have competing uses—to produce more of one good means forgoing the production of another good. The cost of producing a good is measured by the worth of the most valuable alternative that was given up to obtain the resource. As you may recall, this is called the *opportunity cost*.

In Chapter 2, the production possibilities curve highlighted this trade-off. Recall that the opportunity cost of producing additional shelter was the units of food that had to be sacrificed. Other examples of opportunity costs abound: Paper used in this text could have been used in other books or for hundreds of other uses, and the steel used in the construction of a new building could have been used in the production of an automobile or a washing machine.

But what exactly makes up a firm's costs? Let's look at the two distinct components that make up the firm's costs: explicit costs and implicit costs.

Explicit Costs

explicit costs
the opportunity costs of production that require a monetary payment

Explicit costs are the opportunity costs of production that require a monetary payment—the out-of-pocket expenses for labour services, raw materials, fuel, transportation, utilities, advertising, and so on. It is important to note that the explicit costs are opportunity costs to the firm. For example, money spent on electricity cannot be used for advertising. Remember, in a world of scarcity, we are always giving up something to get something else. Trade-offs are pervasive. The costs that we have discussed so far are relatively easy to measure and an economist and an accountant would most likely arrive at the same amounts. But that will generally not be the case.

Implicit Costs

Some of the firm's (opportunity) costs of production are implicit. **Implicit costs** do not require monetary payment. This is where the economist's and the accountant's ideas of costs diverge because accountants do not include implicit costs. For example, whenever an investment is made, opportunities to invest elsewhere are forgone. This lost opportunity is an implicit cost that economists include in the total cost of the firm, even though no money is expended. A typical farmer or small business owner may perform work without receiving formal wages, but the value of the alternative earnings forgone represents an implicit opportunity cost to the individual. Because other firms could have used the resources, what the resources could have earned elsewhere is an implicit cost to the firm. It is important to emphasize that whenever we are talking about costs—explicit or implicit—we are talking about opportunity costs.

To better delineate the difference between explicit and implicit costs, consider whether the following statement is true or false: "A company located in a growing urban area with rising rents can protect itself against these rising costs by owning the building it occupies." This statement is not entirely true. The company is protected against having to pay the rising rents (explicit cost) by owning the building it occupies. However, if the company owns the building and rents increase, so does the opportunity cost of owning the building. That is, by occupying the building, the company is giving up the new higher rents it could receive from renters if it leased out the space. So, even though the company pays zero rent by owning the building, the rent that it could receive by leasing it to another company is a very real economic cost (but not an accounting cost) to the firm.

implicit costs
the opportunity costs of production that do not require a monetary payment

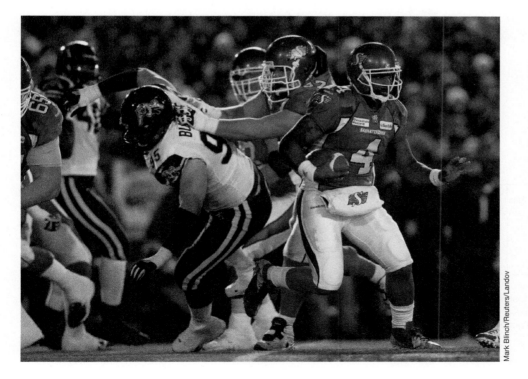

Mark Blinch/Reuters/Landov

Suppose you bought two tickets for $1000 online at eBay for the 101st Grey Cup game in Regina, Saskatchewan. The weather was forecasted to be 10 degrees at game time. However, an unexpected blizzard hits, plunging the wind chill down to −20 on game day. Because you paid so much for the tickets, do you go to the game anyway, even if you would rather watch it at home? What if someone offers you $500 for the two tickets. Would losing $500 necessarily make it a bad decision? The decision to attend the game or not depends on how much you value the $500 and how much you value seeing the game in person.

WHAT ARE PROFITS?

profits
the difference between total revenue and total cost

Economists generally assume that the ultimate goal of the firm is to maximize **profits,** that is, to maximize the difference between total revenue and total cost. In other words, firms try to maximize the difference between what they give up for their inputs—their total costs (explicit and implicit)—and the amount they receive for their goods and services—their total revenue. Like revenues and costs, profits refer to flows over time. When we say that a firm earned $5 million in profits, we must clarify the time period in which the profits were earned—a week, month, year, and so on.

Accounting Profits versus Economic Profits

accounting profits
total revenues minus total explicit costs

economic profits
total revenues minus explicit and implicit costs

A firm can make a profit in the sense that the total revenues that it receives exceed the explicit costs that it incurs in the process of doing business. We call these **accounting profits**—profits as accountants record them are determined by total revenues minus total explicit costs. In other words, accounting profits do not include implicit costs.

Economists prefer an alternative way of measuring profits; **economic profits** are determined by total revenue minus all costs (both explicit and implicit). In calculating a firm's total costs, economists include the implicit costs—as well as the explicit costs.

Summing up, measured in terms of accounting profits like those reported in real-world financial statements, a firm has a profit if its total revenues exceed explicit costs. In terms of economic profits, a firm has a profit if its total revenues exceed its total opportunity cost—both its explicit costs and implicit costs. Exhibit 1 illustrates the difference between accounting profits and economic profits.

A Zero Economic Profit Is a Normal Profit

As we just discussed, an economic profit is less than an accounting profit because economic profits include implicit as well as explicit costs. In fact, an economist considers a zero economic profit to be a normal profit. Recall that zero economic profit means that the firm is covering both explicit and implicit costs—the total opportunity costs of its resources. In other words, the firm's total revenue is sufficient to compensate the time and money that owners have put into the business. For example, suppose you became a farmer and made $80 000 per year. Initially, you had to invest $1 million for the property, seed, and equipment. However, if you had put that money in the bank at, say, 3 percent interest, you would have made $30 000 per year, so you have an implicit cost of $30 000 per year in lost interest. In addition, you have an implicit cost of $50 000 per year because you did not take the job you were offered at the tractor dealership. So an accountant would have you making an economic profit of $80 000, but an economist would say you made zero economic profit because your total revenue minus total costs (explicit + implicit costs) is zero. But even though your profits are driven to zero, your revenue from farming compensates you for your total costs, so you stay in business. This is clearly different from making zero accounting profits, when revenues would cover only the explicit costs. (We will return to this important point in the next chapter.)

section 7.1
Exhibit 1
Accounting Profits versus Economic Profits

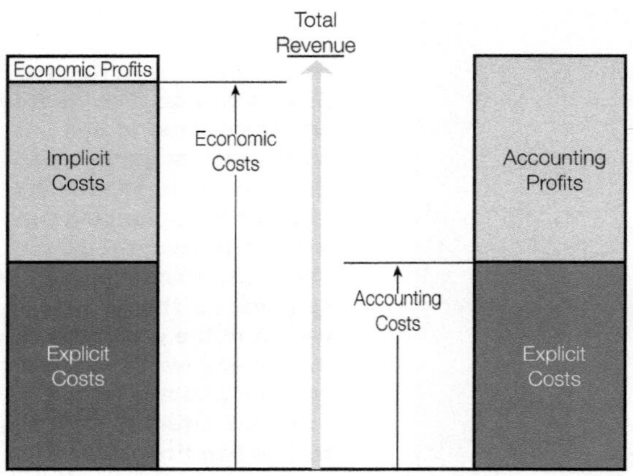

Economic profits equal total revenue minus economic costs (explicit plus implicit costs). Accounting profits equal total revenue minus accounting costs (explicit costs).

WHAT ARE SUNK COSTS?

We have just seen how opportunity costs are often hidden, as in the case of implicit costs. However, there is another type of cost that should be discussed—sunk costs. **Sunk costs** are costs that have already been incurred and cannot be recovered. Suppose, for example, that you bought a DVD that looked interesting, but when you got home and played it you wished you hadn't. Now your friend comes over and says he likes that DVD and will buy it from you for $5. You say "no way" because you paid $15 for the DVD. Are you acting rationally? Economists believe that what you paid for the DVD is now irrelevant. Now, you must decide whether you would rather have the $5 or the DVD. If you decide to keep the DVD, the cost is the $5 you could have received from your friend—the rest is sunk.

Or suppose a doughnut shop has a one-year lease and after three months the owner decides that the shop would do much better by relocating to a new mall that has just opened. Should the doughnut shop just stay put until the end of the year because it is legally obligated to pay the 12-month lease? No, the nonrefundable lease payment is sunk and irrelevant to the decision to relocate. The decision to relocate should be based on the prospects of future profits regardless of the length of the current lease. In short, sunk costs are irrelevant for any future action because they have already been incurred and cannot be recovered.

sunk costs
costs that have been incurred and cannot be recovered

Business *CONNECTION*

THE IMPORTANCE OF WATCHING *ALL* COSTS

Many businesses fail because they focus on revenues and forget to watch and understand all of their costs. The key word here is *all*, because although some costs are obvious and can readily be identified, others are not so apparent. In fact, some time may pass between a business incurring a cost and realizing the impact. In economics, we give the label *explicit costs* to incurred costs that are paid directly with cash, debit, or a cheque and can easily be identified as corresponding to particular units of land, buildings, materials, machinery or equipment, or labour. Sometimes these are also referred to as *accounting costs* because they can be readily identified, measured, recorded, interpreted, and communicated to others—an important role of accounting. Accounting costs reflect historical costs, and planning (or forecasting) requires interpreting historical costs into the future.

There is, however, another set of costs that are not easily identified, that many business operators forget to take into account in making business decisions, and that many students forget about, too. These costs are referred to as *implicit costs*. They are *implicit* because they are not usually apparent unless we carefully consider what we are giving up to obtain a good or service. Take, for example, our education. Our explicit costs include tuition fee payments to the college or university and the cost of textbooks and other school supplies. Our implicit costs—what we gave up to pursue an education—vary, based on individual circumstances. For some of us, the implicit costs include the wages we could have earned working at a job; for others, it's the interest on the savings that we no longer have in the bank.

There is another set of costs, known as *sunk costs*. These are costs that a firm is required to undertake but will not be able to recover, such as the cost of repairing a leaky roof or cleaning up after a flood—costs that are rare and generally cannot be passed on to the customer. If firms do try to pass the costs off, they very well might push the product price into an uncompetitive level.

Business operators who take into account that total economic costs include both explicit and implicit costs, with the reality of sunk costs, realize that over time, if they are really to make a profit, the revenue obtained from their business activities must cover these costs and that they will need to interpret opportunity costs in making decisions on future activities. For example, assume a Canadian toy manufacturer's main plant is close to its operational capacity as it runs two eight-hour shifts. The manufacturer is considering three courses of action: (1) running two ten-hour shifts, (2) building and expanding its plant across town, or (3) outsourcing its manufacturing to Southeast Asia. In considering the explicit costs, it would look at all historical costs and forecast future costs of the overtime in option 1 and construction/transportation costs in option 2. In option 3, it would look at the explicit costs of added transportation and perhaps training, but the manufacturer would also have to compare the opportunity costs of manufacturing in-house versus outsourcing.

(continued)

The possibility of losing control of intellectual property and having to deal with counterfeit production might also be of concern. Looking only at the historical/accounting costs, a firm would limit its success, not putting itself in a position to think of alternatives when the market changes.

Businesspeople who are fully aware of all costs are more likely to set realistic prices for goods and services to ensure that the revenues received cover all explicit and all implicit costs, as well as an amount to provide a profit.

3 to 4 percent per year for a long time. What can business managers do from both the demand side and the supply side to survive (or maybe thrive) if this situation occurs?

1.   Credible data suggest that modern developed economies will probably not see annual growth rates at

2.   As a business owner, you have the choice between adding labour to your organization or mechanizing your production line. Which would you choose and why?

3.   Given the situation in question 2, do you think your decision is sustainable over the long term? Why or why not? If it's not sustainable, what could you do to make your business sustainable? (Think about a particular product or service your company currently produces.)

DEBATE

ARE THE COSTS OF A FORMAL EDUCATION WORTH THE INVESTMENT?

For:
Gone are the days when a high school diploma was the minimum requirement to enter the job market. It's an employers' market now, with many job candidates to choose from, so why should employers take on employees who haven't at least demonstrated a commitment to complete something? Also, many organizations require credentials to meet the necessities of their suppliers or agencies, and certain jobs require credentials for insurance or regulatory reasons. It's not that students without credentials can't do the job, but rather that they're not always legally able to practise. A formal education carries explicit costs, such as tuition, books, and living expenses. It also carries the implicit opportunity cost of what we could have made by forgoing a formal education and starting a job right out of high school. But clearly, those of us who have decided to attend college or university must believe to some extent that a formal education is worth the costs. Are there other reasons why a formal education is worth the investment?

Against:
Many of us arrive at college and university thinking that once we've completed our studies, we will be "educated" to take on a job. The truth is that getting a formal education is just one way to learn skills. We can learn by doing, for example, or through the Internet without having to pay for access to content. If we can demonstrate that we have learned a skill, why do we need credentials to prove it? It's only in recent history that credentials have been accepted as knowledge: Decades ago, practical knowledge was the accepted norm. And now with so many students attending college or university, the value of such credentials is dropping. So it makes sense for students to spend more time getting practical knowledge and then, if required, obtain the credentials once they are sure it's worth the investment. There is recent evidence that the wage gaps between high school-educated and college-educated individuals is narrowing, which helps make a strong argument for only a high school education.[*] Can you elaborate on these arguments or think of others that illustrate why a formal education is not worth the investment?

---

[*]Tavia Grant, "Why the undergrad advantage in wages is vanishing," *The Globe and Mail*, April 28, 2014.

SECTION CHECK
- Total cost consists of explicit costs and implicit costs. Explicit costs are the opportunity costs of production that require a monetary payment, while implicit costs are the opportunity costs that do not represent an outlay of money or a contractual obligation.
- Profits are the difference between the total revenues of a firm and its total costs. Accounting profits are revenues minus explicit costs, while economic profits are revenues minus total opportunity costs—both explicit and implicit.
- Sunk costs are irretrievable and irrelevant to the firm.

Production in the Short Run

- What is the difference between the short run and the long run?
- How does production in the short run behave?

WHAT IS THE DIFFERENCE BETWEEN THE SHORT RUN AND THE LONG RUN?

Of fundamental importance for cost and production behaviour is the extent to which a firm is able to adjust inputs as it varies output. Since it takes more time to vary some inputs than others, we must distinguish between the short run and the long run. The **short run** is defined as a period too brief for some production inputs to be varied. For example, the current size of a plant cannot be altered and new equipment cannot be obtained or built overnight. If demand increases for the firm's product and the firm chooses to produce more output in the short run, it must do so with its existing equipment and factory. Inputs like buildings and equipment that do not change with output are called *fixed* inputs.

The **long run** is a period of time over which all production inputs are variable and can change as output changes. The long run can vary considerably from industry to industry. For a chain of coffeehouses that wants to add a few more stores, the long run may be only a few months. In other industries, like the automobile or steel industry, the long run might be a couple of years, as a new plant or factory in this type of industry will take much longer to build.

short run
a period too brief for some production inputs to be varied

long run
a period over which all production inputs are variable

production function
the relationship between the quantity of inputs and the quantity of outputs produced

total product (*TP*)
the total output of a good produced by the firm

HOW DOES PRODUCTION IN THE SHORT RUN BEHAVE?

Exhibit 1 shows how the quantity of bagels produced by Moe's Bagel Shop per hour varies with the number of workers. This relationship between the quantity of inputs (workers) and the quantity of outputs (bagels) is called the **production function.** Suppose that Moe's Bagel Shop has just one input that is variable, labour, whereas the size of the bagel shop is fixed in the short run. What will happen to **total product (*TP*),** the total amount of output (bagels) generated by Moe's shop, as the level of the variable input, labour, is increased? Common sense suggests that total product will start at a low level and increase—perhaps rapidly at first, and then more slowly—as the amount of the variable input increases. It will continue to increase until the quantity of the variable input (labour) becomes so large in relation to the quantity of other inputs—like the size of the bagel shop—that further increases in output become more and more difficult or even impossible. In the second column of Exhibit 1, we see that as we increase the number of workers in Moe's Bagel Shop, Moe is able to produce more bagels. The addition of the first worker results in a total output of 10 bagels per hour. When Moe adds a

Moe's Production Function with One Variable Input, Labour

Variable Input Labour (workers)	Total Output (bagels per hour) Q	Marginal Product of Labour (bagels per hour) $\Delta Q/\Delta L$
0	0	10
1	10	14
2	24	12
3	36	10
4	46	4
5	50	1
6	51	

second worker, bagel output climbs to 24, an increase of 14 bagels per hour. Total product continues to increase even with the sixth worker hired, but you can see that it has slowed considerably, with the sixth worker increasing total product by only one bagel per hour. Beyond this point, additional workers may even result in a decline in total bagel output as workers bump into each other in the small bagel shop. This outcome is evident both in the table in Exhibit 1, as well as in the total product curve shown in Exhibit 2(a).

Diminishing Marginal Product

marginal product (MP)
the change in total product resulting from a unit change in input

The **marginal product (MP)** of any single input is defined as the change in total product resulting from a unit change in the amount of input used. This concept is shown in the final column in Exhibit 1, and is illustrated by the *MP* curve in Exhibit 2(b). As you can see in Exhibit 2(b), the *MP* curve first rises and then falls.

The Rise in Marginal Product   The initial rise in the marginal product is the result of more effective use of fixed inputs (the bagel shop) as the number of workers increases (due to specialization and division of labour). For example, certain types of capital equipment may require a minimum number of workers for efficient operation, or perhaps any operation at all. With a small number of workers (the variable factors), some machines cannot operate at all, or only at a very low level of efficiency. As additional workers are added, machines are brought into efficient operation, and thus the marginal

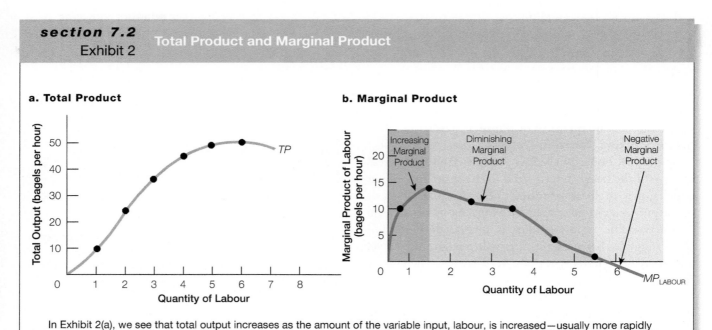

section 7.2
Exhibit 2

Total Product and Marginal Product

a. Total Product

b. Marginal Product

In Exhibit 2(a), we see that total output increases as the amount of the variable input, labour, is increased—usually more rapidly at first and then more slowly. In Exhibit 2(b), we see that the marginal product first rises (increasing marginal product) as workers are added to the fixed input (e.g., a machine), which is thus used more efficiently. Then the marginal product falls; the crowding of the fixed input with more and more workers causes marginal product to fall. Lastly, negative marginal product occurs where additional inputs cause output to fall.

product of the workers rises. Similarly, if one person tried to operate a large department store alone—doing work of all types necessary in the store—her energies would be spread so thinly in so many directions that total output (sales) might be less than if she was operating a smaller store (working with less capital). As successive workers are added, up to a certain number, each worker adds more to total product than the previous one and the marginal product rises. This is seen in the shaded area of Exhibit 2(b), labelled "Increasing Marginal Product."

The Fall in Marginal Product

The Fall in Marginal Product But why does marginal product then fall? The answer is **diminishing marginal product,** which stems from the crowding of the fixed input. Specifically, as the amount of a variable input is increased, the amount of other (fixed) inputs being held constant, a point ultimately will be reached beyond which marginal product will decline. Beyond this point, output increases, but at a decreasing rate. It is the crowding of the fixed input with more and more workers that causes the decline in the marginal product. Too many workers in a store make it more difficult for customers to shop; too many workers in a factory get in each other's way. Adding more and more of a variable input to a fixed input will eventually lead to diminishing marginal product.

The point of this discussion is that production functions conform to the same general pattern as that shown by Moe's Bagel Shop in the third column of Exhibit 1 and illustrated in Exhibit 2(b). In the third column of Exhibit 1, we see that as we increase the number of workers in Moe's Bagel Shop, Moe is able to produce more bagels. The first worker is able to produce 10 bagels per hour. When Moe adds a second worker, total bagel output climbs to 24, an increase of 14 bagels per hour. However, when Moe hires a third worker, bagel output still increases, but a third worker's marginal production (12 bagels per hour) is less than that of the second worker. In fact, the marginal product continues to drop as more and more workers are added to the bagel shop. This is diminishing marginal product at work. Note that it is not because the third worker is not as "good" as the second worker that marginal product fell. Even with identical workers, the increased "crowding" of the fixed input causes marginal output to eventually fall.

A firm never *knowingly* allows itself to reach the point where the marginal product becomes negative, the situation in which the use of additional variable input units actually reduces total product. In such a situation, there are so many units of the variable input—inputs with positive opportunity costs—that efficient use of the fixed input units is impaired. In such a situation, *reducing* the number of workers would actually *increase* total product.

diminishing marginal product
as a variable input increases, with other inputs fixed, a point will be reached where the additions to output will eventually decline

© Christine Gonzalves/Shutterstock

How many workers could be added to this jackhammer and still be productive (not to mention safe)? If more workers were added, how much output would be derived from each additional worker? There may be slightly more total output from the second worker because the second worker will be using the jackhammer while the first worker is taking a break from "the shakes." However, the fifth or sixth worker would clearly not create any additional output, as workers would just be standing around waiting for their turn. That is, the marginal product (additional output) would eventually fall because of diminishing marginal product.

SECTION CHECK

- The short run is defined as a period too brief for some inputs to be varied, whereas the long run is a period of time long enough to allow the firm to adjust all inputs. Inputs like buildings and equipment that do not change with output are called *fixed inputs*.
- Total output increases as variable inputs are increased. Marginal product initially rises, but eventually declines as variable inputs are added. Finally, negative marginal product can occur, indicating a fall in total output.

section 7.3 Costs in the Short Run

- What are fixed costs, variable costs, and total costs?
- What are average costs?
- What is marginal cost?

In the last section we learned about the relationship between a firm's inputs and its level of output. But that is only one part of the discussion; we must also consider how much it will cost the firm to use each of these inputs in production. In this section, we will examine the short-run costs of the firm—what they are and how they vary with the output levels that are produced. The short-run total costs of a business fall into two distinct categories: fixed costs and variable costs.

WHAT ARE FIXED COSTS, VARIABLE COSTS, AND TOTAL COSTS?

fixed costs
costs that do not vary with the level of output

Fixed costs are those that do not vary with the level of output. For example, the rent on buildings or equipment is usually fixed for at least some period of time; whether the firm produces lots of output or little output, the rent stays the same. Insurance premiums, property taxes, and interest payments on debt used to finance capital equipment are other examples of fixed costs—they have to be paid even if no output is produced. In the short run, fixed costs cannot be avoided. The only way a firm can avoid a fixed cost is by going out of business. The sum of the firm's fixed costs is called the **total fixed cost (*TFC*).**

total fixed cost (*TFC*)
the sum of the firm's fixed costs

variable costs
costs that vary with the level of output

Variable costs vary with the level of output. As more variable inputs like labour and raw materials are added, output increases. The variable cost, the expenditures for wages and raw materials, increases as output increases. The sum of the firm's variable costs is called **total variable cost (*TVC*).** The sum of the total fixed costs and total variable costs is called the firm's **total cost (*TC*).**

total variable cost (*TVC*)
the sum of the firm's variable costs

total cost (*TC*)
the sum of the firm's total fixed costs and total variable costs

WHAT ARE AVERAGE COSTS?

average total cost (*ATC*)
a per-unit cost of operation; total cost divided by output

Although we are often interested in the total amount of costs incurred by the firm, sometimes we find it convenient to discuss these costs on a per-unit-of-output, or an average, basis. For example, if Pizza Shack Company has $1600 in total fixed cost and $2400 in total variable cost, its total cost is $4000. If it produces 800 pizzas in the time period in question, its total cost per unit of output equals $5 ($4000 total cost divided by 800 units of output). We call this per-unit total cost the **average total cost (*ATC*)**—total costs divided by output. Likewise, we might talk about the per-unit fixed cost of output, or **average fixed cost (*AFC*)**—fixed costs divided by output. In the case of Pizza Shack, the average fixed cost, or *AFC,* would equal $2 ($1600 is the fixed cost divided by 800 units of output). Similarly, we can speak of per-unit variable cost, or **average variable cost (*AVC*)**—variable costs divided by output. In this example, the average variable cost would equal $3 ($2400 is the variable cost divided by 800 units of output).

average fixed cost (*AFC*)
a per-unit measure of fixed costs; fixed costs divided by output

average variable cost (*AVC*)
a per-unit measure of variable costs; variable costs divided by output

WHAT IS MARGINAL COST?

To this point, six different short-run cost concepts have been introduced: total cost, total fixed cost, total variable cost, average total cost, average fixed cost, and average variable cost. All of these concepts are relevant to a discussion of firm behaviour and profitability. However, the most important single cost concept has yet to be mentioned: marginal (or additional) cost. You may recall this concept from Chapter 1, where we highlighted the importance of using marginal analysis—that is, analysis that focuses on *additional* or marginal choices. Specifically, **marginal cost (*MC*)** shows the change in total costs resulting from a one-unit change in output ($\Delta TC/\Delta Q$). Put a bit differently, marginal cost is the cost of producing one more unit of output. As such, marginal costs are really just a very useful way to view variable costs—costs that vary as output varies. Marginal cost represents the added labour, raw materials, and miscellaneous expenses that are incurred in making an additional unit of output. Marginal cost is the additional, or incremental, cost associated with the "last" unit of output produced.

marginal cost (*MC*)
the change in total costs resulting from a one-unit change in output

The Relationships among the Different Costs

Exhibit 1 summarizes the definitions of the seven different short-run cost concepts introduced in this chapter. To further clarify these concepts and to illustrate the relationships among them, we will now return to our discussion of the costs faced by Pizza Shack.

Exhibit 2 presents the costs incurred by Pizza Shack at various levels of output. Note that the total fixed cost is the same at all output levels and that at very low output levels (four or fewer units in the example), total fixed cost is the dominant portion of total costs. At high output levels (eight or more units in the example), total fixed cost becomes quite small relative to total variable cost. As the firm increases its output, it spreads its total fixed cost across more units; as a result, average fixed cost declines continuously.

It is often easier to understand the cost concepts by examining graphs that show the levels of the various costs at different output levels. The graph in Exhibit 3 shows the first three cost concepts: fixed, variable, and total costs for Pizza Shack. The total fixed cost (*TFC*) curve is always a horizontal line because, by definition, fixed costs are the same at all output levels—even at zero level of output. In Exhibit 3, notice that $TVC = 0$ when $Q = 0$; if there is no output being produced, there are no variable costs.

---

section 7.3
Exhibit 1   **A Summary of the Short-Run Cost Concepts**

Concept	Abbreviation	Definition
Total fixed cost	*TFC*	Costs that are the same at all output levels (e.g., insurance, rent).
Total variable cost	*TVC*	Costs that vary with the level of output (e.g., hourly labour, raw materials).
Total cost	*TC*	The sum of the firm's total fixed costs and total variable costs at a level of output ($TC = TFC + TVC$).
Marginal cost	*MC*	The added cost of producing one more unit of output; change in *TC* associated with one more unit of output ($\Delta TC/\Delta Q$).
Average total cost	*ATC*	*TC* per unit of output; *TC* divided by output (*TC/Q*).
Average fixed cost	*AFC*	*TFC* per unit of output; *TFC* divided by output (*TFC/Q*).
Average variable cost	*AVC*	*TVC* per unit of output; *TVC* divided by output (*TVC/Q*).

section 7.3
    Exhibit 2

section 7.3 Exhibit 2 — Cost Calculations for Pizza Shack Company

Hourly Output (Q)	Total Fixed Cost (TFC)	Total Variable Cost (TVC)	Total Cost (TC = TVC + TFC)	Marginal Cost (MC = ΔTC/ΔQ)	Average Fixed Cost (AFC = TFC/Q)	Average Variable Cost (AVC = TVC/Q)	Average Total Cost (ATC = TC/Q or AFC + AVC)
0	$40	$ 0	$ 40		—	—	—
1	40	10	50	$10	$40.00	$10.00	$50.00
2	40	18	58	8	20.00	9.00	29.00
3	40	25	65	7	13.33	8.33	21.67
4	40	33	73	8	10.00	8.25	18.25
5	40	43	83	10	8.00	8.60	16.60
6	40	56	96	13	6.67	9.33	16.00
7	40	73	113	17	5.71	10.43	16.10
8	40	94	134	21	5.00	11.75	16.75
9	40	120	160	26	4.44	13.33	17.78
10	40	152	192	32	4.00	15.20	19.20

section 7.3 Exhibit 3 — Total, Variable, and Fixed Costs for Pizza Shack

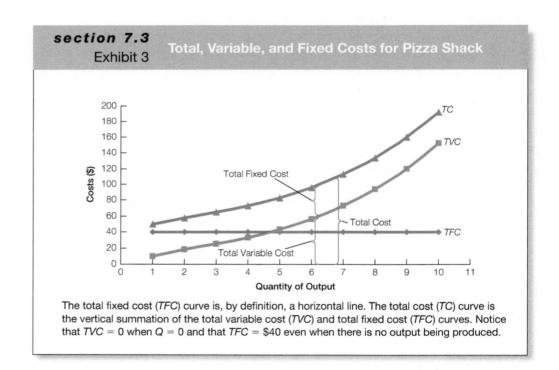

The total fixed cost (*TFC*) curve is, by definition, a horizontal line. The total cost (*TC*) curve is the vertical summation of the total variable cost (*TVC*) and total fixed cost (*TFC*) curves. Notice that *TVC* = 0 when *Q* = 0 and that *TFC* = $40 even when there is no output being produced.

The total cost (*TC*) curve is the summation of the total variable cost (*TVC*) and total fixed cost (*TFC*) curves. Because the total fixed cost curve is horizontal, the total cost curve lies above the total variable cost curve by a fixed (vertical) amount.

Exhibit 4 shows the average fixed cost curve, the average variable cost curve, the average total cost curve, and the associated marginal cost curve for Pizza Shack. In this

section 7.3
Exhibit 4
Average and Marginal Costs for Pizza Shack

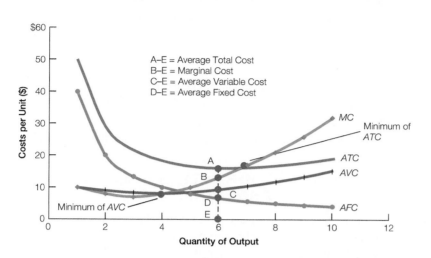

A–E = Average Total Cost
B–E = Marginal Cost
C–E = Average Variable Cost
D–E = Average Fixed Cost

The marginal cost (*MC*) curve always intersects the average total cost (*ATC*) and average variable cost (*AVC*) curves at those curves' minimum points. Average fixed cost (*AFC*) curves always decline and approach but never reach zero. The *ATC* curve is the vertical summation of the *AFC* and *AVC* curves; it reaches its minimum (lowest unit cost) point at a higher output than the minimum point of the *AVC* curve.

exhibit, note how the average fixed cost (*AFC*) curve constantly declines, approaching but never reaching zero. Remember, the *AFC* is simply *TFC/Q*, so as output expands, *AFC* declines because the total fixed cost is being spread over successively larger volumes of output. Also observe how the marginal cost (*MC*) curve crosses the average variable cost (*AVC*) and average total cost (*ATC*) curves at their lowest points. At higher output levels, high marginal costs pull up the average variable cost and average total cost curves, whereas at low output levels, low marginal costs pull the curves down. In the next section, we will explain why the marginal cost curve intersects the average variable cost curve and the average total cost curve at their minimum points.

SECTION CHECK

- Total fixed costs do not change with the level of output, total variable costs change as the level of output changes, and total costs are the sum of total variable costs and total fixed costs.
- Average total cost (*ATC*) is total cost divided by output; average fixed cost (*AFC*) is fixed cost divided by output; and average variable cost (*AVC*) is variable cost divided by output.
- Marginal cost (*MC*) is the added cost of producing one more unit of output; it is the change in total cost associated with one more unit of output. It is this cost that is relevant to decisions to produce more or less.

The Shape of the Short-Run Cost Curves

■ What is the relationship between marginal costs and marginal product?
■ What is the relationship between marginal and average amounts?
■ Why is the average total cost curve U-shaped?
■ What is the relationship between marginal cost and average variable and average total cost?

WHAT IS THE RELATIONSHIP BETWEEN MARGINAL COSTS AND MARGINAL PRODUCT?

The behaviour of marginal costs bears a definite relationship to marginal product (*MP*). Say, for example, that the variable input is labour. Initially, as the firm adds more workers, the marginal product of labour tends to rise. When the marginal product of labour is rising, marginal costs are falling, because each additional worker adds more to the total product than the previous worker. Thus, the increase in total cost resulting from the production of another unit of output—marginal cost—falls. However, when marginal product of labour is declining, marginal costs are rising, because additional workers are adding less to total output.

In sum, if an additional worker's marginal product is lower (higher) than that of previous workers, marginal costs increase (decrease), as seen in Exhibit 1. In area (a) of the two graphs in Exhibit 1, we see that as marginal product rises, marginal costs fall; in area (b), we see that as marginal product falls, marginal costs rise. For example, if we are producing only a few bagels in our bagel shop, we have some idle resources like equipment: toasters, cash registers, and so on. At this point, the marginal product of an extra worker is large and the marginal cost of producing one more bagel is small. However, when the bagel shop is crowded, with many bagels being produced by many workers and the equipment being used to capacity, the marginal product of hiring another worker is low. Why? Because the new worker has to work in crowded conditions where she may be bumping into other workers as she waits to use a toaster or cash register. In short, when the number of bagels produced is high, the marginal product of another worker is low and the marginal cost of an additional bagel is large.

section 7.4
Exhibit 1
Marginal Product and Marginal Costs

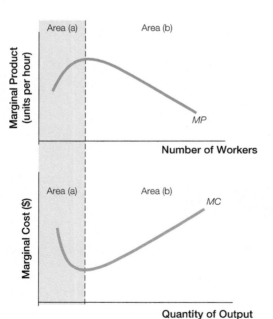

An inverse relationship exists between marginal product (*MP*) and marginal cost (*MC*). When marginal product is rising, marginal cost must fall, and when marginal product falls, marginal cost must rise.

WHAT IS THE RELATIONSHIP BETWEEN MARGINAL AND AVERAGE AMOUNTS?

The relationship between the marginal and the average is simply a matter of arithmetic; when a number (the marginal cost) being added into a series is smaller than the previous average of the series, the new average will be lower than the previous one. Likewise, when the marginal number is larger than the average, the average will rise. For example, if you have taken two economics exams and received 90 percent on your first exam and 80 percent on your second exam, you have an 85 percent average. If after some serious studying, you get 100 percent on the third exam (the marginal exam), what happens to your average? It rises to 90 percent. Because the marginal is greater than the average, it "pulls" the average up. However, if the score on your third (marginal) exam is lower, 70 percent, your average will fall to 80 percent because the marginal is below the average.

WHY IS THE AVERAGE TOTAL COST CURVE U-SHAPED?

The average total cost curve is usually U-shaped, as seen in Exhibit 2. Why is this? At very small levels of output and very large levels of output, average total cost is very high. The reason for the high average total cost when the firm is producing a very small amount of output is the high average fixed cost—when the output rate of the plant is small relative to its capacity, the plant is being underutilized. But as the firm expands output beyond this point, the average total cost falls. Why? Remember that $ATC = AFC + AVC$, and average fixed cost always falls when output expands because the fixed costs are being spread over more units of output. Thus, it is the declining AFC that is primarily responsible for the falling ATC.

The average total cost rises at high levels of output because of diminishing marginal product. For example, as more and more workers are put to work using a fixed quantity of machines, the result may be crowded working conditions and/or increasing maintenance costs as equipment is used more intensively, or older, less efficient machinery is called upon to handle the greater output. In fact, diminishing marginal product sets in at the very bottom of the marginal cost curve, as seen in Exhibit 2. That is, diminishing marginal product causes the marginal cost to increase, eventually causing the average variable cost and the average total cost curves to rise. At very large levels of output, where the plant approaches full capacity, the fixed plant is overutilized, and this leads to high marginal cost that causes a high average total cost.

WHAT IS THE RELATIONSHIP BETWEEN MARGINAL COST AND AVERAGE VARIABLE AND AVERAGE TOTAL COST?

Certain relationships exist between marginal cost and average variable and average total cost. For example, when average variable cost is falling, marginal cost must be less than average variable cost; and when average variable cost is rising, marginal cost is greater than average variable cost. Marginal cost is equal to average variable cost at the lowest point of the average variable cost curve, as seen in Exhibit 3.

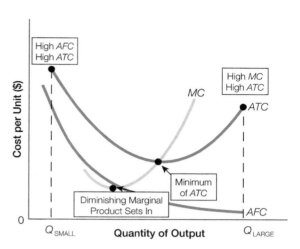

section 7.4 | U-Shaped Average Total Cost Curve
Exhibit 2

At low levels of output, ATC is high because AFC is high—the fixed plant is underutilized. At high levels of output (close to capacity), the fixed plant will be overutilized, leading to high MC and, consequently, high ATC. It is diminishing marginal product that causes the MC, and eventually the AVC and ATC, to rise.

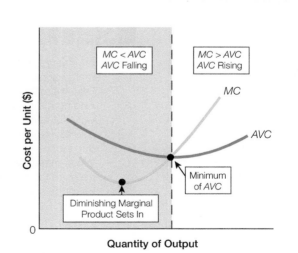

section 7.4 | Marginal Cost and Average Variable Cost
Exhibit 3

The marginal cost curve crosses the average variable cost curve at its minimum point.

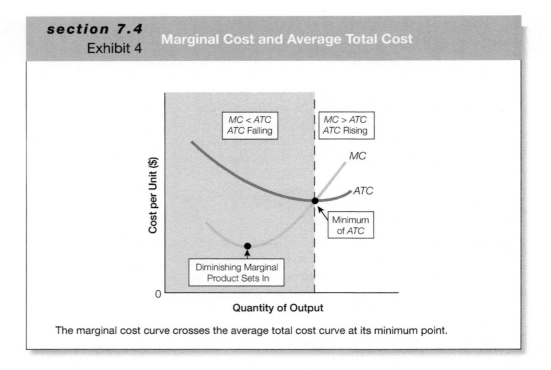

section 7.4
Exhibit 4   **Marginal Cost and Average Total Cost**

The marginal cost curve crosses the average total cost curve at its minimum point.

In the left-hand (shaded) portion of Exhibit 3, marginal cost is less than average variable cost and the average is falling. On the right-hand side, marginal cost is greater than average variable cost and the average is rising. The same relationship holds for the marginal cost curve and the average total cost curve. In the left-hand (shaded) portion of Exhibit 4, marginal cost is less than average total cost and the average is falling. On the right-hand side, marginal cost is greater than average total cost and the average is rising.

SECTION CHECK

- An inverse relationship exists between marginal product and marginal cost—as marginal product increases, marginal cost must fall, and when marginal product falls, marginal cost must rise.
- Adding a marginal amount affects the value of the average amount—the average will rise (fall) when the marginal amount is larger (smaller) than the initial average.
- Average total cost declines with expanding output as average fixed costs decline, but then increases as output expands due to increasing marginal cost.
- When marginal cost is less than (greater than) an average cost, the average cost must be falling (rising); when marginal cost is greater than (less than) an average cost, the average cost must be rising (falling).

Cost Curves: Short Run and Long Run

- How is the long-run average total cost curve created?
- What are economies of scale?
- Why would cost curves shift?

Over long enough periods of time, firms can vary all of their productive inputs. For example, time provides an opportunity to substitute lower-cost capital (like larger plants or newer, more sophisticated equipment) for more expensive labour inputs. However, in the short run, a company cannot vary its plant size and equipment. These inputs are fixed in the short run, so the firm can expand output only by employing more variable inputs (e.g., workers and raw materials) in order to get extra output from the existing factory. For example, if a company has to pay lots of workers overtime wages to get expanded output in the short run, over longer periods, new highly automated machinery may be introduced that conserves on expensive labour. That is, in the long run (perhaps several years), the company can expand the size of its factories, build new ones, or shut down unproductive ones. Of course, the time it takes for a firm to get to the long run varies from firm to firm. For example, it may take only a couple of months to build a new coffee shop, whereas it may take a few years to build a new automobile plant.

HOW IS THE LONG-RUN AVERAGE TOTAL COST CURVE CREATED?

In Exhibit 1, the firm has three possible plant sizes—a small plant, $SRATC_1$, a medium-sized plant, $SRATC_2$, and a large plant, $SRATC_3$. As we move along the $LRATC$ (the blue line) in Exhibit 1, the factory size changes with the quantity of output. Certain relationships among the successive curves should be emphasized. For very small output levels, q_1, costs are lowest with plant size $SRATC_1$, point A. Costs with plant size $SRATC_2$ (the medium plant size) are relatively high for these low levels of output because the plant's fixed costs are far too high for low levels of output; machinery, buildings, and so on would be poorly utilized. In Exhibit 1, we can see that if q_1 output is produced with plant size $SRATC_2$, the plant would be operating below capacity, point B, and the cost would be higher at \$10 per unit rather than at \$8 per unit, at point A. However, if the firm planned to produce output level q_2, costs with plant size $SRATC_2$ are lower than those with $SRATC_1$. If output levels in this range were produced with the smaller plant, $SRATC_1$, the plant would be operating beyond designed capacity, point D, and the cost would be higher at \$8 per unit rather than at \$5 per unit, at point C. That is, plant $SRATC_2$, designed for a larger volume of output than the small plant, would minimize costs for producing quantity q_2.

If a straight line was extended upward from the horizontal output axis on a graph containing the various $SRATC$ curves for different-sized plants, the point at which it first struck an $SRATC$ curve would indicate the relevant value of $LRATC$ for that output level. Thus, in Exhibit 1, for low levels of output, q_1, the lowest average cost point is on curve $SRATC_1$; at output, q_2, it is on $SRATC_2$, and so on. The $LRATC$ curve is

By having several screens in one complex, a cinema company can cut down on advertising and employee costs as well as rent. Because of economies of scale, it may be less expensive to have eight screens in one building with one concession area than eight separate theatres, each with one screen and a concession area.

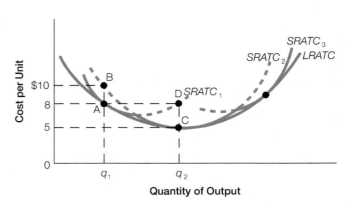

In the short run, some inputs are fixed, like the size of the physical plant or certain machinery. In the long run, firms can increase their capital inputs as well as their inputs that are variable in the short run, in some cases lowering average costs per unit. The curve thus has a shallower U-shape than the short-run average total cost curves. In the long run, all inputs are variable. The *LRATC* is the solid blue line that traces out the three different possible plant sizes, $SRATC_1$, $SRATC_2$, and $SRATC_3$. The *LRATC* shows the lowest average total cost for producing each output in the long run.

economies of scale
occur in an output range where LRATC falls as output increases

constant returns to scale
occur in an output range where LRATC does not change as output varies

diseconomies of scale
occur in an output range where LRATC rises as output expands

identical with *SRATC* at the solid scalloped portion of the three short-run cost curves. When there are many possible plant sizes, the successive *SRATC* curves will be close to one another, and the *LRATC* curve will be smooth and U-shaped like the dark solid blue line in Exhibit 1.

The *LRATC* curve is often called a *planning curve,* since it represents the cost data relevant to the firm when it is planning policy relating to scale of operations, output, and price over a long period of time. At a particular time, a firm already in operation has a certain plant and must base its current price and output decisions on the costs with the existing plant. However, when the firm considers the possibility of adjusting its scale of operations, long-run cost estimates are necessary.

WHAT ARE ECONOMIES OF SCALE?

By examining the long-run average total cost in Exhibit 2, we can see three possible production patterns. When *LRATC* falls as output expands, we say that there are **economies of scale** present. And when the *LRATC* does not vary with output, the firm is facing **constant returns to scale.** And when *LRATC* rises as output expands, we say that the firm is facing **diseconomies of scale.**

section 7.5
Exhibit 2   **A Typical Long-Run *ATC***

All firms are different but most firms will probably have a long-run *ATC* that declines at low levels of output and then remains constant and eventually will rise at the higher levels of output. The minimum efficient scale is the lowest level of output at which average total costs are minimized.

The typical firm in an industry may well experience economies of scale at low levels of output, constant returns to scale at higher levels of output, and diseconomies of scale at still higher levels of output, as seen in Exhibit 2. At the **minimum efficient scale,** a plant has exhausted its economies of scale and constant returns to scale begin. This is shown in Exhibit 2. In this constant returns to scale range (the flat portion of the *LRATC*), firms of differing size can compete on a roughly equal basis as far as costs are concerned—that is, they have no cost advantage over firms that are operating at the minimum efficient scale.

minimum efficient scale
the output level where economies of scale are exhausted and constant returns to scale begin

The Causes of Economies and Diseconomies of Scale

As we have just seen, economies of scale exist when there is a reduction in the firm's long-run average costs as output expands. This may occur because a firm can use mass production techniques like assembly-line production or capture gains from labour specialization that might not be possible if the firm was producing at lower levels of output. For example, workers might experience greater proficiency gains if they concentrated on a few specific tasks rather than on many different tasks; that is, people who try to do everything may end up doing nothing very well. As well, larger firms may also enjoy cost advantages relative to smaller competitors when borrowing money or when purchasing inputs.

Recall that diseconomies of scale exist when there is an increase in the firm's long-run average costs as output expands. This may occur as the firm finds it increasingly difficult to handle the complexities of large-scale management. For example, information and coordination problems tend to increase when a firm becomes very large. As well, workers may feel alienated in a large plant and hence productivity and creativity may be stifled.

WHY WOULD COST CURVES SHIFT?

Any cost curve is based on the assumption that input prices, taxes, regulation, and technology are constant. When these factors change, the cost curves of the firm will shift. For example, in Exhibit 3(a) we see how a per-unit tax increases the marginal cost of each unit of output, shifting the *MC* curve and the *ATC* up by the tax amount. The tax does not affect the firm's fixed cost because it is a tax on units produced. If a licence-to-operate fee increased, it would act like a fixed cost and affect only the average total cost curve—shifting *ATC* up by the amount of the fee increase. Improved technology will reduce marginal costs, shifting *MC* downward along with *ATC*, as in Exhibit 3(b).

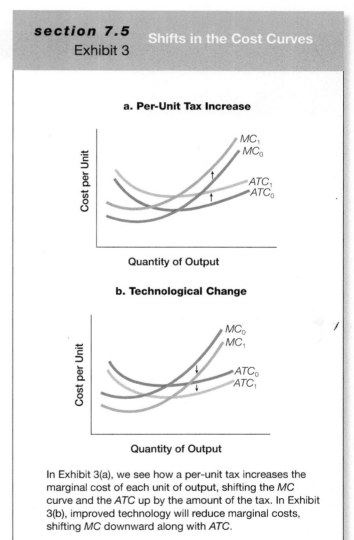

section 7.5
Exhibit 3   Shifts in the Cost Curves

a. Per-Unit Tax Increase

b. Technological Change

In Exhibit 3(a), we see how a per-unit tax increases the marginal cost of each unit of output, shifting the *MC* curve and the *ATC* up by the amount of the tax. In Exhibit 3(b), improved technology will reduce marginal costs, shifting *MC* downward along with *ATC*.

SECTION CHECK

■ In the long run, firms can vary inputs that are fixed in the short run, such as plant size and equipment, and in some cases, lowering average costs per unit. The long-run average total cost curve shows the lowest average total cost for producing each output in the long run.

■ At low output levels, when all inputs can be varied, some firms will experience economies of scale, where their per-unit costs are decreasing as output increases. In intermediate output ranges, firms may exhibit roughly constant returns to scale; in this range, their per-unit costs remain stable as output increases. Firms that expand all inputs beyond a certain point will encounter diseconomies of scale, incurring rising per-unit costs as output grows in the long run.

■ Input prices, taxes, technology, and regulation can shift the cost curves.

For Your Review

Section 7.1

1. The year 2015 marks the tenth anniversary of Ontario's Greenbelt. As the world's largest greenbelt at some 800 000 hectares of working countryside, it spans across the Greater Golden Horseshoe and extends to the tip of the Bruce Peninsula. As the amount of land around Toronto and its adjacent suburbs continues to fall well short of that needed to satisfy both the needs of local agricultural interests and of city dwellers looking for a more affordable place to live, the policy of keeping this productive farmland and environmentally sensitive land officially off-limits to developers has become a growing issue. What happens to the cost of farming and environmental protection as developers continue to offer more and more money for the right to develop this key land resource?

2. As a farmer, you work for yourself using your own tractor, equipment, and farm structures, and you cultivate your own land. Why might it be difficult to calculate your profits from farming?

3. The salmon fishery on Vancouver Island has historically been one of the world's richest. Over the past few years, poor returns of salmon to the island and competition from farm-raised salmon have reduced the economic returns to the anglers. One response to lower revenues has been for anglers to use family members instead of hiring crew "in order to reduce their costs." Evaluate this business strategy. Will employing relatives really keep profits from falling? Under what conditions is this a good strategy?

4. Emily, an energetic ten-year-old, set up a lemonade stand in front of her house. One Saturday, she sold 50 cups of lemonade at 50 cents each to her friends, who were hot and thirsty from playing. These sales generated $25 in total revenues for Emily. Emily was pleased because she knew that her total costs—lemonade mix, cups, and so on—were only $5. As she was closing up shop for the day, her neighbour, an accountant, stopped by to say hello. Emily told him about her successful day. He said, "What a great job! You made a $20 profit!" Excited, Emily rushed into the house to tell her mother, an economist, the great news. Will Emily's mother agree with the accountant's calculation of Emily's profits? If not, why?

Section 7.2

5. Willie's Water Park Short-Run Production Function

Labour (workers)	Total Product (visits per hour)	Marginal Product
0		—
1		10
2		12
3		9
4		8
5		4
6		−2

    a. Fill in the Total Product column.

    b. Willie's Water Park experiences diminishing marginal product beginning with which worker?

    c. Willie's Water Park experiences diminishing total product beginning with which worker?

6. Harry's Hat Company makes hats "for discerning gentlemen."

With Three Machines			With Four Machines		
Labour	Total Product (hats)	Marginal Product (hats)	Labour	Total Product (hats)	Marginal Product (hats)
1 day	8		1 day	9	
2 days	18		2 days	20	
3 days	30		3 days	35	
4 days	45		4 days	55	
5 days	57		5 days	76	
6 days	67		6 days	88	
7 days	72		7 days	95	

    a. Fill in the Marginal Product columns of these tables.

    b. At what point does diminishing marginal product set in with three machines? With four?

    c. Why is the point of diminishing marginal product different in each case?

7. Fill in the rest of the production function for Candy's Candies from the information provided.

Labour (workers)	Total Product (kilograms)	Marginal Product (kilograms)
0		
1	20	
2	44	
3	62	
4		12
5		6
6	78	

a. Candy's Candies begins to experience diminishing marginal product with which worker?

b. Does Candy's Candies ever experience negative marginal product? If so, with the addition of which worker?

8. Draw a typically shaped total product curve and the marginal product curve derived from it, and indicate the ranges of increasing, diminishing, and negative marginal product.

9. Suppose your firm's total product curve includes the following data: One worker can produce 8 units of output; two workers, 20 units; three workers, 34 units; four workers, 50 units; five workers, 60 units; six workers, 70 units; seven workers, 76 units; eight workers, 78 units; and nine workers, 77 units.

a. What is the marginal product of the seventh worker?

b. When does the law of diminishing product set in?

c. Under these conditions, would you ever choose to employ nine workers?

10. Why does the law of diminishing marginal product imply the law of increasing costs?

Section 7.3

Blueprint Problem

Complete the following cost of production table for Carl's Calculators.

Output	TVC	TFC	TC	AVC	AFC	ATC	MC
0			$40.00	—	—	—	—
1			$50.00				
2			$56.00				
3			$60.00				
4			$69.00				
5			$84.00				
6			$106.00				
7			$144.00				

Blueprint Solution

1. The initial value for *TVC* is zero because output is zero. Since variable costs change as output changes, if output is reduced to zero, no variable costs of production are incurred.[1]

2. The initial value for *TFC* is equal to *TC*, because with no variable costs, all of this cost of production is interpreted to be fixed cost.[2]

3. Fixed costs do not change as output changes; therefore, fixed costs remain constant at $40.[3]

4. Having determined *TFC*, *TVC* can be computed as *TVC* = *TC* − *TFC*.[4]

Output	TVC	TFC	TC	AVC	AFC	ATC	MC
0	$0.00[1]	$40.00[2]	$40.00	–	–	–	–
1	$10.00[4]	$40.00[3]	$50.00	$10.00	$40.00	$50.00	$10.00
2	$16.00	$40.00	$56.00	$8.00	$20.00	$28.00	$6.00
3	$20.00	$40.00	$60.00	$6.67	$13.33	$20.00	$4.00
4	$29.00	$40.00	$69.00	$7.25	$10.00	$17.25	$9.00
5	$44.00	$40.00	$84.00	$8.80	$8.00	$16.80	$15.00
6	$66.00	$40.00	$106.00	$11.00	$6.67	$17.67	$22.00
7	$104.00	$40.00	$144.00	$14.86	$5.71	$20.57	$38.00

$$MC = \frac{\Delta TC}{\Delta q}$$

For example, as output increases from 0 to 1 (a change of 1), *TC* increases from $40 to $50 (a change of $10).

$$MC = \frac{\$10}{1} = \$10$$

AVC and *AFC* values are determined by dividing the corresponding total cost value by quantity produced.

Note: The initial values are indeterminate because you cannot divide by zero.

ATC values can be determined in two ways:
1. *TC/q*
2. *AVC* + *AFC*

11. Complete the following table describing the short-run daily costs of the Attractive Magnet Co. for 2014.

Output	Total Fixed Costs	Total Variable Costs	Total Costs	Average Fixed Costs	Average Variable Costs	Average Total Costs	Marginal Costs
1	$100	$30	$130	$100	$30	$130	$30
2					25		
3					20		
4					16		
5					18		
6					21		
7					24		
8		218	318				

12. A one-day ticket to visit the Screaming Coasters theme park costs $36, but you can also get a two-consecutive-day ticket for $40. What is the average cost per day for the two-day ticket? What is the marginal cost of the second consecutive day?

13. As a movie exhibitor, you can choose between paying a flat fee of $5000 to show a movie for a week and paying a fee of $2 per customer. Will your choice affect your fixed and variable costs? How?

14. What is likely to happen to your marginal costs when adding output requires working beyond an eight-hour day, if workers must be paid time-and-a-half wages beyond an eight-hour day?

15. Suppose an oil producer's average total cost of producing a barrel of oil has been $20 a barrel and the oil producer can sell that oil to a distributor for $23 a barrel. On average, this seems like a profitable business. Should the oil producer expand production given this profitability?

16. Fill in the rest of the cost function for Bob's Bowling Balls.

Output	Total Fixed Costs	Total Variable Costs	Total Costs	Average Fixed Costs	Average Variable Costs	Average Total Costs	Marginal Costs
1	$200	$60	$	$	$	$	$
2		100					
3		120					
4		128					
5		180					
6		252					
7		366					
8		536					

17. If your college or university pays lecture note-takers $20 per hour to take notes in your economics class and then sells subscriptions for $15 per student, is the cost of the lecture note-taker a fixed or variable cost of selling an additional subscription?

18. The Lighthouse Safety Vest Co. makes flotation vests for recreational boaters. The company currently employs 50 people and produces 12 000 vests per month. Lighthouse managers know that when they hire one more person, monthly vest production will increase by 200 vests. They pay workers $1600 per month.

   a. What is the marginal product of the 51st worker?

   b. What is the marginal cost to produce one more vest? (*Hint:* Think of the marginal cost as the additional worker's pay divided by the changes in output.)

   c. If labour is the only variable factor of production, will the average variable cost of production rise or fall as a result of hiring a 51st worker? Why?

   d. What happens to the marginal cost of a vest when the 52nd worker is added and the marginal product drops to 160 vests per month?

Section 7.4

19. Use the graph below to answer the following questions.

    a. Curve A represents which cost curve?

    b. Curve B represents which cost curve?

    c. Curve C represents which cost curve?

    d. Curve D represents which cost curve?

    e. Why must curve D pass through the minimum points of both curve B and curve C?

    f. What significance does the point have where curve A intersects curve D?

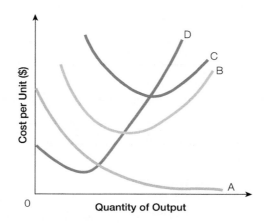

20. Illustrate how the shape of the marginal product curve relates to the shape of the marginal cost curve.

21. Use the following graph to answer the questions below.

    a. At what level is *AVC* at its minimum? Why is it at its minimum at this point?

    b. At what level is *ATC* at its minimum? Why is it at its minimum at this point?

    c. At what level is *MC* at its minimum? Why is it at its minimum at this point?

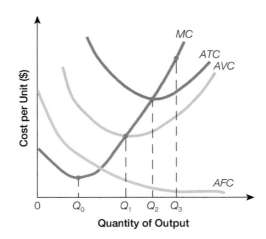

Section 7.5

22. You have the following information about long-run total cost for the following firms:

Quantity	Arnold's Apples LRTC	Belle's Bananas LRTC	Cam's Cantaloupes LRTC
1	120	33	42
2	140	72	68
3	160	117	98
4	180	168	132
5	200	225	170
6	220	288	212
7	240	357	258

    a. Do any of these firms experience constant returns to scale? How do you know?

    b. Do any of these firms experience diseconomies of scale? How do you know?

    c. Do any of these firms experience economies of scale? How do you know?

23. Refer to the cost curve below.

    a. What is the lowest level of output at which the efficient scale of production is reached in the long run?

    b. In the short run described by *SRATC*, what is the efficient output level?

    c. When the firm is producing at the level of output described by D, will it be experiencing constant returns to scale, economies of scale, or diseconomies of scale?

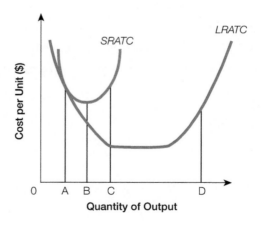

24. Suppose the following table details the cost structure for an Internet modem manufacturer.

Output	TVC_0	TVC_1	AVC_0	AVC_1	MC_0	MC_1
0	0		—		—	
1	10		10		5	
2	18		9		10	
3	21		7		6	
4	26		6.55		5	
5	35		7		9	
6	51		8.5		15	
7	77		11		21	

If the cost of the inputs needed to produce Internet modems increases by 50 percent, calculate TVC_1, AVC_1, and MC_1. Graph the results for AVC_1 and MC_1 against the original AVC and MC curves (AVC_0 and MC_0).

25. Determine the effect (increase, decrease, or unchanged) of the following changes of MC, AVC, and ATC.

Change	AVC	MC	ATC
a. The government imposes a tax that is applied to every unit produced.			
b. The price of rent increases.			
c. New technology that improves productivity is introduced.			
d. The cost of labour increases.			
e. The cost of materials used in manufacturing decreases.			
f. Property taxes increase.			

8

Perfect Competition

section

8.1 The Four Major Market Structures

- What are the four major market structures?
- What are the characteristics of a perfectly competitive market?
- Why is it useful to study the perfectly competitive market structure?

WHAT ARE THE FOUR MAJOR MARKET STRUCTURES?

Economists have identified four major market structures in which firms operate: perfect competition, monopoly, monopolistic competition, and oligopoly. Each structure or environment has certain key characteristics that distinguish it from the other structures. In practice it is sometimes difficult to decide precisely which structure a given firm or industry most appropriately fits, since the dividing line between the structures is not entirely crystal clear.

Perfect Competition

A competitive market is a market situation in which there is a large number of buyers and sellers—perhaps thousands or very conceivably millions. In addition, no single firm produces more than an extremely small proportion of total output. This means that no single firm can influence the market price or quantity. Firms are price takers; they must accept the price for the product as determined by the forces of demand and supply. Individually, they are too small and powerless to alter prices.

Firms in perfect competition sell a homogeneous or standardized product. In the wheat market, which approximates the conditions of perfect competition, it is not possible to determine any significant and consistent qualitative differences in the wheat produced by different farmers. New firms can easily enter the market.

Monopoly

On the other end of the continuum of market environments is pure monopoly. In this market structure, there is one firm (a single seller) that produces a good or service that has no close substitutes, and there are significant barriers to potential entrants into the market. Examples of monopoly include government-owned or government-regulated public utilities (electric, water, and natural gas suppliers) and Facebook as a social networking tool.

Monopolistic Competition

Monopolistic competition falls between perfect competition and monopoly. Monopolistic competition is a market structure where firms have both an element of competition and an element of monopoly power. Because each firm's product is differentiated at least slightly from that of other competitors, it has some monopoly power. For example, in a given city of 100 000 there may be 100 restaurants, each slightly different in the type of food that it sells, the services that it provides, and the hours that it stays open. However, because there are so many competing restaurants vying for your business it also has an element of competitive markets. The same is true for service stations and retail businesses such as furniture stores.

Oligopoly

Like monopolistic competition, oligopoly also falls between perfect competition and monopoly. Oligopoly exists when a *few* firms produce similar or identical goods, as opposed to one firm (monopoly) or many (competitive market). Unlike pure monopoly, oligopoly allows for some competition between firms; unlike competition, firms in oligopolistic environments have a significant share of the total market for the good being produced.

The oligopolist is very conscious of the actions of competing firms. In this respect, the oligopoly structure differs from others. In perfect competition, Farmer Jones does not worry about what Farmer Smith does, since neither of them is big enough to have any influence on overall market conditions. In monopoly, there is no other firm to worry about. In true monopolistic competition, there are many relatively small firms, so again a firm usually does not worry much about the impact on it of the behaviour of a competing firm. In oligopoly, though, a firm's behaviour is closely related to that of its competitors. General Motors' pricing decisions influence the pricing decisions of Ford, Chrysler, and other manufacturers, including ones located in other countries. The oligopolist does have some control over price and thus is a price setter. Note that the oligopoly may involve a standardized product (like steel, aluminum, or crude oil) or a differentiated one (automobiles, refrigerators, personal computers).

Exhibit 1 provides an overview of the various market structures; for added insight, the structures have been placed in order on a continuum (or ruler). While no significance should be attributed to the left versus the right side of the continuum, the positioning of pure monopoly at one end of the continuum and perfect competition at the other is significant. By locating perfect competition and pure monopoly at opposite ends of the continuum, it can be understood that the opposite characteristics that define pure monopoly define perfect competition. For example, looking at the *Number of Firms*

Can the owner of this orchard charge a noticeably higher price for the same quality of apples? What if she charges a lower price for the same-quality apples? How many apples can she sell at the market price?

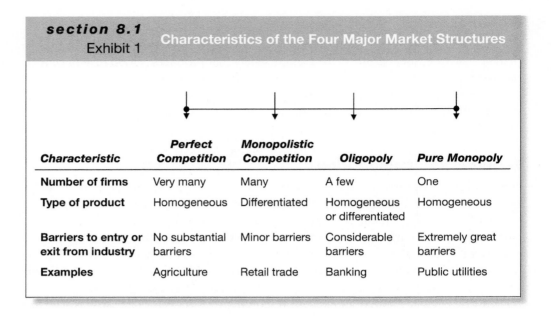

section 8.1
Exhibit 1

Characteristics of the Four Major Market Structures

Characteristic	Perfect Competition	Monopolistic Competition	Oligopoly	Pure Monopoly
Number of firms	Very many	Many	A few	One
Type of product	Homogeneous	Differentiated	Homogeneous or differentiated	Homogeneous
Barriers to entry or exit from industry	No substantial barriers	Minor barriers	Considerable barriers	Extremely great barriers
Examples	Agriculture	Retail trade	Banking	Public utilities

characteristic, the perfectly competitive market consists of very many producers—the largest number of producers of any market structure, while the purely monopolized market consists of one producer—the fewest number of producers of any market structure. This relationship of opposites remains intact for all but one of the characteristics.

Another key feature of Exhibit 1 is the positioning of the oligopoly and monopolistic competition market structures. The oligopoly market structure is located closer to pure monopoly than it is to perfect competition. This tells us that, while the oligopoly market structure is a mixture of monopolistic and competitive principles, it is predominantly monopolistic. Alternatively, the positioning of the monopolistic competition market structure closer to the perfect competition end of the continuum indicates that this structure is predominantly competitive. For example, looking at the *Barriers to entry or exit from industry* characteristic, the monopolistic competition structure exhibits only minor barriers (an increase from the perfectly competitive structure that experiences no substantial barriers to entry or exit), while the oligopolistic market structure experiences considerable barriers (a further increase in this characteristic toward the pure monopoly experience of extremely great barriers to entry or exit).

WHAT ARE THE CHARACTERISTICS OF A PERFECTLY COMPETITIVE MARKET?

This chapter examines perfect competition, a market structure characterized by (1) many buyers and sellers, (2) an identical (homogeneous) product, and (3) easy market entry and exit. Let's examine these characteristics in greater detail.

Many Buyers and Sellers

In **perfect competition**, there are many buyers and sellers, all selling a homogeneous product; market entry and exit is easy, and no one firm can affect the market price. Because each firm is so small in relation to the industry, its production decisions have no impact on the market—each regards price as something over which it has little control. A perfectly competitive firm is called a **price taker** because it takes the price that it is given by the intersection of the market demand and market supply curves.

perfect competition

a market with many buyers and sellers, all selling a homogeneous product; market entry and exit is easy, and no firm can affect the market price

price taker

a perfectly competitive firm takes the price that it is given by the intersection of the market demand and market supply curves

That is, it must take the price given by the market because its influence on price is insignificant. If the price of apples in the apple market is $2 a kilogram, then individual apple farmers will receive $2 per kilogram for their apples. Similarly, no single buyer of apples can influence the price of apples because each buyer purchases only a small amount of the apples traded. We will see how this works in more detail in Section 8.2.

Identical (Homogeneous) Products

Consumers believe that all firms in perfectly competitive markets *sell identical (or homogeneous) products*. For example, in the wheat market, it is not possible to determine any significant and consistent qualitative differences in the wheat produced by different farmers. Another way of describing what firms in a perfectly competitive market sell is to realize their output as perfect substitutes for each other. That is, the wheat produced by Farmer Jones looks, feels, smells, and tastes like that produced by Farmer Smith. In short, a tonne of wheat is a tonne of wheat.

Easy Entry and Exit

Product markets characterized by perfect competition have no significant *barriers to entry or exit*. This means that it is fairly easy for entrepreneurs to become suppliers of the product or, if they are already producers, to stop supplying the product. "Fairly easy" does not mean that any person on the street can instantly enter the business, but rather that the financial, legal, educational, and other barriers to entering the business are modest, so that large numbers of people can overcome the barriers and enter the business in any given time period if they so desire. If buyers can easily switch from one seller to another and sellers can easily enter or exit the industry, then we have met the perfectly competitive condition of easy entry and exit. Because of this easy market entry, perfectly competitive markets generally consist of a large number of small suppliers.

WHY IS IT USEFUL TO STUDY THE PERFECTLY COMPETITIVE MARKET STRUCTURE?

A perfectly competitive market is approximated most closely in highly organized markets for securities such as the Toronto Stock Exchange and the markets for agricultural products such as wheat and corn. For example, there are literally hundreds of thousands of farms across Canada, growing a variety of agricultural products. In 2012 alone, Canadian farmers produced close to 25 million tonnes of wheat, 15 million tonnes of canola, and 5 million tonnes of soybeans. However, whether the corn was grown in Ontario or Quebec, domestic and international consumers considered the output for each individual farm to be virtually identical. The Toronto Stock Exchange (TSX), along with the TSX Venture Exchange (TSXV), lists nearly 4000 companies. Other than the fees associated with "going public," there are few restrictions preventing any company from listing themselves on the TSX/TSXV and therefore entering this market.

You can legitimately ask the question: If perfectly competitive and monopolistic firms are rare and monopolistically competitive and oligopoly firms are common, why do we start our study of market structures with the former first? What we will learn from the perfectly competitive model about costs, entry, exit, and efficiency are important concepts for imperfectly competitive firms. Although all of the criteria for a perfect competitive market are rarely met, a number of markets come close to satisfying them. Even when all the assumptions don't hold, it is important to note that studying the model of perfect competition is useful because there are many markets that resemble perfect competition—that is, markets in which firms face very elastic (flat) demand curves and relatively easy entry and exit. The model also gives us a standard of comparison. In other words, we can make comparisons with the perfectly competitive model to help us evaluate what is going on in the real world.

SECTION CHECK

- There are four major market structures: perfect competition, monopoly, monopolistic competition, and oligopoly.
- A perfectly competitive market has the following characteristics: many buyers and sellers, so that neither buyers nor sellers have control over price; a homogeneous product—consumers believe that all firms sell virtually identical products; no significant barriers to entry or exit.
- Studying the perfectly competitive market structure provides us with important information about how markets operate (entry, exit, costs) that can be applied to imperfect market structures. In addition to this, the perfectly competitive structure can give us a point of comparison to evaluate real-world markets.

section 8.2

An Individual Price Taker's Demand Curve

- What does the individual price taker's demand curve look like?
- What effect will a change in market price have on an individual price taker's demand curves?

WHAT DOES THE INDIVIDUAL PRICE TAKER'S DEMAND CURVE LOOK LIKE?

Perfectly competitive firms are price takers; that is, they must sell at the market-determined price, where the market price and output are determined by the intersection of the market supply and demand curves, as seen in Exhibit 1(a). Individual wheat farmers know that they cannot dispose of their wheat at any figure higher than the current market price; if they attempt to charge a higher price, potential buyers would simply make their purchases from other wheat farmers. And the farmers certainly would not knowingly charge a lower price because they could sell all they want at the market price.

Likewise, in a perfectly competitive market, individual sellers can change their output and it will not alter the market price. This is possible because of the large number of sellers who are selling identical products. Each producer provides such a small fraction of the total supply that a change in the amount it offers does *not* have a noticeable effect on market equilibrium price. In a perfectly competitive market, then, an individual firm can sell as much as it wants to place on the market at the prevailing price; the demand, as seen by the seller, is perfectly elastic.

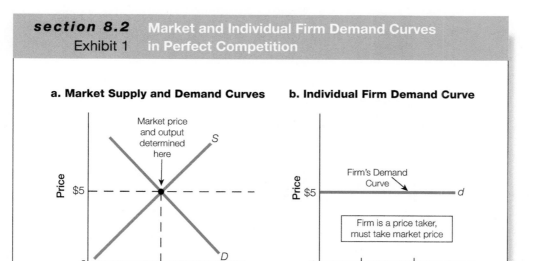

section 8.2 Market and Individual Firm Demand Curves
Exhibit 1 in Perfect Competition

a. Market Supply and Demand Curves

b. Individual Firm Demand Curve

At the market price for wheat, $5, the individual farmer can sell all the wheat he wishes. Because each producer provides only a small fraction of industry output, any additional output will have an insignificant impact on market price. The firm's demand curve is perfectly elastic at the market price.

It is easy to construct the demand curve for an individual seller in a perfectly competitive market. Remember, she won't charge more than the market price because no one will buy the good, and she won't charge less because she can sell all she wants at the market price. Thus, the farmer's demand curve is horizontal over the entire range of output that she could possibly produce. If the prevailing market price of the product is $5, the farmer's demand curve will be represented graphically by a horizontal line at the market price of $5, as shown in Exhibit 1(b).

WHAT EFFECT WILL A CHANGE IN MARKET PRICE HAVE ON AN INDIVIDUAL PRICE TAKER'S DEMAND CURVES?

To say that producers under perfect competition regard price as a given is not to say that price is constant. The *position* of the firm's demand curve varies with every change in the market price. In Exhibit 2, we see that when the market price for wheat increases, perhaps as a result of an increase in market demand, the price-taking firm will receive a higher price for all of its output. Or when the market price decreases, say as a result of a decrease in market demand, the price-taking firm will receive a lower price for all of its output.

In effect, sellers are provided with current information about market demand and supply conditions as a result of price changes. It is an essential aspect of the perfectly competitive model that sellers respond to the signals provided by such price movements, so they must alter their behaviour over time in the light of actual experience, revising their production decisions to reflect changes in market price. In this respect, the perfectly competitive model is very straightforward; it does not assume any knowledge on the part of individual buyers and sellers about market demand and supply—they only have to know the price of the good they sell.

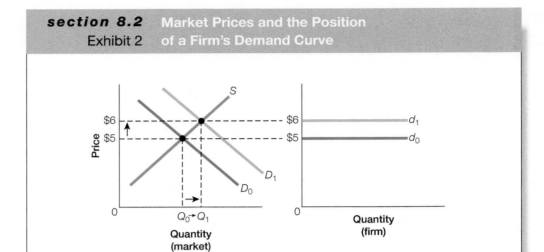

section 8.2   **Market Prices and the Position**
      Exhibit 2   **of a Firm's Demand Curve**

The position of the firm's demand curve will vary with every change in the market price.

SECTION CHECK

■ Individual sellers won't sell at a higher price than the going price because buyers can purchase the same good from someone else at the going price, nor will they sell for less than the going price because they are so small relative to the market that they can sell all they want at the going price. Therefore, the individual price taker's demand curve is horizontal over the entire range of output.

■ The position of the individual firm's demand curve varies directly with the market price.

section 8.3

Profit Maximization

■ What is total revenue?

■ What is average revenue and marginal revenue?

■ How do firms maximize profits?

The objective of the firm is to maximize profits. To maximize profits the firm wants to produce the amount that maximizes the difference between its total revenues and total costs. In this section, we will examine the different ways to look at revenue in a perfectly competitive market: total revenue, average revenue, and marginal revenue.

WHAT IS TOTAL REVENUE?

total revenue (TR)
the product price times the quantity sold

Total revenue (TR) equals the product price (P) times the quantity (q) sold ($TR = P \times q$); it is the revenue that the firm receives from the sale of its product. For example, if a farmer sells 10 tonnes of wheat a day for $5 a tonne, his total revenue is $50 ($5 × 10 tonnes). (Note: We will use the small letter q to denote the single firm's output and reserve the large Q for the output of the entire market. For example, q would be used to represent the output of one potato grower, whereas Q would be used to represent the output of all potato growers in the potato market.)

WHAT IS AVERAGE REVENUE AND MARGINAL REVENUE?

Average revenue (AR) equals total revenue divided by the number of units sold (TR/q, or $[P \times q]/q$). For example, if the farmer sells 10 tonnes at $5 a tonne, total revenue is $50 and average revenue is $5 ($50/10 tonnes = $5 per tonne). So, in perfect competition, average revenue is equal to the price of the good.

Marginal revenue (MR) represents the increase in total revenue that results from the sale of one more unit. In a perfectly competitive market, because additional units of output can be sold without reducing the price of the product, marginal revenue is constant at all outputs and equal to average revenue. For example, if the price of wheat per tonne is $5, the marginal revenue is $5. Because total revenue is equal to price multiplied by quantity ($TR = P \times q$), as we add one additional unit of output, total revenue will always increase by the amount of the product price, $5. Marginal revenue facing a perfectly competitive firm is equal to the price of the good.

The relationship between marginal revenue, price, and average revenue is clearly illustrated in the calculations presented in Exhibit 1. In perfect completion, then, we can draw the following conclusion:

$$P = MR = AR.$$

average revenue (AR)
total revenue divided by the number of units sold

marginal revenue (MR)
the increase in total revenue that results from the sale of one more unit

HOW DO FIRMS MAXIMIZE PROFITS?

Now that we have discussed both the firm's cost curves (Chapter 7) and the firm's revenues, we are ready to see how a firm maximizes its profits. A firm's profits equal its total revenues minus its total costs. But at what output level will a firm produce and sell in order to maximize profits? There are two methods for identifying this output: the marginal approach and the total cost–total revenue approach. In all types of market environments, firms will maximize profits at the output that maximizes the difference between total revenue and total costs, which is at the same output level where marginal revenue equals marginal costs.

Equating Marginal Revenue and Marginal Cost

The importance of equating marginal revenue and marginal costs is seen in Exhibit 2. As output expands beyond zero up to q^*, the marginal revenue derived from each unit of the expanded output exceeds the marginal cost of that unit of output, so the

section 8.3	**Revenues for a Perfectly Competitive Firm**			
Exhibit 1				

Quantity (q)	Price (P)	Total Revenue (TR = P × q)	Average Revenue (AR = TR/q)	Marginal Revenue (MR = ΔTR/Δq)
1	$5	$ 5	$5	$5
2	5	10	5	5
3	5	15	5	5
4	5	20	5	5
5	5	25	5	

section 8.3
Exhibit 2

Finding the Profit-Maximizing Level of Output

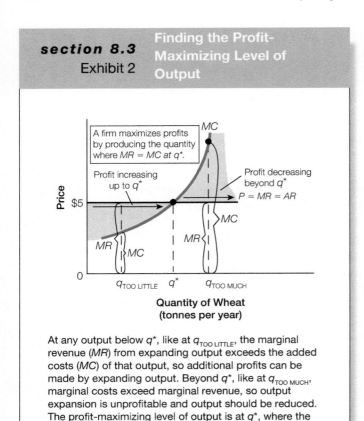

A firm maximizes profits by producing the quantity where *MR* = *MC* at *q**.

Profit increasing up to *q**

Profit decreasing beyond *q**

P = *MR* = *AR*

Price

$5

MR

MC

MC

MR

MC

0

$q_{\text{TOO LITTLE}}$ *q** $q_{\text{TOO MUCH}}$

Quantity of Wheat (tonnes per year)

At any output below *q**, like at $q_{\text{TOO LITTLE}}$, the marginal revenue (*MR*) from expanding output exceeds the added costs (*MC*) of that output, so additional profits can be made by expanding output. Beyond *q**, like at $q_{\text{TOO MUCH}}$, marginal costs exceed marginal revenue, so output expansion is unprofitable and output should be reduced. The profit-maximizing level of output is at *q**, where the profit-maximizing output rule is followed—the firm should produce the level of output where *MR* = *MC*.

expansion of output creates additional profits. This addition to profit is shown as the left-most shaded section in Exhibit 2. As long as marginal revenues exceed marginal costs, profits continue to grow. For example, if the firm decides to produce $q_{\text{TOO LITTLE}}$, the firm sacrifices potential profits because the marginal revenue from producing more output is greater than the marginal cost. Only at *q**, where *MR* = *MC*, is the output level just right—not too large, not too small. Further expansion of output beyond *q** will lead to losses on the additional output (decrease the firm's overall profits) because *MC* > *MR*. For example, if the firm produces $q_{\text{TOO MUCH}}$, the firm incurs losses on that output produced beyond *q**; the firm should reduce its output. Only at output *q**, where *MR* = *MC*, can we find the profit-maximizing level of output. The **profit-maximizing output rule** says a firm should always produce at the level of output where its *MR* = *MC*.

Profit-Maximizing Output Rule

$$MR = MC$$

profit-maximizing output rule

a firm should always produce at the level of output where MR = MC

The Marginal Approach

We can use the data in Exhibit 3 to find Farmer John's profit-maximizing position. In the table in Exhibit 3, columns 5 and 6 show the marginal revenue and marginal cost, respectively. We see that output levels of one and two tonnes produce outputs that have marginal revenues that exceed marginal cost—John certainly wants to produce those units and more. That is, as long as marginal revenue exceeds marginal costs, producing and selling those units adds more to revenues than to costs; in other words, they add to profits. However, once he expands production beyond four units of output, John's marginal revenues are less than his marginal costs and his profits begin to fall. Clearly, Farmer John should not produce beyond four tonnes of wheat.

The Total Cost–Total Revenue Approach

Let us take another look at profit maximization using the table in Exhibit 3. Comparing columns 2 and 3, the calculations of total revenues and total costs, respectively, we see that Farmer John maximizes his profits at output levels of three or four tonnes, where he will make profits of $4. In column 4, "Profit," you can see that there is no higher level of profit at any of the other output levels.

In the next section we will use the profit-maximizing output rule to see what happens when changes in the market cause the price to fall below average total cost and even below average variable costs. We will introduce the four-step method to determine whether the firm is making an economic profit, minimizing its losses, or should temporarily shut down.

section 8.3
Exhibit 3
Cost and Revenue Calculations for a Perfectly Competitive Firm

Quantity (1)	Total Revenue (2)	Total Cost (3)	Profit (TR – TC) (4)	Marginal Revenue ($\Delta TR/\Delta q$) (5)	Marginal Cost ($\Delta TC/\Delta q$) (6)
0	$ 0	$ 2	–$2	$5	
1	5	4	1	5	$2
2	10	7	3	5	3
3	15	11	4	5	4
4	20	16	4	5	5
5	25	22	3		6

SECTION CHECK

■ Total revenue is price times the quantity sold ($TR = P \times q$).
■ Average revenue is total revenue divided by the quantity sold ($AR = TR/q$). Marginal revenue is the change in total revenue from the sale of an additional unit of output ($MR = \Delta TR/\Delta q$). In a competitive industry, $P = AR = MR$.
■ The profit-maximizing output rule says a firm should always produce where $MR = MC$. When $MR > MC$, the seller should expand production because producing and selling those units adds more to revenues than to costs, or increases profits. However, if $MR < MC$, the seller should decrease production.

Short-Run Profits and Losses

■ How do we determine if a firm is generating an economic profit or loss?
■ What is the individual firm's short-run supply curve?
■ Can we review the short-run production decisions of an individual competitive firm?

In the previous section, we discussed two methods of determining the profit-maximizing output level for a perfectly competitive firm. However, producing at this profit-maximizing level does not mean that a firm is actually generating profits; it merely means that a firm is maximizing its profit opportunity at a given price level.

HOW DO WE DETERMINE IF A FIRM IS GENERATING AN ECONOMIC PROFIT OR LOSS?

Determining whether a firm is generating economic profits, economic losses, or zero economic profits at the profit-maximizing level of output, q^*, can be done in four easy steps. First, we will walk through these steps and then, in Exhibit 1, we will apply the method to three different situations for a hypothetical firm in the short run.

The Four-Step Method for Perfect Competition

1. The first step is to find the profit-maximizing level of output (q^*). To do this, find where marginal revenues equal marginal costs and proceed straight down to the horizontal quantity axis to find the profit-maximizing output level.

2. The second step is to determine the total revenue (TR) being generated at q^*. To do this, go straight up from q^* to the demand curve and then to the left to find the market price, P^*. Once you have identified P^* and q^*, you can find total revenue at the profit-maximizing output level, because $TR = P \times q$.

3. The third step is to find total costs (TC) at q^*. Again, go straight up from q^* to the average total cost (ATC) curve and then left to the vertical axis to compute the average total cost *per unit*. If we multiply average total costs by the output level, we can find the total costs ($TC = ATC \times q$).

4. The final step is to determine the amount of either profit or loss at q^*. If total revenue (from step 2) is greater than total costs (from step 3) at q^*, the firm is generating economic profits. However, if total revenue is less than total costs at q^*, the firm is generating economic losses.

Remember, the cost curves include implicit and explicit costs—that is, we are covering the opportunity costs of our resources. So even if there are zero economic profits, no tears should be shed, because the firm is covering both its implicit and explicit costs. Because firms are also covering their implicit costs, or what they could be producing with these resources in another endeavour, economists sometimes call this zero economic profit *a normal rate of return*. That is, the owners are doing as well as they could elsewhere, in that they are getting the normal rate of return on the resources they invested in the firm.

The Four-Step Method in Action

In Exhibit 1, there are three different short-run equilibrium positions; in each case, the firm is producing at a level where marginal revenue equals marginal costs. Each of these alternatives shows that the firm is maximizing profits or minimizing losses in the short run.

Assume that there are three alternative prices for a firm with given costs. In Exhibit 1(a), the firm receives $6 per unit at an equilibrium level of output ($MR = MC$) of 120 units. Total revenue ($P \times q^*$) is $6 × 120, or $720. The average total

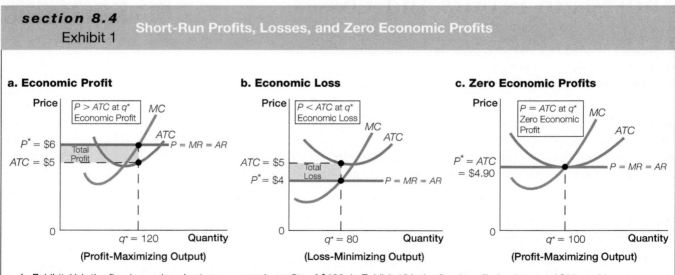

section 8.4

Exhibit 1   Short-Run Profits, Losses, and Zero Economic Profits

a. Economic Profit

b. Economic Loss

c. Zero Economic Profits

In Exhibit 1(a), the firm is earning short-run economic profits of $120; in Exhibit 1(b), the firm is suffering losses of $80; and in Exhibit 1(c), the firm is making zero economic profits, with the price just equal to the average total cost in the short run.

cost at 120 units of output is $5, and the total cost (*ATC* × *q**) is $600. Following the four-step method, we can calculate that this firm is earning total economic profits of $120.

In Exhibit 1(b), the market price has fallen to $4 per unit. At the equilibrium level of output, the firm is now producing 80 units of output at an average total cost of $5 per unit. The total revenue is now $320 ($4 × 80), and the total costs are $400 ($5 × 80). We can see that the firm is now incurring total economic losses of $80.

In Exhibit 1(c), the firm is earning zero economic profits, or a normal rate of return. The market price is $4.90, and the average total cost is $4.90 per unit for 100 units of output. In this case, economic profits are zero because total revenue, $490, minus total cost, $490, is equal to zero. This firm is just covering all its costs, both implicit and explicit.

Evaluating Economic Losses in the Short Run

A firm generating an economic loss faces a tough choice: Should it continue to produce or shut down its operation in the short run? To make this decision, we need to add another variable to our discussion of economic profits and losses: average variable costs. Variable costs are those costs that vary with output, such as wages, raw material, transportation, and electricity. If a firm cannot generate enough revenues to cover its variable costs, then it will have larger losses if it operates than if it shuts down (losses in that case = fixed costs). Thus, a firm will not produce at all unless the price is greater than its average variable costs.

Operating at a Loss   At price levels greater than or equal to average variable costs, a firm may continue to operate in the short run even if average total costs—variable and fixed costs—are not completely covered. That is, the firm may continue to operate even though it is experiencing an economic loss. Why? Because fixed costs continue whether the firm produces or not; it is better to earn enough to cover a portion of fixed costs rather than earn nothing at all.

In Exhibit 2, price is less than average total cost but more than average variable cost. In this case, the firm produces in the short run, but at a loss. To shut down would make this firm worse off because it can cover at least *some* of its fixed costs with the excess of revenue over its variable costs.

The Decision to Shut Down   Exhibit 3 illustrates a situation in which the price a firm is able to obtain for its product is below its average variable costs at all ranges of output. In this case, the firm is unable to cover even its

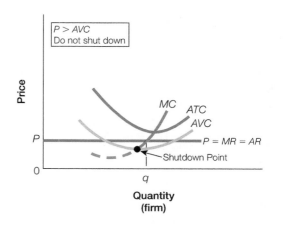

section 8.4
Exhibit 2   Short-Run Losses: Price Above *AVC* but Below *ATC*

In this case, the firm operates in the short run but incurs a loss because *P* < *ATC*. Nevertheless, *P* > *AVC*, and revenues cover variable costs and partially defray fixed costs. This firm will leave the industry in the long run unless prices are expected to rise in the near future, but in the short run it continues to operate at a loss as long as *P* > *AVC*.

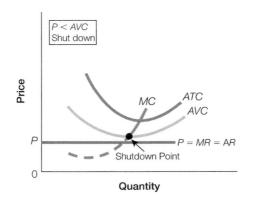

section 8.4
Exhibit 3   Short-Run Losses: Price Below *AVC*

Because its average variable costs exceed price at all levels of output, this firm would cut its losses by discontinuing production.

section 8.4
Exhibit 4
The Firm's Short-Run Supply Curve

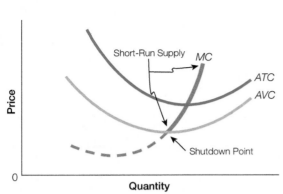

If price is less than average variable costs, the firm's losses would be smaller if it shut down and stopped producing. That is, if $P < AVC$, the firm is better off producing zero output. Hence, the firm's short-run supply curve is the marginal cost curve above average variable cost.

variable costs in the short run. Because the firm is losing even more than the fixed costs it would lose if it shut down, it is more logical for the firm to cease operations. So if $P < AVC$, the firm can cut its losses by shutting down.

WHAT IS THE INDIVIDUAL FIRM'S SHORT-RUN SUPPLY CURVE?

As we have just seen, at all prices above minimum AVC, a firm produces in the short run even if average total cost (ATC) is not completely covered, and at all prices below the minimum AVC, the firm shuts down. The firm produces above the minimum of the AVC even if it is incurring economic losses because it can still earn enough in total revenues to cover all of its average variable costs and a portion of its fixed costs—this is better than not producing, and earning nothing at all.

For an individual competitive seller, the **short-run supply curve,** as a cost relationship, shows the marginal cost of producing any *given output;* as a supply curve, it shows the *equilibrium output* that the firm will supply at various prices in the short run. In graphical terms, the short-run supply curve is identical to the portion of the MC curve that lies above the minimum of the AVC curve. This is illustrated by the thick line in Exhibit 4. The declining portion of the MC curve has no significance for supply, because if the price falls below average variable costs, the firm is better off shutting down—producing no output. Beyond the point of lowest AVC, the marginal costs of successively larger amounts of output are progressively greater, so the firm will supply larger and larger amounts only at higher prices. The absolute maximum that the firm can supply, regardless of price, is the maximum quantity that it can produce with the existing plant.

short-run supply curve
as a cost relationship, this curve shows the marginal cost of producing any given output; as a supply curve, it shows the equilibrium output that the firm will supply at various prices in the short run

Deriving the Short-Run Market Supply Curve

short-run market supply curve
the horizontal summation of the individual firms' supply curves in the market

The **short-run market supply curve** is the horizontal summation of the individual firms' supply curves (i.e., the portion of the firms' MC above AVC) in the market. Because the short run is too brief for new firms to enter the market, the market supply curve is the horizontal summation of *existing* firms. For example, in Exhibit 5, at P_0, each of the 1000 identical firms in the industry produces 50 tonnes of wheat per day at point a, in Exhibit 5(a) and the quantity supplied in the market is 50 000 tonnes of wheat, point A, in Exhibit 5(b). We can again sum horizontally at P_1; the quantity supplied for each of the 1000 identical firms is 80 tonnes of wheat per day at point b in Exhibit 5(a), so the quantity supplied for the industry is 80 000 tonnes of wheat per day, point B in Exhibit 5(b). Continuing this process gives us the market supply curve for the wheat market. In a market of 1000 identical wheat farmers, the market supply curve is 1000 times the quantity supplied by each firm, as long as the price is above AVC.

section 8.4
Exhibit 5   Deriving the Short-Run Market Supply Curve

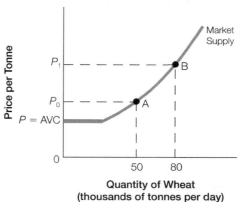

a. Individual Firm Supply Curve for Wheat

b. Market Supply Curve for Wheat

The short-run market supply curve is the horizontal summation of the individual firm's supply curves (the firm's marginal cost curve above *AVC*) in Exhibit 5(a). In a market of 1000 identical wheat farmers, the market supply curve is 1000 times the quantity supplied by each firm in Exhibit 5(b).

CAN WE REVIEW THE SHORT-RUN PRODUCTION DECISIONS OF AN INDIVIDUAL COMPETITIVE FIRM?

Consider the firm represented by the revenue and cost curves presented in Exhibit 6. At the various market prices—P_1, P_2, P_3, and P_4—what would be the firm's short-run output decisions?

At a market price of P_1, the firm would not cover its average variable costs—the firm would produce zero output because the firm's losses would be smaller if it shut down and stopped producing. At a market price of P_2, the firm would produce at the loss-minimizing output of q_2 units. It would operate rather than shut down because it could cover all of its average variable costs and some of its fixed costs. At a market

section 8.4
Exhibit 6   The Short-Run Output Decision

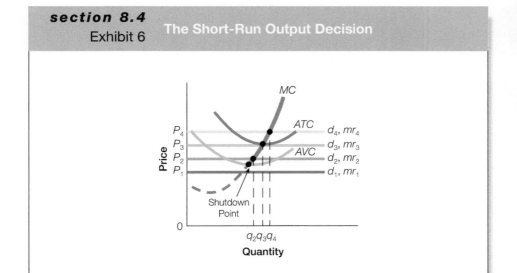

Since the demand for winter activities like skiing will be lower during the off-season, it is likely that revenues may be too low for the ski resort owners to cover their variable costs and the owners will choose to shut down. Remember, the owners will still have to pay the fixed costs: property tax, insurance, and other costs associated with the building and land. However, if the resort is not in operation during the off-season, the owners will at least not have to pay the variable costs: salary for the staff, food, and electricity.

price of P_3, the firm would produce q_3 units of output and make zero economic profits (a normal rate of return). Finally, at a market price of P_4, the firm would produce q_4 units of output and be making short-run economic profits.

Business *CONNECTION*

A KEY FACTOR IN PERFECT COMPETITION— MANAGING COSTS

In economics, we teach perfect competition to illustrate to students that on one end of the economic spectrum is a market where neither consumers nor producers have any power in setting price—the market sets the price. On the other end of the spectrum are pure monopolies, where the power rests with the producer. In perfect competition, we are all price takers and we compete only on price. In fact, perfect competition happens only in theory—can you think of any product or service that is purchased solely on price? The other 3Ps (product, price, and promotion) have no place in the perfectly competitive market.

In business, the basic decisions that owners/managers must make are how many units to produce and at what price. Given that in perfect competition the price decision is made for producers (and consumers) in the market, the only decision left is how much to produce. Remember that a firm's revenue equals price times quantity and profits are revenues less expenses. So for a firm to maximize its profit, it has to produce or sell the amount that achieves the lowest costs. If it makes too many at the given price, it will have a surplus and be forced to lower prices to sell. In this case, it won't be maximizing profit—it will be minimizing losses instead. On the other hand, if it doesn't make as much as the market demands, the market will bid up the price due to the shortage, and in the short term, some other firm will benefit from selling the added quantity.

The biggest mistake entrepreneurs (and new students) make in understanding the basics of business is to think that the more they sell, the more profits they'll make. It's critical to understand that revenues and profits are not the same, and that when businesses are able to make more products on the economies of scale side (where average costs fall because of an increase in the scale of production) or without saturating the market, they will both lower their costs and increase their profits. However, if they produce while on the diseconomies of scale side (where firms expand too much), they will drive up their costs and eventually find themselves making up the loss from their available cash or credit. Once those resources are exhausted, the business may fail.

Success, whether for businesses or for consumers, is not based on increasing revenues but rather on controlling expenses. Businesses in a highly competitive market absolutely need to be aware at what level of production their costs are the lowest, and unless the market changes or they can lower costs further, deviating from that level of production may have dire long-term consequences.

1. Can you think of any business that competes in an absolutely perfectly competitive market in which price is the only deciding factor of the product? Can you describe the attributes of that product?

2. Can you describe why you think firms that are competing strictly on price tend to be large firms? Why can't smaller firms compete with these large firms? Do you see this as a barrier to entry for smaller firms, and if so, how can smaller firms compete (or can they)?

3. If a firm is competing in a perfectly competitive market, which should they be concerned more about—revenues or profits—and why?

SECTION CHECK

■ The profit-maximizing output level is found by equating $MR = MC$ at q^*. If at q^* the firm's price is greater than its ATC, it is making an economic profit. If at q^* the price is less than ATC, the firm is incurring an economic loss. If at q^* the price is equal to ATC, the firm is making zero economic profits; that is, making a normal rate of return.

■ The portion of the MC curve that lies above the minimum of the AVC curve is the short-run supply curve for the individual competitive seller.

■ As market price rises, the output decisions of a competitive firm evolve from not producing at all (shutting down), to operating at an economic loss, to economically breaking even, to generating an economic profit.

Long-Run Equilibrium

- What happens to economic profits and losses in the long run?
- What is the long-run equilibrium for the competitive firm?

WHAT HAPPENS TO ECONOMIC PROFITS AND LOSSES IN THE LONG RUN?

If farmers are able to make economic profits producing wheat, what will their response be in the long run? Farmers will increase the resources that they devote to the lucrative business of producing wheat. Suppose Farmer John is making an economic profit (he is earning an above-normal rate of return) producing wheat. To make even more profits, he may take land out of producing other crops and plant more wheat. Other farmers or people who are holding land for speculative purposes might also decide to plant wheat on their land.

As the word gets out that wheat production is proving profitable, there will be a supply response—the market supply curve will shift to the right as more firms enter the industry and existing firms expand, as in Exhibit 1(a). With this shift, the quantity of wheat supplied at any given price is greater than before. It may take a year or even longer, of course, for the complete supply response to take place, simply because it takes some time for information to spread on profit opportunities, and still more time

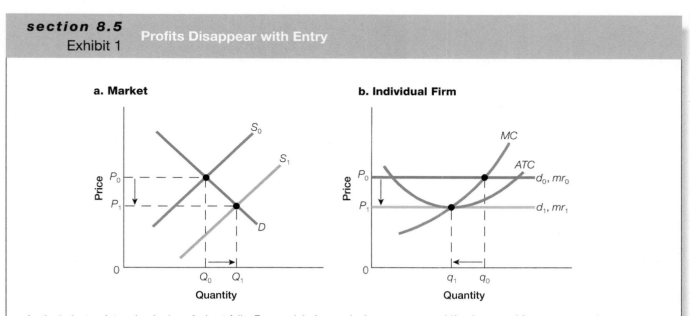

section 8.5
Exhibit 1 — **Profits Disappear with Entry**

a. Market

b. Individual Firm

As the industry-determined price of wheat falls, Farmer John's marginal revenue curve shifts downward from mr_0 to mr_1 in Exhibit 1(b). A new profit-maximizing ($MC = MR$) point is reached at q_1. When the price is P_0, Farmer John is making a profit because $P_0 > ATC$. But when the market supply increases, causing the market price to fall to P_1, Farmer John's profits disappear because $P_1 = ATC$.

to plant, grow, and harvest the wheat. Note that the impact of increasing supply, other things equal, is to reduce the equilibrium price of wheat. Suppose that, as a result of the supply response, the price of wheat falls from P_0 to P_1.

The impact of the change in the market price of wheat, over which John has absolutely no control, is very simple. If his costs have not changed, he will move from making a profit ($P_0 > ATC$) to zero economic profits ($P_1 = ATC$), as seen in Exhibit 1(b). In long-run equilibrium, perfectly competitive firms make zero economic profits. Remember, zero economic profits means that the firm is actually earning a normal return on the use of its capital. Zero economic profits is an equilibrium or stable situation because any positive economic (above-normal) profits signal resources to enter the industry, beating down prices and thus revenues to the firm. Any economic losses signal resources to leave the industry, causing market supply reductions that lead to increased prices and higher firm revenues for the remaining firms. For example, in Exhibit 2 we see a firm that continues to operate despite its losses—ATC is greater than P_0 at q_0. With losses, however, some firms will exit the industry, causing the market supply curve to shift from S_0 to S_1 and driving up the market price to P_1. This price increase reduces the losses for the firms remaining in the industry, until the losses are completely eliminated at P_1. The remaining firms will maximize profits by producing at q_1 units of output, where profits and losses are zero. Only at zero economic profits is there no tendency for firms to either enter or exit the industry.

section 8.5
Exhibit 2

Losses Disappear with Exit

a. Individual Firm

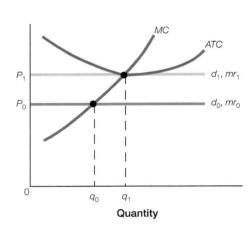

b. Market

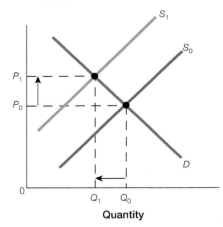

When firms in the industry suffer losses, some firms will exit in the long run, shifting the market supply curve to the left from S_0 to S_1. This causes market price to rise from P_0 to P_1 and market output to fall from Q_0 to Q_1. When the price is P_0 the firm is incurring a loss, because ATC is greater than P_0 at q_0. When the market supply decreases from S_0 to S_1, it causes the market price to rise and the firm's losses disappear, because $P_1 = ATC$.

WHAT IS THE LONG-RUN EQUILIBRIUM FOR THE COMPETITIVE FIRM?

The long-run competitive equilibrium for a perfectly competitive firm is graphically illustrated in Exhibit 3. At the equilibrium point (where $MC = MR$), short-run and long-run average total costs are also equal. The average total cost curves touch the marginal cost and marginal revenue (demand) curves at the equilibrium output point. Because the marginal revenue curve is also the average revenue curve, average revenues and average total costs are equal at the equilibrium point. The long-run equilibrium in perfect competition depicted in Exhibit 3 has an interesting feature. Note that the equilibrium output occurs at the lowest point on the average total cost curve. As you may recall, this occurs because the marginal cost curve must intersect the average total cost curve at the latter curve's lowest point. Hence, the equilibrium condition in the long run in perfect competition is for firms to produce at that output that minimizes average total costs—that is, the firm is operating at its minimum efficient scale. At this long-run equilibrium, all firms in the industry are earning zero economic profit; consequently, new firms have no incentive to enter the market, and existing firms have no incentive to exit the market.

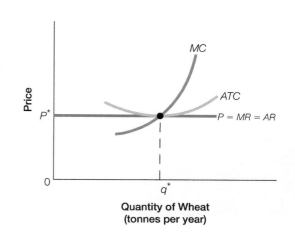

section 8.5
Exhibit 3   The Long-Run Competitive Equilibrium

In the long run in perfect competition, a stable situation or equilibrium is achieved when economic profits are zero. In this case, at the profit-maximizing point where $MC = MR$, short-run and long-run average total costs are equal. Industry-wide supply shifts would change prices and average revenues and wipe out any losses or profits that develop in the short run, leading to the situation depicted above.

DEBATE

IS "PERFECT" COMPETITION IMPERFECT IN THE LONG TERM?

For:
In a perfectly competitive market, goods trade on price alone—not on product differentiation, convenience, or promotional advertising. Innovation raises costs, and there's no incentive for producers to innovate if they can't recover those costs. Those who try to innovate will only increase their costs, and eventually they'll be driven out of the market. Economies that work at this level will sustain themselves only as long as the resource involved is available. When scarcity starts to set in, they are unprepared to adapt. There is a social cost to this approach—greater wealth it based on value-added, and without adding value, an economy develops at less than a socially optimal level. So surely a form of competition that stifles innovation is imperfect in the long term? In this market, the marginal social costs (the costs to society of producing more of the item) exceed the marginal private costs of the producers. Can you provide examples of where these two costs come in conflict and how they might be played out in the market to back up your position?

Against:
One point worth considering is that the goods that trade in perfectly competitive markets tend to be very basic and homogeneous in nature—most likely commodities and raw resources. Economies that generally trade in raw resources are usually not innovative to start with. Over the long term, though, firms have to innovate to lower their costs, and in that way they contribute to long-term economic development. While it may be true that innovation is slower in markets that are perfectly competitive, innovation nevertheless develops. Firms in perfectly competitive markets have found ways to innovate while maintaining competitive margins, and such firms are generally efficient and lower-cost producers. Surely perfect competition is as perfect as those involved want it to be, for the short term as well the long term. Can you provide examples where firms in perfectly competitive markets can innovate and where this has been socially beneficial?

SECTION CHECK

■ Economic profits will encourage entry of new firms, which will shift the market supply curve to the right, driving down prices and revenues to the firm. Any economic losses signal resources to leave the industry, leading to supply reduction, higher prices, and increased revenues.

■ Only at zero economic profits is there no tendency for firms to either enter or exit the industry. This is the long-run equilibrium for the competitive firm.

section
8.6

Long-Run Supply

■ What are constant-cost industries?
■ What are increasing-cost and decreasing-cost industries?
■ How is perfect competition economically efficient?

The preceding sections have considered the costs of an individual, perfectly competitive firm as it varies output, on the assumption that the prices paid for inputs (costs) are given. However, when the output of an entire industry changes, the likelihood is greater of changes occurring in costs. But how will the changes in the number of firms in an industry affect the input costs of individual firms? In this section we develop the long-run supply curve (*LRS*). As we will see, the shape of the long-run supply curve depends on the extent to which input costs change when there is entry or exit of firms in the industry. We will look at two possible types of industries when considering long-run supply: constant-cost industries and increasing-cost industries.

WHAT ARE CONSTANT-COST INDUSTRIES?

constant-cost industry
an industry where input prices (and cost curves) do not change as industry output changes

In a **constant-cost industry,** input prices do not change as industry output changes. The industry may not use inputs in sufficient quantities to affect input prices. For example, say the firms in the industry use a lot of unskilled labour but the industry is small. So, as output expands, the increase in demand for unskilled labour will not cause the market wage for unskilled labour to rise. Similarly, suppose a paper-clip maker decides to double its output. It is highly unlikely that its demand for steel will have an impact on steel prices because its demand for the input is so small.

Once long-run adjustments are complete, by necessity each firm operates at the point of lowest long-run average total costs because supply shifts with entry and exit, eliminating profits. Therefore, each firm supplies the market with the quantity of output that it can produce at the lowest possible long-run average total cost.

In Exhibit 1, we can see the impact of an unexpected increase in market demand. Suppose that recent reports show that blueberries can lower cholesterol, lower blood pressure, and significantly reduce the risk of all cancers. The increase in market demand for blueberries leads to a price increase from P_0 to P_1 as the firm increases output from

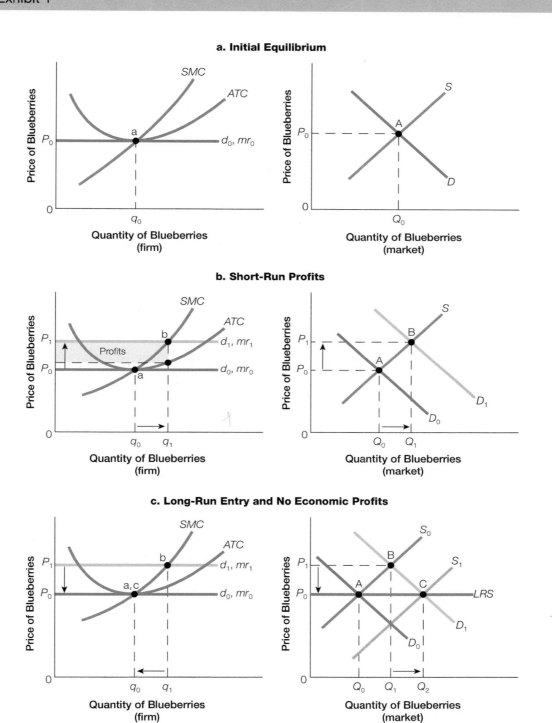

a. Initial Equilibrium

b. Short-Run Profits

c. Long-Run Entry and No Economic Profits

An unexpected increase in market demand for blueberries leads to an increase in the market price at point b. The new market price leads to positive profits for existing firms, which attracts new firms into the industry, shifting market supply from S_0 to S_1 at point c. This increased short-run industry supply curve intersects D_1 at point C. Each firm (of a new larger number of firms) is again producing at q_0 and earning zero economic profit.

q_0 to q_1, and blueberry industry output increases from Q_0 to Q_1, as seen in Exhibit 1(b). The increase in market demand generates a higher price and positive profits for existing firms in the short run. The existence of economic profits will attract new firms into the industry, causing the short-run supply curve to shift from S_0 to S_1 and lowering price until excess profits are zero. This shift results in a new equilibrium, point C in Exhibit 1(c). Because the industry is one of constant costs, industry expansion does not alter firms' cost curves, and the industry long-run supply curve is horizontal. That is, the long-run equilibrium price is at the same level that prevailed before demand increased; the only long-run effect of the increase in demand is an increase in industry output, as more firms enter that are just like existing firms, as Exhibit 1(c) indicates. However, the long-run supply curve does not have to be horizontal. The long-run supply curve is horizontal when the market has free entry and exit, there are a large number of firms with identical costs, and input prices are constant. Because these strong assumptions do not generally hold, we will now discuss when the long-run supply curve has a positive or negative slope. Studies have shown that retail trade may fall into the category of a constant-cost industry because output can be expanded or contracted without a noticeable impact on input prices. The same may be true of publishing and content businesses such as AOL.

WHAT ARE INCREASING-COST AND DECREASING-COST INDUSTRIES?

An Increasing-Cost Industry

increasing-cost industry
an industry where input prices rise (and cost curves rise) as industry output rises

In the **increasing-cost industry,** input prices rise (and cost curves rise) as industry output rises. In this more likely scenario, the cost curves of the individual firms rise as the total output of the industry increases. Increases in input prices (upward shifts in cost curves) occur as larger quantities of factors are employed in the industry. When an industry utilizes a large portion of an input whose total supply is not huge, input prices will rise when the industry uses more of the input.

Increasing cost conditions are typical of "extractive" industries, such as agriculture, fishing, mining, and lumbering, which utilize large portions of the total supply of specialized natural resources such as land and mineral deposits. As the output of such an industry expands, the increased demand for the resources raises the prices that must be paid for their use. Because additional resources of given quality cannot be produced, greater supplies can be obtained (if at all) only by luring them away from other industries or by using lower-quality (and less-productive, thus higher-cost) resources.

Wheat production is a typical example of an increasing-cost industry. As the output of wheat increases, the demand for land suitable for the production of wheat rises, so the price paid for the use of land of any given quality increases.

If there was a construction boom in a fully employed economy, would it be more costly to get additional resources like workers and raw materials? Yes, in an increasing-cost industry, the industry can produce more output only if it gets a higher price, because the firm's costs of production rise as output expands. As new firms enter and output expands, the increase in demand for inputs causes the price of inputs to rise—the cost curves of all construction firms shift upward as the industry expands. Or consider a downtown building boom where the supply of workers who are willing to work on tall skyscrapers is very inelastic; a very steep supply of labour curve. The high demand for these few workers causes their wages to rise sharply and the cost of skyscrapers to rise. The industry can produce more output but only at a higher price, enough to compensate the firm for the higher input costs. In an increasing-cost industry, the long-run supply curve is upward sloping.

For example, in Exhibit 2, we see that an unexpected increase in the market demand for wheat will shift the market demand curve from D_0 to D_1. Consequently, price will increase from P_0 to P_1 in the short run and the industry output will increase from Q_0 to Q_1. The typical firm (farm) will have positive short-run profits and expand output. With the presence of short-run economic profits, new firms will enter the industry, shifting the short-run market supply curve to the right from S_0 to S_1. The prices of inputs, like farmland, fertilizer, seed, farm machinery, and so on, will be bid up by competing farmers, causing the farm's marginal and long-run average cost curves to rise. The cost increases mean that the market supply curve shifts right less than it would in a constant-cost industry. This leads to an upward-sloping long-run industry supply curve, as seen in Exhibit 2.

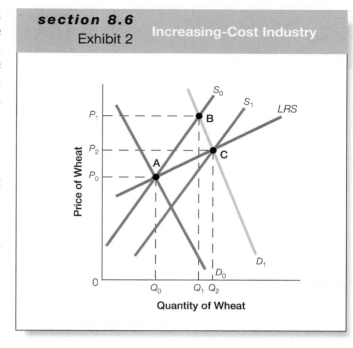

section 8.6
Exhibit 2   **Increasing-Cost Industry**

Another example of an increasing cost industry can be found by looking at the National Hockey League (NHL). The 1990s saw the NHL undergo ambitious expansion with the addition of numerous teams in the southern United States. This growth in turn created increased demand for professional calibre hockey players, as new teams worked to become competitive with existing teams. That is, as the number of professional hockey teams increased, the team's costs increased, *ceteris paribus*. This created the situation of an upward-sloping long-run industry supply curve.

Whether the industry is one of constant cost or increasing cost, the basic point is the same. The long-run supply is usually more elastic than the short-run supply because in the long run, firms can enter and exit the industry.

A Decreasing-Cost Industry

It is also possible that an expansion in the output of an industry can lead to a reduction in input costs and shift the *MC* and *ATC* curves downward, and the market price falls because of *external economies of scale*. We use the term *external* because the cost decreases are external to the firm; no one firm can gain by its own expansion. That is, the gains occur when the total industry's output expands. A **decreasing-cost industry** is an industry where input prices fall (and cost curves fall) as industry output rises. As a result, the new long-run market equilibrium has more output at a lower price—that is, the long-run supply curve is downward sloping.

Consider a new mining region, developed in an area remote from railroad facilities back in the days before motor vehicles. As long as the total output of the mines was small, the ore was hauled by wagon, an extremely expensive form of transportation. But when the number of mines increased and the total output of the region rose substantially, it became feasible to construct a railroad to service the area. The railroad lowered transportation costs and reduced the costs of all firms in the industry. As a practical matter, decreasing-cost industries are rarely encountered, at least over a large range of output. However, some industries may operate under decreasing-cost conditions in the short intervals of output expansion when continued growth makes possible the supply of materials or services at reduced cost. A larger industry might benefit from improved transportation or financial services, for example.

This situation might occur in the computer industry. The firms in the industry may be able to acquire computer chips at a lower price as the industry's demand for computer

decreasing-cost industry
an industry where input prices fall (and cost curves fall) as industry output rises

chips rises. Why? Perhaps it is because the computer chip industry can employ cost-saving techniques that become more economical at higher levels of output. That is, the marginal and average costs of the firm fall as input prices fall because of expanded output in the industry.

HOW IS PERFECT COMPETITION ECONOMICALLY EFFICIENT?

Perfect Competition and Productive Efficiency

In this chapter, we have seen that a firm in a perfectly competitive market produces at the minimum of the *ATC* curve in the long run and charges a price consistent with that cost (recall Section 8.5, Exhibit 3). Because competitive firms are producing using the least-cost method, the minimum amount of resources is being used to produce a given level of output. This leads to lower product prices for consumers. In short, since perfect competition requires a firm to operate at the minimum of its *ATC* curve, perfect competition ensures a good or service is produced at the lowest possible cost—**productive efficiency.**

productive efficiency
where a good or service is produced at the lowest possible cost

Perfect Competition and Allocative Efficiency

Productive efficiency alone does not guarantee that markets are operating efficiently—society must also produce the goods and services that society wants most. This leads us to what economists call **allocative efficiency,** where $P = MC$ and production is allocated to reflect consumer preferences.

At the intersection of market supply and market demand we find the competitive equilibrium price, P^*, and the competitive equilibrium output, Q^*. In competitive

allocative efficiency
where P = MC and production is allocated to reflect consumer preferences

---

section 8.6
Exhibit 3
Allocative Efficiency and Perfect Competition

a. Producing Less Than the Competitive Level of Output Lowers Welfare

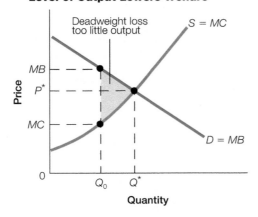

b. Producing More Than the Competitive Level of Output Lowers Welfare

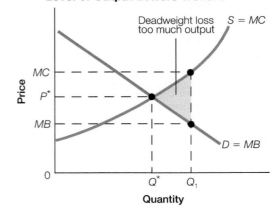

The demand curve measures the marginal benefits to the consumer and the supply curve measures the marginal cost to the sellers. At P^* and Q^*, resources are being allocated efficiently—the marginal benefits of those resources are equal to the marginal cost of those resources. At this point the sum of consumer and producer surplus is maximized. If Q_0 is produced, then the marginal benefits from producing additional units are greater than the marginal costs. Society gains from expanding output up to the point where $MB = MC$ at Q^*. If output is expanded beyond Q^*, $MC > MB$, society gains from a reduction in output, back to Q^*. The firm's losses disappear, because $P_1 = ATC$.

markets, market supply equals market demand and $P = MC$. When $P = MC$, buyers value the last unit of output by the same amount that it cost sellers to produce it. If buyers value the last unit by more than the marginal cost of production, resources are not being allocated efficiently, like at Q_0 in Exhibit 3(a). Think of the demand curve as the marginal benefit curve ($D = MB$) and the supply curve as the marginal cost curve ($S = MC$). According to the rule of rational choice, we should pursue an activity as long as the expected marginal benefits are greater than the expected marginal costs. For example in Exhibit 3(a), if Q_0 is produced, then the marginal benefits from producing additional units are greater than the marginal costs. The shaded area is deadweight loss. That is, at Q_0, resources are not being allocated efficiently, and output should be expanded.

We can also produce too much output. For example, if output is expanded beyond Q^* in Exhibit 3(b) the cost to sellers for producing the good is greater than the marginal benefits to consumers. The shaded area is deadweight loss. Society would gain from a reduction in output back to Q^*. Once the competitive equilibrium is reached, the buyers' marginal benefit equals the sellers' marginal cost; that is, in a competitive market, producers efficiently use their resources (labour, machinery, and other inputs) to produce what consumers want. In this sense, perfect competition achieves *allocative efficiency*.

SECTION CHECK

- In constant-cost industries, the cost curves of the firm are not affected by changes in the output of the entire industry. Such industries must be very small demanders of resources in the market.
- In an increasing-cost industry, the cost curves of the individual firms rise as total output increases, whereas in a decreasing-cost industry, the cost curves decline as total output increases. The increasing-cost case is the most typical.
- Perfect competition long-run equilibrium achieves productive efficiency (production at least-possible cost), allocative efficiency ($P = MC$), and production allocated to reflect consumers' wants, thereby making perfect competition economically efficient.

For Your Review

Section 8.1

1. Which of the following is/are most likely to be perfectly competitive?
   a. the fishing industry
   b. the fast-food industry
   c. the computer software industry
   d. the Toronto Stock Exchange
   e. the clothing industry

2. Based on the information provided in the following table, which of the industries described in the table are perfectly competitive? Check-mark the perfectly competitive market characteristics that each industry possesses and indicate whether it is a perfectly competitive market.

Industry	Many Firms and Buyers	Identical Products	Ease of Entry and Exit	Perfectly Competitive Market
Montreal taxi business: City issues a limited number of permits.				
Commercial aircraft company: The costs of starting such a business are significant.				
Window-washing business: Low cost of entry and limited specialized training.				
Fast-food business: Restaurant chains produce meals that are distinctive.				
Broccoli farming: There are many producers of broccoli, which requires no special growing conditions.				

3. Industry councils promote the consumption of particular types of farm products. These groups urge us to "Drink Milk" and "Get Cracking." Very little advertising is done by individual farmers. Using your understanding of the perfectly competitive market, explain this advertising strategy.

Section 8.2

Use the following exhibit to answer questions 4 and 5.

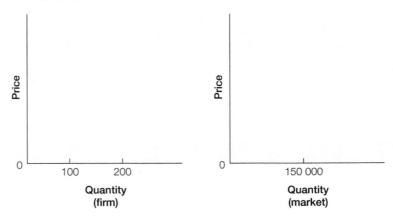

4. Using the above exhibit:
   a. Illustrate the relationship between a perfectly competitive firm's demand curve and the market supply and demand curve.
   b. Illustrate the effects of an increase in market demand on a perfectly competitive firm's demand curve.

5. Using the above exhibit:
   a. Illustrate the relationship between a perfectly competitive firm's demand curve and the market supply and demand curve.
   b. Illustrate the effects of a decrease in market demand on a perfectly competitive firm's demand curve.

6. Suppose Spartan Orchards is one of over a thousand perfectly competitive apple growers in Canada. The following graph shows the market demand and supply curves.

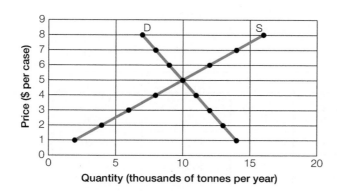

In a properly labelled diagram, draw Spartan Orchard's demand curve for apples. What is the predominant feature of this individual perfectly competitive firm's demand curve?

Blueprint Problem

Suppose the following table describes the costs of production for Carl's Calculators, a perfectly competitive firm.

Output (q)	TVC	TFC	TC	AVC	AFC	ATC	MC
0	$0.00	$40.00	$40.00	—	—	—	—
1	$10.00	$40.00	$50.00	$10.00	$40.00	$50.00	$10.00
2	$16.00	$40.00	$56.00	$8.00	$20.00	$28.00	$6.00
3	$20.00	$40.00	$60.00	$6.67	$13.33	$20.00	$4.00
4	$29.00	$40.00	$69.00	$7.25	$10.00	$17.25	$9.00
5	$44.00	$40.00	$84.00	$8.80	$8.00	$16.80	$15.00
6	$66.00	$40.00	$106.00	$11.00	$6.67	$17.67	$22.00
7	$104.00	$40.00	$144.00	$14.86	$5.71	$20.57	$38.00

a. If Carl sells each calculator for $19, determine profit-maximizing output using the total approach.

b. At the same market clearing price of $19, determine Carl's profit-maximizing output using the marginal approach. Use the four-step method and detail the steps.

Blueprint Solution

a.

> Given that Carl is selling each calculator for $19, total revenue (*TR*) can be determined.
>
> $TR = P \times q$

Output (q)	TR	TC	Total Profit
0	0	$40.00	−$40.00
1	19	$50.00	−$31.00
2	38	$56.00	−$18.00
3	57	$60.00	−$3.00
4	76	$69.00	$7.00
5	95	$84.00	$11.00
6	114	$106.00	$8.00
7	133	$144.00	−$11.00

> By determining total profit (*TR* – *TC*), the total approach reveals that *q** is 5 calculators.

b.

Output	MR	MC	Interpretation
0	—	—	
1	$19.00	$10.00	Produce
2	$19.00	$6.00	Produce
3	$19.00	$4.00	Produce
4	$19.00	$9.00	Produce
5	$19.00	$15.00	Produce
6	$19.00	$22.00	Do not produce
7	$19.00	$38.00	Do not produce

> Being a rational decision maker, Carl will produce only the number of calculators that will give him positive net benefit (*MR* > *MC*). This rational decision rule will lead Carl to produce a total of 5 calculators.

> The individual perfectly competitive firm experiences constant *MR* over the entire range of output.

Step 1: $MR = MC$ at 5 calculators (actually in this example, MR is as close to MC without exceeding it)

Step 2: $TR = P^* \times q^* = \$19 \times 5 = \$95$

Step 3: $TC = ATCq^* \times q^* = \$16.80 \times 5 = \$84$

Step 4: Total profit $= TR - TC = \$95 - \$84 = \$11$

Section 8.3

7. Given the data below, determine *AR, MR, P,* and the short-run profit-maximizing (loss-minimizing) level of output.

Output	Total Cost	Total Revenue
0	$ 30	$ 0
1	45	25
2	65	50
3	90	75
4	120	100
5	155	125

8. Complete the following table for a perfectly competitive firm, and indicate its profit-maximizing output.

Quantity	Price	Total Revenue	Marginal Revenue	Total Cost	Marginal Cost	Total Profit
6	$10	$	$	$30	$3	$30
7				35		
8				42		
9				51		
10				62		
11				75		
12				90		

9. At a price of $5, the profit-maximizing output for a perfectly competitive firm is 1000 units per year. If the average total cost is $3 per unit, what will be the firm's profit? If the average total cost is $6 per unit, what will be the firm's profit? What is the relationship between profit, price, and average total cost?

10. Use the following diagram to answer questions (a) through (d).

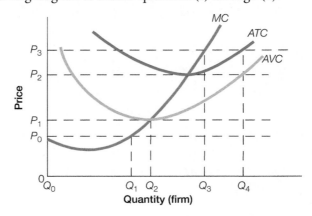

  a. How much would a perfectly competitive firm produce at each of the indicated prices?

  b. At which prices is the firm earning economic profits? Zero economic profits? Negative economic profits?

  c. At which prices would the firm shut down?

  d. Indicate what this firm's supply curve would be.

11. a. Complete the following table and identify the profit-maximizing output.

Quantity	Price	Total Revenue	Marginal Revenue	Marginal Cost	Total Profit
10	$12	$120	$12	$ 8	$25
11	12			9	
12	12			11	
13	12			12	
14	12			14	

  b. What is true about marginal revenue and marginal costs when profit is maximized?

  c. What would be the profit-maximizing level of output if the price fell to $9?

Section 8.4

12. Illustrate the *SRATC, AVC, MC,* and *MR* curves for a perfectly competitive firm that is operating at a loss. What is the output level that minimizes losses? Why is it more profitable to continue producing in the short run rather than shut down?

13. The diagram below applies to a perfectly competitive firm.

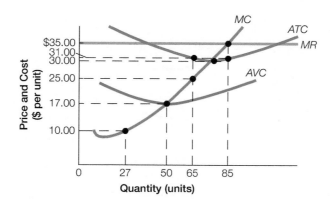

a. According to the diagram, what is the current market clearing price facing this producer and how many units are being produced at this price?

b. At the indicated market clearing price, what are the economic profits or losses of the firm?

c. Suppose the market clearing price falls to $25. What are the economic profits or losses of the firm? Should the firm continue to produce in the short run to maximize profits (or minimize losses)? Explain.

d. Suppose the market clearing price falls to $10. Should the firm continue to produce in the short run to maximize profits (or minimize losses)? Explain.

14. Discuss the following questions.

a. Why must price cover *AVC* if firms are to continue to operate?

b. If the firm is covering its *AVC* but not all its fixed costs, will it continue to operate in the short run? Why or why not?

c. Why is it possible for price to remain above the average total cost in the short run but not in the long run?

15. Evaluate the following statements. Determine whether each is true or false and explain your answer.

a. If economic profits are zero, firms will exit the industry in the long run.

b. A firm cannot maximize profits without minimizing costs.

c. If a firm is minimizing costs, it must be maximizing profits.

Section 8.5

16. Explain why the following conditions are typical under perfect competition in the long run.

a. $P = MC$

b. $P = \text{Minimum } ATC$

17. Describe what would happen to the industry supply curve and the economic profits of the firms in a competitive industry if those firms were currently earning economic profits. What if they were currently earning economic losses?

18. The following graph shows the output for Pat, a profit-maximizing corn farmer.

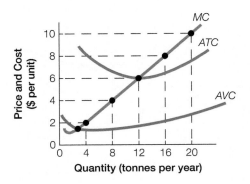

a. Suppose the corn market consists of 1000 farms, including and identical to Pat's. In the table below, determine the market supply in column 2.

b. If the market demand for corn is as shown in column 3 of the table below, at equilibrium price how much will Pat produce? Is she generating a profit or a loss? How much will the market produce? Is the market generating a profit or a loss?

(1)	(2)	(3)
Price ($)	Market Supply (tonnes per year)	Market Demand (tonnes per year)
2		19 000
4		15 000
6		12 000
8		10 000
10		7 000

c. Given the results from part (b), what will happen to the corn market in the long run?

Section 8.6

19. Use the following diagrams to answer (a) and (b).

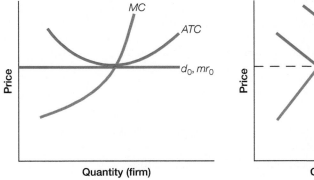

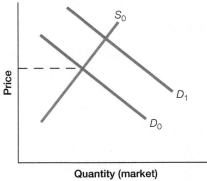

a. Show the effect of an increase in demand on the perfectly competitive firm's price, marginal revenue, output, and profits in the short run.

b. Show the long-run effects of an increase in demand for the industry, and the effects on a perfectly competitive firm's price, marginal revenue, output, and profits for a constant-cost industry.

20. Graph and explain the adjustments to long-run equilibrium when market demand decreases in a constant-cost industry.

21. Given the industry description, identify each of the following as an increasing-cost or constant-cost industry.

a. Major League Baseball: Uses the majority of pitchers. As the number of pitchers used increases, the quality declines.

b. Fast-food restaurants: Use a relatively small share of land and unskilled labour in most cities.

c. Trucking industry: Uses a large number of trained and experienced drivers, especially long-distance drivers.

9

Monopoly

9.1 Monopoly: The Price Maker

■ What is a monopoly?
■ What are the sources of monopoly power?

WHAT IS A MONOPOLY?

This chapter examines monopolies, a market structure that can be characterized by (1) only one seller of a product, (2) no close substitutes, and (3) barriers to entry that prevent competition. Let's examine these characteristics in greater detail.

Single Seller

monopoly
a market with only one seller of a product that has no close substitute and there are natural and legal barriers to entry that prevent competition

price maker
a monopolistic firm that sets the price of its product so as to maximize its profits

A true or pure **monopoly** exists where there is a market with only one seller of a product that has no close substitute and there are natural or legal barriers to entry that prevent competition. In a monopoly, the firm and "the industry" are one and the same. Consequently, the firm sets the price of the good because the firm faces the industry demand curve and can pick the most profitable point on that demand curve.

A monopolist is a **price maker** (rather than a price taker) that sets the price of its product so as to maximize its profits. Take for example the market for cable television in Canada. Depending on where you live in the country, you can get cable television services from only one provider. Whether that provider is Rogers, Shaw, Cogeco, or EastLink, cable companies are prevented from competing with each other within the same market by the Canadian Radio-television and Telecommunications Commission (CRTC). Therefore, due to their single-seller status in the cable television market, cable companies could be considered monopolists.

Unique (Heterogeneous) Product

Since a true monopolist exists alone, without any competition, the good or service that is produced by the monopolist is without any substitute—the product is unique. For example, while other forms of power generation exist, the vast majority of household products (refrigerator, television, computer, etc.) require electricity to operate. Therefore, it could be said that electricity is a product without a reasonable alternative, that it is a unique source of consumer energy. As a result, local electricity utilities, which are the exclusive providers of this very unique product, could be considered to be monopolists.

Barriers to Entry

If a monopolist is to maintain its exclusive ownership of the manufacturing of a particular product and therefore maintain the product's uniqueness in the marketplace, other producers have to be prevented from entering. Monopolists successfully accomplish this through a variety of barriers to entry. For example, the Liquor Control Board of Ontario (LCBO) is (with few exceptions) the only retailer with a licence to sell distilled spirits in the province on Ontario, although bars and restaurants have liquor licences to re-sell beer, wine, and alcohol. The impact of this provincial regulation is that no other producer can enter the distilled spirits market in Ontario, making the LCBO a monopolist.

Pure Monopolies Are Rare

In discussing the key characteristics of monopolies, various examples have been given to illustrate the existence of these features in the marketplace. However, you should remember that few goods and services are actually produced by monopolies. One might think of a small community with a single bank, a single newspaper, or a single grocery store. Even in these situations, however, most people can bank out of town, use a substitute financial institution, buy out-of-town newspapers or read them on the Web, go to a nearby town to buy groceries, and so on. Near-monopoly conditions exist, but absolute total monopoly is rather unusual.

One area where there is typically only one producer of goods and services within a market area is public utilities. In any given market, usually only one company provides natural gas or supplies water. Moreover, governments themselves provide many services for which they are often the sole providers—sewer services, fire and police protection, and military protection. Most of these situations resemble a pure monopoly. Again, however, for most of the goods and services mentioned above, substitute goods and services are available. People heating their homes with natural gas can switch to electric heat (or vice versa). In some areas, one can even substitute home-collected rainwater or well water for that provided by the local water company.

Although the purist might correctly deny the existence of monopoly, the situations where monopoly conditions are closely approximated are numerous enough to make the study of monopoly more than a theoretical abstraction; moreover, the study of monopoly is useful in clarifying certain desirable aspects of perfect competition.

As the sole retailer licensed to sell distilled spirits in the province of Ontario, the LCBO is an example of a monopolist.

DEBATE

IS THE GRANTING OF A MONOPOLY TO THE 407 ETR CONTROLLERS JUSTIFIABLE?

For:

The electronically operated 407 Express Toll Route (ETR) encircling the Greater Toronto Area (GTA) is a monopoly run by the private sector—and for good reason. Gridlock has a real and significant cost to productivity in the GTA and neither level of government can finance the massive undertaking of developing new highways without involving the private sector. In doing so governments must yield to the market controls of a monopoly—in this case, 407 International Inc. The C. D. Howe Institute estimates that gridlock costs the Toronto economy as much as $11 billion annually.* If governments can't justify the $50 billion necessary to alleviate the problem, perhaps private industry can, but it must be given the opportunity to recapture those costs. Through the monopoly mode, these costs can be recaptured over a reasonable period of time. The development of the Canadian economy has relied on monopolies—consider our railway, telephone, and TV systems. Surely, because the public sector can't afford the costs to develop alternative highways and because the productivity of the GTA requires massive investments in transportation infrastructure, the granting of a monopoly to 407 International Inc. is absolutely justifiable.

*Trevor Melanson, "Gridlock is costing Toronto up to $11 billion yearly—Here's how to fix it," *Canadian Business*, July 11, 2013.

Against:

The development of monopolies allows for unfair pricing for consumers. It also causes inefficiencies, by way of dead-weight losses to an economy. Exorbitant profits are also made and ensure that the rich get richer on the backs of consumers. These profits provide greater producer surplus and less consumer surplus—proof that monopolies benefit producers more than consumers. Governments have recognized the power of some monopolies and have moved to regulate that power. So it seems logical to do away with all monopolies and not allow them to compete in a modern economy. There may be short-term benefits to providing a charter to 407 International Inc., but already there is some concern that over the long term this corporation could benefit multiple times more than consumers would benefit. Monopolies extract higher profits from the market simply because they can. They control access to the market, and consumers who want their products are forced to pay a higher price. Surely 407 International Inc. is simply not a good choice for Toronto-area citizens. Are there other arguments why this monopoly is not good for the GTA economy?

WHAT ARE THE SOURCES OF MONOPOLY POWER?

There are several ways that a monopolist may make it virtually impossible for other firms to overcome barriers to entry. For example, a monopolist might prevent potential rivals from entering the market through legal barriers, through economies of scale, or by controlling important inputs.

Legal Barriers

In the case of legal barriers, the government might franchise only one firm to operate an industry, as is the case for postal services in most countries. The government can also provide licensing designed to ensure a certain level of quality and competence. People in many industries require government licensing, such as medical doctors, nurses, electricians, and plumbers.

Also, the government could give a company a patent to encourage inventive activity. It can cost millions of dollars to develop a new drug or a computer chip and without a patent to recoup some of these costs, there would certainly be less inventive activity. As long as the patent is in effect, the company has the potential to enjoy monopoly profits for many years. After all, why would a firm engage in costly research if any other company could free-ride off its discovery and produce and sell the new drug or computer chip?

Economies of Scale

natural monopoly
a firm that can produce at a lower cost than a number of smaller firms could

The situation in which one large firm can provide the output of the market at a lower cost than two or more smaller firms is called a **natural monopoly.** With a natural monopoly, it is more efficient to have one firm produce the good. The reason for the cost advantage is economies of scale; that is, *ATC* falls as output expands throughout the relevant output range, as seen in Exhibit 1. Public utilities, such as water, natural gas, and electricity, are examples of natural monopoly. It is less costly for one firm to lay down pipes and distribute water than for a number of firms to lay down a maze of competing pipes. That is, a single firm can supply water more efficiently than a large number of competing firms.

Control Over an Important Input

Another barrier to entry could occur if a firm had control over an important input. For example, from the late nineteenth century to the early 1940s, the Aluminum Company of America (Alcoa) had a monopoly in the production of aluminum in the United States. Its monopoly power was guaranteed because of its control over an important ingredient in the production of aluminum—bauxite. However, the ownership of key resources is rarely the source of monopoly power. Many goods are traded internationally, and resources are owned by many different people around the world. It is uncommon that a firm would control the worldwide supply of a resource that did not have a close substitute.

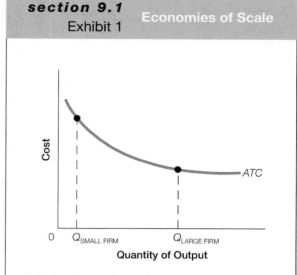

section 9.1
Exhibit 1   Economies of Scale

Exhibit 1 shows a firm that has economies of scale over the relevant range of output with declining average total costs. If one firm can produce the total output at a lower cost than several small firms, it is called a *natural monopoly.*

SECTION CHECK

- A pure monopoly exists where there is only one seller of a product for which no close substitute is available.
- Sources of monopoly power include legal barriers, economies of scale, and control over important inputs.

Demand and Marginal Revenue in Monopoly

- How does the demand curve for a monopolist differ from that of a perfectly competitive firm?
- Why is marginal revenue less than price in a monopoly?
- What is the relationship between the elasticity of demand and total and marginal revenue?

HOW DOES THE DEMAND CURVE FOR A MONOPOLIST DIFFER FROM THAT OF A PERFECTLY COMPETITIVE FIRM?

In monopoly, the market demand curve may be regarded as the demand curve for the firm's product because the monopoly firm *is* the market for that particular product. The demand curve indicates the quantities that the firm can sell at various possible prices. In monopoly, the price for the firm's product declines as additional units are placed on the market—the demand curve is downward sloping. That is, a monopolist can set the price at a desired level and allow consumers to decide how much they will purchase at that price, or alternatively, set production at a desired quantity and allow the market to determine the maximum price it will sell for. Even a monopolist, with its powerful presence in the market, cannot sell a larger quantity at a higher price—the market simply won't allow it. If the monopolist reduces output, the price will rise; if the monopolist expands output, the price will fall.

Recall that in perfect competition, because there are many buyers and sellers of homogeneous goods (resulting in a perfectly elastic demand curve for the firm), competitive firms can sell all they want at the market price. They face a horizontal demand curve. The firm takes the price of its output as determined by the market forces of supply and demand. Monopolists, on the other hand, face a downward-sloping demand curve and if the monopolist wants to expand output, it must accept a lower price. The two demand curves are displayed side by side in Exhibit 1.

WHY IS MARGINAL REVENUE LESS THAN PRICE IN A MONOPOLY?

In Exhibit 2, we see the price of the good, the quantity of the good, the *total revenue* ($TR = P \times Q$), and the *average revenue*, the amount of revenue the firm receives per unit sold ($AR = TR/Q$). The average revenue is just the price per unit sold. We are also given the *marginal revenue*—the amount of revenue the firm receives from selling an additional unit ($MR = \Delta TR/\Delta Q$).

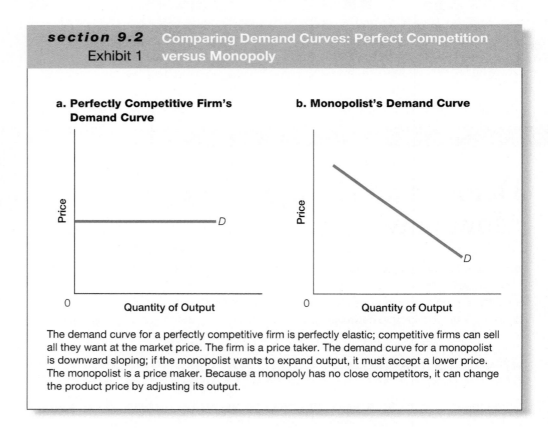

section 9.2   **Comparing Demand Curves: Perfect Competition**
    Exhibit 1   **versus Monopoly**

a. Perfectly Competitive Firm's Demand Curve

Price

0   Quantity of Output   *D*

b. Monopolist's Demand Curve

Price

0   Quantity of Output   *D*

The demand curve for a perfectly competitive firm is perfectly elastic; competitive firms can sell all they want at the market price. The firm is a price taker. The demand curve for a monopolist is downward sloping; if the monopolist wants to expand output, it must accept a lower price. The monopolist is a price maker. Because a monopoly has no close competitors, it can change the product price by adjusting its output.

section 9.2
Exhibit 2 — Total, Marginal, and Average Revenue

Price	Quantity	Total Revenue (TR = P × Q)	Marginal Revenue (MR = ΔTR/ΔQ)	Average Revenue (AR = TR/Q)
$6	0	$0	—	—
5	1	5	$5	$5
4	2	8	3	4
3	3	9	1	3
2	4	8	−1	2
1	5	5	−3	1
0	6	0	−5	0

Taking the information from Exhibit 2, we can create the demand and marginal revenue curves as seen in Exhibit 3. We see that the marginal revenue curve for a monopolist lies below the demand curve. Why is this the case? Suppose the firm initially sets its price at $5. It sells only one unit per day and its total revenue is $5. To increase sales it decides to drop the price to $4. Sales increase to two units per day and total revenue increases to $8 (moving from point A to point B in Exhibit 3). The firm's marginal revenue is only $3. Why? When the firm cuts the price in order to induce the second customer to buy, it now receives only $4 from the first customer even though she is willing to pay $5. That is, because both customers are now paying $4, the company is receiving $4 more from customer two but it is now earning $1 less from customer one. Remember, the first customer was willing to pay $5. So, in order to get revenue from marginal customers, the firm has to lower the price. In Exhibit 3, the marginal revenue of selling a second unit per day is illustrated by point C on the marginal revenue curve.

In order to induce a third daily customer to purchase the good, the firm must cut its price to $3. In doing so, it gains $3 in revenue from the third customer, but it loses $2 in revenue because each of the first two customers are now paying $1 less than previously. The marginal revenue is $1 ($3 − $2), less than the price of the good ($3).

Finally, in order to get a fourth customer, the firm has to cut the price to $2. The firm finds that in doing so, it actually loses revenue, because the new revenue received from the fourth customer ($2) is more than offset by losses in revenues from the first three customers, $3, because each customer pays $1 less than before.

Hence, *the marginal revenue is always less than the price*—that is, the marginal revenue curve will always lie below the demand curve, as shown in Exhibit 3. Recall from Chapter 8 (Perfect Competition) that the firm could sell all it wanted at the market

section 9.2
Exhibit 3 — Demand and Marginal Revenue for the Monopolist

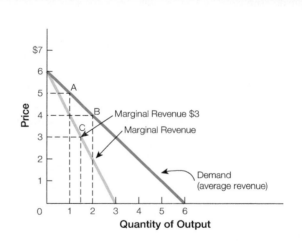

In order to sell more output, the monopolist must accept a lower price on all units sold. This means that the monopolist receives additional revenue from the new unit sold but will receive less revenue on all of the units it was previously selling. Thus, the marginal revenue curve will always lie below the demand curve.

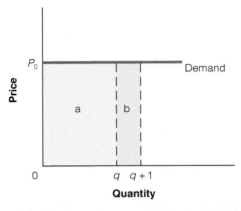

a. Perfectly Competitive Firm's Demand Curve

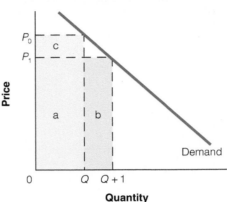

b. Monopolist's Demand Curve

Area b in Exhibit 4(a) represents the marginal revenue from an extra unit of output ($q + 1$) for the firm in perfect competition. The competitive firm's marginal revenue (area b) is equal to the market price. In Exhibit 4(b), we see that the monopolist's marginal revenue from an extra unit ($Q + 1$) is less than the price by area c, because the monopolist must lower its price to sell another unit of output.

price and the price was equal to marginal revenue. However, in monopoly, if the seller wants to expand output, it will have to lower its price on *all* units. This means that the monopolist receives additional revenue from the new unit sold but it will receive less revenue on all of the units it was previously selling. So when the monopolist cuts price to attract new customers, the old customers benefit.

In Exhibit 4, we can compare marginal revenue for the perfectly competitive firm with marginal revenue for the monopolist. The firm in perfect competition can sell another unit of output without lowering its price; hence, the marginal revenue from selling its last unit of output is the market price. However, the monopolist has a downward-sloping demand curve. This means that to sell an extra unit of output, if must lower the price from P_0 to P_1, and the monopolist loses area c in Exhibit 4(b).

It is important to note that although a monopolist can set its price anywhere it wants, it will not set its price as high as possible—be careful not to confuse ability with incentive. As we will see in the next section, some prices along the demand curve will not be profitable for a firm. In other words, profits may be enhanced by either lowering the price or raising it.

WHAT IS THE RELATIONSHIP BETWEEN THE ELASTICITY OF DEMAND AND TOTAL AND MARGINAL REVENUE?

The relationship between the elasticity of demand and total and marginal revenue are shown in Exhibit 5. In Exhibit 5(a), elasticity varies along a linear demand curve. Recall from Chapter 5 that above the midpoint, the demand curve is elastic ($E_D > 1$); below the midpoint, it is inelastic ($E_D < 1$); and at the midpoint, it is unit elastic ($E_D = 1$). How does elasticity relate to total and marginal revenue? In the elastic portion of the curve, when the price falls, total revenue rises in Exhibit 5(b), so that marginal revenue is positive. In the inelastic region of the demand curve, when the price falls, total revenue falls in Exhibit 5(b), so that marginal revenue is negative. At the midpoint of the linear demand curve, the total revenue curve reaches its highest point, as seen in Exhibit 5(b), so that $MR = 0$.

section 9.2   The Relationship between the Elasticity of Demand
Exhibit 5   and Total and Marginal Revenue

a. Demand and Marginal Revenue

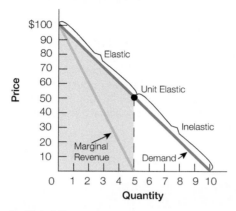

b. Total Revenue

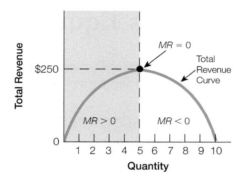

In Exhibit 5(a) we see that along a linear demand curve, the elastic segment lies above the
midpoint, the inelastic segment lies below the midpoint, and at the midpoint the demand is unit
elastic. When demand is elastic, a decline in price will increase total revenue; when demand is
inelastic, a decline in price will lead to a decrease in total revenue. In Exhibit 5(b), we see that
over the range from 0 to 5 units, total revenue is rising, so that marginal revenue is positive. Over
the range from 5 to 10 units, total revenue is falling, so that marginal revenue is negative. At 5
units of output, total revenue is maximized at $250 ($50 × 5), so that marginal revenue is zero.

For example, suppose the price falls on the top half of the demand curve in
Exhibit 5(a) from $90 to $80; total revenue increases from $90 ($90 × 1) to $160
($80 × 2); the marginal revenue is positive at $70. Because a reduction in price leads
to an increase in total revenue, the demand curve is elastic in this region. Now, suppose
the price falls from $20 to $10 on the lower portion of the demand curve; total revenue
falls from $160 ($20 × 8) to $90 ($10 × 9); the marginal revenue is negative at −$70.
Because a reduction in price leads to a decrease in total revenue, the demand curve is
inelastic in this region.

A monopolist will never knowingly operate in the inelastic portion of its demand
curve because increased output will lead to lower total revenue in this region. Not only
are total revenues falling, but total costs will rise as you produce more output. Similarly,
if a monopolist lowered its output, it could increase its total revenue and lower its total
costs (because it costs less to produce fewer units), leading to greater economic profits.

SECTION CHECK

■ The monopolist's demand curve is downward sloping because it is the market demand curve. To produce and sell another unit of output, the firm must lower its price on all units. As a result, the marginal revenue curve lies below the demand curve.

■ The monopolist's marginal revenue will always be less than price because there is a downward-sloping demand curve. In order to sell more output, the monopolist must accept a lower price on all units sold. This means that the monopolist receives additional revenue from the new unit sold but receives less revenue on all of the units it was previously selling.

■ Along the elastic portion of the demand curve, a fall in price leads to an increase in total revenue, making marginal revenue positive. Along the inelastic portion of the demand curve, a fall in price leads to a fall in total revenue, making marginal revenue negative. Therefore, the monopolist will operate in the elastic portion of its demand curve.

section 9.3

The Monopolist's Equilibrium

■ How does the monopolist determine the profit-maximizing output?
■ How do we know if the monopolist is making a profit or a loss?

HOW DOES THE MONOPOLIST DETERMINE THE PROFIT-MAXIMIZING OUTPUT?

In the last section we saw how a monopolist could choose any point along a demand curve. But the monopolist's decision on what level of output to produce depends on more than the marginal revenue derived at various outputs. The firm faces production costs, and the monopolist, like the perfect competitor, will maximize profits at that output where $MR = MC$. This point is demonstrated graphically in Exhibit 1.

As you can see in Exhibit 1, at output level Q_1, the marginal revenue exceeds the marginal cost of that production, so it is profitable for the monopolist to expand output. Profits continue to grow until output Q^* is reached. Beyond that output, say Q_2, the marginal cost of production exceeds the marginal revenue from production, so profits decline. The monopolist should cut production back to Q^*. Therefore, the equilibrium output is Q^*. At this output, marginal costs and marginal revenues are equal.

Four-Step Method for Monopolists

Let's return to the four-step method we introduced in Chapter 8. Determining whether a firm is generating economic profits, economic losses, or zero economic profits at the profit-maximizing level of output, Q^*, can be done in four easy steps.

1. The first step is to find the profit-maximizing level of output (Q^*). To do this, find where marginal revenues equal marginal costs and proceed straight down to the horizontal quantity axis to find the profit-maximizing output level.

2. The second step is to determine the total revenue (TR) being generated at Q^*. To do this, go straight up from Q^* to the demand curve and then to the left to find the market price, P^*. Once you have identified P^* and Q^*, you can find total revenue at the profit-maximizing output level, because $TR = P \times Q$.

3. The third step is to find total costs (*TC*) at *Q**. Again, go straight up from *Q** to the average total cost (*ATC*) curve and then left to the vertical axis to compute the average total cost *per unit*. If we multiply average total costs by the output level, we can find the total costs (*TC = ATC × Q*).

4. The final step is to determine the amount of either profit or loss at *Q**. If total revenue (from step 2) is greater than total costs (from step 3) at *Q**, the firm is generating economic profits. However, if total revenue is less than total costs at *Q**, the firm is generating economic losses.

HOW DO WE KNOW IF THE MONOPOLIST IS MAKING A PROFIT OR A LOSS?

Exhibit 1 does not show what profits, if any, the monopolist is actually making. This is rectified in Exhibit 2, which shows the equilibrium position of a monopolist, this time adding an average total cost (*ATC*) curve. As we just discussed, the firm produces where *MC = MR*, or 100 units of output. At 100 units of output, the demand curve gives us a price of $6 per unit. The firm's total revenue is *P × Q* ($6 × 100), or $600. The firm's total cost is *ATC × Q* ($4 × 100), or $400. Thus, the firm has a total profit of $200.

In perfect competition, profits in an economic sense will persist only in the short run, because in the long run, new firms will enter the industry, increasing industry supply and thus driving down the price of the good. With this, profits are eliminated. In monopoly, however, profits are not eliminated because one of the conditions for monopoly is that barriers to entry exist. Other firms cannot enter, so economic profits persist in the long run.

Losses for a Monopolist

It is easy to imagine a monopolist ripping off consumers by charging prices resulting in long-run economic profits. However, there are also many companies with monopoly power that have gone out of business. Imagine that you received a patent on a bad idea like a roof ejection seat for a helicopter, or that you had the sole rights to turn an economics textbook into a screenplay for a motion picture. Although you may be the sole supplier of a product, that does not guarantee that consumers will demand your product. There may be no close substitute for your product, but there is always competition for the consumer dollar—other goods may provide greater satisfaction.

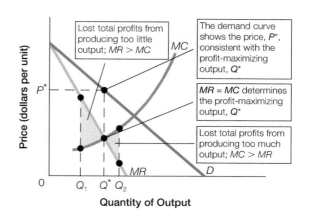

section 9.3 **Equilibrium Output and Price**
Exhibit 1 **for a Pure Monopolist**

The monopolist maximizes profits at that quantity where *MR = MC*, at *Q**. At *Q** the monopolist finds *P** by extending a vertical line up to the demand curve and over to the vertical axis to find the price. Rather than charging a price equal to marginal cost or marginal revenue at their intersection, however, the monopolist charges the price that customers are willing to pay for that quantity as indicated on the demand curve at *P**. At *Q₁*, *MR > MC* and the firm should expand output. At *Q₂*, *MC > MR* and the firm should cut back its production.

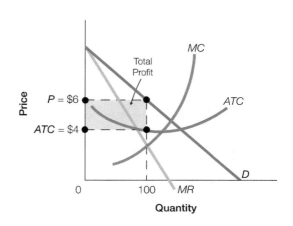

section 9.3
Exhibit 2 **A Monopolist's Profits**

The intersection of *MR* and *MC* determines the profit-maximizing level of output. The demand curve shows the price that can be charged. Total profit is total revenue minus total cost ($600 − 400), or $200.

section 9.3
Exhibit 3   **A Monopolist's Losses**

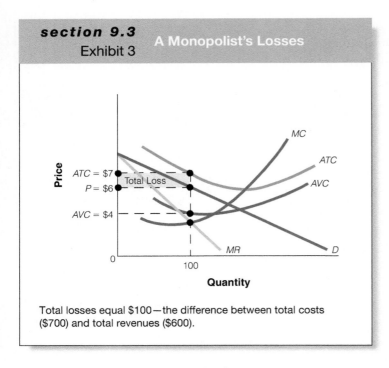

Total losses equal $100—the difference between total costs ($700) and total revenues ($600).

Exhibit 3 illustrates loss in a monopoly situation. In this graph, notice that the demand curve is well below the average total cost curve. In this case, the monopolist will incur a loss because there is insufficient demand to cover average total costs at any price and output combination along the demand curve. Total revenue is $600 ($P \times Q = \$6 \times 100$) and total cost is $700 ($ATC \times Q = \$7 \times 100$), for an economic loss of $100. Notice that the total revenue is great enough to cover the total variable costs of $400 ($TVC = \$4 \times 100$). Thus, the firm can reduce its losses by operating rather than shutting down in the short run. However, in monopoly as in perfect competition, a firm will go out of business in the long run if it cannot generate enough revenue to cover its total costs.

In summary, if total revenue is greater than total costs at Q^*, the firm is generating total economic profits. And if total revenue is less than total costs at Q^*, the firm is generating total economic losses. If total revenue is equal to total costs at Q^*, the firm is earning zero economic profits. Remember, the cost curves include implicit and explicit costs—so in this case, we are covering the total opportunity costs of our resources and are earning a normal profit or rate of return.

Patents

One form of monopoly power conferred by governments is provided by patents and copyrights. A patent puts the government's police power behind the patent holder's exclusive right to make a product for a period of time (in Canada, the period of time is 20 years) without anyone else being able to make an identical product. As Exhibit 4 suggests, this gives the supplier at least temporary monopoly power over that good or service. This allows the firm with the patent to price its product well above marginal costs, at P_M. Notice the marginal cost curve is flat. The reason for this is that most of the cost of drugs, for example, is in the development stage. Once the drug is available for the market, the marginal costs are close to constant—flat. When patents expire, the price of the patented good or service usually falls substantially with the entry of competing firms. The price will fall toward the perfectly competitive price P_{PC} and the output will increase toward $Q_{NO\ PATENT}$.

Why does the government give inventors this limited monopoly power, raising the prices of pharmaceutical drugs and other "vital" goods? The rationale is simple. Without patents, inventors would have little incentive to incur millions of dollars in research and development expenses to create new products (e.g., life-saving drugs) if others could

section 9.3
Exhibit 4   **Impact of Patent Protection on Equilibrium Price and Quality**

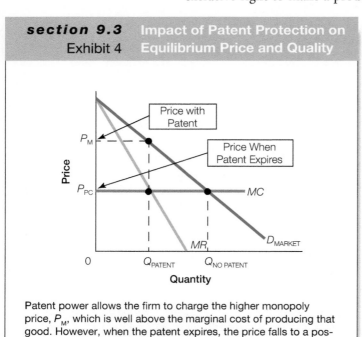

Patent power allows the firm to charge the higher monopoly price, P_M, which is well above the marginal cost of producing that good. However, when the patent expires, the price falls to a position closer to the perfectly competitive price, P_{PC}.

Without patents, would some life-saving drugs have been invented? Some drugs cost millions of dollars in research. Without the protection of a patent, the firm may not have been able to make profits from its inventive activity for very long, which is why the government issues patents that last up to 20 years. However, after the patent expires, many popular drugs soon lose their protection. In most cases, less costly generic drugs hit the market soon after the patent expiration and prices then move closer to the competitive price, although perhaps not all the way to the competitive level, as some companies are able to keep customers through brand loyalty. Pfizer lost its Canadian patent on Viagra in November 2012.

immediately copy the idea and manufacture the products without incurring the research expenses. Similarly, copyrights stimulate creative activity of other kinds, giving writers the incentive to write books that earn royalties and are not merely copied freely. Just as the enormous number of computer programs written for home computers reflects the fact that program writers receive royalties from the sale of each copy sold; that is why they and the firms they work for vehemently oppose unauthorized copying of their work.

SECTION CHECK

- The monopolist, like the perfect competitor, maximizes profits at that output where marginal revenue equals marginal cost. Price is set according to the demand for the product at the profit-maximizing output.
- Monopoly profits can be found by comparing price per unit and average total cost at Q^*. If $P > ATC$, there are economic profits. If $P < ATC$, there are economic losses.

section
9.4

Monopoly and Welfare Loss

- Does monopoly promote inefficiency?
- Does monopoly hinder innovation?

DOES MONOPOLY PROMOTE INEFFICIENCY?

Monopoly is often considered to be bad. But what is the basis in economic theory for concerns about the establishment of monopoly power? There are two main objections to monopoly. First, on equity grounds, many people feel that it is not "fair" for monopoly owners to have persistent economic profits when they do not work harder than other firms. However, to most economists, the more serious objection is that monopolies result in market inefficiencies. That is, monopoly leads to a lower output and to higher

section 9.4   Perfect Competition versus
Exhibit 1   Monopoly

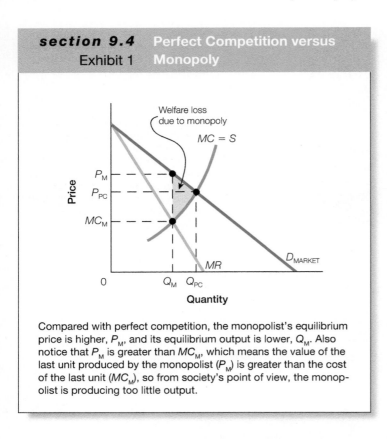

Compared with perfect competition, the monopolist's equilibrium price is higher, P_M, and its equilibrium output is lower, Q_M. Also notice that P_M is greater than MC_M, which means the value of the last unit produced by the monopolist (P_M) is greater than the cost of the last unit (MC_M), so from society's point of view, the monopolist is producing too little output.

prices than would exist under perfect competition. To demonstrate why this is so, see Exhibit 1. In monopoly, the firm produces output Q_M and charges a price of P_M. Suppose, however, that we had perfect competition and that the industry was characterized by many small firms that could produce output with the same efficiency (at the same cost) as one large firm. Then the marginal cost curve shown in Exhibit 1 could be the sum of the individual marginal cost curves of the individual firms, and the upward portion of that curve might be considered the industry supply curve.

Equilibrium price and quantity with perfect competition would be determined where the marginal cost (or supply) curve intersects with the demand curve, at output Q_{PC} and price P_{PC}. Thus, the competitive equilibrium solution provides for more output and lower prices than the solution prevailing in monopoly. This provides the major efficiency objection to monopoly: Monopolists charge higher prices and produce less output. This may also be viewed as "unfair," in that consumers are burdened more than under the alternative competitive arrangement.

Welfare Loss in Monopoly

In addition to the monopolist producing lower levels of output at higher prices, notice that the monopolist produces at an output where the price (P_M) is greater than the marginal cost (MC_M). Because $P > MC$, it means that the value to society from the last unit produced is greater than the cost of the last unit (MC_M). That is, the monopoly is *not* producing enough of the good from society's perspective. We call the shaded area in Exhibit 1 the *welfare loss,* or *deadweight loss, due to monopoly.*

The actual amount of the deadweight loss in monopoly is of considerable debate among economists. Estimates across nations vary between one-tenth of 1 percent and 6 percent of national income. The variation depends on the researchers' estimates of elasticity of demand, whether firm or industry data were used, whether adjustments for profits were made (for the inclusion of royalties and intangibles), and last, whether the researcher included some proxy for scarce resources used in attempting to create a monopoly.

DOES MONOPOLY HINDER INNOVATION?

Another argument against monopoly is that a lack of competition tends to hinder technological advancement. Monopolists become comfortable, reaping their monopolistic profits, so they do not work hard at product improvement, technical advances designed to promote efficiency, and so forth. The railroad industry is sometimes cited as an example of this situation. Early in the last century, railroads had a strong amount of monopoly power, but they did not spend much on research or development; they did not aggressively try to improve rail transport. As a consequence, technical advances in other transport modes—like cars, trucks, and airplanes—led to a loss of monopoly power, as transportation substitutes came into existence.

However, the notion that monopoly hinders all innovation can be disputed. Many near-monopolists are, in fact, important innovators. Companies like Microsoft, IBM,

Google, and Apple have all, at one time or another, had very strong market positions, in some instances approaching monopoly secured by patent protection, but they were also important innovators. Indeed, innovation helps firms initially obtain a degree of monopoly status, as patents can give a monopoly of new products and/or cost-saving technology. Even the monopolist wants more profits, and any innovation that lowers costs or expands revenues creates profits for the monopolist. In addition, because patents expire, a monopolist may be expected to innovate in order to obtain additional patents and preserve its monopoly power. Therefore, the incentive to innovate may well exist in monopolistic market structures.

Business *CONNECTION*

DEREGULATION + PRIVATIZATION = A BETTER ECONOMY

Few businesses operate as monopolies, but it's helpful to understand the motivation and behaviour of companies operating in this extreme market structure.

All businesses, including monopolies, face two major decisions: (1) what price to charge and (2) how many units of goods or services to produce in order to maximize profits. Firms operating in perfect competition decide the level of production, but monopolies can choose both price and production levels. Monopolies always produce less than the market desires, which creates their own market shortage, so they can charge higher prices at all production levels. There is, in fact, a casual disregard for the needs of society or the community unless, of course, regulations demand otherwise.

Demand begins with those who are willing and able to buy, which determines the shape of the industry demand curve. So changes in buyers' tastes, expectations, or income influence shifts of the demand curve. If the monopolist is in the business of providing a good or service that is considered to be a necessity or a near-necessity, the effect of a shift in the demand curve is quite muted. Even though consumers have limited power in a monopoly market, they still hold the ultimate power: whether or not to buy. While having the ability to charge more that the market wants to pay helps to make monopolists profitable, they must also deal with higher costs—because they have to convince buyers of the value of paying the higher price. In essence, they are competing on anything but price—product, place, or promotion—in convincing buyers.

Like any other business, the monopoly has a cost curve that reflects the aggregate and average of the costs of its inputs. But, unlike a business operating in a competitive market structure, monopolists pay less attention to costs and more to getting the highest price they can charge. This lack of motivation to keep costs down leads to serious inefficiencies in the operation of most monopolies and eventually to inefficiencies in the economy. The net effect results in fewer prospective customers getting products or services at reasonable rates, which reflects monopolies' less-than-efficient production methods and processes.

Those who would like to compete with monopolies will argue about monopolies' inefficient cost structure, poor use of available resources, and general disservice to society. The fewer products sold (even at higher prices) has an impact on the numbers of people employed, which affects unemployment rates and tax revenues for governments. When monopolists benefit in excess and to a point that harms society and governments, deregulation and/or privatization can be used to adjust the market balance. Such adjustments do away with or pull apart special privileges that the monopolists have enjoyed, and other businesses are encouraged to compete in the market by offering the same or similar services.

Successful deregulation and privatization of industries leads to more competition, greater industry output, and lower prices. This is good for consumers, for other producers, and for governments in meeting society's needs. Increased innovation is another important result—it leads to many new suppliers and subcontractors hoping to compete in providing better products and processes in revitalized industries. Control of aggressive monopolies can lead to measured growth for all sectors of the economy.

1. Firms such as Microsoft have evolved into natural monopolies. Do you think governments are justified in breaking those monopolies as they have done in the eurozone, or do you think successful companies should be left alone?

2. Imagine yourself as a CEO of a large monopoly and your management has increased market prices to increase profits. Do you think your managers have made a good decision? What further decisions do you think the managers have to make to ensure that your profits grow?

3. Some monopolies have established "company towns," often in remote locations where they are the primary and largest employer. What are the benefits and challenges of the company in operating there? What are the benefits and challenges to the citizens of one of these towns?

SECTION CHECK

■ Monopoly results in smaller output and a higher price than would be the case under perfect competition. Since the monopolist produces at an output where $P > MC$, the value to society of the last unit produced is greater than its cost. In other words, the monopoly is not producing enough output from society's standpoint.

■ Monopoly may lead to greater concentration of economic power and could hinder innovation.

section 9.5

Monopoly Policy

■ What is the objective of anti-combine laws?
■ What is government regulation?
■ What is marginal cost pricing?
■ What is average cost pricing?

Because monopolies pose certain problems with respect to efficiency, equity, and power, the public, through its governments, must decide how to deal with the monopoly phenomenon. Two major approaches to dealing with the monopoly problem are commonly used: anti-combine laws and government regulation. It should be pointed out that in these discussions, the word "monopoly" is sometimes used in a loose, general sense to refer to imperfectly competitive markets, not just to "pure" monopoly.

WHAT IS THE OBJECTIVE OF ANTI-COMBINE LAWS?

The rationale for anti-combine laws is to prevent monopoly, to promote competition, and to enhance economic efficiency. Canada's first anti-combine statute was passed in 1889. Around that time, monopolistic behaviour arose in a number of industries such as twine, sugar, and flour.

Today, Canada's anti-combine laws are covered by the Competition Act of 1986. The act covers business practices that unduly prevent or lessen competition, and it differentiates between criminal and civil offences. Criminal offences are handled by the courts and the standard of evidence is "beyond a reasonable doubt." Penalties range from fines to possible imprisonment of guilty executives.

Criminal offences include conspiracy to fix prices, bid-rigging, and predatory pricing. Bid-rigging occurs when firms that bid on contracts arrange among themselves who will win each contract and at what price. Predatory pricing occurs when a firm temporarily reduces the price of its product below the product's average cost in order to drive the firm's competition out of business.

The federal Competition Bureau is responsible for the administration and enforcement of the Competition Act and other acts. The Bureau investigates complaints and decides whether to proceed with the filing of an application to the Competition Tribunal to hear a complaint. The Tribunal is a strictly adjudicative body that operates independently of any government department. The cases it hears are complex and deal with matters such as mergers (the combining of two organizations into one), misleading advertising, and restrictive trade practices.

If a merger would significantly reduce competition in an industry, the Competition Bureau has the power to stop the merger. On the other hand, if a merger would increase efficiency in an industry and consumers would benefit from the resulting lower prices, it could allow the merger. Abuse of a dominant market position occurs when a firm that controls most of the sales in a market uses its dominant position to engage in anti-competitive behaviour.

A number of high-profile cases have come under the Competition Act. For example, in 2004, an extensive review of the proposed merger between Cineplex Galaxy and Famous Players was conducted by the Competition Bureau. It came to the conclusion that such a merger would result in a substantial lessening of competition of first-run motion pictures in a number of urban areas. As a result of these concerns, Cineplex Galaxy was required to divest itself of theatres in all the affected areas.

In September 2010, the Competition Bureau reached an agreement with The Coca-Cola Company regarding the acquisition of the North American business of its primary bottler, Coca-Cola Enterprises Inc. The Bureau concluded that the proposed acquisition likely would have lessened and/or prevented competition substantially in the supply of soft drinks in Canada. To satisfy the Competition Bureau's concerns, The Coca-Cola Company agreed to certain restrictions regarding commercially sensitive information and access to relevant personnel, with the Bureau appointing an independent monitor to ensure compliance.

In March 2013, the Competition Bureau reached an agreement with BCE Inc. (Bell) regarding Bell's proposed acquisition of Astral Media Inc. Following an extensive review involving both parties and many third parties, the Bureau concluded that Bell's acquisition of Astral's pay and specialty television channels would have likely resulted in higher prices, less innovation, and reduced choice in television programming. The Bureau therefore required Bell to divest itself of Astral's ownership interests in a number of areas. According to the Bureau, the resulting agreement was necessary to preserve competition in the supply of English and French pay and specialty television programming services in Canada.

WHAT IS GOVERNMENT REGULATION?

Government regulation is an alternative approach to dealing with monopolies. Under regulation, a company would not be allowed to charge any price it wants. Suppose the government does not want to break up a natural monopoly in the water or the power industry. Remember that natural monopolies occur when one large firm can produce as much output as many smaller firms but at a lower average cost per unit. The government may decide to regulate the monopoly price, but what price does it let the firm charge? The goal is to achieve the efficiency of large-scale production without permitting the high monopoly prices and low output that can promote allocative *inefficiency*.

The basic policy dilemma that regulators often face in attempting to fix maximum prices can be rather easily illustrated. Consider Exhibit 1. Without regulation, say the profit-maximizing monopolist operates at point A, at output Q_M, and price P_M. At that output, the price exceeds the average total cost, so economic profits exist. However, the monopolist is producing relatively little output and is charging a relatively high price, and it is producing at a point where price is above marginal cost. This is not the best point from society's perspective.

section 9.5
Exhibit 1   Marginal Cost Pricing versus Average Cost Pricing

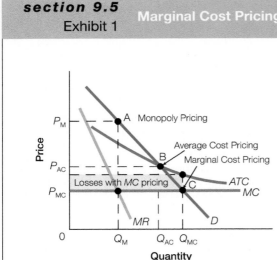

The marginal cost (*MC*) curve is less than the average total cost curve (*ATC*) for a natural monopolist as the average cost falls. If the monopolist is unregulated, it could produce a relatively small level of output, Q_M, at a relatively high price, P_M. If regulators require the natural monopolist to use marginal cost pricing, the monopoly will lose money, because P_{MC} is less than average total costs. Average cost pricing (at point B) would permit firms to make a normal rate of return, where $P_{AC} = ATC$. The monopolist's unregulated output at point A is not optimal from society's standpoint, and the optimal output at point C is not feasible.

WHAT IS MARGINAL COST PRICING?

From society's point of view, what would be the best price and output position? As we discussed in Chapter 8, the best position is at the competitive equilibrium output where $P = MC$, because the equilibrium price represents the marginal value of output. The marginal cost represents society's opportunity costs in making the good as opposed to something else. Where price equals marginal cost, *allocative efficiency* is achieved; that is, society matches marginal value and marginal cost. This is seen at point C in Exhibit 1. The decision to set production where the price of a good equals marginal cost is referred to as **marginal cost pricing.**

marginal cost pricing
the decision to set production where the price of a good equals marginal cost

Operation of the Regulated Monopolist

Unfortunately, the natural monopoly cannot operate profitably at the allocative efficient point, where $P = MC$, indicated at point C in Exhibit 1. At point C, the intersection of the demand and marginal cost curves, average total costs are greater than price. The optimal output, then, is an output that produces losses for the producer. Any regulated business that produced for long at this "optimal" output would go bankrupt; it would be impossible to attract new capital to the industry.

Therefore, the "optimal" output from a welfare perspective really is not viable because losses are incurred. The regulators cannot force firms to price their product at P_{MC} and to sell Q_{MC} output because the firm would go out of business. Indeed, in the long run, the industry's capital would deteriorate as investors failed to replace old capital when it became worn out or obsolete. If the monopolist's unregulated output at point A is not optimal from society's standpoint, and the short-run optimal output at point C is not feasible from the monopolist's standpoint, where should the regulated monopolist be allowed to operate?

One option to solving the problem is that the government could subsidize the losses associated with marginal cost pricing. However, the burden will ultimately fall on the taxpayers, as the government will have to raise the money to pay for the losses.

WHAT IS AVERAGE COST PRICING?

A compromise between monopoly pricing and marginal cost pricing is found at point B in Exhibit 1, output Q_{AC}, which is somewhere between the excessively low output and high prices of an unregulated monopoly and the excessively large output and low prices achieved when prices are equated with marginal cost pricing. At point B, price equals average total costs, a compromise called **average cost pricing.** The monopolist is permitted to price the product where economic profits are zero, meaning that there is a normal economic profit or rate of return, like firms experience in perfect competition in the long run.

In the real world, regulators often permit utilities to receive a "fair and reasonable" return that is a rough approximation to that suggested by average cost pricing, at point B. Point B would seem "fair" in that the monopolist is receiving rewards equal to those that a perfect competitor would ordinarily receive—no more and no less. Point B permits more output at a significantly lower price than would occur if the monopolist was unregulated, point A, even though output is still somewhat less and price somewhat more than that suggested by point C, the social optimum or best position.

average cost pricing
production where the price of a good equals average total cost

Difficulties in Average Cost Pricing

Accurate Calculations of Costs   The actual implementation of a rate (price) that permits a "fair and reasonable" return is more difficult than the analysis suggests. The calculations of costs and values are difficult. In reality, the firm may not know exactly what its demand and cost curves look like. This forces regulatory agencies to use profits, another somewhat ambiguous target, as a guide. If profits are "too high," lower the price, and if profits are "too low," raise the price.

No Incentives to Keep Costs Down   Another problem is that average cost pricing gives the monopolists no incentive to reduce costs. That is, if the firm's costs rise from ATC_0 to ATC_1 in Exhibit 2, the price will rise from P_0 to P_1. And if costs fall, the firm's price will fall. In either scenario, the firm will still be earning a normal rate of return. This is equivalent to saying that if the regulatory agency sets the price at any point where the ATC curve intersects the demand curve, the firm will earn a normal rate of return. So if the agency is going to set the price wherever ATC intersects the demand curve, why not let your average costs rise? Let your employees fly first class and dine in the finest restaurants. While you are at it, why not buy concert tickets and season tickets to sporting events? And if the regulated monopolist knows that the regulators will reduce prices if costs fall, the regulated monopolist does not benefit from lower costs. Regulators have tackled this problem by allowing the regulated firm to keep some of the profits that come from lower costs; that is, they do not adhere strictly to average cost pricing.

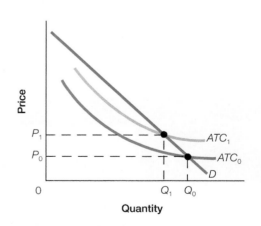

section 9.5
Exhibit 2   **Changes in Average Costs**

An increase in average total costs leads to a higher price and lower output (P_1Q_1); lower average total costs lead to a lower price and greater output (P_0Q_0). However, both situations lead to a normal rate of return. Because the regulated firm has little incentive to minimize costs, average total costs would have a tendency to rise.

Special Interest Groups   In the real world, consumer groups are constantly battling for lower rates, while the utilities themselves are lobbying for higher rates so that they can approach the monopoly profits indicated by point A in Exhibit 1. Decisions are not always made in a calm, objective, dispassionate atmosphere, free of outside involvement. It is precisely the political economy of rate setting that disturbs some critics of this approach to dealing with the monopoly problem. For example, it is possible that a rate-making commissioner could become friendly with a utility company, believing that he can obtain a nice job after his tenure as a regulator is over. The temptation is great for the commissioner to be generous to the utilities. On the other hand, there may be a tendency for regulators to bow to pressure from consumer groups. A politician who wants to win votes can almost always succeed by attacking utility rates and promising rate "reform" (lower rates). If zealous rate regulators listen too closely to the consumer groups and push rates down to a level indicated by point C in Exhibit 1, the industry might be too unstable to attract capital for expansion.

A review of government behaviour in this case would reveal a trend away from regulation toward competition; for example, between 1980 and 1997, the federal government fully deregulated the telecommunications industry, ending Bell Canada's monopoly. Similar instances of deregulation have also occurred in the transportation industry and natural gas market. Technological advances now allow us to separate the production of electric power and natural gas from the distributor, which will ultimately lead to greater competition in these markets.

SECTION CHECK

- Anti-combine laws are designed to reduce the abuses of monopoly power and push production closer to the social optimum.
- Privately owned monopolies may be allowed to operate but under regulation of a government agency.
- Marginal cost pricing sets price equal to marginal cost, where demand intersects marginal cost. This regulation achieves allocative efficiency.
- Average cost pricing sets price equal to average total cost, where the demand curve intersects average total costs.

section
9.6 Price Discrimination

- What is price discrimination?
- Why does price discrimination exist?

price discrimination

the practice of charging different consumers different prices for the same good or service when the cost of providing that good or service is not different for different consumers

WHAT IS PRICE DISCRIMINATION?

Price discrimination is the practice of charging different customers different prices for the same good or service when the cost of providing that good or service does not differ among the customers. For example, kids pay less for the movies than adults; senior citizens get discounts on hotels, restaurants, museums, and zoos; and most vacation travellers fly between places for less than business travellers. Under certain conditions, the monopolist finds it profitable to discriminate among various buyers, charging higher prices to those who are more willing to pay and lower prices to those who are less willing to pay.

Conditions for Price Discrimination

The ability to practise price discrimination is not available to all sellers. In order to practise price discrimination, the following three conditions must hold:

Monopoly Power. Price discrimination is possible only with monopoly or where members of a small group of firms (firms that are not price takers) follow identical pricing policies. When there is a large number of competing firms, discrimination is less likely because competitors tend to undercut the high prices charged by the firms that are engaging in price discrimination.

Market Segregation. Price discrimination can occur only if the demand curves for markets, groups, or individuals are different. If the demand curves are not different, a profit-maximizing monopolist would charge the same price in both markets. In short, price discrimination requires the ability to separate customers according to their willingness to pay.

No Resale. For price discrimination to work, the person buying at a discount must have difficulty in reselling the product to customers being charged more. Otherwise, those getting the items cheaply would want to buy extra amounts of the product at the discounted price and sell it at a profit to others. Price differentials between groups erode if reselling is easy.

WHY DOES PRICE DISCRIMINATION EXIST?

Price discrimination results from the profit-maximization motive. In our graphical analysis of monopoly, we suggested that there was a demand curve for the product and a corresponding marginal revenue curve. Sometimes, however, different groups of people have different demand curves and therefore react differently to price changes. A seller can make more money by charging those different buyers different prices. For example, if the price of a movie is increased from $7 to $10, many kids who would attend at $7 may have to stay home at $10, as they (and perhaps their parents) balk at paying the higher price. The impact on attendance of raising prices may be less, however, for adults, for whom the ticket price may represent a smaller part of the expenses of an evening out.

Thus, there is a different demand curve for those, say, under 16, as opposed to those who are older. Specifically, the elasticity of demand with respect to price is greater for children than for adults. This means that there is a different marginal revenue curve for children than for adults. Assume, for simplicity, that the marginal cost is constant. The profit-maximizing movie-theatre owner will price where the constant marginal costs equal marginal revenue for each group. As you can see in Exhibit 1(a), the demand curve for kids is rather elastic. The adult demand curve, shown in Exhibit 1(b), is more downward sloping at any given price and quantity (relatively inelastic), meaning the marginal revenue curve lies well below the demand curve at most output levels. Thus, the price charged adults is far above the point where marginal revenue equals marginal costs, whereas for kids, the price is not as much above the point where marginal revenue equals marginal costs.

Examples of Price Discrimination

There are other examples of price discrimination in Canada. The following are just a few.

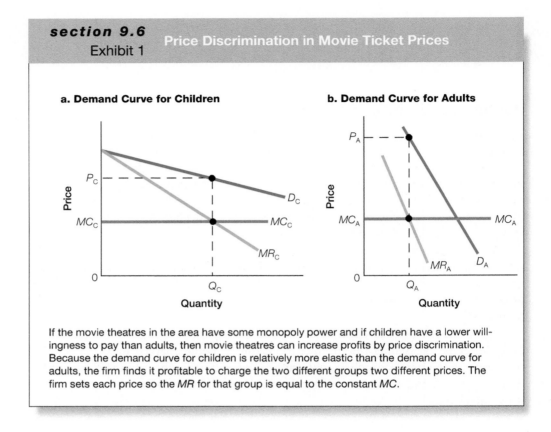

section 9.6
Exhibit 1   Price Discrimination in Movie Ticket Prices

a. Demand Curve for Children

b. Demand Curve for Adults

If the movie theatres in the area have some monopoly power and if children have a lower willingness to pay than adults, then movie theatres can increase profits by price discrimination. Because the demand curve for children is relatively more elastic than the demand curve for adults, the firm finds it profitable to charge the two different groups two different prices. The firm sets each price so the *MR* for that group is equal to the constant *MC*.

Airline Tickets   Seats on airplanes usually go for different prices. There are the high-prices, no-strings-attached fares and there are restricted fares—tickets that require Saturday-night layovers or must be purchased weeks in advance. This airline pricing strategy allows the airlines to discriminate against business travellers, who usually have little advance warning, travel on weekdays, and are not as willing to spend their weekends away from home and family. Because business travellers have a high willingness to pay (a relatively inelastic demand curve), airlines can charge them higher prices. If airlines were to cut prices for these clients, their revenues would fall. On the other hand, the personal traveller (perhaps a vacationer) can choose among many substitutes, such as other modes of transportation and different times. In short, the personal traveller has a lower willingness to pay (a relatively elastic demand curve). Thus, the airlines can clearly make more money by charging a higher price to those who have a higher willingness to pay (less elastic demand) and a lower price to those who have a lower willingness to pay (more elastic demand)—those who are willing to book in advance and stay over on Saturday nights. If airlines charged a higher single price to everyone, those with a lower willingness to pay would not travel; if they charged a lower single price to everyone, they would lose profits by receiving less revenue from those who are willing to pay more.

High-Speed Internet   The key to price discrimination is observing the difference in demand curves for different customers. The business customer, who considers high-speed Internet an essential component of running a business, will probably have a relatively less elastic demand curve than, say, a personal customer who uses the Internet for social networking and entertainment. Consequently, telecommunication providers charge a higher price to business customers, who have a higher willingness to pay (less elastic demand)—and a lower price to those who access the Internet only for personal use (more elastic demand).

Quantity Discounts

Another form of price discrimination occurs when customers buy in large quantities. This is often the case with public utilities and wholesalers, but even stores will sell a six-pack of soft drinks for less than six single cans. Or the local bagel shop might sell you a baker's dozen, where you may get 13 bagels for the price of 12. This type of price discrimination allows the producer to charge a higher price for the first unit than for, say, the twentieth unit. This form of price discrimination is effective because a buyer's willingness to pay declines as additional units are purchased.

SECTION CHECK

- When producers charge different prices for the same good or service when no cost differences exist, it is called *price discrimination*.
- Price discrimination is a result of the profit-maximization motive. If different groups have different demand curves for a good or service, a seller can make more money by charging these different buyers different prices.

For Your Review

Section 9.1

1. Which of the following could be considered a monopoly?
   a. Kate Hudson (an actress)
   b. BC Hydro
   c. the only doctor in a small town
   d. Ford Motor Company

2. Barriers to entry are important in the creation of monopolies because they keep competitors out of the industry. Although many types of barriers exist, historically, ownership of an essential resource, government patents and licences, and large entry costs have served as the primary barriers to entry. For each of the following cases, indicate which type of barrier created the monopoly.
   a. In the 1940s, the Aluminum Company of America owned all of the world's known bauxite deposits.
   b. A local cable TV company had the only government-issued licence to supply services in the area.
   c. The pharmaceutical company, MAXCO, invented and patented a new hair-growth drug.
   d. In the 1960s, Bell Canada provided long-distance telephone service by stringing millions of kilometres of copper wiring across Canada.

3. Evaluate the following statement regarding monopoly behaviour: "Since a monopoly firm is a *price maker*, it can charge whatever price it wants for whatever quantity it wants to sell."

4. Is it optimal for a monopolist to operate on the inelastic portion of the demand curve? Why or why not?

Section 9.2

5. Fill in the missing data for a monopolist in the following table.

Quantity	Price	Total Revenue	Marginal Revenue	Demand Elastic or Inelastic
1	$11			
2	10			
3	9			
4	8			
5	7			
6	6			
7	5			
8	4			
9	3			
10	2			
11	1			

6. Assume that the monopolist in problem 5 had fixed costs of $10 and a constant marginal cost of $4 per unit. In the following table, insert the relevant data in the columns for total cost, marginal cost, and profit.

Quantity	Price	Total Revenue	Marginal Revenue	Demand Elastic or Inelastic	Total Cost	Marginal Cost	Profit
1	$11						
2	10						
3	9						
4	8						
5	7						
6	6						
7	5						
8	4						
9	3						
10	2						
11	1						

7. Suppose Star Phone Company served remote northern Ontario as a government-authorized natural monopoly. The following table describes a portion of the demand curve for long-distance service facing Star Phone Company.

a. Complete the table.

Star Phone Company Demand for Phone Hours				
Quantity	Price	Total Revenue	Marginal Revenue	Elastic or Inelastic?
30	$3.65			
31	3.58			
32	3.51			
33	3.44			
34	3.37			
35	3.30			
36	3.22			
37	3.14			
38	3.06			
39	2.98			
40	2.90			
41	2.82			
42	2.74			
43	2.66			
44	2.58			
45	2.50			
46	2.42			
47	2.34			
48	2.25			
49	2.15			
50	2.04			

b. How does the company's marginal revenue change as the price changes? What is the relationship between marginal revenue and price?

c. At what price does demand become inelastic?

d. What will happen to the elasticity of demand when a new company, NorOnt Phones, starts a competing wireless phone company?

8. The following table shows the demand for water and cost conditions for the New South Springdale Water Utility, a pure monopoly.

a. Complete the table.

Quantity (litres)	Price (per litre)	Total Revenue	Marginal Revenue	Marginal Costs	Average Total Costs	Profit
100	$1.28			$0.15	$1.252	
101	1.27			0.18	1.241	
102	1.26			0.21	1.231	
103	1.25			0.23	1.221	
104	1.24			0.26	1.212	

b. What is true about the relationship between marginal revenue and marginal costs when profit is the greatest?

c. Suppose the government imposed a tax of $103 on the firm that the firm had to pay even if it went out of business. What would be the profit-maximizing level of output? What would happen to profits? Would the firm stay in business?

9. Using the concepts of total revenue and marginal revenue, show why marginal revenue is less than price in a monopoly situation. Suppose a monopolist wants to expand output from one unit to two units. In order to sell two units rather than one, the monopolist must lower its price from $10 to $8—see the table below. Will the marginal revenue be less than the price?

Price	Quantity	Total Revenue	Marginal Revenue
$10	1	$10	
8	2	16	$6
6	3	18	2

Blueprint Problem

Suppose the following table describes revenue and cost of production figures for the monopoly firm Carl's Calculators.

Output	Price	TVC	TFC	TC	AVC	AFC	ATC	MC
0	45	$0.00	$40.00	$40.00	—	—	—	—
1	40	$10.00	$40.00	$50.00	$10.00	$40.00	$50.00	$10.00
2	35	$16.00	$40.00	$56.00	$8.00	$20.00	$28.00	$6.00
3	30	$20.00	$40.00	$60.00	$6.67	$13.33	$20.00	$4.00
4	25	$29.00	$40.00	$69.00	$7.25	$10.00	$17.25	$9.00
5	20	$44.00	$40.00	$84.00	$8.80	$8.00	$16.80	$15.00
6	15	$66.00	$40.00	$106.00	$11.00	$6.67	$17.67	$22.00
7	10	$104.00	$40.00	$144.00	$14.86	$5.71	$20.57	$38.00

a. Determine Carl's profit-maximizing output using the total approach.

b. Determine Carl's profit-maximizing output using the marginal approach. Use the four-step method and describe each step.

Blueprint Solution

a.

> Given that Carl must lower the price in order to sell more calculators, total revenue (*TR*) can be determined.
> $TR = P \times q$

Output	Price	TR	TC	Total Profit
0	$45.00	$0.00	$40.00	−$40.00
1	$40.00	$40.00	$50.00	−$10.00
2	$35.00	$70.00	$56.00	$14.00
3	$30.00	$90.00	$60.00	$30.00
4	$25.00	$100.00	$69.00	$31.00
5	$20.00	$100.00	$84.00	$16.00
6	$15.00	$90.00	$106.00	−$16.00
7	$10.00	$70.00	$144.00	−$74.00

> By determining total profit (*TR − TC*), the total approach reveals that *Q** is 4 calculators

b.

> $$MR = \frac{\Delta TR}{\Delta Q}$$

Output	Price	TR	MR	MC	Interpretation
0	$45.00	0	—	—	
1	$40.00	$40.00	$40.00	$10.00	Produce
2	$35.00	$70.00	$30.00	$6.00	Produce
3	$30.00	$90.00	$20.00	$4.00	Produce
4	$25.00	$100.00	$10.00	$9.00	Produce
5	$20.00	$100.00	$0.00	$15.00	Do not produce
6	$15.00	$90.00	-$10.00	$22.00	Do not produce
7	$10.00	$70.00	-$20.00	$38.00	Do not produce

> Being a rational decision maker, Carl will produce only the number of calculators that will give him positive net benefit (*MR > MC*). This rational decision rule will lead Carl to produce a total of 4 calculators.

Step 1: $MR = MC$ at 4 calculators (actually in this example, *MR* is as close to *MC* without exceeding it)

Step 2: $TR = P^* \times q^* = \$25 \times 4 = \$100$

Step 3: $TC = ATC_{q^*} \times q^* = \$17.25 \times 4 = \$69$

Step 4: Total profit $= TR - TC = \$100 - \$69 = \$31$

Section 9.3

10. Use the following diagram to answer questions (a) through (c).

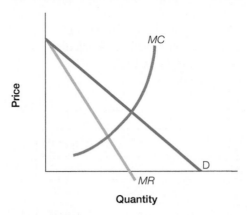

a. Assuming the monopolist indicated in the diagram produced at all, indicate its profit-maximizing quantity and price.

b. Add an *ATC* curve that would show this monopolist earning an economic profit.

c. Add an *ATC* curve that would show this monopolist experiencing an economic loss.

11. If economic profits were zero, would a monopolist ever stay in business? Why might it be possible for a monopolist to earn positive economic profits in the long run?

12. Consider the data in the following table.

Price	Quantity	Fixed Cost	Variable Cost
$100	0	$60	$ 0
90	1	60	25
80	2	60	40
70	3	60	50
60	4	60	70
50	5	60	100
40	6	60	140
30	7	60	190
20	8	60	250

A simple monopolist with these fixed and variable cost schedules maximizes profits at what level of output?

13. Given the data in the following table, determine the short-run profit-maximizing (loss-minimizing) level of output and price for the monopolist. Fixed cost equals $10.

Quantity	Price	Output	Total Cost
4	$35	4	$ 20
5	30	5	30
6	25	6	45
7	20	7	65
8	15	8	100

Section 9.4

14. What is meant by the "welfare loss" of monopoly? Why does no welfare loss occur if a monopolist successfully practises perfect price discrimination?

15. Consider the following graph for a monopolist.

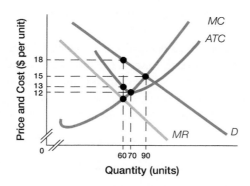

a. At its profit-maximizing price and quantity, how much of a profit or loss is this monopolist realizing?

b. At its profit-maximizing level of output, is this monopolist productively efficient? Explain.

c. At its profit-maximizing level of output, is this monopolist allocatively efficient? Explain.

16. Governments around the world are allowing competition in the production of goods and services that have historically been considered natural monopolies, such as provision of local telephone service and electricity. Why might the introduction of competition increase the efficiency of these industries?

Section 9.5

17. Use the accompanying diagram to answer questions (a) through (c).

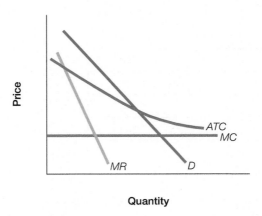

a. Indicate the efficient result on the graph.

b. Illustrate the profits or losses from the efficient result in (a).

c. Show the average cost-pricing solution. What profits are earned with that approach?

18. Suppose an industry experiences decreasing average costs of production over the relevant range of market demand. Discuss the merits of a regulation requiring the natural monopolist to set a price where demand equals marginal cost and to service all willing customers. What about where demand equals average cost? Are any practical difficulties likely to be encountered with either regulatory program?

Section 9.6

19. Explain how each of the following is a form of price discrimination.

a. a student discount at the movie theatre

b. long-distance telephone service that costs 15 cents per minute for the first 10 minutes and 5 cents per minute after 10 minutes

c. a senior citizens' breakfast discount at a local restaurant

d. coupon discounts on laundry detergent

20. In October of 1999, Coca-Cola announced that it was considering testing a new vending machine that was temperature-sensitive. The price of the soft drinks in the machines would be higher on hot days. The *Miami Herald* story read "Soda jerks." How is this practice a form of price discrimination? How can the placement of the vending machines create a monopoly? What if other vending machines are close by and are not owned by Coca-Cola?

21. Does the price schedule below reflect price discrimination? Why or why not?

Super Duper Cuts Hair Salon	
Permanent Price for Haircuts	
Long hair	$100
Short hair	75

22. Explain why a computer store offering significant student discounts may require student buyers to sign an agreement not to purchase another computer from the store for a period of six months.

23. Why do business travellers generally pay more for their flights than vacation travellers?

24. Tara loves to go through the Saturday paper and cut out supermarket coupons. How do you think Tara's coupon-clipping habits apply to the concept of price discrimination?

chapter 10

Monopolistic Competition and Oligopoly

section

10.1 Monopolistic Competition

■ What is monopolistic competition?
■ What are the three basic characteristics of monopolistic competition?

WHAT IS MONOPOLISTIC COMPETITION?

monopolistic competition
a market structure with many firms selling differentiated products

Monopolistic competition is a market structure with many firms selling differentiated products. For example, a restaurant is a monopoly in the sense that it has a unique name, menu, quality of service, location, and so on, but it also has many competitors—others selling prepared meals. That is, monopolistic competition has features in common with both monopoly and perfect competition, even though this may sound like an oxymoron—like "jumbo shrimp" or "press release." As with monopoly, individual sellers in monopolistic competition believe that they have some market power. But monopolistic competition is probably closer to competition than monopoly. Entry into and exit out of the industry is unrestricted, and consequently, there are many independent sellers. In virtue of the relatively free entry of new firms, the long-run price and output behaviour, and zero long-run economic profits, monopolistic competition is similar to perfect competition. However, the monopolistically competitive firm produces a product that is different (i.e., *differentiated* rather than identical or homogeneous) from others, which leads to some degree of monopoly power. In a sense, sellers in a monopolistically competitive market may be regarded as "monopolists" of their own particular brands; however, unlike firms with a true monopoly, there is competition among many firms selling similar (but not identical) brands. Examples of monopolistically competitive markets include retail clothing, real estate, furniture, health and personal care, restaurant meals, running shoes, and music lessons.

WHAT ARE THE THREE BASIC CHARACTERISTICS OF MONOPOLISTIC COMPETITION?

The theory of monopolistic competition is based on three characteristics: (1) many sellers, (2) product differentiation, and (3) free entry.

Many Sellers

When many firms compete for the same customers, any particular firm has little control over or interest in what other firms do. That is, a restaurant may change prices or improve service without a retaliatory move on the part of other competing restaurants because the time and effort necessary to learn about such changes may have marginal costs that are greater than the marginal benefits.

Product Differentiation

One characteristic of monopolistic competition is **product differentiation**—the accentuation of unique product qualities, real or perceived, to develop a specific product identity.

   The significant feature of differentiation is the buyer's belief that various sellers' products are not the same, whether the products are actually different or not. Headache remedies and some brands of over-the-counter cold medicines are examples of products that are very similar or identical but have different brand names. Product differentiation leads to preferences among buyers dealing with or purchasing the products of particular sellers.

Physical Differences   Physical differences constitute a primary source of product differentiation. For example, brands of ice cream (such as Chapmans and Breyers), or fast-food restaurants (such as Wendy's and Burger King) differ significantly in taste to many buyers.

Prestige   Prestige considerations also differentiate products to a significant degree. Many people prefer to be seen using the currently popular brand, whereas others prefer the "off" brand. Prestige considerations are particularly important with gifts—Godiva chocolates, Rolex watches, and so on.

Location   Location is a major differentiating factor in retailing. Shoppers are not willing to travel long distances to purchase similar items, which is one reason for the large number of convenience stores and service station mini-marts. Because most buyers realize there are no significant differences among brands of gasoline, the location of a gas station might influence their choice of gasoline.

Service   Service considerations are also significant for product differentiation. Speedy and friendly service and lenient return policies are important to many people. Likewise,

Restaurants can be very different. A restaurant that sells pizza competes with other Italian restaurants, but it also competes with restaurants that sell burgers and fries. Monopolistic competition has some elements of competition (many sellers) and some elements of monopoly power (differentiated products).

product differentiation
the accentuation of unique product qualities, real or perceived, to develop a specific product identity

Fast, warranty-approved automotive maintenance, all without an appointment, might differentiate one vehicle service depot from others.

speed and quality of service may significantly influence a person's choice of where to take their car for scheduled maintenance.

Free Entry

Entry in monopolistic competition is relatively unrestricted in the sense that new firms may easily start the production of close substitutes for existing products; this is the case for restaurants, lawn care services, barbershops, and many forms of retail activity. Because of relatively free entry, economic profits tend to be eliminated in the long run, as is the case with perfect competition.

SECTION CHECK

- *Monopolistic competition* describes a market structure where many producers of somewhat different products compete with one another.
- The theory of monopolistic competition is based on three primary characteristics: many sellers, product differentiation, and free entry.

section 10.2
Price and Output Determination in Monopolistic Competition

- How is short-run equilibrium determined?
- How is long-run equilibrium determined?

HOW IS SHORT-RUN EQUILIBRIUM DETERMINED?

Because monopolistically competitive sellers are price makers rather than price takers, they do not regard price as given by market conditions as do perfectly competitive firms.

Because each firm sells a slightly different product for which there are many close substitutes, the firm's demand curve is downward sloping but quite flat (elastic). In perfect competition, the demand curve is horizontal because each firm, one of a great many sellers, sells the same homogeneous product. Given the position of an individual firm's demand curve, we can determine short-run equilibrium output and price by using a method similar to that used to determine monopoly output and price.

The cost and revenue curves of a typical seller are shown in Exhibit 1; the intersection of the marginal revenue and marginal cost curves indicates that the short-run profit-maximizing output will be q^*. By observing how much will be demanded at that output level, we find the profit-maximizing price, P^*. That is, at the equilibrium quantity, q^*, we go vertically to the demand curve and read the corresponding price on the vertical axis, P^*, just as we did for monopoly.

section 10.2

Exhibit 1 Short-Run Equilibrium in Monopolistic Competition

a. Determining Profits

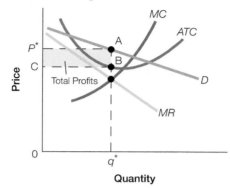

b. Determining Losses

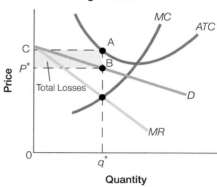

In Exhibit 1(a), the firm is making short-run economic profits because the firm's total revenue, P^*Aq^*0, at output q^* is greater than the firm's total cost, CBq^*0. The firm has a total profit of area P^*ABC. In Exhibit 1(b), the firm is incurring a short-run economic loss because at q^*, price is below average total cost. At q^*, total cost, CAq^*0, is greater than total revenue, P^*Bq^*0, so the firm incurs a total loss of $CABP^*$.

Four-Step Method for Monopolistic Competition

Let us return to the same four-step method we used in Chapters 8 and 9. Determining whether a firm is generating economic profits, economic losses, or zero economic profits at the profit-maximizing level of output, q^*, can be done in four easy steps:

1. The first step is to find the profit-maximizing level of output (q^*). To do this, find where marginal revenues equal marginal costs and proceed straight down to the horizontal "Quantity" axis to find the profit-maximizing output level.
2. The second step is to determine the total revenue (TR) being generated at q^*. To do this, go straight up from q^* to the demand curve and then to the left to find the market price, P^*. Once you have identified P^* and q^*, you can find total revenue at the profit-maximizing output level, because $TR = P \times q$.
3. The third step is to find total costs (TC) at q^*. Again, go straight up from q^* to the average total cost (ATC) curve and then left to the vertical axis to compute the average total cost *per unit*. If we multiply average total costs by the output level, we can find the total costs ($TC = ATC \times q$).
4. The final step is to determine the amount of either profit or loss at q^*. If total revenue (from step 2) is greater than total costs (from step 3) at q^*, the firm is generating economic profits. However, if total revenue is less than total costs at Q^*, the firm is generating economic losses.

Remember, the cost curves include implicit and explicit costs—that is, even at zero economic profits, the firm is covering the total opportunity costs of its resources and earning a normal profit or rate of return.

Short-Run Profits and Losses in Monopolistic Competition

Exhibit 1(a) shows the equilibrium position of a monopolistically competitive firm. As we just discussed, the firm produces where $MC = MR$, at output q^*. At output q^* and price P^*, the firm's total revenue is equal to P^*Aq^*0, which is $P^* \times q^*$. At output q^*, the firm's total cost is CBq*0, which is $ATC \times q^*$. In Exhibit 1(a), we see that total revenue is greater than total cost, so the firm has a total profit of area P*ABC.

In Exhibit 1(b), at q^*, price is below average total cost, so the firm is minimizing its economic loss. At q^*, total cost, CAq*0, is greater than total revenue, P*Bq*0, so the firm incurs a total loss of CABP*. Other than the shape of the demand curve, this is no different from determining the monopolist's price and output in the short run.

HOW IS LONG-RUN EQUILIBRIUM DETERMINED?

The short-run equilibrium situation depicted in Exhibit 1, whether involving profits or losses, will probably not last long, because there is entry and exit in the long run. If market entry and exit are sufficiently free, new firms will enter when there are economic profits, and some firms will exit when there are economic losses.

Economic Profits When Firms Enter the Industry

In Exhibit 2(a), we see the market impact as new firms enter to take advantage of the economic profits. The result of this influx is more sellers of similar products, which means that each new firm will cut into the demand of existing firms. That is, the demand curve for each existing firm will fall. With entry, not only will the firm's demand curve move inward but it also becomes relatively more elastic due to each firm's product having more substitutes (more choices for consumers). We see this situation in Exhibit 2(a) when demand shifts leftward from D_{SR} to D_{LR}. This decline in demand continues to occur until the average total cost (ATC) curve becomes tangent with the demand curve, and economic profits are reduced to zero.

---

section 10.2
Exhibit 2   Achieving Long-Run Equilibrium

a. Firms Enter the Market

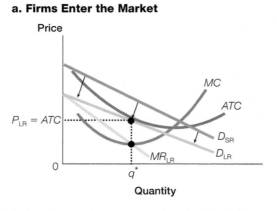

b. Firms Exit the Market

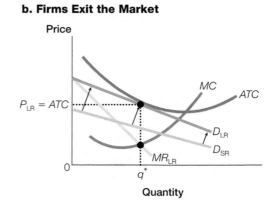

In Exhibit 2(a), excess profits attract new firms into the industry. As a result, the firm's share of the market declines and demand shifts down. Profits are eliminated when $P_{LR} = ATC$, that is, when the ATC curve is tangent to D_{LR}. In Exhibit 2(b), some firms exit because of economic losses. Their exit increases the demand for existing firms, shifting D_{SR} to D_{LR}, where all losses have been eliminated.

Economic Losses When Firms Exit the Industry

When firms are making economic losses, some firms will exit the industry. As some firms exit, it means fewer firms in the market, which increases the demand for the remaining firms' product, shifting their demand curves to the right, from D_{SR} to D_{LR} as seen in Exhibit 2(b). When firms exit, not only will the firm's demand curve move outward but it also will become relatively more inelastic due to each firm's products having fewer substitutes (fewer choices for consumers). The higher demand results in smaller losses for the existing firms until all losses finally disappear where the *ATC* curve is tangent to the demand curve.

Achieving Long-Run Equilibrium

The process of entry and exit will continue until all firms in the industry are making zero economic profits. When the market reaches this long-run equilibrium, no firms have an incentive to enter or exit.

Once entry and exit have driven profits to zero, the demand curve and average total cost curve will be tangent to each other, as seen in Exhibit 3. At the profit-maximizing output level, the firm earns zero economic profits.

In short, the monopolistically competitive producers are a lot like monopolists; they face a downward-sloping demand curve and set marginal revenue to marginal cost to determine the profit-maximizing output level. However, the difference is that at this profit-maximizing level of output, the monopolistically competitive firm cannot make economic profits in the long run because the barriers to entry and exit in this market are assumed to be zero.

As a final note, complete adjustment toward equality of price with average cost may be checked by the strength of reputation built up by established firms. Those firms that are particularly successful in their selling efforts may create such strong consumer preferences that newcomers—even though they are able to enter the industry freely and cover their costs—will not take sufficient business away from the well-established firms to eliminate their excess profits. Thus, a restaurant that has been particularly successful in promoting customer goodwill may continue to earn excess profits long after the entry of new firms has brought about equality of price and average costs for the others, even losses. Adjustments toward a final equilibrium situation involving equality of price and average cost do not proceed with the certainty that is supposed to be characteristic of perfect competition.

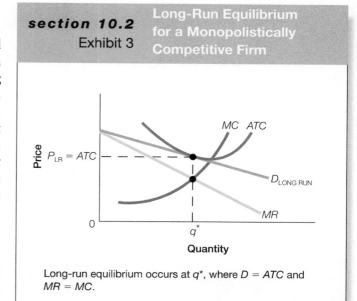

section 10.2
Exhibit 3

Long-Run Equilibrium for a Monopolistically Competitive Firm

Long-run equilibrium occurs at q^*, where $D = ATC$ and $MR = MC$.

SECTION CHECK

- In the short run, a monopolistically competitive firm achieves profit maximization at the intersection of the marginal revenue and marginal cost curves. A monopolistically competitive firm is making short-run economic profits when the equilibrium price is greater than average total costs at the equilibrium output; when equilibrium price is below average total cost at the equilibrium output, the firm is minimizing its economic losses.
- In the long run, equilibrium price equals average total costs. With that, economic profits are zero, so there are no incentives for firms to either enter or exit the industry.

section

10.3

Monopolistic Competition versus Perfect Competition

- What are the differences and similarities between monopolistic competition and perfect competition?
- What are the real costs of monopolistic competition?
- Are the differences between monopolistic competition and perfect competition exaggerated?

© Judy Barranco/iStockphoto.com

WHAT ARE THE DIFFERENCES AND SIMILARITIES BETWEEN MONOPOLISTIC COMPETITION AND PERFECT COMPETITION?

We have seen that both monopolistic competition and perfect competition have many buyers and sellers and relatively free entry. However, product differentiation enables a monopolistic competitor to have some influence over price. Consequently, a monopolistically competitive firm has a downward-sloping demand curve, but because of the large number of good substitutes for its product, the curve tends to be much more elastic than the demand curve for a monopolist.

How much do you value variety in clothing? Imagine a world where everyone wore the same clothes, drove the same cars, and lived in identical houses. Most individuals are willing to pay for a little variety, even if it costs somewhat more.

excess capacity

occurs when the firm produces below the level where average total cost is minimized

Failing to Achieve Productive Efficiency

Because in monopolistic competition the demand curve is downward sloping, its point of tangency with the *ATC* curve will not and cannot be at the lowest level of average cost. What does this mean? It means that even when long-run adjustments are complete, firms are not operating at a level that permits the lowest average cost of production—the efficient scale of the firm. The existing plant, even though optimal for the equilibrium volume of output, is not used to capacity; that is, **excess capacity** exists at that level of output. Excess capacity occurs when the firm produces below the level where average total cost is minimized.

Unlike a perfectly competitive firm, a monopolistically competitive firm could increase output and lower its average total cost, as shown in Exhibit 1(a). However, any attempt to increase output to attain lower average cost would be unprofitable because the price reduction necessary to sell the greater output would cause marginal revenue to fall below the marginal cost of the increased output. As we can see in Exhibit 1(a), to the right of q^*, marginal cost is greater than marginal revenue. Consequently, in monopolistic competition, there is a tendency toward too many firms in the industry, each producing a volume of output less than what would allow lowest cost. Economists call this tendency *a failure to reach productive efficiency*. For example, there may be too many grocery stores or too many service stations, in the sense that if the total volume of business was concentrated in a smaller number of sellers, average cost, and thus price, could in principle be less.

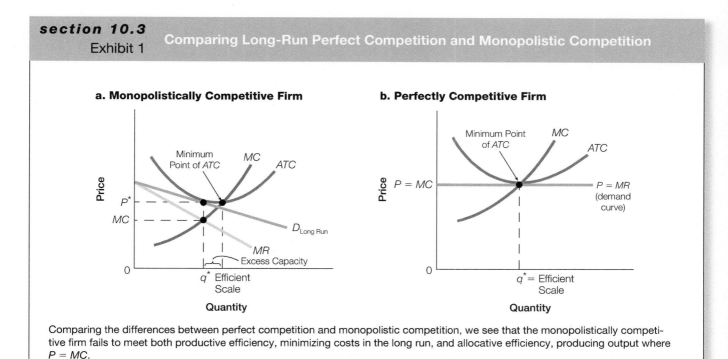

section 10.3
Exhibit 1   Comparing Long-Run Perfect Competition and Monopolistic Competition

a. Monopolistically Competitive Firm

b. Perfectly Competitive Firm

Comparing the differences between perfect competition and monopolistic competition, we see that the monopolistically competitive firm fails to meet both productive efficiency, minimizing costs in the long run, and allocative efficiency, producing output where $P = MC$.

Also Failing to Meet Allocative Efficiency

Productive inefficiency is not the only problem with a monopolistically competitive firm. Exhibit 1(a) shows a firm that is not operating where price is equal to marginal costs. In the monopolistically competitive model, at the intersection of the *MC* and *MR* curves (q^*), we can clearly see that price is greater than marginal cost. This means that society is willing to pay more for the product (the price, P^*) than it costs society to produce it. In this case, the firm is failing to reach allocative efficiency, where price equals marginal cost. In short, this means that the firm is underallocating resources—too many firms are producing, each at output levels that are less than full capacity. Note that in Exhibit 1(b), the perfectly competitive firm has reached both productive efficiency ($P = ATC$ at the minimum point on the *ATC* curve) and allocative efficiency ($P = MC$). However, it is clear that these drawbacks in the monopolistically competitive market would be far greater in monopoly, where the demand curve is more inelastic (steeper).

Further, in defence of monopolistic competition, the higher average cost and the slightly higher price and lower output may simply be the price that firms pay for differentiated products—variety. That is, just because monopolistically competitive firms have not met the conditions for productive and allocative efficiency, it is not obvious that society is not better off.

WHAT ARE THE REAL COSTS OF MONOPOLISTIC COMPETITION?

We have just argued that perfect competition meets the tests of allocative and productive efficiency and that monopolistic competition does not. Can we "fix" a monopolistically competitive firm to look more like an efficient, perfectly competitive firm? One remedy might entail using government regulation, as in the case of a natural monopoly. However, this process would be costly because a monopolistically competitive firm makes no economic profits in the long run. Therefore, asking monopolistically competitive firms to equate price and marginal cost would lead to economic losses because long-run average total cost would be greater than price at $P = MC$. Consequently, the government would have to subsidize the firm. Living with the inefficiencies in monopolistically competitive markets might be easier than coping with the difficulties entailed by regulations and the cost of the necessary subsidies.

We argued that the monopolistically competitive firm does not operate at the minimum point of the *ATC* curve, whereas the perfectly competitive firm does. However, is this a fair comparison? In monopolistic competition, there are differentiated goods and services, whereas in perfect competition, there are not. In other words, the excess capacity that exists in monopolistic competition is the price we pay for product differentiation. Have you ever thought about the many restaurants, movie theatres, and gasoline stations that have "excess capacity"? Can you imagine a world where all firms were working at full capacity? After all, choice is a good, and most of us value some choice.

In short, the inefficiency of monopolistic competition is a result of product differentiation. Since consumers value variety—the ability to choose from competing products and brands—the loss in efficiency must be weighed against the gain in increased product variety. The gains from product diversity can be large and may easily outweigh the inefficiency associated with a downward-sloping demand curve.

ARE THE DIFFERENCES BETWEEN MONOPOLISTIC COMPETITION AND PERFECT COMPETITION EXAGGERATED?

The significance of the difference between the relationship of marginal cost to price in monopolistic competition and in perfect competition can easily be exaggerated. As long as preferences for various brands are not extremely strong, the demand for a firm's products will be highly elastic (very flat). Accordingly, the points of tangency with the *ATC* curves are not likely to be far above the point of lowest cost, and excess capacity will be small, as illustrated in Exhibit 2. Only if differentiation is strong will the difference between the long-run price level and the price that would prevail under perfectly competitive conditions be significant.

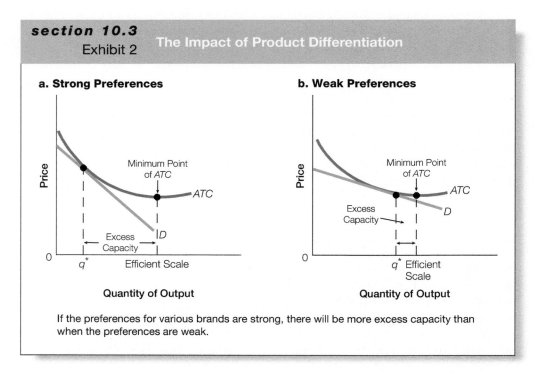

section 10.3
Exhibit 2   **The Impact of Product Differentiation**

a. Strong Preferences

Price / Quantity of Output

Minimum Point of *ATC* / *ATC* / *D* / Excess Capacity / q^* / Efficient Scale

b. Weak Preferences

Price / Quantity of Output

Minimum Point of *ATC* / *ATC* / *D* / Excess Capacity / q^* / Efficient Scale

If the preferences for various brands are strong, there will be more excess capacity than when the preferences are weak.

Remember this little caveat: The theory of the firm is like a road map that does not detail every gully, creek, and hill but does give directions to get from one geographic point to another. Any particular theory of the firm may not tell precisely how an individual firm will operate, but it does provide valuable insight into the ways firms will tend to react to changing economic conditions such as entry, demand, and cost changes.

SECTION CHECK

- While both the competitive firm and the monopolistically competitive firm may earn short-run economic profits, these profits will be eliminated in the long run. Because monopolistically competitive firms face a downward-sloping demand curve, average total cost is not minimized in the long run after entry and exit have eliminated profits. Monopolistically competitive firms fail to reach productive efficiency, producing at output levels less than the efficient output. The monopolistically competitive firm does not achieve allocative efficiency because it does not operate where the price is equal to marginal costs.
- The inefficiencies of monopolistic competition are a by-product of product differentiation and must be weighed against the social benefits of increased product variety.
- The difference between the long-run price level and the price that would prevail under perfect competition varies directly with the strength of product differentiation.

Advertising

- Why do firms advertise?
- Is advertising good or bad from society's perspective?

WHY DO FIRMS ADVERTISE?

Advertising is an important nonprice method of competition that is commonly used in monopolistic competition. Why do firms advertise? The reason is simple: By advertising, firms hope to increase the demand and create a less elastic demand curve for their products, thus enhancing revenues and profits. Advertising is part of our life, whether we are watching television, listening to the radio, reading a newspaper or magazine, or simply driving down the highway. Firms that sell differentiated products can spend between 10 and 20 percent of their revenue on advertising.

Advertising Can Change the Shape and Position of the Demand Curve

Consider Exhibit 1, which shows how a successful advertising campaign can increase demand and change elasticity. If an ad campaign convinces buyers that a firm's product is truly different, the demand curve for that good will become less elastic. Consequently, price changes (up or down) will have a relatively smaller impact on the quantity demanded of the product. The firm hopes that this change in elasticity, ideally coupled with an increase in demand, will increase profits.

section 10.4
Exhibit 1
The Impact of a Successful
Advertising Campaign

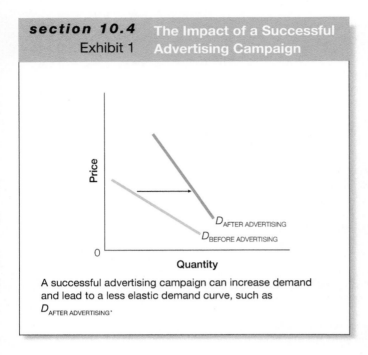

A successful advertising campaign can increase demand
and lead to a less elastic demand curve, such as
$D_{\text{AFTER ADVERTISING}}$.

The degree to which advertising affects demand
will vary from market to market. For example, in the
laundry detergent market, empirical evidence shows that
it is very important to advertise because the demand for
any one detergent critically depends on the amount of
money spent on advertising. That is, if you don't advertise your detergent, you don't sell much of it.

IS ADVERTISING GOOD OR BAD FROM SOCIETY'S PERSPECTIVE?

The Impact of Advertising on Society

Questions about whether advertising's impact on society
is good or bad elicit sharply different responses. Some
have argued that advertising manipulates consumer tastes
and wastes billions of dollars annually creating "needs" for
trivial products. Advertising helps create a demonstration
effect, whereby people have new urges to buy products
that were previously unknown to them. In creating additional demands for private goods, the ability to provide
needed public goods (for which there is little advertising
to create demand) is potentially reduced. Moreover, sometimes advertising is based on
misleading claims, so people find themselves buying products that do not provide the
satisfaction or results promised in the ads. Finally, adver-
tising itself requires resources that raise average costs.

On the other hand, who is to say that the purchase of any product is frivolous or unnecessary? If one
believes that people are rational and should be permitted
freedom of expression, the argument against advertising
loses some of its force.

Furthermore, defenders of advertising argue that
firms use advertising to provide important information
about the price and availability of a product, the location and hours of store operation, and so on. This allows
for customers to make better choices and allows markets
to function more efficiently.

section 10.4
Exhibit 2
Advertising and
Economies of Scale

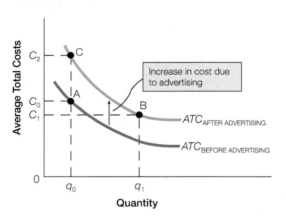

The average total cost before advertising is shown as
$ATC_{\text{BEFORE ADVERTISING}}$. After advertising, the curve shifts to
$ATC_{\text{AFTER ADVERTISING}}$. If the increase in demand resulting from
advertising is significant, economies of scale from higher
output levels may offset the advertising costs, lowering
average total cost. The movement from point A to point B
allows the firm to sell its product at a lower price. However,
when two firms engage in an advertising war, it is possible
that neither will gain market share (increased output) but
each will incur higher advertising costs. This is shown as
a movement from point A to point C in Exhibit 2—output
remains at q_0, but average total cost rises from C_0 to C_2.

Advertising and Costs

Although it is true that advertising may raise the average
total cost, it is possible that when substantial economies of
scale exist, the average production cost will decline more
than the amount of the per-unit cost of advertising. In
other words, average total cost, in some situations, actually declines after extensive advertising. This can happen
because advertising may allow the firm to operate closer to
the point of minimum cost on its ATC curve. Specifically,
notice in Exhibit 2 that the average total cost curve before
advertising is $ATC_{\text{BEFORE ADVERTISING}}$. After advertising,
the curve shifts upward to $ATC_{\text{AFTER ADVERTISING}}$. If the
increase in demand resulting from advertising is significant, economies of scale from higher output levels may

offset the advertising costs. Average total cost may fall from C_0 to C_1, a movement from point A to point B, and allow the firm to sell its product at a lower price. Toys "R" Us versus a smaller owner-operated toy store provides an example.

However, it also is possible that an advertising war between two firms, say Burger King and McDonald's, will result in higher advertising costs for both and no gain in market share (increased output) for either. This is shown as a movement from point A to point C in Exhibit 2. Output remains at q_0, but average total cost rises from C_0 to C_2.

Firms in monopolistic competition are not likely to experience substantial cost reductions as output increases. Therefore, they probably will not be able to offset advertising costs with lower production costs, particularly if advertising costs are high. Even if advertising does add to total cost, however, it is true that advertising conveys information. Through advertising, customers become aware of the options available to them in terms of product choice. Advertising helps customers choose products that best meet their needs, and it informs price-conscious customers about the costs of products. In this way, advertising lowers information costs, which is one reason that the Competition Bureau opposes bans on advertising.

Advertising and Competition

If advertising reduces information costs, this leads to some interesting economic implications. For example, say that as a result of advertising, we know about more products that may be substitutes for the products we have been buying for years. That is, the more goods that are advertised, the more consumers are aware of "substitute" products, which leads to increasingly competitive markets. Studies in the eyeglass, toy, and drug industries have shown that advertising has increased competition and led to lower prices in these markets.

Business *CONNECTION*

AN ECONOMIC TAKE ON ADVERTISING

Businesses that operate in perfectly competitive markets compete only on price and those that operate as a monopoly compete on anything but price, so where do those that operate in the middle compete? Simply put, those that have products or services that are highly, but not perfectly, competitive will compete more on price and to a lesser degree on the other 3Ps (product, place, or promotion). In oligopolies, with a few sellers offering similar or identical services, businesses strive to behave like a monopoly, but there is still limited competition, so there is a lot of competition on product, place, and promotion. Price has a place somewhere, but more in terms of justifying the higher prices than about having to lower prices just to get into the game.

To succeed, new businesses need to understand—really understand—where their products or services fit into the market continuum. If they don't know where they are or how they'll compete, they will leave money on the table, waste valuable time and resources, rack up increasing costs, and not see the expected returns for their efforts.

For businesses operating in monopolistic competitive or oligopolistic environments, promotion (advertising) is extremely important. Obviously advertising ads cost, but the key is to bring about additional benefits to offset the costs. In the language of economics, effective advertising shifts a firm's demand curve rightward. From the business viewpoint, that usually means that consumers are willing and able to buy the same number of products over time at higher prices because the firm is increasing consumers' perceived value of the product and in the process is increasing consumer surplus. Recall that any time producers can increase consumer surplus, the greater the likelihood is that consumers will offer up their hard-earned cash. Basically, they are prepared to pay a premium for the company's products.

Sometimes the features of a firm's product meet or exceed the market needs but are not understood or appreciated. In such situations, promotion makes more sense than changing the product itself. At other times the firm wants to

(continued)

enhance either its customer loyalty to the brand or its company's reputation. In either case, advertising builds value for buyers who are prepared to buy despite higher prices. These are all examples of shifting the demand curve rightward, *ceteris paribus*, which leads to increased revenues resulting from price increases.

Another effect that advertising has on the rightward shift of the demand curve is to gain market share. Firms often want to compare their products to those of close substitutes to help illustrate to consumers that their product is superior. If they are successful (think how car manufacturers compare their offerings to autos in similar classes), they gain market share and additional marginal revenues from the increased sales.

A rightward shift of a firm's demand curve signals a higher number of potential consumers who can sustain higher product prices. Couple that with increased unit sales and it turns into increases in overall revenue. For managers, the question often arises: To what extent will the resulting increases in revenue support increases in profit? Managers have to analyze at what levels of increased sales the firm can keep up the increased costs.

Firms try to come up with reliable forecasts of costs and profits. They have two main considerations: (1) Do increases in output achieve economies of scale and so reduce average unit cost, or will diseconomies of scale lead to increasing average unit costs? (2) Is this an increasing-cost,

constant-cost, or decreasing-cost industry? Smart business operators know that effective advertising moves more than just buyers—it basically moves the firm's demand curve, with major implications for profits.

Remember that added revenue will not always produce higher profits. Consider what happens if a car manufacturer overestimates sales forecasts: At the end of the year, those unsold units increase costs dramatically, sometimes as sunk costs. This is why you'll often see car companies offering rebates or incentives that actually are greater than they can get for the car. Here they are increasing their costs just to sell the car and realize some revenue. Again, it's not about maximizing profits, but minimizing losses!

1. A number of small and medium-sized enterprises state that they cannot afford to invest in advertising—it's too expensive and they cannot see the desired results. From an economics perspective, what advice would you give them if you were their consultant?

2. Which to do think is more beneficial to a firm, advertising focusing on the product or focusing on the firm? Which would have the most benefit in shifting the demand curve over the longer term, and why?

3. Can you think of specific ideas or methods of using online marketing or e-commerce that would oligopolies could use in achieving higher profits?

SECTION CHECK

- With advertising, a firm hopes it can alter the elasticity of the demand for its product, making it more inelastic and causing an increase in demand that will enhance profits.
- To some, advertising manipulates consumer tastes and creates "needs" for trivial products. Where substantial economies of scale exist, it is possible that average production costs will decline more than the amount of per-unit costs of advertising in the long run. By making consumers aware of different "substitute" products, advertising may lead to more competitive markets and lower consumer prices.

section
10.5   Oligopoly

- What is oligopoly?
- Why do oligopolies exist?
- Why is it so difficult for the oligopolist to determine its profit-maximizing price and output?

WHAT IS OLIGOPOLY?

oligopoly
a market structure with only a few sellers offering similar or identical products

As we first stated in Chapter 8, an **oligopoly** is a market structure with only a few sellers offering similar or identical products. While the goods and services produced by oligopolists can be either homogeneous or differentiated, the barriers to entry are often high, which makes it difficult for firms to enter the industry. Consequently, long-run economic profits may be earned by firms in the industry. Examples of oligopolistic markets include commercial airlines, oil, automobiles, steel, breakfast cereals, computers, tobacco, and beer. For all these products, the market is dominated by anywhere from a few to several big companies, although they may have many different brands.

In Canada specifically, a number of industries could be considered to be oligopolistic. The Canadian banking sector is dominated by six large financial institutions: Bank of Nova Scotia, Royal Bank, TD Canada Trust, the Canadian Imperial Bank of Commerce, the Bank of Montreal, and National Bank, controlling over 90 percent of total banking assets in Canada. As of 2011, three telecommunication service providers (Rogers, Bell, and Telus) shared over 90 percent of the Canadian wireless industry. Finally, five major Internet service providers (ISPs) account for over 75 percent of market share (based on revenue). The five major ISPs are Rogers, Telus, Bell, Shaw, and Quebecor.

Mutual Interdependence

Oligopoly is characterized by **mutual interdependence** among firms; that is, each firm shapes its policy with an eye to the policies of competing firms. Oligopolists must strategize, much like good chess or bridge players, who are constantly observing and anticipating the moves of their rivals. Oligopoly is likely to occur whenever the number of firms in an industry is so small that any change in output or price on the part of one firm appreciably impacts the sales of competing firms. In this situation, it is almost inevitable that competitors will respond directly to each other's actions in determining their own policies.

mutual interdependence
when a firm shapes its policy with an eye to the policies of competing firms

WHY DO OLIGOPOLIES EXIST?

Primarily, oligopoly is a result of the relationship between the technological conditions of production and potential sales volume. For many products, a firm cannot obtain a reasonably low cost of production unless it is producing a large fraction of the market output. In other words, substantial economies of scale are present in oligopoly markets. Automobile and steel production are classic examples of this. Because of legal concerns such as patents, large start-up costs, and the presence of pronounced economies of scale, the barriers to entry are quite high in oligopoly.

Economies of Scale as a Barrier to Entry

Economies of large-scale production make operation on a small scale extremely unprofitable during a new firm's early years. A firm cannot build up a large market overnight; in the interim, average total cost is so high that losses are heavy. Recognition of this fact discourages new firms from entering the market, as illustrated in Exhibit 1. We can see that if an automobile company produces quantity Q_{LARGE} rather than Q_{SMALL}, it will be able to produce cars at a significantly lower cost. If the average total cost to a potential entrant is equivalent to point A on the *ATC* curve and the price of automobiles is less than P_0, a new firm would be deterred from entering the industry.

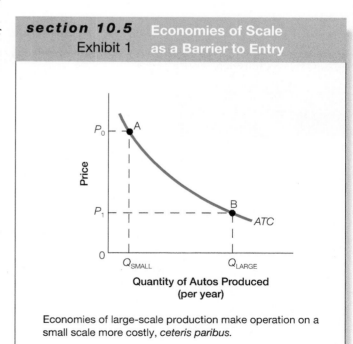

section 10.5
Exhibit 1
Economies of Scale as a Barrier to Entry

Economies of large-scale production make operation on a small scale more costly, *ceteris paribus*.

© ARTEKI/Shutterstock

WHY IS IT SO DIFFICULT FOR THE OLIGOPOLIST TO DETERMINE ITS PROFIT-MAXIMIZING PRICE AND OUTPUT?

It is difficult to predict how firms will react when there is mutual interdependence. No firm knows what its demand curve looks like with any degree of certainty, and therefore it has a very limited knowledge of its marginal revenue curve. To know anything about its demand curve, the firm must know how other firms will react to its prices and other policies. In the absence of additional assumptions, then, equating marginal revenue and marginal cost is relegated to guesswork. Thus, it is difficult for an oligopolist to determine its profit-maximizing price and output.

Do you think economies of scale are important in this industry? Unlike home-cooked meals, few cars are "homemade." The barriers to entry in the auto industry are formidable. A new entrant would have to start out as a large producer (investing billions of dollars in plant, equipment, and advertising) to compete with existing firms, which have lower average total costs per unit because of economies of large-scale production.

SECTION CHECK

- Oligopolies exist where relatively few firms control all or most of the production and sale of a product. The products may be homogeneous or differentiated, but the barriers to entry are often very high and, consequently, there may be long-run economic profits.
- In oligopoly markets, economies of large-scale production make operation on a small scale extremely unprofitable. Recognition of this fact discourages new firms from entering the market and is the primary reason why oligopolies exist.
- Because in oligopoly the pricing decision of one firm influences the demand curve of competing firms, the oligopolist faces considerable uncertainty as to the location and shape of its demand and marginal revenue curves. Thus, it is difficult for an oligopolist to determine its profit-maximizing price and output.

section 10.6 Collusion and Cartels

- Why do firms collude?
- What is joint profit maximization?
- Why are most collusive oligopolies short-lived?

The uncertainties of pricing decisions are substantial in oligopoly. The implications of misjudging the behaviour of competitors could prove to be disastrous. An executive who makes the wrong pricing move may force the firm to lose sales or, at a minimum, be forced to back down in an embarrassing fashion from an announced price increase. Because of this uncertainty, some believe that oligopolists change their prices less frequently than perfect competitors, whose prices may change almost continually. The empirical evidence, however, does not clearly indicate that prices are in fact always slow to change in oligopoly situations.

WHY DO FIRMS COLLUDE?

Because the actions and profits of oligopolists are so dominated by mutual interdependence, the temptation is great for firms to **collude**—act together to restrict competition. If firms believe they can increase their profits by coordinating their actions, they will be tempted to collude. Collusion reduces uncertainty and increases the potential for monopoly profits. From society's point of view, however, collusion has the same disadvantages monopoly does; namely, it creates a situation in which goods very likely become overpriced and underproduced, with consumers losing out as the result of a misallocation of resources.

collude
when firms act together to restrict competition

Collusion Is Like a Monopoly

From the standpoint of pricing and output decisions, a truly collusive oligopoly that involves all the firms in an industry could act as the equivalent of one large firm with several plants. Acting in this manner, the economic effect of the collusive oligopoly would be exactly the same as that of a monopoly: A single demand curve would exist for the group of companies. Once the profit-maximization price was determined, they could agree on how much output each firm in the group would offer for sale.

cartel
a collection of firms that agree on sales, pricing, and other decisions

WHAT IS JOINT PROFIT MAXIMIZATION?

Agreements between or among firms on sales, pricing, and other decisions are usually referred to as *cartel agreements*. A **cartel** is a collection of firms that agree on sales, pricing, and other decisions.

Cartels may lead to what economists call **joint profit maximization:** the determination of price based on the marginal revenue function derived from the market demand schedule and the marginal cost schedule of the firms in the industry. Exhibit 1 illustrates this. With outright agreements—necessarily secret because of anti-combine laws (in Canada, at least)—firms that make up the market will attempt to estimate demand and cost schedules and then set optimum price and output levels accordingly.

joint profit maximization
determination of price based on the marginal revenue derived from the market demand schedule and marginal cost schedule of the firms in the industry

Equilibrium price and quantity for a collusive oligopoly, like those for a monopoly, are determined according to the intersection of the marginal revenue curve (derived from the market demand curve) and the horizontal sum of the short-run marginal cost curves for the oligopolists. As shown in Exhibit 1, the resulting equilibrium quantity is Q^* and the equilibrium price is P^*. Collusion facilitates joint profit maximization for the oligopoly. Like monopoly, if the oligopoly is maintained in the long run, it charges a higher price, produces less output, and fails to maximize social welfare, relative to perfect competition, because $P^* > MC$ at Q^*.

The manner in which total profits are shared among firms in the industry depends in part on the relative costs and sales of the various firms. Firms with low costs and large supply capabilities will obtain the largest profits because they have greater bargaining power. Sales, in turn, may depend in large measure on consumer preferences for various brands if there is product differentiation. With outright collusion, firms may agree on market shares and the division of profits. The division

section 10.6
Exhibit 1   **Collusion in Oligopoly**

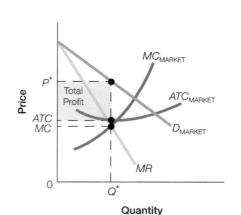

In collusive oligopoly, the producers would restrict joint output to Q^*, setting their price at P^*. The price and output situation is identical to that for monopoly. The members of the collusive oligopoly would share the profits in the shaded area.

of total profits will depend on the relative bargaining strength of each firm, influenced by its relative financial strength, ability to inflict damage (through price wars) on other firms if an agreement is not reached, ability to withstand similar actions on the part of other firms, relative costs, consumer preferences, and bargaining skills.

Organization of the Petroleum Exporting Countries

The most spectacularly successful example of a collusive oligopoly able to earn monopoly-type profits is the Organization of the Petroleum Exporting Countries (OPEC) cartel. Although organized in 1960, it didn't become successful as a collusive oligopoly until 1973.

For 20 years before 1973, the price of crude oil had hovered around US$2 per barrel. Then, in 1973, OPEC members agreed to quadruple oil prices in nine months; later price increases pushed the cost of a barrel of oil to more than US$20.

The share of the world's proven oil reserves produced by companies that are OPEC members has steadily increased, from around 20 percent produced in the early 1940s to more than 80 percent by 2012. While ongoing world events have seen the price of a barrel of oil fluctuate, OPEC has had remarkable success at managing world price for the benefit of its member states. In 2013, a barrel of oil was selling for approximately US$100.

DEBATE

DO COMPANIES COLLUDE ON THE PRICE OF GAS?

For:

There seems to be ample evidence that gas companies collude to gouge customers over prices. When one company's station raises prices, for example, the station across the street also raises prices. Gas prices of all companies seem to rise as weekends and holidays approach, and they all drop afterward. The fact is that relatively few companies control the gas inventories. "Big Oil" companies control all levels of distribution and without any real competition, they behave like monopolies and charge whatever the market will bear—regardless of the laws of supply and demand. If there were true competition, when one station increased its price the others would have a competitive advantage in keeping their prices stable. It's also worth noting that gas stations don't buy their supplies at the same time, so there must be differences in margins based on their individual costs. Proving collusion in court is difficult and the oil companies are so wealthy that potential legal costs have been prohibitive. In effect, oil companies are regarded as too big to prosecute. Governments have no incentive to investigate because they reap huge profits from high gas prices through taxes. Isn't it clear that companies collude on the price of gas? Can you provide other evidence of collusion on gas prices?

Against:

Those in the oil companies' camp argue that the price of gasoline follows the market forces of demand and supply. They also argue that the prices of gasoline, diesel, and other fuels are loosely associated with the costs of crude oil and that comparing prices of crude to the other products is not a good indicator of market forces. Gas companies say that they raise prices for the holidays and lower them afterward only in response to expectations of supply and demand. They know that the demand for gas will be much higher during long weekends and that stations will have a limited supply, so they are justified in raising and lowering prices as the demand shifts. Also, customers can choose from countless retail gas outlets, so gas companies have to charge prices that pay for the convenience that consumers demand and also reinvest millions in making stations competitive by adding convenience stores and car washes. Different oil companies also offer loyalty programs. These extras and other consumer incentives provide value-added services for the consumer, so there *is* evidence of competition. Can you explain why these are all good reasons showing the markets at work? Can you think of other reasons to confirm that companies aren't colluding on the price of gas?

WHY ARE MOST COLLUSIVE OLIGOPOLIES SHORT-LIVED?

Collusive oligopolies are potentially highly profitable for participants but detrimental to society. Fortunately, most strong collusive oligopolies are rather short-lived, for two reasons. First, in Canada and in some other nations, collusive oligopolies are strictly illegal under anti-combine laws. For example, in March of 2013, three more individuals were found guilty of conspiring to fix the price of retail gasoline in Sherbrooke and Magog, Quebec. To date, 33 individuals and 7 companies have pleaded guilty or have been found guilty by the courts in connection with this one instance of price fixing. Second, for collusion to work, firms must agree to restrict output to a level that will support the profit-maximizing price. At that price, firms can earn positive economic profits. Yet there is great temptation for firms to cheat on the agreement of the collusive oligopoly, and because collusive agreements are illegal, the other parties have no way to punish the offender. Why do they have a strong incentive to cheat? Because any individual firm could lower its price slightly and thereby increase sales and profits, as long as it goes undetected. Undetected price cuts could bring in new customers, including rivals' customers. In addition, there are nonprice methods of defection— better credit terms, rebates, prompt delivery service, and so on.

SECTION CHECK

- The mutual interdependence of oligopolists tempts them to collude in order to reduce uncertainty and increase potential for monopoly profits.
- Joint profit maximization requires the determination of price based on the market demand for the product and the marginal costs of the various firms.
- Most strong collusive oligopolies are rather short-lived for two reasons: (1) Collusive oligopolies are strictly illegal under Canadian anti-combine laws, and (2) there is great temptation for firms to cheat on the agreement of the collusive oligopoly.

Game Theory and Strategic Behaviour

- What is game theory?
- What are cooperative and noncooperative games?
- What about repeated games?
- What are network externalities?

In some respects, noncollusive oligopoly resembles a military campaign or a poker game. Firms take certain actions not because these actions are necessarily advantageous in themselves but because they improve the position of the oligopolist relative to its competitors and may ultimately improve its financial position. For example, a firm may deliberately cut prices, sacrificing profits either to drive competitors out of business or to discourage them from undertaking actions contrary to the interests of other firms.

WHAT IS GAME THEORY?

game theory
firms attempt to maximize profits by acting in ways that minimize damage from competitors

Some economists have suggested that the entire approach to oligopoly equilibrium and output should be recast. They replace the analysis that assumes that firms attempt to maximize profits with one that examines firm behaviour in terms of a strategic game. This point of view, called **game theory,** stresses how firms attempt to maximize profits by acting in ways that minimize damage from competitors. This approach involves a set of alternative actions (with respect to price and output levels, for example); the action that would be taken in a particular case depends on the specific policies followed by each firm. The firm may try to figure out its competitors' most likely countermoves to its own policies and then formulate alternative defensive measures.

Each firm will react to the price, quantity, and quality of rival firms. Because each firm is interdependent, each must observe the moves of its rivals.

WHAT ARE COOPERATIVE AND NONCOOPERATIVE GAMES?

cooperative game
collusion by two firms in order to improve their profit maximizations

noncooperative game
each firm sets its own price without consulting other firms

Games, in interactions between oligopolists, can either be cooperative or noncooperative. A **cooperative game** involves collusion by two firms in order to improve their profit maximizations. However, as discussed earlier, enforcement costs are usually too high to keep all firms from cheating on collusive agreements. Consequently, most games are **noncooperative games,** in which each firm sets its own price without consulting other firms. The primary difference between cooperative and noncooperative games is the contract. For example, players in a cooperative game can talk and set binding contracts, while those in noncooperative games are assumed to act independently, with no communication and no binding contracts. Because Canadian competition laws forbid firms to collude, we will assume that most strategic behaviour in the marketplace is noncooperative.

The Prisoners' Dilemma

A firm's decision makers must map out a pricing strategy based on a wide range of information. They must also decide whether their strategy will be effective and whether it will be affected by competitors' actions. A strategy that will be optimal regardless

A quarterback wants to run a play that will surprise the defence. The defence knows that the quarterback wants to fool them. So what play does the quarterback run, knowing the defence expects the quarterback to fool them? Is this a game with strategic interaction?

The Canadian Press Images/CFL PHOTO/D. Chidley

of the opponents' actions is called a **dominant strategy.** The classic game that has a dominant strategy and demonstrates the basic problem confronting noncolluding oligopolists is known as the *prisoners' dilemma.*

Imagine that a bank robbery occurs and two suspects are caught. The suspects are placed in separate jail cells and are not allowed to talk to each other. Four results are possible in this situation: both prisoners confess, neither confesses, Prisoner A confesses but Prisoner B doesn't, or Prisoner B confesses but Prisoner A doesn't. In Exhibit 1, we see the **payoff matrix,** a summary of the possible outcomes from the various strategies. Looking at the payoff matrix, we can see that if each prisoner confesses to the crime, each will serve two years in jail. However, if neither confesses, each prisoner may only get one year because of insufficient evidence. Now, if Prisoner A confesses and Prisoner B does not, Prisoner A will get six months (because of his cooperation with the authorities and his evidence) and Prisoner B will get six years. Alternatively, if Prisoner B confesses and Prisoner A does not, Prisoner B will get six months and Prisoner A will get six years. As you can see, then, the prisoners have a dilemma. What should each prisoner do?

Looking at the payoff matrix, we can see that if Prisoner A confesses, it is in the best interest for Prisoner B to confess. If Prisoner A confesses, he will get either two years or six months, depending on what Prisoner B does. However, Prisoner B knows the temptation to confess facing Prisoner A, so confessing is also the best strategy for Prisoner B. A confession would mean a lighter sentence for Prisoner B—two years rather than six years.

It is clear that both would be better off confessing *if* they knew for sure that the other was going to remain silent, because that would lead to a six-month sentence for each.

dominant strategy

will be optimal regardless of the opponents' actions

payoff matrix

a summary of the possible outcomes from the various strategies

---

section 10.7
Exhibit 1　　**The Prisoners' Dilemma Payoff Matrix**

		Prisoner B	
		Confesses	Doesn't Confess
Prisoner A	**Confesses**	2 years (A) / 2 years (B)	6 months (A) / 6 years (B)
	Doesn't Confess	6 years (A) / 6 months (B)	1 year (A) / 1 year (B)

The sentence depends on each prisoner's decision to confess or remain silent. When the prisoners follow their dominant strategy and confess, both will be worse off than if each had remained silent—hence, the prisoners' dilemma.

Fisun Ivan/Shutterstock.com

However, in each case, can the prisoner take the chance that the co-conspirator will not talk? The dominant strategy, although it may not lead to the best joint outcome, is to confess. That is, the prisoners know that confessing is the way to make the best of a bad situation. No matter what their counterpart does, the maximum sentence will be two years for each, and each understands the possibility of being out in six months. In summary, when the prisoners follow their dominant strategy and confess, both will be worse off than if each had remained silent—hence, the "prisoners' dilemma."

Firms in an oligopoly often behave like the prisoners in the prisoners' dilemma, carefully anticipating the moves of their rivals in an uncertain environment. For example, should a firm cut its prices and try to gain more sales by luring customers away from its competitors? What if the firm keeps its price stable and competitors all lower their prices? What if all of the firms decide to raise their prices? Each of these situations will have vastly different implications for an oligopolist, so it must carefully watch and anticipate the moves of its competitors.

Profits under Different Pricing Strategies

To demonstrate how the prisoners' dilemma can shed light on oligopoly theory, let us consider the pricing strategy of two firms. In Exhibit 2, we present the payoff matrix—the possible profits that each firm would earn under the different pricing strategies. Assume that each firm has total production costs of $1 per unit. When both firms set their price at $10 and each sells 1000 units per week, then each earns a profit of $9000 a week. If each firm sets its price at $9, each sells 1100 units per week for a profit of $8800 [($9 − $1) × 1100]. However, what if one firm charges $10 and the other firm charges $9? The low-price firm increases its profits through additional sales. It now sells, say, 1500 units for a profit of $12 000, while the high-price firm sells only 600 units per week for a profit of $5400.

Nash equilibrium

firms that are interacting with one another each chooses its best strategy given the strategies of the other firms

When the two firms each charge $9 per unit, they are said to have reached a Nash equilibrium (named after the Nobel prize-winning economist and mathematician John Nash, who was the subject of the movie *A Beautiful Mind*). At a **Nash equilibrium,**

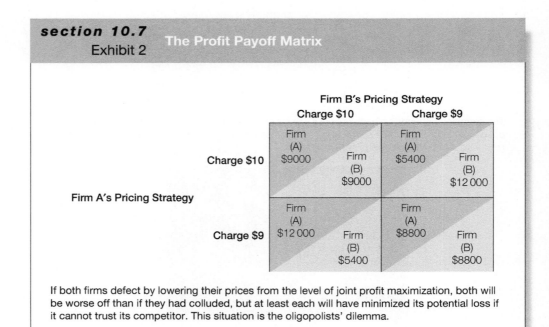

section 10.7
Exhibit 2   The Profit Payoff Matrix

If both firms defect by lowering their prices from the level of joint profit maximization, both will be worse off than if they had colluded, but at least each will have minimized its potential loss if it cannot trust its competitor. This situation is the oligopolists' dilemma.

firms that are interacting with one another each chooses its best strategy given the strategies of the other firms. For example, if each firm believes the other is going to charge $9, then the best strategy for both firms is to charge $9. In this scenario, if Firm A charges $9, the worst possible outcome is a profit of $8800. However, if Firm A prices at $10 and Firm B prices at $9, Firm A will have a profit of only $5400. Hence, the choice that minimizes the risk of the worst scenario is $9. The same is true for Firm B; it too minimizes risk of the worst scenario by choosing to price at the Nash equilibrium, $9. In this case, the Nash equilibrium is also the dominant strategy. The Nash equilibrium takes on particular importance because it is a self-enforcing equilibrium. That is, neither firm has an incentive to move.

In sum, we see that if the two firms were to collude and set the price at $10, it would be in their best interest. However, each firm has a strong incentive to lower its price to $9 if this pricing strategy goes undetected by its competitor. However, if both firms defect by lowering their prices from the level of joint profit maximization, both will be worse off than if they had colluded, but at least each will have minimized its potential loss if it cannot trust its competitor. This situation is the oligopolists' dilemma.

Advertising

Advertising can lead to a situation like the prisoners' dilemma. For example, perhaps the decision makers of a large firm are deciding whether to launch an advertising campaign against a rival firm. According to the payoff matrix in Exhibit 3, if neither company advertises, the two companies split the market, each making $100 million in profits. They also split the market if they both advertise, but their net profits are smaller, $75 million, because they would both incur advertising costs that are greater than any gains in additional revenues from advertising. However, if one advertises and the other does not, the company that advertises takes customers away from the rival. Profits for the company that advertises would be $125 million, and profits for the company that does not advertise would be $50 million.

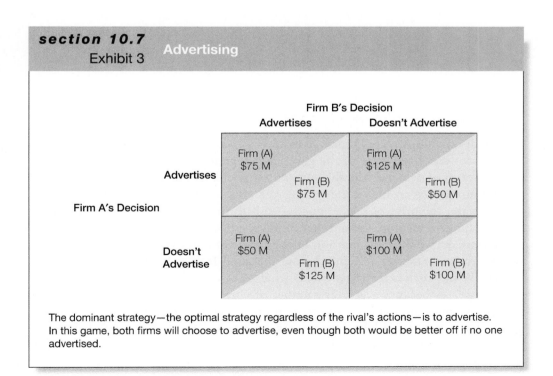

section 10.7
Exhibit 3   Advertising

	Firm B's Decision	
	Advertises	**Doesn't Advertise**
Firm A's Decision — Advertises	Firm (A) $75 M / Firm (B) $75 M	Firm (A) $125 M / Firm (B) $50 M
Firm A's Decision — Doesn't Advertise	Firm (A) $50 M / Firm (B) $125 M	Firm (A) $100 M / Firm (B) $100 M

The dominant strategy—the optimal strategy regardless of the rival's actions—is to advertise. In this game, both firms will choose to advertise, even though both would be better off if no one advertised.

The dominant strategy—the optimal strategy regardless of the rival's actions—is to advertise. In this game, both firms will choose to advertise, even though both would be better off if no one advertised. But one company can't take a chance and not advertise, because if its competitor then elects to advertise, the competitor could have a big year, primarily at the expense of the firm that doesn't advertise.

WHAT ABOUT REPEATED GAMES?

In the one-shot prisoners' dilemma game in Exhibit 1, we saw that the best strategy was to confess regardless of what your opponent does—your behaviour does not influence the other player's behaviour. In one-shot prisoners' dilemma games, self-interest prevents cooperative behaviour and leads to an inferior joint outcome for the participants. However, cooperation is not impossible, because most oligopolistic interactions are not one-shot games. Instead they are repeated games. Most firms assume that they will have repeat customers. For example, if a grocery store fails to provide fresh produce, customers can punish the store by shopping elsewhere in the future. These future consequences change the incentives from those in a one-shot game. All stores might have gained short-run profits from low-quality (and low-cost) produce, but all may offer high-quality produce because of the adverse future effects of offering lower quality produce. In a repeated game, cooperation occurs as long as others continue to cooperate.

Suppose two firms are both going to be in business for many years. Several studies have shown that, in this type of situation, the best strategy is to do what your opponent did to you earlier. This form of strategic behaviour is called **tit-for-tat strategy**—a strategy used in repeated games, where one player follows the other player's move in the previous round, often leading to greater cooperation.

A repeated game allows the firm to establish a reputation of cooperation. Cooperation may mean maintaining a high price or a certain advertising budget, providing that the other firm did the same in the previous round. In short, a firm has an incentive to cooperate now, so there is greater cooperation in the future. However, if your opponent cheats, you cheat in the next round to punish your opponent for a lack of cooperation. You do what your opponent did in the previous round. In the tit-for-tat game, both firms will be better off if they stick to the plan rather than cheating—that is, failing to cooperate. Many cartels appear to employ the tit-for-tat strategy. In short, the most effective strategy to promote cooperation is tit-for-tat.

WHAT ARE NETWORK EXTERNALITIES?

In our discussion of supply and demand (Chapter 3), we assumed that demand was a function of the price of the good (a change in quantity demanded) and the determinants of demand (the shifters that cause changes in demand). For example, the amount of ice cream we are willing and able to buy is a function of the price of ice cream, the price of related goods—substitutes like yogurt and complements like hot fudge—income, the number of buyers, tastes, and expectations. However, a determinant we did not mention at the time was a **network externality**—when the number of other people purchasing the good influences quantity demanded. A **positive network externality** occurs when a consumer's quantity demanded for a good increases because a greater number of consumers purchase the same good. A **negative network externality** occurs if the consumer's quantity demanded for a good increases because fewer consumers are purchasing the same good. In other words, sometimes an individual's demand curve is influenced by the other people purchasing the good.

tit-for-tat strategy
used in repeated games, where one player follows the other player's move in the previous round; leads to greater cooperation

network externality
when the number of other people purchasing the good influences quantity demanded

positive network externality
when a consumer's quantity demanded for a good increases because a greater number of consumers purchase the same good

negative network externality
when a consumer's quantity demanded for a good increases because fewer consumers are purchasing the same good

Positive Network Externalities

Many examples of network externalities can be found in the communications area, such as with fax machines, telephones, and the Internet. Imagine you had a telephone, but nobody else did; it would be relatively worthless without others with whom to talk. It is also true that if you were the only one to own a Blu-ray player, it would make little sense for manufacturers to make Blu-ray discs and your Blu-ray player would be of little value.

The software industry has many examples of positive network externalities. For example, it is a lot easier to coordinate work if people are using the same software on their computers. It is also a lot easier (less costly) to get help if you need it because many people are familiar with the product, which may be a lot easier (less costly) than calling the software supplier for help. Another example is Apple's FaceTime application—others have to have this video calling software (not to mention an Apple product to run it on). In short, our demand increases as the number of users increases.

Another type of positive network externality is called the **bandwagon effect,** where a consumer's demand for a product increases because other consumers own it. In recent years, we watched people get on the bandwagon in the toy industry with Beyblades, Silly Bandz, Bratz, Tickle Me Elmo, and Furbies, among others. It can happen in the clothing industry, too (e.g., lululemon athletic clothes or UGG boots).

bandwagon effect
a positive network externality where a consumer's demand for a product increases because other consumers own it

Negative Network Externalities

Other goods and services are subject to negative network externalities, which may be a result of the snob effect. The snob effect is a negative network externality, where a consumer wants to own a unique good. For example, a rare junior hockey card of Wayne Gretzky, a Model T car, a Vincent Van Gogh painting, a Rolex watch, or an expensive sports car may qualify as snob goods, where the quantity that a particular individual demanded of a good increases when fewer other people own it. Firms seek to achieve a snob effect though marketing and advertising, knowing that if they can create a less elastic demand curve for their product they can raise price.

Negative network externalities can arise from congestion too. For example, if you are a member of a health club, a negative network externality may occur because too many people are in the gym working out at the same time. Even though I may prefer a ski resort with shorter lift lines, others may view these goods as a positive externality and would increase their quantity demanded if more people were in the gym, on the beach, or on the ski slopes. Perhaps they do not want to work out alone, hang out on a lonely beach, or ride up on the chair lift by themselves. That is, whether it is a positive or negative externality may depend on the consumer's tastes and preferences.

Switching Costs

Along with the possible advantages of joining a larger network from capturing positive network externalities, you may also encounter costs if you leave. **Switching costs** are the costs involved in changing from one product to another brand or in changing suppliers. For example, costs are associated with switching to a new social networking site. If you were very familiar with Facebook and had established an extensive network of "friends," it would be costly to switch to Google+ and start over again. Network externalities and switching costs are two of the reasons that eBay and Amazon.com have done so well. The first firm in a market, where everybody in its large customer base is familiar with the operation, gains huge advantages. Other potential competitors recognize this advantage and, as a result, are leery of entering into the business.

switching costs
the costs involved in changing from one product to another brand or in changing suppliers

In short, in industries that see significant positive network effects, oligopoly is likely to be present. That is, a small number of firms may be able to secure most of the market. Consumers tend to choose the products that everyone else is using. Thus, behaviour may allow these firms to increase their output and achieve economies of scale that smaller firms cannot obtain. Hence, the smaller firms will go out of business or be bought out by larger firms.

SECTION CHECK

- Game theory stresses the tendency of various parties to minimize damage from opponents. A firm may try to figure out its competitors' most likely countermoves to its own policies and then formulate alternative defensive measures.
- Players in cooperative games can talk and set binding contracts, while those in noncooperative games are assumed to act independently with no communications and no binding contracts. The prisoners' dilemma is an example of a noncooperative game.
- In one-shot games, the participants' self-interest tends to prevent cooperative behaviour, but in repeated games, cooperation occurs as long as others continue to cooperate (a tit-for-tat strategy).
- Positive (negative) network externality occurs when a consumer's quantity demanded increases (decreases) because a greater (smaller) number of consumers purchase the same good.

For Your Review

Section 10.1

1. Which of the following markets is/are perfectly competitive or monopolistically competitive? Why?
   a. soy market
   b. retail clothing stores
   c. CUT Steakhouse in Halifax
2. List three ways in which a grocery store might differentiate itself from its competitors.
3. What might make you choose one gas station over another?
4. If Frank's hot dog stand was profitable when he first opened, why should he expect those profits to fall over time?
5. Can you explain why some restaurants are highly profitable while other restaurants in the same general area are going out of business?
6. Suppose that half of the restaurants in a city are closed so that the remaining eateries can operate at full capacity. What "cost" might restaurant patrons incur as a result?
7. How does Starbucks differentiate its product? Why does Starbucks stay open until late at night but a doughnut or bagel shop might close at noon?

8. Product differentiation is a hallmark of monopolistic competition, and the text lists four sources of such differentiation: physical differences, prestige, location, and service. How do firms in the industries listed below differentiate their products? How important is each of the four sources of differentiation in each case? Give the most important source of differentiation in each case.

   a. fast-food restaurants

   b. espresso shops/carts

   c. hair stylists

   d. soft drink company

   e. wine merchant

Section 10.2

9. Draw a graph showing a monopolistically competitive firm in a short-run equilibrium where it is earning positive economic profits. What must be true of price versus average total cost for such a firm? What will happen to the firm's demand curve as a result of the short-run profits?

10. Draw a graph showing a monopolistically competitive firm in a short-run equilibrium where it is earning economic losses. What must be true of price versus average total cost for such a firm? What will happen to the firm's demand curve as a result of the short-run losses?

11. How is price related to marginal cost and average total cost for monopolistically competitive firms in the following situations?

   a. a short-run equilibrium where it is earning positive economic profits

   b. a short-run equilibrium where it is earning economic losses

   c. a short-run equilibrium where it is earning zero economic profits

   d. a long-run equilibrium

12. The following graph shows the long-run equilibrium for a monopolistically competitive firm.

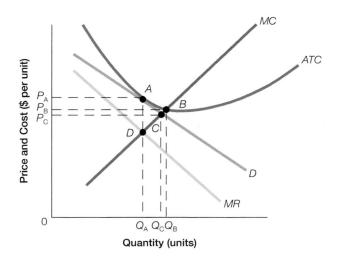

   a. For this monopolistically competitive firm, what is the profit-maximizing output level and at what price will it sell this output?

   b. At profit maximization, explain why this firm is considered to be in long-run equilibrium.

13. The following table displays the daily quantity sold, prices, and costs for an automotive oil-change business. While competing with several other companies that offer similar services, this operation differentiates itself by offering warranty-approved service without having to make an appointment.

Quantity (number of oil changes)	Price	MC	ATC
0	$50.00		
1	45.00	$13.00	$30.50
2	40.00	18.00	26.75
3	35.00	23.00	24.75
4	30.00	28.00	26.25
5	25.00	33.00	28.75
6	20.00	38.00	32.50

a. Why would this automotive oil-change business be considered monopolistically competitive?

b. In the short run, what would be the profit-maximizing number of oil changes? What price would this monopolistically competitive firm charge in the short run?

c. Determine whether our monopolistically competitive firm is generating economic profits in the short run. If so, how much?

Section 10.3

14. Refer to the diagram in question 12. Explain why this monopolistically competitive firm, despite being in long-run equilibrium, has failed to achieve either productive or allocative efficiency.

15. How are monopolistically competitive firms and perfectly competitive firms similar? Why don't monopolistically competitive firms produce the same output in the long run as perfectly competitive firms, which face similar costs?

16. What is meant by the *price of variety*? Graph and explain.

17. As you know, perfect competition and monopolistic competition differ in important ways. Show your understanding of these differences by listing the following terms below under either "Perfect Competition" or "Monopolistic Competition."

	Perfect Competition	Monopolistic Competition
Standardized product		
Differentiated product		
Allocative efficiency		
Excess capacity		
Productive efficiency		
Horizontal demand curve		
Downward-sloping demand curve		
No control over price		

Section 10.4

18. Why is advertising more important for the success of chains such as Toys "R" Us and Office Depot than for the corner barbershop?

19. Think of your favourite ads on television. Do you think that these ads have an effect on your spending? These ads are expensive; do you think they are a waste from society's standpoint?

20. In what way is the use of advertising another example of Adam Smith's "invisible hand," according to which entrepreneurs pursuing their own best interest make consumers better off?

21. How does advertising intend to shift demand? How does it intend to change the elasticity of demand?

22. Why is it so important for monopolistically competitive firms to advertise?

Section 10.5

23. Which of the following markets are oligopolistic?
    a. corn
    b. funeral services
    c. airline travel
    d. hamburgers
    e. oil
    f. breakfast cereals

24. Which of the following are characteristic of oligopolistic industries?
    a. a large number of firms
    b. few firms
    c. a high degree of product differentiation
    d. high barriers to entry
    e. free entry and exit
    f. mutual interdependence

25. Explain how the long-run equilibrium under oligopoly differs from that of perfect competition.

26. Important differences exist between perfect competition and oligopoly. Show your understanding of these differences by listing the following terms under either "Perfect Competition" or "Oligopoly" in the table below.

allocative efficiency	high barriers to entry	downward-sloping demand curve
large economies of scale	horizontal demand curve	
many small firms	few large firms	no control over price
productive efficiency	mutual interdependence	

Perfect Competition	Oligopoly

Section 10.6

27. Suppose Farmer Smith from Saskatchewan and Farmer Jones from Alberta agree to restrict their combined output of wheat in an attempt to increase the price and profits. How likely do you think the Smith–Jones cartel is to succeed? Explain.

28. Explain how the joint profit-maximizing price of colluding firms under oligopoly is determined? How about output?

29. One of the world's most successful cartels has been the De Beers Central Selling Organization (CSO), which controls about three-quarters of the world's diamonds. This collusive oligopoly has kept diamond prices high by restricting supply. The CSO has also promoted the general consumption of diamonds through advertising and marketing. New supplies of diamonds have been found in Canada and Russia. These new mines, which are outside the direct control of the CSO, want to sell their diamonds on the open market.

    a. How might the CSO cartel be in jeopardy if these new mines in Canada and Russia do not cooperate with the cartel and instead supply their diamonds to the market outside the collusive agreement established by the CSO?

    b. Given the situation described in part (a), what do you think would happen to CSO diamond advertising?

30. Suppose your professor announced that each student in your large lecture class who receives the highest score (no matter how high) on the take-home final exam will get an A in the course. The professor points out that if the entire class colludes successfully, everyone could get the same score. Is it likely that everyone in the class will get an A?

Section 10.7

31. Two firms compete in the breakfast cereal industry producing Wheat Krinkles and Rice Krinkles cereal, respectively. Each manufacturer must decide whether to promote its product with a large or small advertising budget. The potential profits for these firms are as shown below (in millions of dollars).

		Firm A **Wheat Krinkles Cereal**	
		Small Advertising Budget	**Large Advertising Budget**
Firm B Rice Krinkles Cereal	**Small Advertising Budget**	Firm (A) $50 M Firm (B) $50 M	Firm (A) $30 M Firm (B) $100 M
	Large Advertising Budget	Firm (A) $140 M Firm (B) $20 M	Firm (A) $150 M Firm (B) $150 M

Describe the nature of the mutual interdependence of the two firms. Is a Nash equilibrium evident?

32. Suppose Pepsi is considering an ad campaign aimed at rival Coca-Cola. What is the dominant strategy if the payoff matrix is similar to the one shown in Exhibit 3 in Section 10.7?

33. The following payoff matrix shows the possible sentences that two suspects, arrested on suspicion of car theft, could receive. The suspects are interrogated separately and are unable to communicate with one another. Use the payoff matrix to answer the questions that follow it.

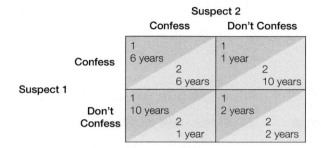

For the information given in the payoff matrix above:

a. Is there is a dominant strategy? If so, what is it?

b. Is there a Nash equilibrium? How do you know?

34. Why are repeated games more likely to be more cooperative than one-shot games?

35. Why might shirking on a team project in school be a dominant strategy, but not shirking on a team project at work?

chapter

11

Labour Markets and the Distribution of Income

section 11.1 Labour Markets

- What determines the price paid to workers?
- What is derived demand?

WHAT DETERMINES THE PRICE PAID TO WORKERS?

Approximately 70 percent of net national income goes to wages and salaries for labour services. After labourers take their share, the remaining 30 percent of net national income is compensation received by the owners of land and capital and the entrepreneurs who employ those resources to produce valued goods and services. In this chapter we will see how supply and demand in the labour market determines the salary levels among different workers.

In labour markets, actor Mike Myers was paid $25 million to make one movie. Singer Celine Dion's income is many times larger than that of the average college professor or medical doctor. Female models make more than male models, yet male basketball players make more than female basketball players. Why is this the case? To understand why some workers receive such vastly different compensation for their labour than others, we must focus on the workings of supply and demand in the labour market.

WHAT IS DERIVED DEMAND?

Input markets are the markets for the factors of production used to produce output. Output (goods and services) markets and input markets have one major difference. In input or factor markets, the demand for an input is called a **derived demand.** That is, the demand for an input like labour is derived from the consumer demand for the good or service. So consumers do *not* demand the labour directly—it is the goods and services that labour produces that consumers demand. For example, the chef at a

derived demand
the demand for an input is derived from the consumer's demands for a good or service

restaurant is paid for her skills, which are in demand because she produces what the customer wants—a meal. The "price" of any productive factor is directly related to consumer demand for the final good or service.

SECTION CHECK

■ Supply and demand determine the prices paid to workers.
■ In factor or input markets, demand is derived from consumers' demand for the final good or service that the input produces.

Supply and Demand in the Labour Market

■ Will hiring that extra worker add more to revenue than to costs?
■ Why is the labour demand curve downward sloping?
■ How many workers will an employer hire?
■ What is the shape of the labour supply curve?

marginal revenue product (*MRP*)
the additional revenue that a firm obtains from one more unit of input

marginal resource cost (*MRC*)
the amount that an extra input adds to the firm's total costs

WILL HIRING THAT EXTRA WORKER ADD MORE TO REVENUE THAN TO COSTS?

Because firms are trying to maximize their profits, they try to make the *difference* between total revenue and total cost as large as possible. An input's attractiveness, then, varies with what the input can add to the firm's revenues relative to what the input adds to costs. The demand for labour is determined by its **marginal revenue product (*MRP*)**—the additional revenue that a firm obtains from one more unit of input. Why? Suppose a worker adds $500 per week to a firm's sales by his productivity; he produces 100 units that add $5 each to firm revenue. In order to determine if the worker adds to the firm's profits, we would need to calculate the marginal resource cost associated with the worker. The **marginal resource cost (*MRC*)** is the amount that an extra input adds to the firm's total costs. In this case, the marginal resource cost is the wage the employer has to pay to entice an extra worker. Assume that the marginal resource cost of the worker, the market wage, is $350 per worker a week. In our example, the firm would find its profits growing by adding one more worker, because the marginal benefit (*MRP*) associated with the worker, $500, would exceed the marginal cost (*MRC*) of the worker, $350. So we can see that just by adding another worker to its labour force, the firm would increase its weekly profits by $150 ($500 − $350). Even if the market wage was $490 per week, the firm

Restaurant owners are willing to pay a wage to workers because the owners expect to be able to sell the food and services produced at a price high enough to cover workers' wages and all other costs of production.

Sean Gallup/Getty Images News/Thinkstock

could slightly increase its profits by hiring the employee because the marginal revenue product, $500, is greater than the added labour cost, $490. At wage payments above $500, however, the firm would not be interested in adding the worker because the marginal resource cost would exceed the marginal revenue product, making additional hiring unprofitable.

WHY IS THE LABOUR DEMAND CURVE DOWNWARD SLOPING?

The downward-sloping demand curve for labour indicates a negative relationship between the wage and the quantity of labour demanded. Higher wages will decrease the quantity of labour demanded, whereas lower wages will increase the quantity of labour demanded. But why does this relationship exist?

The major reason for the downward-sloping demand curve for labour (illustrated in Exhibit 1) is the law of diminishing marginal product. Remember that the law of diminishing marginal product states that as increasing quantities of some variable input (say, labour) are added to fixed quantities of another input (say, land or capital), output will rise, but at some point it will increase by diminishing amounts.

Consider a farmer who owns a given amount of land. Suppose he is producing wheat, and the relationship between his output and his labour force requirements is that indicated in Exhibit 2. Output expands as more workers are hired to cultivate the land, but the growth in output steadily slows, meaning the added output associated with one more worker declines as more workers are added. For example, in Exhibit 2 when a third worker is hired, total wheat output increases from 5500 tonnes to 7000 tonnes, an increase of 1500 tonnes in terms of marginal product. However, when a fourth worker is added, total wheat output increases from 7000 tonnes to only 8000 tonnes, or a marginal increase of 1000 tonnes. Note that the reason for this is *not* that the workers being added are steadily inferior in terms of ability or quality relative to the first workers. Indeed, for simplicity, we assume that each worker has exactly the same skills and productive capacity. But as more workers are added, each additional worker has fewer of the fixed resources with which to work, and marginal product falls. For example, the fifth worker might just cultivate the same land more intensively. The work of the fifth worker, then, might only slightly improve output. That is, the marginal product (*MP*)—the number of physical units of added output from the addition of one additional unit of input—falls.

As we discussed earlier, the marginal revenue product (*MRP*) is the change in total revenue associated with an additional unit of input. The marginal

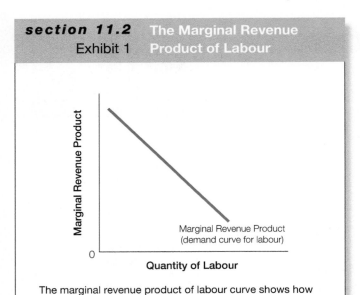

section 11.2
Exhibit 1

The Marginal Revenue Product of Labour

The marginal revenue product of labour curve shows how the marginal revenue product depends on the number of workers employed. The curve is downward sloping because of the diminishing marginal product of labour.

section 11.2
Exhibit 2

Diminishing Marginal Productivity on a Hypothetical Farm

Units of Labour Input (workers)	Total Wheat Output (tonnes per year)	Marginal Product of Labour (tonnes per year)
0	—	—
1	3000	3000
2	5500	2500
3	7000	1500
4	8000	1000
5	8500	500
6	8800	300
7	9000	200

revenue product is equal to the marginal product, the units of output added by a worker, multiplied by marginal revenue, in this case the price of the output (e.g., $10 per tonne of wheat).

$$MRP = MP \times P$$

(Note that in this case the price of the output, wheat, is the same at all levels of output because the farmer is a price taker in a competitive wheat market.)

The marginal revenue product of labour declines because of the diminishing marginal product of labour when additional workers are added. This is illustrated in Exhibit 3, which shows various output and revenue levels for a wheat farmer using different quantities of labour. We see in Exhibit 3 that the marginal product, or the added physical volume of output, declines as the number of workers grows because of diminishing marginal product. Thus, the fifth worker adds only 60 tonnes of wheat per week, compared with 100 tonnes for the first worker.

HOW MANY WORKERS WILL AN EMPLOYER HIRE?

Profits are maximized if the firm hires only to the point where the wage equals the expected marginal revenue product. Because the demand curve for labour and the value of the marginal revenue product show the quantity of labour that a firm demands at a given wage in a competitive labour market, we say that the marginal revenue product (*MRP*) is the same as the demand curve for labour for a competitive firm.

Using the data in Exhibit 3, if the market wage is $500 per week, it would pay for the grower to employ six workers. The sixth worker's marginal revenue product ($500) equals the wage, so profits are maximized. Adding a seventh worker would be unprofitable, though, as that worker's marginal revenue product of $400 is less than the wage of $500. Hiring the seventh worker would reduce profits by $100.

But what if the market wage increases from $500 to $700? In this case, the firm would employ only four workers, since the fourth worker's marginal revenue product ($700) equals the wage ($700), so profits are maximized. That is, a higher wage rate, *ceteris paribus,* lowers the employment levels of individual firms.

section 11.2
Exhibit 3 Marginal Revenue Product, Output, and Labour Inputs

Quantity of Labour	Total Output (tonnes per week)	Marginal Product of Labour (tonnes per week)	Product Price (dollars per tonne)	Marginal Revenue Product of Labour	Wage Rate (MRC) (dollars per week)
0	0	100	$10	$1000	$500
1	100	90	10	900	500
2	190	80	10	800	500
3	270	70	10	700	500
4	340	60	10	600	500
5	400	50	10	500	500
6	450	40	10	400	500
7	490	30	10	300	500
8	520				

section 11.2
Exhibit 4   The Competitive Firm's Hiring Decision

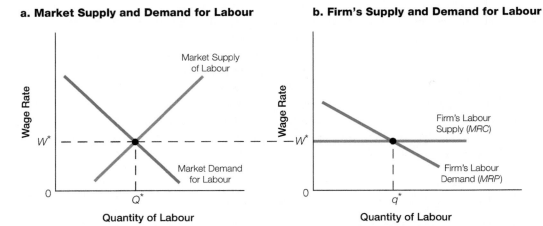

a. Market Supply and Demand for Labour

b. Firm's Supply and Demand for Labour

A competitive firm can hire any number of potential workers at the market-determined wage; it is a wage taker. At employment levels less than q^*, additional workers add profits. At employment levels beyond q^*, additional workers are unprofitable; at q^*, profits are maximized.

In a competitive labour market, many firms are competing for workers and no single firm is big enough by itself to have any significant effect on the level of wages. The intersection of the market supply of labour and the market demand for labour determines the competitive market wage, as shown in Exhibit 4(a). The firm's ability to hire all the workers it wants at the prevailing wage is similar to perfect competition in output markets, where a firm could sell all it wanted at the going price.

In Exhibit 4, when the firm hires fewer than q^* workers, the marginal revenue product exceeds the market wage, so adding workers expands profits. With more than q^* workers, though, the "going wage" exceeds marginal revenue product, and hiring additional workers lowers profits. With q^* workers, profits are maximized.

In this chapter, we assume that labour markets are competitive—there are many buyers and sellers of labour, with no individual firm or no individual worker having an impact on wages. This is generally a realistic assumption because in most labour markets, firms compete with each other to attract workers and workers can choose from many possible employers.

WHAT IS THE SHAPE OF THE LABOUR SUPPLY CURVE?

How much work effort are individuals collectively willing and able to supply in the marketplace? This is the essence of the market supply curve. Just as was the case in our earlier discussion of the law of supply, a positive relationship exists between the wage rate and the quantity of labour supplied. As the wage rate rises, the quantity of labour supplied increases, *ceteris paribus;* as the wage rate falls, the quantity of labour supplied falls, *ceteris paribus*. This positive relationship is consistent with the actual empirical evidence that the total quantity of labour supplied by *all* workers increases as the wage rate increases, as shown in Exhibit 5.

An Individual's Labour Supply Curve

Will the quantity of labour supplied by an individual be greater at higher wages than lower wages? The answer is by no means obvious because workers have another use for their time—leisure. Furthermore, wage increases have two conflicting effects on the quantity of labour supplied:

1. *Substitution effect:* At a higher wage rate, the cost of forgoing labour time to gain more leisure time increases, producing a tendency to substitute labour for leisure. In other words, a higher wage rate makes leisure more expensive—its opportunity cost rises.
2. *Income effect:* At a higher wage rate, the quantity of labour supplied tends to decrease because many individuals consider leisure a normal good. So when income increases, people demand more leisure. That is, at some wage rate, some workers feel that they can afford more leisure.

Thus, the individual's labour supply curve might be backward-bending. At a lower wage rate, as wages increase, the worker might supply more hours of work to obtain as much money income as possible (the substitution effect dominates the income effect), resulting in an upward-sloping labour supply curve. However, above a certain wage rate, a worker might prefer to work less and enjoy more leisure (the income effect dominates the substitution effect), resulting in a **backward-bending labour supply curve.** That is, if the substitution effect is stronger than the income effect, the individual's labour supply curve is upward sloping. If the income effect is stronger than the substitution effect, the individual's labour supply curve is backward-bending.

For example, a student working during the summer to earn money for the school year might quit her job once she has reached a certain level of earnings; she then concentrates on leisure for the rest of the summer. In this case, the student's labour supply curve might appear as shown in Exhibit 6. Actually, the market supply curve might also bend backward, too, but at a much higher wage rate than currently exists. In the rest of this chapter, therefore, we will assume that the market supply curve is upward sloping, at least in the relevant range.

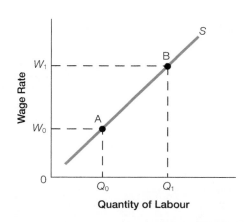

section 11.2
Exhibit 5
The Market Supply
Curve of Labour

An increase in the wage rate, from A to B, leads to an increase in the quantity of labour supplied, *ceteris paribus*. A decrease in the wage rate, from B to A, leads to a decrease in the quantity of labour supplied, *ceteris paribus*.

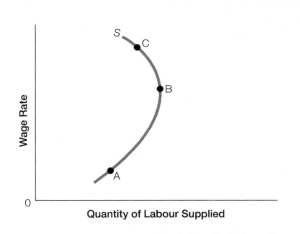

section 11.2
Exhibit 6
An Individual Backward–
Bending Labour Supply Curve

The movement of A → B results from the substitution effect being stronger than the income effect. The movement of B → C results from the income effect being stronger than the substitution effect.

backward-bending labour supply curve
above a certain wage rate, a worker might prefer to work less and enjoy more leisure (the income effect dominates the substitution effect)

SECTION CHECK

- Whether an additional unit of labour is hired depends on the unit's marginal revenue product (*MRP*) and its marginal resource cost (*MRC*).
- The demand curve for labour is downward sloping because of diminishing marginal product. That is, if additional labour is added to a fixed quantity of land or capital equipment, output will increase, but eventually by smaller amounts.
- Profits are maximized if the firm hires only up to the point where the wage equals the expected marginal revenue product.
- Along a market supply curve, a higher wage rate will increase the quantity of labour supplied and a lower wage rate will decrease the quantity of labour supplied.

section
11.3   Labour Market Equilibrium

- How is equilibrium determined in a competitive labour market?
- What shifts the labour demand curve?
- What shifts the labour supply curve?
- What is a monopsony?

section 11.3   **Supply and Demand**
Exhibit 1   **in the Labour Market**

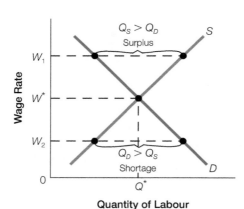

Equilibrium prices and quantities in the labour market are determined in the same way that prices and quantities of goods and services are determined: by the intersection of demand and supply. At wages above the equilibrium wage, like W_1, quantity supplied exceeds quantity demanded, and potential workers will be willing to supply their labour services for an amount lower than the prevailing wage. At a wage lower than W^*, like W_2, potential demanders will overcome the resulting shortage of labour by offering workers a wage greater than the prevailing wage. In both cases, wages are pushed toward the equilibrium value.

HOW IS EQUILIBRIUM DETERMINED IN A COMPETITIVE LABOUR MARKET?

The equilibrium wage and quantity in the labour market is determined by the intersection of labour demand and labour supply. Referring to Exhibit 1, the equilibrium wage, W^*, and equilibrium employment level, Q^*, are found at that point where the quantity of labour demanded equals the quantity of labour supplied. At any wage higher than W^*, like at W_1, the quantity of labour supplied exceeds the quantity of labour demanded, resulting in a surplus of labour. In this situation, unemployed workers would be willing to undercut the established wage in order to get jobs, pushing the wage down and returning the market to equilibrium. Likewise, at a wage below the equilibrium level, like at W_2, quantity demanded would exceed quantity supplied, resulting in a labour shortage. In this situation, employers would be forced to offer higher wages in order to hire as many workers as they would like. Note that only at the equilibrium wage are both suppliers and demanders able to exchange the quantity of labour they desire.

WHAT SHIFTS THE LABOUR DEMAND CURVE?

In Chapter 3, we demonstrated that changes in the determinants of demand can shift the demand curve for a good or service. In the case of an input such as labour, two important factors can shift the demand curve: increases in labour productivity, such as those due to technological advances, or changes in the output price of the good, such as those due to increased demand for the firm's product. Exhibit 2 highlights the impact of these changes.

Changes in Labour Productivity

Workers can increase productivity if they have more capital or land with which to work, if technological improvements occur, or if they acquire additional skills or experience. This increase in productivity will increase the marginal product of the labour and shift the demand curve for labour to the right from D_0 to D_1 in Exhibit 2(a). However, if labour productivity falls, then marginal product will fall and the demand curve for labour will shift to the left, as shown in Exhibit 2(b).

Changes in the Demand for the Firm's Product

The greater the demand for the firm's product, the greater the firm's demand for labour or any other variable input (the "derived demand" discussed earlier). This is because the higher demand for the firm's product increases the firm's marginal revenue, which increases marginal revenue product. That is, the greater demand for the product will cause prices to rise, and the price of the product is part of the value of the labour to the firm ($MRP = MP \times P$)—so the rising product price shifts the labour demand curve to the right. Of course, if demand for the firm's product falls, the labour demand curve will shift to the left as marginal revenue product falls.

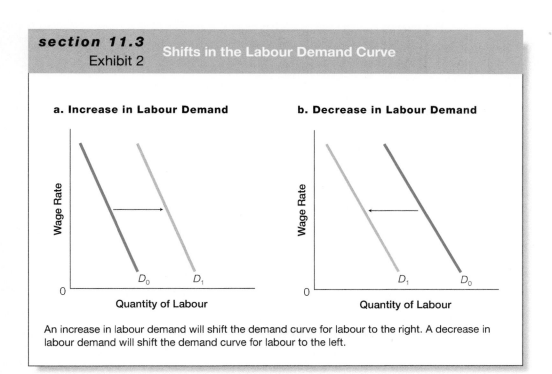

section 11.3
Exhibit 2   **Shifts in the Labour Demand Curve**

a. Increase in Labour Demand

Wage Rate

Quantity of Labour

D_0 D_1

0

b. Decrease in Labour Demand

Wage Rate

Quantity of Labour

D_1 D_0

0

An increase in labour demand will shift the demand curve for labour to the right. A decrease in labour demand will shift the demand curve for labour to the left.

WHAT SHIFTS THE LABOUR SUPPLY CURVE?

In Chapter 3, we learned that changes in the determinants of supply can shift the supply curve for goods and services to the right or left. Likewise, several factors can cause the labour supply curve to shift. These factors include immigration and population growth, the number of hours workers are willing to work at a given wage (worker tastes or preferences), nonwage income, and amenities. Exhibit 3 illustrates the impact of these factors on the labour supply curve.

Immigration and Population Growth

If new workers enter the labour force, it will shift the labour supply curve to the right, as from S_0 to S_1 in Exhibit 3(a). Of course, if workers leave the country or the labour force population declines, it will cause the supply curve to shift to the left, as shown in Exhibit 3(b).

Number of Hours People Are Willing to Work (Worker Preferences)

If people become willing to work more hours at a given wage (due to changes in worker tastes or preferences), the labour supply curve will shift to the right, shown in the movement from S_0 to S_1 in Exhibit 3(a). If they become willing to work fewer hours at a given wage (e.g., as they approach retirement age), then the labour supply curve will shift to the left, as shown in Exhibit 3(b).

Nonwage Income

Increases in income from sources other than employment can cause the labour supply curve to shift to the left. For example, if you just won $20 million in the lottery, you might decide to take yourself out of the labour force. Likewise, a decrease in nonwage

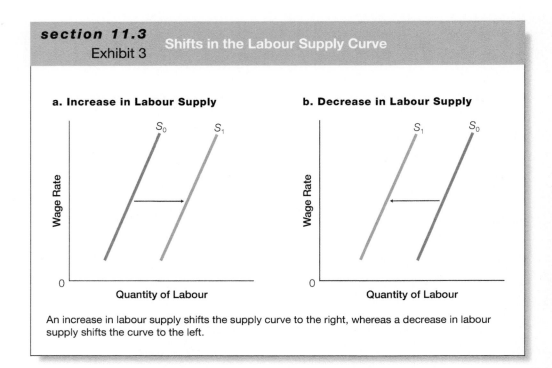

section 11.3
Exhibit 3   **Shifts in the Labour Supply Curve**

a. Increase in Labour Supply

Wage Rate / Quantity of Labour

S_0 S_1

b. Decrease in Labour Supply

Wage Rate / Quantity of Labour

S_1 S_0

An increase in labour supply shifts the supply curve to the right, whereas a decrease in labour supply shifts the curve to the left.

income (say, if pension benefits were reduced) might push a person back into the labour force, thus shifting the labour supply curve to the right.

Amenities

Amenities associated with a job or a location—like good fringe benefits, safe and friendly working conditions, a child-care centre, and so on—will make for a more desirable work atmosphere, *ceteris paribus*. These amenities would cause an increase in the supply of labour, resulting in a rightward shift, such as from S_0 to S_1 in Exhibit 3(a). If job conditions deteriorated, it would lead to a reduction in the labour supply, shifting the labour supply curve to the left, as shown in Exhibit 3(b).

WHAT IS A MONOPSONY?

So far our discussion has assumed that the labour market is competitive—many buyers of labour and many sellers of labour, with no one having a marked impact on wages. Recall that, in the case of a single seller of a product or input, we say that a **monopsony** exists. When the market involves a single buyer, however, we say that a monopsony exists. While monopsony could exist in any single-buyer situation, the situation considered most relevant in the real world is the labour market. Monopsony usually refers, then, to circumstances where only one employer is bidding for the services of many labourers. Where monopsony is present, the buyer of labour may have market power and may be able to affect wages. However, pure monopsony, like pure monopoly, is rare. For example, monopsony may arise because a person within a given locality has only a relatively few choices of where to work. However, if the individual was willing to move or if the number of buyers increased, then the role of a monopsony would be diminished. So, monopsony power is more likely to be present where movement and search costs impede workers from seeking employment in different locales.

monopsony
a market with a single buyer

In the nineteenth century, one or two lumber mills often dominated northern Ontario towns; in other areas, a single mining or manufacturing firm dominated the community to the point that it might be called a *company town*. Monopsony power existed in such situations and increased the opportunities for monopsonistic exploitation. Even though no fences around the town kept workers from leaving, high transportation costs and the expense involved in investigating job opportunities elsewhere made it expensive, sometimes prohibitively so, for workers to move to another locale. Economic theory suggests that where monopsony exists, fewer will be hired at lower wages than if perfect competition prevailed in the labour market. That is, the monopsony firm moves down along the positively sloped labour supply curve it faces, lowering the wages it pays and increasing profits. In short, workers will work for less than their marginal revenue product—they are in this sense exploited.

Today, an example of monopsony power is the situation in some professional sports, where drafted players are assigned to teams until they are eligible to be free agents (after six years in baseball). Because other teams cannot compete for these players, the outcome is lower salaries, as team owners exercise their monopsony power. However, for the most part, in most occupations, many potential employers in many different locations compete for workers.

Business *CONNECTION*

IS A RETAIL GIANT HEALTHY FOR THE ECONOMY?

Historically, there has been much debate in economic circles about market inefficiencies resulting from monopolies. Governments too have considered the costs and benefits of monopolies, but there has been little serious concern about monopsonies—markets with a single buyer. Why? To date, markets just haven't experienced situations where there is a single buyer that has any significant impact on the market. As markets mature, though, we see ever-increasing economic concentration through international mergers and acquisitions. Walmart has come to have a dominant position in the retail sector, and even though it doesn't technically have monopsony power, it's acting as if it does because of the concentration and power it exerts on its suppliers. Should governments review Walmart's market dominance with thoughts of bringing in new regulations?

Walmart has competition in the market from a number of other large retailers, but in the United States, it's bigger than Home Depot, Sears, Costco, Target, Kmart, and Kroger combined. At Walmart in the United States, the average family of four spends over $4000 a year, and one out of every four grocery dollars; the company does $474.88 billion a year in sales.* With these numbers, Walmart controls both access to the retail customer and what suppliers can charge to get access to that market.

At what cost does the economy accept this control? For one, suppliers' margins are squeezed, not to be competitive, but to get access to the market. Fewer dollars are available to suppliers for innovation and product development. Suppliers also have to squeeze their workforce in order to reduce costs, which means fewer jobs and those that remain are likely part-time positions with fewer hours and benefits. These supply companies used to be able to provide reasonable benefits, but now they can't, which means employees are forced to seek publicly funded, low-quality benefits—in essence, governments are funding Walmart's employee costs.

*Barry Ritholtz, "Always Low Wages? Wal-Mart's Other Choices," *Bloomberg View*, December 18, 2013, www.bloombergview.com/articles/2013-12-18/always-low-wages-wal-mart-s-other-choices.

With fewer suppliers, Walmart is contributing to the destruction of small and medium-sized enterprises (SMEs), which are the backbone of the North American manufacturing base and the backbone of a healthy economy. It's not only the SMEs that are under siege from Walmart, but even large multinationals that have relied on so much concentrated revenue coming from Walmart that they have no leverage to increase prices for fear of losing the Walmart account. (Walmart, with its market power, could easily contract third-party suppliers to manufacture house-brand products at higher margins than name brands have traditionally held.)

The long-term health of the retail sector depends on fair and open competition. Governments took aim at firms that amassed market power by being the sole producer. They now need to rewrite their anti-trust laws to reflect market conditions where one firm amasses power by being the controlling buyer and restricting access to the consumer market.

In its defence, Walmart has so far successfully argued that it has reduced prices for consumers and been one of North America's largest and most consistent employers. It's been able to provide many jobs and offer the chance of corporate advancement while other companies were cutting back on opportunities. Where Walmart stores act as anchor retailers, other retailers benefit from the traffic that Walmart generates. Walmart says it's not taking market share, but rather is growing the overall retail market. In the end, Walmart has continually argued that it is a net benefit to society.

1. You are the owner of a small hardware store in a town close to where a big box store is located. How do you think you can compete with the big box store?

2. Do you think big box stores have more impact on the supply-side or on the demand-side of the economy? Is your opinion the same when you think about the problem over the different economic terms (short versus long term)?

3. You are living in a town that has a big box retailer. You want to open a business and you don't want to leave town. What type of business would you open and how would you compete?

SECTION CHECK

- ■ The intersection of the labour demand curve and the labour supply curve determines the equilibrium wage and employment in competitive labour markets.
- ■ The labour demand curve can shift if there is a change in productivity or a change in the demand for the final product.
- ■ The labour supply curve can shift if there are changes in immigration or population growth, workers' preferences, nonwage income, or amenities.
- ■ Any market with a single buyer is a monopsony; the labour market represents the most relevant situation.

Labour Unions

- Why do labour unions exist?
- What is the impact of unions on wages?
- Can unions increase worker productivity?

WHY DO LABOUR UNIONS EXIST?

The supply and demand curves for labour can help us better understand the impact of labour unions. Labour unions like the Canadian Auto Workers (CAW) and the United Food and Commercial Workers (UFCW) were formed to increase their members' wages and to improve working conditions. Negotiations between representatives of employers and unions (on behalf of union members) is a process called **collective bargaining.** Why is this necessary? The argument is that when economies begin to industrialize and urbanize, firms become larger and often the "boss" becomes more distant from the workers. In small shops or on farms, workers usually have a close relationship with an owner–employer, but in larger enterprises, the workers may know only a supervisor and have no direct contact with either the owner or upper management. Workers realize that acting together, as a union of workers, gives them more collective bargaining power than acting individually.

collective bargaining
negotiations between representatives of employers and unions

Labour Unions in Canada

On average, just over 4.3 million employees belonged to a union in Canada during the first half of 2011, up 80 000 from the same period last year. With a labour force of 14.5 million paid employees, that means about 30 percent of employees were unionized. Employees in the public sector (government, Crown corporations, schools, hospitals) were over four times as likely to belong to a union than employees in the private sector (71 percent versus 16 percent). Low union rates were found for 15- to 24-year-olds (15 percent) compared to 45- to 54-year-olds (36 percent). Geographically, the highest union rate was in Newfoundland and Labrador (38 percent), whereas the lowest union rate was in Alberta (22 percent).

Wide variation in union rates is observed across different industries. Industries with high rates of unionization include education (68 percent), public administration (67 percent), utilities (64 percent), health care and social assistance (53 percent), and transportation and warehousing (41 percent). Low rates of unionization are found in agriculture (5 percent); professional, scientific, and technical industries (4 percent); accommodation and food (7 percent); and finance, insurance, real estate, and leasing (9 percent). The size of the firm also has an impact on union rates, with small firms (those with under 20 employees) having a 13 percent union rate, and large firms (those with over 500 employees) having a 53 percent union rate.

WHAT IS THE IMPACT OF UNIONS ON WAGES?

Labour unions influence the quantity of union labour hired and the wages at which they are hired primarily through their ability to alter the supply of labour services from what would exist if workers acted independently. One way to do this, of course, is by raising barriers to entry into a given occupation. For example, by restricting membership, unions can reduce the quantity of labour supplied to industry employers from what it otherwise would be, and as a result, wages in that occupation would increase from W_0 to W_1, as shown in Exhibit 1(a). As you can see in the shift from Q_0 to Q_1 in Exhibit 1(a), although some union workers will now receive higher wages, others will become unemployed. Many economists believe that this is why wages are approximately 10–25 percent higher in union jobs, even when nonunion workers have comparable skills. Of course, some of these gains will be appropriated by the unions in the form of union dues, initiation fees, and the like, so the workers themselves will not receive the full benefit.

Wage Differences for Similarly Skilled Workers

Suppose you had two labour sectors: the union sector and the nonunion sector. If unions are successful in obtaining higher wages either through bargaining, threatening to strike, or by restricting membership, wages will rise and employment will fall in the union sector, as seen in Exhibit 1(a). With a downward-sloping demand curve for labour, higher wages mean that less labour is demanded in the union sector. Those workers that are equally skilled but are unable to find union work will seek nonunion work, thus increasing supply in that sector and, in turn, lowering wages in the nonunion sector. This effect is shown in Exhibit 1(b). Thus, comparably skilled workers will experience higher wages in the union sector (W_1) than in the nonunion sector (W_2).

CAN UNIONS INCREASE WORKER PRODUCTIVITY?

Harvard University economists Richard Freeman and James Medoff argue that unions might actually increase worker productivity. Their argument is that unions provide a collective voice that workers can use to communicate their discontents

---

section 11.4
Exhibit 1   **The Effect of Unions on Wages**

a. Union Sector

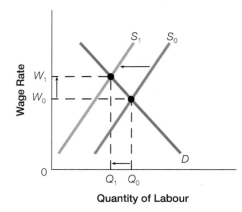

b. Nonunion Sector

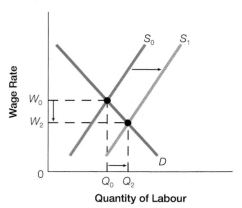

Through restrictive membership practices and other means, a union can reduce the labour supply in its industry, thereby increasing the wage rate workers can earn (from W_0 to W_1) but reducing employment (from Q_0 to Q_1), as shown in Exhibit 1(a). However, as workers unable to get jobs in the union sector join the nonunion sector, the supply of labour in the nonunion sector increases (from Q_0 to Q_2), lowering wages in those industries (from W_0 to W_2), as shown in Exhibit 1(b).

more effectively. This might lower the number of union workers that quit their jobs. Resignations can be particularly costly for firms, because they have often invested in training and job-specific skills for their employees. In addition, by handling workers' grievances, unions may increase worker motivation and morale. The combined impact of fewer resignations and improved morale could boost productivity.

However, this improvement in worker productivity in the union sector should show up on the bottom line—the profit statement of the firm. Although the empirical evidence is mixed, it appears that unions may lower the profitability of firms, not raise it.

DEBATE

AS LABOUR MARKETS EVOLVE, SHOULD COLLEGE ATHLETES GET UNION RIGHTS?

For:

North American college athletes have begun seeking power through union representation—at a time when governments around the world have been moving to limit the powers of unions. Scholarship student athletes at Northwestern University in Illinois have been spearheading this new drive to seek compensation for the work and risks that the athletes take on.* Central to the college athletes' argument for union representation is the idea that they are employees of their colleges. As employees, the law would give them the right to form a union if the majority votes for union representation. While history has proved that unions have protected workers' rights and ensured safe work places, these safeguards have never been in place to protect college athletes, who may be injured during their college careers to the point where they are unable to realize a potential pro career. Further, while the colleges have negotiated multi-billion dollar sponsorships and media contracts, none of those dollars are reaching the relatively few athletes themselves. What's worse is that athletes are actually barred from receiving any form of compensation for their participation in the sport and for their images that are being used by video game developers. The only benefits they receive are their scholarships and exposure to pro teams. Surely, considering the benefits that members of a union typically get and the financial gains that athletes bring to others, it makes sense for college athletes to be labelled employees and allowed union representation. Can you think of other reasons why college athletes should be represented by a union?

*Ben Strauss and Steve Eder, "College Players Granted Right to Form Union," *The New York Times*, March 26, 2014, www.nytimes .com/2014/03/27/sports/ncaafootball/national-labor-relations-board -rules-northwestern-players-are-employees-and-can-unionize.html

Against:

Some argue that unions provide the foundations for fair working wages that benefit workers, employers, and society as a whole. But athletes in college are not employees in the eyes of the law—or at least that is the argument that college administrators have been making to defend against unions organizing their players. Administrators believe that they have offered scholarships to attract students to attend their institutions, not as compensation for playing football. The players have argued that playing on a team has rules and policies that are in essence similar to those of other employees within the colleges, but the administrators say that team rules can't be compared with terms of employment—they are there to build team unity, not to serve as rules for employment. A key argument against unionization of athletes is that if it went ahead, only a small group of high-profile athletes would benefit and unionization would actually act as a hindrance to lower-level athletes or athletes of lower-profile sports. Many of these students enter college by using sport scholarships as their main way of getting an affordable education. Many of these athletes could lose out if colleges were forced to offer equal or equitable terms for all athletes. In recent times, the courts in some parts of the world have heard appeals aimed at trying to save collective bargaining rights, but there have been few instances where people have sought union membership. The college athletes seem to be going against labour market trends. Surely they are clearly not employees. What are some other reasons you can think of that would support those who are against unionization?

SECTION CHECK

■ Workers realize that acting together gives them collective bargaining power; this is the primary reason why unions exist. Labour unions try to increase their members' wages and improve working conditions.

■ Through restrictive membership, a union can reduce the labour supply in the market for union workers, thus reducing employment and raising wages. This increases the supply of workers in the nonunion sector, shifting supply to the right and lowering wages for nonunion workers.

■ By reducing discontent and increasing worker retention, some economists argue that unions can actually increase worker productivity.

section 11.5   Income Distribution

■ What has happened to income distribution since 1951?
■ How much income inequality exists in other countries?
■ Are we overstating the disparity in the distribution of income?
■ Why do some earn more than others?
■ How can we remedy discrimination?

The ultimate purpose of producing goods and services is to satisfy the material wants of people. Up to this point, we have examined the process by which society decides which wants to satisfy in a world characterized by scarcity; we have examined the question of how goods are produced; and we have examined the question of how society can fully utilize its productive resources. We have not, however, looked carefully into the question of for whom society produces consumer goods and services. Why are some people able to consume much more than others?

WHAT HAS HAPPENED TO INCOME DISTRIBUTION SINCE 1951?

Exhibit 1 shows a breakdown of mean (average) household income before tax. Economists rank Canadian households by income and then divide them into five groups (quintiles) based on their income levels. The average income of the richest fifth of Canadian households, at $171 900, is over eleven times greater than that of the poorest fifth of Canadian households, at $15 200.

The Record Since 1951

Exhibit 2 illustrates the distribution of income in Canada since 1951. The series in Exhibit 2 represents the shares of the total before-tax income in Canada going to each fifth (quintile) of Canadian households. For example, in 2010 the fifth of Canadian households with the lowest incomes received only about 4 percent of the total before-tax income in Canada. The highest fifth (20 percent) of Canadian households received

section 11.5
Exhibit 1   Mean Household Income by Quintile (Year 2010)

Quintile	Income
Lowest quintile	$ 15 200
Second quintile	34 900
Third quintile	55 700
Fourth quintile	85 900
Highest quintile	171 900

SOURCE: Statistics Canada, Income in Canada June 2012

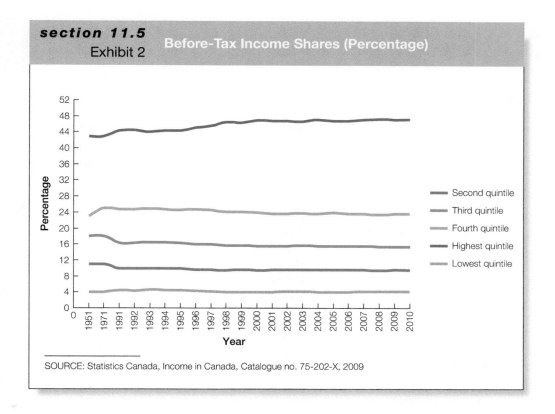

section 11.5
Exhibit 2   Before-Tax Income Shares (Percentage)

SOURCE: Statistics Canada, Income in Canada, Catalogue no. 75-202-X, 2009

more than 47 percent of the total before-tax income. In other words, the income share of the highest fifth of Canadian households is over eleven times greater than the income share of the lowest fifth of households.

Looking at the distribution of income in Canada since 1951, it is interesting to note that the income shares have remained relatively stable over that period. The share of income going to the lowest fifth of households is about 4 percent over the whole period, whereas the share of income going to the middle fifth of households is roughly 15 to 18 percent over the same period. One does notice, however, that the share of income going to the highest fifth of Canadian households has risen from about 43 percent to over 47 percent, suggesting that the rich are getting richer.

HOW MUCH INCOME INEQUALITY EXISTS IN OTHER COUNTRIES?

Is Canada typical of advanced, industrialized nations with respect to the distribution of income among its population? This is a difficult question to answer with absolute certainty, given international differences in defining income, difficulties in measuring the impact of taxes, the problem of nonmonetary payments, and so on. Despite these obstacles, international comparisons of income distribution have been made.

Exhibit 3, constructed with data from the World Bank, shows that income inequality is greater in Canada and the United States than in Sweden and Japan. Japan's ratio of 4.5 means that the richest 10 percent of the population makes 4.5 times as much income as the bottom 10 percent. In Brazil, the richest 10 percent of the population makes a staggering 40.6 times as much income as the bottom 10 percent. However, Exhibit 3 also shows that some of the greatest disparities in income are found in developing countries such as South Africa, Argentina, and Brazil.

section 11.5
Exhibit 3   Global Income Inequalities

Income Inequality	Country	Gap between Rich and Poor (ratio)
Most Equal	Japan	4.5
	Sweden	6.2
	Germany	6.9
	India	8.6
	France	9.1
	Canada	9.4
	Russia	11.0
	China	13.2
	United Kingdom	13.8
	United States	15.9
	Nigeria	16.3
	Mexico	21.0
	Argentina	31.6
	Chile	33.0
	South Africa	35.1
Least Equal	Brazil	40.6

The ratio of the richest 10 percent to the poorest 10 percent gives us the gap between rich and poor. A smaller ratio indicates a greater degree of income equality in that country.

SOURCE: The World Bank: *World Development Report*.

Although income inequality within nations is often substantial, it is far less than income inequality among nations. The majority of global income inequality comprises differences in living standards among countries rather than disparities within nations.

ARE WE OVERSTATING THE DISPARITY IN THE DISTRIBUTION OF INCOME?

Failing to take into consideration differences in age, certain demographic factors, and government taxation and transfer programs, which have all been identified as elements that influence income distribution data, suggests that we might be overstating inequality.

Differences in Age

At any moment in time, middle-aged people tend to have higher incomes than both younger and older people. At middle age most people are at their peak in terms of productivity, and participate in the labour force to a greater extent than the very old or very young. Put differently, if every individual earned exactly the same total income over his or her lifetime, there would still be some observed inequality at any given moment in time, simply because people earn more in middle age.

Other Demographic Trends

Other demographic trends, like the increased number of divorced couples and the rise of two-income families, have also caused the measured distribution of income (which is measured in terms of household income) to appear more unequal. For example, in the 1950s, the majority of families had single incomes. Today, many households have two breadwinners instead of one. Suppose their incomes rise from $50 000 a year to roughly $100 000; these households thus move into a higher-income quintile and create greater apparent income inequality. At the same time, divorces create two households instead of one, lowering income per household for divorced couples; thus, they move into lower-income quintiles, also creating greater apparent income inequality.

The contrasts between rich and poor are more extreme in Brazil than in almost any other country in the world. According to the UN Development Program, nearly half of Brazil's population lives in absolute poverty. Those who are unable to make a living as vendors of newspapers or lottery tickets, shoeshine boys, guards for parked cars, or the like are often forced to earn a living illegally. The number of children who work on the streets, or even live there permanently, is estimated to have reached 10 million.

Government Activities

The impact of government activity should be considered in evaluating the measured income distribution. Government-imposed taxes burden different income groups in different ways. Most importantly, Canada has a progressive income tax system, which means that higher-income individuals pay a larger proportion of their income in tax than lower-income individuals. The progressivity of the tax system results in the after-tax income distribution being more equal than the before-tax income distribution. In 2010, for example, the shares of after-tax income going to each of the five quintiles were 5 percent, 11 percent, 16 percent, 24 percent, and 44 percent, respectively. As you can see when comparing to the before-tax shares in Exhibit 2, the share of after-tax income going to each of the lower two quantiles is greater, whereas the after-tax share of the quantiles is lower.

Also, government programs benefit some groups of income recipients more than others. For example, it has been argued that government-subsidized higher education has benefited the high- and middle-income groups more than the poor (because far more students from these income groups go to university or college), as have such things as government subsidies to airports, operas, and art museums. Some programs, though, clearly aid the poor more than the rich. Food banks, school lunch programs, housing subsidies, day-care subsidies, and several other programs provide recipients with **in-kind transfers**—that is, transfers of goods and services (nonmonetary) rather than cash (monetary). Many economists conclude that these in-kind transfers have served to reduce levels of inequality from the levels suggested by aggregate income statistics.

in-kind transfers
transfers of goods and services rather than cash

WHY DO SOME EARN MORE THAN OTHERS?

There are many reasons why some people make more income than others. Some reasons for the differences in income include differences in age, skill, education and training, preferences with respect to risk and leisure, and discrimination.

Age

The amount of income people earn varies over their lifetimes. Younger people with few skills tend to make little income when they begin their working careers. Income rises as workers gain experience and on-the-job training. As productivity increases, workers can command higher wages. These wage earnings generally increase up to the age of 50 and fall dramatically at retirement age, around 65.

Skills and Human Capital

Some workers are just more productive than others and therefore earn higher wages. The greater productivity may be a result of innate skills or of improvements in human capital, such as training and education. Still others, like star athletes and rock stars, have specialized talents that are in huge demand, so they make more money than those with fewer skills or with skills that are in less demand.

Worker Preferences

Aside from skills, education, and training, people have different attitudes about and preferences regarding their work. Workaholics work longer hours and so they earn more than others with comparable skills. Some earn more because they work more intensely than others. Still others may choose jobs that pay less but have more amenities—flexible hours, favourable job location, generous benefit programs, child care, and so on. And some may choose to work less and spend more time pursuing leisure activities, like travelling, hobbies, or spending time with family and friends. It is not for us to say that one preference is better than another but simply to recognize that these choices lead to differences in earnings.

Job Preferences

Some of the differences in income are the result of the risks or undesirable features of some occupations. Police officers and firefighters are paid higher wages because of the dangers associated with their jobs. Nickel miners and garbage collectors are paid more than other workers with comparable skill levels because of the unpleasantness of the jobs. In short, some workers have higher earnings because they are compensated for the difficult, risky, or unappealing nature of their jobs.

Discrimination

Finally, some of the differences in income result from employment and wage discrimination. Employment discrimination occurs when a worker is denied employment or promotion on the basis of some feature, such as gender, age, religion, or race, without any regard to his or her productivity. Wage discrimination occurs when a worker is given employment at a wage lower than that of other workers based on an attribute other than productivity. These types of discrimination are illegal but, because they can be difficult to detect, still sometimes occur.

Discrimination is one factor in explaining why men, on average, earn more than women. Studies have shown that even after accounting for a wide range of factors that determine incomes, such as education, training, experience, seniority, and hours worked, a male–female wage gap remains that can be attributed to discrimination in the labour market. Moreover, it is important to note that discrimination outside of the labour market may also contribute to male–female wage inequality. Because women, on average, perform a greater share of household responsibilities, especially child-rearing, this impacts the labour market choices women make in areas such as occupational choice, mobility, training, absenteeism, and hours worked.

HOW CAN WE REMEDY DISCRIMINATION?

In Canada, the problem of employment discrimination is addressed primarily through the Employment Equity Act (1996, amended in 2005). This federal legislation requires or encourages Canadian employers to give preferential treatment in employment practices to a list of designated groups—specifically women, persons with disabilities, Aboriginal peoples, and visible minorities.

Applying only to companies in federally regulated industries (such as banking, tele-communications, and the airline industry, to name a few) and those corporations that are controlled by two or more provincial governments, the act ultimately has limited coverage. Although some provincial governments have chosen to incorporate employment equity standards into their provincial-level human rights legislation, no province has preferential employment practices equivalent to those in the Employment Equity Act.

Policies designed around the concepts of *pay equity* and *pay equality* are intended to address the existence of wage discrimination in Canada. Pay equality, or equal pay for equal work, is required by law in Canada. The principle of pay equality works as follows: Suppose an organization employs both male and female truck drivers, with reasonable allowances for differences in skill or seniority, the female truck drivers would have to be paid the same as the male truck drivers.

Alternatively, pay equity legislation, or equal pay for work of equal value, exists only in certain jurisdictions in Canada (e.g., in Ontario, pay equity is guaranteed through the Ontario Pay Equity Act). The principle of pay equity works as follows: Suppose an organization's nurses are seen as doing a job that is equal in importance to its plumbers; they must all then be paid the same.

Employment equity programs are controversial. Employment equity may increase the probability that someone will be hired on some basis other than productivity. Although this may be desirable from the standpoint of equalizing opportunities among demographic groups, it also can serve to lower society's output and firms' profits. Furthermore, some critics have raised the "reverse discrimination" equity argument. For example, with respect to productivity, a firm may be forced to hire a worker from one of the designated groups with a marginal revenue product of $80 instead of a nondesignated worker whose marginal revenue product may be $100 (perhaps because of more years of schooling). Society ultimately loses $20 of output (the difference in the value of marginal output). Moreover, if the firm that hires the worker from one of the designated groups has to pay the prevailing wage (say, $90) to avoid wage discrimination charges, hiring that worker will lower profits. With that, the firm might decide not to hire anyone, knowing that employment equity will prevent it from hiring the profitable nondesignated worker (whose marginal revenue product exceeds the prevailing wage by $10) instead of the worker from one of the designated groups (whose hiring will reduce profits by $10).

Employers' actions to protect profits, then, might negate some or all of the expected gains from employment equity. One alternative to using implicit quotas would be to subsidize employers for hiring members from one of the designated groups. Opponents to this approach regard it as a gift or bailout for business enterprise more than a help to under-represented workplace groups. The subsidy approach would, however, provide employers with greater incentives to increase job opportunities for designated group members.

SECTION CHECK

- Since 1951, the distribution of income in Canada has been relatively stable.
- Income inequality among nations is substantial.
- Demographics and government programs affect the disparity in income inequality. Not taking these issues into consideration when evaluating income distribution could result in the inequality being overstated.
- Differences in ages, skill, education and training, preferences related to risk and leisure, and discrimination are all possible reasons why some people make more money than others.
- In Canada, the problem of employment discrimination is addressed primarily through the Employment Equity Act (2005).

section
11.6   Poverty

- How do we define poverty?
- How many people live in poverty?
- What government programs help to reduce poverty?

At several points in this chapter, the words "rich" and "poor" have been used without being defined. Of particular interest is the question of poverty. Our concern over income distribution largely arises because most people believe that those with low incomes have lower satisfaction than those with higher incomes. Thus, the "poor" people are those who, in a material sense, suffer relative to other people. It is desirable, therefore, to define and measure the extent of poverty in Canada.

HOW DO WE DEFINE POVERTY?

poverty
a state in which a family's income is too low to be able to buy the quantities of food, shelter, and clothing that are deemed necessary

low-income cut-off (LICO)
income level at which a family may be in straitened circumstance because it has to spend a greater proportion of its income on the basics (food, clothing, and shelter) than the average family of similar size

Poverty refers to a state in which a family's income is too low to be able to buy the quantities of food, shelter, and clothing that are deemed necessary. In Canada, poverty is measured on a relative income basis, that is, if someone's income is lower than is socially acceptable as compared to others Canadians, that person is considered to be poor. Officially, however, there is no measure of poverty.

Based on this above concept, Statistics Canada has been able to create a measure called a **low-income cut-off (LICO),** which is the income level at which a family may be in straitened circumstance because it has to spend a greater proportion of its income on the basics (food, clothing, and shelter) than the average family of similar size. This low-income cut-off depends on the number of people that live in the household as well as the size of the community that the household lives in. Exhibit 1 shows

section 11.6
Exhibit 1   Low-Income After-Tax Cut-Offs, 2010

		Community Size			
	Rural Area	**Urban Areas**			
		Less than 30 000	**30 000–99 999**	**100 000–499 999**	**500 000 and over**
Size of Family Unit		**$**			
1 person	12 271	14 044	15 666	15 865	18 759
2 persons	14 936	17 094	19 069	19 308	22 831
3 persons	18 598	21 283	23 744	24 043	28 430
4 persons	23 202	26 554	29 623	29 996	35 469
5 persons	26 421	30 237	33 732	34 157	40 388
6 persons	29 301	33 534	37 410	37 881	44 971
7 or more persons	32 182	36 831	41 087	41 604	49 195

SOURCE: Statistics Canada. Table 202-0801 - Low income cut-offs before and after tax by community and family size, 2010 constant dollars, annual (dollars), CANSIM (database). <http://www5.statcan.gc.ca/cansim/a26?lang=eng&retrLang=eng&id=2020801&pattern=2020801&csid=> (June 19, 2013)

the low-income cut-offs for various household sizes and various community sizes. The LICO for a single-person household living in a large Canadian city is $18 759, whereas, if a family of three lives in a rural area, the LICO is $18 598.

At this point, it is important to emphasize that Statistics Canada's low-income cut-off is a relative measure of poverty, not an absolute measure of poverty. For example, a household right at the low-income cut-off point would still have a proportion of its after-tax income to spend on goods and services other than food, shelter, and clothing. Thus, it would not be poor in an absolute sense, especially when compared to households in countries such as Zimbabwe or the Congo. It is poor, however, in the sense that its income falls to a specified degree below the income of an average comparable household. An absolute measure of poverty is based on whether a household's income is sufficient to provide the basic necessities of life in minimum quantities.

HOW MANY PEOPLE LIVE IN POVERTY?

Based on Statistics Canada's low-income cut-off, we can measure the incidence of poverty as the percentage of households whose income falls below the low-income cut-off. Exhibit 2 provides a summary of poverty rates among households based on selected characteristics of the household.

Unattached individuals have a 26.9 percent incidence of low income, whereas only 5.9 percent of married couples with children are poor. A single-parent family headed by a female experiences a poverty rate of 21.8 percent.

The age of the major income earner in the household makes a significant difference to a household's income and to the risk of poverty. In families where the major income earner is 24 years old or younger, the incidence of low income is 33.3 percent, considerably higher than the 6.7 percent of persons who experience low income in families where the major income earner is 45 to 54 years old.

Education also makes a huge impact on the incidence of poverty. Households headed by someone with a university degree have a poverty rate of 10.3 percent, whereas those headed by someone with less than a high school education have a 22.5 percent incidence of low income.

Overall then, how many Canadian families are considered poor, and is the problem getting better or worse? The incidence of poverty in Canada, as defined by the percentage

section 11.6 Exhibit 2 — The Incidence of Low Income by Selected Household Characteristics, 2010

Characteristic	Percentage of Households below LICO
Married couples with children	5.9
Single-parent families (female head)	21.8
Unattached individuals	26.9
Major income earner 24 years old or younger	33.3
Major income earner 45 to 54 years old	6.7
Household head has less than a high school education	22.5
Household head has a university degree	10.3

SOURCE: Statistics Canada, Income in Canada, 75-202-XIE2009000, June 2011; http://www.statcan.gc.ca/bsolc/olc-cel/olc-cel?catno=75-202-XIE&lang=eng#formatdisp

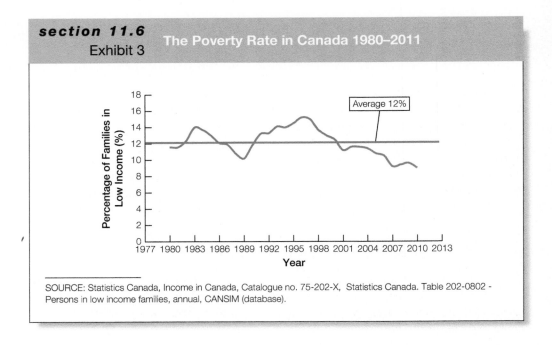

section 11.6
Exhibit 3

The Poverty Rate in Canada 1980–2011

SOURCE: Statistics Canada, Income in Canada, Catalogue no. 75-202-X, Statistics Canada. Table 202-0802 - Persons in low income families, annual, CANSIM (database).

of persons with low income as determined by the after-tax low income cut-off, is illustrated in Exhibit 3. Commonly referred to as the *poverty rate,* the measure has most recently ranged between a high of just over 15 percent in 1996 to a low of just over 9 percent in 2007. While the current poverty rate is below the average rate of 12 percent, there appears to be no defined trend in poverty.

WHAT GOVERNMENT PROGRAMS HELP TO REDUCE POVERTY?

A variety of government programs are designed to reduce poverty and redistribute income. We examine several of them here.

Taxes

progressive tax system
as a person's income rises, the amount of his or her tax as a proportion of income rises

One way to redistribute income to reduce disparities among individuals is through federal and provincial income taxes. The federal income tax (and the majority of provincial income tax) is designed to be a **progressive tax system**—as a person's income rises, the amount of tax as a proportion of income rises. For example in 2014 (federally), an individual would pay 15 percent tax on the first $43,953 of taxable income, 22 percent on the next $43,954 of taxable income, 26 percent on the next $48,363 of taxable income, and 29 percent of taxable income over $136,270.

Social Insurance Programs

cash transfer
direct cash payment such as public pensions, social assistance, and Employment Insurance benefits

A second means by which income redistribution can be carried out by the government is through social insurance programs operated by the federal government, the provinces and territories, and municipalities. These programs are often referred to as Canada's social safety net and consist of both in-kind transfers and cash transfers. In-kind transfers are direct transfers of goods and services such as food banks and school lunch programs, whereas **cash transfers** are direct cash payments such as public pensions, social assistance, and Employment Insurance (EI) benefits.

Public pension payments are a cash transfer program that provides income to persons over the age of 65. Health care is an in-kind transfer that covers medical care and hospitalization—financed by the provincial and territorial governments with funding from the federal government. Neither of these programs are considered welfare programs because one does not have to be poor to receive benefits. Benefits for the unemployed in the form of Employment Insurance are also a cash transfer payment. All three of these social insurance programs are event-based—old age, illness, or job loss.

Known by such names as "social assistance," "income support," "income assistance," and "welfare assistance," these programs of last resort are targeted toward people with little or no income. For example, the Federal-Provincial/Territorial Child Benefit Program is designed to help low-income families provide for their children, and the federal Guaranteed Income Supplement (GIS) is a program that provides additional money (above that provided by the Old Age Security pension) to low-income seniors.

Government Subsidies

A third way that governments can help the less affluent is by using government revenues to provide low-cost public services. Inexpensive public housing, subsidized public transportation, and even public parks are services that probably serve the poor to a greater extent than the rich. "Free" public education is viewed by many as an equalizing force in that it opens up opportunities for children of less prosperous members of society to obtain employment that could improve their economic status. Of course, not all government programs benefit the relatively poor at the expense of the rich. For example, provincial government subsidies to universities may help middle-income and upper-income groups more than the poor. In addition, there are agricultural subsidies that often provide large benefits to farmers who may already have sufficient incomes.

Minimum Wage

Can a higher minimum wage ease the burden on the poor? We discussed the minimum wage in Chapter 4. You may recall that the minimum-wage law forbids employers from paying a wage less than the minimum wage. In Canada, provinces and territories administer their own minimum-wage legislation—for example, the minimum-wage in Nunavut is $11.00 (effective January 1, 2011).

Almost all economists would agree that a large increase in the minimum wage — say, to $20—would have a devastating effect on the unskilled labour market: Many small businesses would have to shut their doors, leaving many unskilled workers without jobs. There is some debate among economists over the elasticity of the demand curve for labour. If the demand curve for labour is relatively inelastic, an increase in the minimum wage leads to only a small reduction in employment. However, if the demand curve for labour is relatively elastic, the reduction in employment is larger.

Critics of a higher minimum wage argue that it is poorly targeted if its object is to reduce poverty, because many of the recipients of the minimum wage are teenagers living in households that are not facing poverty. Some argue that a policy focusing on subsidizing the wages of the poor would go much further in reducing poverty. That is, society needs to find more effective policies for low-wage workers—perhaps job-training programs.

SECTION CHECK

■ In Canada, poverty is defined on a relative income basis. If a household's income is too low to afford the necessary quantities of food, shelter, and clothing, it is classified as being poor.

■ The incidence of low income varies depending on the characteristics of the household, such as family type, age, and education.

■ A variety of government programs are designed to reduce poverty: progressive income tax, cash transfer, in-kind transfers, social assistance, and minimum wages.

For Your Review

Section 11.1

1. What would happen to the demand for unskilled labour if there was an increase in the demand for hamburgers and fries?

2. The following figure illustrates the market for apple pickers.

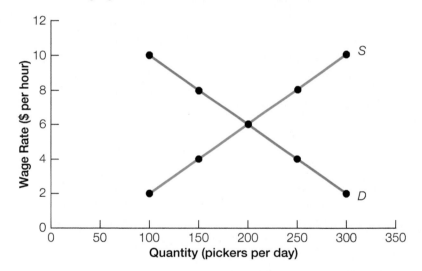

a. What is the wage rate paid to apple pickers?

b. How many apple pickers have been hired?

c. If the demand for apples increases, resulting in 100 more apple pickers per day being hired, what would be the new wage rate paid to pickers?

Section 11.2

Blueprint Question

Consider a company operating in a perfectly competitive market. It sells it output for $26 a unit and pays its workers $250 a day. The following table shows the marginal productivity of each worker.

Number of Workers	Marginal Productivity (number of units/day)
0	
1	16
2	13
3	9
4	6
5	2

What is the profit-maximizing number of workers that this company should hire at this market wage rate?

Blueprint Solution

Notice that in this question you are given the marginal productivity (*MP*) of each worker. Had you been given total productivity (*TP*), you would have needed to compute *MP* (to see how to do this, consult the Blueprint Problem in Chapter 1).

Profit-maximizing decision rule for firm: Hire workers until $MRP = MRC$

A	B	C	D	E
Number of Workers	Marginal Productivity (number of units/day)	Marginal Revenue of Product (*MRP*) of Labour ($ per day)	Marginal Resource Cost (*MRC*) (Wage per day)	Profit-Maximizing Decision, Firm
0				
1	16	$416	$250	Hire
2	13	$338	$250	Hire
3	9	$234	$250	Do not hire
4	6	$156	$250	Do not hire
5	2	$52	$250	Do not hire

The *MRP* of labour (per day) = $MP \times P$

The company's demand curve for labour is given by the downward-sloping portion of the marginal revenue of product (*MRP*) curve. A profit-maximizing firm will add labour as long as *MRP* > wage. By referring to column E, you can see that the firm will choose to hire two workers.

Use the following table to answer questions 3 and 4.

Quantity of Labour	Total Output/Week	Marginal Product of Labour	Marginal Revenue Product of Labour
0	–		
1	250		
2	600		
3	900		
4	1125		
5	1300		
6	1450		
7	1560		

3. The table above shows the total output each week of workers in a perfectly competitive apple orchard. The equilibrium price of a kilogram of apples is $4. Complete the Marginal Product of Labour and the Marginal Revenue Product of Labour columns in the table.

4. Using the same table, how many workers will the owner hire if the equilibrium wage rate is $550 per week? $650 per week?

5. Fill in the missing data in the following table.

Workers	Total Corn Output	Marginal Product of Labour
1	4 000	
2	10 000	
3	15 000	
4		3000
5		1000
6		−1000

6. If all individuals have backward-bending labour supply curves, is the labour supply curve for a particular industry or occupation also backward-bending?

7. Fill in the missing data for a perfectly competitive firm in the following table.

Workers	Total Output	Marginal Product	Price	Marginal Revenue Product
1	200		$20	
2	380		20	
3	540		20	
4	680		20	
5	800		20	
6	900		20	
7	980		20	
8	1040		20	

8. Would the owner of University Pizza Parlour hire another worker for $60 per day if that worker added 40 pizzas a day and each pizza added $2 to University Pizza Parlour's revenues? Why or why not?

Section 11.3

9. If a competitive firm is paying $8 per hour (without fringe benefits) to its employees, what would tend to happen to its equilibrium wage if the company began to give on-the-job training or free dental insurance to its workers? What would happen to its on-the-job training or dental insurance for its workers if the government mandated a minimum wage of $9 an hour?

10. Professional athletes command and receive higher salaries than teachers. Yet teachers, not athletes, are considered essential to economic growth and development. If this is in fact the case, why do athletes receive higher salaries than teachers?

11. The availability of jobs at higher real wages motivates many people to migrate to Canada. Other things equal, what impact would a large influx of immigrants have on Canadian real wages?

12. The dean of Anara University knows that poets generally earn less than engineers in the private market; that is, the equilibrium wage for engineers is higher than that for poets—in the same way that professional athletes command and receive higher salaries than teachers do. The administration at Anara University believes that salaries should be equal across all disciplines because its professors work equally hard and because all of the professors have similar qualifications. As a result, Anara University opts to pay all of its professors a mid-range wage. Suppose that all colleges and universities, except Anara University, paid their professors according to their potential private market wage. What do you think is likely to happen to the engineering and poetry programs at Anara University?

13. Use the following diagram to answer questions (a) through (i).

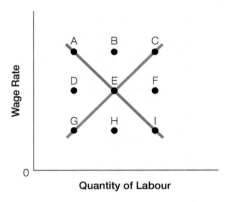

Indicate which point could correspond to the equilibrium wage and quantity hired

   a. at the initial equilibrium.

   b. if the price of the output produced by the labour increased.

   c. if the price of the output produced by the labour decreased.

   d. with an increase in immigration.

   e. with a reduction in the quality of workplace amenities.

   f. if worker productivity increased and workers' nonwage incomes increased.

   g. if worker productivity decreased and population decreased.

   h. if the price of output produced by the labour increased and the number of hours that workers were willing to work increased.

   i. if the price of output produced by the labour decreased and workers' nonwage incomes decreased.

14. How would each of the following affect the demand or supply of workers? In each case, determine the impact on equilibrium wage and quantity.

   a. Immigration increases dramatically.

   b. Demand for Canadian manufactured goods declines.

   c. New computerized technology increases the productivity of Canadian workers.

   d. Canadian firms increase job amenities for workers.

   e. Canadian workers choose more leisure.

Section 11.4

15. Use the following diagrams to answer questions (a) through (c).

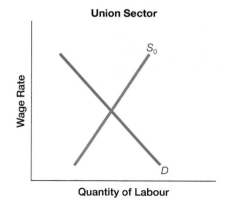

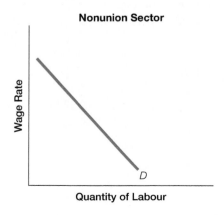

a. If unions are unable to have any effect on wages, draw the supply curve for the nonunion market.

b. If unions become able to restrict the supply of labour in the union sector, indicate what would happen in both the union and nonunion sectors.

c. What happens to the union wage and the number of union workers hired in (b)? What happens to the nonunion wage and the number of nonunion workers hired in (b)?

16. Explain why some economists believe that labour unions are responsible for increasing workplace productivity.

Section 11.5

17. Explain at least three reasons why the official data on the distribution of income may overstate the actual degree of income inequality.

18. In 2010, average earnings for Canadian males was $46 500, but it was only $31 700 for Canadian women. Provide some possible explanations for this difference in annual earnings.

19. How might each of the following affect the distribution of income in the near term?

a. a massive influx of low-skilled immigrants

b. a new baby boom occurs

c. the babies in (b) enter their twenties

d. the babies in (b) reach age 65 or older

20. The following table contains income distributions from five nations—divided into quintiles (20 percent segments of the population).

Income Distribution Data by Country, 2008					
	Switzerland	Peru	Sweden	Mexico	Honduras
Highest quintile	38.7	54.8	33.4	54.9	58.4
Fourth quintile	22.4	20.8	22.7	19.8	20.4
Third quintile	17.3	13.0	18.7	12.8	12.1
Second quintile	13.2	7.8	15.2	8.3	6.7
Lowest quintile	8.4	3.6	10	4.2	2.5

a. Based on the evidence presented in the table, which country displays the greatest degree of income inequality (the greatest difference between the top quintile and the bottom quintile)?

b. Based on the evidence presented in the table, which country displays the lowest degree of income inequality (the least difference between the top quintile and the bottom quintile)?

21. If every individual earned the same total income over his or her lifetime, why would we still see inequality at a given point in time?

22. How might a significant reduction in the divorce rate affect the distribution of income?

Section 11.6

23. Can economic growth reduce poverty? How does the answer depend on whether we are using an absolute or relative measure of poverty?

24. Refer to Section 11.6, Exhibit 1, to answer this question. Ryan and Trisha live in Thunder Bay (population 110 000) with their three children, who are all under the age of 18. Ryan works as a factory labourer and earns $37 000 a year. Trisha is a stay-at-home mother.

    a. According to the 2010 Statistics Canada low-income cut-offs (LICOs), are Ryan and Trisha "poor"? Explain.

    b. Suppose Ryan is killed in a tragic industrial accident. With no insurance settlement, Trisha is forced to find work to support her family. After some time, Trisha finds a part-time job teaching art at a local grade school. She earns a total of $26 000 a year. According to Statistics Canada's 2010 LICOs, are Trisha and her three children "poor"? Explain.

25. What are the main characteristics of those people in Canada who earn low incomes?

chapter 12

Market Failure and the Environment

Externalities

- What are externalities?
- What are negative externalities?
- What are positive externalities?
- What can the government do to correct for positive externalities?
- Are there nongovernmental solutions to externalities?

WHAT ARE EXTERNALITIES?

Even if the economy is competitive, it is still possible that the market system fails to produce the efficient level of output because of side effects that economists call *externalities*. An **externality** is a benefit or cost from consumption or production that spills over onto those that are not consuming or producing the good. Externalities are caused by economic agents—producers and consumers—receiving the wrong signals. That is, the free market works well in providing most goods but does less well without regulations, taxes, and subsidies in providing others.

externality
a benefit or cost from consumption or production that spills over onto those that are not consuming or producing the good

WHAT ARE NEGATIVE EXTERNALITIES?

A **negative externality** occurs when costs spill over to an outside party that is not involved in producing or consuming the good. The classic example of a negative externality, which we will be investigating in the next section, is pollution from an air-polluting factory, such as a steel mill. If the firm uses clean air in production and returns dirty air to the atmosphere, it has created a negative externality. The polluted air has "spilled over" to outside parties. Now people in the neighbouring communities may experience higher incidences of disease, dirtier houses, and other property damage. Such damages are real costs, but because no one owns the air, the firm does not have

negative externality
when costs spill over to an outside party that is not involved in producing or consuming the good

to pay for its use, unlike the other resources the firm uses in production. A steel mill has to pay for labour, capital, energy, and raw materials because it must compensate the owners of those inputs for their use. If a firm can avoid paying the cost it imposes on others—the external costs—it has lowered its own costs of production, but not the true cost to society.

Examples of negative externalities are numerous: the roommate who plays his stereo too loud at 2:00 A.M.; the neighbour's dog that barks all night long or leaves "messages" on your front lawn; the commuter who talks loudly on her cellphone while riding on a crowded bus. Driving our cars may be another area in which people don't bear the full costs of their choices. We pay the price to purchase cars, as well as to maintain, insure, and fuel them—those are the private costs. But do we pay for all of our external costs such as emissions, congestion, wear and tear on our highways, and the possible harm to those driving in cars smaller than ours?

WHAT ARE POSITIVE EXTERNALITIES?

positive externality
when benefits spill over to an outside party that is not involved in producing or consuming the good

A **positive externality** occurs when benefits spill over to an outside party that is not involved in producing or consuming the good. So, unlike negative externalities, positive externalities benefit others. For some goods, the individual consumer receives all of the benefits. If you buy a hamburger, for example, you get all of its benefits. But take, for example, a company that landscapes its property with beautiful flowers and sculptures. The landscaping may create a positive externality for those who walk or drive by the company grounds. Or consider education. Certainly, when you "buy" an education, you receive many of its benefits: greater future income, more choice of future occupations, and the consumption value of knowing more about life as a result of classroom (and extracurricular) learning. These benefits, however, great as they may be, are not all of the benefits associated with your education. You may be less likely to be unemployed or commit crimes, or you may end up curing cancer or solving some other social problem. These nontrivial benefits are the positive external benefits of education.

The government frequently subsidizes education. Why? Presumably because the private market does not provide enough. It is argued that the education of a person benefits not only that person, but all of society, because a more informed citizenry can make more intelligent collective decisions that benefit everyone. Another example: Why do public-health departments sometimes offer free inoculations against certain communicable diseases, such as influenza? Partly because by protecting one group of citizens, everyone gets some protection; if the first citizen does not get the disease, it prevents that person from passing it on to others. Many governmental efforts in the field of health and education are justified on the basis of perceived positive externalities. Of course, because positive externalities are often difficult to measure, it is hard to empirically demonstrate whether many governmental educational and health programs achieve their intended purpose.

In short, the presence of positive externalities interferes with reaching economic efficiency because of the tendency for the market to underallocate (produce too little) of this good.

Graphing Positive External Benefits

Let's take the case of a new vaccine against the common cold. The market for the vaccine is shown in Exhibit 1. The demand curve $D_{PRIVATE}$ represents the prices and quantities that buyers would be willing to pay for in the private market to reduce their

FALL IS THE TIME TO GET YOUR FLU SHOT.

Because the sooner you get it, the sooner you're protected. You'll also be protecting those around you. Get it from your doctor, a participating pharmacy or a clinic near you.

GET YOUR FLU SHOT EARLY.

@ONThealth

ontario.ca/flu • 1-877-844-1944 • TTY 1-800-387-5559

Ontario

The government of Ontario will once again spend hundreds of millions of dollars on free seasonal flu vaccines. According to a recent report, Ontario's model helped deliver positive results for not only the health of Ontarians, but for the health system in general. The annual flu prevention program was attributed with preventing 300 influenza-related deaths, 1000 hospitalizations, 30 000 visits to the emergency department, and 200 000 visits to doctors' offices in 2012 alone.

probability of catching the common cold. The supply curve shows the amounts that suppliers would offer for sale at different prices. However, at the equilibrium market output, Q_{MARKET}, we are far short of the socially optimum level of output for vaccinations, Q_{SOCIAL}. Why? Many people benefit from the vaccines, including those who do not have to pay for them; they are now less likely to be infected because others took the vaccine. If we could add the benefits derived by nonpaying consumers, the demand curve would shift to the right, from $D_{PRIVATE}$ to D_{SOCIAL}. The greater level of output, Q_{SOCIAL}, which would result if D_{SOCIAL} was the observed demand, reflects the socially optimal output level. However, because producers are unable to collect payments from all of those who are benefiting from the good or service, the market has a tendency to underproduce. In this case, the market is not producing enough vaccinations from society's standpoint, so there is an *underallocation* of resources because from society's standpoint we are producing too little of this good or service, producing Q_{MARKET} rather than Q_{SOCIAL}.

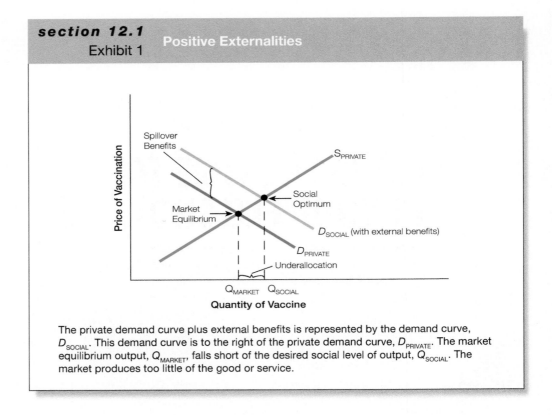

Positive Externalities

The private demand curve plus external benefits is represented by the demand curve, D_{SOCIAL}. This demand curve is to the right of the private demand curve, $D_{PRIVATE}$. The market equilibrium output, Q_{MARKET}, falls short of the desired social level of output, Q_{SOCIAL}. The market produces too little of the good or service.

WHAT CAN THE GOVERNMENT DO TO CORRECT FOR POSITIVE EXTERNALITIES?

How could society correct for this market failure? Two particular methods of achieving the higher preferred output are subsidies and regulation.

Subsidies

Government could provide a subsidy to achieve the higher preferred output—either give refunds to individuals who receive an inoculation or provide an incentive for businesses to give their employees "free" inoculations at the office. If the subsidy was exactly equal to external benefits of inoculation, the demand curve would shift from $D_{PRIVATE}$ to D_{SOCIAL}, resulting in an efficient level of output, Q_{SOCIAL}.

Regulation

The government could also pass a regulation requiring each person to get an inoculation. This would also shift the demand curve to the right toward the efficient level of output.

In summary, when there are positive externalities, the private market supplies too little of the good in question (such as education or inoculations for communicable diseases). When there are negative externalities, the market supplies too much. In either case, buyers and sellers are receiving the wrong signals. The free market works fine in providing most goods because most goods do not have externalities. When there are externalities, the market fails to allocate resources efficiently.

Ints Vikmanis/Shutterstock, Inc.

People might take steps on their own to minimize negative externalities. For example, to lower pollution, some people might use battery-powered mowers, or even old-fashion push mowers, rather than gasoline mowers.

ARE THERE NONGOVERNMENTAL SOLUTIONS TO EXTERNALITIES?

Sometimes the externality problems can be handled by individuals without the intervention of government, and people may decide to take steps on their own to minimize negative externalities. Moral and social codes may prevent some people from littering, driving gas-guzzling cars, or using gas-powered mowers. The same self-regulation also applies to positive externalities. Philanthropists, for example, frequently donate money to universities and colleges. In part, this must be because they view the positive externalities from education as a good buy for their charitable dollars.

SECTION CHECK

- Externalities are the costs or benefits from either production or consumption that spill over onto those that are not producing or consuming the good.
- If a market activity has a negative physical impact on an outside party, that side effect is called a *negative externality*.
- If a market activity has a positive physical impact on an outside party, that side effect is called a *positive externality*.
- The government can provide subsidies or other forms of regulation to correct the underallocation problem associated with positive externalities.
- Nongovernment solutions to externalities are possible as people self-regulate personal behaviour to either prevent negative externalities or to promote positive externalities.

Negative Externalities and Pollution

- ■ What are social costs?
- ■ Can externalities be accurately measured?

WHAT ARE SOCIAL COSTS?

As we learned in the previous section, whenever an economic activity has benefits or costs that are shared by individuals other than the demanders or suppliers of a good or service, an externality is involved. If the activity imposes costs on individuals other than the demanders or suppliers of a good or service, it is said to have negative externalities. Put another way, negative externalities exist anytime the social costs of producing a good or service exceed the private costs. Social costs refer to costs that spill over to other members of society. Private costs refer to costs incurred only by the producer of the good or service.

Negative Externalities and Pollution

The classic example of a negative externality is pollution. When a steel mill puts soot into the air as a by-product of making steel, it imposes costs on others not connected with the steel mill or with buying or selling steel. The soot requires nearby homeowners to paint their houses more often, entailing costs. Studies show that respiratory diseases are more prevalent in areas with high air pollution, imposing substantial costs and often shortening lives. In addition, the steel mill might discharge chemicals or overheated water into a stream, killing wildlife, ruining business for those who make a living fishing, spoiling recreational activities for the local population, and so on.

In deciding how much to produce, the steelmakers are governed by demand and supply. They do not worry (unless forced to) about the external costs imposed on members of society, and in all likelihood, the steelmakers would not even know the full extent of those costs.

Consider the hypothetical steel industry in Exhibit 1. It produces where demand and supply intersect, at output $Q_{PRIVATE}$ and $P_{PRIVATE}$. Let us assume that the marginal social cost of producing the product is indicated by the marginal social cost (*MSC*) curve, lying above the supply curve, which represents the industry's marginal private costs (*MPC*). The marginal social costs of production are higher at all output levels, as those costs include all of the industry's private costs plus the costs that spill over to other members of society from the pollution produced by the industry—that is, the external costs.

section 12.2
Exhibit 1   **The Effect of a Negative Externality**

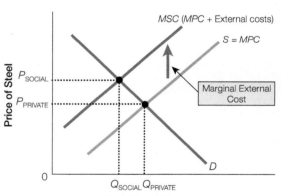

The industry would normally produce where demand equals supply (where supply is equal to the marginal private costs), at output Q_{SOCIAL} and charging price $P_{PRIVATE}$. If, however, the industry was forced to also pay those external costs imposed on others, the industry would produce where demand equals marginal social costs, at output Q_{SOCIAL} and price P_{SOCIAL}. Where firms are not forced to pay for negative externalities, output tends to be larger and prices lower than at the optimal output, where the marginal benefits to society (as measured by demand) equal the marginal costs to society.

At output Q_{SOCIAL}, the marginal social costs to society equal the marginal social benefits (as indicated by the demand curve) from the sale of the last unit of steel. At that output, the price of steel is P_{SOCIAL}. If the firm was somehow forced to compensate people who endure the costs of its pollution, the firm would produce at output Q_{SOCIAL} and price steel at P_{SOCIAL}. When an industry is forced to compensate those enduring some negative externality caused by its production, the industry is said to have **internalized externalities.** When negative externalities are internalized, steel firms produce less output (Q_{SOCIAL} instead of $Q_{PRIVATE}$) and charge higher prices (P_{SOCIAL} instead of $P_{PRIVATE}$). Optimal output occurs where the marginal social costs are equal to the marginal social benefits. When firms do not pay all of the social costs they incur, and therefore produce too much output, the result is too much pollution. The output of pollution is directly related to the output of the primary goods produced by the firm.

internalized externalities
when an industry is forced to compensate those enduring some negative externality caused by its production

Besides polluting the air, this factory is polluting water downstream from it, creating a negative externality for those who fish downstream. It is possible that the people who fish could try to bargain with the factory, perhaps even pay it to pollute less. However, sometimes private bargaining does not work and the government can provide a solution through regulation or pollution taxes.

Business *CONNECTION*

CAPITALISM IN TRANSITION

One challenge of the capitalistic model of economics is that growth is necessary for it to continue over the long run. Over the past millennia, attaining growth has never been a real problem, but doing so at the right levels has—and it's been left to economists and politicians to debate what those levels are.

Also at the forefront of decision making is how to distribute the fruits of growth: in an efficient manner or in an equitable manner? Choosing efficiency means extracting the greatest amount of growth for the least amount of cost. In this model, profits are of the greatest importance, and the economists argue that once we achieve the highest profits or the greatest growth, there is more to distribute to the wider economy. In essence, this is the building of a bigger pie. But building a bigger pie has its limits, and now both business and society are having to rethink the profit-maximizing model.

Many businesses (and countries) are recognizing that there is a limit to the resources that the earth has to offer, as well as a limit to the demand for products that consumers want and are able to buy. There are now concerns that the capitalism model can't hold up, given current conventional thought. This doesn't necessarily mean the end of capitalism, but perhaps a revised edition is coming! How would businesses respond or what would they need to do to survive in this new form of capitalism?

We already see some evidence of progressive companies changing their goals and missions. Instead of operating their businesses to make the most profit, they're operating in a socially responsible and sustainable manner. Instead of reaping the highest profits for distribution to shareholders, these corporations suggest that they have a responsibility to keep going in the long term.. This might mean they will limit profits and redirect funds back into the business for hiring employees (who in turn buy the products they make) or invest in the environment so that the resources that the company uses will be there for millennia. It may also change the way that they view waste: At one time, waste was seen as a cost, but now corporations are looking at waste as a beneficial resource.

Other companies are looking at changes to their manufacturing systems with a view of conserving resources. For example, BMW is designing parts not only for functionality, but for how the company can conserve capital in manufacturing those parts. When a part fails, with most manufacturers the whole part is scrapped even though just a component within the part fails. BMW is looking at ways to change the design on the part so that it's more modular, and when a part fails it's replaced with a new one for the owner, but the old part is sent back to production for the modules to be replaced. This has higher short-term costs but lower long-term costs, especially when the company considers internalizing the externality costs of waste.

In the near future, these companies will opt for longer-term solutions and benefits over the shorter-term answers.

(continued)

They will also be considering the benefits and costs to all stakeholders (which is society at large), not just the shareholders. So we will be looking at what is good for the masses and finding ways to make it good for individuals as well. This is not socialism—it's sustainable capitalism—but it will require an acceptance of looking at our problems from a different perspective. Nothing is more effective at forcing markets to function differently than when they are confronted with scarcity. Perhaps corporations of the future will act in a socially responsible manner, not because they are forced politically to do so, but because it just makes good business sense.

1. To encourage companies to be more economically sustainable, what do you think consumers can do that would have an impact on the companies' decisions?

2. What are some ideas you have that companies could undertake on the supply-side to promote sustainable capitalism? What could they do on the demand-side?

3. What do you think are the biggest challenges businesses face in attempting to change into more socially responsible organizations?

4. Remember that demand is based on want and ability to purchase. Do you think consumers would be willing to pay higher prices in order for socially responsible firms to be able to survive? Do you think prices are the primary motivator on the demand-side? Are prices the primary inhibitor on the supply-side? Explain your comments.

CAN EXTERNALITIES BE ACCURATELY MEASURED?

It is generally accepted that in the absence of intervention, the market mechanism will underproduce goods and services with positive externalities, such as education, and overproduce those with negative externalities, such as pollution. But the exact extent of these market misallocations is quite difficult to establish in the real world because the divergence between social and private costs and benefits is often difficult to measure. For example, exactly how much damage at the margin does a steel mill's air pollution do to nonconsumers of the steel? No one really knows because no market fully measures those costs. Indeed, the costs are partly nonpecuniary, meaning that no outlay of money occurs. Even though we pay dollars to get medicine for respiratory ailments and pay dollars for paint to repair pollution-caused paint peeling of homes in the vicinity of plants, we do not make explicit money payments for the visual pollution and undesirable odours that the mill might produce as a by-product of making steel. Nonpecuniary

Can skyscrapers be good for the environment? People who live in the city usually drive less, use more public transportation, and also use less electricity and home heating because they tend to live in smaller living spaces compared to suburbanites. As a result, central city residents may emit less carbon into the atmosphere than suburbanites.

Crocodile Images/Thinkstock

costs are real costs and potentially have a monetary value that can be associated with them, but assessing that value in practical terms is immensely difficult. You might be able to decide how much you would be willing to pay to live in a pollution-free world, but no current mechanism allows anyone to express the perceived monetary value of having clear air to breathe and smell. Even some pecuniary, or monetary, costs are difficult to truly measure: How much respiratory disease is caused by pollution and how much by other factors such as secondhand cigarette smoke? Environmental economists continue to make progress in valuing these difficult damages.

DEBATE

ARE THE TAR SANDS WORTH THE ENVIRONMENTAL COSTS FOR CANADA?

For:

The strongest argument for the ongoing development of the Alberta tar sands centres on the revenues they create for the Canadian economy—revenues that are shared among a wide range of stakeholders. This industry creates hundreds of thousands of jobs, mainly in western Canada but also across the nation and across borders. Think about how much Alberta, British Columbia, and Saskatchewan have grown over the past 40 years. This means jobs not only in the oil industry, but also in virtually every facet of a modern economy—housing, manufacturing, and transportation. So vast is this employment need that workers literally fly across Canada to meet the demand. Think also of the R&D that has been done in relation to the tar sands, the results of which have been used in faraway regions. The need for low-cost fuel justifies the development of key transportation links, such as Keystone and Northern Gateway developments; once completed, they will provide an almost endless supply of secure oil to refineries around North America and the world. While it's recognized that the tar sands development does some harm, that actually occurs in a remote area, with limited impact. What has to be considered is the greatest good for the greatest number of people, and the remoteness of this development provides a strong argument for its continued growth. The Alberta tar sands have replaced the manufacturing engine of central Canada. If environmentalists slow down the tar sands development, the impact on the Canadian GDP and federal and provincial coffers will be great, with higher unemployment rates, higher tax rates to offset the declining royalties, and lower levels of public service across the nation. Surely it's clear that continued development of the tar sands is worth the environmental costs for Canada. Can you look in more detail at some of the issues raised and investigate other arguments? Think about private and social benefits.

Against:

The fact that the tar sands have been developed in a remote area of the country is tragic—most people have experienced only the benefits. But this development is not a clean technology and there has been little regard so far for the costs to our environment. It's not just the land that's affected, but the health and vitality of the whole ecosystem, including human welfare. The land where the oil sands are located is boreal forest and muskeg and it acts as a key ecological area in water and forestation. Recovering the bitumen from the sands requires vast amounts of water and natural gas, because water is heated into steam and injected into the ground to unlock the viscous oil. Three to five cubic metres of water are needed to recover a single cubic metre of oil. The key watershed is the Athabasca River, from which this water is drawn. Once the water has been drawn and used, it is polluted and has to be either treated and released or stored as tailing pond water. Vast ponds have been created, but they fill to capacity in short order and cannot be truly contained, which means thousands of cubic metres of toxic tailings entering back into the watershed. These tailing contain highly toxic components that even in trace concentrations have dire consequences to human and animal health in the areas. The tar sands also release some of the world's largest concentrations of CO_2 deposits into the atmosphere, which will grow with increased U.S. and Asian demand for a secured oil source. In 1990, Canada agreed to the Kyoto target of reducing its greenhouse emissions 6 percent by 2012, but in fact Canada increased its emissions by 24 percent, of which the tar sands accounted for about 7 percent of the Canadian total. That doesn't seem like much, but in 1990, the tar sands contributed just over 1 percent of the Canadian total. Over the medium and longer term, these increases in greenhouse emissions will have a dramatic effect on global warming and on our climate. Surely it's clear that the ongoing development of the tar sands isn't worth the environmental costs. Can you find other arguments to support this position?

section 12.3 Public Policy and the Environment

■ Why is a clean environment not free?
■ What can be done to reduce pollution?
■ What is an ideal pollution-control policy?

WHY IS A CLEAN ENVIRONMENT NOT FREE?

In many respects, a clean environment is no different from any other desirable good. In a world of scarcity, we can improve our environment only by giving up something else. The problem that we face is choosing the combination of goods that does the most to enhance human well-being. Few people would enjoy a perfectly clean environment if they were cold, hungry, and generally destitute. On the other hand, an individual choking to death in smog is hardly to be envied, no matter how great his or her material wealth.

Only by considering the additional cost as well as the additional benefit of increased consumption of all goods, including clean air and water, can decisions on the desirable combination of goods to consume be made properly.

The Costs and Benefits of Pollution Control

It is possible, even probable, that pollution elimination, like nearly everything else, is subject to diminishing returns. Initially, a large amount of pollution can be eliminated fairly inexpensively, but getting rid of still more pollution may prove more costly. Likewise, it is also possible that the benefits from eliminating soot from the air might decline as more and more pollution is eliminated. For example, perhaps some pollution elimination initially would have a profound impact on health costs, home repair expenses, and so on, but as pollution levels fall, further elimination of pollutants brings fewer marginal benefits.

The cost–benefit trade-off just discussed is illustrated in Exhibit 1, which examines the marginal social benefits and marginal social costs associated with the elimination of air pollution. In the early 1960s, we had few regulations as a nation on pollution control, and as a result, private firms had little incentive to eliminate the problem. In the context of Exhibit 1, we may have spent Q_1 on controls, meaning that the marginal social benefits of greater pollution-control expenditures exceeded the marginal costs associated with having the controls. Investing more capital and labour to reduce pollution is efficient in such a situation.

Optimum pollution control occurs when Q^* of pollution is eliminated. As indicated in Exhibit 1, Q^* is achieved where the marginal social benefits of greater pollution-control expenditures are equal to the marginal social costs of having them; that is, $MSB = MSC$. Overly stringent regulations force companies to control pollution to the level indicated by Q_2 in Exhibit 1, where the additional costs from the controls far outweigh the additional environmental benefits. It should be noted, however, that increased concerns about pollution have probably caused the marginal social benefit curve to shift to the right over time, increasing the optimal amount of pollution control. Because of measurement problems, however, it is difficult to state whether we are generally below, at, or above the optimal pollution level.

WHAT CAN BE DONE TO REDUCE POLLUTION?

Even though measuring externalities, both negative and positive, is often nearly impossible, it does not necessarily mean that it is better to ignore the externality and allow the market solution to continue. As already explained in the previous section, the market-determined solution will almost certainly result in excessive output by polluters unless some intervention occurs. What form should the intervention take?

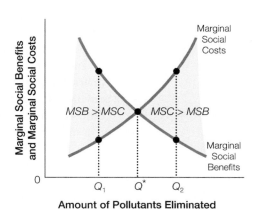

section 12.3 **Costs and Benefits**
Exhibit 1 **of Pollution Controls**

With the principles of diminishing marginal utility and increasing marginal cost at work, the marginal benefits of further expenditures on pollution control will, at some point, fall below the marginal costs to society imposed by still stricter controls. At output Q_1, pollution control is inadequate; on the other hand, elimination of Q_2 pollution will entail costs that exceed the benefits. Only at Q^* is pollution-control expenditure at an optimum level. Of course, in practice, it is difficult to know exactly the position and slope of these curves.

Environmental Regulation

One approach to dealing with externalities is to regulate behaviour in response to the externality. The range of environmental regulations is significant, as the government can choose to prohibit certain activities that cause pollution, dictate maximum permissible levels of pollution, or require producers to adopt certain pollution-control technology. In Canada, environmental policy is the joint responsibility of all three levels of government (federal, provincial/territorial, and municipal), with Environment Canada as the central department responsible for developing and enforcing regulations designed to protect the environment.

Evidence suggests that pollution levels have declined in recent years, although these statistics do not measure exactly what Environment Canada's impact has been, as other things were also changing. However, it does appear that the regulatory approach adopted by Environment Canada to limit key pollutants has led to a reduction in pollution levels. For example, the phasing-out of leaded gasoline, which started in the 1980s, has dramatically reduced the levels of lead in the atmosphere.

Pollution Taxes

Another means of solving the misallocation problem (relatively too many polluting goods) posed by the existence of externalities is for the government to create incentives for firms to internalize the external costs resulting from their activities. For example, returning to the case of pollution, suppose that the marginal private cost of making steel was $150 a tonne. Suppose further that at the margin, each tonne of steel caused $40 in environmental damages per tonne. If the government was then to levy a

pollution tax—a tax levied by government on a firm for environmental pollution—on the steelmaker equal to $40 per tonne, the manufacturer's marginal private cost would rise from $150 to $190; the $190 figure would then be equal to the true marginal social cost of making steel. The firm would accordingly alter its output and pricing decisions to take into account its higher marginal cost, leading ultimately to reduced output (and pollution) and higher prices. The firm also has an incentive to seek new, less pollution-intensive methods of making steel.

In July of 2007, the Alberta government became the first jurisdiction in North America to put a price on CO_2 emissions—$15 for each tonne of carbon released in the province. The actual implementation of the program, however, was considerably more complex. Only firms that emitted more than 100 000 tonnes of greenhouse gas annually were subject to the policy and even then, companies were subject to the $15-per-tonne policy only if they failed to reduce their "carbon intensity" by the required 12 percent. Quebec introduced a carbon tax in October 2007, the first North American province or state to do so. The tax required oil companies to pay 0.8 cents per litre of gasoline distributed in the province and 0.938 cents for each litre of diesel fuel.

In 2008, the province of British Columbia implemented a carbon tax of $10 per tonne on carbon dioxide equivalent (CO_2e) emissions (2.41 cents per litre on gasoline)—the most significant carbon tax in the western hemisphere. This *carbon tax* is based on greenhouse gas emissions (GHG) generated from the burning of fossil fuels, particularly on the amount of carbon in the fuel. It puts a price on each tonne of GHG emitted, effectively sending a price signal to the economy that the government intends to reduce emissions. In July of 2012, the British Columbia government implemented the final scheduled increase in its carbon tax program. Currently, the total tax is $30 per tonne.

Using taxes to internalize external costs is appealing because it allows the relatively efficient private sector to operate according to market forces in a manner that takes socially important spillover costs into account. A major objection to the use of such taxes is that, in most cases, it is difficult to measure externalities with any precision. Choosing a tax rate involves some guesswork, and poor guessing might lead to a solution that is far from optimal. But it is likely to be better than ignoring the problem. In spite of the severe difficulties in measurement, however, many economists would like to see greater effort made to force internalization of externalities through taxes rather than using regulation. Why? We know that firms will seek out the least expensive (in terms of using society's scarce resources) approaches to cleanup because they want more profits. This plan is good for them and good for society because we can have more of everything that way, including environmental quality.

Transferable Pollution Rights: Cap and Trade

Economists see an opportunity to control pollution through a government-enforced system of property rights. **Transferable pollution rights** are rights given to a firm to discharge a specified amount (smaller than the uncontrolled amount) of pollution. In this plan, firms have an incentive to lower their levels of pollution because they can sell their permits if they go unused. Specifically, firms that can lower their emissions at the lowest costs will do so and trade their pollution rights to firms that cannot reduce their pollution levels as easily. That is, each polluter—required either to reduce pollution to the level allowed by the number of rights it holds or to buy more rights—will be motivated to eliminate all pollution that is cheaper than the price of pollution rights. The crucial advantage to the pollution rights approach comes from the fact that the rights are private property and can be sold.

It is worth emphasizing that this least-cost pattern of abatement does not require any information about the techniques of pollution abatement on the part of the government—more specifically, Environment Canada. Environment Canada does not need to know the cheapest abatement strategy for each and every polluter. Faced with a positive price for pollution rights, each polluter has every motivation to discover and use the cheapest way to reduce pollution. Nor does Environment Canada need to know anything about the differences in abatement costs among polluters. Each polluter is motivated to reduce pollution as long as the cost of reducing one more unit is less than the price of pollution rights. The information and incentives generated by private ownership and market exchange of these pollution rights automatically leads to the desirable pattern of pollution abatement—namely, having those best at cleaning up doing all the cleanup.

The pulp and paper industry is one of the largest and most polluting industries in North America. One of the primary environmental concerns is the use of chlorine-based bleaches and resultant toxic emissions to air, water, and soil.

The pollution rights approach also creates an incentive for polluters to develop improved pollution abatement technologies.

The prospect of buying and selling pollution permits would allow firms to move into an area that is already as polluted as allowed by Environment Canada standards. Under the tradable permits policy, the firm can set up operation by purchasing pollution permits from an existing polluter in the area. This type of exchange allows the greatest value to be generated with a given amount of pollution. It also encourages polluters to come up with cheaper ways of reducing pollution, because the firm that reduces pollution is able to sell its pollution credits to others, making pollution reduction profitable. An example of transferrable pollution rights in action is the Western Climate Initiative (WCI), a nonprofit corporation involved in the administration and implementation of state and provincial greenhouse gas emission trading programs. Currently, WCI includes officials from the provinces of Quebec and British Columbia, and the state of California.

WHAT IS AN IDEAL POLLUTION-CONTROL POLICY?

What would be the objectives of an ideal pollution-control policy? First, and most obviously, we want pollution reduced to the efficient level—the level that maximizes the value of all of our resources. This goal would involve continuing to reduce pollution by one more unit only as long as the value of the improved environmental quality is greater than the value of ordinary goods that are sacrificed.

A second related objective is to reduce pollution as cheaply as possible. Two separate considerations are important here. If pollution is to be reduced as cheaply as possible, it is obvious that each pollution source has to abate at minimum cost. Of the many ways to cut back on pollution, not all are equally costly. But even if all polluters are abating as cheaply as possible, it does not necessarily mean that pollution overall is being reduced at least cost.

The pattern of pollution abatement over all sources is of great importance here. Because some polluters will be more efficient at pollution reduction than others, the least-cost abatement pattern will require some polluters to clean up more than others.

A third objective of a pollution-control policy is to establish incentives that will motivate advances in pollution abatement technology. Over the long run, this objective may be even more important than the first two. For example, the cost of controlling pollution can be significantly reduced over time, even if the second objective is not fully realized, if consistent advances are made in the technology of pollution control.

It should be clear that these three objectives—(1) achieving the efficient level of pollution, (2) achieving pollution reduction at least cost, and (3) motivating advances in abatement technology—may never be fully realized, especially the first objective.

Because we cannot own and control identifiable and separate portions of the atmosphere, we are not in a position to require that a price be paid in exchange for fouling clean air that we each consider ours alone. Without such exchanges and prices, we have no way of knowing the value people place on clean air. Without this information, it is not possible to determine the efficient level of air pollution. Likewise, private ownership of identifiable and separate portions of water in our lakes, rivers, and oceans is not possible, leaving no precise ways of determining the efficient level of water pollution. In the absence of market exchange, we rely on the political process to determine the efficient level of pollution.

In a democratic political order, the presumption is that the information provided by voting and lobbying will keep the political process at least somewhat responsive to the preferences of the citizens. To the extent that this presumption is justified, the hope is that political decision makers will arrive at a level of pollution near the efficient level.

SECTION CHECK

- In a world of scarcity, we can improve our environment only by giving up something else—the opportunity cost of environmental policy.
- Environmental regulations force companies to find less pollution-intensive ways of producing goods and services. Pollution taxes can be used to force firms to internalize externalities and allow the relatively efficient private sector to operate according to market forces in a manner that takes socially important spillover costs into account. The transferable pollution rights policy encourages polluters to come up with cheaper ways of reducing pollution because the firm that reduces pollution is able to sell its remaining pollution credits to others.
- The objectives of pollution-control policies are to achieve the efficient level of pollution, achieve pollution reduction at least cost, and motivate advances in abatement technology.

Section 12.4   Property Rights

- What is the relationship between externalities and property rights?
- What is the Coase theorem?

WHAT IS THE RELATIONSHIP BETWEEN EXTERNALITIES AND PROPERTY RIGHTS?

The existence of externalities and the efforts to deal with them in a manner that will enhance the social good can be considered a question of the nature of property rights. If Environment Canada limits the soot that a steel company emits from its smokestack, then the property rights of the steel company with respect to its smokestack have been altered or restricted. Similarly, zoning laws restrict how property owners can use their property. Sometimes, to deal with externalities, governments radically alter arrangements of property rights.

Indeed, the entire matter of dealing with externalities ultimately evolves into a question of how property rights should be altered. If no externalities existed in the world, reasons for prohibiting property owners from using their property in any manner they voluntarily chose would be few. Ultimately, then, externalities involve an evaluation of the legal arrangements under which we operate our economy and thus illustrate one area where law and economics merge.

WHAT IS THE COASE THEOREM?

In a classic paper, Nobel laureate Ronald Coase observed that when the benefits are greater than the costs for some course of action (say, environmental cleanup), potential transactions can make some people better off without making anyone worse off. Formally known as the **Coase theorem,** it states that where

property rights are defined in a clear-cut fashion, externalities are internalized. To appreciate this important insight, consider the following problem: A cattle rancher lives downstream from a paper mill. The paper mill dumps waste into the stream, which injures the rancher's cattle. If the rancher is not compensated, an externality exists. The question is, why does the externality persist? Suppose the courts have established (perhaps because the paper mill was there first) that the property rights to use (or abuse) the stream reside with the mill. If the benefits of cleanup are greater than the costs, the rancher should be willing to pay the mill owner to stop polluting. Let's assume that the rancher's benefits (say $10 000) from the cleanup undertaken by the mill are greater than the cost (say $5000). If the rancher was to offer $7500 to the mill owner to clean up the stream, both the rancher and the mill owner would be better off than with continued pollution. If, on the other hand, the rancher had the property rights to the stream and the mill owner received a sufficiently high benefit from polluting the river, then it would be rational for the mill owner to pay the rancher up to the point where the marginal benefit to the mill owner of polluting equalled the marginal damage to the rancher from pollution.

If a rancher lives downstream from a polluting factory and the courts have given the rights to the factory to pollute, economists say that the property rights to pollute are well defined. However, the rancher may be able to negotiate privately and pay the polluting firm to reduce the amount of pollution—and make both parties better off.

Coase theorem
states that where property rights are defined in a clear-cut fashion, externalities are internalized

Transaction Costs and the Coase Theorem

The mill owner and rancher example hinges critically on low transaction costs. Transaction costs are the costs of negotiating and executing an exchange, excluding the cost of the good or service bought. For example, when buying a car, it is usually rational for the buyer to spend some time searching for the "right" car and negotiating a mutually agreeable price.

Suppose instead that the situation involved 1000 ranchers and 10 mill owners. Trying to coordinate the activity between the ranch owners and mill owners would be almost impossible. Now imagine the complexities of more realistic cases: Over 6 million people live in the Greater Toronto Area (GTA). Each of them is damaged a little by a large number of firms and other consumers (e.g., automobile drivers) in the GTA.

It thus becomes apparent why the inefficiencies resulting from pollution control are not eliminated by private negotiations. First is the issue of ambiguity regarding property rights in air, water, and other environmental media. Firms that have historically polluted resent controls, giving up their rights to pollute only if bribed, yet consumers feel they have the right to breathe clean air and use clean bodies of water. These conflicting positions must be resolved in court, with the winner being, of course, made wealthier. Second, transaction costs increase greatly with the number of transactors, making it next to impossible for individual firms and citizens to negotiate private agreements. Finally, the properties of air or water quality (and similar public goods) are such that additional people can enjoy the benefits at no additional cost and cannot be excluded from doing so. Hence, in practice, private agreements are unlikely to solve many problems of market failure.

It is, however, too easy to jump to the conclusion that governments should solve any problems that cannot be solved by private actions. No solution may be possible, or all solutions may involve costs that exceed benefits. In any event, the ideas developed in this chapter should enable you to think critically about such problems and the difficulties in formulating appropriate policies.

SECTION CHECK

- In a world with no externalities, property owners with only a few exceptions, could use their property in any manner they desired. Ultimately, then, externalities involve an evaluation of the legal arrangements in which we operate our economy.
- The Coase theorem states that when property rights are defined in a clear-cut fashion, externalities are internalized. This condition holds when information and transaction costs are close to zero.

Section
12.5 Public Goods

- What are private goods versus public goods?
- What is the free-rider problem with public goods?
- Why does the government provide public goods?
- What is a common resource?

WHAT ARE PRIVATE GOODS VERSUS PUBLIC GOODS?

public good
a good that is nonrivalrous in consumption and nonexcludable

Externalities are not the only cause of market failure. A public good is another source of market failure. As used by economists, this term refers not to how particular goods are purchased—by a government agency rather than some private economic agent—but to the properties that characterize them. Specifically, the term **public good** refers to a good that is nonrivalrous in consumption and nonexcludable. In this section, we learn the difference between private goods, public goods, and common resources.

Private Goods

private good
a good with rivalrous consumption and excludability

A **private good** is a good with rivalrous consumption and excludability (such as a cheeseburger). First, a cheeseburger is rival in consumption because if one person eats a particular cheeseburger, nobody else can eat the same cheeseburger. Second, a cheeseburger is excludable. It is easy to keep someone from eating your cheeseburger by not giving it to them. Most goods in the economy like food, clothing, cars, and houses are private goods that are rival and excludable.

Public Goods

The consumption of public goods, unlike private goods, is neither excludable nor rival. A public good is not rival because everyone can consume the good simultaneously; that is, one person's use of it does not diminish another's ability to use it. A public good is likewise *not excludable* because once the good is produced, it is prohibitively costly to exclude anyone from consuming the good. Consider national defence. Once the military has its defence in place, everyone enjoys the benefits of national defence (not rival) and it would be prohibitively costly to exclude anyone from consuming national defence (not excludable).

Another example of a public good is the environment (fresh air, clean water). An environmental protection program would allow all of the people who live in the jurisdiction governed by the program to enjoy the protection of the new program simultaneously. It would be very difficult to exclude someone who lived in the middle of the jurisdiction who said she did not want to pay. Like national defence, the good is neither rival nor excludable in consumption. Other examples of public goods include outdoor fireworks displays and flood-plain projects.

WHAT IS THE FREE-RIDER PROBLEM WITH PUBLIC GOODS?

The fact that a public good is not rival and not excludable makes the good difficult to produce privately. Some people would know they could derive the benefits from the good without paying for it because once it is produced, it is too difficult to exclude anyone. That is, some people try to be a **free rider**—derive benefits from something *without paying for it.*

Let's return to our public good example of national defence. Suppose national defence is actually worth $100 to you. Assume that 10 million households in Canada are each willing to make a $100 contribution for national defence. This would add up to $1 billion. You might write a cheque for $100. Or you might reason as follows: "If I don't give $100 and everybody else does, I will be equally well protected plus derive the benefits of the $100 in my pocket." Taking the latter course represents a rational attempt to be a free rider. The rub is that if everyone attempts to take a free ride, the ride will not exist.

The free-rider problem prevents the private market from supplying the efficient quantity of public goods. That is, little incentive exists for individuals in the private sector to provide public goods because it is too difficult to make a profit. Therefore, the government provides important public goods such as national defence.

free rider
a party that derives benefits from something without paying for it

Eugene Berman/Shutterstock.com

Government provides important public goods, such as national defence. Voters may disagree on whether we have too much or too little national defence, but most agree that we must have it. If national defence was provided privately and people were asked to pay for the use of national defence, many would free-ride, knowing they could derive the benefits of the good without paying for it.

WHY DOES THE GOVERNMENT PROVIDE PUBLIC GOODS?

Everything the government provides has an opportunity cost. What is the efficient level of national defence? More national defence means less of something else that society may value more, like health care or education. To be efficient, public goods must also follow the rule of rational choice—pursue additional government activities only if the expected marginal benefits exceed the expected marginal costs. It all comes back to the saying "There are no free lunches."

In addition, there is also the problem of assessing the value of these goods. Consider the case of a new highway. Before it builds the highway, the appropriate government agency will undertake a benefit–cost analysis of the situation. In this case, it must evaluate consumers' willingness to pay for the highway against the costs that will be incurred for construction and maintenance. However, those individuals who want the highway have an incentive to exaggerate their desire for it. At the same time, individuals who will be displaced or otherwise harmed by the highway have an incentive to exaggerate the harm that will be done to them. Together, these elements make it difficult for the government to assess benefits and costs accurately. Ultimately, government evaluations are reduced to educated guesses about the net impact of the highway on all parties concerned.

WHAT IS A COMMON RESOURCE?

In many cases we do not have exclusive private-property rights to things such as the air around us or the fish in the sea. They are common resources—goods that are owned by everyone and therefore not owned by anyone. When a good is not owned by anyone, individuals feel little incentive to conserve or use the resource efficiently.

common resource
a rival good that is not excludable

A **common resource** is a rival good that is not excludable; that is, nonpayers cannot be easily excluded from consuming the good, and when one unit is consumed by one person, it means that it cannot be consumed by another. Fish in the vast ocean waters are a good example of a common resource. They are rival because fish are limited—a fish taken by one person is not available for others. They are not excludable because it is prohibitively costly to keep anyone from catching them—almost anyone with a boat and a fishing rod could catch one.

The failure of private incentives to provide adequate maintenance to common resources can lead to their degeneration and ultimate extinction; that is, common resources can lead to a tragedy of the commons. While there is no shortage of examples of such tragedies in modern society, the one that could potentially impact us the greatest is the digital commons—the Internet. The current problem with the vast majority of the digital information on the Internet is that no effective market exists for its economic exchange. Information is often poorly catalogued and unorganized, with little or no commercial value. The information that is well organized and of value is separated from the rest through various revenue-generating channels. If the Internet is to remain a useful tool for society, solutions to this market disconnect need to be developed.

SECTION CHECK

- ■ A public good is both nonrivalrous in consumption (one person's usage of it does not diminish another's ability to use it) and nonexclusive (no one can be excluded from using it), whereas a private good is both rivalrous and excludable.
- ■ Despite their demand, because public goods are not rival and not excludable, there is little incentive for private individuals to produce them.
- ■ The free-rider problem prevents the private market from supplying the efficient quantity of public goods, whereas a private good is both rivalrous and excludable.
- ■ A common resource good is rival in consumption but not excludable.

Section 12.1

1. Indicate which of the following activities create a positive externality, a negative externality, or no externality at all:

   a. During a live-theatre performance, an audience member's cellphone rings loudly.

   b. You are given a flu shot.

   c. You purchase and drink a soft drink during a break from class.

   d. A local youth group cleans up trash along a two-kilometre stretch of highway.

   e. A firm dumps chemical waste into a local stream.

   f. The person down the hall in your residence plays a Britney Spears CD loudly while you are trying to sleep.

2. Draw a standard supply and demand diagram for widgets, and indicate the equilibrium price and output. Assuming that the production of widgets generates external benefits, illustrate the effect of a subsidy equal to the external benefits generated, and indicate the equilibrium output.

Section 12.2

3. Say that the last tonne of steel produced by a steel company imposes three types of costs: labour costs of $25, additional equipment costs of $10, and the cost of additional "crud" dumped into the air of $15. What costs will the steel company consider in deciding whether to produce another tonne of steel?

4. Why can a homeowner make a better argument for compensation for noise pollution if a local airport was built after he moved in than if it was already there when he moved in? Would it matter whether he knew it was going to be built?

5. A newly released study demonstrates that populated areas with significant air pollution caused by diesel engines experience a much higher incidence of cancer. If diesel engines were then banned, what sorts of results would you expect?

6. Draw a standard supply and demand diagram for widgets, and indicate the equilibrium price and output.

7. a. Why does internalizing externalities with taxes or subsidies sometimes increase the prices of goods and sometimes decrease them?

   b. When would workers in an industry benefit from internalizing its externalities?

8. Many communities have launched programs to collect recyclable materials but have been unable to find buyers for the salvaged materials. If the government was to offer a subsidy to firms using recycled materials, how might this affect the market for recycled materials? Illustrate using a demand and supply diagram.

Section 12.3

9. Discuss the incentive effects of each of these policies to reduce air pollution:

   a. a higher tax on gasoline

   b. an annual tax on automobiles based on average emissions

   c. an annual tax on total emissions from a particular model of car

10. If a firm can reduce its sulphur dioxide emissions for $30 per tonne but it owns tradable emissions permits that are selling for $40 per tonne, what will the firm want to do if it is trying to maximize profits?

11. Compare a pollution-reduction program that permits a certain level of pollution using emissions standards with one that permits the same level of pollution using tradable emissions permits.

12. Evaluate the following statement: "Public health is at stake when drinking water is contaminated by pollution. Local governments should take all measures necessary to ensure that zero pollutants contaminate the water supply."

13. Evaluate the following statement: "If people do not use paper or if they recycle paper, there is less incentive for lumber companies to plant trees on private land."

14. If an industry created both external benefits and external losses, would a tax or subsidy be appropriate? Why would someone be hurt by either one?

Section 12.4

15. A chemical factory dumps pollutants into a nearby river (permissible under the existing laws). In lieu of dumping into the river, the factory could pay for the pollution to be hauled to a toxic waste dump site at a cost of $125 000 per year. A vacation resort located downstream from the factory suffers damages estimated at $200 000 per year. Evaluate whether a change in law is necessary to achieve an efficient outcome in this situation.

16. A factory releases air pollutants that have a negative impact on the adjacent neighbourhood (populated by 2000 households). If the government could assign property rights to the air to either the factory or to the residents of the neighbourhood, would this make a difference in the quantity of pollution generated? Explain.

Section 12.5

17. For each of the goods below, indicate whether they are nonrival and/or nonexclusive. Also indicate whether they are private or public goods.
    a. hot dogs
    b. cable TV
    c. broadcast TV
    d. automobiles
    e. national defence
    f. pollution-control device
    g. parking spot in a parking structure
    h. a sunset
    i. admission to a theme park

18. Is a lighthouse a public good if it benefits many ship owners? What if it primarily benefits ships going to a port nearby?

19. Why do you think buffalo became almost completely extinct on the Great Plains but cattle did not? Why is it possible to buy buffalo burgers in a store or restaurant today?

20. How does a TV broadcast have characteristics of a public good? What about specialty cable services such as the Discovery Channel?

13

Introduction to the Macroeconomy

Macroeconomic Goals

- What are the three major macroeconomic goals in Canada?
- Are these macroeconomic goals universal?

WHAT ARE THE THREE MAJOR MACROECONOMIC GOALS IN CANADA?

Recall from Chapter 1 that macroeconomics is the study of the whole economy—the study of the forest, not the trees. A macroeconomist may study the changes in the inflation rate or the unemployment rate, the impact of changing monetary policy or fiscal policy on output and inflation, or alternative policies that may contribute to long-term economic growth.

Nearly every society has been interested in three major macroeconomic goals:

1. **Employment**: By maintaining employment of human resources at relatively high levels, jobs are relatively plentiful and financial suffering from lack of work and income is relatively uncommon.
2. **Price-level stability**: By keeping prices relatively stable, consumers and producers can make better decisions.
3. **Economic growth**: By achieving a high rate of growth in real output over time, standards of living improve.

While each goal is valid in its own right, of greater importance for effective macroeconomic management is how to strike a balance among all three. An economy with perfectly stable prices but no jobs and no growth is vastly inferior to an economy that is able to promote appropriate levels of economic growth and job creation while maintaining acceptable levels of price-level stability. A society will experience true economic benefit with the achievement of all three goals—a problem with no easy solution.

real gross domestic product (RGDP) *the total value of all final goods and services produced in a given time period, such as a year or a quarter, adjusted for inflation*

The statistic **real gross domestic product (RGDP)** measures the total value of all final goods and services produced in a given time period, such as a year or a quarter, adjusted for inflation. The word *real* is used to indicate that the output is adjusted for general increases in prices over time. We use real gross domestic product to measure the level of output or production in the entire economy.

Exhibit 1 provides data on Canada's macroeconomic performance 1993. Economic growth increased sharply after 1997, which helped to lower Canada's unemployment rate from relatively high levels in the early 1990s. For the 2008–12 period, however, economic growth averaged only 1.0 percent per year. This lower rate of growth is one reason why the unemployment rate has experienced a gradual increase. Throughout the 1993–2012 period, the inflation rate remained below 3 percent per year.

ARE THESE MACROECONOMIC GOALS UNIVERSAL?

In addition to these primary goals, concern has been expressed at various times and places about other economic issues, some of which are essentially microeconomic in character. For example, concern about the "quality of life" has prompted some societies to try to reduce "bads" such as pollution and crime, and increase goods and services such as education and health services. Another goal has been "fairness" in the distribution of income or wealth. Still another goal pursued in many nations at one time or another has been self-sufficiency in the production of certain goods or services, such as food and energy.

The Impact of Value Judgments on Economic Goals

In stating that nations have economic goals, we must acknowledge that nations are made up of individuals. Individuals within a society may differ considerably in their evaluation of the relative importance of certain issues, or even whether certain "problems" are really problems after all. For example, economic growth, viewed positively

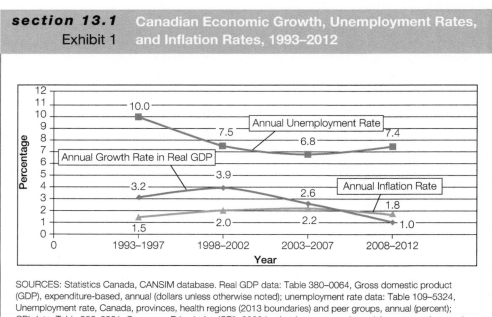

section 13.1   Canadian Economic Growth, Unemployment Rates,
Exhibit 1   and Inflation Rates, 1993–2012

SOURCES: Statistics Canada, CANSIM database. Real GDP data: Table 380–0064, Gross domestic product (GDP), expenditure-based, annual (dollars unless otherwise noted); unemployment rate data: Table 109–5324, Unemployment rate, Canada, provinces, health regions (2013 boundaries) and peer groups, annual (percent); CPI data: Table 326–0021, Consumer Price Index (CPI), 2009 basket (percentage change) (year-to-year), annual (2002 = 100 unless otherwise noted).

by most people, is not considered as favourably by others. Although some citizens may think that income distribution is just about right, others might think it provides insufficient incomes to the poorer members of society; still others think it involves taking too much income from the relatively well-to-do and thereby reduces incentives to carry out productive, income-producing activities.

SECTION CHECK

- The three major macroeconomic goals for Canada are full employment, price stability, and economic growth.
- People have their own reasons for valuing certain goals more than others. As a result, there is debate as to what is most important for an economy.

section
13.2

Employment and Unemployment

- What is the unemployment rate?
- Are unemployment statistics accurate reflections of the labour market?
- What are the categories of unemployment?
- What is the labour force participation rate?

News of lower unemployment usually sends stock prices higher, and the news of higher unemployment usually sends stock prices lower. Politicians are also concerned about unemployment figures because elections often hinge precariously on whether unemployment has been rising or falling.

Nearly everyone agrees that it is unfortunate when a person who wants a job cannot find one, and the loss of a job can mean financial insecurity and a great deal of anxiety. High rates of unemployment in a society can increase tensions and despair. A family without income undergoes great suffering; as its savings fade, it wonders where it is going to obtain the means to survive. Society loses some potential output of goods when some of its productive resources—human or nonhuman—remain idle, and potential consumption is also reduced. Clearly, then, there is a loss in efficiency when people willing to work and productive equipment remain idle. That is, other things equal, relatively high rates of unemployment are viewed almost universally as undesirable.

WHAT IS THE UNEMPLOYMENT RATE?

When discussing unemployment, economists and politicians refer to the unemployment rate. In order to calculate the unemployment rate, you must first understand another important concept—the labour force. The **labour force** is the number of persons 15 years of age and over who are employed or are unemployed and seeking work. Exhibit 1 shows the population categories used by Statistics Canada in its analysis of the labour market. First, it calculates the population 15 years of age and over, which was 28 314.7 thousand people in 2012. This population is broken down into two categories: those in the labour force and those not in the labour force. Those not in the labour force, 9438.6 thousand people, are people who are not working and are not

labour force *persons 15 years of age and over who are employed or are unemployed and seeking work*

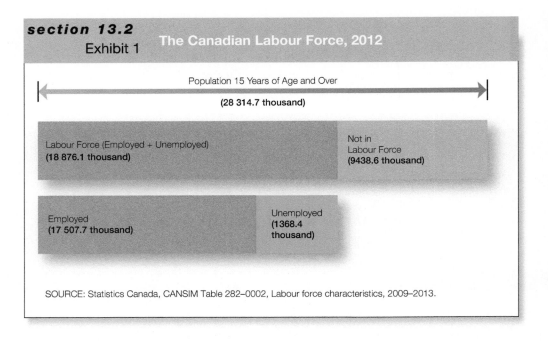

section 13.2
Exhibit 1   The Canadian Labour Force, 2012

Population 15 Years of Age and Over
(28 314.7 thousand)

Labour Force (Employed + Unemployed)
(18 876.1 thousand)

Not in
Labour Force
(9438.6 thousand)

Employed
(17 507.7 thousand)

Unemployed
(1368.4
thousand)

SOURCE: Statistics Canada, CANSIM Table 282–0002, Labour force characteristics, 2009–2013.

unemployment rate *the percentage of the people in the labour force who are unemployed*

seeking work. For example, they may be retired persons, full-time homemakers, or full-time students. Those in the labour force, 18 876.1 thousand people, are people who are employed or are unemployed and seeking work.

The **unemployment rate** is defined as the percentage of the people in the labour force who are unemployed. To calculate the unemployment rate, we divide the number of unemployed people by the number of people in the labour force:

$$\text{Unemployment rate} = (\text{Number of unemployed}/\text{Labour force}) \times 100$$

In 2012, 1368.4 thousand people were unemployed from a labour force of 18 876.1 thousand people:

$$\text{Unemployment rate} = (1368.4 \text{ thousand}/18\,876.1 \text{ thousand}) \times 100$$
$$= 0.072 \times 100$$
$$= 7.2 \text{ percent}$$

The Worst Case of Canadian Unemployment

By far the worst employment downturn in Canadian history was the Great Depression, which began in late 1929 and continued until 1939. Unemployment rose from only 2.9 percent of the labour force in 1929 to more than 19 percent in the early 1930s, and double-digit unemployment persisted through 1939. Some economists would argue that modern macroeconomics, with its emphasis on the determinants of unemployment and its elimination, truly began in the 1930s.

Variations in the Unemployment Rate

Exhibit 2 shows the unemployment rate since 1976. Unemployment has ranged from a high of 11.9 percent in 1983 to a low of 6.0 percent in 2007. Unemployment varies not only over time, it also varies between different segments of the population and by regions of the country. Unemployment tends to be much greater among teenagers, and female unemployment tends to be slightly lower than male unemployment. As Exhibit 3 indicates, the unemployment rate for teenagers

section 13.2
Exhibit 2
Unemployment Rate

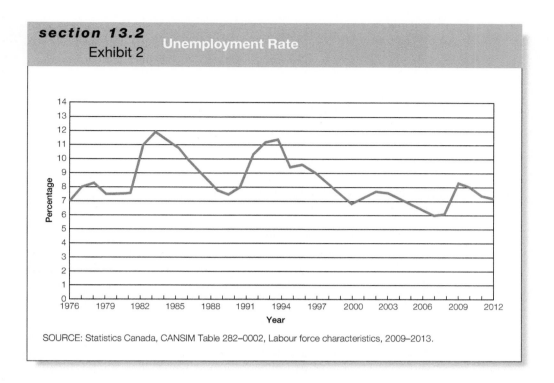

SOURCE: Statistics Canada, CANSIM Table 282–0002, Labour force characteristics, 2009–2013.

section 13.2
Exhibit 3
Unemployment in Canada by Age, Sex, and Region, 2012

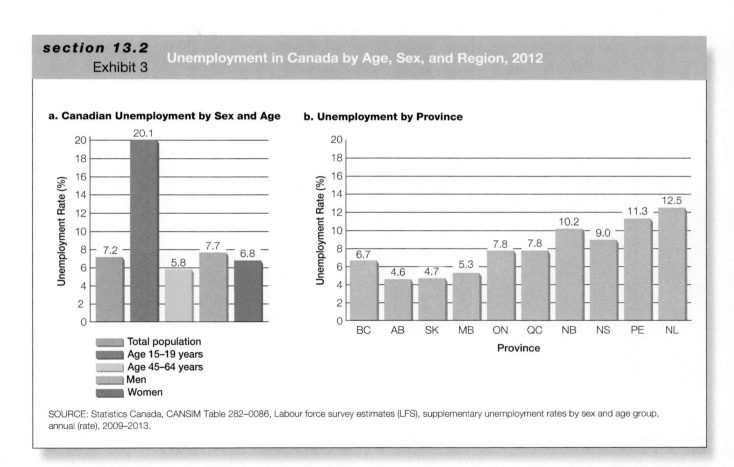

a. Canadian Unemployment by Sex and Age

Legend:
- Total population
- Age 15–19 years
- Age 45–64 years
- Men
- Women

Values: 7.2, 20.1, 5.8, 7.7, 6.8

b. Unemployment by Province

Province	Rate
BC	6.7
AB	4.6
SK	4.7
MB	5.3
ON	7.8
QC	7.8
NB	10.2
NS	9.0
PE	11.3
NL	12.5

SOURCE: Statistics Canada, CANSIM Table 282–0086, Labour force survey estimates (LFS), supplementary unemployment rates by sex and age group, annual (rate), 2009–2013.

(20.1 percent) is three times greater than the unemployment rate for workers aged 45 to 64 (5.8 percent). The difference in unemployment rates for men and women is smaller, with a female unemployment rate of 6.8 percent versus a male unemployment rate of 7.7 percent.

Provincial unemployment rates show considerable variation: from a high of 12.5 percent in Newfoundland and Labrador to a low of 4.7 percent in Saskatchewan. It is also clear from Exhibit 3(b) that, on average, the unemployment rate tends to rise as one moves from west to east across the country.

ARE UNEMPLOYMENT STATISTICS ACCURATE REFLECTIONS OF THE LABOUR MARKET?

In periods of prolonged economic recession and high unemployment, some individuals think that the chances of landing a job are so bleak that they quit looking. People who have left the labour force because they could not find work are called **discouraged workers.** Individuals who have not actively sought work are not counted as unemployed; instead, they fall out of the labour force. Also, people looking for full-time work who grudgingly settle for a part-time job are counted as "fully" employed, yet they are only "partly" employed. However, at least partially balancing these two biases in official employment statistics are a number of jobs in the underground economy (drugs, prostitution, gambling, and so on) that are not reported at all. In addition, many people may claim they are actually seeking work when, in fact, they may just be going through the motions so that they can continue to collect Employment Insurance or receive other government benefits.

discouraged workers *people who have left the labour force because they could not find work*

job loser *an individual who has been laid off or fired*

job leaver *a person who quits his or her job*

re-entrant *an individual who worked before and is now re-entering the labour force*

new entrant *an individual who has not held a job before but is now seeking employment*

WHAT ARE THE CATEGORIES OF UNEMPLOYMENT?

There are four main categories of unemployed workers: **job losers** (laid off or fired), **job leavers** (quit), **re-entrants** (worked before and are now re-entering the labour force), and **new entrants** (entering the labour force for the first time—primarily teenagers). It is a common misconception that the only reason workers become unemployed is because they have lost their jobs. Although job losers can typically account for 50 to 60 percent of the unemployed, a sizable proportion of unemployment is due to job leavers, new entrants, and re-entrants. Job leavers are typically the smallest source of unemployment.

CP PHOTO/Paul Chiasson

In Canada, teenagers have the highest rates of unemployment. A shortage of marketable skills and a lack of workplace experience are seen as two major reasons for this unequal burden.

Reducing Unemployment

Although unemployment is painful to those who have no source of income, reducing unemployment is not costless. In the short run, a reduction in unemployment may come at the expense of a higher rate of inflation, especially if the economy is close to full capacity, where resources are almost fully employed. Also, trying to match employees with jobs quickly may lead to significant inefficiencies because of mismatches between the worker's skill level and the level of skill required for a job. For example, the economy would be wasting resources subsidizing education if people with a Ph.D. in biochemistry were driving taxis or tending bar. That is, situations in which workers have skills higher than necessary for a job are what economists call **underemployment.** Alternatively, employees may be placed in jobs beyond their abilities, which would also lead to inefficiencies.

underemployment *a situation in which workers have skills higher than necessary for a job*

The Average Duration of Unemployment

The *duration* of unemployment is equally as important as the amount of unemployment. The financial consequences of a head of household being unemployed for four or five weeks are usually not extremely serious, particularly if the individual is covered by Employment Insurance. The impact becomes much more serious if a person is unemployed for many months. Therefore, it is useful to look at the average duration of unemployment to discover what percentage of the labour force is unemployed for more than a certain time period, say, 13 weeks. Canadian data indicate that long-term unemployment (greater than 13 weeks) accounts for approximately 40 to 50 percent of total unemployment.

Exhibit 4 shows the unemployment duration for Canada from 1997–2012. According to the exhibit, the average duration of unemployment has fallen from 26.5 weeks in 1997 to a low of 14.8 weeks in 2008. However, the economic downturn that followed the global financial crisis, with its slow recovery, has seen the duration of unemployment return to over 20 weeks on average. The duration of unemployment tends to be greater when the amount of unemployment is high and smaller when the amount of unemployment is low. Unemployment of any duration, of course, means a potential loss of output. This loss of current output is permanent; it is not made up when unemployment starts falling again.

WHAT IS THE LABOUR FORCE PARTICIPATION RATE?

The percentage of the population aged 15 years and over that is in the labour force is what economists call the **labour force participation rate.** Since 1976, the labour force participation rate has increased from 61.5 to around 67.0 percent. The increase in the labour force participation rate can be attributed in large part to the entry of the baby boomers into the labour force and a 17 percentage point increase in the women's labour force participation rate.

labour force participation rate *the percentage of the population (aged 15 years and over) in the labour force*

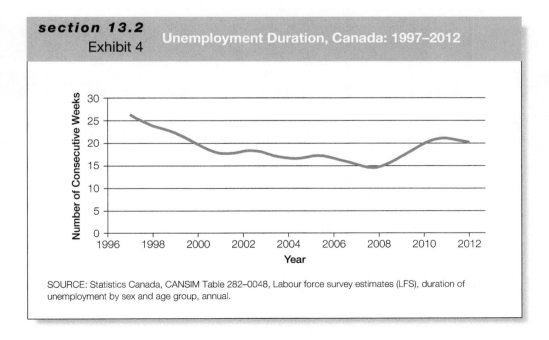

section 13.2 Exhibit 4 — Unemployment Duration, Canada: 1997–2012

SOURCE: Statistics Canada, CANSIM Table 282–0048, Labour force survey estimates (LFS), duration of unemployment by sex and age group, annual.

	1976	*1986*	*1996*	*2007*	*2010*	*2012*
Total	61.5%	66.0%	64.7%	67.6%	67.0%	66.8%
Men	77.6	76.8	72.2	72.7	71.1	71.5
Women	45.7	55.5	57.5	62.7	62.4	62.3

section 13.2 Exhibit 5 — Labour Force Participation Rates for Men and Women

SOURCE: Statistics Canada. CANSIM Table 282–0002, Labour force characteristics, 1976–2013.

Since 1976, the number of women working has shifted dramatically, reflecting the changing role of women in the workforce. In Exhibit 5, we see that in 1976 only 46 percent of women were working or looking for work. Today that figure is more than 62 percent. In 1976, over 77 percent of men were working or looking for work. Today the labour force participation rate for men has fallen to roughly 72 percent, as many men stay in school longer or opt to retire earlier.

SECTION CHECK

- The unemployment rate is found by taking the number of people officially unemployed and dividing by the number in the labour force. Unemployment rates are higher for teenagers, men, and those living in eastern Canada.
- The overall accuracy of the unemployment rate is impacted by factors such as discouraged workers, the treatment of part-time work statistics, and the underground economy.
- There are four main categories of unemployed workers: job losers, job leavers, re-entrants, and new entrants.
- Labour force participation measures the percentage of the adult population that is participating in the labour force. In Canada, women's labour force participation has increased dramatically since 1976.

section 13.3 Different Types of Unemployment

- What is frictional unemployment?
- What is structural unemployment?
- What is cyclical unemployment?
- What is the natural rate of unemployment?

In examining the status of and changes in the unemployment rate, it is important to recognize that there are numerous types of unemployment. In this section, we will examine frictional, structural, and cyclical unemployment and evaluate the relative impact of each on the overall unemployment rate.

WHAT IS FRICTIONAL UNEMPLOYMENT?

In a dynamic economy where people are constantly losing or leaving their jobs, some unemployment is always present. Specifically, **frictional unemployment** is the temporary unemployment that results from workers searching for suitable jobs and firms looking for suitable workers. People seeking work do not usually take the first job offered to them. Likewise, firms do not usually take the first person they interview. People and firms engage in a search to match up skills and interests. While the unemployed are looking, they are frictionally unemployed.

For example, consider an advertising executive who was laid off and is now actively looking for similar work. Of course, not all unemployed workers were laid off from their jobs; some may have voluntarily quit their jobs, while still others are without a job because they have just entered the labour market (such as recent college and university graduates). In any case, frictional unemployment is short term and results from normal turnover in the labour market, as when people change from one job to another.

Some unemployment occurs because certain types of jobs are seasonal in nature; this type of unemployment is called *seasonal unemployment*. For example, a ski instructor in British Columbia might become seasonally unemployed when the skiing season is over. Or a roofer in Nova Scotia may become seasonally unemployed during the winter months. In agricultural areas, employment increases during the harvest season and falls after harvesting is finished. Even a forest firefighter in a provincial park might be employed only during the months when forest fires are more likely to occur. Because the seasonal unemployment rate is of course higher in the off-season, Statistics Canada also publishes a seasonally adjusted unemployment rate.

Frictional Unemployment—A Sign of Economic Health

A certain amount of frictional unemployment might be good for the economy because workers who are temporarily unemployed might find jobs that are better suited to their skill level, increasing output in society as well as the wage income of the mover. Hence, frictional unemployment, although not good in itself, can be viewed as a by-product of a healthy phenomenon, and because it is often short-lived, it is generally not viewed as a serious problem. Actually, frictional unemployment tends to be somewhat greater in periods of low unemployment, when job opportunities are plentiful. This high level of job opportunity stimulates mobility, which, in turn, creates some frictional unemployment.

WHAT IS STRUCTURAL UNEMPLOYMENT?

A second type of unemployment is structural unemployment. Like frictional unemployment, structural unemployment is related to occupational movement or mobility, or in this case, to a lack of mobility. Specifically, **structural unemployment** refers to unemployment that occurs due to a lack of skills necessary for available jobs. For example, if a machine operator in a manufacturing plant loses his job, he could remain unemployed despite the fact that there are openings for computer programmers in his community. The quantity of unemployed workers conceivably could equal the number of job vacancies, but the unemployment persists because the unemployed lack the appropriate skills for some of the job vacancies. Given the existence of structural unemployment, it is wise to look at both unemployment and job vacancy statistics in assessing labour market conditions. Structural unemployment, like frictional unemployment, reflects the dynamic dimension of a changing economy. Over time, new jobs open up that require new skills, whereas old jobs that required different skills disappear. It is not surprising, then, that many people advocate government-subsidized retraining programs as a means of reducing structural unemployment.

frictional unemployment *the temporary unemployment that results from workers searching for suitable jobs and firms looking for suitable workers*

structural unemployment *unemployment that occurs due to a lack of skills necessary for available jobs*

Jules Frazier/Photodisc/Getty One Images

What type of unemployment would occur if these miners lost their jobs as a result of a reduction in demand for their output and needed retraining to find other employment? Usually structural unemployment occurs because of a lack of required skills or long-term changes in demand. Consequently, it generally lasts for a longer period of time than frictional unemployment. In this situation, both might come into play.

Another reason for structural unemployment is that low-skilled workers are frequently unable to find desirable long-term employment. Some low-skilled jobs do not last long and involve little job training, so workers may soon be looking for a new job. Because these workers acquired no new skill from the old job, they may be stuck without long-term secure work. That is, structural workers cannot be said to be "between jobs," like those who are frictionally unemployed. Structural unemployment is more long term and serious than frictional unemployment because these workers do not have marketable skills.

The dimensions of structural unemployment are debatable, in part because of the difficulty in precisely defining the term in an operational sense. Structural unemployment varies considerably—sometimes it is low and at other times, like in the 1970s and 1980s, it is high. To some extent, in this latter period, jobs in the traditional sectors like manufacturing and mining gave way to jobs in the computer and financial services sectors. Consequently, structural unemployment was higher.

Some Unemployment Is Unavoidable

Some unemployment is actually normal and important to the economy. Frictional and structural unemployment are simply unavoidable in a vibrant economy. To a considerable extent, one can view both frictional and structural unemployment as phenomena resulting from imperfections in the labour market. For example, if individuals seeking jobs and employers seeking workers had better information about each other, the level of frictional unemployment would be considerably lower. It takes time for suppliers of labour to find the demanders of labour services, and it takes time and money for labour resources to acquire the necessary skills. But because information is not costless, and because job search also is costly, the bringing of demanders and suppliers of labour services together does not occur instantaneously.

WHAT IS CYCLICAL UNEMPLOYMENT?

cyclical unemployment *unemployment due to short-term cyclical fluctuations in the economy*

Often, unemployment is composed of more than just frictional and structural unemployment. In years of relatively low economic activity some unemployment may be due to short-term cyclical fluctuations in the economy. We call this **cyclical unemployment.** Whenever the unemployment rate is greater than the natural rate, or during a recession, there is cyclical unemployment.

The Costs of Cyclical Unemployment

When the unemployment rate is high, numerous economic and social hardships result. The economic costs are the forgone output when the economy is not producing at its potential level. According to Okun's law (really, a rule of thumb), a 1 percent increase in cyclical unemployment reduces output by 2 percentage points, so we can actually estimate the economic costs of not producing at our potential output. The costs are particularly high for those groups with the least skills—the poorly educated and teenagers with little work experience.

WHAT IS THE NATURAL RATE OF UNEMPLOYMENT?

It is interesting to observe that over the period in which annual unemployment data are available, the unemployment rate has never been zero; that is, some level of unemployment has always existed within a dynamic economy. Some economists call this unavoidable amount of unemployment the **natural rate of unemployment** and equate it to the sum of frictional and structural unemployment when they are at a maximum. The current rate of unemployment (May 2013) is 7.1 percent, which is above what is currently believed to Canada's natural rate of unemployment of 6 percent. The natural rate does not necessarily mean that it is the desirable rate; it merely refers to the rate that the economy normally experiences. There will always be some people without jobs, even when the economy is performing well. Some will be transitioning between jobs, others will have lost jobs, and still others may have quit to look for better jobs.

natural rate of unemployment *the amount of unemployment that is unavoidable, equal to the sum of frictional and structural unemployment when they are at a maximum*

When unemployment rises well above the natural rate, we have abnormally high unemployment; when it falls well below the natural rate, we have abnormally low unemployment. Since the natural rate of unemployment roughly equals the sum of frictional and structural unemployment when they are at a maximum, we can view unemployment rates below the natural rate as reflecting the existence of below-average levels of frictional and structural unemployment. When unemployment rises above the natural rate, however, it reflects the existence of cyclical unemployment. In short, the natural rate of unemployment is the unemployment rate when the economy is experiencing neither a recession nor a boom. The natural rate of unemployment is also called the *full-employment rate of unemployment*.

The natural rate of unemployment can change over time as technological, demographic, institutional, and other conditions vary. For example, as baby boomers age, the natural rate falls because middle-aged workers generally experience lower unemployment rates than do younger workers. In addition, the Internet and job placement agencies have improved access to employment information and allowed workers to find jobs more quickly. Also, the restructuring of Canada's Employment Insurance program is believed to have increased the number of people with jobs. Thus, the natural rate is not fixed, because it can change with demographic changes over time.

In fact, it is estimated that the natural rate was as low as about 5 percent in the 1960s, and then rose to over 8 percent in the 1980s and early 1990s. Today, most economists estimate the natural rate of unemployment to lie in a range of between 6 and 7 percent.

Full Employment and Potential Output

The amount of real output that an economy produces when its resources—labour, land, and capital—are fully employed is considered to be that economy's **potential output**; that is, the amount of output at the natural rate of unemployment. Literal full employment of labour means that the economy is providing employment for all who are willing and able to work, with no cyclical unemployment. It also means that capital and land are fully employed. That is, at the natural rate of unemployment, all resources are fully employed and the economy is producing its potential output and there is no cyclical unemployment. This does not mean the economy will always be producing at its potential output of resources. For example, when the economy is experiencing cyclical unemployment, the unemployment rate is greater than the natural rate. It is also possible that the economy's output can temporarily exceed the potential output as workers take on overtime or moonlight by taking on extra employment.

potential output *the amount of real output the economy would produce if its labour and other resources were fully employed—that is, at the natural rate of unemployment*

Will new technology in one industry displace workers in the whole economy? No. There may be some job loss of specific jobs or within certain industries, but the overall effect of technological improvements is the release of scarce resources for the expansion of output and employment in other areas and ultimately more economic growth and a higher standard of living.

Employment Insurance and the Natural Rate of Unemployment

Losing a job can lead to considerable hardship, and Employment Insurance (EI) is designed to partially offset the severity of the unemployment problem. That is, EI allows unemployed workers to maintain some income and spending, reducing hardship and the severity of a recession. The program does not cover those who quit their jobs. To qualify, recipients must have worked a certain length of time. Although the program is intended to ease the pain of unemployment, it also leads to more frictional unemployment, as job seekers stay unemployed for longer periods of time while searching for new jobs.

For example, some unemployed people may show little drive in seeking new employment, because EI lowers the opportunity cost of being unemployed. For example, a worker making $600 a week when employed receives $330 in compensation when unemployed; as a result, the cost of losing his job is not $600 a week in forgone income, but only $270.

Without EI, job seekers would more likely take the first job offered even if it did not match their preferences or skill levels. A longer job search might mean a better match but at the expense of lost production and greater amounts of tax dollars.

Of course, that does not mean that EI is necessarily a bad program. It still serves its desired goal of reducing income uncertainty. Workers who turn down unattractive jobs have an opportunity to find jobs that may be better suited to their tastes and skills. In summary, most economists believe that eliminating EI could reduce unemployment but they disagree on whether economic well-being is reduced or enhanced by such a change in policy.

Technological Change and the Natural Rate of Unemployment

Although many believe that technological advances inevitably result in the displacement of workers, this is not necessarily the case. New inventions are generally cost-saving, and these cost savings will generally generate higher incomes for producers and lower prices and better products for consumers, benefits that will ultimately result in the growth of other industries. If the new equipment is a substitute for labour, then it might displace workers. For example, many fast-food restaurants have substituted self-service beverage bars for workers. However, new capital equipment requires new workers to manufacture and repair the new equipment. The most famous example of this is the computer, which was supposed to displace thousands of workers. Although it did displace workers, the total job growth it generated exceeded the number of lost jobs. The problem is that it is easy to see just the initial effect of technological advances (displaced workers), without recognizing the implications of that invention for the whole economy over time.

SECTION CHECK

- Frictional unemployment results when a person moves from one job to another as a result of normal turnover in the economy.
- Structural unemployment results when people who are looking for jobs lack the required skills for the jobs that are available or a long-term change in demand occurs.
- Cyclical unemployment is due to short-term cyclical fluctuations in the economy, such as recessions.
- When cyclical unemployment is eliminated, our economy is said to be operating at full employment, or at a natural rate of unemployment.

Inflation

■ Why is the overall price level important?
■ How is inflation measured using the Consumer Price Index (CPI)?
■ Who are the winners and losers during inflation?
■ What are the costs of inflation?
■ What is the relationship between inflation and interest rates?

WHY IS THE OVERALL PRICE LEVEL IMPORTANT?

Just as full employment brings about economic security of one kind, stable prices increase another form of security. Most prices in the Canadian economy tend to rise over time and economists use a statistic known as a *price level* to measure this change. A **price level** measures the average level of prices in the economy. A continuous rise in the *overall* price level is called **inflation**. Even when the level of prices is stable, some prices will be rising while others are falling. However, when inflation is present, the goods and services with rising prices will outweigh the goods and services with falling prices. Without stability in the price level, consumers and producers will experience more difficulty in coordinating their plans and decisions. When the *overall* price level is falling, there is **deflation.**

In general, the only thing that can cause a *sustained* increase in the price level is a high rate of growth in money, a topic we will discuss thoroughly in the coming chapters.

price level *the average level of prices in the economy*

inflation *a continuous rise in the overall price level*

deflation *a decrease in the overall price level*

HOW IS INFLATION MEASURED USING THE CONSUMER PRICE INDEX (CPI)?

We often use the term *purchasing power* when we discuss how much a dollar can buy of goods and services. In times of inflation, a dollar cannot buy as many goods and services. Thus, the higher the inflation rate, the greater the rate of decline in purchasing power.

In periods of high and variable inflation, households and firms have a difficult time distinguishing between changes in the **relative price** of individual goods and services (the price of a specific good compared to the prices of other goods) and changes in the general price level of all goods and services. Suppose the price of milk rises by 5 percent between 2012 and 2013, but the overall price level (inflation rate) increases by only 2 percent during that period. Then we could say that between 2012 and 2013, the relative price of milk rose only 3 percent (5 – 2 percent). The next year, the price of milk might increase 5 percent again, but the general inflation rate might be 6 percent. That is, between 2012 and 2013, the relative price of milk might actually fall by 1 percent (5 – 6 percent).

Remember, the relative price is the price of a good relative to all other goods and services. Because of this difficulty in establishing relative prices, inflation distorts the information that flows from price signals. Does the good have a higher price because it has become relatively more scarce and therefore more valuable relative to other goods, or did the price rise along with all other prices because of inflation?

This muddying of price information undermines good decision making, so we need a method to measure inflation. We adjust for the changing purchasing power of the dollar by constructing a price index. Essentially, a **price index** is a measure of the trend in prices for a certain bundle of goods and services over a given time period.

relative price *the price of a specific good compared to the prices of other goods*

price index *a measure of the trend in prices for a certain bundle of goods and services over a given time period*

Consumer Price Index (CPI) *a measure of the prices of a basket of consumable goods and services that serves to gauge inflation*

There are many different types of price indices. The best-known price index, the **Consumer Price Index (CPI)** is a measure of the prices of a basket of consumable goods and services that serves to gauge inflation. Constructing the Consumer Price Index is complicated. Since literally thousands of consumer goods and services are involved, attempting to include all of them in the index would be cumbersome and make the index expensive to compute; in addition, it would take a long time to gather the necessary price data. Therefore, Statistics Canada bases the CPI on a basket of over 600 consumer goods and services, in 175 basic goods and services classes, that are purchased by a typical Canadian household. Each month, the prices of these goods and services are recorded all across Canada. The eight major components of the CPI appear in Exhibit 1. The weight for each component is represented as a proportion of the total expenditures for the CPI basket.

Calculating the CPI—A Simplified Example

Suppose a consumer typically buys 24 loaves of bread and 12 kilograms of oranges in a year. The following table indicates the prices of bread and oranges and the cost of the consumer's typical market basket in the years 2011 through 2013.

Year	Price of Bread	Price of Oranges	Cost of Market Basket
2011	$1.00	$2.00	(24 × $1.00) + (12 × $2.00) = $48.00
2012	1.15	2.10	(24 × 1.15) + (12 × 2.10) = 52.80
2013	1.40	2.20	(24 × 1.40) + (12 × 2.20) = 60.00

section 13.4
Exhibit 1   2011 CPI Weights by Major Component, Canada

Consumer Price Index and Major Components, Canada

	Relative importance
	%
All-items CPI	100.00
Food	16.60
Shelter	26.26
Household operations, furnishings, and equipment	12.66
Clothing and footwear	5.82
Transportation	19.98
Health and personal care	4.93
Recreation, education, and reading	10.96
Alcoholic beverages and tobacco products	2.79

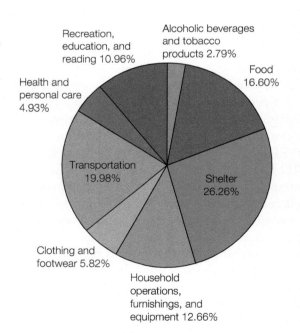

Statistics Canada divides the typical Canadian household's spending among various categories of goods and services.

SOURCE: Statistics Canada, Consumer Price Index, *The Daily*, May 17, 2013.

We calculate the CPI by comparing the cost of the market basket in the current year to the cost of the market basket in the base year. The base year is arbitrarily chosen; in our example, we will designate 2011 as the base year. The CPI for each year is calculated using the following formula:

$$\text{CPI} = \frac{\text{Cost of market basket in current year}}{\text{Cost of market basket in base year}} \times 100$$

The following table shows the CPI from 2011 through 2013. In 2011, the base year, the CPI equals 100. In 2012 and 2013, the CPI is 110 and 125, respectively, meaning that the average price level has risen in each of these two years.

Year	Consumer Price Index
2011	$48/$48 × 100 = 100.0
2012	$52.80/$48 × 100 = 110.0
2013	$60/$48 × 100 = 125.0

A comparison of the CPI shows that between 2011 and 2012, prices increased an average of 10 percent. Between 2011 and 2012, 25 percent inflation occurred. And between 2012 and 2013, the inflation rate was 13.6 percent, $(125 - 110)/110 \times 100$.

The CPI is not a completely accurate measure of the cost of living since three factors cause the CPI to overestimate changes in the cost of living. First, goods and services change in quality over time but the CPI is not able to adjust for the quality of all products, so the observed price change may, in reality, reflect a quality change in the product rather than a change in the purchasing power of the dollar. A $300 television set today is dramatically bigger and better than a television set in 1950 that cost $499. Second, new products come on the market and occasionally old products disappear. For example, colour TV sets did not exist in 1950 but are a major consumer item now. How do you calculate changes in prices over time when some products did not even exist in the earlier period? Third, the CPI measures the price changes of a fixed basket of goods and services. Thus, the CPI does not capture the fact that consumers are able to keep their cost of living down by substituting those goods whose prices have risen relatively less for those goods whose prices have risen relatively more.

The Price Level over the Years

Unanticipated and sharp changes in the price level are almost universally considered to be "bad" and to require a policy remedy. What is the historical record of changes in the overall Canadian price level? Exhibit 2 shows changes in the Consumer Price Index, the standard measure of inflation, from 1915 to 2012. As you can see from the chart, the Canadian economy experienced deflation in the early 1920s and the early 1930s. High rates of inflation, on the other hand, were experienced in the mid-1970s and early 1980s. Notice that since 1992, the annual inflation rate has remained below 3 percent, implying a substantial period of relatively low and stable inflation. Remember, however, that even when the inflation rate is only 3 percent per year, prices on average are rising, and the price level will double in 24 years.

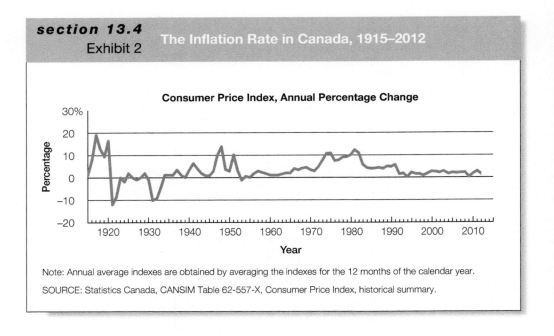

section 13.4
Exhibit 2   The Inflation Rate in Canada, 1915–2012

Consumer Price Index, Annual Percentage Change

Note: Annual average indexes are obtained by averaging the indexes for the 12 months of the calendar year.

SOURCE: Statistics Canada, CANSIM Table 62-557-X, Consumer Price Index, historical summary.

Anticipated versus Unanticipated Inflation

Before we can determine the effects of inflation, we must distinguish between anticipated and unanticipated inflation. If the annual inflation rate has been 3 percent for
several years and people anticipate that the inflation rate will remain at 3 percent, then
there is anticipated inflation. Anticipated inflation causes few problems. For the most
part, people see it coming and prepare for it.

Unanticipated inflation occurs when people don't see it coming and have failed to
prepare for it. Suppose people anticipate a 3 percent inflation rate, but the inflation
rate unexpectedly jumps to 10 percent. When inflation is unanticipated, people are
less able to protect themselves from its costs. But that does not mean that everybody
is worse off. Unanticipated inflation leads to arbitrary gains and losses as wealth and
income are redistributed from one group to another. In addition, it makes it more difficult to make long-term plans, and forces people to focus more on money and prices
and less on efficient choices about production and consumption in order to protect
themselves from eroding purchasing power.

WHO ARE THE WINNERS AND LOSERS DURING INFLATION?

Inflation brings about changes in people's purchasing power, and these changes may
be either desirable or undesirable. Suppose you retire on a fixed pension of $3000
per month. Over time, the $3000 will buy less and less if prices generally rise. Your
real income—your income adjusted to reflect changes in purchasing power—falls.
Inflation lowers income in real terms for people on fixed-dollar incomes. Likewise,
inflation can hurt creditors.

For example, suppose that in the early 1960s (a period of low inflation), a bank
loaned someone money for a house at a 4 percent fixed rate for 20 years. However,
the 1970s was a period of high inflation rates (roughly 10 percent per year). In this
scenario, because the lender did not correctly anticipate the higher rate of inflation, the
lender is the victim of unanticipated inflation. That is, the borrower is paying back with
dollars that have much less purchasing power than those dollars that were borrowed in
the early 1960s.

Another group that sometimes loses from inflation, at least temporarily, are people whose incomes are tied to long-term contracts. For example, if inflation begins shortly after a labour union signs a three-year wage agreement, it may completely eat up the wage gains provided by the contract. The same applies to businesses that agree to sell a quantity of something, say, phone service, for a fixed price for a given number of years.

If some people lose because of unanticipated inflation, others must gain. The debtor pays back dollars worth less in purchasing power than those she borrowed. Corporations that can quickly raise the prices on their goods may have revenue gains greater than their increases in costs, providing additional profits. Wage earners sometimes lose as a result of inflation because wages may rise at a slower rate than the price level. The redistributional impact of inflation is not the result of conscious public policy—it just happens.

WHAT ARE THE COSTS OF INFLATION?

The uncertainty that unanticipated inflation creates can also discourage investment and economic growth. When inflation rates are high, they also tend to vary considerably, which creates a lot of uncertainty. This uncertainty complicates planning for businesses and households, which is vital to capital formation, as well as adding an inflation risk premium to long-term interest rates.

Moreover, inflation can raise one nation's price level relative to that in other countries. In turn, this can make that nation's goods and services less competitive in international markets or can decrease the value of the national currency relative to that of other countries.

Costs of High Inflation

Predictable low rates of inflation, while still a problem, are considerably better than high and variable inflation rates. A slow predictable rate of inflation makes predicting future price increases relatively easy, so setting interest rates will be an easier task and the redistribution effects of inflation will be minimized. High and variable inflation rates make it almost impossible to set long-term contracts, however, because prices and interest rates may be changing by the day or even by the hour in the case of **hyperinflation**—extremely high rates of inflation for a sustained period of time.

In its extreme form, inflation can lead to a complete erosion of faith in the value of the pieces of paper we commonly call money. In Germany after both world wars, prices rose so fast that people in some cases finally refused to take paper money, insisting instead on payment in goods or metals, whose prices tend to move predictably with inflation. Unchecked inflation can feed on itself and ultimately can lead to hyperinflation of 300 percent or more per year. We saw these rapid rates of inflation in Argentina and Brazil in the 1990s, when the inflation rate toped 2000 percent per year. Most economists believe we can live quite well in an environment of low, steady inflation, but no economist believes we can prosper with high, variable inflation.

hyperinflation *extremely high rates of inflation for a sustained period of time*

Unanticipated Inflation Distorts Price Signals

In periods of high and variable inflation, households and firms have a difficult time distinguishing between changes in the relative prices of individual goods and services and changes in the general price level of all goods and services. Inflation distorts the information that flows from price signals. Does the good have a higher price because it has become relatively more scarce, and therefore more valuable relative to other goods, or did the price rise along with all other prices because of inflation? This muddying of price information undermines good decision making.

Menu and Shoe-Leather Costs

menu costs *the costs incurred by a firm as a result of changing its listed prices*

Whether inflation is anticipated or not, firms incur costs as a result of the need to change prices more frequently. For example, a restaurant may have to print new menus, or a department or mail-order store may have to print new catalogues to reflect changing prices. These costs are called **menu costs**—the costs incurred by a firm as a result of changing its listed prices. In some South American economies in the 1980s, inflation increased at over 300 percent per year, with prices changing on a daily, or even hourly, basis in some cases. Imagine how large the menu costs could be in an economy such as that!

shoe-leather cost *the time and inconvenience cost incurred when individuals reduce their money holdings because of inflation*

There is also the **shoe-leather cost** of inflation: the time and inconvenience cost incurred when individuals reduce their money holdings because of inflation. Specifically, high rates of inflation erode the value of a currency, which means that people will want to hold less currency—perhaps going to the ATM once a week rather than twice a month, thus wearing out the leather of their shoes going to and from the ATM. That is, higher inflation rates lead to higher nominal interest rates, which may induce more individuals to put money in the bank rather than allowing it to depreciate in their pockets. The effects of shoe-leather costs of inflation, like those of menu costs, are modest in countries with low inflation rates but can be quite large in countries where inflation is anticipated and substantial.

Unanticipated Deflation

The effects of unanticipated deflation are generally opposite to those for unanticipated inflation. As the overall price level declines with deflation, it has the effect of raising people's purchasing power, so people on fixed-dollar incomes will benefit. Savers will also discover that the purchasing power of their savings has increased, possibly stimulating additional savings at the expense of additional spending. Deflationary pressures will benefit creditors, as opposed to debtors, as the money that is repaid to lenders is worth more (in terms of purchasing power) than the money that was initially loaned out, possibly leading to a drop in bank lending.

A final note relates to the impact of deflation on wages. As the economy's price level falls, companies will find it increasingly difficult to maintain profits. As profits are reduced, an argument can be made that this can lead to rising unemployment and falling wages.

WHAT IS THE RELATIONSHIP BETWEEN INFLATION AND INTEREST RATES?

nominal interest rate *the reported interest rate that is not adjusted for inflation*

real interest rate *the nominal interest rate minus the inflation rate*

The interest rate that is usually reported is not adjusted for inflation. This is the **nominal interest rate.** We determine the actual **real interest rate** by taking the nominal rate of interest minus the inflation rate:

$$\text{Real interest rate} = \text{Nominal interest rate} - \text{Inflation rate}$$

For example, if the nominal interest rate was 5 percent and the inflation rate was 3 percent, then the real interest rate would be 2 percent.

If people can correctly anticipate inflation, they will behave in a manner that will largely protect them against loss. Consider the creditor who believes that the overall price level will rise 6 percent a year, based on immediate past experience. Would that creditor lend money to someone at a 5 percent rate of interest? No. A 5 percent rate of interest means that a person borrowing $1000 now will pay back $1050 ($1000 plus 5 percent of $1000) one year from now. But if prices go up 6 percent, it will take $1060 to buy what $1000 does today. (That is, $1060 is 6 percent more than $1000.) Thus, the person who lends at 5 percent will be repaid an amount ($1050) that is less than the purchasing power of the original loan ($1060). The real interest rate, then, would actually be negative. Hence, to protect themselves, lenders will demand a rate of interest large enough to compensate for the deteriorating value of money.

Creditors Don't Always Lose from Inflation

Usually lenders are able to anticipate inflation with reasonable accuracy. For example, in the early 1980s when the inflation rate was over 10 percent a year, nominal interest rates on a three-month Treasury bill were relatively high. Since 2000, with low inflation rates, the nominal interest rate has been relatively low. If the inflation rate is anticipated accurately, new creditors will not lose nor will debtors gain from a change in the inflation rate. However, nominal interest rates and real interest rates do not always run together. For example, in periods of high *unexpected* inflation, the nominal interest rates can be very high whereas the real interest rates may be very low or even negative.

DEBATE

SHOULD THE GOVERNMENT STAY FOCUSED ON INFLATION RATHER THAN UNEMPLOYMENT RATES?

For:

Although governments have three major macroeconomic goals that they try to keep in balance, they tend to zero in on one at a time. The goals are (1) to keep employment rates at relatively high levels, (2) to keep prices at relatively stable levels, and (3) to achieve high rates of growth. These are competing forces that act against each other—for example, if growth increases at too high a rate, prices (inflation) will likely rise, and if growth isn't meeting expected levels, unemployment rises. As this book goes to press, the Canadian economy is recovering from the effects of the Great Recession, and growth and inflation are meeting their targets. Stable prices of goods and service, in both the consumer and the factor markets, are of top importance to a strong economy. Stable prices ensure that investment and interest rates are at manageable levels, which will ensure that growth continues and people are employed. By managing inflation rates, the government benefits in meeting the other goals without having to directly intervene. In an open, capitalist economy, the less government intervention, the better. It can be argued that changing the dominant policy may be premature—it's too early to conclude one way or the other that the current dominant policy target is not the right policy. Surely the government should not change its dominant policy from inflation to unemployment rates under these circumstances. What are the consequences if the government changes the dominant policy too soon? What about if it changes too late? Can you think of other reasons why the government would chose inflation over the other goals?

Against:

The government's choice to control inflation came at a time when rising prices were a concern. During the late 1970s and early 1980s, the government concentrated on growth and the policies that were put in place certainly achieved growth, but as a result, inflation rates rose to around 20 percent. At that point, the key goal changed from targeting growth to targeting inflation, so both growth and inflation rates dropped to more manageable and productive levels. The country had undergone a period when high inflation was causing high interest rates and therefore impeded growth. At the time, targeting inflation was the proper policy. However, since the start of the Great Recession and its recovery, we have seen growth and inflation rates slightly below target levels, but corresponding increases in longer-term unemployment rates to the point where there is debate that the natural rate of unemployment has moved 2 to 3 percentage points higher than the target 6 to 7 percent rate. This means that the economy is performing relatively well in terms of productivity but there are fewer workers employed. So, under the current economic conditions, there are more important concerns than inflation, in fact, such as putting people back to work. Further, if the unemployment rate is too high, growth is impeded and the government will be paying higher costs for social programs. Surely the Government should concentrate on employment rates over rising prices in this situation. Can you think of other reasons why the government should reconsider its primary target?

Protecting Ourselves from Inflation

Some groups try to protect themselves from inflation by using cost-of-living clauses in contracts. In labour union contracts with these clauses, workers automatically get wage increases that reflect rising prices. The same is true of some private pension plans that are adjusted for inflation, as well as the government-run Canada Pension Plan. Personal income taxes also are now indexed (adjusted) for inflation. However, some of the tax laws are still not indexed for inflation. This can affect the incentives to work, save, and invest.

Some economists have argued that we should go one step further and index everything, meaning that all contractual arrangements would be adjusted frequently to take changing prices into account. Such an arrangement might reduce the impact of inflation, but it would also entail additional contracting costs. An alternative approach has been to try to stop inflation through various policies relating to the amount of government spending, tax rates, or the amount of money created.

SECTION CHECK

- A continuous rise in the price level defines the case of inflation, whereas a fall in the overall price level defines the case for deflation.
- A price index allows us to compare prices paid for goods and services over time. The Consumer Price Index (CPI) is the best-known price index.
- Inflation generally hurts creditors and those on fixed incomes and pensions; debtors generally benefit from inflation.
- Unanticipated inflation causes unpredictable transfers of wealth and reduces the efficiency of the market system by distorting price signals.
- The nominal interest rate is the actual amount of interest you pay. The real interest rate is the nominal rate minus the inflation rate. Inflationary expectations tend to increase nominal interest rates.

section 13.5

Economic Fluctuations

- What are short-term economic fluctuations?
- What are the four phases of a business cycle?
- How long does a business cycle last?

WHAT ARE SHORT-TERM ECONOMIC FLUCTUATIONS?

business cycles *short-term fluctuations in the economy relative to the long-term trend in output*

The aggregate amount of economic activity in Canada and most other nations has increased markedly over time, even on a per capita basis, indicating long-term economic growth. Short-term fluctuations in the economy relative to the long-term trend in output are referred to as **business cycles.** Exhibit 1 illustrates the distinction between long-term economic growth and short-term economic fluctuations. Over a long period of time, the line representing economic activity slopes upward, indicating increasing real output. Over short time periods, however, there are downward, as well as upward, output changes. Business cycles are the short-term ups and downs in economic activity, not the long-term trend in output, which in modern times has been upward.

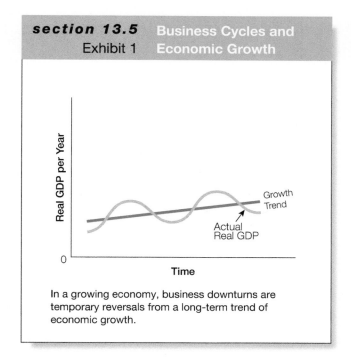

section 13.5
Exhibit 1
Business Cycles and
Economic Growth

In a growing economy, business downturns are temporary reversals from a long-term trend of economic growth.

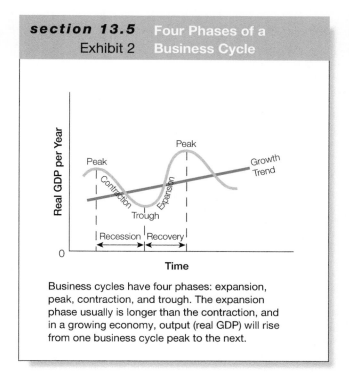

section 13.5
Exhibit 2
Four Phases of a
Business Cycle

Business cycles have four phases: expansion, peak, contraction, and trough. The expansion phase usually is longer than the contraction, and in a growing economy, output (real GDP) will rise from one business cycle peak to the next.

WHAT ARE THE FOUR PHASES OF A BUSINESS CYCLE?

A business cycle has four phases—expansion, peak, contraction, and trough—as illustrated in Exhibit 2. The period of **expansion** occurs when output (real GDP) is rising significantly. Usually during the expansion phase, unemployment is falling and both consumer and business confidence is high. Thus, investment spending by firms is rising, as well as expenditures for expensive durable consumer goods, such as automobiles and household appliances. The **peak** is the point in time when the expansion comes to an end, when output is at the highest point in the cycle. The **contraction** is a period of falling real output, and is usually accompanied by rising unemployment and declining business and consumer confidence. The contraction phase is measured from the peak to the trough. Investment spending by firms and expenditures on consumer durable goods fall sharply in a typical contraction. This contraction phase is also called **recession,** a period of significant decline in output and employment (lasting at least six months). The **trough** is the point in time when output stops declining; it is the moment when business activity is at its lowest point in the cycle. Unemployment is relatively high at the trough, although the actual maximum amount of unemployment may not occur exactly at the trough. Often, unemployment remains fairly high well into the expansion phase. The expansion phase is measured from the trough to the peak.

Exhibit 3 shows the growth in Canadian real GDP over the 1962–2012 period. On an annual basis, you can see that there were three major recessions during this period; 1982, 1991, and 2009. In the 1982 recession, the economy declined by 3.0 percent, whereas in 1991, the economy contracted by 2.1 percent. As for the 2009 recession, the Canadian economy experienced a 2.7 percent decline in real GDP. Of the three recessions, the sharp drop in output in 1982 was the deepest recession the economy had experienced since the Great Depression of the 1930s. Both the 1982 and 1991 recessions were accompanied by sharp rises in unemployment, which rose from 7.6 percent (1981) to 12.0 percent (1983), and from 8.1 percent (1990) to 11.4 percent (1993). The 2009 recession, however, was different in that the unemployment rate remained relatively low at around 8.3 percent (2009), the rate being 6.1 percent in 2008.

expansion *when output (real GDP) is rising significantly—the period between the trough of a recession and the next peak*

peak *the point in time when the expansion comes to an end, when output is at the highest point in the cycle*

contraction *when the economy's output is falling—measured from the peak to the trough*

recession *a period of significant decline in output and employment*

trough *the point in time when output stops declining; it is the moment when business activity is at its lowest point in the cycle*

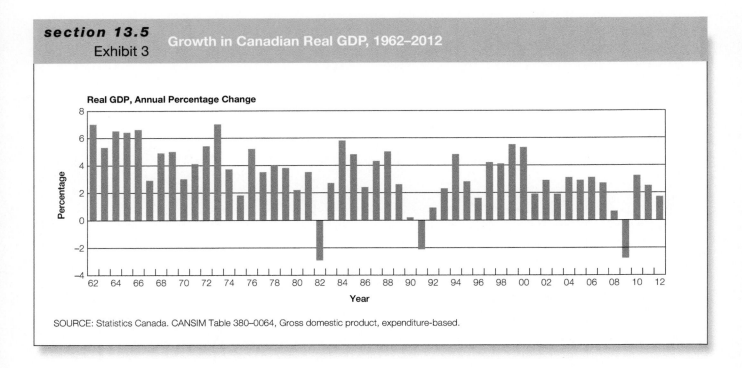

section 13.5
Exhibit 3   Growth in Canadian Real GDP, 1962–2012

SOURCE: Statistics Canada. CANSIM Table 380–0064, Gross domestic product, expenditure-based.

Another factor you will notice from Exhibit 3 is that the 1991 recession was more prolonged than either the 1982 or 2009 recessions. With the 1991 recession, the economy actually began to experience negative real GDP growth in the second half of 1990, which then lasted throughout 1991. It was only in 1992 that the economy began to show signs of positive growth in real GDP, albeit very small amounts. By comparison, in the years that immediately followed the 1982 recession, the economy was already exhibiting significant growth (2.6 percent and 5.6 percent in 1983 and 1984, respectively). In terms of the 2009 recession, the economy did initially exhibit this same "bounce back," with economic growth reaching 3.4 percent in 2010. Unfortunately, the recovery somewhat slowed, with real GDP growth rates of 2.5 percent and 1.7 percent in 2011 and 2012, respectively. The prolonged nature of the 1991 recession also impacted unemployment, with the unemployment rate remaining above 10 percent through 1994, even as the economy entered the expansion phase, which is a characteristic of unemployment that we discussed previously.

You will also notice that the expansion phase of the business cycle is characterized by varying rates of economic growth. In 1962 and 1973, for example, the economy grew at a very rapid pace of 7 percent per year. In other years, economic growth can be much more sluggish, as in 1975 and 2003 when the economy grew by less than 2 percent each year.

HOW LONG DOES A BUSINESS CYCLE LAST?

As you can see from Exhibit 3, there is no uniformity to a business cycle's length. Because it does not have the regularity that the term *cycle* implies, economists often use the term *economic fluctuation* rather than *business cycle*. In addition, economic fluctuations are almost impossible to predict. Severe recessions are called **depressions.** Likewise, a prolonged expansion in economic activity is sometimes called a **boom.** For example, during the Great Depression, real GDP contracted for four consecutive years,

depression *a severe recession*

boom *prolonged expansion in economic activity*

from 1930 to 1933. An economic boom occurred during the 1960s when real GDP grew by about 6 percent a year on average over that decade.

Seasonal Fluctuations Affect Economic Activity

The determinants of cyclical fluctuations in the economy are the major thrust of the next several chapters, and some fluctuations in economic activity reflect seasonal patterns. Business activity, whether measured by production or by the sale of goods, tends to be high in the two months before the winter holidays and somewhat lower in the summer, when families often are on vacation. Within individual industries, of course, seasonal fluctuations in output are often extremely pronounced, agriculture being the best example.

Often, key economic statistics, such as unemployment rates, are seasonally adjusted, meaning that the numbers are modified to account for normal seasonal fluctuations. Thus, seasonally adjusted unemployment rates in summer months are below actual unemployment rates, because employment is normally high in the summer due to the inflow of school-aged workers into the labour force.

Forecasting Cyclical Changes

The farmer and the aviator rely heavily on weather forecasters for information on climatic conditions in planning their activities. Similarly, businesses, government agencies, and, to a lesser extent, consumers rely on economic forecasts to learn of forthcoming developments in the business cycle. If it looks like the economy will continue in an expansionary phase, businesses might expand production to meet a perceived forthcoming need; if it looks like contraction is coming, perhaps they will be more cautious.

Forecasting Models Using theoretical models, which will be discussed in later chapters, economists gather statistics on economic activity in the immediate past, including, for example, consumer expenditures, business inventories, the supply of money, governmental expenditures, and tax revenues. Using past historical relationships between these factors and the overall level of economic activity (which form the basis of economic theories), they formulate *econometric models*. Statistics from the immediate past are plugged into the model and forecasts are made. Because human behaviour changes and we cannot correctly make assumptions about certain future developments, our numbers are imperfect and our econometric models are not always accurate. Like the weather forecasts, although the econometric models are not perfect, they are helpful.

Leading Economic Indicators One less sophisticated but very useful forecasting tool is watching trends in **leading economic indicators**—factors that typically change before changes in economic activity. Statistics Canada has identified ten such leading indicators: furniture and appliance sales, other durable goods sales, length of the average workweek, new orders in manufacturing, shipments-to-inventory ratio, housing starts, business and personal services employment, index of stock prices, money supply, and the U.S. leading indicator. Statistics Canada combines all of these into a composite index of leading indicators. If the index rises sharply for two or three months, it is likely (but not certain) that increases in the overall level of activity will follow.

Although the leading economic indicators do provide a warning of a likely downturn, they do not provide accurate information on the depth or the duration of the downturn.

leading economic indicators *factors that typically change before changes in economic activity*

Business *CONNECTION*

WHAT BUSINESS GETS FROM MACROECONOMICS

In introductory economics, we learn both *microeconomics* (how individuals, businesses, and sometimes governments make decisions) and *macroeconomics* (once those decisions are made, how does the economy perform?). Individual business managers usually focus on the micro side, because they're interested in making decisions that will increase their firms' performance. In making these decisions, they adjust both the marketing factors (price, product, place, and promotion) and the operation factors (e.g., input costs, operational efficiency levels, and capacity). Business is also concerned with the macro side of economics, but arguably less so than the micro side. Why? Because on the macro side, managers have to make their decisions on how the market presents itself: Is the economy growing or are we in a recession? Are workers available and at what price? What are interest rates and is it wise to take on more debt? In macroeconomics, managers can't change the data they get—they just have to work with them.

When making business decisions, managers often use a PEST analysis to assess their current situation. PEST, of course, stands for political, economic, social, and technological factors—all of which are external to the business. While economics is contained within the PEST analysis, it's also essential to the individual PEST factors. For example, political decisions generally follow economics problems, not the other way around. Politicians don't make policy decisions that are divorced from economic issues—they make decisions to correct or adjust economic realities. So it's critical for managers to understand the economic environment they will operate in.

The main goal for business is to maximize profits. In order to do so, firms need to know if what they make will sell. Generally, they follow the demand of the market, but demand often changes due to external factors of the business or the product. For example, demand for products changed greatly during the Great Recession of 2009. If you were in housing construction, it's highly likely that your company suffered—maybe even folded—due to the crisis. Millions of people lost their jobs, so they couldn't afford the products you were making. Chances are your inventories grew, which added

costs and lowered your profits. If you had to cut production because demand dropped, you probably laid off part of your workforce and those who had the opportunity to stay may have offered wage concessions just to keep their jobs. You probably did away with all the perks you'd offered your employees when times were good. Back in your role as a student, what do you think happened to company morale?

There would be a positive side to this story if the company's finances were well managed and the firm had money in the bank. Because the whole economy suffered, virtually every company was willing to make pricing concessions just to sell products—that kept their production lines moving, although not as fast as a few years earlier. If a company wanted to upgrade its machinery, there was no better time because prices were dropping, and if the firm was strong enough to be able to finance a machinery purchase, the interest rate for the loan was much lower than during the boom years. Then, when the economy rebounded in 2012–13, the firm could produce more products at a lower unit cost with its new machinery than it could have with its previous number of employees. That would help it to be competitive going forward and likely would have positive effects on profits in the future.

So for business managers, reading macroeconomic signals is like reading the tea leaves of the business—the information is all there, and a good manager just has to do his or her best to interpret the data.

1. If you were to become a business manager, where would you look to find information on the macroeconomy?

2. What do you think comes first: low levels of inflation that lead to low levels of growth, or low levels of growth that result in low inflation? Knowing which comes first, what is the benefit in business decisions?

3. Assume your company is undertaking a new strategic direction and you have to choose among growth, profits, or employing individuals. Which would be your primary target and why? How do you think your choice would impact the overall economy?

SECTION CHECK

■ Business cycles (or economic fluctuations) are short-term fluctuations in the amount of economic activity relative to the long-term growth trend in output.

■ The four phases of a business cycle are expansion, peak, contraction, and trough.

■ Recessions occur during the contraction phase of a business cycle. Severe, long-term recessions are called *depressions,* while prolonged expansions are referred to as *booms.* The economy often goes through short-term contractions even during a long-term growth trend. Overall, the duration of any one business cycle is uncertain.

Section 13.1

1. Visit the Statistics Canada website at www.statcan.gc.ca. Review the links listed under "Latest indicators" (on the left-hand side of the page). Based on the most recent information, how is the Canadian economy doing in terms of the macroeconomic goals of maintaining prices, maintaining employment, and achieving a high rate of economic growth?

2. Numerous African nations have targeted food self-sufficiency as their primary economic goal. How can this fact coexist with the three primary economic goals discussed in the chapter?

Section 13.2

3. What would be the labour force participation rate if
   a. The population = 200 million, the labour force = 160 million, and employment = 140 million?
   b. The population = 200 million, the labour force = 140 million, and employment = 120 million?
   c. Starting from the situation in (a), what would happen to the labour force participation rate if 30 million people lost their jobs and all of them exited the labour force?
   d. Starting from the situation in (a), what would happen to the labour force participation rate if employment rose from 140 to 150 million?

4. Answer the following questions about unemployment.
   a. If a country had an adult population (those 15 years of age and over) of 200 million and a labour force of 160 million, and 140 million people were employed, what would be its labour force participation rate and its unemployment rate?
   b. If 10 million new jobs were created in the country and it attracted into the labour force 20 million of the people who were previously not in the labour force, what would be its new labour force participation rate and its unemployment rate?
   c. Beginning from the situation in (a), if 10 million unemployed people became discouraged and stopped looking for work, what would be the country's new labour force participation rate and its unemployment rate?
   d. Beginning from the situation in (a), if 10 million current workers retired but their jobs were filled by others still in the labour force, what would be the country's new labour force participation rate and its unemployment rate?

5. Which of the following individuals would economists consider unemployed?
   a. Sam looked for work for several weeks, but has now given up his search and is going back to university.
   b. A 12-year-old wants to mow lawns for extra cash but is unable to find neighbours willing to hire her.

   c. A factory worker is temporarily laid off but expects to be called back to work soon.

   d. A receptionist who works only 20 hours per week would like to work 40 hours per week.

   e. A high-school graduate spends his days backpacking across the country rather than seeking work.

6. Answer the following questions about reasons for unemployment.

   a. In a severe recession, explain what would tend to happen to the number of people in each of the following categories:

      job losers

      job leavers

      re-entrants

      new entrants

   b. In very good economic times, why might the number of job leavers, re-entrants, and new entrants all increase?

7. Each of the individuals described below is considered to be unemployed. Categorize each as either a job loser, a job leaver, a re-entrant, or a new entrant.

   a. Karl is planning to start his new career as a mechanic, having recently completed a government-sponsored training program in small engine repair.

   b. Following a series of poor workplace evaluations that resulted in David being fired from his job at a local fast-food restaurant, he is looking for a new job.

   c. Adam, a recent college graduate with a diploma in marketing, is sending out his résumé for the first time.

   d. Olivia, a customer service representative for a large retail store, is looking for a new job after tendering her resignation.

Section 13.3

8. Identify whether each of the following reflects structural, frictional, or cyclical unemployment.

   a. A real estate agent is laid off due to slow business after housing sales fall.

   b. An automotive worker is replaced by robotic equipment on the assembly line.

   c. A salesperson quits a job in Ontario and seeks a new career after moving to Alberta.

   d. An employee is fired for poor job performance and searches the want ads each day for work.

9. Which type of unemployment would be affected by the following changes? Would it go up or down?

   a. increased employment benefits

   b. a heavy snowfall in Saskatchewan

   c. more effective online job search

   d. a large, permanent decrease in the demand for coal

   e. more retraining of people to develop new skills

   f. a sharp fall in demand for goods and services in the economy

10. a. What is the relationship between the natural rate of unemployment and frictional, structural, and cyclical unemployment?

    b. What would happen to both unemployment and the natural rate of unemployment if

       i. cyclical unemployment increases.

       ii. frictional unemployment increases.

       iii. structural unemployment falls and cyclical unemployment rises by the same amount.

       iv. structural unemployment increases and cyclical unemployment decreases by a larger amount.

       v. frictional unemployment decreases and structural unemployment increases by the same amount.

11. Most economists consider Canada's current natural rate of unemployment to be around 6 percent.

    a. Suppose the actual rate of unemployment was 8 percent. What could be concluded about what types of unemployment are occurring?

    b. Suppose the actual rate of unemployment was 4 percent. What could be concluded about what types of unemployment are occurring?

12. Employment insurance benefits in the United States tend to be both less generous and available for shorter periods of time than in Canada. What impact do you think this is likely to have on the unemployment rate in the United States? Why?

13. How can the existence of unions result in higher unemployment rates? How would the results differ for someone who wants to be employed in the union sector than for someone who currently has a job in the union sector?

14. Why isn't it true that technological advances inevitably displace workers?

Section 13.4

15. Answer the following questions about inflation.

    a. What would be the effect of unexpected inflation on each of the following?
       retirees on fixed incomes
       workers
       debtors
       creditors
       shoe-leather costs
       menu costs

    b. How would your answers change if the inflation was expected?

16. Answer the following questions about the nominal and real interest rate.

    a. What would be the real interest rate if the nominal interest rate was 14 percent and the inflation rate was 10 percent? If the nominal interest rate was 8 percent and the inflation rate was 1 percent?

    b. What would happen to the real interest rate if the nominal interest rate went from 9 to 15 percent when the inflation rate went from 4 to 10 percent? If the nominal interest rate went from 11 to 7 percent when the inflation rate went from 8 to 4 percent?

17. Calculate a price index for 2011, 2012, and 2013 using the following information about prices. Let the market basket consist of one pizza, two sodas, and three video rentals. Let the year 2011 be the base year (with an index value of 100).

Year	Price of a Pizza	Price of a Soda	Price of a Video Rental
2011	$ 9.00	$0.50	$2.00
2012	9.50	0.53	2.24
2013	10.00	0.65	2.90

How much inflation occurred between 2011 and 2012? Between 2011 and 2013? Between 2012 and 2013?

18. You borrow money at a fixed rate of interest to finance your university education. If the rate of inflation unexpectedly slows down between the time you take out the loan and the time you begin paying it back, is there a redistribution of income? What if you already expected the inflation rate to slow at the time you took out the loan? Explain.

19. How does a variable rate mortgage agreement protect lenders against inflation? Who bears the inflation risk?

Blueprint Problem

The following table contains prices for items consumed by a typical college student over time.

Year	Pizza/Slice	Energy Drink/Can	Internet
2010	$3.50	$2.00	$30.00
2011	3.95	3.00	28.00
2012	4.50	4.00	26.00

Let the market basket consist of three slices of pizza, two energy drinks, and one Internet connection.

   a. Based on the information presented above, calculate the Consumer Price Index for 2010, 2011, and 2012 if 2010 is designated as the base year.

   b. How much inflation occurred during 2010–2011, and 2011–2012?

Blueprint Solution

The first step in determining a CPI style index is to determine the cost of each "market basket." Notice that the basket remains the same from year to year, only the prices change.

The next step is to determine the price index for each year. Recall the formula:

$$CPI = \frac{\text{Cost of market basket in current year}}{\text{Cost of market basket in base year}} \times 100$$

Note that since the base year remains constant over the period of observation, the denominator in the formula does not change. Also, don't forget to multiply each index calculation by 100.

Year	Market Basket Costs (3 energy drinks, 2 slices of pizza, 1 Internet connection)	Price Index	Inflation Rate
2010	= (3 × $3.50) + (2 × $2.00) + (1 × $30) = $44.5	= ($44.50/44.50) × 100 = 100	
2011	= (3 × $3.95) + (2 × $3.00) + (1 x $28) = $45.85	= ($45.85/$44.50) × 100 = 103	= (103 − 100)/100 = 3%
2012	= (3 × $4.50) + (2 × $4.00) + (1 x $26) = $47.50	= ($47.50/$44.5) × 100 = 107	= (107 − 103)/103 = 3.6%

Once price index values have been calculated for each year, inflation rates can be determined. Recall the formula:

$$\text{Inflation rate} = \frac{CPI_1 - CPI_0}{CPI_0}$$

Unlike the price index calculations, which use a static base year for comparison, inflation rates are typically calculated year on year.

20. Say that the bundle of goods purchased by a typical consumer in the base year consisted of 20 litres of milk at a price of $1 per litre and 15 loaves of bread at a price of $2 per loaf. What would be the price index in a year in which

   a.   milk cost $2 per litre and bread cost $1 per loaf?

   b.   milk cost $3 per litre and bread cost $2 per loaf?

   c.   milk cost $2 per litre and bread cost $4 per loaf?

Section 13.5

21. Suppose the hypothetical economy of Ecoland is characterized by the following economic data. Where along the business cycle would the economy of Ecoland be located?

Variable	Value (%)	Trend
Unemployment rate	8	Decreasing
Natural rate of unemployment	5	—
Inflation rate	1	Increasing
Real gross domestic product (growth rate)	2	Increasing

22. Evaluate the following statement regarding business cycles: "Typically, unemployment and inflation move in opposite directions as the economy travels through its business cycle."

23. Suppose a country experiences the following annual percentage changes in real GDP over a 10-year period.

Year	1	2	3	4	5	6	7	8	9	10
% Δ real GDP	2	3	5	3	1	−2	−3	1	2	3

a. Which year(s) best illustrate(s) the peak phase of the business cycle?

b. Which year(s) best illustrate(s) the recessionary (contractionary) phase of the business cycle?

c. Which year(s) best illustrate(s) the trough phase of the business cycle?

d. Which year(s) best illustrate(s) the expansionary phase of the business cycle?

14 Measuring Economic Performance

National Income Accounting: Measuring Economic Performance

- Why do we measure our economy's performance?
- What is gross domestic product (GDP)?

WHY DO WE MEASURE OUR ECONOMY'S PERFORMANCE?

There is a great desire to measure the success, or performance, of our economy. Are we getting "bigger" (and hopefully better) or "smaller" (and worse) over time? Aside from intellectual curiosity, the need to evaluate the magnitude of our economic performance is important to macroeconomic policymakers who want to know how well the economy is performing so that they can set goals and develop policy recommendations.

Measurement of the economy's performance is also important to private businesses because inaccurate measurement can lead to bad decision making. Traders in stocks and bonds are continually checking economic statistics—buying and selling in response to the latest economic data.

National Income Accounting

To fulfill the desire for a reliable method of measuring economic performance, **national income accounting**—a uniform means of measuring economic performance—was born early in the twentieth century. The establishment of these accounting rules for economic performance was such an important accomplishment that one of the first Nobel Prizes in economics was given to the late Simon Kuznets, a pioneer of national income accounting in the United States.

national income accounting
a uniform means of measuring economic performance

Several measures of aggregate national income and output have been developed, the most important of which is gross domestic product (GDP). We will examine GDP and other indicators of national economic performance in detail later in this chapter.

WHAT IS GROSS DOMESTIC PRODUCT (GDP)?

The measure of aggregate economic performance that receives the most attention in the popular media is **gross domestic product (GDP),** which is defined as the value of all final goods and services produced in a country during a given period of time. By convention, that period of time is almost always one year. But let's examine the rest of this definition. What is meant by "value" and "final goods and services"?

Measuring the Value of Goods and Services

Value is determined by the market prices at which goods and services sell. Underlying the calculations, then, are the various equilibrium prices and quantities for the multitude of goods and services produced.

Final Goods and Services

The word "final" means that the good is ready for its designated ultimate use. Many goods and services are intermediate goods or services; that is, they are used in the production of other goods. For example, suppose Magna International produces auto parts that it sells to General Motors for use in making an automobile. If we counted the value of the parts used in making the car as well as the full value of the finished auto in the GDP, we would be adding the value of auto parts twice, first in their raw intermediate form and second in their final form, the automobile. This type of error in accounting is referred to as **double counting**—adding the value of a good or service twice by mistakenly counting intermediate goods and services in GDP.

Measuring Gross Domestic Product

Economic output can be calculated primarily in two ways: the expenditure approach and the income approach. Although these methods differ, their result, GDP, is the same, apart from minor "statistical discrepancies." In the following two sections, we will examine each of these approaches in turn.

gross domestic product (GDP)
the measure of economic performance based on the value of all final goods and services produced in a country during a given period of time

double counting
adding the value of a good or service twice by mistakenly counting intermediate goods and services in GDP

The paper used in this book is an intermediate good; it is the book, the final good, that is included in the GDP.

© JANIS CHRISTIE/PHOTODISC/GETTY ONE IMAGES

Production, Income, and the Circular Flow Model

When we calculate GDP in the economy, we are measuring the value of total production—our total expenditures. However, we are also measuring the value of total income because every dollar of spending by some buyer ends up being a dollar of income for some seller. In short, expenditures (spending) must equal income. And this is true whether it is a household, firm, or a government that buys the good or service. The main point in that when we spend (the value of total expenditure) it ends up as someone's income (the value of total income). Buyers have sellers.

In Exhibit 1, we reintroduce the circular flow model to show the flow of money in the economy. For example, households use some of their income to buy domestic goods and services and some to buy foreign goods and services (imports). Households also use some of their income to pay taxes and invest in financial markets (company shares, bonds, saving accounts, and other financial assets). When income flows into the financial system as saving, it makes it possible for consumers, firms, and governments to borrow. This market for saving and borrowing is vital to a well-functioning economy.

section 14.1
Exhibit 1   The Expanded Circular Flow Model

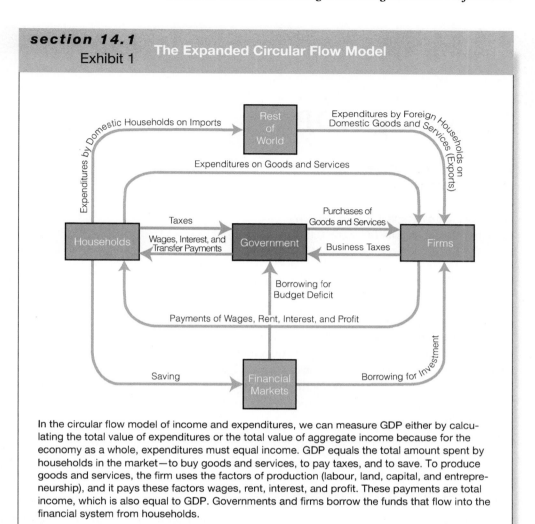

In the circular flow model of income and expenditures, we can measure GDP either by calculating the total value of expenditures or the total value of aggregate income because for the economy as a whole, expenditures must equal income. GDP equals the total amount spent by households in the market—to buy goods and services, to pay taxes, and to save. To produce goods and services, the firm uses the factors of production (labour, land, capital, and entrepreneurship), and it pays these factors wages, rent, interest, and profit. These payments are total income, which is also equal to GDP. Governments and firms borrow the funds that flow into the financial system from households.

Firms sell their goods and services to domestic and foreign consumers and foreign firms and governments. Firms use their factors of production (labour, land, capital, and entrepreneurship) to produce goods and services. Firms pay wages to workers, interest for the use of capital, and rent for land. Profits are the return to entrepreneurs for taking the risk of producing the goods and services. Wages, rent, interest, and profit comprise aggregate income in the economy. Governments provide transfer payments such as Employment Insurance payments. Whether we add up the aggregate expenditure on final goods and services, or the value of aggregate income (wages, rent, interest, and profit) we get the same GDP. For an economy as a whole, expenditures and income are the same. Actually, while the two should be exactly the same, there may be a slight variation because of data issues.

SECTION CHECK

- We measure our economy's status in order to see how its performance has changed over time. These economic measurements are important to government officials, private businesses, and investors.
- Gross domestic product (GDP) is the value of all final goods and services produced in a country during a given time period. The two different ways to measure GDP are the expenditure approach and the income approach.

section 14.2
The Expenditure Approach to Measuring GDP

■ What is the expenditure approach to measuring GDP?
■ What is consumption (*C*)?
■ What is investment (*I*)?
■ What are government purchases (*G*)?
■ What are net exports (*X* – *M*)?

WHAT IS THE EXPENDITURE APPROACH TO MEASURING GDP?

expenditure approach
calculation of GDP by adding up how much market participants spend on final goods and services over a period of time

One approach to measuring GDP is the **expenditure approach.** With this method, GDP is calculated by adding up how much market participants spend on final goods and services over a period of time. For convenience and for analytical purposes, economists usually categorize spending into four categories: consumption, identified symbolically by the letter *C;* investment, *I;* government purchases, *G;* and net exports, which equals exports (*X*) minus imports (*M*), or (*X* – *M*). Following the expenditure method, then

$$GDP = C + I + G + (X - M)$$

WHAT IS CONSUMPTION (*C*)?

consumption (C)
purchases of consumer goods and services by households

Consumption refers to the purchase of consumer goods and services by households. For most of us, a large percentage of our income in a given year goes for consumer goods and services. The consumption category does not include purchases by business or government. As Exhibit 1 indicates, in 2012 consumption expenditures totalled $1015 billion. This figure was 56 percent of GDP.

Consumption spending, in turn, is usually broken down into four subcategories: nondurable goods, semi-durable goods, durable goods, and services.

section 14.2 Exhibit 1	2012 Canadian GDP by Type of Spending	
Category	**Amount (billions of current dollars)**	**Percentage of GDP**
Gross domestic product	$1820	
Consumption (*C*)	1015	55.8%
Investment (*I*)	369	20.3
Government purchases (*G*)	472	25.9
Net exports of goods and services (*X* – *M*)	−36	−2.0

Note: This exhibit is the result of source data and author calculations.

SOURCE: Statistics Canada, CANSIM Table 380–0064, Gross domestic product, expenditure-based.

Goods

Nondurable goods include tangible consumer items that are typically consumed or used only once (or retain little value once used). Food and gasoline are examples, as are drugs, magazines, soap, and toys. Nearly everything purchased in a supermarket or drugstore is a nondurable good. In 2012, nondurable goods accounted for nearly 25 percent of total consumer expenditure.

Semi-durable goods include consumer items that can be used more than once and have an expected lifetime of around one year. Clothing and footwear are both common examples of semi-durable goods. In 2012, semi-durable goods accounted for nearly 7 percent of total consumer expenditure.

Durable goods include those consumer goods that can be used repeatedly for more than one year. The most important single category of durable goods is automobiles and other consumer vehicles. Appliances, consumer electronics like cellphones, and furniture are also included in the durable goods category. On occasion, it is difficult to decide whether a good is durable, semi-durable, or nondurable, and the definitions are, therefore, somewhat arbitrary.

The distinction between durables and nondurables is important because consumer buying behaviour is somewhat different for each of these categories of goods. In boom periods, when GDP is rising rapidly, expenditures on durables often increase dramatically, whereas in years of stagnant or falling GDP, sales of durable goods often plummet. By contrast, sales of nondurables like food tend to be more stable over time because purchases of such goods are more difficult to shift from one time period to another. You can "make do" with your car for another year, but not your lettuce.

Services

Services are intangible items of value provided to consumers, as opposed to physical goods. Legal services, dental services, recreational services, automobile repair, haircuts, airplane transportation—all of these are services. In recent years, service expenditures have been growing faster than spending on goods; the share of total consumption going for services reached 54 percent in 2012. As incomes have risen, service industries such as health, education, financial, and recreation have grown dramatically.

WHAT IS INVESTMENT (*I*)?

Investment (*I*), as used by economists, refers to the creation of capital goods to augment future production, that is, inputs like machines and tools whose purpose is to produce other goods. This definition of investment deviates from the popular use of that term. It is common for people to say that they invested in stocks, meaning that they have traded money for a piece of paper, called a stock certificate, that says they own a share in some company. Such transactions are not investment as defined by economists (i.e., an increase in capital goods), even though they might provide the enterprises selling the shares with the resources for new capital goods, which *would* be counted as investment by economists.

There are two categories of investment purchases measured in the expenditures approach: fixed investment and inventory investment.

Fixed Investments

Fixed investments include all new spending on capital goods by producers—sometimes called **producer goods**—such as machinery, tools, and factory buildings. All of these goods increase future production capabilities. Residential construction is also included as an investment expenditure in GDP calculations. The construction of a

nondurable goods
tangible consumer items that are typically consumed or used only once, such as food

semi-durable goods
consumer items that can be used more than once and have an expected lifetime of around one year, such as clothing

durable goods
consumer goods that can be used repeatedly for more than one year, such as automobiles

investment (*I*)
the creation of capital goods to augment future production

fixed investments
all new spending on capital goods by producers

producer goods
capital goods that increase future production capabilities

house allows for a valuable consumer service—shelter—to be provided, and is thus considered an investment. Residential construction is the only part of investment that is tied directly to household expenditure decisions.

Inventory Investment

inventory investment
all purchases by businesses that add to the stocks of goods kept by the firm to meet consumer demand

Inventory investment includes all purchases by businesses that add to the stocks of goods kept by firms to meet customer demands. Every business needs inventory and, other things equal, the greater the inventory, the greater the amount of goods and services that can be sold to a consumer in the future. Thus, inventories are considered a form of investment. Consider a grocery store. If the store expands and increases the quantity and variety of goods on its shelves, future sales can rise. An increase in inventory, then, is presumed to increase the firm's future sales, and this is why we say it is an investment.

Gross versus Net Investment

The concept of Investment that we have discussed so far—fixed investment plus inventory investment—is more accurately described as *gross investment*. The term *gross* refers to the fact that this measure of investment includes all forms of investment goods. That is, gross investment includes both investment goods that are new additions to the stock of capital as well as investment goods that are a replacement for plant and equipment worn out over the current period.

In contrast to gross investment, economists define *net investment* as the amount of investment that is new, the amount of investment that adds to the stock of capital in an economy. Specifically, net investment is defined as

$$\text{Net investment} = \text{Gross investment} - \text{Depreciation}$$

where depreciation (or capital consumption allowance) refers to the amount of capital that is used up over the year through the production of goods and services.

Usually the amount of gross investment is greater than the amount of depreciation. In this case, net investment is positive and the economy's capital stock is increasing. However, in cases where gross investment is less that depreciation, net investment becomes negative and an economy's capital stock declines.

The Stability of Investment Expenditures

In recent years, investment expenditures have generally been around 20 percent of gross domestic product. Investment spending is the most volatile category of GDP, however, and tends to fluctuate considerably with changing business conditions. When the economy is booming, investment purchases tend to increase dramatically. In downturns, the reverse happens. In addition, investment expenditure often increases in advance of an economic recovery, as firms look to position themselves for the return of economic demand. Again, the opposite happens in economic downturns. Because investment in capital goods is directly tied to a nation's future production capabilities, in those countries where expenditures on capital goods represent a smaller proportion of GDP, such as the United States, there is concern about GDP growth.

WHAT ARE GOVERNMENT PURCHASES (*G*)?

Expenditures on goods and services are the government purchases that are included in GDP. For example, the government (which includes all four levels of government: federal, provincial/territorial, regional, and municipal) must pay the salaries of its employees, and it must also make payments to the private firms with which it contracts to provide various goods and services, such as highway construction companies and computer companies. All of these payments would be included in GDP. However, transfer payments (such as Employment Insurance benefits and Canada Pension Plan payments) are not included in government purchases because that spending does not go to purchase newly produced goods or services. Transfer payments are merely a transfer of income among that country's citizens (which is why such expenditures are called *transfer payments*). The government purchase proportion of GDP, at 26 percent, has grown over the last 50 years, in part because of rising spending on publicly funded health care.

WHAT ARE NET EXPORTS (*X* – *M*)?

Some of the goods and services that are produced in Canada are exported for use in other countries. The fact that these goods and services were made in Canada means that they should be included in a measure of Canadian production, so we include the value of exports when calculating GDP. At the same time, however, some of our expenditures in other categories (consumption and investment in particular) are for foreign-produced goods and services. These imports must be excluded from GDP in order to obtain an accurate measure of Canadian production. Thus, GDP calculations measure net exports, which equals total exports (X) minus total imports (M).

In 2012, Canada's net exports were −\$36 billion, or −2 percent of GDP. However, exports of goods and services themselves were \$547 billion, or 30 percent of GDP. Likewise, imports of goods and services were \$583 billion, or 32 percent of GDP. These numbers mean that about 30 percent of all Canadian production of goods and services is sold to foreigners, whereas about 32 percent of all Canadian expenditure is on foreign-produced goods and services. These high proportions reflect the fact that Canada is very much an "open" economy; that is, the Canadian economy is highly dependent on foreign markets in terms of both buying and selling goods and services. In some years, the value of Canada's exports is greater than the value of its imports, net exports are a positive number, and Canada runs a trade surplus. However, in 2012, the value of imports exceeded the value of exports, net exports were a negative number, and Canada ran a trade deficit.

Business *CONNECTION*

NUANCES OF THE GDP

The measuring of gross domestic product (GDP) is much discussed in macroeconomics. This key economic indicator may, in fact, be understated. It's often observed that the existence of an underground economy leads to distortions in achieving more accurate measures of GDP, and how do you capture the value of nonmarket transactions such as homemade meals, housework, and home-grown vegetables and flowers in the measure of GDP? So should business disregard GDP?

A basic understanding of the make-up of the GDP, using the expenditure approach, indicates four components: (1) the consumer spending of individuals and households, (2) the capital spending by businesses, mainly to expand their productive capacity and build up inventory levels, (3) the spending by various levels of government, and (4) the spending by those who bought goods and services produced by Canadians less the amounts Canadians spent to buy goods and services from abroad. While the exact measure of GDP may be in question, we can learn much by simply observing the direction and change in each component of GDP over time.

In Canada, using the expenditure approach, consumer spending accounts for more than 55 percent of the GDP measure. Businesses that rely strongly on consumer spending will at the least have a great deal of interest in the change in direction of this element—if not in the absolute magnitude of the GDP. If at a point in time, increases in consumer spending are expected to provide the main fuel for economic growth—essentially increases in GDP—businesses that depend on consumers can expect growth in demand for the consumer products they sell or produce, presenting an opportunity to increase revenues. At other times, the growth in GDP may be a result of an increase in foreign buyers' demand for

(continued)

Canadian goods and services, often natural resources such as oil or lumber. When this is the case, those sectors of the economy can expect increases in revenues.

Another component of GDP, government spending—which accounts for about 22 percent of GDP expenditure—is somewhat constrained by government dependence on tax collection. Still, at times when it appears that economic growth might slow or the economy might dip into a recession (two consecutive periods of negative growth), governments often borrow funds to increase their capacity to spend, and so soften a drop in economic growth. Here again, without considering the absolute measure or completeness of the GDP indicator, business operators can gain a sense of the economy's performance and what that means for revenue growth and profits. So the rate of change of GDP may be more significant than its absolute measure.

1. You're a business owner and you've been offered cash (which you likely won't report as income) to complete the transaction? If many businesses accepted cash, how would it impact the microeconomy and the macroeconomy?

2. There is an argument that *per capita* GDP is not a good indicator in general of a country's well-being. What would you add or remove when measuring GDP that would be a better indicator of the quality of life of a country's citizens? Why?

3. There is significant discussion about cutting back on purchasing products from afar and instead buying Canadian-made products. Knowing the benefits of trade, do you think the classic arguments against "buy Canadian" still hold?

SECTION CHECK

- The expenditure approach to measuring GDP involves adding up the purchases of final goods and services by market participants. Four categories of spending are used in the GDP calculation: consumption (*C*), investment (*I*), government purchases (*G*), and net exports (*X* – *M*).
- Consumption includes spending on nondurable consumer goods—tangible items that are usually consumed in a short period of time; semi-durable goods—items that are used for an intermediate period of time; durable consumer goods—longer-lived consumer goods; and services—intangible items of value.
- Fixed investment includes all spending on capital goods, such as machinery, tools, and buildings. Inventory investment includes the net expenditures by businesses to increase their inventories.
- Purchases of goods and services are the only part of government spending included in GDP. Transfer payments are not included in these calculations because that spending is not a payment for a newly produced good or service.
- Net exports are calculated by subtracting total imports from total exports.

section 14.3

The Income Approach to Measuring GDP

- What is the income approach to measuring GDP?
- What do personal income and disposable income measure?

WHAT IS THE INCOME APPROACH TO MEASURING GDP?

income approach
calculation of GDP based on the summation of incomes received by the owners of resources used in the production of goods and services

In the last section, we outlined the expenditure approach to GDP calculation. There is, however, an alternative method called the *income approach*. The **income approach** is a calculation of GDP based on the summation of incomes received by the owners of resources used in the production of goods and services.

When someone makes an expenditure for a good or service, that spending creates income for someone else. For example, if you spend $10 on groceries at the local supermarket, your $10 of spending creates $10 in income for the grocery store owner. The owner, then, must buy more goods to stock her shelves as a consequence of your consumer purchases; in addition, she must pay her employees, her electricity bill, and so on. Consequently, much of the $10 spent by you will eventually end up in the hands of someone other than the grocer. The basic point, however, is that someone (one person or many) receives the $10 you spent, and that receipt of funds is called *income.* Therefore, by adding up all of the incomes received by producers of goods and services, we can also calculate the gross domestic product, because output creates income of equal value.

Factor Payments

Factor payments are the wages (salaries), rent, interest payments, and profits paid to the owners of productive resources; that is, the incomes received by people providing goods and services. Factor payments include wages for labour services; rent for land; payments for the use of capital goods in the form of interest; and profits for entrepreneurs who put labour, land, and capital together. Exhibit 1 presents the income approach to measuring GDP. Exhibit 1 presents the income approach to measuring GDP. "Compensation of employees" is the payment for labour services, which includes wages and salaries as well as the employer's social contributions. This category of factor payment totalled $923 billion, or 51 percent of GDP. "Net operating surplus: Corporations" is the corporation's profits before tax. "Net mixed income" comprises the earnings of farmers and proprietors from their own businesses. The sum of these three categories of income is called **net domestic income at factor cost,** which totalled $1329 billion in 2012.

We have to make two adjustments to net domestic income at factor cost to arrive at GDP. Net domestic income is the cost of the factor payments, but GDP is the value of the output at market prices. Therefore, the first adjustment we have to make to net domestic income is to add indirect taxes and subtract subsidies. An indirect tax is a tax paid by consumers when they buy goods and services (such as provincial sales taxes, the GST, and excise taxes). Because of indirect taxes, the market price of a product bought by consumers (e.g., $1 plus 7 percent tax = $1.07) is greater than the factor payments to the owners of the resources who produced the good ($1). A subsidy is a payment by the government to producers (such as payments to airplane manufacturers or grain farmers).

factor payments
wages (salaries), rent, interest payments, and profits paid to the owners of productive resources

net domestic income at factor cost
a measure of income earned by the owners of factors of production

section 14.3
Exhibit 1   2012 Canadian GDP by Type of Income

Category	Amount (billions of current dollars)	Percentage of GDP
Gross domestic product	$1820	
Compensation of employees	923	50.7%
Net operating surplus: Corporations	246	13.5
Net mixed income	160	8.8
Indirect taxes less subsidies	184	10.1
Depreciation	307	16.9

Note: This exhibit is the result of source data and author calculations.

SOURCE: Statistics Canada, CANSIM Table 380—0063, Gross domestic product, income-based.

Because of subsidies, the market price of a product bought by consumers is less than the cost of the factor payments.

The second adjustment to net domestic income is to add depreciation (or capital consumption allowances). When firms purchase capital equipment, the cost of such goods must be allocated over the time that the capital equipment will be used, possibly 10 to 20 years for some types of equipment. The cost allocated, which is called *depreciation,* is an estimate of the amount of the equipment being used up each year in production. Depreciation is a cost of production and is included in the market value of output, but it is not part of any factor's income and is not included in net domestic income.

Adding indirect taxes less subsidies, $184 billion, and depreciation, $307 billion, to net domestic income at factor cost gives us GDP.

WHAT DO PERSONAL INCOME AND DISPOSABLE INCOME MEASURE?

personal income
the amount of income received by households before taxes

disposable income
the personal income available after taxes

Often, we are interested in the income people *receive* rather than the income they *earn,* because the income received reflects the total amount available for spending before taxes. **Personal income** measures the amount of income received by households (including transfer payments) before income taxes. **Disposable income** is the personal income available after taxes. Disposable income can be used by households in two ways: consumption or saving.

SECTION CHECK

■ The income approach to measuring GDP involves adding together the incomes received by the producers of goods and services. These payments to the owners of productive resources are also known as *factor payments.* The income approach to GDP adds together compensation of employees, net operating surplus: corporations, and net mixed income to get net domestic income at factor cost. Adding indirect taxes less subsidies and depreciation to net domestic income gives us GDP.

■ Personal income measures the amount of income received by households (including transfer payments) before taxes. Disposable income is the personal income available after taxes.

section
14.4
Issues with Calculating an Accurate GDP

■ What are the problems with GDP in measuring output?
■ How is real GDP calculated?
■ What is real GDP per capita?

WHAT ARE THE PROBLEMS WITH GDP IN MEASURING OUTPUT?

The primary problem in calculating accurate GDP statistics becomes evident when attempts are made to compare the GDP over time. Between 1971 and 1976, a period of relatively high inflation, GDP in Canada rose over 100 percent. What great progress! Unfortunately, however, the measure used in adding together the values of different products, the Canadian dollar, also changed in value over this time period. A dollar in 1976, for example, would certainly not buy as much as a dollar in 1971, because the *overall* price level for goods and services increased.

One solution to this problem would be to use physical units of output—which, unlike the Canadian dollar, don't change in value from year to year—as our measure of total economic activity. The major problem with this approach is that different products have different units of measurement. How do you add together tonnes of steel, bushels of wheat, kilowatts of electricity, litres of paint, cubic metres of natural gas, kilometres of air passenger travel, number of games of bowling, and number of magazines sold? In order to compare GDP values over time, a common or standardized unit of measure, which only money can provide, must be used in the calculations.

The dollar, then, is the measure of value that we can use to correct the inflation-induced distortion of the GDP. We must adjust for the changing purchasing power of the dollar by constructing a price index. As we discussed in the last chapter, a price index attempts to provide a measure of the trend in prices paid for a certain bundle of goods and services over time. The price index can be used to deflate the nominal or current dollar GDP values to a real GDP expressed in dollars of constant purchasing power.

There are many different types of price indices. In the last chapter, we calculated the Consumer Price Index (CPI), which measures the trend in the prices of certain goods and services purchased for consumption purposes. The CPI may be the most relevant price index to households trying to evaluate their changing financial position over time. Another price index, the **GDP deflator,** corrects GDP statistics for changing prices. The GDP deflator is a price index that measures the average level of prices of all final goods and services produced in the economy.

GDP deflator
a price index that helps to measure the average price level of all final goods and services produced in the economy

HOW IS REAL GDP CALCULATED?

To correct the nominal or current dollar GDP values for inflation, the appropriate price index to use is the GDP deflator. Once the GDP deflator has been calculated, the actual procedure for adjusting nominal, or current dollar, GDP to get real GDP is not complicated. Remember, real GDP gives us a measure of GDP in constant dollars that have been corrected for inflation.

The formula for converting any year's nominal GDP into real GDP (in constant dollars) is as follows:

$$\text{Real GDP} = \frac{\text{Nominal GDP}}{\text{GDP deflator}} \times 100$$

Exhibit 1 presents data on nominal GDP, real GDP, and the GDP deflator for the Canadian economy for the 2000–12 period. The base year for the GDP deflator is 2007 (2007 = 100), so real GDP is expressed in billions of 2007 dollars, and the GDP deflator for 2012 of 109.53 means that prices were 9.53 percent higher in 2012 than they were in 2007. Now, in order to correct the 2012 nominal GDP, we take the nominal GDP figure for 2012, $1820.0 billion, and divide it by the GDP deflator, 109.53, which results in a quotient of $16.616 billion. We then multiply this number by 100, giving us $1661.6 billion, which is the 2012 GDP in 2007 dollars (that is, 2012 real GDP, in terms of a 2007 base year). Or to correct the 2000 nominal GDP into real GDP, take the nominal GDP figure for 2000, $1098.2 billion and divide it by the GDP deflator (83.23), which results in a quotient of $13.194 billion. We then multiply this number by 100, giving us $1319.4 billion, which would be the 2000 GDP in 2007 dollars (that is, 2000 real GDP, in terms of the 2007 base year).

section 14.4
Exhibit 1

section 14.4
Exhibit 1   Nominal GDP, Real GDP, and the GDP Deflator

Year	Nominal GDP (billions of current dollars)	GDP Deflator (2007 = 100)	Real GDP (billions of 2007 dollars)
2000	$1098.2	83.23	$1319.4
2001	1134.8	84.58	1341.7
2002	1181.0	85.62	1379.3
2003	1243.8	88.47	1405.9
2004	1324.9	91.37	1450.0
2005	1410.7	94.30	1495.9
2006	1486.9	96.86	1535.1
2007	1565.9	100.00	1565.9
2008	1646.0	103.89	1584.3
2009	1567.0	101.66	1541.4
2010	1662.8	104.36	1593.4
2011	1760.0	107.74	1633.6
2012	1820.0	109.53	1661.6

SOURCE: Statistics Canada, CANSIM Table 380–0064, Gross domestic product, expenditure-based, annual (dollars unless otherwise noted).

Notice that nominal GDP (in current dollars) increased from $1098.2 billion in 2000 to $1646.0 billion in 2008, an increase of 49.9 percent. However, over the same time period, the GDP deflator rose from 83.23 to 103.89, an increase of 24.8 percent. This means that the average price level of all the final goods and services produced in the economy increased by 25 percent, meaning the economy experienced 25 percent inflation over this eight-year period. This inflation was one of the factors that led to the growth in nominal (current dollar) GDP. The other factor was growth in real GDP, or the economy's actual physical production of final goods and services. As we can see, real GDP (measured in 2007 dollars) increased from $1319.4 billion in 2000 to $1584.3 billion in 2008, an increase of 20.1 percent. This is the economy's "real" economic growth.

Finally, notice that during the years after the base year (2007), real GDP is less than nominal GDP. This means that the price level has risen since 2007 (2009 being an exception), lowering the purchasing power of the dollar. Prior to 2007, nominal GDP was less than real GDP; the purchasing power of the dollar was higher relative to the base year (2007). Also, notice that nominal GDP rises more rapidly than real GDP because inflation is included in the nominal GDP figures. When there is inflation, the adjustment of nominal (current dollar) GDP to real GDP (measured in constant dollars) will reduce the growth in GDP suggested by the nominal GDP figures. Thus, it is important when comparing GDP over time that we use real GDP as our measure of the economy's production of final goods and services, as this measure corrects nominal GDP for the distortions caused by inflation.

Real GDP Has Not Always Been Less Than Nominal GDP

In modern times, inflation has been prevalent. For many readers of this book, the price level (as measured by the consumer price index) has risen in every year of their lifetime, because the last year with a negative price level was 1953. Therefore, the adjustment of nominal (money) GDP to real GDP will tend to reduce the growth in GDP suggested by nominal GDP figures. Given the distortions introduced by inflation, most news reports about GDP today speak of real GDP changes, although this distinction is not always made explicit.

WHAT IS REAL GDP PER CAPITA?

The measure of economic well-being, or standard of living, most often used is **real gross domestic product per capita**—real output of goods and services per person. We use a measure of real GDP for reasons already cited. To calculate real GDP per capita, we divide the real GDP by the total population to get the value of real output of final goods and services per person. *Ceteris paribus,* people prefer more goods to fewer, so a higher GDP per capita would seemingly make people better off, improving their standard of living. Economic growth, then, is usually considered to have occurred anytime the real GDP per capita has risen. In Exhibit 2, we see that in Canada, the real gross domestic product per capita more than doubled between 1968 and 2012.

real gross domestic product per capita

real output of goods and services per person

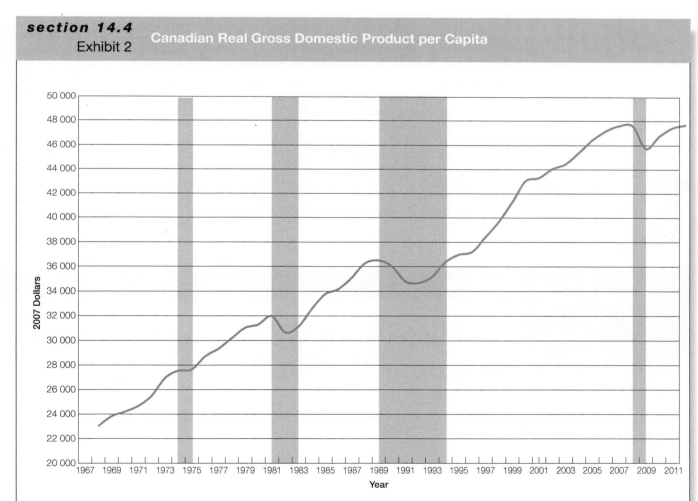

section 14.4
Exhibit 2   Canadian Real Gross Domestic Product per Capita

SOURCES: Statistics Canada, CANSIM Table 380–0064, Gross domestic product, expenditure-based, annual (dollars unless otherwise noted); survey or program details: National gross domestic product by income and by expenditure accounts, 1901; real GDP (prior to 1981): CAMSIN Table 380–0017, Gross domestic product (GDP), expenditure-based, annual (dollars unless otherwise noted); population statistics: CAMSIN Table 051–0005, Estimates of population, Canada, provinces and territories, annual (persons); underground economy statistic: *The Daily*, September 21, 2012, The underground economy in Canada, 1992 to 2009.

However, the growth in real GDP per capita was not steady, as seen by the shaded areas that represent recessions in Exhibit 2. Falling real GDP per capita can bring on many human hardships, such as rising unemployment, lower profits, stock market losses, and bankruptcies. Note, in particular, the prolonged stagnation in standard of living during the early 1990s, when real GDP per capita was at the same level in 1994 as it was in 1989.

Because one purpose of using GDP is to relate output to human desires, we need to adjust for population change. If we do not take population growth into account, we can be misled by changes in real GDP values. For example, in some less-developed countries in some time periods, real GDP has risen by perhaps 2 percent a year but the population has grown just as fast. In these cases, the real output of goods and services per person has remained virtually unchanged, but this would not be apparent in an examination of real GDP trends alone.

While real GDP per capita is therefore a superior indicator of how well-off individuals are in a given economy, as compared to just real GDP alone, it is important to recognize that it does not say anything about the distribution of output and income. For example, a country could have extraordinary growth in per capita output and yet the poor might make little or no improvement in their standard of living. That is, it is possible that income group would make little or no gain.

SECTION CHECK

- It is difficult to compare nominal GDP over time because of the changing value of money over time.
- The GDP deflator is a price index that measures the average level of prices of all final goods and services produced in the economy. It is used to convert nominal measures of GDP into equivalent real measures of GDP.
- Per capita real GDP is the real output of goods and services per person. In some cases, real GDP may increase but per capita real GDP may actually drop as a result of population growth.

section 14.5

Problems with GDP as a Measure of Economic Welfare

- What are some of the deficiencies of GDP as a measure of economic welfare?

WHAT ARE SOME OF THE DEFICIENCIES OF GDP AS A MEASURE OF ECONOMIC WELFARE?

As we noted earlier, real GDP is often used as a measure of the economic welfare of a nation. The accuracy of this measure for that purpose is, however, questionable because several important factors are excluded from its calculations. These factors include nonmarket transactions, the underground economy, leisure, externalities, and the quality of the goods purchased.

Nonmarket Transactions

Nonmarket transactions include the provision of goods and services outside of traditional markets for which no money is exchanged. We simply do not have reliable enough information on this output to include it in the GDP. The most important single nonmarket transaction omitted from the GDP is the work of housewives (or househusbands). These services are not sold in any market, so they are not entered into the GDP, but they are nonetheless performed. For example, if a single woman hires a tax accountant, those payments enter into the calculation of GDP. Suppose, though, that the woman marries her tax accountant. Now the woman no longer pays

her husband for his accounting services. Reported GDP falls after the marriage, although output does not change.

In less-developed countries, where a significant amount of food and clothing output is produced in the home, the failure to include nonmarket economic activity in GDP is a serious deficiency. Even in Canada, homemade meals, housework, and the vegetables and flowers produced in home gardens are excluded, even though they clearly represent an output of goods and services.

Are her household production efforts included in GDP? If a family hires someone to clean the house, provide child care, mow the lawn, or cook, this is included in GDP; when members of the household provide these services, it is not. Neglecting household production in GDP distorts measurements of economic growth and leads to potential policy problems. Is it time to include household activities in GDP? An estimate of the value of these services could be obtained by calculating the cost to buy these services in the marketplace.

The Underground Economy

It is impossible to know for sure the magnitude of the underground economy, which includes unreported income from both legal and illegal sources. For example, illegal drug dealing and prostitution are not included in the GDP, leading to underreporting of an unknown dimension. The reason these activities are excluded, however, has nothing to do with the morality of the services performed, but rather results from the fact that the payments made for these services are not reported to governmental authorities. Likewise, cash payments made to employees "under the table" slip through the GDP net. The estimates of the size of the underground economy vary considerably. For example, one figure published by Statistics Canada estimated an upper limit for total underground activity in Canada of $35 billion for 2009. It also appears that a good portion of this unreported income comes from legal sources, such as self-employment.

Measuring the Value of Leisure

The value that individuals place on leisure is omitted in calculating GDP. Most of us could probably get a part-time job if we wanted to, earning some additional money by working in the evening or on weekends. Yet we choose not to do so. Why? The opportunity cost is too high—we would have to forgo some leisure. If you work on Saturday nights, you cannot visit your friends, go to parties, see concerts, watch television, or go to the movies. The opportunity cost of the leisure is the income forgone by not working. For example, if people start taking more three-day weekends, GDP will surely fall, but can we necessarily say that the standard of living will fall? GDP will fall but economic well-being may rise.

Leisure, then, has a positive value that does not show up in the GDP accounts. To put leisure in the proper perspective, ask yourself if you would rather live in Country A, which has a per capita GDP of $25 000 a year and a 30-hour workweek, or Country B, with a $25 000 per capita GDP and a 50-hour workweek. Most would choose Country A. The problem that this omission in GDP poses can be fairly significant in international comparisons, or when one looks at one nation over time.

GDP and Externalities

Economists have observed that side effects can accompany the production of some goods and services. These additional impacts (in the form of either benefits or costs) are referred to as *externalities*. As a result of these positive and negative externalities, the equilibrium prices of goods and services—the figures used in GDP calculations—do not reflect their true value to society (unless the externality has been internalized). For example, if a steel mill produces 100 000 more tonnes of steel, GDP increases; GDP does not, however, decrease to reflect damages from the air pollution that results from the production of that additional steel. Likewise, additional production of a vaccine would be reflected in the GDP, but the positive benefit to members of society—other than the purchaser—would not be included in the calculation. In other words, while GDP measures the goods and services produced, it does not adequately measure the "goods" and "bads" that result from the production processes.

In addition to the inability of GDP calculations to properly address the existence of externalities, there is the issue of sustainability. GDP is a measure of historical economic activity, not necessarily a projection of an economy's ability to sustain economic growth in the future. An economy that has been able to achieve GDP growth through unsustainable treatment of natural resources and misallocated investment would appear to be no different (in terms of its value of GDP) from an economy that accomplished its GDP growth through thoughtful natural resource management and investment strategies with a long-term planning horizon.

Quality of Goods

GDP calculations can also miss important improvements in the *quality* of goods and services. For example, there is a huge difference between the quality of a computer bought today and one that was bought ten years ago, but it will not lead to an increase in measured GDP. The same is true of many goods, from cellular phones to automobiles to medical care.

Other Measures of Economic Well-Being

Even if we included some of these statistics that are difficult to measure, such as non-market transactions, the underground economy, leisure, externalities, and the quality of products, GDP would still not be a precise measure of economic well-being. Many other indices of well-being should be considered: life expectancies, infant mortality rates, education and environmental quality, levels of discrimination and fairness, health care, low crime rates, and minimum traffic congestion, to name just a few. One example of an index that attempts to incorporate these other indicators of well-being is the Human Development Index (HDI) first published by the United Nations Development Programme in 1990. The HDI, a composite measure of health, income, and education, has become the most widely cited and generally accepted measure of its kind. In closing, while GDP is solely a measure of economic production and not a measure of economic well-being, we must also remember that greater levels of GDP can lead to economic and social improvements because society would then be able to afford better education and health care and a cleaner, safer environment.

DEBATE

SHOULD GOVERNMENTS WORRY ABOUT THE UNDERGROUND ECONOMY?

For:

In the underground economy (or black market), there is illegal trade in goods or services such as drugs, prostitution, weapons, and ivory. Underground economies are a fact of life—but governments should still try to get rid of them or at least control them. Left unreported, purchases made in the underground market mean that the economic activity taking place within the country is underestimated, employment rates are underrepresented, and governments lose tax revenues. Tax compliance is a cornerstone of the effective and equitable operation of government. When citizens feel they don't have to pay taxes, the system breaks down—think of what happened when citizens of Greece decided not to pay their income taxes and took part in many underground economies. It's not just the explicit costs to the system—the implicit and opportunity costs also take their toll. Governments have an obligation to those who choose to live in a legal manner to go after those who don't. Completely eliminating underground economies is probably an expensive, unachievable goal, but controlling the black market through enforcement to ensure it doesn't get out of hand is a reasonable approach. Surely it makes sense for governments to worry about the underground economy. Can you think of other arguments in favour of that view?

Against:

Governments that don't concern themselves with the underground economy probably have a "live and let live" economic structure. When they discover the existence of underground economies, instead of trying to enforce compliance, they may try to deal with the reasons why people are turning to these economies. For example, instead of banning the use of marijuana, some governments are considering making its use legal and taxing it fairly, much like fair taxes on alcohol. This is the approach that Colorado has taken. The Netherlands has decriminalized or legalized underground markets like the sex trade and recreational drug use for two reasons: (1) to capture some tax, but mostly (2) to try to regulate better health care for those who engage in those markets. Most well-run economies are based on the trust the citizens have in the system. Those who earn income are expected to pay taxes on those earnings. When citizens believe that the system is fair and have an expectation that cheaters will be punished, a solid foundation is provided for a well-run economy. When individuals perceive that the costs of taxes are unreasonable or unfair, they opt for the black market, and governments have to use scarce resources to recapture those unpaid taxes—and the cost of compliance rises dramatically for the government. In fact, governments may not even know that the economies exist because they are "underground." Many would argue that monitoring and enforcement costs outweigh the loss of tax revenue and that when the cost of compliance is so high that it can't be offset by added revenues to the government, it becomes useless for the government to try and force compliance. The "War on Drugs" might be a good example. Over the long run, costs of running the system are less when individuals generally police themselves, with occasional stern penalties when people cheat by not paying taxes. Surely it's now clear that it is better that governments generally not worry about the underground economy. Can you think of other reasons why?

SECTION CHECK

- Several factors make it difficult to use GDP as a welfare indicator, including nonmarket transactions, the underground economy, leisure, and externalities. Nonmarket transactions are the exchanges of goods and services that do not occur in traditional markets, so no money is exchanged. The underground economy is the unreported production and income that come from legal and illegal activities. The presence of positive and negative externalities also make it difficult to measure GDP accurately.

For Your Review

Section 14.1

1. Which of the following are included in Canadian GDP calculations?
   a. cleaning services performed by a cleaning company
   b. washing your own car
   c. drugs sold illegally on a local street corner
   d. prescription drugs manufactured in Canada and sold at a local pharmacy
   e. a rug woven by hand in Turkey
   f. air pollution that diminishes the quality of the air you breathe
   g. toxic waste cleanup performed by a local company
   h. car parts manufactured in Canada for assembly of a car in Mexico
   i. a purchase of 1000 shares in a Canadian-owned high-tech company
   j. a monthly Canada Pension Plan payment received by a retiree

2. Answer the following questions about GDP.
   a. What is the definition of GDP?
   b. Why does GDP measure only the final value of goods and services?
   c. Why does GDP measure only the value of goods and services produced within a country?
   d. How does GDP treat the sales of used goods?
   e. How does GDP treat sales of corporate shares from one shareholder to another?

3. Explain how the determination of GDP via the expenditure approach is equivalent to the determination of GDP via the income approach.

4. The expenditures on tires by the Ford Motor Company of Canada are not included directly in GDP statistics, whereas consumer expenditures on replacement tires are included. Why?

Section 14.2

5. To which Canadian GDP expenditure category does each of the following correspond?
   a. Ministry of Transportation snow-clearing services
   b. automobiles exported to Europe
   c. a refrigerator
   d. a newly constructed four-bedroom house
   e. a restaurant meal
   f. additions to inventory at a furniture store
   g. purchases of new computers by Statistics Canada
   h. a new steel mill

6. Using any relevant information below, calculate GDP via the expenditure approach.

Inventory investment	$ 50 billion
Fixed investment	120 billion
Consumer durables	420 billion
Consumer nondurables	275 billion
Interest	140 billion
Indirect business taxes	45 billion
Government wages and salaries	300 billion
Government purchases of goods and services	110 billion
Imports	80 billion
Exports	40 billion
Consumer semi-durables	185 billion
Profits	320 billion
Consumer services	600 billion

7. Fill in the missing data for the following table (in millions).

Consumption	_____
Consumption of durable goods	$1200
Consumption of semi-durable goods	1100
Consumption of nondurable goods	1800
Consumption of services	2400
Investment	_____
Fixed investment	800
Inventory investment	600
Government expenditures on goods and services	1600
Government transfer payments	500
Exports	500
Imports	650
Net exports	_____
GDP	_____

8. Answer these questions about durable goods and GDP:

   a. Do consumer nondurable or durable goods tend to change more over the course of a business cycle?

   b. How are consumer durables like investments?

   c. Can either fixed investment or inventory be negative in a given year?

   d. Why isn't all of government spending part of GDP?

9. Why do you think economic forecasters focus so much on consumption purchases and their determinants?

Section 14.3

10. What basic principle proves that the income approach to calculating gross domestic product is valid?

11. Following is a list of national income figures for a given year. All figures are in millions. Using this data, determine GDP by both the expenditure and income approaches. The answer arrived at by each method should be the same.

Government current purchases of goods and services	$ 60
Indirect taxes (less subsidies)	35
Compensation of employees	210
Corporation profits before taxes	62
Exports	10
Net mixed income	21
Gross investment	100
Undistributed corporate profits	12
Capital consumption allowances (depreciation)	32
Net investment	68
Imports	20
Personal consumption expenditures	210

Section 14.4

12. Nominal GDP in Nowhereland in 2012 and 2013 was as follows:

Nominal GDP 2012	Nominal GDP 2013
$400 billion	$440 billion

Can you say that the production of goods and services in Nowhereland increased between 2012 and 2013? Why or why not?

Blueprint Problem

The following table contains partial national income accounting data for a hypothetical country.

Year	Nominal GDP (in millions)	GDP Deflator	Real GDP (in millions)
2007	$245 689	92.8	
2008	268 375		$281 611
2009		95.9	300 857
2010	298 402		298 402
2011	307 329	103.5	
2012	315 386		293 929
2013	322 437	110.3	

a. Fill in the missing data in the above table.

b. What conclusion can be made regarding the economy's production of goods and services over the 2007–13 time period?

Blueprint Solution

a.

> Use the following formula:
>
> $$\text{Real GDP} = \left(\frac{\text{Nominal GDP}}{\text{GDP deflator}} \right) \times 100$$
>
> Each year's amount of nominal GDP (current dollar output) has now been converted into real GDP (constant dollar output—output measured using 2010 prices).

Year	Nominal GDP (in millions)	GDP Deflator	Real GDP (in millions)
2007	$245 689	92.8	$264 751
2008	268 375	95.3	281 611
2009	288 522	95.9	300 857
2010	298 402	100	298 402
2011	307 329	103.5	296 936
2012	315 386	107.3	293 929
2013	322 437	110.3	292 327

> Use the following formula:
>
> $$\text{Nominal GDP} = \left(\frac{\text{Real GDP} \times \text{GDP deflator}}{100} \right)$$
>
> Each year's real GDP (constant dollar output—measured in 2010 prices) has now been converted to nominal GDP (current dollar output—measured in current prices).

> Use the following formula:
>
> $$\text{GDP deflator} = \left(\frac{\text{Nominal GDP}}{\text{Real GDP}} \right) \times 100$$
>
> The GDP deflator is a price index (like the CPI). An increase in this value indicates a rise in the overall level of prices in the economy—that is, inflation.

b. When making any observation about the ability of an economy to produce goods and services over time, you must first look at the correct information. Real GDP has been adjusted to account for any distortions caused by price level changes. Therefore, it is each year's real GDP amount that must be interpreted as that year's true measure of production. With this distinction between nominal GDP and real GDP clear, we observe that real GDP increased from 2007 to 2009, then declined from 2009 to 2013—therefore indicating that our economy experienced first an increase then a decline in its ability to produce goods and services between 2007 and 2013. So it is important when comparing GDP over time that we use real GDP as our measure of the economy's production of final goods and services, as this measure corrects nominal GDP for the distortions caused by inflation.

13. Calculate real GDP for the years 2009 to 2013 using the following information:

Year	Nominal GDP (in billions)	GDP Deflator	Real GDP
2009	$720	100	
2010	750	102	
2011	800	110	
2012	900	114	
2013	960	120	

What was the real economic growth rate in 2013?

14. Fill in the missing data in the following table.

Year	GDP Deflator	Nominal GDP (in billions)	Real GDP (in billions)
2009	90.9	$ 700	
2010	100.0		$ 800
2011		1000	800
2012	140.0	1400	
2013	150.0		1200

15. The table below contains national income data for a hypothetical economy.

Year	Nominal GDP (in millions)	GDP Deflator	Real GDP (in millions)
2008	$3237.0	93.3	
2009	3156.4		$3247.3
2010		100	2995.3
2011	3376.2		3271.5
2012	3517.6	101.4	
2013	3797.3		3701.1

a. Fill in the missing data in the table.
b. Which year is the base year and what role does this year play in determining real GDP?
c. How would you describe the behaviour of production for this economy over the 2008–13 time period?

16. Population and real GDP in Country A are as follows:

Year	Population (in millions)	Real GDP (in millions)
1990	1.25	$4000
2000	1.60	6750
2010	1.80	9000

Calculate real GDP per capita in 1990, 2000, and 2010. Does real output per person increase or decrease over time?

Section 14.5

17. Answer these questions about GDP:

    a. Could next year's real GDP exceed next year's nominal GDP?

    b. Could real GDP grow at the same time that real GDP per capita falls?

    c. Could people's real consumption possibilities expand at the same time that real GDP per capita falls?

    d. How does changing the amount of leisure complicate comparisons of real well-being over time?

18. Evaluate the following statement: "Real GDP in the United States is higher than real GDP in Canada. Therefore, the standard of living in the United States must be higher than that in Canada."

19. How would the existence of a high level of nonmarket activities in one country impact real GDP comparisons between it and other countries?

20. How do pollution and crime affect GDP? How do pollution-control and crime-control programs funded by various levels of government impact GDP?

chapter

15

Economic Growth in the Global Economy

section

15.1   Economic Growth

- How does economic growth differ from the business cycle?
- What is economic growth?
- What is the Rule of 70?

HOW DOES ECONOMIC GROWTH DIFFER FROM THE BUSINESS CYCLE?

John Maynard Keynes, one of the most influential economic thinkers of all time, once said that "in the long run, we are all dead." Keynes said this because he was primarily concerned with explaining and reducing short-term fluctuations in the level of business activity. He wanted to smooth out the business cycle, largely because of the implications that cyclical fluctuations had for buyers and sellers in terms of unemployment and price instability. No one would deny that Keynes's concerns were important and legitimate.

At the same time, however, Keynes's flippant remark about the long run ignores the fact that human welfare is greatly influenced by long-term changes in a nation's capacity to produce goods and services. Emphasis on short-run economic fluctuations ignores the longer-term dynamic changes that affect output, leisure, real incomes, and lifestyles.

Economists distinguish between the short-run variations in economic activity that they call *business cycles* and long-run economic growth. In Chapter 13, we discussed the short-run economic fluctuations of business cycles. Here in Chapter 15, our focus will be on the long-run trend rate of growth—that is, economic growth. Exhibit 1 is provided to distinguish between short-run economic fluctuations and long-run economic growth.

What are the determinants of long-run economic growth? What are some of the consequences of rapid economic change? Why are some nations rich whereas others are poor? Does growth in output improve our economic welfare? These are a few questions that we need to explore.

WHAT IS ECONOMIC GROWTH?

Economic growth refers to an upward trend in the real per capita output of goods and services (real GDP per capita). In Chapter 2, we introduced the production possibilities curve. Along the production possibilities curve, the economy is producing at its potential output. How much the economy will produce at its potential output, sometimes called its *natural rate of output,* depends on the quantity and quality of an economy's resources, including labour, capital (like factories, machinery, and tools), land (fish, lumber, and so on), and entrepreneurial activity. In addition, technology can increase the economy's production capabilities. As shown in Exhibit 2, improvements in and greater stocks of land, labour, capital, and entrepreneurial activity will shift the production possibilities curve outward. Another way of saying that economic growth has shifted the production possibilities curve outward is to say that it has increased potential output.

WHAT IS THE RULE OF 70?

If Nation A and Nation B start off with the same size of population and the same level of real GDP but grow at only slightly different rates over a long period of time, will it make much of a difference? Yes. In the first year or two, the differences will be small but even over a decade, the differences will be large and, after 50 to 100 years, the differences will be huge. The final impact will be a much higher standard of living in the nation with the greater economic growth, *ceteris paribus.*

A simple formula, called the *Rule of 70,* shows how long it will take a nation to double its output at various growth rates. If you take a nation's growth rate and divide it into 70, you will have the approximate time it will take to double the income level. For example, if a nation grows at 3.5 percent per year, then the economy will double every 20 years (70/3.5). However, if an economy grows at only 2 percent per year, then the economy will double every 35 years (70/2). And at a 1 percent annual growth rate, it will take 70 years to double income (70/1). So even a small change in the growth rate of a nation will have a large impact over a lengthy period.

In Exhibit 3, we see the growth in real GDP for Canada since 1968. The exhibit shows that Canadian real GDP per capita (measured in 2007 dollars) grew from $23 002.73 in 1968 to $47 708.89 in 2012. That is, Canadians today, on average, can purchase more than twice the amount of goods and services purchased 45 years ago.

In Exhibit 4, we see a comparison of selected industrial countries. Because of differences in growth rates, some countries will become richer than others over time. With relatively slower economic growth, today's richest countries will not be the richest for very long. On the other hand, with even slight improvements in economic growth, today's poorest countries will not remain poor for long. Ireland, for example, once one

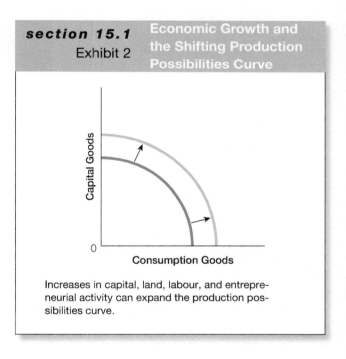

section 15.1
Exhibit 1 — Short-Run versus Long-Run Economic Growth

Short-run fluctuations in economic activity occur around the long-run trend rate of growth. It is this long-run trend rate that economists refer to when discussing economic growth.

section 15.1
Exhibit 2 — Economic Growth and the Shifting Production Possibilities Curve

Increases in capital, land, labour, and entrepreneurial activity can expand the production possibilities curve.

economic growth
an upward trend in the real per capita output of goods and services

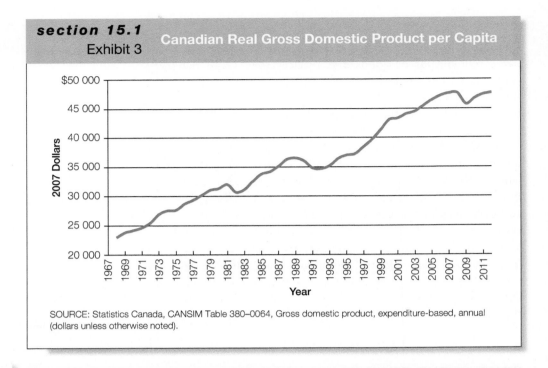

section 15.1
Exhibit 3   Canadian Real Gross Domestic Product per Capita

SOURCE: Statistics Canada, CANSIM Table 380–0064, Gross domestic product, expenditure-based, annual (dollars unless otherwise noted).

section 15.1
Exhibit 4   Annual Growth Rates in Real GDP per Capita, Selected Countries

	Period Averages	
	1992–2002	*2003–13*
Industrialized Economies		
Canada	2.45%	0.72%
United States	2.20	0.71
Japan	0.54	0.85
Germany	1.18	1.38
France	1.54	0.32
Italy	1.56	−0.83
United Kingdom	3.10	0.34
Ireland	6.93	0.07
Greece	2.11	−1.35
Emerging Markets and Developing Economies		
China	8.83%	9.68%
India	3.78	6.07
Haiti	−1.54	0.27
Democratic Republic of the Congo	−5.80	3.36
Zimbabwe	n/a	−0.90
Cameroon	0.10	0.80
Central African Republic	0.84	2.55
Niger	0.62	4.44
Republic of Congo	1.16	4.45

SOURCE: *World Economic Outlook,* April 2013. International Monetary Fund.

of the poorest countries in Western Europe, is now one of the richest. China and India have both experienced spectacular economic growth over the past 20 years. Because of this economic growth, much of the world is now poorer than these two heavily populated countries.

Because of past economic growth, the "richest" or "most-developed" countries today have many times the market output per person of the "poorest" or "least-developed" countries. Put differently, the most-developed countries produce and market more output per person per day than the least-developed countries do in a year. The international differences in income, output, and wealth are indeed striking and have caused a great deal of friction between developed and less-developed countries. Canada, the United States, Japan, and the nations of the European Union have had sizable increases in real output over the past two centuries, but even in 1900 most of these nations were better off in terms of real GDP per capita than impoverished countries such as Ethiopia, India, or Nepal are today.

BRICS

BRICS is an acronym that refers to the economies of **B**razil, **R**ussia, **I**ndia, **C**hina, and **S**outh Africa. According to some, this association of rapidly emerging economies has the potential to become the new superpower in the global economy. While the current level of per capita real GDP level for each member economy within BRICS is far less than Canada's, each of these economies has exhibited rates of economic growth that could dramatically change things in the future.

Brazil, with the world's fifth-largest population, has the world's seventh-largest economy in international terms (as determined by purchasing power parity calculations). A wealth of natural resources has been central to Brazil's rapid growth and new international recognition. Prior to the global financial crisis, the Brazilian economy was growing at over 5 percent annually (2005–08). More recently, however, growth rates have slowed (3.2 percent per year for 2008–12), primarily due to lower global demand for raw materials.

India is the world's second-most populous nation and its third-largest economy in international terms. Experiencing an average growth rate of over 9 percent per year from 2004–07, India's economic growth rate slowed in 2008–09 as a result of the global financial crisis. By 2010, however, the Indian economy had recorded economic growth of nearly 10 percent.

China, the world's most populous country, has the world's second-largest economy in international terms. China is growing at about 10 percent per year. Foreign investment in China has helped to spur output of both domestic and export goods. China grew only 9.6 percent in 2008, its slowest growth rate since 2001. The global financial crisis had a large impact on China due to its heavy reliance on exports. Exports account for about one-third of China's GDP. Since economic liberalization began in 1978, China's investment and export-led economy has grown 70 times larger and is the fastest-growing major economy in the world. While China's per capita income is still low, surpassed by roughly a hundred other countries, its rapid economic growth has pulled millions out of poverty.

The most recent member to join BRICS, South Africa (South Africa became a member of BRICS in 2010) is considered an upper-middle income economy. The largest and most developed economy in Africa, South Africa has the world's 25th-largest economy in international terms. Current rates of economic growth have the South African economy growing at a rate of 2.5 percent per year (2012). This figure is down from the growth rates experienced prior to the global financial crisis, when the South African economy was growing at over 5.5 percent per year.

section
15.2

Determinants of Economic Growth

■ What factors contribute to economic growth?

productivity

the amount of goods and services a worker can produce per hour

Will the standard of living in Canada rise, level off, or even decline over time? The answer depends on productivity growth. **Productivity** is the amount of goods and services a worker can produce per hour. Productivity is especially important because it determines a country's standard of living. For example, slow growth of capital investment can lead to lower labour productivity and, consequently, lower wages. On the other hand, increases in productivity and higher wages can occur as a result of carefully crafted economic policies, such as tax policies that stimulate investment or programs that encourage research and development.

The link between productivity and the standard of living can most easily be understood by recalling our circular flow model in Section 6.1. The circular flow model showed that aggregate expenditures are equal to aggregate income. In other words, the aggregate values of all final goods and services produced in the economy must equal the payments made to the factors of production—the wages and salaries paid to workers, the interest payment to capital, the profits, and so on. That is, the only way an economy can increase its rate of consumption in the long run is if it increases the amount it produces. But why are some countries so much better than others at producing goods and services? We will see the answer in this section as we examine the determinants of productivity—physical capital, quantity and quality of labour resources, natural resources, and technology.

WHAT FACTORS CONTRIBUTE TO ECONOMIC GROWTH?

Many explanations of the process of economic growth have been proposed. Which is correct? None of them, by themselves, can completely explain economic growth. However, each of the explanations may be part of a more complicated reality. Economic growth is a complex process involving many important factors, not one of which completely dominates. We can list at least several factors that nearly everyone would agree have contributed to economic growth in some or all countries:

1. Physical capital inputs (machines, tools, buildings, inventories)
2. Quantity and quality of labour resources (labour and human capital)

3. Increase in the use of inputs provided by the land (natural resources)
4. Technological knowledge (new ways of combining given quantities of labour, natural resources, and capital inputs), allowing greater output than previously possible

Physical Capital

Recall that physical capital includes goods such as tools, machinery, and factories that have already been produced and are now producing other goods and services. Combining workers with more capital makes workers more productive, so capital investment can lead to increases in labour productivity. Even in primitive economies, workers usually have some rudimentary tools to further their productive activity. Consider the farmer who needs to dig a ditch to improve drainage in his fields. If he used just his bare hands, it might take a lifetime to complete the job. If he used a shovel, he could dig the ditch in hours or days. But with a big earth-moving machine, he could do it in minutes. Most economists agree that capital formation has played a significant role in the economic development of nations.

Per-Worker Production Function Since resources are scarce, in order to invest in new capital, society must sacrifice some current consumption. To save more now, we need to consume less now. Ultimately, this will allow society to consume more in the future. In Exhibit 1, we see how the amount of capital per worker influences the amount of output per worker. This positively sloped curve is called the *per-worker production function*. Holding the other determinants of output constant (human capital, natural resources, and technology), we see that moving up along the production function, when the quantity of capital per worker rises, so does the amount of output per worker, but at a diminishing rate—the curve eventually becomes flatter as more capital per worker is added. That is, capital is subject to diminishing marginal returns. If the economy has a very low level of capital, an extra unit of capital leads to a relatively large increase in output—a movement from point A to point B in Exhibit 1. If the economy already has a great deal of capital, an extra unit of capital leads to a relatively smaller increase in output—a movement from point C to point D in Exhibit 1.

Imagine that you owned a small company and you had 10 employees and one computer. As you added more computers, output per worker rose, but only up to a point. What if you added 20 computers for your workforce of 10? Adding more computers (capital) still adds to output but by smaller and smaller additional amounts. This is what is called *diminishing marginal returns to capital*—in the long run, *ceteris paribus*, the benefits of a higher saving rate and additional capital stock become smaller and the rate of growth slows.

Some economists believe diminishing marginal returns to capital can help explain the variation in growth rates between rich and poor countries. In poor countries, where there is little capital, small increases in capital investment can lead to relatively large increases in productivity. In rich countries, where workers already have large amounts of capital, increases in capital investment may have a very small additional effect on productivity. Economists call this the *catch-up effect.*

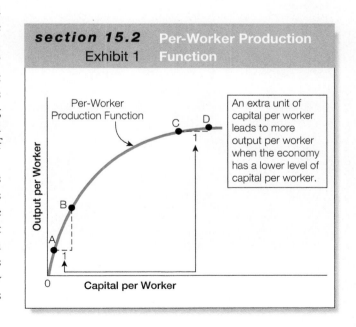

section 15.2   **Per-Worker Production**
Exhibit 1   **Function**

An extra unit of capital per worker leads to more output per worker when the economy has a lower level of capital per worker.

Labour

We know that labour is needed in all forms of productive activity but, *ceteris paribus*, an increase in the quantity of labour inputs does not necessarily increase output per capita. For example, if the increase in the quantity of labour input is due to an increase in population, per capita growth might not occur because the increase in output could be offset by the increase in population. However, if a greater proportion of the population works (that is, the labour force participation rate rises) or if workers put in longer hours, output per capita will increase—assuming that the additional work activity adds something to output.

When workers acquire qualitative improvements (learning new skills, for example), output increases. Workers with a large stock of human capital are more productive than those with small stocks of human capital. Indeed, it has become popular to view labour skills as human capital—the productive knowledge and skill people receive from education and on-the-job training. Like physical capital, human capital must be produced, usually by means of teachers, classrooms, libraries, computer labs, and time devoted to studying. Human capital may be more important than physical capital as a determinant of economic growth. It certainly can increase labour productivity. Human capital also includes improvements in health. Better health conditions allow workers to be more productive.

Countries that do not keep up with technology will generally be unable to keep up their economic growth and standard of living. If a country is technologically backward, it will lose global competitiveness and often rely on a narrow range of exports that will eventually lose their profitability in the global economy. For example, a country that relies on exporting copper may lose its market as other countries around the world convert their phone and cable lines to fibre optics.

Natural Resources

An abundance of natural resources, such as fertile soil, and other raw materials, such as timber and oil, can enhance output. Many scholars cite the abundance of natural resources in Canada as one reason for its historical success. Resources are, however, not the whole story; for example, Japan and Hong Kong have had tremendous economic success despite having relatively few natural resources. In addition, Kuwait and Saudi Arabia are rich because they sit on top of large pools of oil. On the other hand, Brazil has a large and varied natural resource base, yet its income per capita is relatively low compared with many developed countries. It appears that a natural resource base can affect the initial development process but sustained growth is influenced by other factors. However, most economists would agree that a limited resource base does pose an important obstacle to economic growth.

© Lawrence Lowery/PhotoDisc/Getty One Images

Technological Advances

Most economists believe that progress in technology drives productivity, that technology allows workers to produce more. Technological change can lead to better machinery and equipment, increases in capital, and better organization and production methods. Technological advances stem from human ingenuity and creativity in developing new ways of combining the factors of production to enhance the amount of output from a given quantity of resources. The process of technological advance involves invention and innovation. **Innovation** refers to the application of new knowledge that creates new products or improves existing products. For example, the invention and innovation of the combine machine in agriculture, the assembly line in manufacturing, and the railroad were important stimuli to economic growth. New technology, however, must be introduced into productive use by managers or entrepreneurs who must weigh the perceived estimates of benefits of the new technology against estimates of costs. So the entrepreneur is an important economic factor in the growth process.

Technological advance permits us to economize on one or more inputs used in the production process. It can permit savings of labour, such as when a new machine does the work of many workers. When this happens, technology is said to be embodied in capital and to be labour saving. Technology, however, can also save land (natural resource) or even capital. For example, nuclear fission has permitted us to build power plants that economize on the use of coal, a natural resource. The reduction in transportation time that accompanied the invention of the railroad allowed businesses to reduce the capital they needed for inventories. Because goods could be obtained more quickly, businesses could reduce the stock kept on their shelves.

And inventions can come in all sizes. Obviously, the semiconductor chip made a huge impact on productivity and growth, but so did the Post-it Note that was introduced in the early 1980s, the laptop computer, and bar-code scanners, which were first introduced in Walmart stores. We have also seen huge advances in communication (the Internet) and medicines.

In short, better methods of organization and production can lead to increases in labour productivity. When fewer workers are needed in a grocery store or a department store due to better methods of organization, or new machinery and equipment, labour productivity rises.

In Exhibit 2, we see that technological change can shift the per-worker production curve upward, producing more output per worker with the same amount of capital per worker. Technological change allows the economy to escape the full impact of diminishing marginal returns to capital. So, in the long run, *ceteris paribus*, an economy must experience technological advance in order to improve its standard of living and overcome the diminishing marginal returns to capital.

innovation

applications of new knowledge that create new products or improve existing products

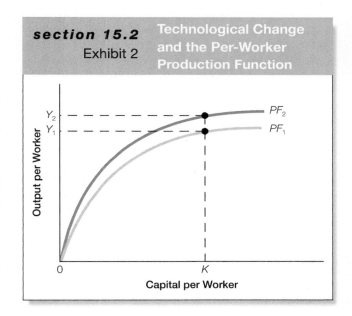

section 15.2
Exhibit 2

Technological Change and the Per-Worker Production Function

SECTION CHECK

■ The factors that contribute to economic growth are the same factors that determine growth in productivity. They include physical capital, quantity and quality of labour, increased use of natural resources, and technology.

section
15.3

Public Policy and Economic Growth

■ What policies can a nation pursue to increase economic growth?
■ Can rates of economic growth between different economies converge?

WHAT POLICIES CAN A NATION PURSUE TO INCREASE ECONOMIC GROWTH?

Economic growth means more than an increase in the real income (output) of the population. A number of other important changes accompany changes in output. Some have even claimed that economic growth stimulates political freedom or democracy, but the correlation here is far from conclusive. Although there are rich democratic societies and poor authoritarian ones, the opposite also holds. That is, some features of democracy, such as majority voting and special-interest groups, may actually be growth retarding. For example, if the majority decides to vote in large land reforms and wealth transfers, this will lead to higher taxes and market distortions that will reduce incentives for work, investment, and ultimately economic growth. In this section, we will investigate the major policies and institutional structures that help to promote economic growth.

The Importance of Savings

One of the most important determinants of economic growth is the saving rate. In order to consume more in the future, we must save more now. Generally speaking, higher levels of saving will lead to higher rates of investment and capital formation and, therefore, to greater economic growth. Individuals can either consume or save their disposable income. If individuals choose to consume all of their disposable income, there will be nothing left for saving, which businesses could use for investment purposes to build new plants or replace worn-out or obsolete equipment. With little investment in capital stock, there will be little economic growth. Capital can also increase as a result of capital injections from abroad (foreign direct investments), but the role of national saving rates in economic growth is of particular importance. However, investment alone does not guarantee economic growth. Economic growth hinges on the quality and type of investment as well as on investments in human capital and improvements in technology.

The Importance of Infrastructure

Infrastructure (e.g., highways, ports, bridges, power lines, airports, and information technology) is critical to economic coordination and activity. Some infrastructure is private and some is public. In the past several decades, the amount of government investment in Canadian infrastructure has fallen. Some economists argue that improvements in infrastructure could lead to higher productivity. Others argue that the causality runs in the other direction, that higher productivity leads to greater infrastructure. In addition, a special-interest problem concerns favoured jurisdictions with political clout that end up as the recipients of improved infrastructure—which may not be an efficient solution. Most would agree, however, that poor infrastructure is a major deterrent to economic growth.

The Importance of Research and Development

Some scholars believe that the importance of research and development is understated. **Research and development (R&D)** are activities that are undertaken to create new products and processes that will lead to technological progress. The concept of R&D is broad indeed—it can include new products, management improvements, production innovations, or simply learning-by-doing. However, it is clear that investing in R&D and rewarding innovators with patents have paid big dividends in the past 50 to 60 years. Some would argue that even larger rewards for research and development would spur even more rapid economic growth. Some types of scientific research may have far-reaching benefits that cannot be captured by a private firm. Such a case presents a compelling argument for government support of basic research. GPS satellite systems in cars, for example, were originally designed for military purposes.

In addition, an important link exists between research and development and capital investment. As already noted, when capital depreciates over time, it is replaced with new equipment that embodies the latest technology. Consequently, R&D may work hand in hand with investment to improve growth and productivity. Lastly, there is the benefit of R&D to foreign countries to consider as they import goods and services from technologically advanced countries. Adoption or adaptation of some of these advances might make their firms more efficient.

research and development (R&D)
activities undertaken to create new products and processes that will lead to technological progress

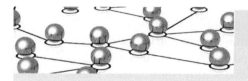

Business *CONNECTION*

GROWING IN A SLOW ECONOMY

Should individual businesses care about the country's growth? Whether oriented as business-to-consumer (B2C) or business-to-business (B2B), a firm will want to be aware when GDP numbers are reported because the figures show where and what sectors of the economy are performing, as well as the aggregate totals. While GDP looks at longer-trend numbers, businesses plan in shorter terms, so they need to know where they are operating in the business cycle. Smart businesses conserve and protect capital during periods of slow growth and recessions, and look for opportunities to expand or pay down debt during periods of higher growth.

In simple terms, what growth in the economy means for business is expansion—the "pie" is getting bigger. In growth periods, firms can increase their revenues by selling more product if the demand is there. Individual demand grows on a macro scale if more people are added to the economy or if incomes rise—which allows people to buy more products. Businesses that grow during these times benefit in the short term, but may find themselves challenged when there's a change in demographics or a slowdown in the economy. Many Western economies aren't growing at historical rates because of demographic changes in which older populations are retiring and buying less and younger citizens are not replacing the deficiencies. Also, businesses may find demand falling because of the way periods of low or declining growth affect individual

incomes. When the pie isn't growing, businesses have to deal with challenges to their productivity so that they can survive.

Productivity is a measure of the value of outputs relative to inputs. A firm can increase productivity in one of two ways: First, it can reduce its costs by increasing the number of outputs at the same or lower cost. (This is often done through automation—by replacing higher-cost labour inputs with lower-cost mechanical or automated processes.) Second, the firm can increase the value of its outputs relative to its inputs—it can increase consumer surplus by raising the perceived value of the good rather than by lowering the actual selling price. (This is achieved through investment in R&D and entrepreneurship, which drives innovation and the development and creation of new goods and services. New and innovative goods introduced to the market have higher perceived value.)

Businesses must actively adapt to the current economic climate, which includes periods of slower growth, but eventually the business cycle will change and the economy will start to grow. Once this happens, firms that have improved their productivity will enjoy higher rates of returns than those that just tried to weather the storm. Not only will the improved firms be able to capture greater market share with new and competitive products, but with the rise in revenues, they should be in a position to pay down any accumulated debt they took on during the slower-growth periods. As economic

(continued)

conditions improve, progressive firms also accumulate capital and prepare for the next downturn, where they can again invest in productivity improvements and stay well ahead of their competition.

1. Credible data suggest that modern developed economies will likely not see annual growth rates at 3 to 4 percent per year for a long time. What can business managers do from both the demand-side and the supply-side to survive (or maybe thrive) if this situation occurs?

2. As a business owner, you have the choice between adding workers to your organization or mechanizing your production line. Which would you choose and why?

3. Given the situation in question 2, do you think your decision is sustainable over the long term? Why or why not? If it's not sustainable, what could you do to make your business sustainable? (Think about a particular product or service your company currently produces.)

The Importance of Property Rights

Economic growth rates tend to be higher in countries where the government enforces property rights. Property rights give owners the legal right to keep or sell their property—land, labour, or capital. In addition, intellectual property (IP) rights are the legal rights that result from intellectual activity in the industrial, scientific, literary, and artistic fields. IP rights protection can take many forms; patents, copyrights, and trademarks are some examples. Without property and IP rights, life would be a huge free-for-all, where people could take whatever they wanted; in this scenario, protection for private property, such as alarm systems and private security services, would have to be purchased and intellectual property would be fair game for anyone. Economists call the government's ability to protect private property and IP rights and to enforce contracts the *rule of law*.

In most developed countries, property and IP rights are effectively protected by the government. However, in developing countries, this is not usually the case, and if the government is not enforcing these rights, the private sector must respond in costly ways that stifle economic growth. For example, an unreliable judiciary system means that entrepreneurs are often forced to rely on informal agreements that are difficult to enforce. As a result, they may have to pay bribes to get things done, and even then, they may not get the promised services. Individuals will have to buy private security or pay organized crime for protection against crime and corruption. In addition, landowners and business owners might be fearful of coups or takeovers from a new government, which might confiscate their property altogether. In short, if government is not adequately protecting property and IP rights, the incentive to invest will be hindered, and political instability, corruption, and lower rates of economic growth will be likely.

Free trade and a stable monetary environment are important to economic growth, but governance is important too. The government has to protect private property and individual rights and enforce contracts, otherwise globalization can lead to corruption and violence. Russians have high levels of education, but the failure of the legal system has led to a dismal economic performance.

Cayuwe Kulzer/iStockphoto.com

The Importance of Free Trade

Allowing free trade can also lead to greater output because of the principle of comparative advantage. Essentially, the principle of comparative advantage suggests that if two nations or individuals with different resource endowments and production capabilities specialize in producing a smaller number of goods and services and engage in trade, both parties will benefit. Total output and consumption will rise. This will be discussed in greater detail in Chapter 22. However, it is important to note that for a country like Canada, which is a significantly open economy that trades considerably with the rest of the world, international trade has played a central role in its economic growth over the last half-century.

The Importance of Education

Education, an investment in human capital, may be just as important as improvements in physical capital. At any given time, an individual has a choice between current work and investment activities like education that can increase future earning power. People accept reductions in current income to devote current effort to education and training. In turn, a certain return on the investment is expected, because in later years they will earn a higher wage rate (the amount of the increase depending on the nature of the education and training as well as individual natural ability). For example, in Canada, a person with a college or university degree can be expected to earn almost twice as much per year as a high-school graduate.

Better education is a relatively inexpensive method to enrich the lives of those in poorer countries. Education allows these countries to produce more advanced goods and services and enjoy the wealth created from trading in the global economy. Taiwan, India, and Korea are now all part of the high-tech global economy, but most of Africa, with the lowest levels of education, has been left behind.

One argument for government subsidizing education is that this investment can increase the skill level of the population and raise the standard of living. However, even if the individual does not benefit financially from increased education, society may benefit socially and in other respects from having its members highly educated. For example, more education may lead to lower crime rates, new ideas that may benefit the society at large, and more informed voters.

With economic growth, illiteracy rates fall and formal education grows. Improvements in literacy stimulate economic growth by reducing barriers to the flow of information; when information costs are high, ignorance often results in many resources flowing to or remaining in uses that are rather unproductive. Moreover, education imparts skills that are directly useful in raising labour productivity, whether it is mathematics taught to a salesclerk, engineering techniques taught to a college or university graduate, or just good ideas that facilitate production and design.

Many economists believe that the tremendous growth in East Asia (South Korea, Taiwan, Hong Kong, and Singapore) in the last half of the twentieth century was a result of good basic education for many of the countries' citizens. This reason was one of many factors that contributed to growth, including high rates of saving and a large increase in labour force participation.

However, in developing poor countries, the higher opportunity costs of education present an obstacle. Children in developing countries are an important part of the labour force starting at a young age. But children who are attending school cannot help in the field—planting, harvesting, fence building, and many other tasks that are so important in the rural areas of developing countries. A child's labour contribution to the family is far less important in a developed country. Thus, the higher opportunity cost of an education in developing countries is one of the reasons that school enrollments are lower.

Education may also be a consequence of economic growth, because as incomes rise, people's tendency to consume education increases. People increasingly look to education for more than the acquisition of immediately applicable skills. Education becomes a consumption good as well as a means of investing in human capital.

There are also a number of factors that can lead to slower economic growth. Countries that fail to enforce the rule of law, experience wars and revolutions, have poor education and health systems and low rates of saving and investment are not likely to grow very rapidly.

CAN RATES OF ECONOMIC GROWTH BETWEEN DIFFERENT ECONOMIES CONVERGE?

Many economists believe that, holding other things equal, countries with lower real GDP per capita will grow faster than countries with higher real GDP per capita. However, other things, including infrastructure, the extent to which the rule of law is followed, and the level of education are not equal. Adjusting for such additional variables, there is a tendency for poorer countries to grow faster. This has certainly been true of South Korea, Taiwan, and Singapore, which have invested in technology and human resources, but many poor countries of Africa and Latin America continue to be poor. So, there is no guarantee that being poorer leads to greater economic growth.

What are some of the factors that impact the ability of developing nations to achieve economic growth? First, they can adopt existing technology from developed countries. Second, developed economies may be subject to diminishing marginal returns to capital—a concept we discussed earlier in the chapter. Third, population growth is higher in developing counties, leading to lower levels of per capita consumption for a given level of economic output. For example, in Western Europe and Canada, population growth rates are currently roughly 1 percent per year, while in some of the poorer African countries, they can approach 3 percent per year or more. Finally, while technology is portable, the ability to use that technology is not. With low literacy rates and educational attainment, as in sub-Saharan African nations, countries can lack the human capital to adopt and use the new technology.

In summary then, the issue of economic growth in the developing world is both complex and conflicting—its difficulty evidenced by the sheer number of countries that struggle with finding a winning recipe for success.

SECTION CHECK

- Generally speaking, greater economic growth is fostered by those policies and institutional structures that promote higher levels of saving, more research and development, better protection of private property rights, freer trade, and more education.
- While certain factors such as the ability to adopt existing technology would seem to allow developing nations to grow faster than developed nations, population growth and low literacy rates tend to have the opposite effect. Therefore, there seems to be no clear indication that rates of economic growth between economies will converge.

section 15.4

Population and Economic Growth

- What is the effect of population growth on per capita economic growth?
- What is the Malthusian prediction?

WHAT IS THE EFFECT OF POPULATION GROWTH ON PER CAPITA ECONOMIC GROWTH?

At the beginning of the English Industrial Revolution (c. 1750), the world's population was perhaps 700 million. It took 150 years (to 1900) for that population to slightly more than double to 1.6 billion. Just 64 years later (in 1964), it had doubled again to 3.2 billion.

After another 41 years (in 2005), the population doubled yet again to more than 6.4 billion. At the end of October 2011, the United Nations Population Fund announced that the world's population had reached 7 billion. According to United Nations estimates, world population should reach approximately 9 billion by 2050 and then level off. Most of this population growth will occur in developing countries—industrialized countries will see very little growth in population. Economic development occurred amidst all of the past growth in population, but what role does population play in economic growth?

The effect of population growth on per capita economic growth is far from obvious. If population was to expand faster than output, per capita output would fall; population growth would inhibit growth. With a larger population, however, comes a larger labour force. Also, economies of large-scale production may exist in some forms of production, so larger markets associated with greater populations lead to more efficient-sized production units.

The general feeling, however, is that in many of the developing countries today, rapid population growth threatens the possibility of attaining sustained economic growth. These countries are predominantly agricultural with modest natural resources, especially land. The land–labour ratio is low. Why is population growth a threat in these countries? One answer was provided nearly two centuries ago by an English economist, the Reverend Thomas Malthus.

WHAT IS THE MALTHUSIAN PREDICTION?

Malthus formulated a theoretical model that predicted that per capita economic growth would eventually become negative and that wages would ultimately reach equilibrium at a subsistence level, or just large enough to provide enough income to stay alive. To create this model, Malthus made three assumptions: (1) the economy was agricultural, with goods produced by two inputs, land and labour; (2) the supply of land was fixed; and (3) human sexual desires worked to increase population.

The Law of Diminishing Returns

As population increases, the number of workers increases, and with greater labour inputs available, output also goes up. At some point, however, output will increase by diminishing amounts because of the law of diminishing returns, which states that if you add variable amounts of one input (in this case, labour) to fixed quantities of another input (in this case, land), output will rise but by diminishing amounts (because as the land–labour ratio falls, less land is available per worker). For example, a rapid growth in the labour force might make it more difficult to equip each worker with sufficient capital, and lower amounts of capital per worker lead to lower productivity and a lower real GDP per capita. In short, the increase in the one factor of production, labour, might cause the other factors of production to be spread too thinly.

Avoiding Malthus's Prediction

Fortunately, Malthus's theory proved spectacularly wrong for much of the world. Although the law of diminishing returns is a valid concept, Malthus's other assumptions were unrealistic. The quantity or quality of tillable land is not completely fixed. Irrigation, fertilizer, and conservation techniques effectively increase arable land. More important, Malthus implicitly neglected the potential for technological advances and ignored the real possibility that improved technology, often embodied in capital, could overcome the impact of the law of diminishing returns. Further, the Malthusian assumption that sexual desire would necessarily lead to population increase is not accurate. True, sexual desire will always be with us, but the number of births can be reduced by birth control techniques.

Economic Growth and Fertility

Economists have also found that as countries become richer, family sizes tend to become smaller. This has been the case in Canada, Western Europe, and the United States. As a nation becomes richer, families have access to better medical care and do not require as many children to provide for them as they age. Another reason that birth rates fall as nations become richer is that, as women achieve better access to education and jobs, their opportunity costs of raising children rise and fertility rates fall. So one possible policy approach for developing countries struggling with an exploding population is to provide more equal treatment for women.

DEBATE

SHOULD CANADA STOP FINANCING ITS BRAIN DRAIN?

For:

One of the benefits of living in Canada is our access to lower-cost, high-quality education. But many students, especially those in the professions (scientists, engineers, doctors/nurses, etc.) move to the United States in search of higher wages after they graduate. The loss of these individuals and what they contribute to the Canadian economy is known as the "brain drain" and has been a particular concern to Canadian governments. Part of the social contract that Canadians have with their government and society is that all individuals benefit from social programs during their lives and help pay for those programs by paying taxes. These taxes partly cover the individuals' benefits, but also help fund benefits for future generations. Those who leave for the United States represent a great cost to the Canadian economy for two reasons: (1) the best and brightest—those with higher degrees—tend to leave,* which down the road can affect innovation and research and so have longer-term costs to our productivity and economy, and (2) because those who leave generally have higher (potential) income, there's a major loss of tax revenues. (Those with incomes over $150 000 are seven times more likely to leave than those with less income; those with incomes between $100 000 and $150 000 are five times more likely to leave.**) The remaining population will be expected to pay higher tax rates to replace what is lost. So isn't it obvious that the brain drain produces a net cost to Canadian society and Canada should stop financing it?

Against:

There are sound financial reasons why individuals leave Canada for other opportunities, but there are other reasons why people leave that aren't financially based and so are less likely to have a net cost to the economy. For example, some people leave for health or climate benefits. Those who leave for health reasons are not as big a cost to the Canadian health system if they are not consuming those services in Canada. Others who leave for climate benefits probably have an insignificant cost effect on the Canadian economy. Then there are our free-trade agreements: No matter whether individuals work in the United States or in Canada, North American economies as a whole benefit; exactly where the individuals live in these two countries is immaterial. It's known that for developing countries, a net brain drain can actually have a positive benefit for the country that loses individuals when they develop skills and return home. Canada has benefitted from such migration and should seek ways to encourage individuals to leave and return at a later date. (Can you think of ways to encourage these workers to return to Canada?) It can also be argued that Canadians who leave for the United States raise the awareness of Canadian academic quality and that can have employment benefits for all Canadians, especially those who remain in Canada and want to work for U.S. firms. This could increase Canada's productivity rates. What are some other arguments that can be used to prove that the brain drain does not provide a net loss to the Canadian economy and so doesn't need to stop? Think in terms of short term versus long term and micro versus macro benefits.

*D. D. John Zhao, Knowledge Workers on the Move, *Perspectives*, 2000, Summer, Catalogue No. 75 001 XPE, pp. 32–46.
**S. Uhm, The Brain Drain: The Loss of Canada's Brightest Minds to the United States. *Western Undergraduate Economics Review 2003*, pp. 3–25.

To complicate matters even further, some economists believe that population growth can lead to greater economic growth. In some countries, a larger population may lead to more entrepreneurs, engineers, and scientists who will contribute to even greater economic growth through technological progress. These factors turn Malthus's theory on its head; instead of population being the villain, it could actually turn out to be the hero.

Developing Countries and Malthus's Prediction

Unfortunately, however, the Malthusian assumptions don't vary widely from reality for several developing countries today. Some developing nations of the world are having substantial population increases, with a virtually fixed supply of land, slow capital growth, and few technological advances. For example, in some African nations, the population growth rate is 3 percent per year, whereas food output is growing at only 2 percent per year. In these cases, population growth causes a negative effect on per capita output because the added output derived from having more workers on the land is small.

In fact, some developing countries have tried to reduce the rate of population growth to achieve greater economic growth per capita and higher standards of living. For example, China tried to reduce its population growth rate through laws regulating the number of children a family may have. It is true that in many poor countries, the population growth rate is much higher, nearly 3 percent per year, than in richer countries, about 1 percent per year. High population growth rates may be one explanation for lower standards of living, but many non-Malthusian explanations help explain the recurring poverty that exists in developing countries today, such as political instability, the lack of defined and enforceable property rights, and inadequate investment in human capital.

SECTION CHECK

- Population growth may increase per capita output in resource-rich countries such as Canada, the United States, Australia, and Saudi Arabia, because these countries have more resources for production use by each labourer. Such countries are more likely to be able to take advantage of economies of large-scale production and are also more likely to have rapidly expanding technology.
- The Malthusian prediction was that, due to limited productive resources and rapid population growth, eventually per capita economic growth would become negative.

For Your Review

Section 15.1

1. Answer the following questions.

   a. According to the Rule of 70, how many years would it take a country to double its output at each of the following annual growth rates?

0.5 percent:	_____ years	2.8 percent:	_____ years
1.0 percent:	_____ years	3.5 percent:	_____ years
1.4 percent:	_____ years	7.0 percent:	_____ years
2.0 percent:	_____ years		

b. If a country had $100 billion of real GDP today, what would its real GDP be in 50 years if it grew at an annual growth rate of

1.4 percent?   _____

2.8 percent?   _____

7.0 percent?   _____

2. Explain how choosing between consumer goods and capital goods in the current period can impact the availability of choices between present and future consumption.

3. Answer the following questions about real GDP per capita:

a. If Country A had four times the initial level of real GDP per capita of Country B and it was growing at 1.4 percent a year, while real GDP was growing at 2.8 percent in Country B, how long would it take before the two countries had the same level of real GDP per capita?

b. If two countries had the same initial level of real GDP per capita and Country A grew at 2.8 percent while Country B grew at 3.5 percent, how would their real per capita GDP levels compare over the span of a century?

4. Suppose that two poor countries experience different growth rates over time. Country A's real GDP per capita grows at a rate of 7 percent per year on average, while Country B's real GDP per capita grows at a rate of only 3 percent per annum. Predict how the standard of living will vary between these two countries over time as a result of divergent growth rates.

5. Which of the following best measures economic growth?

a. the change in nominal GDP

b. the change in real GDP

c. the annual percentage change in nominal GDP per capita

d. the annual percentage change in real GDP per capita

6. Which of the following will shift the Canadian production possibilities curve outward?

a. the discovery of new oil reserves

b. increased immigration of scientists and engineers to Canada

c. a nuclear war that destroys both people and structures

d. producing fewer pizzas in order to produce more tractors

e. producing fewer strawberries in order to produce more corn

Section 15.2

7. Would a shift from investment in capital goods to investment in education increase or decrease the growth rate of real GDP per capita?

8. What is the difference between "labour" and "human capital"? How is human capital increased?

9. Which of the following are likely to improve the productivity of labour and thereby lead to economic growth?

a. on-the-job experience

b. college education

c. a decrease in the amount of capital per worker

d. improvements in management of resources

10. How is Hong Kong a dramatic example of why abundant natural resources are not necessary for rapid economic growth?

Sections 15.2 and 15.3

11. Which direction would the following changes alter GDP growth and per capita GDP growth in a country (increase, decrease, or indeterminate), other things being equal?

	Real GDP Growth	Real GDP Growth per Capita
An increase in population	_____	_____
An increase in labour force participation	_____	_____
An increase in population and labour force participation	_____	_____
An increase in current consumption	_____	_____
An increase in technology	_____	_____
An increase in illiteracy	_____	_____
An increase in tax rates	_____	_____
An increase in productivity	_____	_____
An increase in tariffs on imported goods	_____	_____
An earlier retirement age in the country	_____	_____
An increase in technology and a decrease in labour force participation	_____	_____
An earlier retirement age and an increase in the capital stock	_____	_____

Section 15.3

12. What is the implication for an economic system with weak enforcement of patent and copyright laws? Why does weak property right enforcement create an incentive problem?

13. How could permanently lower marginal tax rates increase the capital stock, the level of education, the level of technology, and the amount of developed natural resources over time?

14. Why would you expect an inverse relationship between self-sufficiency and real GDP per capita?

Section 15.4

15. Answer these questions about GDP:

    a. How could real GDP grow, while, over the same period, real GDP per capita falls?

    b. If Country A has a 4 percent annual growth rate of real GDP and a 2 percent annual rate of population growth, while Country B has a 6 percent annual growth rate of real GDP and a 5 percent annual rate of population growth, which country will have a higher growth rate of real GDP per capita?

16. Could a country experience a fall in population and a rise in real GDP at the same time? Could an increase in labour force participation allow that?

17. How did Malthus's prediction on population growth follow from the law of diminishing returns?

chapter
16
Aggregate Demand

The Determinants of Aggregate Demand

- What is aggregate demand?
- What is consumption?
- What is investment?
- What are government purchases?
- What are net exports?

WHAT IS AGGREGATE DEMAND?

Aggregate demand (*AD*) is the total demand for all final goods and services in the economy. It can also be seen as the quantity of real GDP demanded at different price levels. The four major components of aggregate demand are consumption (C), investment (I), government purchases (G), and net exports ($X - M$). Aggregate demand, then, is equal to $C + I + G + (X - M)$.

aggregate demand (*AD*)
the total demand for all final goods and services in the economy

WHAT IS CONSUMPTION?

Consumption (C) is by far the largest component in aggregate demand. Expenditures for consumer goods and services typically absorb almost 60 percent of total economic activity, as measured by GDP. Understanding the determinants of consumption, then, is critical to an understanding of the forces leading to changes in aggregate demand, which in turn, change total output and income.

The Impact of Higher Income on Consumption

The notion that the higher a nation's income, the more it spends on consumer items, has been validated empirically. At the level of individuals, most of us spend more

DEBATE

SHOULD ONTARIO DEVELOP A NEW RETIREMENT PENSION PLAN?

For:

Thoughts of an Ontario Retirement Pension Plan (ORPP) grew out of concern that workers weren't saving enough for their retirements. With no modification of the federal Canada Pension Plan (CPP) in the pipeline, Ontario wanted to develop a parallel plan that other provinces could administer for their citizens, too. Without an increase in CPP deductions, the argument for an ORPP is this: Canada is going to have to increase social payments in some form to ensure people are able to meet their needs, and higher levels of social programs will be needed in the future, which means higher future taxes for those of working age, who wouldn't get many benefits from their money. The argument is that this would transfer the costs of benefits to future generations, which would be unfair. Those who argue for the development of the ORPP suggest that funds generated by the taxpayer belong to the taxpayer and would not be a "tax," but a contribution to an arm's-length board to manage the funds. They argue that the contributions would be a form of savings in which contributions are matched by employers, and just like contributions made to the CPP, could be deducted as an expense on tax returns. Finally, proponents note that there is widespread support for the new plan. Surely Ontario needs to develop a new retirement pension plan. What other points or arguments can you make in this regard?

Against:

Increasing CPP or instituting ORPP deductions can be viewed as essentially short-term taxes, because they reduce resources that can be reinvested or distributed to investors. Further, these marginal tax increases affect the small-business sector the most—the sector that the policy is actually supposed to help. Increasing these "taxes" reduces the wealth of individuals and firms. Increasing or establishing new taxes further affects consumption and investment, and so limits the growth of the economy. Also, the ORPP would be a regional plan that if enacted would provide a barrier to economic freedom, as it may limit where individuals could work if they can't transfer their contributions to other provincial plans, or can't continue to contribute to their accounts if they live outside Ontario. While there is some interest in other provinces adapting or participating in the ORPP, the fact that it would not be available across Canada, as the CPP is, strengthens this counterargument. Many argue that it is up to individuals—not the state or the employer—to look after their own financial future. They point to the many other investment vehicles that are there for individuals to save for their retirement—such as RRSPs, private and public workplace pensions, and tax-free savings accounts—and they say there's nothing that the ORPP could offer that isn't already being offered. Surely it's clear that the ORPP should not be developed. What are other consequences that impact savings, investment, and consumption when a nation's taxes are increased? What are other arguments you can use to defend shelving the ORPP?

money when we have higher incomes. But what matters most to us is not our total income but our after-tax or *disposable income.* Moreover, other factors might explain consumption. Some consumer goods are "lumpy"; that is, the expenditures for these goods must come in big amounts rather than in small dribbles. So, in years in which a consumer buys a new car, takes the family on a European trip, or goes to college or university, consumption may be much greater in relation to income than in years in which the consumer does not buy such high-cost consumer goods or services. Interest rates also affect consumption because they affect savings. At higher real interest rates, people save more and consume less. At lower real interest rates, people save less and consume more.

average propensity to consume (*APC*) *the fraction of total disposable income that households spend on consumption*

The Average and Marginal Propensity to Consume

Households typically spend a large portion of their disposable income and save the rest. The fraction of their total disposable income that households spend on consumption is called the **average propensity to consume (*APC*)**. For example, a household that consumes $450 out of $500 disposable income has an *APC* of 0.9 ($450/$500). However, households tend to behave differently with additional income than with their income as a whole. How much increased consumption results from an increase in income? That depends on the **marginal propensity to consume (*MPC*)**, which is the additional consumption resulting from an additional dollar of disposable income. If consumption goes from $450 to $600 when disposable income goes from $500 to $700, what is the marginal propensity to consume out of disposable income? First, we calculate the change in consumption: $600 − $450 = $150. Next, we calculate the change in income: $700 − $500 = $200. The marginal propensity to consume, then, equals change in consumption divided by change in disposable income. In this example,

marginal propensity to consume (*MPC*) *the additional consumption resulting from an additional dollar of disposable income*

$$MPC = \frac{\text{Change in consumption}}{\text{Change in disposable income}} = \frac{150}{200} = \frac{3}{4} = 0.75$$

For each additional dollar in after-tax income over this range, this household consumes three-fourths of the addition, or 75 cents.

WHAT IS INVESTMENT?

Because investment (*I*) spending (purchases of investment goods) is an important component of aggregate demand, which in turn is a determinant of the level of GDP, changes in investment spending are often responsible for changes in the level of economic activity. If consumption is determined largely by the level of disposable income, what determines the level of investment expenditures? As you may recall, investment expenditure is the most unstable category of GDP; it is sensitive to changes in economic, social, and political variables. In 2012, investment was 20 percent of GDP.

Many factors are important in determining the level of investment. Good business conditions "induce" firms to invest because a healthy growth in demand for products in the future is likely based on current experience. In the next section, we will consider the key variables that influence investment spending.

open economy *a type of model that includes international trade effects*

If firms expect higher sales and profits, they will increase investment spending on capital goods, such as factories, machinery, and equipment.

WHAT ARE GOVERNMENT PURCHASES?

Government purchases (*G*), another component of aggregate demand, are purchases by federal, provincial and territorial, and local governments of new goods and services produced. Government purchases include expenditures on health, education, highways, and police protection. In 2012, government purchases accounted for 25 percent of total spending. Although dramatic shifts in government purchases are less frequent and volatile than shifts in investment spending, they do occasionally occur, most recently in response to the global financial crisis.

WHAT ARE NET EXPORTS?

The interaction of the Canadian economy with the rest of the world is becoming increasingly important. Models that include international trade effects are called **open economy** models.

Remember, exports are Canadian-made goods and services that we sell to foreign customers, like lumber, wheat, and telecommunications equipment; imports are goods and services that we buy from foreign companies, like BMWs, French wine, and Sony TVs. Exports and imports can alter aggregate demand. It makes no difference to Canadian sellers if buyers are in this country or in some other country. A buyer is a buyer, foreign or domestic, so exports (X) must be added to the demand side of our equation. But what about goods and services that are consumed here but not produced by the domestic economy? When Canadian consumers, firms, or the government buy foreign goods and services, there is no direct impact on the total demand for Canadian goods and services, so imports (M) must be subtracted from our equation.

net exports *the difference between the value of exports and the value of imports*

The difference between the value of exports and the value of imports is what we call **net exports** ($X - M$ = Net exports). If exports are greater than imports, we have positive net exports ($X > M$). If imports are greater than exports, net exports are negative ($X < M$).

The impact that net exports have on aggregate demand is similar to the impact that government purchases have on aggregate demand. Suppose that Canada has no trade surplus and no trade deficit—zero net exports. Now say that foreign consumers start buying more Canadian goods and services whereas Canadian consumers continue to buy imports at roughly the same rate. This will lead to *positive net exports* ($X > M$) and result in greater demand for Canadian goods and services, a higher level of aggregate demand. From a policy standpoint, this might explain why countries that are currently in a recession might like to run a trade surplus by increasing exports.

Of course, it is also possible that a country could run a trade deficit. Again let us assume that the economy was initially in a position with zero net exports. A trade deficit, or *negative net exports* ($X < M$), *ceteris paribus,* would lower Canadian aggregate demand.

SECTION CHECK

- Aggregate demand is the sum of the demand for all final goods and services in the economy. It can also be seen as the quantity of real GDP demanded at different price levels.
- Consumption—the purchases of consumer goods and services by households—is the largest component of aggregate demand. Empirical evidence suggests that consumption increases directly with any increase in income.
- Investment spending refers to the purchases of investment goods such as machinery and equipment. Changes in investment spending are often responsible for changes in the level of economic activity.
- Government purchases are made up of federal, provincial/territorial, and local purchases of goods and services.
- Net exports are the difference between the value of exports and the value of imports. Trade deficits lower aggregate demand, other things equal; trade surpluses increase aggregate demand, other things equal.

The Investment and Saving Market

- What is the investment demand curve?
- What is the saving supply curve?
- How is equilibrium determined in the investment and saving market?
- What effect do budget surpluses and budget deficits have on the investment and saving market?

Exhibit 1 shows the breakdown of real GDP into its individual components since 2000. While each category of expenditure exhibits some variability from one year to the next, the volatility of investment spending is clearly evident. It is this significant variability along with the sizable contribution of investment spending to total GDP that necessitates we take a closer look at the investment and saving market.

WHAT IS THE INVESTMENT DEMAND CURVE?

If we put the investment demand for the whole economy and national savings together, we can establish the real interest rate in the saving and investment market. We begin by revisiting investment, and then follow with the introduction of the saving supply curve and equilibrium.

Exhibit 2 shows the investment demand curve for all the firms in the whole economy. The investment demand (*ID*) curve is downward sloping, reflecting the fact that investment spending varies inversely with the real interest rate—the amount

section 16.2
Exhibit 1   **Individual Components of Real GDP**

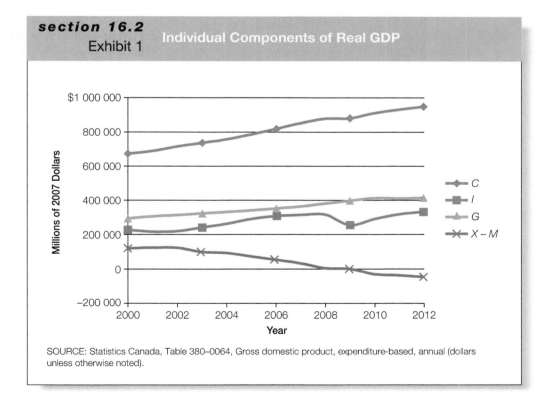

SOURCE: Statistics Canada, Table 380–0064, Gross domestic product, expenditure-based, annual (dollars unless otherwise noted).

section 16.2   The Investment Demand
Exhibit 2   Curve

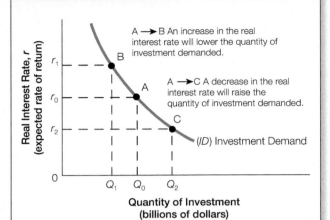

There is an inverse relationship between the
real interest rate and the quantity of investment
demanded. As the real interest rate rises, the
quantity of investment demanded falls, and as the
real interest rate falls, the quantity of investment
demanded rises.

section 16.2   Shifts in the Investment
Exhibit 3   Demand Curve

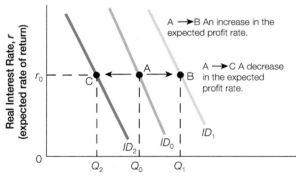

Investment demand depends on the expected rates
of profit. For example, a higher expected profit
rate will cause an increase in investment demand,
shifting the *ID* curve to the right from point A to
point B. A lower expected profit rate will cause a
decrease in investment demand, shifting the *ID*
curve to the left from point A to point C. Any change
in technology, inventories, expectations, and
business taxes can cause the investment demand
curve to shift.

borrowers pay for their loans. At higher real interest rates, firms will pursue only those few investment activities with even higher expected rates of return, causing the quantity of investment demand to fall—a movement from point A to point B in Exhibit 2. As the real interest rate falls, additional projects with lower expected rates of return become profitable for firms, and the quantity of investment demanded rises—a movement from point A to point C in Exhibit 2. In other words, the investment demand curve shows the dollar amount of investment forthcoming at different real interest rates. Because lower interest rates stimulate the quantity of investment demanded, governments often try to combat recessions by lowering interest rates.

Shifting the Investment Demand Curve

Several other determinants will shift the investment demand curve. If firms expect higher rates of return on their investments, for a given interest rate, the *ID* curve will shift to the right, from point A to point B, as seen in Exhibit 3. If firms expect lower rates of return on their investments, for a given interest rate, the *ID* curve will shift to the left, from point A to point C, also seen in Exhibit 3. Possible investment demand curve shifters include changes in technology, inventories, expectations, and business taxes.

Technology   Product and process innovation can cause the *ID* curve to shift rightward. For example, the development of new machines that can improve the quality and the quantity of products or lower the costs of production will increase the rate of return on investment, independent of the interest rate. The same is true for new products like hand-held computers, the Internet, genetic applications in medicine, or HDTV. Imagine how many different firms increased their investment demand during the computer revolution.

Inventories   When inventories are high and goods are stockpiled in warehouses all over the country, there is a lower expected rate of return on new investment—*ID* shifts to the left. Firms with excess inventories of finished goods have very little incentive to invest in new capital. Alternatively, if inventories are depleted below the levels desired by firms, the expected rate of return on new investment increases, as firms look to replenish their shelves to meet the growing demand—*ID* shifts to the right.

Expectations   If sales and profit rates are expected to be higher in the future, firms will invest more in plant and equipment now, causing the *ID* curve to shift to the right—more investment will be desired at a given interest rate. If lower sales and profits are forecast, the *ID* curve shifts to the left—fewer investments will be desired at a given interest rate.

Business Taxes　If business taxes are lowered—such as with an investment tax credit—potential after-tax profits on investment projects will increase and shift the *ID* curve to the right. Higher business taxes will lead to lower potential after-tax profits on investment projects and shift the *ID* curve to the left.

WHAT IS THE SAVING SUPPLY CURVE?

There are two types of saving—private and public. **Private saving** is the amount of income that households have left over after consumption and taxes. So private savings (S_{private}) is equal to the amount of total income (GDP) that remains after people have paid for consumption (C) and taxes (T):

$$S_{\text{private}} = \text{GDP} - C - T$$

private saving
the amount of income that households have left over after consumption and taxes

Public saving is the amount of income the government has left over after paying for its spending. Therefore, public saving (S_{public}) is equal to the amount of tax revenues (T) that the government has left over after paying for government purchases (G):

$$S_{\text{public}} = T - G$$

public saving
the amount of income that the government has left over after paying for its spending

National saving in an economy is the sum of both private and public saving:

$$S = (\text{GDP} - C - T) + (T - G)$$

national saving
the sum of both private and public saving

Most people are familiar with the idea that households and firms can save but are less familiar with the idea that the government can also save. If the government collects more in taxes than it spends ($T > G$), it runs a surplus and public saving is positive. If the government spends more than it collects in taxes ($G < T$), it runs a deficit and public saving is negative. In the next section, we use the tools of supply and demand to examine how budget surpluses and budget deficits affect the real interest rate, national saving, and investment.

The supply curve of savings, as seen in Exhibit 4, is upward sloping, indicating a positive relationship between the real interest rate and the quantity of saving supplied. At a higher real interest rate, a greater quantity of savings is supplied—the movement from point A to point B in Exhibit 4. At a lower real interest rate, a lower quantity of saving is supplied—the movement from point A to point C in Exhibit 4. Think of the interest rate as the reward for saving and supplying funds to financial markets.

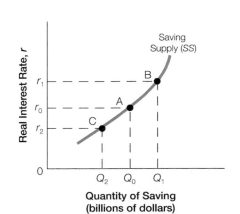

There is a positive relationship between the real interest rate and the quantity of saving supplied. At a higher real interest rate, there is a greater quantity of saving. At a lower real interest rate, there is a lower quantity of saving.

Shifting the Saving Supply Curve

As with the investment demand curve, there are noninterest determinants of the saving supply curve. Two such saving supply curve shifters are disposable (after-tax) income and future expected earnings.

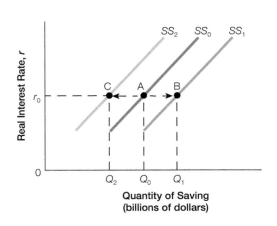

An increase in disposable income or lower expected future earnings shifts the saving supply curve to the right, from point A to point B. A decrease in disposable income and higher expected future earnings will shift the saving supply curve to the left, from point A to point C.

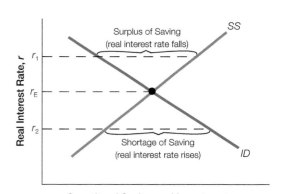

Desired investment equals desired national saving at the intersection of the investment demand curve and the saving supply curve, the equilibrium in the saving and investment market. The intersection of these two curves shows the real equilibrium interest rate. If the real interest rate, r_1, is above the equilibrium real interest rate, r_E, a surplus of savings occurs. If the real interest rate, r_2, is below the equilibrium real interest rate, r_E, a shortage of saving occurs.

Disposable Income   If taxes are lowered—allowing disposable income to increase—the supply of saving would shift to the right, from point A to point B in Exhibit 5—more saving would occur at any given interest rate. If taxes increased, causing disposable income to decline, there would be less saving at any given interest rate and the supply of saving would shift to the left, from point A to point C in Exhibit 5.

Earnings Expectation   If you expected lower future earnings, you would tend to save more now at any given interest rate—shifting the saving supply curve to the right, from point A to point B. If you expected higher future earnings, you would tend to consume more and save less now, knowing that more income is right around the corner—shifting the saving supply curve to the left, from point A to point C in Exhibit 5.

HOW IS EQUILIBRIUM DETERMINED IN THE INVESTMENT AND SAVING MARKET?

In equilibrium, desired investment equals desired national saving at the intersection of the investment demand curve and the saving supply curve. The real equilibrium interest rate is shown by the intersection of these two curves, as seen in Exhibit 6. If the real interest rate, r_1, is above the equilibrium real interest rate, r_E, forces within the economy would tend to restore the equilibrium. At a higher-than-real equilibrium interest rate, the quantity of savings supplied would be greater than the quantity of investment demanded—there would be a surplus of savings at this real interest rate. As savers (lenders) compete against each other to attract investment demanders (borrowers), the real interest rate falls. Alternatively if the real interest rate, r_2, is below the equilibrium real interest rate, r_E, the quantity of investment demanded is greater than the quantity of saving supplied at that interest rate—a shortage of saving occurs. As investment demanders (borrowers) compete against each other for the available saving, the real interest rate is bid up to r_E.

WHAT EFFECT DO BUDGET SURPLUSES AND BUDGET DEFICITS HAVE ON THE INVESTMENT AND SAVING MARKET?

First, let's see how a budget surplus affects the real interest rate and the amount of saving and investment. In Exhibit 7, suppose that the government has a balanced budget, the saving supply curve is SS_0, and the investment demand curve is ID_0, resulting in an equilibrium real interest rate equal to r_0 and an equilibrium quantity of saving and

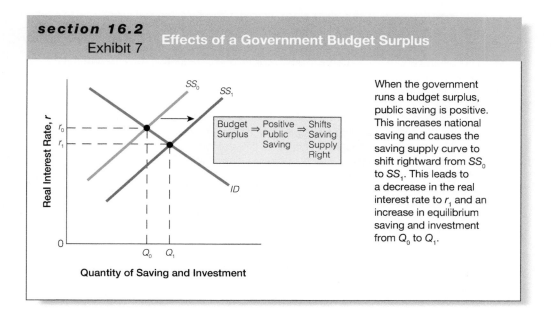

section 16.2
Exhibit 7   **Effects of a Government Budget Surplus**

When the government runs a budget surplus, public saving is positive. This increases national saving and causes the saving supply curve to shift rightward from SS_0 to SS_1. This leads to a decrease in the real interest rate to r_1 and an increase in equilibrium saving and investment from Q_0 to Q_1.

investment equal to Q_0. If the government now runs a budget surplus—the government receives more in tax revenues than it spends—there is an increase in public saving, assuming that private saving is unchanged. Because national saving is the sum of private saving and public saving, national saving increases, shifting the saving supply curve from SS_0 to SS_1.

What impact does this budget surplus (government saving) have on the real interest rate, saving, and investment? The increase in the saving supply from SS_0 to SS_1 leads to a decrease in the real interest rate to r_1 and an increase in equilibrium saving and investment from Q_0 to Q_1, as shown in Exhibit 7. The budget surplus leads to an increase in the saving supply, a lower real interest rate, and a larger amount of saving and investment. This increase in capital formation will tend to increase long-term economic growth.

When the government spends more than it receives in tax revenues, it experiences a budget deficit; the government is actually **dissaving**—consuming more than total available income. This negative saving or borrowing will cause national saving to decrease. That is, the budget deficit reduces the national supply of saving, shifting the saving supply curve leftward from SS_0 to SS_1 in Exhibit 8. At the new equilibrium, there is a higher real interest rate and a lower amount of saving and investment.

When the real interest rate rises because of the government budget deficit, private investment decreases. Economists call this the *crowding-out effect,* a topic we will expand on in Chapter 18, "Fiscal Policy." In sum, when the government runs a budget deficit, it reduces national saving, which leads to a higher real interest rate and lower investment. Because investment is critical for capital formation, long-term economic growth is reduced by budget deficits.

dissaving *consuming more than total available income*

section 16.2
Exhibit 8   **Effects of a Government Budget Deficit**

When the government runs a budget deficit, public saving is negative. This lowers the supply of national saving, shifting the saving supply curve leftward from SS_0 to SS_1. At the new equilibrium, there is a higher real interest rate and a lower amount of saving and investment.

SECTION CHECK

■ The investment demand curve is downward sloping, reflecting the fact that the quantity of investment demanded varies inversely with the real interest rate. Technology, inventories, expectations, and business taxes can shift the investment demand curve at a given real interest rate.

■ The supply of national saving is composed of both private saving and public saving. The supply curve of saving is upward sloping, reflecting the fact that the quantity of savings is positively related to the real interest rate. Two noninterest determinants of the saving supply curve are disposable (after-tax) income and expected future earnings.

■ In equilibrium, desired investment equals desired national saving at the intersection of the investment demand curve and the saving supply curve. A surplus of saving will occur at real interest rates above equilibrium and shortages of saving will occur at real interest rates below equilibrium.

■ Budget surpluses lead to an increase in national saving, a lowering of the real interest rate, and an increase in the quantity of saving and investment. Budget deficits reduce national saving, increase the real interest rate, and lower the quantity of saving and investment.

section 16.3

The Aggregate Demand Curve

■ How is the quantity of real GDP demanded affected by the price level?
■ Why is the aggregate demand curve negatively sloped?

The aggregate demand curve reflects the total amount of real goods and services that all groups together want to purchase in a given time period. In other words, it indicates the quantities of real gross domestic product (RGDP) demanded at different price levels. Note that this is different from the demand curve for a particular good presented in Chapter 3, which looked at the relationship between the relative price of a good and the quantity demanded. Because we are dealing with the economy as a whole, we need an explanation for why the aggregate demand curve is downward sloping and why the short-run aggregate supply curve is upward sloping.

HOW IS THE QUANTITY OF REAL GDP DEMANDED AFFECTED BY THE PRICE LEVEL?

aggregate demand curve
a graphical representation that shows the inverse relationship between the price level and RGDP demanded

The **aggregate demand curve** is a graphical representation that shows the inverse (or opposite) relationship between the price level and real gross domestic product demanded. Exhibit 1 illustrates this relationship, where the quantity of RGDP demanded is measured on the horizontal axis and the overall price level is measured on the vertical axis. As we move from point A to point B on the aggregate demand curve, we see that an increase in the price level causes RGDP demanded to fall. Conversely, if there is a reduction in the price level, a movement from point B to point A, quantity demanded of RGDP increases. Why do purchasers in the economy demand less real output when the price level rises, and more real output when the price level falls?

WHY IS THE AGGREGATE DEMAND CURVE NEGATIVELY SLOPED?

Three complementary explanations exist for the negative slope of the aggregate demand curve: the real wealth effect, the interest rate effect, and the open economy effect.

The Real Wealth Effect: Changes in Consumer Spending

If you had $1000 in cash stashed under your bed while the economy suffered a serious bout of inflation, the purchasing power of your cash would be eroded by the extent of the inflation. That is, an increase in the price level reduces real wealth and would consequently decrease your planned purchases of goods and services, lowering the quantity of RGDP demanded.

In the event that the price level falls, the reverse would hold true. A falling price level would increase the real value of your cash assets, increasing your purchasing power and increasing RGDP. The connection can be summarized as follows:

$\uparrow$Price level $\Rightarrow$ $\downarrow$Real wealth $\Rightarrow$ $\downarrow$Purchasing power $\Rightarrow$ $\downarrow$RGDP demanded

and

$\downarrow$Price level $\Rightarrow$ $\uparrow$Real wealth $\Rightarrow$ $\uparrow$Purchasing power $\Rightarrow$ $\uparrow$RGDP demanded

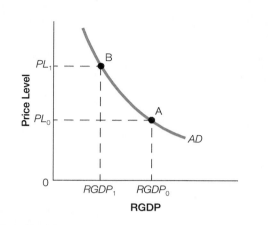

section 16.3   **The Aggregate Demand**
Exhibit 1   **Curve**

The aggregate demand curve slopes downward, reflecting an inverse relationship between the overall price level and the quantity of real GDP demanded. When the price level increases, the quantity of RGDP demanded decreases; when the price level decreases, the quantity of RGDP demanded increases.

The Interest Rate Effect: A Change in Investment

If the price level falls, households and firms will need to hold less money to conduct their day-to-day activities. Firms will need to hold less money for such inputs as wages and taxes; households will need to hold less money for such purchases as food, rent, and clothing. At a lower price level, households and firms will shift their "excess" money into interest-earning assets such as bonds or savings accounts. This will increase the supply of funds to the loanable funds market, leading to lower interest rates. As interest rates fall, households and firms will borrow more and buy more goods and services, so the quantity of RGDP demanded will increase.

If the price level rises, households and firms will need to hold more money to buy goods and services and conduct their daily activities. Households and firms will need to borrow money, and this increased demand for loanable funds will result in higher interest rates. At higher interest rates, consumers may give up plans to buy new cars or houses, and firms may delay investments in plant and equipment. We can summarize this process as follows:

$\uparrow$Price level $\Rightarrow$ $\uparrow$Interest rate $\Rightarrow$ $\downarrow$Investment $\Rightarrow$ $\downarrow$RGDP demanded

and

$\downarrow$Price level $\Rightarrow$ $\downarrow$Interest rate $\Rightarrow$ $\uparrow$Investment $\Rightarrow$ $\uparrow$RGDP demanded

The Open Economy Effect: Changes in Net Exports

Many goods and services are bought and sold in global markets. If the price level in Canada rises relative to the price level in other countries, Canadian exports will become relatively more expensive and foreign imports will become relatively less expensive. As a result, some Canadian consumers will shift from buying domestic goods to buying foreign goods (imports) and some foreign consumers will stop buying Canadian goods. Canadian exports will fall and Canadian imports will rise. This means that net exports will fall, reducing the amount of RGDP purchased in Canada. A lower price level makes Canadian exports less expensive and foreign imports more expensive. So Canadian consumers will buy more domestic goods, and foreign consumers will buy more Canadian goods. This will increase net exports, increasing the amount of RGDP purchased in Canada. This relationship can be shown as follows:

$$\uparrow \text{Price level} \Rightarrow \downarrow \text{Demand for domestic goods} \Rightarrow \downarrow \text{RGDP demanded}$$

and

$$\downarrow \text{Price level} \Rightarrow \uparrow \text{Demand for domestic goods} \Rightarrow \uparrow \text{RGDP demanded}$$

SECTION CHECK

■ An aggregate demand curve shows the inverse relationship between the amounts of real goods and services (RGDP) that are demanded at each possible price level.

■ The aggregate demand curve is downward sloping because of the real wealth effect, the interest rate effect, and the open economy effect.

section
16.4 Shifts in the Aggregate Demand Curve

■ What variables cause the aggregate demand curve to shift?
■ Can we review the determinants that change aggregate demand?

As with the supply and demand curves in microeconomics (see Chapter 3), there can be both shifts in and movements along the aggregate demand curve. In the previous section, we discussed three factors—the real wealth effect, the interest rate effect, and the open economy effect—that result in the downward slope of the aggregate demand curve. Each of these factors, then, generates a movement *along* the aggregate demand curve because the general price level changed. In this section, we will discuss some of the many factors that can cause the aggregate demand curve to shift to the right or left.

WHAT VARIABLES CAUSE THE AGGREGATE DEMAND CURVE TO SHIFT?

The whole aggregate demand curve can shift to the right or left, as seen in Exhibit 1. Put simply, if some nonprice-level determinant causes total spending to increase, then the aggregate demand curve will shift to the right. If a nonprice-level determinant causes the level of total spending to decline, then the aggregate demand curve will shift to the left. More specifically, an increase in any component of GDP (C, I, G, or $X - M$) can cause the aggregate demand curve to shift rightward. Conversely, decreases in C, I, G, or ($X - M$) will shift aggregate demand leftward. Now let's look at some specific factors that could cause the aggregate demand curve to shift.

Changing Consumption

A whole host of changes could alter consumption (C) patterns. For example, an increase in consumer confidence, an increase in wealth, or a tax cut can each increase consumption and shift the aggregate demand curve to the right. An increase in population will also increase the aggregate demand because more consumers will be spending more money on goods and services. A lower interest rate can also spur consumption spending.

Of course, the aggregate demand curve could shift to the left due to decreases in consumption demand. For example, if consumers sensed that the economy was headed for a recession or if the government imposed a tax increase, this would result in a leftward shift of the aggregate demand curve. Because consuming less is saving more, an increase in saving, *ceteris paribus,* will shift aggregate demand to the left. High levels of accumulated consumer debt may also be a reason that some consumers might put off additional spending.

section 16.4   Shifts in the Aggregate
Exhibit 1   Demand Curve

Price Level / *RGDP*

Left Decrease ← → Right Increase

AD_2 AD_0 AD_1

An increase in aggregate demand shifts the curve to the right (from AD_0 to AD_1). A decrease in aggregate demand shifts the curve to the left (from AD_0 to AD_2).

Changing Investment

Investment (I) is also an important determinant of aggregate demand. Increases in the demand for investment goods occur for a variety of reasons. For example, if business confidence increases or real interest rates fall, business investment will increase and aggregate demand will shift to the right. A reduction in business taxes would also shift the aggregate demand curve to the right because businesses would now retain more of their profits to invest. However, if interest rates or business taxes rise, we would expect to see a leftward shift in aggregate demand.

Business *CONNECTION*

STAYING AHEAD OF CHANGES IN GDP

We know that when the economy is in a broadly based expansionary phase, aggregate demand is increasing. This means that on average, consumers, business, and all levels of government—along with foreign buyers—are probably increasing their demand for Canadian goods and services. In expansionary phases, businesses often experience rises in sales revenues and are encouraged to make capital expenditures to increase operating capacity and output. We also know that business reacts to changes in demand, so usually supply lags behind changes in demand.

Business operators need to understand the nature and business implications of an expansionary phase of the economy if they want to benefit most from the growth. The key is to monitor several leading indicators in such expansions. Expansions often start with the consumer sector, which accounts for 58 percent of economic growth. One positive development or a combination of such developments often signal the coming of such growth—these include lower personal taxes, a rise in consumer confidence, greater stock market wealth, a reduction in interest rates, or/and an

(continued)

increase in transfer payments. When these conditions are present, there is every indication that consumer demand will increase, *ceteris paribus*. Firms that fail to recognize or acknowledge these leading indicators could miss opportunities for increased revenues and profits.

To take advantage of the impending growth in consumer demand for goods and services that these indicators signal, businesses must often expand their capacity by hiring and training workers, getting new capital equipment, or starting new processes. (While businesses expand during this growth stage, it's also an expensive time to do so due to inflationary pressures. Companies that can prepare for expansion during slower growth periods are able to do so at lower costs and conserve precious capital.) Such changes often take the form of projects that require considerable time to plan and implement. Businesses that mainly serve individuals and households must often complete capacity expansion projects before, or coincident with, the predicted growth in consumer spending. Failure to properly time or estimate increases in aggregate demand can result in severe overcapacity, inventory buildups, and higher costs.

Businesses that rely on governments or industry sectors as customers must also watch for certain leading indicators. These include (1) increases in government spending; (2) in the case of investments, the lowering of interest rates or optimistic business forecasts; or (3) proposed lower business taxes. Businesses leaders recognize that government spending should not be leading the economy—rather, the most prudent government spending happens when the economy needs stimulation. It is in this period that firms look for opportunities that government can participate in, and firms are more competitive in their prices in order to win government contracts.

While an expanding economy presents opportunities for increases in revenues, a contracting economy almost always presents the challenge of dealing with high and stubborn fixed operating costs in the face of falling production levels—a situation that could end up posing serious threats to profitability. To avoid such unfavourable developments, firms must closely follow the leading indicators that communicate changes in aggregate demand across all four components of the GDP. Then they may stay ahead of the curve and remain profitable.

1. North American economies rely on consumerism to drive their economies, whereas developing economies such as China rely on exports and the government side. In your opinion, which is the preferred distribution and why?

2. One of the challenges that China's GDP faces is its dependence on exports. Why is this an issue for China and what issues would you as a business manager consider when making decisions?

3. Assume your company is a manufacturer of a durable product, such as appliances, furniture, or automobiles, and interest rates have increased. What impact would the increased rates have on your company and how would you respond?

Changing Government Purchases

Government purchases (G) are also part of total spending and therefore must impact aggregate demand. An increase in government purchases, other things equal, shifts the aggregate demand curve to the right, whereas a reduction shifts aggregate demand to the left.

Changing Net Exports

Global markets are also important in a domestic economy. For example, in 2009, when Canada's major trading partner, the United States, fell into a major recession, Canadian exports of goods and services to the United States fell by nearly 27 percent, causing overall Canadian exports to decline by close to 25 percent. This dramatic reduction in exports was the leading cause of net exports ($X - M$) falling by more than $50 billion in 2009, shifting the aggregate demand curve for Canada to the left. Alternatively, an economic boom in the U.S. economy might lead to an increase in our exports to the United States, causing net exports ($X - M$) to rise and aggregate demand to increase.

Another factor that has an important effect on net exports is the exchange rate. The exchange rate is the price of one unit of a country's currency in terms of another country's currency. For example, if it takes US$0.84 to buy one Canadian dollar (as was the case on October 10, 2008), then the exchange rate is US$0.84 per Canadian dollar. When the Canadian dollar appreciates in value (to, say, US$1.05 per Canadian dollar—as was the case on July 26, 2011), it is more expensive for foreigners to buy Canadian dollars, and therefore more expensive for foreigners to buy Canadian goods and services (which are priced in Canadian dollars). At the same time, it becomes less expensive for

Canadians to buy U.S. dollars, and therefore less expensive for Canadians to buy U.S. goods and services (which are priced in U.S. dollars). As a result, Canadian exports decline and Canadian imports increase. Therefore, an appreciation of the Canadian dollar decreases Canadian net exports and shifts the aggregate demand curve to the left. On the other hand, when the Canadian dollar depreciates in value (to, say, US$0.97 per Canadian dollar—as was the case on March 19, 2013), Canadian net exports increase, and the aggregate demand curve shifts to the right.

CAN WE REVIEW THE DETERMINANTS THAT CHANGE AGGREGATE DEMAND?

Any aggregate demand category that has the ability to change total purchases in the economy will shift the aggregate demand curve. That is, changes in consumption purchases, investment purchases, government purchases, or net export purchases shift the aggregate demand curve. The effects of some of the determinants that cause a change in aggregate demand (shifters) are reviewed in Exhibit 2.

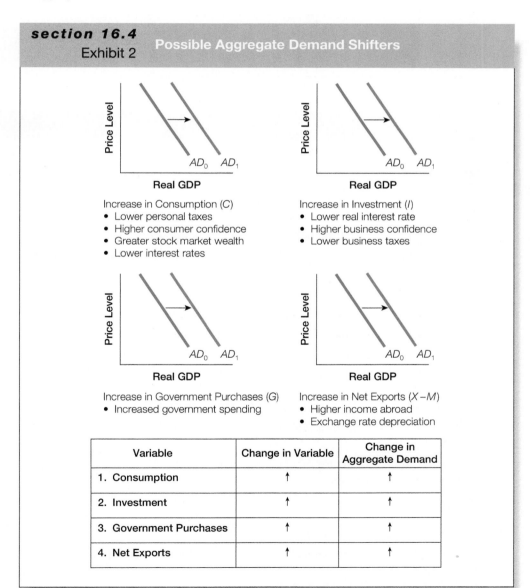

section 16.4
Exhibit 2   **Possible Aggregate Demand Shifters**

Increase in Consumption (C)
• Lower personal taxes
• Higher consumer confidence
• Greater stock market wealth
• Lower interest rates

Increase in Investment (I)
• Lower real interest rate
• Higher business confidence
• Lower business taxes

Increase in Government Purchases (G)
• Increased government spending

Increase in Net Exports (X−M)
• Higher income abroad
• Exchange rate depreciation

Variable	Change in Variable	Change in Aggregate Demand
1. Consumption	↑	↑
2. Investment	↑	↑
3. Government Purchases	↑	↑
4. Net Exports	↑	↑

SECTION CHECK

■ A change in the price level causes a movement along the aggregate demand curve, not a shift in the aggregate demand curve. Aggregate demand is made up of total spending, or $C + I + G + (X - M)$. Any change in these factors will cause the aggregate demand curve to shift.

Variable	Change in Variable	Change in Aggregate Demand
1. Consumption (C)	↑	↑
2. Investment (I)	↑	↑
3. Government purchases (G)	↑	↑
4. Exports (X)	↑	↑
5. Imports (M)	↑	↓
6. Net exports ($X - M$)	↑	↑

For Your Review

Section 16.1

1. Assume that Melanie had $200 000 of disposable income and spent $180 000 on consumption in 2012, and had $300 000 of disposable income and spent $240 000 on consumption in 2013.

    a. What was Melanie's average propensity to consume in 2012?

    b. What was Melanie's average propensity to consume in 2013?

    c. What was Melanie's marginal propensity to consume?

    d. If Melanie's income went up to $400 000 in 2014, how much would she be likely to spend on consumption that year? What would be her average propensity to consume?

    e. If Melanie's income went down to $100 000 in 2014, how much would she be likely to spend on consumption that year? What would be her average propensity to consume?

2. How can the amount of net exports be positive or negative? How do positive net exports and negative net exports impact aggregate demand?

Section 16.2

3. In the saving and investment market,

    a. what happens to the investment demand curve when the real interest rate declines?

    b. what happens to the investment demand curve when firms' inventories are rising above what the firms desire?

   c. what happens to the investment demand curve when technological advances give rise to popular new products?

   d. what happens to the saving supply curve when the real interest rate increases?

   e. what happens to the saving supply curve when disposable income increases?

4.

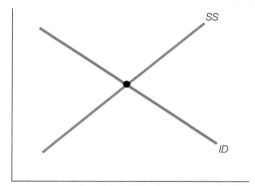

Label the axes for the saving and investment market. Then explain and illustrate what would happen in the saving and investment market if

   a. businesses became more optimistic about future business conditions.

   b. individuals became less optimistic about their future incomes.

   c. business taxes increased.

   d. individuals' disposable incomes increased.

5. What would happen to the saving supply curve if there was both an increase in current disposable income and a decrease in new technologies creating investment opportunities?

6. Other things equal, in which direction will an increasing budget deficit change the equilibrium interest rate, the saving supply curve, the level of saving and investment in the economy, and the likely rate of economic growth, other things equal?

7. Why does GDP − C − G = S in a simple, closed economy?

8. If net taxes rise, what happens to private saving? To public saving?

Section 16.3

9. Fill in the blanks in the following explanations.

   a. The real wealth effect is described by the following: An increase in the price level leads to a(n) _____ in real wealth, which leads to a(n) _____ in purchasing power, which leads to a(n) _____ in RGDP demanded.

   b. The interest rate effect is described by the following: A decrease in the price level leads to a(n) _____ in money demand, which leads to a(n) _____ in the interest rate, which leads to a(n) _____ in investments, which leads to a(n) _____ in RGDP demanded.

   c. The open economy effect is described by the following: An increase in the domestic price level leads to a(n) _____ in the demand for domestic goods, which leads to a(n) _____ in RGDP demanded.

10. Evaluate the following statement: A higher price level decreases the purchasing power of the dollar and reduces RGDP.

11. What is the wealth effect, and how does it imply a downward-sloping aggregate demand curve?

12. What is the interest rate effect, and how does it imply a downward-sloping aggregate demand curve?

13. What is the open economy effect, and how does it imply a downward-sloping aggregate demand curve?

Section 16.4

14. Describe what the effect on aggregate demand would be, other things being equal, if
    a. exports increase.
    b. both imports and exports decrease.
    c. consumption decreases.
    d. investment increases.
    e. investment decreases and government purchases increase.
    f. the price level increases.
    g. the price level decreases.

15. Suppose retailers like Canadian Tire and Target find that their inventories are being depleted. What type of change in aggregate demand (a rightward or leftward shift) could be seen as responsible? What are the likely consequences for output and investment of this type of change in aggregate demand?

16. Which of the following both decreases consumption and shifts the aggregate demand curve to the left?
    a. an increase in financial wealth
    b. an increase in taxes
    c. an increase in the price level
    d. a decrease in interest rates

17. Predict how each of the following would impact investment expenditures.
    a. Inventory levels are depleted.
    b. Banks scrutinize borrower credit more carefully and interest rates rise.
    c. Profit rates have decreased over the past few quarters.
    d. Factories operate at 60 percent capacity, down from 80 percent.

18. Identify which expenditure category each of the following will directly impact, and also in which direction the Canadian aggregate demand curve will shift as a result.
    a. Income increases abroad.
    b. There is a decrease in interest rates.
    c. Parliament passes a permanent tax cut.
    d. Firms become more optimistic about the outlook for the economy.
    e. Stocks traded on the Toronto Stock Exchange lose 40 percent of their value in one month's time.

19. Explain how the most recent recession in the United States affected aggregate demand in the Canadian economy.

17

Aggregate Supply and Macroeconomic Equilibrium

The Aggregate Supply Curve

- What is the aggregate supply curve?
- Why is the short-run aggregate supply curve positively sloped?
- Why is the long-run aggregate supply curve vertical at the natural rate of output?

WHAT IS THE AGGREGATE SUPPLY CURVE?

The **aggregate supply (AS) curve** is a graphical representation that shows the positive relationship between the price level and real gross domestic product supplied. It illustrates the relationship between the overall price level and the total quantity of final goods and services that suppliers are *willing* and *able* to produce. In fact, there are two aggregate supply curves—a short-run aggregate supply curve and a long-run aggregate supply curve. The **short-run aggregate supply (SRAS) curve** is the graphical relationship between *RGDP* and the price level when output prices can change but input prices are unable to adjust. For example, nominal wages are assumed to adjust slowly in the short run. The **long-run aggregate supply (LRAS) curve** is the graphical relationship between *RGDP* and the price level when output prices and input prices can fully adjust to economic changes.

WHY IS THE SHORT-RUN AGGREGATE SUPPLY CURVE POSITIVELY SLOPED?

In the short run, the aggregate supply curve is upward sloping, as shown in Exhibit 1. This means that at a higher price level, producers are willing to supply more real output, and at lower price levels, they are willing to supply less real output. Why would producers be willing to supply more output just because the price level increases? There are two possible explanations: the profit effect and the misperception effect.

aggregate supply (AS) curve *a graphical representation that shows the positive relationship between the price level and real gross domestic product supplied*

short-run aggregate supply (SRAS) curve *the graphical relationship between RGDP and the price level when output prices can change but input prices are unable to adjust*

long-run aggregate supply (LRAS) curve *the graphical relationship between RGDP and the price level when output prices and input prices can fully adjust to economic changes*

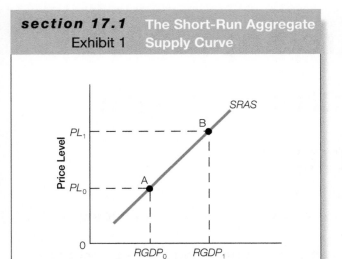

The short-run aggregate supply (*SRAS*) curve is
upward sloping. Suppliers are willing to supply
more RGDP at higher price levels and less at
lower price levels, other things equal.

The Profit Effect

To many firms, input costs—like wages and rents—are relatively constant in the short run. Workers and other material input suppliers often enter into long-term contracts with firms at prearranged prices. Thus, the slow adjustments of input prices are due to contracts that do not adjust quickly to output price level changes. So when the price level rises, output prices rise relative to input prices (costs), raising producers' short-run profit margins. That is, a higher price level leads to a higher profit per unit of output and higher RGDP supplied because wages and other input prices can be slow to adjust in the short run. With this short-run profit effect, the increased profit margins make it in the producers' self-interest to expand production and sales at higher price levels.

If the price level falls, output prices fall and producers' profits tend to fall. That is, a lower price level leads to a lower profit per unit of output and lower RGDP supplied because wages and other input prices can be slow to adjust in the short run. Again, this is because many input costs, such as wages and other contracted costs, are relatively constant in the short run. When output price levels fall, producers find it more difficult to cover their input costs and, consequently, reduce their level of output.

The Misperception Effect

The second explanation of the upward-sloping short-run aggregate supply curve is that producers can be fooled by price changes in the short run. That is, changes in the overall price level can temporarily mislead producers about what is taking place in their particular market. For example, say a wheat farmer sees the price of wheat rising. Thinking that the *relative price* of his wheat is rising (i.e., that wheat is becoming more valuable in real terms), the wheat farmer supplies more. Suppose, however, that wheat was not the only thing for which prices were rising. What if the prices of many other goods and services were rising at the same time as a result of an increase in the price level? The relative price of wheat, then, was not actually rising, although it appeared so in the short run. In this case, the producer was fooled into supplying more based on the *short-run misperception* of relative prices. In other words, producers may be fooled into thinking that the relative price of the item they are producing is rising, so they increase production. Similarly, if the overall price level falls, many wheat farmers may mistakenly believe that the relative price of wheat has fallen. This could fool these farmers into temporarily producing less wheat.

Workers can also be fooled. If the price level is rising, the first thing they may notice is that their nominal wages—expressed in current dollars—are rising. So they may mistakenly believe that the reward for working has risen and increase the quantity of labour they supply. Only later do they realize that the price of the goods and services they buy are also rising; that is, their real wages (wages that are adjusted for inflation) have not risen. They have been fooled into supplying more of their labour into the market. The key in all of these cases is that short-run misperceptions about relative prices temporarily fool the supplier into producing more as the overall price level rises and producing less as the overall price level falls. This leads to an upward-sloping short-run aggregate supply curve.

WHY IS THE LONG-RUN AGGREGATE SUPPLY CURVE VERTICAL AT THE NATURAL RATE OF OUTPUT?

Along the short-run aggregate supply curve, we assume that wages and other input prices are constant. This is not the case in the long run, which is a period long enough for the price of all inputs to fully adjust to changes in the economy. When we move along the long-run aggregate supply curve, we are then looking at the relationship between RGDP produced and the price level, once input prices have been able to respond to changes in output prices. Along the long-run aggregate supply (*LRAS*) curve, two sets of prices are changing—the price of outputs and the price of inputs. That is, along the *LRAS* curve, a 10 percent increase in the price of goods and services is matched by a 10 percent increase in the price of inputs. The long-run aggregate supply curve, then, is insensitive to the price level. As you can see in Exhibit 2, the *LRAS* curve is drawn as perfectly vertical, reflecting the fact that the level of RGDP producers are willing to supply is not affected by changes in the price level. Note that the ver-

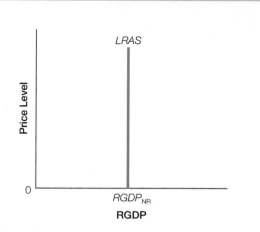

section 17.1
Exhibit 2

The Long-Run Aggregate Supply Curve

Along the long-run aggregate supply curve, the level of RGDP does not change with the price level. The position of the *LRAS* curve is determined by the natural rate of output, $RGDP_{NR}$, which reflects the levels of capital, land, labour, and technology in the economy.

tical long-run aggregate supply curve will always be positioned at the natural rate of output, where all resources are fully employed ($RGDP_{NR}$). That is, in the long run, firms will always produce at the maximum level allowed by their capital, land, labour, and technology, regardless of the price level.

The long-run equilibrium level is where the economy will settle when undisturbed and when all resources are fully employed. Remember that the economy will always be at the intersection of short-run aggregate supply and aggregate demand, but that will not always be at the natural rate of output, $RGDP_{NR}$. Long-run equilibrium will occur only where the short-run aggregate supply and aggregate demand curves intersect along the long-run aggregate supply curve at the natural, or potential, rate of output.

SECTION CHECK

- The aggregate supply curve is the relationship between the overall price level and the total quantity of final goods and services that suppliers are *able* and *willing* to produce.
- The short-run aggregate supply curve measures how much RGDP suppliers are willing to produce at different price levels when input prices are unable to adjust. For this reason, producers can make a profit by expanding production when the price level rises. Producers also may be fooled into thinking that the relative price of the item they are producing is rising, so they increase production.
- In the long run, the aggregate supply curve is vertical. In the long run, input prices change proportionally with output prices. The position of the *LRAS* curve is determined by the level of capital, land, labour, and technology at the natural rate of output, $RGDP_{NR}$.

Shifts in the Aggregate Supply Curve

■ What factors of production affect the short-run and the long-run aggregate supply curves?
■ What factors exclusively shift the short-run aggregate supply curve?
■ Can we review the determinants that change aggregate supply?

WHAT FACTORS OF PRODUCTION AFFECT THE SHORT-RUN AND LONG-RUN AGGREGATE SUPPLY CURVES?

We will now examine the determinants that can shift the short-run and the long-run aggregate supply curves to the right or left, as shown in Exhibit 1. Any change in the quantity of any factor of production available—capital, land, labour, or entrepreneurship—can cause a shift in both the long-run and short-run aggregate supply curves. We will now see how these factors can change the position of both types of aggregate supply curves.

How Capital Affects Aggregate Supply

Changes in the stock of capital—the amount of equipment and structures to aid production—will alter the amount of goods and services the economy can produce. Investing in capital improves the quantity and quality of the capital stock, which lowers the cost of production in the short run. This in turn shifts the short-run aggregate supply curve rightward, and allows output to be permanently greater than before, shifting the long-run aggregate supply curve rightward, *ceteris paribus*.

Changes in human capital can also alter the aggregate supply curve. Investments in human capital may include educational or vocational programs and/or on-the-job training. All of these investments in human capital cause productivity to rise. As a result, the short-run aggregate supply curve shifts to the right because a more skilled workforce lowers the cost of production; in turn, the *LRAS* curve shifts to the right because greater output is achievable on a permanent, or sustainable, basis, *ceteris paribus*.

Land (Natural Resources)

Remember that, in economics, *land* is an all-encompassing definition that includes all natural resources. An increase in natural resources, such as successful oil exploration in Alberta, would presumably lower the costs of production and expand the economy's sustainable rate of output, shifting both the short-run and long-run aggregate supply curves to the right. Likewise, a decrease in natural resources available would result in a leftward shift of both the short-run and long-run aggregate supply curves.

The Labour Force

The addition of workers to the labour force, *ceteris paribus*, can increase aggregate supply. For example, during the 1960s and 1970s, women and baby boomers entered the labour force in large numbers. More recently, however,

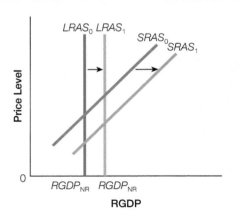

section 17.2
Exhibit 1 Shifts in Both Short-Run and Long-Run Aggregate Supply

Increases in any of the factors of production—capital, land, labour, or entrepreneurship—can shift both the *LRAS* and *SRAS* curves to the right. Decreases in any of the factors of production can shift both the *SRAS* and *LRAS* curves to the left.

immigrants have become a major contributor to Canada's labour force—accounting for over 20 percent of Canada's labour force. This increase tended to depress wages and increase short-run aggregate supply, *ceteris paribus*. The expanded labour force also increased the economy's potential output, increasing long-run aggregate supply. Japan's aging population is causing a decrease in the labour force in recent years—a leftward shift in the short-run and long-run aggregate supply curves, *ceteris paribus.*

Entrepreneurship and Technology

The online *Business Dictionary* defines entrepreneurship as "the capacity and willingness to develop, organize, and manage a business venture along with any of its risks in order to make a profit." Combining entrepreneurship with the other factors of production (capital, land, and labour) and adding technology can lead to significant rewards, as in the cases of Bill Gates of Microsoft, Ted Rogers of Rogers Communications, and Michael Lazaridis of Research in Motion (RIM). Their innovative technological developments, such as computers and specialized software, have led to many cost savings for all types of businesses—ATMs, bar-code scanners, biotechnology, and increased productivity across the board. These activities shift both the short-run and long-run aggregate supply curves outward by lowering costs and expanding real output possibilities.

Government Regulations

Increases in government regulations can increase production costs, resulting in a leftward shift of the short-run aggregate supply curve; a reduction in society's potential output shifts the long-run aggregate supply curve to the left as well. Likewise, a reduction in government regulations on businesses would lower the costs of production and expand potential real output, causing both the *SRAS* and *LRAS* curves to shift to the right.

WHAT FACTORS EXCLUSIVELY SHIFT THE SHORT-RUN AGGREGATE SUPPLY CURVE?

Some factors shift the short-run aggregate supply curve but do not impact the long-run aggregate supply curve. The most important of these factors are changes in wages and other input prices, productivity, and unexpected supply shocks. Exhibit 2 illustrates the impact of these factors on short-run aggregate supply.

Wages and Other Input Prices

The price of factors, or inputs, that go into producing outputs will affect only the short-run aggregate supply curve if they don't reflect permanent changes in the supplies of some factors of production. For example, if money or nominal wages increase without a corresponding increase in labour productivity, then it will become more costly for suppliers to produce goods and services at every price level, causing the *SRAS* curve to shift to the left. Long-run aggregate supply will not shift because with the same supply of labour as before, potential output does not change. If the price of steel rises, automobile producers will find it more expensive to do business because their production costs will rise, again resulting in a leftward shift in the short-run aggregate supply curve. The *LRAS* curve will not shift, however, as long as the capacity to make steel has not been reduced.

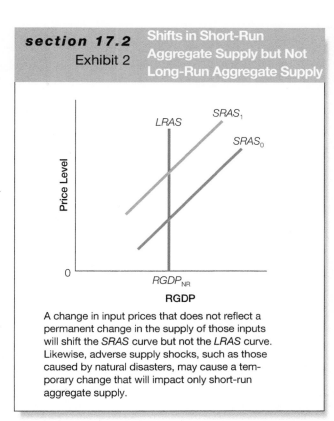

section 17.2
Exhibit 2
Shifts in Short-Run Aggregate Supply but Not Long-Run Aggregate Supply

A change in input prices that does not reflect a permanent change in the supply of those inputs will shift the *SRAS* curve but not the *LRAS* curve. Likewise, adverse supply shocks, such as those caused by natural disasters, may cause a temporary change that will impact only short-run aggregate supply.

Temporary natural disasters like droughts can destroy crops and leave land parched. This may shift the *SRAS* curve but not the *LRAS* curve.

Temporary Supply Shocks

Supply shocks are unexpected temporary events that can either increase or decrease aggregate supply. For example, negative supply shocks like major widespread flooding, earthquakes, droughts, and other natural disasters can increase the costs of production, causing the short-run aggregate supply curve to shift to the left, *ceteris paribus*. However, once the temporary effects of these disasters have been felt, no appreciable change in the economy's productive capacity has occurred, so the long-run aggregate supply doesn't shift as a result. Other temporary supply shocks, such as disruptions in trade due to war, electric power blackouts, or labour strikes, will have similar effects on short-run aggregate supply. However, positive supply shocks such as favourable weather conditions or temporary price reductions of imported resources like oil can shift the short-run aggregate supply curve rightward. During the mid- to late 1990s, Canada experienced a positive supply shock as the Internet, and information technology in general, gave a huge boost to productivity.

CAN WE REVIEW THE DETERMINANTS THAT CHANGE AGGREGATE SUPPLY?

The factors detailed in Exhibit 3 can shift the short-run aggregate supply curve, the long-run aggregate supply curve, or both, depending on whether the effects are temporary or permanent.

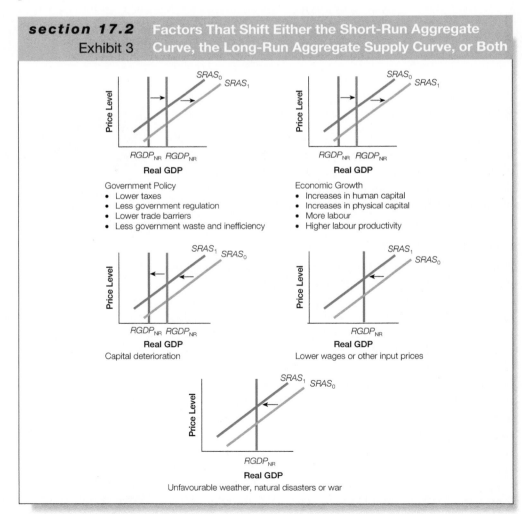

section 17.2
Exhibit 3

Factors That Shift Either the Short-Run Aggregate Curve, the Long-Run Aggregate Supply Curve, or Both

Government Policy
• Lower taxes
• Less government regulation
• Lower trade barriers
• Less government waste and inefficiency

Economic Growth
• Increases in human capital
• Increases in physical capital
• More labour
• Higher labour productivity

Capital deterioration

Lower wages or other input prices

Unfavourable weather, natural disasters or war

SECTION CHECK

- Any increase in the quantity of any of the available factors of production—capital, land, labour, or entrepreneurship—will cause both the long-run and short-run aggregate supply curves to shift to the right. A decrease in any of these factors will shift both of the aggregate supply curves to the left.
- Changes in wages and other input price, productivity, and temporary supply shocks shift the short-run aggregate supply curve but do not affect the long-run aggregate supply curve.

Variable	Change in Variable	Change in *SRAS*	Change in *LRAS*
1. Costs			
• Wages	↑	↓	n/c*
• Other input prices	↑	↓	n/c*
2. Government policy			
• Taxes	↑	↓	↓
• Regulatory framework	↑	↓	↓
• Trade barriers	↑	↓	↓
• Waste and inefficiency	↑	↓	↓
3. Economic growth			
• Quantity of human capital	↑	↑	↑
• Quantity of physical capital	↑	↑	↑
• Technology and entrepreneurship	↑	↑	↑
• Labour productivity	↑	↑	↑
4. Other			
• Unfavourable weather	↑	↓	n/c*
• Natural disasters, war	↑	↓	n/c*

n/c*—The curve does not shift unless the variable change is permanent.

Macroeconomic Equilibrium

section

17.3

- How is macroeconomic equilibrium determined?
- What are recessionary and inflationary gaps?
- How can the economy self-correct to a recessionary gap?
- How can the economy self-correct to an inflationary gap?

HOW IS MACROECONOMIC EQUILIBRIUM DETERMINED?

The *short-run* equilibrium level of real output and the price level are given by the intersection of the aggregate demand curve and the short-run aggregate supply curve. When this equilibrium occurs on the long-run aggregate supply curve, as seen in Exhibit 1, the *long-run* equilibrium level of real output and the price level is achieved. At the long-run equilibrium, the economy is operating at its full employment level of RGDP. That is, when the short-run equilibrium occurs on the long-run aggregate supply curve, the economy is at its potential, or natural, rate of output ($RGDP_{NR}$). Only a short-run equilibrium that is at potential output is also a long-run equilibrium.

section 17.3
Exhibit 1   **Long-Run Macroeconomic Equilibrium**

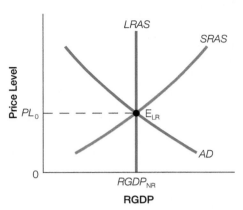

Long-run macroeconomic equilibrium occurs at the level where short-run aggregate supply and aggregate demand intersect at a point on the long-run aggregate supply curve. At this level, real GDP will equal potential GDP at full employment ($RGDP_{NR}$).

shocks
unexpected aggregate supply or aggregate demand changes

Short-run equilibrium can change when the aggregate demand curve or the short-run aggregate supply curve shifts rightward or leftward, but the long-run equilibrium level of RGDP changes only when the *LRAS* curve shifts. Sometimes, these supply or demand changes are anticipated; at other times, however, the shifts occur unexpectedly. Economists call these unexpected aggregate supply or aggregate demand changes **shocks.**

WHAT ARE RECESSIONARY AND INFLATIONARY GAPS?

As we just discussed, equilibrium will not always occur at full employment. In fact, equilibrium can occur at less than the potential output of the economy, $RGDP_{NR}$, temporarily beyond $RGDP_{NR}$, or at potential GDP. Exhibit 2 shows these three possibilities. In Exhibit 2(a) we have a recessionary gap at the short-run equilibrium, E_{SR}, at $RGDP_0$. An output gap that occurs when actual output ($RGDP$) is less than potential output ($RGDP_{NR}$) is a **recessionary gap**—aggregate demand is insufficient to fully employ all of society's resources, so unemployment will be above the natural rate. In Exhibit 2(c) we have an inflationary gap at the short-run equilibrium, E_{SR}, at $RGDP_2$. An output gap that occurs when the actual output ($RGDP$) is greater than the potential output ($RGDP_{NR}$) is an **inflationary gap.** In this case, aggregate demand is so high that the economy is temporarily operating beyond full capacity ($RGDP_{NR}$), which will usually lead to

section 17.3
Exhibit 2   **Recessionary and Inflationary Gaps**

a. Recessionary Gap

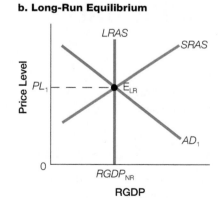

c. Inflationary Gap

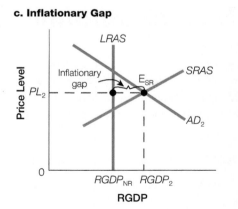

In Exhibit 2(a), the economy is currently in short-run equilibrium at E_{SR}. At this point, $RGDP_0$ is less than $RGDP_{NR}$; that is, the economy is producing less than its potential output and the economy is in a recessionary gap. In Exhibit 2(c), the economy is currently in short-run equilibrium at E_{SR}. At this point $RGDP_2$ is greater than $RGDP_{NR}$. The economy is temporarily producing more than its potential output and we have an inflationary gap. In Exhibit 2(b) the economy is producing its potential output at the $RGDP_{NR}$. At this point the economy is in long-run equilibrium and is not experiencing an inflationary or recessionary gap.

inflationary pressure, so unemployment will be below the natural rate. In Exhibit 2(b) the economy is just right, where AD_1 and $SRAS$ intersect at $RGDP_{NR}$—the long-run equilibrium position.

Demand-Pull Inflation

Demand-pull inflation occurs when the price level increases due to an increase in aggregate demand. Consider the case in which an increase in consumer optimism results in a corresponding increase in aggregate demand. Exhibit 3 shows that an increase in aggregate demand causes an increase in the price level and an increase in real output. The movement is along $SRAS$ from point E_0 to point E_1. This causes an inflationary gap. Recall that there is an increase in output as a result of the increase in the price level in the short run because firms have an incentive to increase real output when the prices of the goods they are selling are rising faster than the costs of the inputs they use in production.

Note that E_1 in Exhibit 3 is positioned beyond $RGDP_{NR}$—an inflationary gap. It seems peculiar that the economy can operate beyond its potential, but this is possible, temporarily, as firms encourage workers to work overtime, extend the hours of part-time workers, hire recently retired employees, reduce frictional unemployment through more extensive searches for employees, and so on. However, this level of output and employment *cannot* be sustained in the long run.

Cost-Push Inflation

The mid-1970s to early 1980s witnessed a phenomenon known as **stagflation,** a situation in which lower growth and higher prices occurred together. Some economists believe that this was caused by a leftward shift in the short-run aggregate supply curve, as seen in Exhibit 4. If the aggregate demand curve did not increase considerably but the price level increased significantly, then the inflation was caused by supply-side forces. This is called **cost-push inflation**—a price level increase due to a negative supply shock or increase in input prices.

recessionary gap *an output gap that occurs when the actual output is less than the potential output*

inflationary gap *an output gap that occurs when the actual output is greater than the potential output*

demand-pull inflation *a price level increase due to an increase in aggregate demand*

stagflation *a situation in which lower growth and higher prices occur together*

cost-push inflation *a price level increase due to a negative supply shock or increase in input prices*

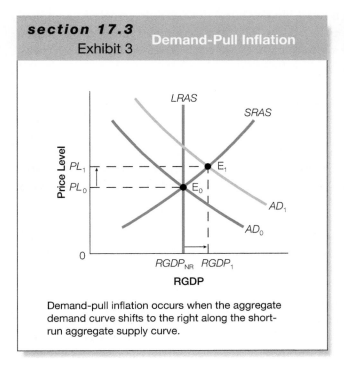

section 17.3 Exhibit 3 — **Demand-Pull Inflation**

Demand-pull inflation occurs when the aggregate demand curve shifts to the right along the short-run aggregate supply curve.

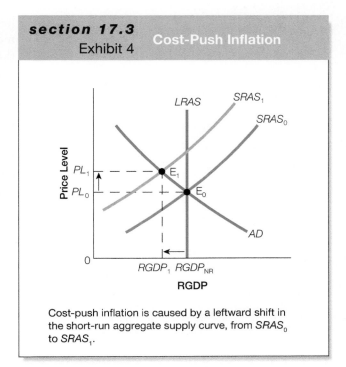

section 17.3 Exhibit 4 — **Cost-Push Inflation**

Cost-push inflation is caused by a leftward shift in the short-run aggregate supply curve, from $SRAS_0$ to $SRAS_1$.

The increase in oil prices was the primary culprit responsible for the leftward shift in the aggregate supply curve. As we discussed in the last section, an increase in input prices can cause the short-run aggregate supply curve to shift to the left, and this spelled big trouble for the Canadian economy—higher price levels, lower output, and higher rates of unemployment. The impact of cost-push inflation is illustrated in Exhibit 4.

In Exhibit 4, we see that the economy is initially at full employment equilibrium at point E_0. Now suppose there is a sudden increase in input prices, such as the increase in the price of oil. This increase would shift the *SRAS* curve to the left—from $SRAS_0$ to $SRAS_1$. As a result of the shift in short-run aggregate supply, the price level rises to PL_1 and real output falls from $RGDP_{NR}$ to $RGDP_1$ (point E_1). Now firms demand fewer workers as a result of the higher input costs that cannot be passed on to the consumers. The result is higher prices, lower real output, and more unemployment—and it leads to a recessionary gap. These supply shocks can change RGDP significantly, but temporarily, away from potential aggregate output at $RGDP_{NR}$. In 2007–08, the price of many raw materials shot up globally—a global negative supply shock. Many countries around the world, including Canada, felt the effects of the negative supply shock.

A Decrease in Aggregate Demand and Recessions

Just as cost-push inflation can cause a recessionary gap, so can a decrease in aggregate demand. For example, consider the case in which consumer confidence plunges and the stock market crashes. As a result, aggregate demand would fall, shown in Exhibit 5 as the shift from AD_0 to AD_1, and the economy would be in a new short-run equilibrium at point E_1. Now, households are buying fewer goods and services at every price level. In response to this drop in demand, output would fall from $RGDP_{NR}$ to $RGDP_1$, and the price level would fall from PL_0 to PL_1. So in the short run, this fall in aggregate demand causes higher unemployment and a reduction in output—and it too can lead to a recessionary gap.

Most of the post-war recessions have been caused by negative demand shocks. Negative supply shocks have been relatively few but quite severe in terms of unemployment rates. The 2008–09 recession appears to have been the product of both negative demand and supply shocks. During the financial crisis of 2008, both consumers and firms reduced their spending and this caused the aggregate demand curve to shift to the left, in turn leading to a recessionary gap. In short, financial market wealth decreased and precautionary saving by consumers increased as confidence fell, obtaining credit became more difficult, and both households and firms adopted a "wait and see" attitude. The rate of inflation slowed and GDP fell by nearly 3 percent in a year.

In an attempt to stave off what some feared was the onset of the next great depression, the Bank of Canada increased the money supply and lowered interest rates. In addition, the Canadian government enacted a number of extraordinary measures to stimulate consumption, investment, and government spending. This helped to shift the aggregate demand curve to the right and RGDP and the price level rose by the end of 2009. We will discuss this in much more detail in our chapters on fiscal policy and monetary policy.

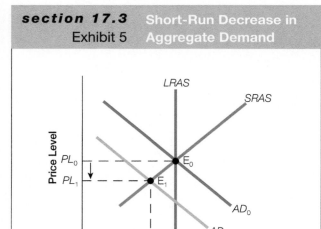

section 17.3   Short-Run Decrease in
Exhibit 5   Aggregate Demand

A fall in aggregate demand from a drop in consumer confidence can cause a short-run change in the economy. The decrease in aggregate demand (shown in the movement from point E_0 to E_1) causes lower output and higher unemployment in the short run.

HOW CAN THE ECONOMY SELF-CORRECT TO A RECESSIONARY GAP?

Many recoveries from a recessionary gap occur because of increases in aggregate demand—perhaps consumer and business confidence picks up or the government lowers taxes and/or lowers interest rates to stimulate the economy. That is, there is eventually a rightward shift in—the aggregate demand curve that takes the economy back to potential output—$RGDP_{NR}$.

However, it is possible that the economy could *self-correct* through declining wages and prices. In Exhibit 6, at point E_1, the intersection of PL_1 and $RGDP_1$, the economy is in a recessionary gap—the economy is producing less than its potential output. At this lower level of output, firms lay off workers to avoid inventory accumulation. In addition, firms may cut prices to increase sales for their products. Unemployed workers and other input suppliers may also bid down wages and prices. That is, labourers and other input suppliers are now willing to accept lower wages and prices for the use of their resources, and the resulting reduction in production costs shifts the short-run supply curve from $SRAS_0$ to $SRAS_1$. Eventually, the economy returns to a long-run equilibrium at E_2 at $RGDP_{NR}$ and a lower price level, PL_2.

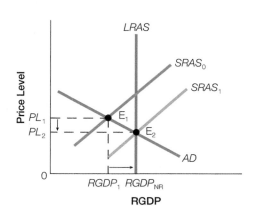

section 17.3 **Self-Correcting to a**
Exhibit 6   **Recessionary Gap**

At point E_1, the economy is in a recessionary gap. However, the economy may self-correct as labourers and other input suppliers are now willing to accept lower wages and prices for the use of their resources. This results in a reduction in production costs that shifts the short-run supply curve from $SRAS_0$ to $SRAS_1$. Eventually, the economy returns to a long-run equilibrium at point E_2, at $RGDP_{NR}$, and a lower price level, PL_2.

Self-Correction to a Recessionary Gap Can Be Slow

Many economists believe that wages and prices may be slow to adjust, especially downward. The tendency for prices and wages to only adjust slowly downward to changes in the economy is referred to as **wage and price inflexibility.** The significance of this inflexibility is that it may lead to prolonged periods of a recessionary gap.

For example, in Exhibit 6 we see that the economy is in a recession at E_1 at $RGDP_1$. The economy will eventually self-correct to $RGDP_{NR}$ at E_2, as workers and other input owners accept lower wages and prices for their inputs, shifting the $SRAS$ curve to the right from $SRAS_0$ to $SRAS_1$. However, if wages and other input prices are sticky, the economy's adjustment mechanism might take many months, or even a few years, to totally self-correct.

Japan witnessed several recessionary gaps in the 1990s and even experienced deflation as the self-adjustment mechanism predicts. However, the adjustment out of the recessionary gap was slow and painful.

wage and price inflexibility
the tendency for prices and wages to only adjust slowly downward to changes in the economy

The Causes of Sticky Wages and Prices

Empirical evidence supports several reasons for the downward stickiness of wages and prices. Firms may not be able to legally cut wages because of long-term labour contracts (particularly with union workers) or a legal minimum wage. Efficiency wages may also limit a firm's ability to lower wage rates. Menu costs may cause price inflexibility as well.

Efficiency Wages

In economics, it is generally assumed that as productivity rises, wages will rise, and that workers can raise their productivity through investments in human capital like education and on-the-job training. However, some economists believe that in some cases, *higher wages will lead to greater productivity.*

In the efficiency wage model, employers pay their employees more than the equilibrium wage as a means to increase efficiency. Proponents of this theory suggest that higher-than-equilibrium wages may attract the most productive workers, lower job turnover and training costs, and improve morale. Because the efficiency wage rate is greater than the equilibrium wage rate, the quantity of labour that would be willingly supplied is greater than the quantity of labour demanded, resulting in greater amounts of unemployment.

However, aside from creating some additional unemployment, it may also cause wages to be inflexible downward. For example, in the event that there is a decrease in aggregate demand, firms that pay efficiency wages may be reluctant to cut wages in the fear that it could lead to lower morale, greater absenteeism, and general productivity losses. In short, if firms are paying efficiency wages, they may be reluctant to lower wages in a recession, leading to downward wage inflexibility.

Menu Costs

As we explained in Chapter 13, there is a cost to changing prices in an inflationary environment. Thus the higher price level in an inflationary environment is often reflected slowly, as restaurants, mail-order houses, and department stores change their prices gradually so that they incur fewer *menu costs* (the costs of changing posted prices) in printing new catalogues, new mailers, new advertisements, and so on. Since businesses are not likely to change these prices instantly, we can say that some prices are sticky, or slow to change. For example, many outputs, like steel, are inputs in the production of other products, like automobiles. As a result, these prices are slow to change.

Suppose that there was an unexpected reduction in the money supply that led to a decrease in aggregate demand. This could lower the price level. Although some firms may adjust to the change quickly, others may move more slowly because of menu costs. The potential result is that their prices may become too high (above equilibrium); sales and output will fall, causing a potential recession.

If some firms are not responding quickly to changes in demand, there must be a reason, and to some economists, menu costs are at least part of that reason.

HOW CAN THE ECONOMY SELF-CORRECT TO AN INFLATIONARY GAP?

In Exhibit 7, the economy is currently in an inflationary gap at E_1, where $RGDP_0$ is greater than $RGDP_{NR}$. Because the price level, PL_1, is now higher than workers anticipated, PL_0, workers become disgruntled with wages that have not yet adjusted to it (if prices have risen, but wages have not risen as much, real wages have fallen). Recall that along the *SRAS* curve, wages and other input prices are assumed to be constant. Therefore, workers' and input suppliers' purchasing power falls as output prices rise. Real (adjusted for inflation) wages have fallen. Consequently, workers and

---

section 17.3
Exhibit 7

Self-Correction to an Inflationary Gap

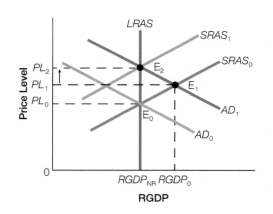

The economy is currently in an inflationary gap at E_1, where $RGDP_0$ is greater than $RGDP_{NR}$. Because the price level is now higher than workers anticipated (i.e., it is PL_1 rather than PL_0), workers and other suppliers demand higher prices. As input prices respond to the higher level of output prices, the short-run aggregate supply curve shifts to the left, from $SRAS_0$ to $SRAS_1$. Suppliers will continually seek higher prices for their inputs until they reach the long-run equilibrium, at point E_2. At point E_2, input suppliers' purchasing power is now restored at the natural rate, $RGDP_{NR}$, at a new higher price level, PL_2.

other suppliers demand higher prices, to be willing to supply their inputs. As input prices respond to the higher level of output prices, the short-run aggregate supply curve shifts to the left, from $SRAS_0$ to $SRAS_1$. Suppliers will continually seek higher prices for their inputs until they reach the long-run equilibrium, at point E_2 in Exhibit 7. At point E_2, input suppliers' purchasing power is now restored at the long-run equilibrium, at $RGDP_{NR}$, and a new higher price level, PL_2.

PRICE LEVEL AND RGDP OVER TIME

In Exhibit 8, we trace the pattern of RGDP versus the price level from 1981 to 2012. According to Statistics Canada, both the price level and RGDP have been rising over the last 32 years. So what is responsible for the changes? The answer is both aggregate demand and aggregate supply. Aggregate demand has risen because of growing population (which impacts consumption and investment spending), rising income, increases in government purchases, and increases in the money supply. Aggregate supply has generally been increasing as well, including increases in the labour force and improvements in labour productivity and technology.

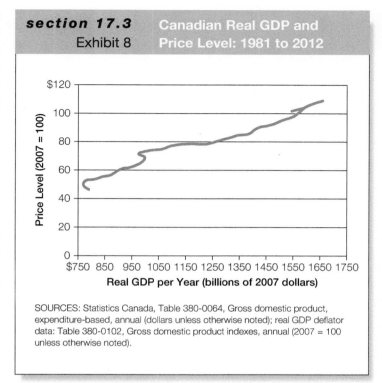

section 17.3
Exhibit 8

Canadian Real GDP and Price Level: 1981 to 2012

SOURCES: Statistics Canada, Table 380-0064, Gross domestic product, expenditure-based, annual (dollars unless otherwise noted); real GDP deflator data: Table 380-0102, Gross domestic product indexes, annual (2007 = 100 unless otherwise noted).

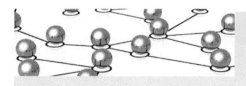

Business *CONNECTION*

FACING THE STORM CLOUDS: LOW INFLATION AND DEFLATION

Recent economic history has always addressed fears of higher rates of inflation. There are two sources of inflation: (1) *demand-pull inflation*, or inflation fuelled by aggregate demand, which occurs when the price level for goods and services in the economy increases because aggregate demand is growing at a greater rate than aggregate supply, and (2) *cost-push inflation*, which usually occurs when input costs for the factors of production increase, which in turn feed into the costs of a host of basic goods and services. This type of inflation forces suppliers in the affected industries to increase prices or, at worst, to leave the industry entirely, resulting in a reduction in aggregate supply.

Inflation usually occurs during high growth rates in the economy, but what happens when the economy is experiencing a recession or a period of prolonged stagnant growth? This situation, triggered by either a fall in wages or a depression in consumer demand, may actually cause prices to contract—a condition that economists call *deflation*. For business, low inflation or deflation ultimately means losses in revenues and profits that many firms will not survive.

Firms need to recognize that they may not be able to do much where demand is greatly influenced by demographic issues. These are challenges to the economy as a whole and there isn't much opportunity to change that at the micro level. Still, firms can look at their product mix and decide whether changes in demographics would adversely affect their products. For example, a firm producing baby diapers might consider changing to adult diapers.

Firms will also have to pay particular attention to their inventory levels. They need to recognize that falling prices send a message to consumers to wait to buy, because prices will be lower in the future. For inventories that are perishable or could be a challenge to sell once they're outdated, it's imperative that firms reduce their inventories and order smaller quantities—more frequently too. They can reduce their input costs by being proactive in their ordering patterns.

Firms will also need to look at all of their operating costs to find any specific reductions they can make to help reduce their product or service costs. This might mean looking into longer-term contracts that have favourable prices and

(continued)

becoming more flexible on contracts for inputs that tend to be commodities. If firms are successful, they can still be profitable if they are forced to lower prices in the market.

When there's downward pressure on prices, firms need to find ways to compete on anything but price. This means increasing the value-added on their products and avoiding competition in markets where their products are viewed as commodities. This might mean investing more in R&D. Firms should recognize that they will get great value from these investments because individuals will likely be willing to work for less (or produce more) just to keep their jobs or contracts. It also helps firms to invest in technology that was too expensive in an expanding market—suppliers are just as anxious to pare down their inventories during deflationary periods, which can mean considerable access and savings to a firm that is trying to increase productivity.

All in all, competing in periods of low inflation or deflation poses extreme challenges to firms, but a careful and well-managed firm will find opportunities while others will fall by the wayside.

1. As a business manager, which is more volatile for your business: demand-pull inflation or cost-push inflation?

2. In a period of "lowflation" or deflation, do you think a business manager would care whether the cause is lower prices or lower demand? What could the manager do differently if the cause of the lowflation was lower prices as opposed to lower demand?

3. When growth starts to slow and inflation lags, many firms' first response is to lay off high-cost sales personnel. In your opinion, is this a good strategy, and why?

SECTION CHECK

▪ Short-run macroeconomic equilibrium is shown by the intersection of the aggregate demand curve and the short-run aggregate supply curve. A short-run equilibrium is also a long-run equilibrium only if it is at potential output on the long-run aggregate supply curve.

▪ If short-run equilibrium occurs at less than the potential output of the economy, $RGDP_{NR}$, there is a recessionary gap. If short-run equilibrium temporarily occurs beyond $RGDP_{NR}$, there is an inflationary gap.

▪ It is possible for the economy to self-correct from a recessionary gap through declining wages and prices. The short-run aggregate supply curve eventually increases, returning the economy to the long-run equilibrium, at $RGDP_{NR}$, at a lower price level.

▪ It is possible for the economy to self-correct from an inflationary gap through increasing wages and prices. The short-run aggregate supply curve ultimately decreases, returning the economy to the long-run equilibrium, at $RGDP_{NR}$, at a higher price level.

For Your Review

Section 17.1

1. You operate a business in which you manufacture furniture. You are able to increase your furniture prices by 5 percent this quarter. You assume that the demand for your furniture has increased and begin increasing furniture production. Only later do you realize that prices in the macroeconomy are rising generally at a rate of 5 percent per quarter. This is an example of what effect? What does it imply about the slope of the short-run aggregate supply curve?

2. Explain why the following statements are false.

   a. The long-run aggregate supply curve is vertical because economic forces do not affect the long run.

   b. If firms adjusted their prices every day, the short-run aggregate supply curve would be horizontal.

3. Why is focusing on producers' profit margins helpful in understanding the logic of the short-run aggregate supply curve?

Section 17.2

4. How will each of the following changes alter aggregate supply?

Change	Short-Run Aggregate Supply	Long-Run Aggregate Supply
An increase in aggregate demand	_____	_____
A decrease in aggregate demand	_____	_____
An increase in the stock of capital	_____	_____
A reduction in the size of the labour force	_____	_____
An increase in input prices (that does not reflect permanent changes in their supplies)	_____	_____
A decrease in input prices (that does reflect permanent changes in their supplies)	_____	_____
An increase in usable natural resources	_____	_____
A temporary adverse supply shock	_____	_____
Increases in the cost of government regulations	_____	_____

5. What would each of the following do to the short-run aggregate supply curve?
   a. a decrease in wage rates
   b. passage of more stringent environmental and safety regulations affecting businesses
   c. technological progress
   d. an increase in consumer optimism
   e. an electric power blackout in Ontario

6. What would each of the following do to the long-run aggregate supply curve?
   a. advances in medical technologies
   b. increased immigration of skilled workers
   c. an increase in wage rates
   d. an epidemic involving a new strain of the flu kills hundreds of thousands of people

7. Indicate whether the following events affect short-run aggregate supply or long-run aggregate supply. Identify the direction of impact.
   a. Unusually cold weather in Saskatchewan reduces the wheat crop.
   b. A devastating earthquake in British Columbia destroys hundreds of buildings and kills thousands of people.
   c. Economy-wide wage increases are made.
   d. Advances in computers and wireless technologies improve the efficiency of production.

8. How can a change in input prices change the short-run aggregate supply curve but not the long-run aggregate supply curve? How could it change both long-run and short-run aggregate supply?

Section 17.3

Blueprint Problem

Use the following diagram to answer questions (a) and (b).

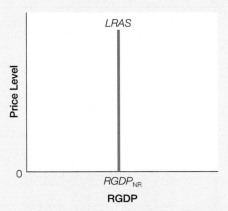

a.   On the diagram provided, illustrate the short-run effects of an increase in aggregate demand. What happens to the price level, real output, employment, and unemployment?

b.   On the diagram provided, illustrate the long-run effects of an increase in aggregate demand. What happens to the price level, real output, employment, and unemployment?

Blueprint Solution

a.

> Use the same three-question procedure used to perform demand–supply analysis in Chapter 4.
>
> Step 1: Establish model in long-run equilibrium (E_0). Note: When doing this type of *AD/AS* analysis, remember to always start from a position of long-run equilibrium.
>
> Step 2: Increase aggregate demand (rightward shift).
>
> Step 3: Re-establish model in the temporary short-run equilibrium E_1. This equilibrium is considered to be short run since it is achieved by the intersection of the *AD* and the *SRAS* curves. The assumption is that, at this point, the economy has not had sufficient time to self-correct to the increase in aggregate demand (that is, the short run).

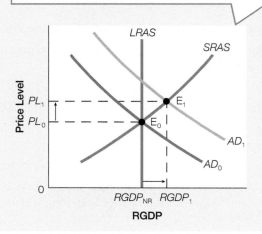

Short-Run Impact Analysis (Comparing E_0 and E_1):

a. Price level is higher ($PL_1 > PL_0$).

b. Real GDP is higher (now above $RGDP_{NR}$, therefore economy is experiencing an inflationary gap ($RGDP_1 - RGDP_{NR}$).

c. Some of the increase in real GDP will come from the existing employed working longer hours and overtime (therefore, no impact on employment or unemployment rates). However, at least some of the increase would presumably come from new-job creation—a reduction in either structural or frictional unemployment (therefore, a rise in employment and reduction in unemployment).

b.

What distinguishes this analysis from that done in part (a) is that this question is looking for the impact of the increase in *AD*, assuming that the economy has had sufficient time to adjust (that is, the long run).

Because the initial increase in *AD* has increased the price level above what is anticipated (PL_2 as opposed to PL_1), workers and other input suppliers will *eventually* demand higher prices. These higher prices will shift the *SRAS* leftward—restoring the economy back to long-run equilibrium ($RGDP_{NR}$), at a higher price level (PL_2).

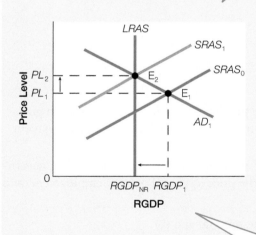

Long-Run Impact Analysis (Comparing E_1 and E_2):

a. Price level is higher ($PL_2 > PL_1$).

b. Real GDP has declined (real output has returned to the natural rate).

c. As real output returns to its natural rate, unemployment will also return to its natural rate—necessarily causing the unemployment rate to increase from below the natural rate back to the natural rate (the rate of employment decreasing as a result).

9. Use the following diagram to answer questions (a) and (b).

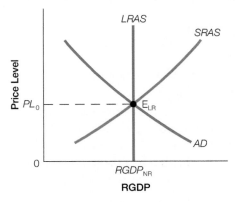

   a. On the diagram provided, illustrate the short-run effects of an increase in consumer confidence. What happens to the price level, real output, employment, and unemployment?

   b. On the diagram provided, illustrate the long-run effects of an increase in consumer confidence. What happens to the price level, real output, employment, and unemployment?

10. Use the following diagram to answer questions (a) and (b).

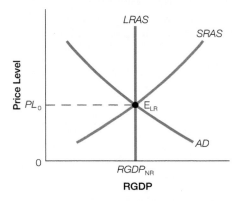

   a. On the diagram provided, illustrate the short-run effects of a decrease in government purchases. What happens to the price level, real output, employment, and unemployment?

   b. On the diagram provided, illustrate the long-run effects of a decrease in government purchases. What happens to the price level, real output, employment, and unemployment?

11. Use the following diagram to answer questions (a) and (b).

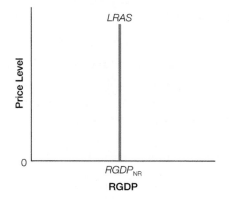

a. Illustrate a recessionary gap on the diagram provided.

b. Given the illustration in (a), illustrate and explain the eventual long-run equilibrium in this case.

12. Use the following diagram to answer questions (a) and (b).

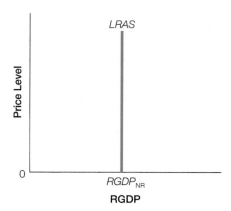

a. Illustrate an inflationary gap on the diagram provided.

b. Given the illustration in (a), illustrate and explain the eventual long-run equilibrium in this case.

13. Distinguish cost-push from demand-pull inflation. Provide an example of an event or shock to the economy that would cause each.

14. Is it ever possible for an economy to operate above the full-employment level in the short term? Explain.

15. How does an increase in aggregate demand affect output, unemployment, and the price level in the short run? How does a decrease in short-run aggregate supply affect output, unemployment, and the price level in the short run?

16. Which of the following leads to stagflation, assuming the economy is currently operating at full employment?

a. an increase in government spending on education

b. large nominal wage increases demanded and received by striking workers

c. a decrease in federal spending on national defence

d. a temporary increase in oil production from the Organization of the Petroleum Exporting Countries (OPEC)

e. a temporary decrease in OPEC oil production

17. The following table shows the initial level of aggregate demand (AD_0) and aggregate supply (AS_0) for the economy of Adanac. The full-employment level of output is $500 billion.

Price Index	AD_0 (billions)	AS_0 (billions)	AD_1 (billions)
60	$875	$250	$
70	800	300	
80	725	350	
90	650	400	
100	575	450	
110	500	500	
120	425	550	
130	350	600	
140	275	650	

a. Draw the corresponding initial aggregate demand and aggregate supply curves (AD_0 and AS_0).

b. What is the initial equilibrium price level and level of real GDP?

c. At this initial equilibrium (AD_0 and AS_0), is Adanac experiencing either a recessionary or inflationary gap? If so, how large a gap exists?

d. Suppose the aggregate demand in Adanac declines for $125 billion at every price level. In the above table, compute the new quantity of aggregate demand in the column labelled AD_1. Add AD_1 to the diagram from part (a). What is the new equilibrium price level and quantity of real GDP?

e. At the new equilibrium (AD_1 and AS_0) is Adanac experiencing either a recessionary or inflationary gap? If so, how large a gap exists?

Appendix

The Keynesian Aggregate
Expenditure Model

THE SIMPLE KEYNESIAN AGGREGATE EXPENDITURE MODEL

The Keynesian aggregate expenditure model is based on the condition that the components of aggregate demand (consumption, investment, government spending, and net exports) must equal total output. Recall from Chapter 15 that Keynes was concerned with explaining and reducing short-term fluctuations in the economy. Keynes believed that total spending was a critical determinant of the overall level of economic activity. When total spending increases, firms increase their output and hire more workers. Even though Keynes ignored an important economic component—aggregate supply—his model still provides a great deal of information about aggregate demand.

Why Do We Assume the Price Level Is Fixed?

Keynes believed wages and prices were inflexible in the short run, so in this appendix we will assume that the price level is fixed or constant. If the price level is fixed, then changes in nominal income will be equivalent to changes in real income. That is, when we assume the price level is fixed, we do not have to distinguish real variable changes from nominal variable changes. Keynes believed that prices and wages were rigid or fixed until full employment is reached. But let us begin by looking at the most important aggregate demand determinant—consumption spending.

What Are the Autonomous Factors That Influence Consumption Spending?

Even though income is given for the representative household, other economic factors that influence consumption spending are not. When consumption (or any of the other components of spending, such as investment) does not depend on income, we call it *autonomous* (or independent). Let's look at some of these other autonomous factors and see how they would change consumption spending.

Real Wealth   The larger the value of a household's real wealth (the money value of wealth divided by the price level, which indicates the amount of consumption goods that the wealth could buy), the larger the amount of consumption spending, other things being equal. Thus, in Exhibit 1, an increase in real wealth would raise consumption to C_2, at point D, for a given level of current income. Similarly, something that would lower the value of real wealth, such as a decline in property values or a stock market decline would tend to lower the level of consumption to C_1, at point B in Exhibit 1.

Interest Rate   A higher interest rate tends to make the consumption items that we buy on credit more expensive, which reduces expenditures on those items. An increase in the interest rate increases the monthly payments made to buy such things as automobiles, furniture, and major appliances and reduces our ability to spend out of a given income. This shift is shown as a decrease in consumption from point A to point B in Exhibit 1. Moreover, an increase in the interest rate provides a higher future return from reducing current spending, which motivates increasing savings. Thus, a higher interest rate in the

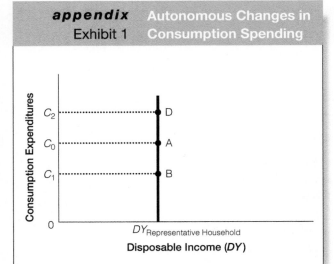

An increase in real wealth would raise consumption spending to C_2, at point D. A decrease in real wealth would tend to lower the level of consumption spending to C_1, at point B. A higher interest rate tends to cause a decrease in consumption spending from point A to point B. As household debt increases, other things equal, consumption spending would fall from point A to point B. In general, an increase in consumer confidence would act to increase household spending (a movement from point A to point D) and a decrease in consumer confidence would act to decrease household spending (a movement from point A to point B).

current period would likely motivate an increase in savings today, which would permit households to consume more goods and services at some future date.

Household Debt   Remember when that friend of yours ran up his credit card obligations so high that he stopped buying goods except the basic necessities? Well, our average household might find itself in the same situation if its outstanding debt exceeds some reasonable level relative to its income. So, as debt increases, other things being equal, consumption expenditure would fall from point A to point B in Exhibit 1.

Expectations   Just as in microeconomics, decisions to spend may be influenced by a person's expectations of future disposable income, employment, or certain world events. Based on monthly surveys conducted that attempt to measure consumer confidence, an increase in consumer confidence generally acts to increase household spending (a movement from point A to point D in Exhibit 1) and a decrease in consumer confidence would act to decrease spending (a movement from point A to point B in Exhibit 1).

Tastes and Preferences   Of course, each household is different. Some are young and beginning a working career; some are without children; others have families; still others are older and perhaps retired from the workforce. Some households like to save, putting dollars away for later spending, whereas others spend all their income, or even borrow to spend more than their current disposable income. These saving and spending decisions often vary over a household's life cycle.

As you can see, many economic factors affect consumption expenditures. The factors already listed represent some of the most important. All of these factors are considered **autonomous determinants of consumption expenditures;** that is, those expenditures that are not dependent on the level of current disposable income.

autonomous determinants of consumption expenditures
expenditures not dependent on the level of current disposable income

CONSUMPTION IN THE KEYNESIAN MODEL

In our first model, we looked at the economic variables that affected consumption expenditures when disposable income was fixed. This assumption is clearly unrealistic, but it allows us to develop some of the basic building blocks of the Keynesian expenditure model. Now we'll look at a slightly more complicated model in which consumption also depends on disposable income.

If you think about what determines your own current consumption spending, you know that it depends on many factors previously discussed, such as your age, family size, interest rates, expected future disposable income, wealth, and, most importantly, your current disposable income. Recall from earlier chapters, disposable income is your after-tax income. Your personal consumption spending depends primarily on your current disposable income. In fact, empirical studies confirm that most people's consumption spending is closely tied to their disposable income.

Revisiting Marginal Propensity to Consume and Save

What happens to current consumption spending when a person earns some additional disposable income? Most people will spend some of their extra income and save some of it. The additional consumption resulting from an additional dollar of disposable income is what economists call your **marginal propensity to consume (MPC).** That is, MPC is equal to the *change* in consumption spending (ΔC) divided by the *change* in disposable income (ΔDY):

$$\text{MPC} = \Delta C / \Delta DY$$

For example, suppose you won a lottery prize of $1000. You might decide to spend $750 of your winnings today and save $250. In this example, your marginal propensity to consume is 0.75 (or 75 percent) because out of the extra $1000, you decided to spend 75 percent of it (0.75 × $1000 = $750).

The term *marginal propensity to consume* has two parts: (1) *marginal* refers to the fact that you received an extra amount of disposable income—in addition to your income, not your total income; and (2) *propensity to consume* refers to how much you tend to spend on consumer goods and services out of your additional income.

The flip side of the marginal propensity to consume is the **marginal propensity to save (MPS)**—the additional saving that results from an additional dollar of disposable income. That is, MPS is equal to the *change* in savings (ΔS) divided by the change in disposable income (ΔDY):

$$\text{MPS} = \Delta S / \Delta DY$$

In the earlier lottery example, your marginal propensity to save is 0.25, or 25 percent, because you decided to save 25 percent of your additional disposable income (0.25 × $1000 = $250). Because your additional disposable income must be either consumed or saved, the marginal propensity to consume plus the marginal propensity to save must add up to 1, or 100 percent.

Let's illustrate the marginal propensity to consume in Exhibit 2. Suppose you estimated that you had to spend $8000 a year, even if you earned no income for the year, for necessities such as food, clothing, and shelter. And suppose for every $1000 of added disposable income you earn, you spend 75 percent of it and save 25 percent of it. So if your disposable income is $0, you spend $8000 (that means you have to borrow or reduce your existing savings just to survive). If your disposable income is $20 000, you'll spend $8000 plus 75 percent of $20 000 (which equals $15 000), for total spending of $23 000. If your disposable income is $40 000, you'll spend $8000 plus 75 percent of $40 000 (which equals $30 000), for total spending of $38 000.

What's your marginal propensity to consume? In this case, if you spend 75 percent of every additional $1000 you earn, your marginal propensity to consume is 0.75 or 75 percent. And if you save 25 percent of every additional $1000 you earn, your marginal propensity to save is 0.25.

In Exhibit 2, the slope of the line represents the marginal propensity to consume. To better understand this concept, look at what happens when your disposable income rises

marginal propensity to consume (MPC)
the additional consumption resulting from an additional dollar of disposable income

marginal propensity to save (MPS)
the additional saving that results from an additional dollar of income

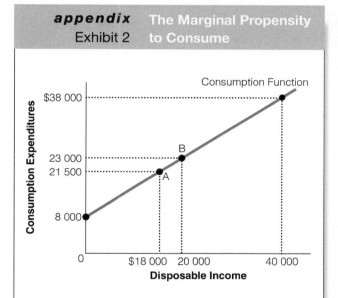

appendix **The Marginal Propensity**
Exhibit 2 **to Consume**

The slope of the line represents the marginal propensity to consume. At a disposable income of $18 000, you spend $8000 plus 75 percent of $18 000 (which is $13 500), for total spending of $21 500. If your disposable income rises to $20 000, you spend $8000 plus 75 percent of $20 000 (which is $15 000), for total spending of $23 000. So when your disposable income rises by $2000 (from $18 000 to $20 000), your spending goes up by $1500 (from $21 500 to $23 000). Your marginal propensity to consume is $1500 (the increase in spending) divided by $2000 (the increase in disposable income), which equals 0.75, or 75 percent. But notice that this MPC calculation is also the calculation of the slope of the line from point A to point B.

from $18 000 to $20 000. At a disposable income of $18 000, you spend $8000 plus 75 percent of $18 000 (which is $13 500), for total spending of $21 500. If your disposable income rises to $20 000, you spend $8000 plus 75 percent of $20 000 (which is $15 000), for total spending of $23 000. So when your disposable income rises by $2000 (from $18 000 to $20 000), your spending goes up by $1500 (from $21 500 to $23 000). Your marginal propensity to consume is $1500 (the increase in spending) divided by $2000 (the increase in disposable income), which equals 0.75, or 75 percent. But notice that this calculation is also the calculation of the slope of the line from point A to point B in the exhibit. Recall that the slope of the line is the rise (the change on the vertical axis) over the run (the change on the horizontal axis). In this case, that's $1500 divided by $2000, which makes 0.75 the marginal propensity to consume. So the marginal propensity to consume is the same as the slope of the line in our graph of consumption and disposable income.

Now, let's take this same logic and apply it to the economy as a whole. If we add up, or aggregate, everyone's consumption and everyone's income, we'll get a line that looks like the one in Exhibit 2, but that applies to the entire economy. This line or functional relationship is called a *consumption function*. Let's suppose consumption spending in the economy is $1 billion plus 75 percent of income.

Now, with consumption equal to $1 billion plus 75 percent of income, consumption is partly autonomous (the $1 billion part, which people would spend no matter what their income, which depends on the current interest rate, real wealth, debt, and expectations), and partly *induced*, which means it depends on income. The induced consumption is the portion that's equal to 75 percent of income.

What is the total amount of expenditure in this economy? Because we've assumed that investment, government purchases, and net exports are zero, aggregate expenditure is just equal to the amount of consumption spending represented by our consumption function.

EQUILIBRIUM IN THE KEYNESIAN MODEL

The next part of the Keynesian aggregate expenditure model is to examine what conditions are needed for the economy to be in equilibrium. This discussion also tells us why the Keynesian expenditure model is sometimes called a *Keynesian-cross model*. In order to determine equilibrium, we need to show (1) that income equals output in the economy, and (2) that in equilibrium, aggregate expenditure (or consumption in this example) equals output. First, income equals output because people earn income by producing goods and services. For example, workers earn wages because they produce some product that is then sold on the market, and owners of firms earn profits because the products they sell provide more income than the cost of producing them. So any income that is earned by anyone in the economy arises from the production of output in the economy. From now on, we'll use this idea and say that income equals output; we'll use the terms *income* and *output* interchangeably.

The second condition needed for equilibrium (aggregate expenditure in the economy equals output) is the distinctive feature of the Keynesian expenditure model. Just as income must equal output (because income comes from selling goods and services), aggregate expenditure equals output because people can't earn income until the products they produce are sold to someone. Every good or service that is produced in the economy must be purchased by someone or added to inventories. Exhibit 3 plots aggregate expenditure against output. As you can see, it's a 45-degree line (slope = 1). The 45-degree line shows that the number on the horizontal axis, representing the amount of output in the economy, real GDP (Y), is equal to the number on the vertical axis, representing the amount of real aggregate expenditure (*AE*) in the economy. If output is $5 billion, then in equilibrium, aggregate expenditure must equal $5 billion. All points of macroeconomic equilibrium lie on the 45-degree line.

DISEQUILIBRIUM IN THE KEYNESIAN MODEL

What would happen if, for some reason, output was lower than its equilibrium level, as would be the case if output was Y_1 in Exhibit 4?

Looking at the vertical dotted line, we see that when output is Y_1, aggregate expenditure (shown by the consumption function) is greater than output (shown by the 45-degree line). This amount is labelled the distance AB on the graph. So, people would be trying to buy more goods and services (*A*) than were being produced (*B*), which would cause producers to increase the amount of production, which would increase output in the economy. This process would continue until output reached its equilibrium level, where the two lines intersect. Another way to think about this disequilibrium is that consumers would be buying more than is currently produced, causing a decrease in inventories on shelves and in warehouses from their desired levels. Clearly, profit-seeking businesspeople would increase production to bring their inventory stocks back up to the desired levels. In doing so, they would move production to the equilibrium level.

Similarly, if output was above its equilibrium level, as would occur if output was Y_2 in Exhibit 4, economic forces would act to reduce output. At this point, as you can see by looking at the graph above point Y_2 on the horizontal axis, aggregate expenditure (D) is less than output (C). People wouldn't want to buy all the output that is being produced, so producers would want to reduce their production. They would keep reducing their output until the equilibrium level was reached. Using the inventory adjustment process, inventories would be bulging from shelves and warehouses and firms would reduce output and production until inventory stocks returned to the desired level. For example, automobile companies might close plants to reduce inventories.

This basic model—in which we've assumed that consumption spending is the only component of aggregate expenditure (i.e., we've ignored investment, government spending, and net exports) and that some consumption spending is autonomous—is quite simple, yet it is the essence of the Keynesian-cross model. Equilibrium in this model, and in more complicated versions of the model, always occurs where one line representing aggregate expenditure crosses another line that represents the equilibrium condition where aggregate expenditure equals output (the 45-degree line).

Now let's put Exhibits 2 and 3 together to find the equilibrium in the economy, shown in Exhibit 4. As you might guess, the point where the two lines cross is the equilibrium point. Why? Because it is only at this point that aggregate expenditure is equal to output. Aggregate expenditure is shown by the flatter line (Aggregate expenditure = Consumption). The equilibrium condition is shown by the 45-degree line ($Y = AE$). The only point for which consumption spending equals aggregate expenditure equals output is the point where those two lines intersect, labelled "Equilibrium." Because these points are on the 45-degree line, equilibrium output equals equilibrium aggregate expenditure.

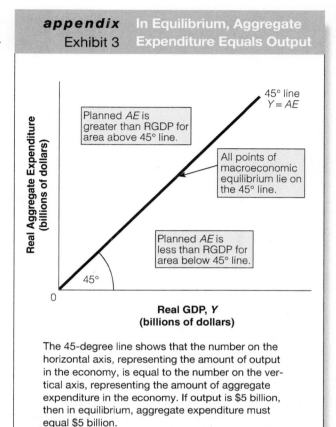

**appendix
Exhibit 3** In Equilibrium, Aggregate Expenditure Equals Output

Planned *AE* is greater than RGDP for area above 45° line.

All points of macroeconomic equilibrium lie on the 45° line.

Planned *AE* is less than RGDP for area below 45° line.

45° line $Y = AE$

Real Aggregate Expenditure (billions of dollars)

45°

0

**Real GDP, *Y*
(billions of dollars)**

The 45-degree line shows that the number on the horizontal axis, representing the amount of output in the economy, is equal to the number on the vertical axis, representing the amount of aggregate expenditure in the economy. If output is $5 billion, then in equilibrium, aggregate expenditure must equal $5 billion.

appendix
Exhibit 4 **Disequilibrium and Equilibrium In the Keynesian Model**

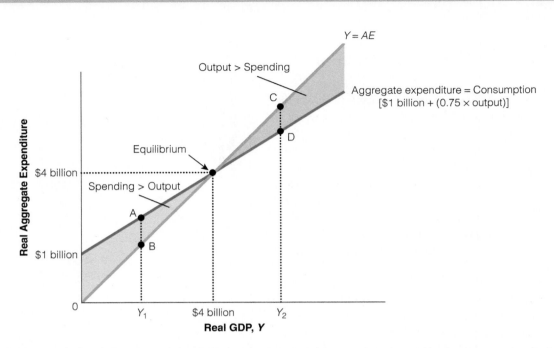

When RGDP is Y_1, aggregate expenditure is greater than output—distance AB on the graph. Consumers are trying to buy more goods and services (A) than are being produced (B), which causes producers to increase the amount of production, increasing output in the economy. This process continues until output reaches its equilibrium level, where the two lines intersect. If RGDP is at Y_2, aggregate expenditure (D) is less than output (C). Consumers wouldn't want to buy all the output that is being produced, so producers would want to reduce their production. They would keep reducing their output until the equilibrium level of output was reached. The only point for which consumption spending equals real aggregate planned expenditure equals output is the point where those two lines intersect. Because these points are on the 45-degree line, equilibrium output equals equilibrium aggregate expenditure.

ADDING INVESTMENT, GOVERNMENT PURCHASES, AND NET EXPORTS

Now we can complicate our model in another important way by adding in the other three major components of expenditure in the economy: investment, government purchases, and net exports. We'll add these components to the model but assume that they are autonomous, that is, they don't depend on the level of income or output in the economy.

Suppose that consumption depends on the level of income or output in the economy, but investment, government purchases, and net exports don't; instead, they depend on other things in the economy, such as interest rates, political considerations, or the condition of foreign economies. Now, aggregate expenditure (AE) consists of consumption (C) plus investment (I) plus government purchases (G) plus net exports (NX):

$$AE \equiv C + I + G + NX$$

This equation is nothing more than a definition (indicated by the $\equiv$ rather than $=$): Aggregate expenditure equals the sum of its components.

When we add up all the components of aggregate expenditure, we'll get an upward-sloping line, as we did in the previous section because consumption increases as income increases. But because we're now allowing for investment, government purchases, and net exports, the autonomous portion of aggregate expenditure is larger. Thus, the intercept of the aggregate expenditure line is higher, as shown in Exhibit 5.

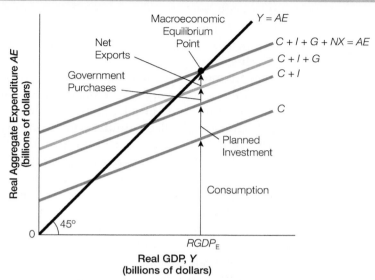

Adding $I + G + NX$ leads to a larger intercept of the aggregate expenditure line. Because consumption is the only component of aggregate expenditure that depends on income, the slope of the line is the same as the slope of the line in Exhibit 4. The new equilibrium occurs where the two lines cross, where the aggregate expenditure line, which has a slope of 0.75, intersects the equilibrium line, which is the 45-degree line.

What is the new equilibrium? As before, the equilibrium occurs where the two lines cross, that is, where the aggregate expenditure line intersects the equilibrium line, which is the 45-degree line.

Now that we've added in the other components of spending, especially investment spending, we can begin to discuss some of the more realistic factors related to the business cycle. This discussion of what happens to the economy during business cycles is a major element of Keynesian theory, which was designed to explain what happens in recessions.

If you look at historical economic data, you'll see that investment spending fluctuates much more than overall output in the economy. In recessions, output declines, and a major portion of the decline occurs because investment falls sharply. In expansions, investment is the major contributor to economic growth. The two major explanations for the volatile movement of investment over the business cycle involve planned investment and unplanned investment.

The first explanation for investment's strong business cycle movement is that *planned* investment responds dramatically to perceptions of future changes in economic activity. If business firms think that the economy will be good in the future, they'll build new factories, buy more computers, and hire more workers today, in anticipation of being able to sell more goods in the future. On the other hand, if firms think the economy will be weak in the future, they'll cut back on both investment and hiring. Economists find that planned investment is extremely sensitive to firms' perceptions about the future. And if firms desire to invest more today, it generates ripple effects that make the economy grow even faster.

The second explanation for investment's movement over the business cycle is that businesses encounter *unplanned* changes in investment as well. The idea here is that recessions, to some extent, occur as the economy is making a transition, before it reaches equilibrium. We'll use Exhibit 6 to illustrate this idea. In the exhibit, equilibrium occurs

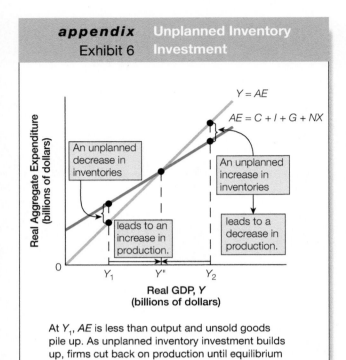

appendix
Exhibit 6
Unplanned Inventory Investment

At Y_1, *AE* is less than output and unsold goods pile up. As unplanned inventory investment builds up, firms cut back on production until equilibrium output is restored at Y_0. At Y_2, *AE* is greater than output: Consumers want to buy more than firms are producing. Inventories become depleted and firms increase production until inventories are restored and output returns to equilibrium at Y_0.

at output of Y_0. Now, consider what would happen if, for some reason, firms produced too many goods, bringing the economy to output level Y_1. At output level Y_1, aggregate expenditure is less than output because the aggregate expenditure line is below the 45-degree line at that point. When people aren't buying all the products that firms are producing, unsold goods begin piling up. In the national income accounts, unsold goods in firms' inventories are counted in a subcategory of investment—inventory investment. The firms didn't plan for this to happen, so the piling up of inventories reflects **unplanned inventory investment.** Of course, once firms realize that inventories are rising because they've produced too much, they cut back on production, reducing output below Y_1. This process continues until firms' inventories are restored to normal levels and output returns to Y_0.

Now let's look at what would happen if firms produced too few goods, as occurs when output is at Y_2. At output level Y_2, aggregate expenditure is greater than output because the aggregate expenditure line is above the 45-degree line at that point. People want to buy more goods than firms are producing, so firms' inventories begin to decline or become depleted. Again, this change in inventories shows up in the national income accounts, this time as a decline in firms' inventories and thus a decline in investment. Again, the firms didn't plan for this situation, so once they realize that inventories are declining because they haven't produced enough, they'll increase production beyond Y_2. Equilibrium is reached when firms' inventories are restored to normal levels and output returns to Y_0. So, our Keynesian aggregate expenditure model helps to explain the process of the business cycle, working through investment.

unplanned inventory investment *collection of inventory that results when people do not buy the products firms are producing*

Shifts in Aggregate Expenditure and the Multiplier

What happens if one of the components of aggregate expenditure increases for reasons other than an increase in income? Remember that we called these components or parts *autonomous*. Households' expectations might become more optimistic, or households may find credit conditions easier as interest rates decline, or their real wealth might increase as the stock market rises. All of these factors increase autonomous consumption, so total consumption at every level of income increases. Firms might increase their investment (especially if their productivity rises or the interest rate declines), government might increase its spending, or net exports could rise as foreign economies improve their economic health. Any of these things would increase aggregate expenditure for any given level of income, shifting the aggregate expenditure curve up, as shown in Exhibit 7.

Suppose that firms optimistic about their future profitability increase their planned investment spending on plants, factories, and machines by $100 million. In Exhibit 7, we see that the increase in planned investment spending shifts the aggregate expenditure curve upward and results in a $400 million gain in equilibrium real GDP, the difference between the equilibrium real GDP at point A and the equilibrium real GDP at point Z. How did the $100 million increase in autonomous investment raise real GDP demanded by $400 million? This result might seem amazing—that an increase in

expenditure multiplier *the multiplier that considers only the impact of consumption changes on aggregate expenditures* planned investment spending of a $100 billion can result in a $400 million increase in real GDP—but it merely reflects a well-understood process, known as the **expenditure multiplier**—the multiplier that considers only the impact of consumption changes on aggregate expenditures.

A caution here: Do not assume that the multiplier applies only to changes in planned investment spending. Multipliers apply to any increase in autonomous expenditure. As an example, if the stock market went up to increase the amount of autonomous household spending by $100 million, the level of output would go up the same $400 million as found in the preceding example. The idea of the multiplier is that permanent increases in spending in one part of the economy lead to increased spending by others in the economy as well. When firms increase investment spending, private resource owners earn more wages, interest, rents, and profits, so they spend more. The higher level of economic activity encourages even more spending, until a new equilibrium with higher output is reached, Y_1 rather than Y_0. In this example, the increase in output is four times as large as the initial increase in investment spending that started the cycle. Let's see how this process works in more detail.

Exhibit 8 shows what happens along the way. We begin at point A, with output of $14 billion. The increase in investment spending of $100 million directly increases aggregate expenditure by that amount, represented by point B. Firms

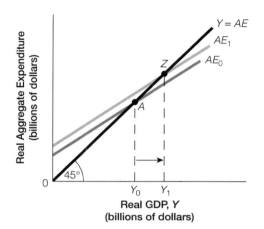

appendix Exhibit 7 Increases in the Autonomous Components of Aggregate Expenditure

If one of the "autonomous" components of aggregate expenditure increases for reasons other than an increase in income (such as optimistic consumer or business expectations, a decrease in the interest rate, or real wealth increases), government might increase its spending or net exports could rise as foreign economies improve their economic health. Any of these things would increase aggregate expenditure for any given level of income, shifting the aggregate expenditure curve up, as shown in this exhibit.

appendix Exhibit 8 Aggregate Expenditures and the Multiplier Process

At point A, output is $14 billion and the increase in investment spending of $100 million directly increases aggregate expenditure by that amount, represented by point B. Firms observe the increase in aggregate expenditure and produce more output, moving the economy to point C, with output of $14.1 billion. But now consumers have an extra $100 million in income and they want to spend three-fourths of it (the MPC is 0.75). Three-fourths of $100 million is $75 million, so consumers now spend an additional $75 million, increasing aggregate expenditure to $14.175 billion at point D. Again, firms observe the increase in expenditure and increase output, bringing the economy to point E. This process continues until the economy eventually reaches point Z, at which output is $14.4 billion. The process is not accomplished immediately, but over the course of several quarters.

observe the increase in aggregate expenditure (perhaps because they see their inventories declining), so over the next few months, they produce more output, moving the economy to point C, with output of $14.1 billion. But now consumers have an extra $100 million in income and they want to spend three-fourths of it (because the marginal propensity to consume is 0.75). Three-fourths of $100 million is $75 million, so consumers now spend an additional $75 million, increasing aggregate expenditure to $14.175 billion at point D. Again, firms observe the increase in expenditure, so over the next few months, they increase output, bringing the economy to point E. This process continues until the economy eventually reaches point Z, at which output is $14.4 billion.

You can see on the graph how the economy reaches its new equilibrium at point Z. We can also calculate it numerically by adding up an infinite series of numbers in the following way. The first increase in output was $100 million, which comes directly from the increase in investment spending. Then consumers, with higher incomes of $100 million, want to spend three-fourths of it, so they increase spending: $100 million × 3/4 = $75 million. Now, with incomes higher by $75 million, consumers want to spend an additional three-fourths of it: $75 million × 3/4 = $56 million. Again, incomes are higher, so consumers will spend more, this time in the amount $56 million × 3/4 = $42 million. The process continues indefinitely. To find the total increase in output (or income), we simply need to add up all these amounts. It turns out that an infinite sum with this pattern is exactly $100 million/(1 − 3/4) = $400 million. So output increases by $400 million from $14 billion to $14.4 billion.

This calculation of the sum of all of the increases to output can be written in a convenient way. As you saw in this example, the multiplier depends on how much consumers spend out of any additions to their income. So in this model in which consumption spending is the only component of aggregate expenditure that depends on income, the multiplier is equal to 1/(1 − MPC), where MPC is the marginal propensity to consume. In the previous example, MPC = 3/4, so the multiplier is 1/(1 − 3/4) = 4. The same multiplier holds whether the increase in aggregate expenditures arises from an increase in investment spending, as in the example, or from an increase in other autonomous elements of spending, such as government purchases, net exports, or the autonomous portion of consumption spending. The larger (smaller) the MPC the larger (smaller) the multiplier. For example, if the MPC is 0.8 (1/[1 − 0.8] or 1/0.2 = 5) then the multiplier would be 5. If the MPC is 0.5 (1/[1 − 0.5] or 1/0.5 = 2), then the multiplier would be reduced to 2. The true multiplier is usually smaller because of complications that we will discuss in the chapter on fiscal policy.

The multiplier can operate in both directions. During the Great Depression, both consumption spending and planned investment fell, causing a decrease in aggregate expenditure. As sales fell, workers were laid off and falling levels of production and income led to further declines in consumption spending as the economy fell into a downward spiral. The downturn can also start in a certain sector and then spread via the multiplier to other sectors of the economy. Recall, the information technology recession of 2001. The initial impact of the decline in investment spending was felt in the computer and telecommunications industries, but eventually the declines in production, income, and spending spread into other industries, such as those for automobiles, furniture, appliances, airlines, and restaurants. And the financial crisis of 2008 started in the U.S. housing and financial sectors and was quickly felt throughout the Canadian economy.

(Chapter 17 Appendix) *For Your Review*

1. Which of the following are likely to cause a reduction in consumption?

   a. an increase in interest rates

   b. an increase in the value of stock market portfolios

   c. a decrease in disposable income

   d. an increase in income taxes

   e. deflation

2. Identify the most volatile component of aggregate expenditure. Identify its largest component.

3. Which of the following will cause the aggregate expenditure schedule to increase?

   a. an increase in consumer optimism

   b. an increase in the purchase of imports

   c. an increase in the sale of exports

   d. pessimism by business owners about the outlook of the economy

   e. an increase in government spending due to the outbreak of war

4. What would happen to autonomous consumption if household debt fell and the interest rate rose over the same time period?

5. What would happen to autonomous consumption if real wealth increased and expectations of the future became more optimistic?

6. Consumption equals $32 000 when disposable income equals $40 000. Consumption increases to $38 000 when disposable income increases to $50 000. What is the marginal propensity to consume? The marginal propensity to save? What is the value of the spending multiplier?

7. If the marginal propensity to save increases, what happens to the consumption function?

8. If MPC was equal to 0.5, would doubling your income double your consumption spending?

9. Why can't an economy with an MPC greater than 1 reach a stable equilibrium in the aggregate expenditure model?

10. Why are unplanned inventory changes the key to predicting future changes in real GDP in the aggregate expenditure model?

11. Why would an increase in planned investment increase real GDP, but an unplanned increase in inventory investment decrease real GDP, in the aggregate expenditure model?

12. If the economy is a net importer, what will that do to the aggregate expenditure function and equilibrium level of real GDP?

13. Why are planned and unplanned investment unlikely to both increase over the same period of time?

14. Why do the aggregate expenditure function and the aggregate demand curve both shift upward at the same time?

15. Evaluate the following statement: The Keynesian assumption of wage and price rigidity best corresponds to the steepest portion of the aggregate supply curve, where factories are operating below capacity.

■ What is fiscal policy?
■ How does fiscal policy affect the government's budget?

WHAT IS FISCAL POLICY?

fiscal policy

use of government spending and/or taxes to alter RGDP and the price level

Fiscal policy is the use of government spending and/or taxes to alter RGDP and the price level. Sometimes it is necessary for the government to use fiscal policy to stimulate the economy during a contraction (or recession) or to try to curb an expansion in order to bring inflation under control. In the early 1980s, the U.S. government implemented large tax cuts, which helped the U.S. economy out of a recession. In 2001 and 2003, tax cuts were again implemented to combat an economic slowdown and promote long-term economic growth. In the 1990s, Japan used large government spending programs to help pull itself out of a recessionary slump.

Beginning in the early 2000s, the federal government in Canada began cutting income taxes to promote long-term economic growth, a policy objective it continued in subsequent budgets. The 2009 budget, however, marked a dramatic departure from the fiscal restraint illustrated in earlier budgets, as the government began to deal with the global economic crisis. The first year of Canada's Economic Action Plan saw the government provide almost $30 billion in support of the Canadian economy. In total, this was equivalent to 1.9 percent of total spending in the Canadian economy in 2009. The 2010 budget confirmed an additional $19 billion in new federal spending under year 2 of Canada's Economic Action Plan, stimulus that was accompanied by additional tax relief measures designed to augment the already substantial tax relief provided by the government since 2006. The tax relief provided to individuals and families was estimated to be about $160 billion throughout 2008–09 and the following five fiscal years.

With the 2011 budget, as planned, the vast majority of initiatives first announced in the 2009 budget were concluded. The conclusion of this first phase of Canada's Economic Action Plan—the stimulus phase—marked the commencement of the second phase of the Plan—the low-tax plan for jobs and growth phase. This second phase would see the government return to the sustainable low-tax environment and growth-friendly policies it had first introduced in 2006. In the 2012 and 2013 versions of Canada's Economic Action Plan, the government maintained its focus on low-tax fiscal policies, emphasizing a return to balanced budgets, job creation, growth, and long-term prosperity. When should the government use such policies? How well do they work? These are just a couple of the questions we will answer in this chapter.

When government spending (for purchases of goods and services and for transfer payments to individuals, like EI benefits) exceeds tax revenues for a given fiscal year, there is a **budget deficit.** When tax revenues are greater than government spending for a given fiscal year, a **budget surplus** exists. A balanced budget, where government expenditures equal tax revenues, may seldom occur unless efforts are made to deliberately balance the budget as a matter of public policy.

HOW DOES FISCAL POLICY AFFECT THE GOVERNMENT'S BUDGET?

When the government wants to stimulate the economy by increasing aggregate demand, it will use **expansionary fiscal policy** and increase government spending on goods and services, lower taxes, or use some combination of these approaches. Any of those options will increase a budget deficit (or reduce a budget surplus). Thus, expansionary fiscal policy is associated with increased government budget deficits. Likewise, if the government wants to dampen a boom in the economy by reducing aggregate demand, it will use **contractionary fiscal policy** and reduce its spending on goods and services, increase taxes, or use some combination of these approaches. Thus, contractionary fiscal policy will tend to increase a budget surplus (or reduce a budget deficit).

budget deficit
government spending exceeds tax revenues for a given fiscal year

budget surplus
tax revenues are greater than government expenditures for a given fiscal year

expansionary fiscal policy
use of fiscal policy tools to foster increased output by increasing government spending and/or lowering taxes

contractionary fiscal policy
use of fiscal policy tools to reduce output by decreasing government spending and/or increasing taxes

SECTION CHECK

- Fiscal policy is the use of government spending on goods and services and/or taxes to affect aggregate demand and to alter RGDP and the price level.
- Expansionary fiscal policies will increase a budget deficit (or reduce a budget surplus) through greater government spending, lower taxes, or both. Contractionary fiscal policies will increase a budget surplus (or reduce a budget deficit) through reduced government spending, higher taxes, or both.

section
18.2

Government: Spending and Taxation

- What are the major categories of government spending?
- What are the major sources of government revenue?

WHAT ARE THE MAJOR CATEGORIES OF GOVERNMENT SPENDING?

In 2011–12, the federal government spent $271.4 billion on goods and services and on transfer payments to individuals. The provincial and territorial governments combined spent $329.7 billion on goods and services and on transfer payments to individuals.

According to Exhibit 1(a), 25 percent of federal government spending in 2011–12 was accounted for under major transfers to persons, including Employment Insurance and Old Age Security programs. Transfers of money from the federal government to other levels of government (for spending on postsecondary education and health care) amounted to 21 percent of federal government expenditure. Interest payments that the federal government makes on its outstanding debt account for 11 percent of total spending, whereas national defence accounts for 8 percent. Expenses associated with the operation of Crown corporations and other federal departments and agencies accounted for 3 percent and 18 percent of total spending, respectively. The remaining 13 percent of federal government spending (other transfers) includes foreign affairs and international aid, the environment, recreation and culture, resource conservation, and industrial development.

WHAT ARE THE MAJOR SOURCES OF GOVERNMENT REVENUE?

Governments have to pay their bills like any person or institution that spends money. But how do they obtain revenue? Two major avenues are taxation and borrowing. When the government runs a budget deficit, spending exceeds tax revenue and therefore part

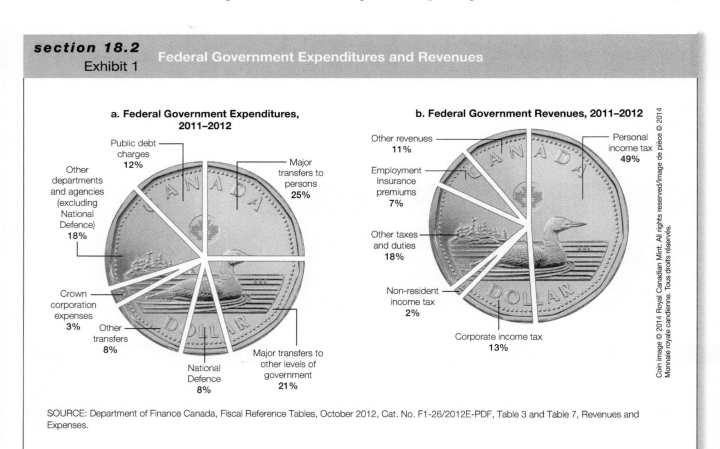

section 18.2
Exhibit 1   Federal Government Expenditures and Revenues

a. Federal Government Expenditures, 2011–2012

Public debt charges 12%
Other departments and agencies (excluding National Defence) 18%
Crown corporation expenses 3%
Other transfers 8%
National Defence 8%
Major transfers to other levels of government 21%
Major transfers to persons 25%

b. Federal Government Revenues, 2011–2012

Other revenues 11%
Employment Insurance premiums 7%
Other taxes and duties 18%
Non-resident income tax 2%
Corporate income tax 13%
Personal income tax 49%

SOURCE: Department of Finance Canada, Fiscal Reference Tables, October 2012, Cat. No. F1-26/2012E-PDF, Table 3 and Table 7, Revenues and Expenses.

Business **CONNECTION**

CORPORATE TAX SAVINGS BRING RESPONSIBILITY

There's no question that one of the main roles of government is to help increase real GDP. Only with increases in economic growth can a country improve its standard of living, characterized and measured by per capita real GDP. The ability to increase real GDP depends on the four engines of the economy: consumer spending (*C*); business investment (*I*) spending; government spending and taxation (*G*); and net exports, or exports less imports (*X* – *M*).

Generally speaking, consumers and business drive the economy, and government involvement should be limited to stabilization and stimulation. Many consumers and businesses feel that the less government involvement in the economy, the better—but we rarely hear those sentiments in recessionary periods when consumers aren't spending and business isn't investing due to consumer lethargy. It's left to governments to stimulate their economies when the other engines can't or won't contribute. Despite this debate, business operators should understand how government involvement affects their revenues, costs, and net profits, in both the short and longer terms.

Governments must balance their involvement between consumers and business, but also between the choices of taxes and spending. For every dollar that government invests on the consumer side, significantly more are required on the business side to get the equivalent results. Many business owners feel that governments should reduce corporate tax rates to allow for increased business investment, but the impact that this strategy has on economic stimulation is debatable.

Over the past decade, corporate taxes in some provinces have been reduced to record lows, with little in the way of positive results to show for it in growth or employment. In fact, evidence has shown that many corporations are not reinvesting their tax savings and, in many cases, the tax savings have resulted in increased profits being redistributed to shareholders, resulting in opportunity costs to the wider economy (i.e., the benefits that would have been gained if the savings had been reinvested). Governments are put in a

very difficult position: If corporate taxes are not reinvested into the economy, the result can be lower production and fewer jobs. This also requires governments to increase their debt, because less revenue is being generated from corporate and consumer taxes. Over the long term, consumers are left to make up the tax shortage. Some firms are sitting on record levels of cash and one proposed solution is to unlock those funds and get them back into circulation by taxing the unused portions. This will force firms to either use it or lose it, and ensures that shareholders don't benefit from the sacrifices that other sectors in the economy make in trying to stimulate growth.

Business needs to appreciate that there's a limit to government's ability to spend, and that the government is constrained by its ability to raise funds. Governments raise funds from taxation or borrowing. In both cases, consumers will end up pay higher taxes to fund government spending. If corporations don't pay their fair share, it falls to consumers, which in turn affects their ability to buy the goods that firms produce. In an ideal world, firms would share their responsibility for the overall health of the economy. But what's good for the individual is not necessarily good for the masses, and without regulation, individuals (or firms) will opt for individual benefit over society's benefit. If this is the case, government will have no choice but to regulate more to ensure economic stability and growth.

1. Many business owners believe government intervention is bad for an economy. What is your opinion and what are the foundations that shape your opinions?

2. As a business owner, would you rather see greater government assistance for consumers or for businesses? Why?

3. Many governments attempt to gain support from businesses by lowering the corporate tax rate. Do you think this is a good policy? Why or why not? What effects would lowering personal taxes rather than corporate taxes have on the economy?

of the spending must be financed by borrowing. When the budget is balanced, all spending is financed by tax revenue and there is no necessity to borrow.

In 2010–11, the federal government made $245.2 billion in revenue. Exhibit 1(b) shows the revenue sources for the federal government. At the federal level, the majority of revenue, 64 percent, comes in the form of income taxes on individuals, corporations, and non-residents. Consumption taxes, such as the Goods and Services Tax (GST) and federal excise taxes on gasoline, alcohol, and tobacco products, account for 18 percent of federal revenue. Social security contributions, like Employment Insurance premiums paid by both employees and employers, amount to 8 percent of federal government revenue. Other revenue, at 11 percent, comes largely from investment income and sales of goods and services.

A Progressive Tax

One impact of substantial taxes on personal income is that the effective take-home income of Canadians is significantly altered by the tax system. A **progressive tax** is designed so that the amount of an individual's tax rises as a proportion of income, as the person's income rises. With progressive taxes, of which the federal personal income tax is one example, those with higher incomes pay a greater proportion of their income in taxes. A progressive tax is one tool that the government can use to redistribute income.

Another way of identifying a tax as being progressive is if its marginal tax rate (the amount of tax paid on an additional dollar of taxable income) is greater than its average tax rate (the average amount of tax paid out of your total taxable income). For example, suppose you have $55 000 in taxable income, with the first $10 000 taxed at 10 percent, the next $15 000 taxed at 15 percent, and the remainder taxed at 20 percent. The marginal tax rate would be determined by the third tax bracket (in this example, 20 percent), since your total taxable income exceeds the upper limits of both the first and second brackets ($10 000 and $25 000, respectively).

To determine the average tax rate, we first need to calculate your total tax liability, remembering that each tax rate applies to only a proportion of your taxable income. In this example, the total tax liability is determined as follows: the 10 percent tax rate applies to the first $10 000 of taxable income—generating $1000 of tax liability ($10 000 × 10 percent); the 15 percent tax rate applies to the next $15 000 of taxable income—generating $2250 of tax liability ($15 000 × 15 percent); finally, the 20 percent tax rate applies to the remaining amount of taxable income ($30 000 in this example)—generating a tax liability of $6000 ($30 000 × 20 percent). Adding together the tax liabilities from each tax bracket generates a total tax liability of $9250 ($1000 + $2250 + $6000). Once we know our total tax liability, the average tax rate can be calculated by determining what percentage of your total taxable income that your total tax liability represents. For this example, the average tax rate is 16.8 percent ($9250/$55 000). Therefore, since the marginal tax rate, 20 percent, is greater than the average tax rate, 16.8 percent, the tax is confirmed as progressive.

A Regressive Tax

Some people consider an **excise tax**—a sales tax on individual products such as alcohol, tobacco, and gasoline—to be the most unfair type of tax because it is generally the most regressive. A **regressive tax** is designed so that the amount of an individual's tax falls as a proportion of income, as the person's income rises. A regressive tax takes a greater proportion of the income of lower-income groups than of higher-income groups. This type of tax on specific items will impose a far greater burden, as a percentage of income, on the poor and middle class than on the wealthy, because low-income families pay a greater proportion of their income on these taxes than do high-income families.

In addition, excise taxes may lead to economic inefficiencies. By isolating a few products and subjecting them to discriminatory taxation, consumption taxes expose economic choices to political manipulation and lead to inefficiency. Regressive taxes can also be described as a tax where the marginal tax rate is less than the average tax rate.

Proportional Tax

Sometimes referred to as a *flat tax*, a **proportional tax** is designed so that all tax payers are subject to the tax rate regardless of earnings. In the case of a proportional tax

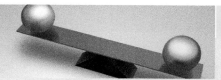

DEBATE

SHOULD CANADA RAISE CORPORATE TAXES?

For:

Western economies have been rebounding slowly since the end of the Great Recession, although below target levels of growth, inflation, and unemployment. Raising corporate taxes would go against conventional wisdom, which favours lowering taxes to try to stimulate the economy. Consistently, governments have lowered corporate tax rates in the belief that raising these taxes would stifle growth and cause unemployment rates to be above targets: Why would firms invest in employees if they had to pay higher taxes? There are those who would argue that the benefits of low tax rates have actually intensified lower rates of corporate investment. They say that if corporations don't use the high amounts of capital they are sitting on (see this chapter's Business Connection feature), the government may as well tax corporations at a higher level to entice them to use this capital, or if left idle, tax those funds and use the proceeds to invest back into the economy through infrastructure investment or other public uses. Since this theoretical model supports raising corporate taxes, surely that is what Canada should do for the benefit of the economy. Can you think of other arguments that you could use to defend the economic benefits of raising corporate taxes?

Against:

The foundations of fiscal policy are based on government's use of spending, taxation, and transfer payments. Since Ronald Regan's term of office as U.S. president, politicians have commonly believed that lowering tax rates benefits the economy in two ways: (1) more total revenues are actually generated for governments (a relationship known as the *Laffer curve*—see the Chapter 1 Appendix), and (2) there is a *trickle-down effect*, which is best explained by the author of the phrase, humourist Will Rogers, who during the Depression stated that "money was all appropriated for the top in hopes that it would trickle down to the needy." If governments subscribe to these theories, the premise in developing fiscal policy would be to lower corporate taxes. In the current economic climate, where the economy demands to be stimulated, there can be no reason to raise corporate taxes—that would lead to lower investment by corporations and ultimately lower employment and lower profits. Even the most conservative economists recognize that stimulation requires lower taxes and higher spending until the economy shows evidence of consistent growth and lowering unemployment. Then and only then will raising corporate taxes be justified, to help pay back the deficits that will have developed. Can you think of any other reasons why raising corporate taxes during the recovery stage would be detrimental to the Canadian economy? What other arguments could you use to bolster your position?

system, marginal and average tax rates would be equal. In 1998, the government of Alberta began the transition from a progressive tax system to a proportional tax system. Currently (2012), the singular tax rate for all taxpayers in Alberta is 10 percent of taxable income.

SECTION CHECK

- Major transfers to persons, such as Employment Insurance and Old Age Security programs, account for 25 percent of federal government spending. Other major expenditures are transfers to other levels of government (21 percent) and expenditures associated with the operation of other departments and agencies (18 percent).
- The largest source of federal revenue is income taxes on individuals and corporations (49 percent and 13 percent, respectively). Other taxes and duties collected by the federal government account for 10 percent of revenue.

section 18.3

The Multiplier Effect

- ◼ What is the multiplier effect?
- ◼ What impact does the multiplier effect have on the aggregate demand curve?
- ◼ What impact does the multiplier effect have on tax cuts?
- ◼ What factors can potentially reduce the size of the multiplier?

Recall from our earlier discussion that any one of the major spending components of aggregate demand (C, I, G, or $X - M$) can initiate changes in aggregate demand, thereby producing a new short-run equilibrium. If policymakers are unhappy with the present short-run equilibrium GDP, perhaps they consider unemployment too high because of a current aggregate demand shortfall. If government increased its purchases of jet fighters, highways, and schools, this increased spending would lead to an increase in aggregate demand. That is, governments can deliberately manipulate the level of their purchases to obtain a new short-run equilibrium value. But how much new additional government purchasing is necessary?

WHAT IS THE MULTIPLIER EFFECT?

multiplier effect
a chain reaction of additional income and purchases that results in total purchases that are greater than the initial increase in purchases

Usually when an initial increase in purchases of goods or services occurs, the ultimate increase in total purchases will tend to be greater than the initial increase; this chain reaction of additional income and purchases that result in total purchases that are greater than the initial increase in purchases is called the **multiplier effect.** But how does this effect work? Suppose the federal government increases its Department of National Defence budget by $100 million to buy new search-and-rescue helicopters. When the government purchases the helicopters, not only does it add to the total demand for goods and services directly, it also provides $100 million in added income to the companies that actually construct the helicopters. Those companies will then hire more workers and buy more capital equipment and other inputs in order to produce the new output. The owners of these inputs therefore receive more income because of the increase in government purchases. And what will they do with this additional income? Although behaviour will vary somewhat among individuals, collectively they will probably spend a substantial part of the additional income on additional consumption purchases, pay some additional taxes incurred because of the income, and save a bit of it as well. The marginal propensity to consume (*MPC*) is the fraction of additional disposable income that a household consumes rather than saves.

The Multiplier Effect at Work

Suppose that out of every dollar in *added* disposable income generated by increased government purchases, individuals collectively spend 75 cents on consumption purchases. In other words, the *MPC* is 0.75. The initial $100 million increase in government purchases causes both a $100 million increase in aggregate demand and an income increase of $100 million to suppliers of the inputs used to produce helicopters; the owners of those inputs, in turn, will spend an additional $75 million (75 percent of $100 million) on additional consumption purchases.

section 18.3
Exhibit 1   **The Multiplier Process**

Change in government purchases	$100 million—direct effect on *AD*
First change in consumption purchases	75 million (0.75 of 100)
Second change in consumption purchases	56.25 million (0.75 of 75)
Third change in consumption purchases	42.19 million (0.75 of 56.25)
Fourth change in consumption purchases	31.64 million (0.75 of 42.19)
Fifth change in consumption purchases	23.73 million (0.75 of 31.64)

The sum of the indirect effect on *AD*, through induced additional consumption purchases, is equal to $300 million.

$400 million = Total effect on purchases (*AD*)

As Exhibit 1 illustrates, a chain reaction has been started with each new round of purchases providing income to a new group of people who in turn increase their purchases. As successive changes in consumption purchases occur, the feedback becomes smaller and smaller. The added income generated and the number of resulting consumer purchases become smaller because some of the increase in income goes to savings and tax payments that do not immediately flow into greater investment or government expenditure. For example, as Exhibit 1 indicates, the fifth change in consumption purchases is indeed much smaller than the first change in consumption purchases. What is the total impact of the initial increase in purchases on additional purchases and income? We can find that out using the multiplier formula, calculated as follows:

$$\text{Multiplier} = \frac{1}{1 - MPC}$$

In this case,

$$\text{Multiplier} = 1/(1 - 0.75) = 1/(0.25) = 4$$

An initial increase in purchases of goods or services of $100 million will increase total purchases by $400 million ($100 million × 4), as the initial $100 million in government purchases also generates an additional $300 million in consumption purchases.

Changes in the *MPC* Affect the Multiplier Process

Note that the larger the marginal propensity to consume, the larger the multiplier effect, because relatively more additional consumption purchases out of any given income increase generate relatively larger secondary and tertiary income effects in successive rounds of the process. For example, if the *MPC* is 0.80, the multiplier is 5:

$$\text{Multiplier} = 1/(1 - 0.8) = 1/(0.2) = 5$$

If the *MPC* is only 0.50, however, the multiplier is 2:

$$\text{Multiplier} = 1/(1 - 0.50) = 1/(0.50) = 2$$

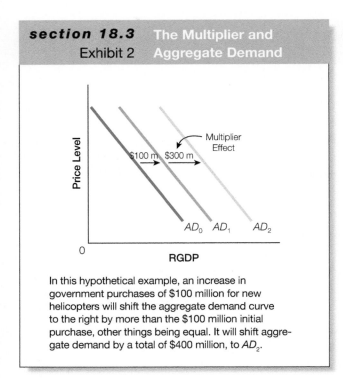

In this hypothetical example, an increase in
government purchases of $100 million for new
helicopters will shift the aggregate demand curve
to the right by more than the $100 million initial
purchase, other things being equal. It will shift aggregate demand by a total of $400 million, to AD_2.

WHAT IMPACT DOES THE MULTIPLIER EFFECT HAVE ON THE AGGREGATE DEMAND CURVE?

As we discussed earlier, when the Department of
National Defence decides to buy additional helicopters,
it increases aggregate demand. The initial effect is that it
increases the incomes of owners of inputs used to make
the helicopters, including profits that go to owners of
the firms involved. The secondary effect, the greater
income that results, will lead to increased consumer purchases. So the initial effect of the government's purchases
will tend to have a multiplier effect on the economy. In
Exhibit 2, we see that the initial impact of a $100 million
additional purchase by the government directly shifts
the aggregate demand curve from AD_0 to AD_1. The multiplier effect then causes the aggregate demand to shift
out $300 million further, to AD_2. The total effect on
aggregate demand of a $100 million increase in govern-
ment purchases is therefore $400 million, if the mar-
ginal propensity to consume equals 0.75.

It is important to note that the multiplier is most
effective when it brings idle resources into production.
If all resources are already fully employed, the expan-
sion in demand and the multiplier effect will lead to a higher price level, not
increases in employment and RGDP.

WHAT IMPACT DOES THE MULTIPLIER EFFECT HAVE ON TAX CUTS?

If the government finds that it needs to use fiscal stimulus to move the economy to the
natural rate, increased government spending is only one alternative. The government
can also stimulate business and consumer spending through tax cuts. Both Canada
(2000, 2003, and again in 2008–09) and the United States (2001, 2003, and 2012)
have employed tax cuts to stimulate their economies.

How much of an *AD* shift do we get from a change in taxes? As in the case of
government spending, it depends on the marginal propensity to consume. However,
the tax multiplier is smaller than the government spending multiplier because government spending has a direct impact on aggregate demand, whereas a tax cut has only an
indirect impact on aggregate demand. Why? Because consumers will save some of their
income from the tax cut. So if the *MPC* is 0.60, then when their disposable income rises
by $1000, households will increase their consumption by $600 ($1000 × 0.60) while
saving $400 of the added income.

To compare the multiplier effect of a tax cut with an increase in government purchases, suppose there was a $100 million tax cut and that the *MPC* was 0.75. The
initial increase in consumption spending from the tax cut would be 0.75 × 100 million
(*MPC* − tax cut) = $75 million. Because in this case people would save 25 percent of
their tax-cut income, the effect on aggregate demand of the change in taxes would be
smaller than that of a change of equal size in government spending. The cumulative
change in spending (the increase in *AD*) due to the $100 million tax cut can be found
by plugging the initial effect of the changed consumption spending into our earlier formula: 1/(1 − *MPC*) × $75 million, which is 4 × $75 = $300 million. So the initial

tax cut of $100 million leads to a stimulus of $200 million in consumer spending. Although this is less than the $400 million from government spending, it is easy to see why tax cuts and government spending are both attractive policy prescriptions for a slow economy.

An alternative technique for determining the cumulative change in spending due to a tax cut is to use the *tax multiplier* formula, calculated as follows:

$$\text{Tax multiplier} = \frac{MPC}{1 - MPC}$$

Returning to our earlier example, if the *MPC* is 0.75, the tax multiplier is 3:

$$\text{Tax multiplier} = \frac{MPC}{1 - MPC} = \frac{0.75}{1 - 0.75} = \frac{0.75}{0.25} = 3$$

An initial tax cut of $100 million will increase total purchases by $300 million ($100 million × 3).

Taxes and Investment Spending

Taxes can also stimulate investment spending. For example, if a cut in corporate profit taxes leads to expectations of greater after-tax profits, it could fuel additional investment spending. That is, tax cuts designed for consumers and investors can stimulate both the *C* and *I* components of aggregate demand. A number of governments have used this strategy to stimulate aggregate spending and shift the aggregate demand curve to the right: Canada (2003 and 2008–09), the United States (2000, 2003, and 2009), and South Korea (2008).

Spending Cuts and Tax Increases

Spending cuts and tax increases are magnified by the multiplier effect, too. Suppose there was a cutback in the public sector. Not only would it decrease government purchases directly, but civil servants would be laid off and unemployed workers would cut back on their consumption spending; this would have a multiplier effect throughout the economy, leading to an even greater reduction in aggregate demand. Similarly, tax hikes would leave consumers with less disposable income, so they would cut back on their consumption. This would lower aggregate demand and set off the multiplier process, leading to an even larger cumulative effect on aggregate demand.

WHAT FACTORS CAN POTENTIALLY REDUCE THE SIZE OF THE MULTIPLIER?

The multiplier process is not instantaneous. If you get an additional $100 in income today, you may spend two-thirds of that on consumption purchases eventually, but you may wait six months or even longer to do it. Such time lags mean that the ultimate increase in purchases resulting from an initial increase in purchases may not be achieved for a year or more. The extent of the multiplier effect evident within a short time period will be less than the total effect indicated by the multiplier formula. In addition, saving, taxes, and money spent on import goods (which are not part of aggregate demand for domestically produced goods and services) will reduce the size of the multiplier because each of them reduces the fraction of a given increase in income that will go to additional purchases of domestically produced consumption goods.

It is also important to note that the multiplier effect is not restricted to changes in government purchases. The multiplier effect can apply to changes that alter spending in any of the components of aggregate demand: consumption, investment, government purchases, or net exports.

SECTION CHECK

- The multiplier effect is a chain reaction of additional income and purchases that results in a final increase in total purchases that is greater than the initial increase in purchases.
- Initially the *AD* curve shifts rightward by the amount of the original increase in expenditure. The multiplier effect has the effect of shifting the *AD* curve farther rightward.
- Because taxes have only an indirect impact on aggregate demand, the tax multiplier is smaller than the government spending multiplier.
- Because of a time lag, the full impact of the multiplier effect on GDP may not be felt until a year or more after the initial purchase. Also, the ultimate size of the multiplier may be reduced by increases in saving rates, taxes, and money spent on imported goods.

section 18.4

Fiscal Policy and the *AD/AS* Model

- How can fiscal policy alleviate a recessionary gap?
- How can fiscal policy alleviate an inflationary gap?

HOW CAN FISCAL POLICY ALLEVIATE A RECESSIONARY GAP?

The primary tools of fiscal policy, government spending and taxes, can be presented in the context of the aggregate supply and demand model. In Exhibit 1, we have used the *AD/AS* model to show how the government can use fiscal policy as an expansionary tool to help control the economy.

Budget Deficits and Fiscal Policy

As we discussed earlier, when the government spends more, and/or taxes less, the size of the government's budget deficit will grow, or the size of the budget surplus will fall. Although budget deficits are often thought to be bad, a case can be made for using budget deficits to stimulate the economy when it is operating at less than full capacity. Such expansionary fiscal policy may have the potential to move an economy out of a contraction (or a recession) and closer to full employment.

Expansionary Fiscal Policy at Less Than Full Employment   If the government decides to spend more and/or cut taxes, other things constant, total purchases will rise. That is, increased government spending and tax cuts can increase consumption, investment, and government purchases, shifting the aggregate demand curve to the right. The effect of this increase in aggregate demand depends on the position of the macroeconomic equilibrium prior to the government stimulus. For example, in Exhibit 1, the initial equilibrium is at E_0, a recession scenario, with real output below potential RGDP. Starting at this point and moving along the short-run aggregate supply curve, an increase in government spending and/or a tax cut would increase the size of the budget deficit and lead to an increase in aggregate demand, ideally from AD_0 to AD_2. The result of such a change would be an increase in the price level, from PL_0 to PL_2, and an increase in RGDP, from $RGDP_0$ to $RGDP_{NR}$. We must remember, of course, that some of this increase in aggregate demand is caused by the multiplier process (from AD_1 to AD_2), so the magnitude of the change in aggregate demand will be larger than the magnitude of the stimulus package of tax cuts and/or government spending (from AD_0 to AD_1). If the policy change is of the right magnitude and timed appropriately, the expansionary fiscal policy might stimulate the economy, pull it out of the contraction and/or recession, and result in full employment at $RGDP_{NR}$. The recessionary gap is then closed.

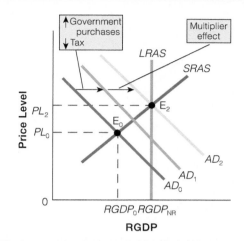

section 18.4
Exhibit 1
Expansionary Fiscal Policy in a Recessionary Gap

The increase in government spending or tax decrease causes an increase in aggregate demand from AD_0 to AD_1. This triggers the multiplier effect (AD_1 to AD_2) and the result is a new equilibrium at E_2, reflecting a higher price level and a higher RGDP. Because this result is on the *LRAS* curve, it is a long-run, sustainable equilibrium.

The 2008–09 Recession   The 2008–09 recession, while not the worst recession in Canadian history, did trigger a massive fiscal expansion. In January 2009, the federal government introduced Canada's Economic Action Plan in response to the global financial crisis. Among other stimulus measures, the plan contained significant tax relief—$20 billion in personal income tax relief over 2008–09 and the next five fiscal years—in addition to unprecedented government spending initiatives—$12 billion in new infrastructure stimulus funding over two years. Many other countries around the world, most notably the United States, also increased the size of their budget deficits by cutting taxes and increasing government spending in response to the financial crisis.

In terms of the *AD/AS* model, the impact of this type of expansionary fiscal policy is clear: a rightward shift of the aggregate demand curve from AD_0 to AD_1 as shown in Exhibit 1. There is, however, debate among economists as to the effectiveness of fiscal policy to stimulate the economy, and much of that debate depends on the size of the multiplier. A multiplier of 1 means that an increase in government purchases of $100 million would increase aggregate demand and lead to an increase of $100 million in RGDP. The economy could now have new highways, bridges, public arenas, and fighter jets without sacrificing other components of aggregate demand, like private consumption and investment. How is this possible? The answer is that these are idle resources that are now being put to use. If a multiplier is greater than 1, it is even more magical: RGDP rises by more than the increase in government spending.

Despite a lack of uniform agreement on the size of the expenditure multiplier, economists do agree that the multiplier is very small—close to zero—when the economy is at or near full employment and that the effectiveness of fiscal policy

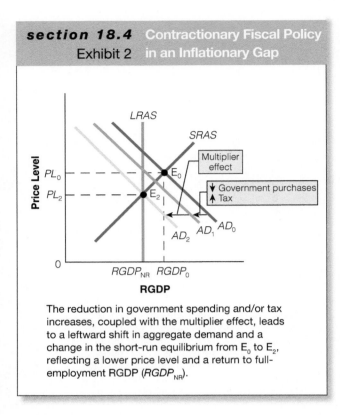

section 18.4 Contractionary Fiscal Policy
Exhibit 2   in an Inflationary Gap

The reduction in government spending and/or tax increases, coupled with the multiplier effect, leads to a leftward shift in aggregate demand and a change in the short-run equilibrium from E_0 to E_2, reflecting a lower price level and a return to full-employment RGDP ($RGDP_{NR}$).

depends on the type of action taken. For example, the short-run effect of government spending on infrastructure like highways and bridges tends to be greater than, say, that of a tax cut where individuals will save a large portion of their tax windfall. Tax cuts for poorer people may be more effective than those for richer people because the poor tend to spend a larger proportion of their additional (marginal) incomes. Economists also agree that tax multipliers are much higher when taxes are permanent than when they are temporary and that fiscal multipliers will be lower in heavily indebted economies than in prudent ones.

HOW CAN FISCAL POLICY ALLEVIATE AN INFLATIONARY GAP?

When the government spends less and/or taxes more, the size of the government's budget deficit will fall or the size of the budget surplus will rise, other things being equal. Sometimes such a change in fiscal policy may help "cool off" the economy when it has overheated and inflation has become a serious problem. Then, contractionary fiscal policy has the potential to offset an overheated, inflationary boom.

Contractionary Fiscal Policy beyond Full Employment

Suppose that the price level is at PL_0 and that short-run equilibrium is at E_0, as shown in Exhibit 2. Say that the government decides to reduce its spending and increase taxes. A government spending change may directly affect aggregate demand. A tax increase on consumers will reduce households' disposable incomes, thus reducing purchases of consumption goods and services, and higher business taxes will reduce investment purchases. The reductions in consumption, investment, and/or government spending will shift the aggregate demand curve leftward, ideally from AD_0 to AD_2. This lowers the price level from PL_0 to PL_2 and brings RGDP back to the full-employment level at $RGDP_{NR}$, resulting in a new short- and long-run equilibrium at E_2.

SECTION CHECK

■ A government decision to spend more and/or cut taxes would increase total purchases and shift out the aggregate demand curve. If the correct magnitude of expansionary fiscal policy is used in a recession, it could potentially bring the economy to full employment at a higher price level.

■ If the correct magnitude of contractionary fiscal policy is used in an inflationary boom, it could potentially bring the economy back to full employment at a lower price level.

Automatic Stabilizers

■ What are automatic stabilizers?
■ How does the tax system stabilize the economy?

WHAT ARE AUTOMATIC STABILIZERS?

Some changes in government spending and taxes take place automatically as business cycle conditions change, without deliberations in Parliament. Changes in government spending or tax collections that automatically help counter business cycle fluctuations are called **automatic stabilizers.**

automatic stabilizers
changes in government spending or tax collections that automatically help counter business cycle fluctuations

HOW DOES THE TAX SYSTEM STABILIZE THE ECONOMY?

The most important automatic stabilizer is the tax system. For example, with the personal income tax, as incomes rise, tax liabilities also increase automatically. Progressive personal income taxes vary directly in amount with income and, in fact, rise or fall by greater percentage terms than income itself. Big increases and big decreases in GDP are both lessened by automatic changes in income tax receipts. In addition, there is the corporate profit tax. Because incomes, earnings, and profits all fall during a recession, the government collects less in taxes. This reduced tax burden partially offsets the magnitude of the recession.

Beyond this, the Employment Insurance program is another example of an automatic stabilizer. During recessions, unemployment is usually high and Employment Insurance benefits increase, providing income that will be consumed by recipients. During boom periods, such benefit payments will fall as the number of unemployed declines. The system of social assistance (welfare) payments tends to be another important automatic stabilizer because the number of low-income persons eligible for some form of social assistance grows during recessions (stimulating aggregate demand) and declines during booms (reducing aggregate demand).

Automatic stabilizers work without legislative action. The stabilizers serve as a shock absorber to the economy. But the key is that they do it quickly.

Perhaps the Great Depression would not have been so "great" if automatic stabilizers had been in place. Many had to dig into their savings and cut back on their spending, which made matters worse. Automatic stabilizers are not strong enough to completely offset a serious recession. However, they certainly reduce the severity of a recession, without the problems associated with lags that were discussed in the last section.

Despite the shortcomings of traditional fiscal policy, it provides policymakers with another option in the event of a severe downturn. The use of fiscal policy can reassure investors and consumers that the government realizes it has the potential to make up for insufficient demand, especially if the economy is far from its potential output.

BRIGITTE BOUVIER, PMO

SECTION CHECK

- Automatic stabilizers are changes in government transfer payments or tax collections that happen automatically and with effects that vary inversely with business cycles.
- The tax system is the most important automatic stabilizer; it has the greatest ability to smooth out swings in GDP during business cycles. Other automatic stabilizers are Employment Insurance and social assistance payments.

<table>
<tr><td>section
18.6</td><td></td></tr>
</table>

Possible Obstacles to Effective Fiscal Policy

- How does the crowding-out effect limit the economic impact of expansionary fiscal policy?
- How do time lags in fiscal policy implementation affect policy effectiveness?

HOW DOES THE CROWDING-OUT EFFECT LIMIT THE ECONOMIC IMPACT OF EXPANSIONARY FISCAL POLICY?

The multiplier effect of an increase in government purchases implies that the increase in aggregate demand will tend to be greater than the initial fiscal stimulus, other things being equal. However, because all other things will not tend to stay equal in this case, the multiplier effect may not hold true. For example, when an increase in government purchases stimulates aggregate demand, it also drives up the interest rate. In particular, when the federal government's borrowing competes with private borrowers for available savings, it drives up interest rates. As a result of the higher interest rate, consumers may decide against buying a car, a home, or other interest-sensitive good, and businesses may cancel or scale back plans to expand or buy new capital equipment. In short, the higher interest rate will choke off private investment spending, and as a result, the impact of the increase in government purchases may be smaller than we first assumed. Economists call the theory that government borrowing drives up the interest rate, lowering consumption by households and investment spending by firms, the **crowding-out effect.** The crowding-out effect happened in Canada in the late 1980s and early 1990s, when record levels of government borrowing contributed, in part, to interest rates rising above 12 percent.

crowding-out effect
theory that government borrowing drives up the interest rate, lowering consumption by households and investment spending by firms

In Exhibit 1, suppose there was an initial $100 million increase in government purchases. This by itself would shift aggregate demand right by $100 million times the multiplier, from AD_0 to AD_1. However, when the government borrows in the money market to pay for increases in government purchases, the interest rate increases. The higher interest rate crowds out investment spending. This causes the aggregate demand curve to shift left, from AD_1 to AD_2. Because both of these processes are taking place at the same time, the net effect is an increase in aggregate demand from AD_0 to AD_2 rather than AD_0 to AD_1.

The multiplier and crowding-out effect can also impact the size of the shift in aggregate demand from a tax change. Recall that when tax cuts stimulate consumer spending, earnings and profits rise, which further stimulates consumer spending—the multiplier effect. But the higher income leads to an increase in the demand for money, which tends to lead to higher interest rates. The higher interest rates make borrowing more costly and reduce investment spending—the crowding-out effect. Also, remember that if households view tax cuts as permanent, they are more likely to increase spending by a larger amount than if they viewed the tax as temporary.

Critics of the Crowding-Out Effect

Critics of the crowding-out effect argue that the increase in government spending, particularly if the economy is in a severe recession, could actually improve consumer and business expectations and actually encourage private investment spending. It is also possible that the monetary authorities could actually increase the money supply to offset the higher interest rates from the crowding-out effect.

The Crowding-Out Effect in the Open Economy

Another form of crowding out can take place in international markets. For example, when the government increases purchases, it tends to drive up interest rates (assuming the money supply is unchanged). This is the basic crowding-out effect. However, the higher Canadian interest rate will attract funds from abroad. In order to invest in the Canadian economy, foreigners will have to first convert their currencies into Canadian dollars. The increase in the demand for dollars relative to other currencies will cause the dollar to appreciate in value. This will cause net exports $(X - M)$ to fall for two reasons. One, because of the higher relative price of the Canadian dollar, imports become cheaper for those in Canada, and imports will increase. Two, because of the higher relative price of the dollar, Canadian-made goods become more expensive to foreigners, so exports fall. The increase in imports and the decrease in exports causes a reduction in net exports and a fall in aggregate demand. The net effect is that to the extent net exports are crowded out, fiscal policy has a smaller effect on aggregate demand than it would otherwise.

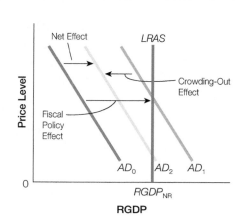

section 18.6
Exhibit 1   The Crowding-Out Effect

Government borrowing to finance a budget deficit leads to a higher interest rate and lower levels of private investment spending. The lower levels of private spending can crowd out the fiscal policy effect, shifting aggregate demand to the left from AD_1 to AD_2; the net effect of the fiscal policy is AD_0 to AD_2, not the larger increase, AD_0 to AD_1.

HOW DO TIME LAGS IN FISCAL POLICY IMPLEMENTATION AFFECT POLICY EFFECTIVENESS?

It is important to recognize that in a democratic country, fiscal policy is implemented through the political process, and that process takes time. Often, the lag between the time that a fiscal response is desired and the time an appropriate policy is implemented and its effects felt is considerable. Sometimes a fiscal policy designed to deal with a contracting economy may actually take effect during a period of economic expansion, or vice versa, resulting in a stabilization policy that actually destabilizes the economy.

The Recognition Lag

Suppose the economy is beginning a downturn. It may take from three to six months before enough data are gathered to indicate the actual presence of a downturn. This is called the *recognition lag*. Sometimes a future downturn can be forecast through econometric models or by looking at the index of leading indicators, but usually decision makers are hesitant to plan policy on the basis of forecasts that are not always accurate.

The Implementation Lag

At some point, however, policymakers may decide that some policy change is necessary. If, for example, a tax cut is recommended, what form should the cut take and how large should it be? Across-the-board income tax reductions? Reductions in corporate taxes? More generous exemptions and deductions from the income tax (e.g., for child care, education)? In other words, who should get the benefits of lower taxes? Likewise, if the decision is made to increase government expenditures, which programs should be expanded or initiated and by how much? These are questions with profound political consequences, so reaching a decision is not always easy and usually involves much compromise and a great deal of time.

Finally, once the budget is formulated by the staff at the Department of Finance, the finance minister presents the budget to Parliament, which must eventually give approval to the budget. This is all part of what is called the *implementation lag*.

In recognition of this lag, the federal government, through Canada's Economic Action Plan, streamlined the federal approval processes so that more provincial, territorial, and municipal projects under the Building Canada Plan could start in 2009 and 2010. Prior to these changes, the infrastructure approval process was subject to significant duplication and administrative inefficiencies, leading to unnecessary project delays. With changes now in place, the time needed to provide federal approvals for major projects was shortened by up to 12 months, allowing construction to begin more quickly.

The Impact Lag

Even after legislation is passed, it takes time to bring about the actual fiscal stimulus desired. If the legislation provides for a reduction in income taxes, for example, it might take a few months before the changes actually show up in workers' paycheques. With respect to changes in government purchases, the delay is usually much longer. If the government increases spending for public works projects like sewer systems, new highways, or urban transit systems, it takes time to draw up plans and get permissions, to advertise for bids from contractors, to get contracts, and then to begin work. And there may be further delays because of government regulations. For example, an environmental impact assessment must be completed before most public works projects can begin, a process that often takes many months or even years. This is called the *impact lag*.

Timing Is Critical

The timing of fiscal policy is crucial. Because of the significant lags before the fiscal policy has its impact, the increase in aggregate demand may occur at the wrong time. For example, imagine that we are initially at E_0 in Exhibit 2. The economy is currently suffering from low levels of output and high rates of unemployment.

---

section 18.6 **Timing Expansionary**
Exhibit 2   **Fiscal Policy**

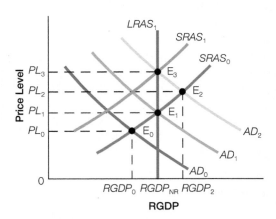

Initially, the macroeconomy is at equilibrium at point E_0. With high unemployment (at $RGDP_0$), the government decides to increase government purchases and cut taxes to stimulate the economy. This shifts aggregate demand from AD_0 to AD_1 over time, perhaps 12 to 16 months. In the meantime, if consumer confidence increases, the aggregate demand curve might shift to AD_2, leading to much higher prices (PL_3) in the long run, rather than at the target level, E_1, at price level PL_1.

In response, policymakers decide to increase government purchases and implement a tax cut. But from the time when the policymakers recognized the problem to the time when the policies had a chance to work themselves through the economy, business and consumer confidence increased, shifting the aggregate demand curve rightward from AD_0 to AD_1—increasing RGDP and employment. Now when the fiscal policy takes effect, the policies will have the undesired effect of causing inflation, with little permanent effect on output and employment. This is seen in Exhibit 2, as the aggregate demand curve shifts from AD_1 to AD_2. At E_2, input owners will require higher input prices, shifting the *SRAS* leftward from $SRAS_0$ to $SRAS_1$ to the new long-run equilibrium at E_3.

SECTION CHECK

- The crowding-out effect states that as the government borrows to finance the budget deficit, it drives up the interest rates and crowds out private investment spending. If crowding out causes a higher Canadian interest rate, it will attract foreign funds. In order to invest in the Canadian economy, foreigners will have to first convert their currencies into Canadian dollars. The increase in the demand for dollars relative to other currencies will cause the dollar to appreciate in value, making imports relatively cheaper in Canada and Canadian exports relatively more expensive in other countries. This will cause net exports $(X - M)$ to fall. This is the crowding-out effect in the open economy.
- The lag time between when a fiscal policy may be needed and when it eventually affects the economy is considerable. Time lags are generally grouped in three classifications: recognition lags, implementation lags, and impact lags.

section
18.7

The Federal Government Debt

- How is the budget deficit financed?
- What has happened to the federal budget balance?
- What is the impact of reducing a budget deficit?
- How much is the burden of government debt in Canada?

HOW IS THE BUDGET DEFICIT FINANCED?

For many years, the Canadian government ran budget deficits and built up a large federal debt. How did it finance those budget deficits? After all, it has to have some means of paying out the funds necessary to support government expenditures that are in excess of the funds derived from tax payments. One thing the federal government can do is simply print money. However, printing money to finance activities is highly inflationary and also undermines confidence in the government. Typically, the budget deficit is financed by issuing debt. The federal government in effect borrows an amount necessary to cover the deficit by issuing bonds, or IOUs, payable typically at some maturity date. The sum total of the values of all bonds outstanding constitutes the federal government debt.

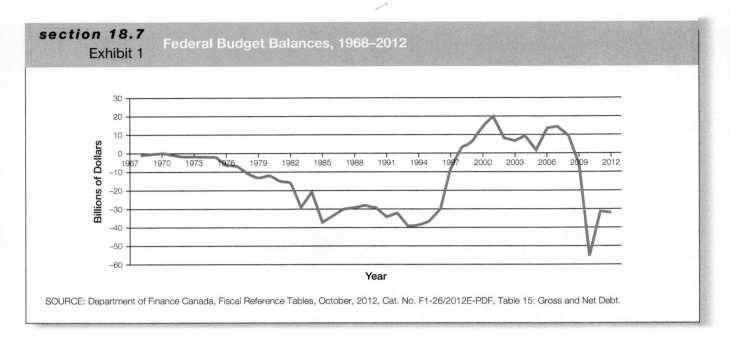

SOURCE: Department of Finance Canada, Fiscal Reference Tables, October, 2012, Cat. No. F1-26/2012E-PDF, Table 15: Gross and Net Debt.

WHAT HAS HAPPENED TO THE FEDERAL BUDGET BALANCE?

Exhibit 1 shows the improvement in the federal budget balance since the early 1990s as a result of economic growth, increased tax revenue, and the efforts of the federal government to control the growth of government spending. Indeed, the improvement in federal government finances is quite remarkable. The yearly budget deficit increased steadily from 1989 to 1994, reaching a record $40 billion in both 1993 and 1994. In 1998, however, the government ran its first budget surplus in almost 25 years, and succeeded in posting annual budget surpluses for 12 consecutive years, to 2009.

WHAT IS THE IMPACT OF REDUCING A BUDGET DEFICIT?

Budget deficits can be important because they provide the federal government with the flexibility to respond appropriately to changing economic circumstances. For example, the government may run deficits in times of special emergencies like military involvement, earthquakes, fires, or floods. The government may also use a budget deficit to avert an economic downturn.

Historically the largest budget deficits and a growing government debt occur during war years when defence spending escalates and taxes typically do not rise as rapidly as spending. For example, during World War II, the federal government debt increased by over 300 percent between 1940 and 1946. The federal government will also typically run budget deficits during recessions as tax revenue falls and government spending increases. Throughout the 1980s, however, deficits and subsequently debt soared in a relatively peaceful and prosperous time. The result was huge budget deficits and growing federal debt that continued through the 1990s, as illustrated by the negative budget balances in Exhibit 1. This mounting public debt led to growing pressure on the government to change its budgetary philosophy, and beginning in 1994, deficits began to diminish, eventually turning into surpluses in 1998.

In 2008, the Canadian economy began to experience the impact of the global financial crisis. In response to these events, the Canadian government again began to run deficits as tax revenues declined and expenditures skyrocketed. The government launched its Economic Action Plan in 2009, a plan that consisted largely of pumping billions of dollars of stimulus into the economy. As a result of these government's efforts to stave off the ever worsening global recession, the federal government posted its largest budget deficit ever in 2009–10, $55.4 billion. Following this unprecedented period of fiscal policy, the government has undertaken significant efforts to return to a more balanced budget situation—as evidenced by the dramatically lower budget deficits in both 2010–11 and 2011–12.

Recall that when the government borrows to finance a budget deficit, it causes the interest rate to rise. The higher interest rate will crowd out private investment by households and firms. But we know that higher private investment and increases in capital formation are critical in a growing economy. So what would happen if the government reduced the budget deficit? In the short run, deficit reduction is the same as running contractionary fiscal policy; either tax increases and/or a reduction in government purchases will shift the aggregate demand curve to the left from AD_0 to AD_1, as seen in Exhibit 2. Unless this is offset by expansionary monetary policy (see Chapter 21), this will lead to a lower price level and lower RGDP. That is, in the short run an aggressive program of deficit reduction can lead to a recession.

In the long run, however, the story is different. Lowering the budget deficit, or running a larger budget surplus, leads to lower interest rates, which increase private investment and stimulate higher growth in capital formation and economic growth. In fact, this is what happened in the late 1990s as the budget deficit was reduced and finally turned into a budget surplus. The reduction in the deficit increased the natural rate of output, shifting the *SRAS* and *LRAS* curves rightward in Exhibit 3. The final effect was a higher RGDP and a lower price level than would have otherwise prevailed. Both

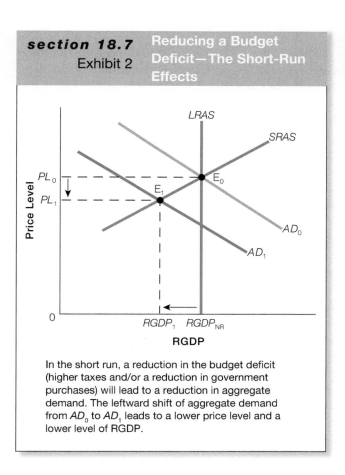

section 18.7
Exhibit 2

Reducing a Budget Deficit—The Short-Run Effects

In the short run, a reduction in the budget deficit (higher taxes and/or a reduction in government purchases) will lead to a reduction in aggregate demand. The leftward shift of aggregate demand from AD_0 to AD_1 leads to a lower price level and a lower level of RGDP.

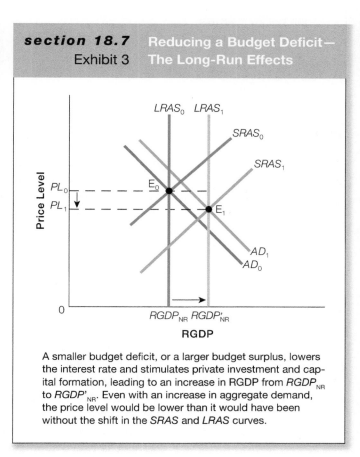

section 18.7
Exhibit 3

Reducing a Budget Deficit—The Long-Run Effects

A smaller budget deficit, or a larger budget surplus, lowers the interest rate and stimulates private investment and capital formation, leading to an increase in RGDP from $RGDP_{NR}$ to $RGDP'_{NR}$. Even with an increase in aggregate demand, the price level would be lower than it would have been without the shift in the *SRAS* and *LRAS* curves.

investment and RGDP grew as the budget deficit shrank. The long-run effects of the deficit reduction are greater economic growth and a lower price level, *ceteris paribus.* The short-run recessionary effects of a budget deficit reduction can be avoided through the appropriate monetary policy, as we will explore in Chapter 21.

What to Do with a Budget Surplus

When Canada has a budget surplus, policymakers have to decide what to do with it. Some favour paying down the government debt, arguing this might drive interest rates down further and stimulate private investment and economic growth. Others think that we should cut taxes since economic theory indicates that taxes can lead to a misallocation of resources. Still others believe the surplus should be used for improvements in education, health care, and research and development that will lead to greater economic growth.

HOW MUCH IS THE BURDEN OF GOVERNMENT DEBT IN CANADA?

The burden of the federal government debt is a topic that has long interested economists, particularly whether the debt falls on present or future generations. Exhibit 4 shows the level of the outstanding federal government debt and the debt expressed as a percentage of GDP from 1930 to 2012. The debt–GDP ratio measures the size of the debt in relation to the size of our national income. The lower the debt–GDP ratio, the smaller the burden of the debt, because less of our national income goes to the federal government in taxes so that the government can service the debt (i.e., make interest payments to the bondholders). Conversely, the higher the debt–GDP ratio, the greater the burden of the debt, because more of our national income goes to the federal government in taxes so that the government can service the debt.

section 18.7 Exhibit 4	Federal Government Debt, Selected Years	
Year	Debt (billions of dollars)	Debt as a Percentage of GDP
1930	$ 2.2	39%
1940	3.3	49
1950	11.6	63
1960	12.0	31
1970	18.1	20
1980	72.6	23
1990	362.9	53
2000	590.1	54
2001	571.7	50
2002	565.3	48
2003	559.6	45
2004	551.0	42
2005	549.6	39
2006	537.0	36
2007	523.9	33
2008	516.3	31
2009	525.2	34
2010	582.5	35
2011	616.9	35
2012	650.1	36

SOURCES: Adapted from Statistics Canada, Table 380-0064, Gross domestic product, expenditure-based, annual (dollars unless otherwise noted); and Department of Finance, Fiscal Reference Tables. October 2012, Cat. No. F1-26/2012E-PDF, Table 15, Gross and Net Debt.

It is interesting to note that between 1930 and 1950, the debt–GDP ratio increased sharply from 39 to 63 percent, as the growth in the debt (caused largely by the Great Depression in the 1930s and World War II in the 1940s) far exceeded the growth in GDP. Although the debt continued to rise to $73 billion in 1980, the debt–GDP ratio fell to 23 percent as strong economic growth reduced the debt in relation to the size of the economy. Between 1980 and 2000, large budget deficits added almost $500 billion in additional debt, bringing the debt to $572 billion and the debt–GDP ratio up to a burdensome 54 percent. The debt–GDP ratio peaked, in fact, in 1996 at 69 percent.

On a more positive note, the budget surpluses that the federal government was able to post between 2000 and 2008 were, at least in part, used to pay down some of the debt. This in combination with good economic growth over this same period of time enabled the government to lower the debt–GDP ratio to 33 percent by 2008. This trend has since reversed as the Canadian economy struggles to recover from the recent global economic crisis. The most recent data show Canada's debt–GDP ratio at 36 percent.

Arguments can be made that the generation of taxpayers living at the time that the debt is issued shoulders the true cost of the debt, because the debt permits the government to take command of resources that might be available for other, private uses. In a sense, the resources it takes to purchase government bonds might take away from private activities, such as private investment financed by private debt. There is no denying, however, that the issuance of debt does involve some intergenerational transfer of incomes. Long after federal debt is issued, a new generation of taxpayers is making interest payments to people of the generation that bought the bonds issued to finance that debt. If public debt is created intelligently, however, the burden of the debt should be less than the benefits derived from the resources acquired as a result; this is particularly true when the debt allows for an expansion in real economic activity or for the development of vital infrastructure for the future. The opportunity cost of expanded public activity may be very small in terms of private activity that must be forgone to finance the public activity, if unemployed resources are put to work. The real issue of importance is whether the government's activities have benefits that are greater than costs; whether taxes are raised, money is printed, or deficits are run are for the most part financing issues.

Parents can offset some of the intergenerational debt by leaving larger bequests. In addition, if the parents save now to bear the cost of the burden of future taxes, the reduced consumption and increased savings will lower interest rates or, more precisely, offset the higher interest rate caused by the budget deficit. Many parents might not respond that way, but some might.

It is possible that if the budget deficits led people to believe there would be higher future taxes, a budget surplus might lead them to think there would be lower future taxes—and perhaps they would save less and consume more. So do we pay down the debt or cut taxes? They may be equivalent policy prescriptions since each tends to lead to increases in consumption spending.

A look internationally at federal, or central, government indebtedness shows us that Canada's situation is by no means an exception—see Exhibit 5. The reality of public finances around the world is that all central governments are to some extent in debt; the issue is the *amount* of government debt. The recent global economic crisis has increased the debt–GDP ratios of virtually every economy in the world. The central concern now is that, for those economies that already had significant ratios of debt to GDP, recent events have pushed them dangerously higher.

section 18.7 Central Government Debt:
Exhibit 5 Selected Economies

Country	Central Government Debt as a Percentage of GDP
Australia	11.0%
Switzerland	20.2
Norway	26.1
Mexico	27.5
Canada	**36.1**
Germany	44.4
Ireland	60.7
United States	61.3
France	67.4
United Kingdom	85.5
Italy	109.0
Greece	147.8

SOURCE: Based on data from *Central Government Debt* under *Finance* from OECD. Stat Extracts, http://stats.oecd.org.

SECTION CHECK

- The budget deficit is financed by issuing debt.
- Improvement in the federal budget balance since the mid-1990s resulted from economic growth, increased tax revenues, and the efforts of the federal government to control the growth of government spending.
- In the short run, reducing a budget deficit can lead to a recession if not offset by expansionary monetary policy. In the long run, however, deficit reduction increases economic growth and lowers the price level.
- With greater fiscal responsibility and increased economic growth, Canada has managed to lower its debt–GDP ratio (the international measure of debt burden).

For Your Review

Section 18.1

1. Answer the following questions.
   a. If there is currently a budget surplus, what would an increase in government purchases do to it?
   b. What would that increase in government purchases do to aggregate demand?
   c. When would an increase in government purchases be an appropriate fiscal policy?

2. Are increases in both government purchases and net taxes at the same time expansionary or contractionary? Would both changes together increase or decrease the federal government deficit?

3. Answer the following questions.
   a. If there is currently a budget deficit, what would an increase in taxes do to it?
   b. What would that increase in taxes do to aggregate demand?
   c. When would an increase in taxes be an appropriate fiscal policy?

4. What is a recessionary gap? What would be the appropriate fiscal policy to combat or offset one? What is an inflationary gap? What would be the appropriate fiscal policy to combat or offset one?

Section 18.2

5. Excise taxes make up the bulk of the retail price of cigarettes and alcohol in Canada. Explain how excise taxes such as these are regressive and unfairly target lower-income individuals.

6. How does Canada's federal government make money?

Section 18.3

7. What would the multiplier be if the marginal propensity to consume was 0.25, 0.5, and 0.75? How would the value for the tax multiplier differ?

8. If there was a $2 billion increase in government spending, other things being equal, what would be the resulting change in aggregate demand, and how much of the change would be a change in consumption, if the *MPC* was
   a. 0.20?
   b. 0.5?
   c. 2/3?
   d. 0.75?
   e. 0.8?

9. Could the multiplier be written as 1 divided by the marginal propensity to save (*MPS*)?

10. Why does it take a larger reduction in taxes to create the same increase in *AD* as a given increase in government purchases?

Section 18.4

Blueprint Problem

An economy with an *MPC* = 0.8 is experiencing a recessionary gap of $100 million.

    a. What amount of government spending would be necessary to bring the economy up to full employment?

    b. What amount of tax reduction would be necessary to bring the economy up to full employment?

Blueprint Solution

a.

> The first step in solving this problem is to calculate the size of the expenditure multiplier.

$$\text{Expenditure multiplier} = \frac{1}{1 - MPC} = \frac{1}{1 - 0.8} = 5$$

> Next, recall the operation of the multiplier effect; an initial change in spending has a magnified (or multiplied) effect on the overall amount of economic activity. In terms of a formula, this effect can be expressed as follows:
>
> Aggregate economic activity = Initial change in spending × Expenditure multiplier
>
> Now enter the given information in the question into this formula.

$100 million = Initial change in spending × 5

> Solving for the "initial change in spending" reveals that a $20 million government injection would be the necessary catalyst to trigger an $80 million multiplier effect. Together, the initial injection and multiplier effect would be sufficient to close the $100 million recessionary gap.

Initial change in spending = $20 million

b.

As with the first part of this question, the first step in the solution is to determine the relevant multiplier—in this case, the tax multiplier.

$$\text{Tax multiplier} = \frac{MPC}{1 - MPC} = \frac{0.8}{1 - 0.8} = 4$$

Next, substitute the given information in the question into the multiplier identity, solving for the necessary "change in taxes."

$$\$100 \text{ million} = \text{Change in taxes} \times 4$$

$$\text{Change in taxes} = -\$25 \text{ million}$$

Finally, notice that the final solution is displayed as a negative value—indicating a reduction in taxes of $25 million. Had the government been looking to resolve an inflationary gap, an increase in taxes would have been required, making this final step unnecessary.

11. Predict the potential impact on real GDP of each of the following events.
    a. an increase in government spending of $5 billion in order to build new highways
    b. a decrease in federal spending of $1 billion due to peacetime military cutbacks
    c. consumer optimism leading to an $8 billion spending increase
    d. gloomy business forecasts leading to a $12 billion decline in investment spending

12. The economy is experiencing a recessionary gap of $30 billion. If the $MPC = 0.75$, what government spending stimulus would you recommend to move the economy back to full employment? If the $MPC = 0.66$?

13. Review the information in question 12. Suppose that instead of using government spending to close the recessionary gap, the government decided to reduce taxes. What amount of tax reduction would be recommended to move the economy back to full employment, if the $MPC = 0.75$? If the $MPC = 0.66$?

14. The economy is experiencing a $225 million inflationary gap. If the government decided to solve this macroeconomic disequilibrium using a change in taxes, would you recommend an increase or decrease in taxes? If the *MPC* = 0.9, what magnitude of tax change would be appropriate?

15. The economy is experiencing a $25 billion inflationary gap. Absent government intervention, what can you predict will happen to the economy in the long run? (Use aggregate demand–aggregate supply analysis in your answer.) If the government decides to intervene using changes in spending, would you recommend a spending increase or decrease? Of what magnitude?

16. Illustrate the impact of a tax cut using aggregate demand–aggregate supply analysis when the economy is operating above full employment. Is this a wise policy? Why or why not?

17. Use the following diagram to answer questions (a) through (f).

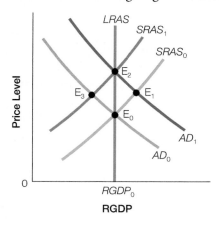

a. At what short-run equilibrium point might expansionary fiscal policy make sense to help stabilize the economy?

b. What would be the result of appropriate fiscal policy in that case?

c. What would be the long-run result if no fiscal policy action was taken in that case?

d. At what short-run equilibrium point might contractionary fiscal policy make sense to help stabilize the economy?

e. What would be the result of appropriate fiscal policy in that case?

f. What would be the long-run result if no fiscal policy action was taken in that case?

Section 18.5

18. How do automatic stabilizers affect budget deficits and surpluses? How would automatic stabilizers be affected by an annually balanced budget rule?

19. Why do automatic stabilizers minimize the lag problems with fiscal policy?

20. What happens to the following variables during an expansion?

a. Employment Insurance benefits

b. welfare payments

c. income tax receipts

d. government budget deficit (surplus)

21. How does the tax system act as an automatic stabilizer?

Section 18.6

22. Can government spending that causes crowding out be detrimental to long-run economic growth? Explain.

23. Answer the following questions:

    a. Describe the crowding-out effect of an increase in government purchases.

    b. Why does the magnitude of the crowding-out effect depend on how responsive interest rates are to increased government borrowing and how responsive investment is to changes in interest rates?

    c. How would the size of the crowding-out effect affect the size of the change in aggregate demand that would result from a given increase in government purchases?

24. How do time lags affect the effectiveness of fiscal policy?

Section 18.7

25. Illustrate diagrammatically the short-run effects of a government budget deficit.

26. Illustrate diagrammatically the long-run effects of a government budget deficit. Describe the mechanism that makes these effects different from the short-run effects described in question 25.

27. What are the intergenerational effects of government debt?

chapter
19

Money and the Banking System

What Is Money?

- ■ What is money?
- ■ What are the four functions of money?

WHAT IS MONEY?

Money is anything that is generally accepted in exchange for goods or services. Hundreds of years ago, commodities such as tobacco and furs were sometimes used as money. At some times and in some places, even cigarettes and playing cards have been used as money. But commodities have several disadvantages when used as money, the most important of which is that many commodities deteriorate easily after a few trades. Precious metal coins were used for money for millennia, partly because of their durability.

money
anything generally accepted in exchange for goods or services

WHAT ARE THE FOUR FUNCTIONS OF MONEY?

Money has four important functions in the economy: as a medium of exchange, a store of value, a unit of account, and a means of deferred payment. Let's examine the four important functions of money to see how they are different from the functions of other assets in the economy, such as stocks, bonds, art, real estate, and comic book collections.

1. Money as a Medium of Exchange

The primary function of money is to serve as a **medium of exchange,** to facilitate transactions, and to lower transactions costs; that is, sellers will accept it as payment in a transaction. However, money is not the only medium of exchange; rather, it is the only medium that is generally accepted for most transactions. How would people trade with one another in the absence of money? They would **barter** for goods and services they desire, that is, transactions would involve the direct exchange of goods and services without the use of money.

medium of exchange
the primary function of money, which is to facilitate transactions and lower transactions costs

barter
direct exchange of goods and services without the use of money

In the seventeenth century, in the absence of coinage, British and French colonists used individual pieces of wampum (polished shells) as lawful money. Tobacco was once used as money in colonial America and the ancient Chinese used chisels for money. Still other societies have used fish and cattle and, of course, gold coins as money.

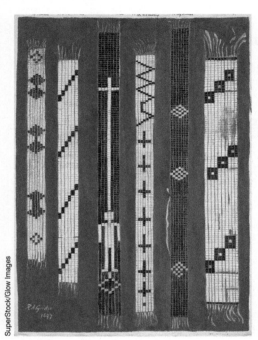

SuperStock/Glow Images

measure of value
money as a common "ruler" of worth allowing for the comparison of diverse goods and services

store of value
how money provides a means of saving or accumulating purchasing power from the present and transferring it to the future

The Barter System Is Inefficient   Under a barter system, individuals pay for goods or services by offering other goods and services in exchange. Suppose you are a farmer who needs some salt. You go to the merchant selling salt and offer her 30 kilograms of wheat for 2 kilograms of salt. The wheat that you use to buy the salt is not money, because the salt merchant may not want wheat and therefore may not accept it as payment. That is one of the major disadvantages of barter: The buyer may not have appropriate items of value to the seller. The salt merchant may reluctantly take the wheat that she does not want, later bartering it away to another customer for something that she does want. In any case, barter is inefficient because several trades may be necessary in order to receive the desired goods.

Moreover, barter is extremely expensive over long distances. What would it cost a customer living in Saskatchewan to send wheat to Toronto in return for an item in the Sears catalogue? It is much cheaper to mail a cheque. Finally, barter is time-consuming because of difficulties in evaluating the value of the product that is being offered for barter. For example, the person who is selling the salt may want to inspect the wheat first to make sure that it is pure and not filled with dirt or other unwanted items.

Barter, in short, is expensive, inefficient, and generally prevails only where limited trade is carried out over short distances, which generally means in relatively primitive economies. The more complex the economy (e.g., the higher the real per capita GDP), the greater the economic interactions between people, and consequently, the greater the need for one or more universally accepted assets serving as money. Only in a Robinson Crusoe economy, where people live in isolated settlements and are generally self-sufficient, is the use of money unnecessary.

2. Money as a Measure of Value

Besides serving as a medium of exchange, money is also a **measure of value**—a common "ruler" of worth allowing for the comparison of diverse goods and services. With a barter system, one does not know precisely what 30 kilograms of wheat are worth relative to 2 kilograms of salt. With money, a common "ruler" exists so that the values of diverse goods and services can be very precisely compared. So if wheat costs 50 cents a kilogram and salt costs $1 a kilogram, we can say that a kilogram of salt is valued precisely two times as much as a kilogram of wheat ($1 divided by 50 cents = 2). By providing a universally understood measure of value, money serves to lower the information costs involved in making transactions. Without money, a person might not know what a good price for salt is, because so many different commodities can be bartered for it. With money, there is but one price for salt, and that price is readily available as information to the potential consumer.

3. Money as a Store of Value

Money also serves as a **store of value;** that is, money provides a means of saving or accumulating purchasing power from the present and transferring it to the future. The farmer in a barter society who wants to save for retirement might accumulate enormous inventories of wheat, which he would then gradually trade away for other goods in his old age. This is a terribly inefficient way to save. Storage buildings would have to be constructed to hold all of the wheat, and the interest payments that the farmer would earn on the wheat would actually be negative, as rats will eat part of the wheat or it will otherwise deteriorate. Most important, physical goods of value would be tied up in unproductive use for many years. With money, the farmer saves pieces of paper that can be used to purchase goods and services after retirement. It is both cheaper and safer to store paper rather than wheat.

4. Money as a Means of Deferred Payment

Finally, the attribute of money that makes it easier to borrow and to repay loans is money as a **means of deferred payment.** With barter, lending is cumbersome and subject to an added problem. What if a wheat farmer borrows some wheat and agrees to pay it back in wheat next year, but the value of wheat soars because of a poor crop resulting from drought? The debt will be paid back in wheat that is far more valuable than that borrowed, causing a problem for the borrower. Of course, fluctuations in the value of money can also occur, and indeed, inflation has been a major problem in our recent past and continues to be a problem in many countries. But the value of money fluctuates far less than the value of many individual commodities, so lending money poses fewer risks to buyers and sellers than lending commodities.

means of deferred payment
the attribute of money that makes it easier to borrow and to repay loans

SECTION CHECK

■ Money is anything that is generally accepted in exchange for goods or services.
■ The four important functions of money are money as a medium of exchange, money as a store of value, money as a unit of account, and money as a means of deferred payment.

Measuring Money

■ What is currency?
■ What are demand and savings deposits?
■ What is liquidity?
■ How is the money supply measured?
■ What backs the money supply?

WHAT IS CURRENCY?

Currency consists of coins and banknotes that an institution or government has created to be used in the trading of goods and services and the payment of debts. Currency in the form of metal coins is still used as money throughout the world today but metal currency has a disadvantage: It is bulky. Also, certain types of metals traditionally used in coins, like gold and silver, are not available in sufficient quantities to meet our demands for a monetary instrument. For these reasons, metal coins were supplemented first by paper currency and now by polymer currency. In Canada, the Bank of Canada issues Bank of Canada notes in various denominations, and this polymer currency, along with coins, provides the basis for most transactions of relatively modest size in Canada today.

currency
consists of coins and banknotes that an institution or government has created to be used in the trading of goods and services and the payment of debts

Currency as Legal Tender

In Canada and in most other nations of the world, metal coins and banknotes are the only forms of legal tender. **Legal tender** refers to coins and banknotes officially

legal tender
refers to coins and banknotes officially declared to be acceptable for the settlement of debts incurred in financial transactions

declared to be acceptable for the settlement of debts incurred in financial transactions. In effect, the government says, "We declare these instruments to be money, and citizens are expected to accept them as a medium of exchange." Legal tender is **fiat money**—a means of exchange that has been established not by custom and tradition or because of the value of the metal in a coin, but by government fiat, or declaration.

fiat money
a means of exchange established by government declaration

WHAT ARE DEMAND AND SAVINGS DEPOSITS?

Most of the money that we use for day-to-day transactions, however, is not official legal tender. Rather, it is a monetary instrument that has become generally accepted in exchange over the years and has now, by custom and tradition, become money. What is this instrument? It is balances in chequing accounts in financial institutions, more formally called *demand deposits*. **Demand deposits** are defined as balances in financial institution accounts that depositors can access on demand by simply writing a cheque or using a debit card. That is, demand deposits are convertible to currency on demand. Some other forms of accounts in financial institutions also have virtually all of the attributes of demand deposits. For example, other chequable deposits earn interest but have some restrictions, such as higher monthly fees or minimum balance requirements. Practically speaking, funds in these accounts are the equivalent of demand deposits and have become an important component in the supply of money.

demand deposits
balances in bank accounts that depositors can access on demand

Why are financial institution balances that depositors have access to by writing cheques or using debit cards the most popular form of money in Canada, as well as in most other well-developed nations? The answer is simple really: Demand deposits offer all the benefits of coins and banknotes in terms of liquidity without the danger and inconvenience of having to carry around large sums of money to facilitate daily transactions.

The Popularity of Demand Deposits

Demand deposits have replaced banknotes and metal currency as the major source of money used for larger transactions in Canada and in most other relatively well-developed nations for several reasons, including ease and safety of transactions, lower transaction costs, and transaction records.

STRABLE/Horizontal/Jutta Klee/2009 Canadian Press Images

Ease and Safety of Transactions Paying for goods and services with a cheque is less risky than paying with banknotes, which are readily transferable: If someone takes a $20 bill from you, it is gone and the thief can use it to buy goods with no difficulty. If, however, someone steals a cheque that you have written to the telephone company to pay a monthly bill, that person probably will have great difficulty using it to buy goods and services, because the individual has to be able to identify himself as a representative of the telephone company. If your chequebook is stolen, a person can use your cheques as money only if she can successfully forge your signature and provide some identification. Hence, transacting business by cheque is much less risky than using legal tender; an element of insurance or safety exists in the use of demand deposits instead of currency.

Lower Transaction Costs Suppose you decide that you want to buy a compact disc player that costs $81.28 from the current Sears mail-order catalogue. It is much cheaper, easier, and safer for you to send a cheque for $81.28 rather than four $20 bills, a $1 coin, a quarter, and three pennies. Demand deposits are popular precisely because they lower transaction costs compared with the use of metal or polymer currency. In very small transactions, the gains in safety and convenience of cheques are outweighed by the time and cost required to write and process them; in these cases, transaction costs are lower with banknotes and metal currency. For this reason, it is unlikely that the use of banknotes or metal currency will disappear entirely.

Transaction Record   Another useful feature of demand deposits is that they provide a record of financial transactions. Each month, the financial institution provides the depositor with a statement recording the deposit and withdrawal of funds. In an age where detailed records are often necessary for tax purposes, this is a useful feature. Of course, this feature of transaction records could be a negative for some types of business activities, whose participants might prefer that no records exist. In these cases, banknote transactions could be preferred because they do not leave a paper trail for the government or authorities to follow.

Credit Cards

A credit card is generally acceptable in exchange for goods and services. At the same time, however, a credit card payment is actually a guaranteed loan available on demand to the cardholder, which merely defers the cardholder's payment for a transaction using a demand deposit. After all, the word "credit" means you are receiving money today with a promise to pay it back in the future—it really is a short-term loan. Ultimately, an item purchased with a credit card must be paid for with a cheque; monthly payments on a credit card account are required for continued use of the card. A credit card, then, is not money but rather a convenient tool for carrying out transactions that minimize the physical transfer of cheques or currency. In this sense, it is a substitute for the use of money and allows cardholders to use any given amount of money in future exchanges.

A debit card lets you access the money in your chequing account, but the card is not money. They are called *debit cards* because they debit your bank account directly when you use them. People often prefer to use debit cards to writing a cheque because it is more convenient—no chequebook is required. It may be safer than a credit card, too, because debit cards require a personal identification number (PIN) for their use. However, there is no grace period, and the transaction immediately reduces the amount of money in your bank account. Consequently, consumers have less leverage if disputing a purchase; with a cheque, you can stop payment and with a credit card you have a grace period between purchase and payment.

Electronic Payment

Advancements in technology and the spread of the Internet have impacted not only how people buy things, but how they pay for their purchases as well. Electronic banking services, widely available throughout Canada and the United States, now enable people to pay bills and transfer funds with a few clicks of the computer mouse. No longer do you have to mail a cheque or line up at an ATM to pay your bills; financial institutions now provide online services that allow you to transmit your payments electronically. The simplicity and security associated with electronic payment systems has made them increasingly popular with consumers.

Savings Deposits

Coins, banknotes, and demand deposits are certainly forms of money, because all are accepted as direct means of payment for goods and services. Money also includes

savings deposits
financial institution accounts containing funds that cannot be used directly for payment

savings deposits, which are financial institution accounts containing funds that cannot be used directly for payment, such as by writing cheques. If these funds cannot be used directly as a means of payment, then why do people hold such accounts? People use these accounts primarily because they generally pay higher interest rates than demand deposits.

Money Market Mutual Funds

Money market mutual funds are interest-earning accounts provided by brokers who pool funds into investments such as Treasury bills. These funds are invested in short-term securities, and depositors are allowed to write cheques against their accounts subject to certain limitations. This type of fund experienced tremendous growth over the last 20 years. Money market mutual funds are highly liquid assets. While not technically considered money, these funds are important because they are relatively easy to convert into money for the purchase of goods and services.

Stocks and Bonds

Virtually everyone agrees that many other forms of financial assets, such as stocks and bonds, are not money. Suppose you buy 1000 shares of common stock in Microsoft at $30 per share, for a total of $30 000. The stock is traded daily on the Toronto Stock Exchange and elsewhere; you can readily sell the stock and get paid in legal tender or a demand deposit. Why, then, is this stock not considered money? First, it will take a few days for you to receive payment for the sale of stock; you cannot turn the asset into cash as you can a savings deposit in a financial institution. Second, and more importantly, the value of the stock fluctuates over time, and as an owner of the asset, you have no guarantee that you will be able to obtain its original nominal value at any time. Thus, stocks and bonds are not generally considered to be money.

WHAT IS LIQUIDITY?

liquidity
the ease with which one asset can be converted into another asset or into goods and services

Money is an asset that we generally use to buy goods or services. In fact, it is so easy to convert money into goods and services that we say it is the most liquid of assets. When we speak of **liquidity** we are speaking about the ease with which one asset can be converted into another asset or into goods and services. For example, to convert a stock or bond into goods and services would prove to be somewhat more difficult—contacting your broker or going online, determining at what price to sell your stock, paying the commission, and waiting for the completion of the transaction. Clearly, stocks and bonds are not as liquid an asset as money. But other assets are even less liquid, like converting your oil paintings or your hockey card collection into other goods and services.

HOW IS THE MONEY SUPPLY MEASURED?

M2
currency outside chartered banks plus demand and savings deposits at chartered banks

M2+
M2 plus demand and savings deposits at trust companies, mortgage loan companies, credit unions, caisses populaires, and other financial institutions

There is no unique official measure of the Canadian money supply. The most common definition of the money supply is called **M2,** which consists of currency held outside chartered banks plus demand and savings deposits at chartered banks. Exhibit 1 shows that in May 2013, the M2 measure of the money supply in Canada was $1186 billion, comprising $63.2 billion of currency held outside chartered banks plus $1123.1 billion of demand deposits and savings deposits at the chartered banks. A broader definition of the money supply is called **M2+,** which consists of M2 plus demand and savings deposits at trust companies, mortgage loan companies, credit unions, caisses populaires, and other financial institutions. M2+ totalled $1549 billion in May 2013.

section 19.2
Exhibit 1 — Two Definitions of the Money Supply: M2 and M2+

Currency held outside chartered banks	$ 63.2 billion
Demand deposits and savings deposits at chartered banks	1123.1 billion
M2	1186.3 billion
Deposits at other financial institutions	362.7 billion
M2+	1549.0 billion

SOURCE: Bank of Canada, Weekly Financial Statistics, July 26, 2013, Table E1, Seasonally adjusted figures.

Of these two different definitions of the money supply, it is the M2 measurement that is more commonly used as the official money supply.

WHAT BACKS THE MONEY SUPPLY?

Until fairly recently, coins in most nations were largely made from precious metals, usually gold or silver. These metals had considerable intrinsic worth: If the coins were melted down, the metal would be valuable for use in jewellery, industrial applications, dentistry, and so forth. Until 1929 (with the exception of the World War I period of 1914–1926), Canada was on an internal **gold standard,** a monetary system that defined the value of the dollar as equivalent in value to a certain amount of gold, thereby allowing direct convertibility from currency to gold. Under this system, the quantity of gold purchased by the government determines the monetary reserves and therefore the supply of money in the economy.

In 1929, Canada effectively went off the gold standard. Excessive monetary expansion in the 1920s, which lowered the ratio of gold reserves to Dominion notes, in addition to a reluctance by Canadian authorities to accept the constraints on the gold standard, were seen as major contributing factors leading to this decision.

gold standard
a monetary system that defines the value of the dollar as equivalent in value to a certain amount of gold, thereby allowing direct convertibility from currency to gold

What Backs Our Money Has Changed

Canadian dollars are no longer convertible into gold, so today no meaningful precious metal gives our money value. Why, then, do people accept currency in exchange for goods? After all, a $20 bill is just a piece of polymer with virtually no inherent utility or worth. Do we accept these bills because it states on the front of the bills that "This note is legal tender"? Perhaps, but we accept demand deposits without that statement.

The true backing behind money in Canada is faith that people will take it in exchange for goods and services. People accept with great eagerness these small pieces of coloured polymer simply because we believe that they will be exchangeable for goods and services with an intrinsic value. If you were to drop two pieces of polymer of equal size on the floor in front of 100 students, one a blank piece of polymer and the other a $100 bill and then leave the room, the group would probably start fighting for the $100 bill while the blank piece of polymer would be ignored. As long as people have confidence in something's convertibility into goods and services, money will exist and no further backing is necessary.

Because governments represent the collective will of the people, they are the institutional force that traditionally defines money in the legal sense. People are willing to accept pieces of paper as money only because of their faith in the government. When people lose

faith in the exchangeability of pieces of paper that the government decrees as money, even legal tender loses its status as meaningful money. Something is money only if people will generally accept it. Although governments play a key role in defining money, much of it is actually created by chartered banks. A majority of Canadian money, whether M2 or M2+, is in the form of deposits at privately owned financial institutions.

People who hold money, then, must have faith not only in their government, but also in banks and other financial institutions. If you accept a cheque drawn on a bank, you believe that bank or, for that matter, any financial institution will be willing to convert that cheque into legal tender (currency), enabling you to buy goods or services that you want to have. Thus, you have faith in the bank as well. In short, our money is money because of the confidence that we have in private financial institutions as well as in our government.

What makes this money valuable? Banknotes are valuable if they are acceptable to people who want to sell goods and services. Sellers must be confident that the money they accept is also acceptable at the place where they want to buy goods and services. Imagine if money in Alberta was not accepted as money in Ontario or Nova Scotia. It would certainly make it more difficult to carry out transactions.

SECTION CHECK

- *Currency* refers of the coins and banknotes that are issued by institutions and governments to facilitate the trading of goods and services and the payment of debts. Canadian currency consists of banknotes and coins issued by the Government of Canada, and demand and savings deposits held in various financial institutions.
- Demand and savings deposits are two types of bank accounts. Demand deposits are balances in financial institution accounts that depositors can access on demand, while savings deposits are deposited funds that cannot be used directly for payment.
- The ease with which one asset can be converted into another asset or goods and services is called *liquidity*.
- M2 is made up of currency outside chartered banks plus demand and savings deposits at chartered banks. M2+ includes M2 plus demand and savings deposits at trust companies, mortgage loan companies, credit unions, caisses populaires, and other financial institutions.
- Money is backed by our faith that others will accept it from us in exchange for goods and services.

iStock/Thinkstock, bank notes images used with the permission of the Bank of Canada.

section
19.3   How Banks Create Money

- What types of financial institutions exist in Canada?
- How do banks create money?
- What does a bank balance sheet look like?
- What is a desired reserve ratio?

WHAT TYPES OF FINANCIAL INSTITUTIONS EXIST IN CANADA?

Financial intermediaries in Canada can be classified into three general categories: depository institutions, contractual savings institutions, and investment intermediaries. Each type of institution is unique in terms of where it obtains its funds (primary liability) and how it uses those funds (primary asset). For example, customer deposits are a depository institution's largest liability (source of funds), while the loans and mortgages it grants to its customers are its largest asset (source of funds). Alternatively, consider pension plans that are established by an employer for the purpose of organizing employee retirement contributions (source of funds). Since most companies do not administer their own pension plans, financial institutions receive this money and invest it in corporate stocks and bonds (use of funds).

Exhibit 1 shows the relative size of the major types of financial institutions in Canada in terms of total financial assets. *Deposit-taking institutions,* a category that includes chartered banks, control over 75 percent of all financial assets in Canada.

Canada's Banking System

Canada's banking system is widely considered to be the most efficient and safest in the world. The biggest players in the Canadian banking industry are its six large **chartered banks,** financial institutions that accept deposits and make loans. The "Big Six" includes the Bank of Montreal, Bank of Nova Scotia, Canadian Imperial Bank of Commerce, National Bank of Canada, Royal Bank of Canada, and Toronto-Dominion Bank. These banks hold over 90 percent of the financial assets in the banking industry and approximately 70 percent of the total domestic assets held by the financial services sector. While chartered banks dominate the financial landscape, there are thousands of other financial institutions offering a variety of financial services in Canada.

chartered banks
financial institutions that accept deposits and make loans

By comparison, the structure of Canada's banking industry is dramatically different than that used in the United States. While Canada had a total of 80 banks as of August 2013, the United States had over 7000 commercial banks, far more than any other country in the world. In addition to the extraordinary number of banks, another distinguishing feature of the U.S. banking industry is the fact that the majority of the banks are small: 90 percent have assets under $1 billion and 30 percent have assets under $100 million.

The Functions of Banks

Banks offer a large number of financial functions. For example, they often will pay an individual's monthly bills by automatic withdrawals, provide financial planning services, rent safe-deposit boxes, and so on. Most important, though, they accept demand deposits and savings deposits from individuals and firms. They can create money by making loans. In making loans, financial institutions act as intermediaries (the middle persons) between savers, who supply funds, and borrowers, who demand funds.

section 19.3   Relative Shares of Financial Institutions in
     Exhibit 1   Canada—2011–12

Type of Institution	Number	Total Assets (in billions)	Percentage (%)
Deposit-taking institutions	152	$ 3658	74.7
Life insurance companies	93	967	19.7
Property and casualty companies	177	134	2.7
Federally regulated private pension plans	1354	142	2.9
Total	**1776**	**$4901**	**100.0**

SOURCE: Office of the Superintendent of Financial Institutions, *OSFI Annual Report, 2011–2012.*

HOW DO BANKS CREATE MONEY?

As we have already learned, most money, narrowly defined, is in the form of demand deposits, assets that can be directly used to buy goods and services. But how did the balance in, say, a chequing account get there in the first place? Perhaps it was through a loan made by a chartered bank. When a bank lends to a person, it does not typically give the borrower cash (banknotes and metal currency). Rather, it gives the person the funds by a cheque or by adding funds to an existing chequing account of the borrower. If you go into a bank and borrow $1000, the bank probably will simply add $1000 to your chequing account at the bank. In doing so, a new demand deposit—money—is created.

Bank Profits

Banks make loans and create demand deposits in order to make a profit. How do they make their profit? By collecting higher interest payments on the loans they make than the interest they pay their depositors for those funds. If you borrow $1000 from Loans R Us National Bank, the interest payment you make, less the expenses the bank incurs in making the loan, including its costs of acquiring the funds, represents profit to the bank.

Fractional Reserve System

Because the way to make more profit is to make more loans, banks want to make a large volume of loans. Shareholders, or owners, of banks want the largest profits possible, so what keeps banks from making nearly infinite quantities of loans? A prudent bank would put some limit on its loan (and therefore deposit) volume. For people to accept demand deposits as money, the cheques written must be generally accepted in exchange for goods and services. People will accept cheques only if they know that they are quickly convertible at par (face value) into legal tender. For this reason, banks must have adequate cash reserves on hand to meet the needs of customers who wish to convert their demand deposits into currency.

fractional reserve system
a system in which banks hold reserves equal to some fraction of their demand deposits

Our banking system is sometimes called a **fractional reserve system** because banks hold reserves equal to some fraction of their demand deposits. If a bank were to create $100 in demand deposits for every $1 in cash reserves that it had, the bank might well find itself in difficulty before too long. Why? Consider a bank with $10 000 000 in demand deposits and $100 000 in cash reserves. Suppose a couple of large companies with big accounts decide to withdraw $120 000 in cash on the same day. The bank would be unable to convert into legal tender all of the funds requested. The word would then spread that the bank's deposits are not convertible into lawful money. This would cause a so-called "run on the bank." The bank would have to quickly convert some of its other assets into currency, or it would be unable to meet its obligations to convert its demand deposits into currency, and it would have to close.

Therefore, few banks would risk maintaining fewer reserves on hand than they thought prudent for their amount of deposits (particularly demand deposits). Although banks must maintain a prudent level of reserves, they do not want to keep any more of their funds as additional reserves than necessary for safety, because cash reserves do not earn any interest for the bank.

In Canada, if a financial intermediary should fail, depositors are insured against financial loss by the federal government. The Canadian Deposit Insurance Corporation (CDIC), a federal Crown corporation, is the most important government agency that provides this type of insurance. Specifically, deposits at member deposit-taking financial institutions are insured up to $100 000 per account. CDIC members are required to make contributions into the CDIC fund, which is then used to reimburse depositors in the case of a member bank's failure. With some exceptions, virtually all deposit-accepting financial institutions in Canada are members of the CDIC.

WHAT DOES A BANK BALANCE SHEET LOOK LIKE?

Earlier in this chapter, we learned that money is created when banks make loans. We will now look more closely at the process of bank lending and its impact on the stock of money. In doing so, we will take a closer look at the structure and behaviour of our hypothetical bank, the Loans R Us National Bank. To get a good picture of the size of the bank, what it owns, and what it owes, we look at its **balance sheet,** which is sort of a financial photograph of the bank at a single moment in time. Exhibit 2 presents a balance sheet for the Loans R Us National Bank.

balance sheet
a financial record that indicates the balance between a bank's assets and its liabilities plus capital

Assets

The assets of a bank are those things of value that the bank owns (e.g., cash reserves, bonds, and its buildings), including contractual obligations of individuals and firms to pay funds to the bank (loans). The largest asset item for most banks is loans. Banks maintain most of their assets in the form of loans because interest payments on loans are the primary means by which they earn revenue. Some assets are kept in the form of noninterest-bearing cash reserves, to meet the cash demands of customers. Banks also keep some assets in the form of bonds (usually Government of Canada bonds) that are quickly convertible into cash if necessary, but also earn interest revenue.

Liabilities

All banks have substantial liabilities, which are financial obligations that the bank has to other people. The predominant liability of virtually all banks is deposits. If you have money in a demand deposit account, you have the right to demand cash for that deposit at any time. Basically, the bank owes you the amount in your chequing account. Savings deposits similarly constitute a liability of banks.

Capital

For a bank to be healthy and solvent, its assets, or what it owns, must exceed its liabilities, or what it owes to others. In other words, if the bank was liquidated and all the assets converted into cash and all the obligations to others (liabilities) paid off, there would still be some cash left to distribute to the owners of the bank, its shareholders. This difference between a bank's assets and its liabilities constitutes the bank's capital.

section 19.3
Exhibit 2 — Balance Sheet, Loans R Us National Bank

Assets		Liabilities and Capital	
Cash reserves	$ 900 000	Demand deposits	$ 5 000 000
Loans	7 200 000	Savings deposits	4 000 000
Bonds	1 500 000	Total Liabilities	$ 9 000 000
		Capital	1 000 000
Bank building, equipment, fixtures	400 000		
Total Assets	**$10 000 000**	**Total Liabilities and Capital**	**$10 000 000**

Note that this definition of capital differs from the earlier definition, which described capital as goods used to further production of other goods (machines, structures, tools, etc.). As you can see in Exhibit 2, capital is included on the right side of the balance sheet so that both sides (assets and liabilities plus capital) are equal in amount. Anytime the aggregate amount of bank assets changes, the aggregate amount of liabilities and capital also must change by the same amount, by definition.

WHAT IS A DESIRED RESERVE RATIO?

desired reserve ratio
the percentage of deposits that a bank chooses to hold as cash reserves

excess reserves
cash reserves that are in excess of desired reserves

Suppose for simplicity that the Loans R Us National Bank wants to hold cash reserves equal to 10 percent of its deposits. That percentage of deposits that a bank chooses to hold as cash reserves is often called the **desired reserve ratio.** But what does a desired reserve ratio of 10 percent mean? This means that the bank *wants to* keep cash on hand equal to one-tenth (10 percent) of its deposits. For example, if the desired reserve ratio was 10 percent, banks would want to hold $100 000 in reserves for every $1 million in deposits. The remaining 90 percent of cash, the cash reserves that are in excess of desired reserves, is called **excess reserves.**

In Canada, the section of the Bank of Canada Act that required banks to hold a specified amount of cash reserves has since been repealed. In June of 1994, banks in Canada were allowed to determine their own reserve requirements, that is, their reserves were subject to a desired reserve ratio. Currently, Canadian banks typically keep about 4.5 percent reserves.

Reserves in the form of vault cash earn no revenue for the bank; no profit is made from holding vault cash. Whenever excess reserves appear, banks will invest the excess reserves in interest-earning assets, sometimes bonds but usually loans.

Loaning Excess Reserves

Let's see what happens when someone deposits $100 000 at the Loans R Us National Bank. We will continue to assume that the desired reserve ratio is 10 percent. That is, the bank wants to hold $10 000 in reserves for this new deposit of $100 000. The remaining 90 percent, or $90 000, becomes excess reserves, and most of this will likely become available for loans for individuals and businesses. Notice that at this point, the money supply (M2) is unchanged. Demand deposits have increased by $100 000 while currency outside the chartered banks has decreased by $100 000, as the currency is now stored in the bank's vault.

However, this is not the end of the story. Let us say that the bank loans all of its new excess reserves of $90 000 to an individual who is remodelling her home. At the time that the loan is made, the money supply will increase by $90 000. Specifically, no one has less money—the original depositor still has $100 000 and the bank now adds $90 000 to the borrower's chequing account (demand deposit). A new demand deposit, or chequing account, of $90 000 has been created. *Since demand deposits are money, the issuers of the new loan have created money.*

Furthermore, borrowers are not likely to keep the money in their chequing accounts for long, since you usually take out a loan to buy something. If that loan is used for remodelling, then the borrower pays the construction company, whose owner will likely deposit the money into his account at another bank to add even more funds for additional money expansion. This whole process is summarized in Exhibit 3.

Money Creation Is Not Wealth Creation

When banks create more money by putting their excess reserves to work, they make the economy more liquid. There is clearly more money in the economy after the loan, but is the borrower any wealthier? The answer is no. Although borrowers have more money to buy goods and services, they are not any richer because the new liability, the loan, has to be repaid.

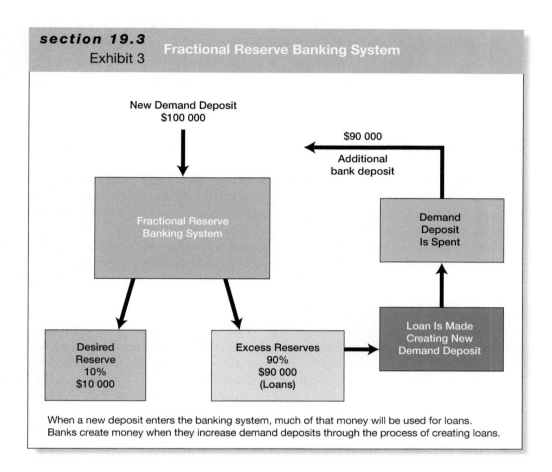

section 19.3
Exhibit 3 **Fractional Reserve Banking System**

New Demand Deposit
$100 000

Fractional Reserve
Banking System

$90 000

Additional
bank deposit

Demand
Deposit
Is Spent

Desired
Reserve
10%
$10 000

Excess Reserves
90%
$90 000
(Loans)

Loan Is Made
Creating New
Demand Deposit

When a new deposit enters the banking system, much of that money will be used for loans.
Banks create money when they increase demand deposits through the process of creating loans.

In short, banks create money when they increase demand deposits through the process of creating loans. However, the process does not stop here. In the next section, we will see how the process of loans and deposits has a multiplying effect throughout the banking industry.

Leverage and the 2008–09 Financial Crisis

To what extent, if any, are financial institutions regulated in their ability to generate loans? To best answer this question, we first need to understand the concept of **leverage**—the use of borrowed money for the purpose of investing. As a business practice, leverage is a common way in which enterprises finance investment projects; that is, it is not uncommon to see businesses finance an investment using debt as opposed to their own capital. For banks, leverage is central to their ability to operate successfully since their business centres around the actions of borrowing and lending funds.

In banking, the ratio of total assets (recall that for a bank assets consist primarily of loans) to bank capital—referred to as the **leverage ratio**—is a common measurement of the degree to which an institution is leveraged. For example, looking back at Exhibit 2, Loans R Us National Bank has a leverage ratio of 10 ($10 000 000/$1 000 000), meaning that for every dollar of capital supplied by the bank owners, the bank has $10 of assets.

To help appreciate the impact of leverage on banking operations, let us continue with the example from Exhibit 2 and consider what happens to bank capital when the value of total assets increases by 10 percent. A 10 percent increase in total assets increases their value to $11 000 000, and since total liabilities remain unchanged, bank capital increases to $2 000 000. That is, since Loans R Us Bank has a leverage ratio of 10, the 10 percent increase in total assets generates a 100 percent increase in bank capital. Alternatively,

leverage
the use of borrowed money for the purpose of investing

leverage ratio
the ratio of total assets to bank capital

if total assets decrease in value by 10 percent, total assets would fall by $1 000 000 (to $9 000 000) and bank capital would be reduced by 100 percent to a value of zero!

In summary, when a bank has total assets that far exceed their capital, their leverage ratio is high, an indication of not only the bank's aggressive business model, but also an indication of the potential risk of failure of the bank. The multiple of assets to capital, that is the degree of leverage that Canadian financial institutions can pursue, is regulated by the Office of the Superintendent of Financial Institutions (OSFI). By restricting how much debt securities a bank can issue, the OSFI effectively controls how much leverage a financial institution can take on.

Beginning in the early 1960s until 1980, the average leverage ratios of major Canadian banks steadily increased from around 20 to a high of over 40. That is, over a 20-year period, Canadian banks went from having $20 of total assets (primarily loans) for each dollar of bank capital to over $40 of total assets (primarily loans) to each dollar of bank capital. In response to this rise in leverage (and the related financial risk it placed on the banking system), a regulatory limit of 30 was imposed on the leverage ratios of large banks beginning in 1982 until 1991. This regulatory limit was further reduced to 20 in 1991 where it remained until 2000. Presently, banks that meet specific preconditions are eligible for a maximum leverage ratio of 23. These lower leverage ratios and the higher capital reserves they generated have been seen as a major reason why Canadian banks weathered the 2008–09 financial crisis so successfully. U.S. and European banks were widely viewed as being dangerously over leveraged in the years leading up to the global financial crisis—a position that is being cited as a major contributing factor to the global financial crisis of 2008.

From an international perspective, it is important to note that few countries have formal leverage constraints. In response to this and the global financial crisis, the Third Basel Accord (*Basel III*) was negotiated in 2010–11 and is now being phased in, which will require central banks to impose lower leverage ratios on their national banks. The impact of *Basel III* on Canadian financial institutions is expected to be minimal, as the new requirements are largely in line with current OSFI regulations. For the United States and Europe, adherence to the tighter regulations will be considerably more difficult.

Business *CONNECTION*

DANCING WITH DEBT AND THE MONEY SUPPLY

In reality, business has little impact on money and the banking system (unless of course the business is banking!). But it's useful for business owners to understand the relationship of business, the money supply, and debt.

Many consumers believe that the money supply is literally a creation of the government's print shop, while business owners appreciate that, in fact, the vast amount of money created stems from the fractional reserves and creation of loans within the banking system. Businesses outside the financial sector have little impact on the money supply, but they do have an indirect effect through the financing of their products. Consider the following example.

About 20 years ago, North American companies started losing some of their share of the car market. Consumers were turning away from domestic cars in favour of foreign ones that were of higher quality and had more features. In an attempt to keep market share, the domestic auto industry started to address product issues, but that required

major investment of capital and time. In the meantime, the domestic industry turned to the financial markets for assistance. Specifically, the car companies began to subsidize the cost of loans to consumers by "buying down" interest rates and taking greater equity positions (or investments) in car leases. In any event, this resulted in more vehicles being sold and more loans to consumers.

As you've learned, the more loans that banks make, the greater the creation of the money supply, so in offering financial incentives to consumers to buy cars, the industry was contributing to inflation. At the same time the industry was contributing to various debt levels within the economy. The auto industry took on significant debt to finance its retooling and to finance the consumer incentives. Consumers took on extra debt by buying cars they might have not been able or willing to buy without taking on debt. Over the short and medium term, this had little effect on the economy—especially when the economy was growing. (Growth hides demons within the economy!)

(continued)

The net effect of this growing debt is that it has produced unparalleled levels of consumption—this has been a perceived benefit for business and consumers (and business and governments). This increase in growth and consumption has in turn put upward pressure on inflation rates. But, since the start of the Great Recession of 2008, growth has been hampered by this unsustainable level of debt and inflation has been reduced to near-record low levels—to the point where deflation is a major concern. All levels of the economy have been burdened by debt, which has to be paid before further demand for products and services can recover. Until debt levels are reduced, inflation rates will struggle to get to healthy levels.

So, while business has not been directly responsible for the increases in debt and the money supply, it has contributed to them. Sensible business owners need to be aware of the dance among themselves, the money supply, infla-tion, and debt—these are short-term decisions affecting the health of the economy in the longer term.

1. As a business owner, do you think the level of consumer debt is an issue for business? For the economy at large? Why or why not?

2. As a business owner, do you think the level of govern-ment debt is an issue for business? For the economy at large? Why or why not?

3. One of the concerns of governments is that the busi-ness sector is sitting on a tremendous amount of cash that is not being reinvested into the economy. One suggested solution is to tax corporations that are not investing that cash. As a business owner, what is your opinion about such a policy?

SECTION CHECK

- While a variety of financial intermediaries exist in the Canadian financial system, the sector is dominated by deposit-accepting institutions—banks. The Canadian banking industry itself is dominated by six large chartered banks. The "Big Six" hold the majority of the financial assets in the banking industry.
- Money is created when banks make loans. Borrowers receive newly created demand deposits.
- A balance sheet is a financial record that indicates the balance between a bank's assets and its liabilities plus capital. A bank's largest asset is loans and its largest liability is deposits.
- A desired reserve ratio is the percentage of deposits a bank chooses to keep on hand in the form of cash reserves.

The Money Multiplier

section
19.4

- How does the multiple expansion of the money supply process work?
- What is the money multiplier?
- Why is it only "potential" money creation?

HOW DOES THE MULTIPLE EXPANSION OF THE MONEY SUPPLY PROCESS WORK?

We have just learned that banks can create money (demand deposits) by making loans and that the monetary expansion of an individual bank is limited to its excess reserves. Although this is true, it ignores the further effects of a new loan and the accompanying expansion in the money supply. New loans create new money directly, but they also create excess reserves in other banks, which leads to still further increases in both loans and the money supply. There is a multiple expansion effect, where a given volume of bank reserves creates a multiplied amount of money.

New Loans and Multiple Expansions

To see how the process of multiple expansion works, let us extend our earlier example. Say Loans R Us National Bank receives a new cash deposit of $100 000. For convenience, say the bank wants to keep new cash reserves equal to one-tenth (10 percent) of new deposits. With that, Loans R Us chooses to hold $10 000 of the $100 000 deposit for reserves. Thus, Loans R Us now has $90 000 in excess reserves as a consequence of the new cash deposit.

The Loans R Us National Bank, being a profit maximizer, will probably put its newly acquired excess reserves to work in some fashion, earning income in the form of interest. Most likely, it will make one or more new loans totalling $90 000.

When the borrowers from Loans R Us National Bank get their loans, the borrowed money will almost certainly be spent on something—such as new machinery, a new house, a new car, or larger store inventories. The new money will lead to new spending.

The $90 000 spent by people borrowing from Loans R Us National Bank likely will end up in bank accounts in still other banks, such as Bank A shown in Exhibit 1. Bank A now has a new deposit of $90 000 with which to make more loans and create still more money. So Bank A's T-account now looks like this:

Bank A

Assets		Liabilities	
Reserves	$9000	Chequing deposits	$90 000
Loans	$81 000		

After the deposits, Bank A has liabilities of $90 000. Thus, Bank A creates $81 000 of money. Now if the money deposited in Bank A is made available for a loan and is then deposited in Bank B, the T-account for Bank B will be

Bank B

Assets		Liabilities	
Reserves	$8100	Chequing deposits	$81 000
Loans	$72 900		

This process continues with Bank C, Bank D, Bank E, and others. Loans R Us National Bank's initial cash deposit, then, has a chain-reaction impact that ultimately involves many banks and a total monetary impact that is far greater than suggested by the size of the original deposit of $100 000; that is, every new loan gives rise to excess reserves, which lead to still further lending and deposit creation. Of course, each round of lending is smaller than the preceding one because some (we are assuming 10 percent) of the new money created will be kept as desired reserves.

WHAT IS THE MONEY MULTIPLIER?

money multiplier *measures the potential amount of demand deposit money that the banking system generates with each dollar of reserves*

The **money multiplier** measures the potential amount of demand deposit money that the banking system generates with each dollar of reserves. To determine the size of the money multiplier we simply divide 1 by the desired reserve ratio, as indicated by the following formula:

$$\text{Money multiplier} = \frac{1}{\text{Desired reserve ratio}}$$

The larger the desired reserve ratio, the smaller the money multiplier. Thus, a desired reserve ratio of 25 percent means a money multiplier of 4. Likewise, a desired reserve ratio of 10 percent means a money multiplier of 10.

The next formula can be used to measure the potential impact on demand deposits of an initial change in deposits:

$$\text{Potential money creation} = \text{Initial deposit} \times \text{Money multiplier}$$

In the example in Exhibit 1, where Loans R Us National Bank (with a 10 percent desired reserve ratio) receives a new $100 000 cash deposit, initial deposit equals $100 000. Potential demand deposit creation, then, equals $100 000 (initial deposit) multiplied by 10 (the money multiplier), or $1 000 000. Using the money multiplier, we can calculate that the total potential impact of the initial $100 000 deposit is some $1 000 000 in demand deposit money being created. What is the final impact on the money supply (M2)? Demand deposits at the chartered banks are up by $1 000 000, but currency outside the chartered banks is down by $100 000 (as the initial deposit is in the banks' vaults), so the money supply has increased by $900 000.

WHY IS IT ONLY "POTENTIAL" MONEY CREATION?

Note that the expression "potential" money creation was used in describing the impact of creating loans and deposits out of excess reserves. Why "potential"? Because it is possible that some banks will choose not to lend all of their excess reserves. Some banks may simply be extremely conservative and keep some extra newly acquired cash assets in that form. When that happens, the chain reaction effect is reduced by the amount of excess reserves not loaned out.

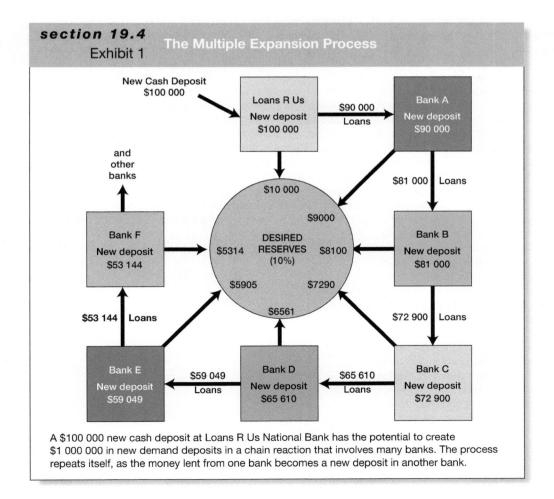

section 19.4
Exhibit 1   The Multiple Expansion Process

A $100 000 new cash deposit at Loans R Us National Bank has the potential to create $1 000 000 in new demand deposits in a chain reaction that involves many banks. The process repeats itself, as the money lent from one bank becomes a new deposit in another bank.

Moreover, some borrowers may not spend all of their newly acquired bank deposits, or they may wait a considerable period of time before doing so. Others may choose to keep some of their loans as currency in their pockets. Such leakages and time lags in the bank money expansion process usually mean that the actual monetary impact of an initial deposit created out of excess reserves within a short time period is less than indicated by the money multiplier. Still, the multiplier principle does work, and a multiple expansion of deposits will generally occur in a fractional reserve banking system.

DEBATE

SHOULD THE GOVERNMENT REGULATE HIGHER LEVELS OF BANK RESERVES?

For:

The fractional reserve system allows for the banks (not the central bank) to "create" money through the process of granting loans. The loaning and reinvesting expands the GDP. But the creation of money, through the multiplier effect, is paralleled by the creation of debt. Those who advocate for the elimination of the fractional system point to the recurring of the boom-and-bust cycles as a result of easy credit and inflation, and they note that with each subsequent boom/bust cycle the magnitude of the cycles increase greatly. The cycles ensure that bank bailouts will eventually be inevitable, all at the expense of the taxpayer. So it's the taxpayer who is left holding the risk and responsibility for the consequences of the fractional reserve system, and therefore it's taxpayers (or their agent, the government) who should protect themselves through tighter regulations on the amount of reserves—notably, regulating higher levels of reserves. Even the massive growth that China has gone through this past decade is at risk through the creation of phantom money and debt.* Another argument addresses the consequences of the debt produced through the fractional reserve system. The per capita debt in Canada, not including mortgages, sits at just under $30 000 as this book goes to press. That's a staggering amount that consumers have to service through the paying of interest—for a family of four it amounts to between about $800 and $1000 a month, just on interest (that's not even reducing the principle!). With this amount of personal debt, there is no way the country, let alone individuals, can grow their wealth. In essence, they literally are working for the banks, and long-term growth for the economy will be suppressed. The solution is not just to make it harder to get a loan (on the demand-side), but make it harder to give a loan (on the supply-side), and one way that's done is by regulating the fractional reserve system so that bank reserves are higher.

Surely it's clear that the government should regulate higher levels of reserves that banks withhold in their vaults. Can you think of other arguments for this position and other consequences of low bank reserves to support increasing reserves in the fractional system? How do you think the system could be regulated to the benefit of society, and what do you think would be the short- and long-term consequences?

*Nathan VanderKlippe and Eric Reguly. "China's Ticking Time Bomb," *The Globe and Mail*, May 3, 2014, pp. B6–7.

Against:

Those who are in favour of the fractional reserve system justify it based on the benefits of growth to citizens and firms alike. The fractional system played a major role in creating the increasingly rapid growth and wealth of the last half-century, which most developed economies have benefitted from. While the perils of the system are significant, the impacts are rarely felt over generations, and these might be the acceptable "costs" for reaching greater levels of wealth. Those who advocate for greater regulation of the fractional reserves don't appreciate the considerable impact to the economy. While arguing for more regulation is one thing, it's a completely different thing to change reserve levels when individuals and firms are faced with the consequences of reducing their wealth. In practical terms, it would never be done, so there ought to be other ways to deal with the consequences that are more palatable for citizens. Another argument is that while the fractional reserve system creates more debt, the debt itself is not bad—it's who holds that debt and their ability to pay it back. Perhaps the better approach is to more strictly regulate who can qualify for loans, not limit the amount of loans for those who can demonstrate they can pay. Surely the arguments against regulating higher levels of bank reserves are compelling. Can you think of ways to regulate the system to ensure it works to society's benefit?

SECTION CHECK

- New loans mean new money (demand deposits), which can increase spending as well as the money supply.
- The money multiplier is equal to 1 divided by the desired reserve ratio.
- The banking system as a whole can potentially create new money equal to several times the amount of new reserves—as determined by the money multiplier. However, due to various leakages and time lags, the actual monetary impact of an initial deposit created out of excess reserves within a short period of time will be less than that calculated by the money multiplier.

For Your Review

Section 19.1

1. Explain the difficulties that an economics professor might face in purchasing a new car using the barter system.

2. Why do people who live in countries experiencing rapid inflation often prefer to hold another country's currency (e.g., U.S. dollars) rather than their own country's currency? Explain.

3. Why does the advantage of monetary exchange over barter increase as an economy becomes more complex?

Section 19.2

4. Which one of each of the following pairs of assets is most liquid?

   a. Air Canada shares or a savings deposit

   b. a 30-year bond or a six-month Treasury bill

   c. a term deposit or a demand deposit

   d. a savings account or residential real estate

5. Why have ATMs and online banking made savings accounts more liquid than they used to be?

6. What would each of the following changes do to M2 and M2+?

Change	M2	M2+
An increase in currency in circulation		
An increase in demand deposits		
An increase in savings deposits		
A transfer of demand deposit balances from credit unions to chartered banks		

7. How have interest-earning chequing accounts and overdraft protection led to a relative decline in demand deposits?

Section 19.3

8. Indicate whether each of the following belong on the asset or liability side of a bank's balance sheet.

   a. loans

   b. holdings of government bonds

   c. demand deposits

   d. vault cash

   e. savings deposits

   f. bank buildings

   g. term deposits

9. Why do you think asking whether money is an asset or a liability is a trick question in economics?

10. If the Bank of Canada paid interest for bank reserves held at the Bank of Canada, would banks still want to avoid holding excess reserves?

11. Suppose you found $10 000 while digging in your backyard and you deposited it in the bank. How would your new demand deposit account create a situation of excess reserves at your bank?

Section 19.4

12. Assume there was a new $100 000 deposit into a demand deposit at a bank.

    a. What would be the resulting excess reserves created by that deposit if banks faced a desired reserve ratio of 10 percent, 20 percent, 25 percent, and 50 percent? Display using a T-account.

    b. How many additional dollars could that bank lend out as a result of that deposit if banks faced a desired reserve ratio of 10 percent, 20 percent, 25 percent, and 50 percent? Display using a T-account.

    c. How many additional dollars of demand deposit money could the banking system as a whole create in response to such a new deposit if banks faced a desired reserve ratio of 10 percent, 20 percent, 25 percent, and 50 percent?

13. Answer the following questions.

    a. If a bank had reserves of $30 000 and demand deposits of $200 000 (and no other deposits), how much could it lend out if it had a desired reserve ratio of

       10 percent?   _____

       15 percent?   _____

       20 percent?   _____

    b. If the bank then received a new $40 000 deposit in a customer's demand deposit account, how much could it now lend out (including the amount in question (a) if it had a desired reserve ratio of

       10 percent?   _____

       15 percent?   _____

       20 percent?   _____

14. Calculate the money multiplier when the desired reserve ratio is

    a. 10 percent.

    b. 2 percent.

c. 20 percent.

d. 8 percent.

15. If the desired reserve ratio is 10 percent, calculate the potential change in demand deposits in the banking system under the following circumstances.

   a. You take $5000 from under your mattress and deposit it in your bank.

   b. You withdraw $50 from the bank and leave it in your wallet for emergencies.

   c. You write a cheque for $2500 drawn on your bank (CIBC) to an auto mechanic, who deposits the funds in his bank (TD Bank).

16. Calculate the magnitude of the money multiplier if banks were to hold 100 percent of deposits in reserve. Would banks be able to create money in such a case? Explain.

Blueprint Problem

Examine the following balance sheet for a bank.

Bank Balance Sheet			
Assets		**Liabilities**	
Reserves	$1 000 000	Demand deposits	$6 000 000
Loans	5 000 000		
Buildings	2 000 000	Capital	2 000 000
Total Assets	**$8 000 000**	**Total Liabilities and Capital**	**$8 000 000**

   a. If this banking system had a desired reserve ratio of 10 percent, what amount of excess reserves does it have, if any?

   b. Assume the banking system lends out its excess reserves. Redesign the systems balance sheet to reflect the ultimate impact of this lending.

Blueprint Solution

   a. The banking system would need $600 000 in reserves to meet its 10 percent desired reserve requirement. Since it currently has $1 million in reserves, it necessarily has $400 000 in excess reserves.

By definition, in a fractional reserve banking system, the institutions have only a fraction of the money they are responsible for (their depositors' demand deposits) on hand in the form of reserves. What determines how much banks will hold in reserves is the desired reserve ratio, in this case, 10 percent. To determine the necessary amount of reserves, calculate 10 percent of the demand deposits:

$$\text{Desired reserves} = \text{Demand deposits} \times \text{Desired reserve ratio}$$

$$\text{Desired reserves} = \$6\ 000\ 000 \times 0.1$$

$$\text{Desired reserves} = \$600\ 000$$

b.

> The first step to solving this problem is to calculate the size of the money multiplier

$$\text{Money multiplier} = \frac{1}{\text{Desired reserve requirement}} = \frac{1}{0.1} = 10$$

> Next, recall the operation of the money multiplier process; when banks have excess reserves, they are able to generate loans. When these loans are redeposited, additional excess reserves are created and additional lending results. In terms of a formula, this effect can be expressed as follows:
>
> Potential money creation = Excess reserves × Money multiplier

Potential money creation = $400 000 × 10

> Solving for "Potential money creation" reveals that from the initial $400 000 in initial excess reserves present in the banking system, $4 million in potential money creation would be possible.

Potential money creation = $4 million

> Finally, revisit the banking systems balance sheet and make the necessary updates to reflect this potential money creation. Remember, when a bank makes a loan available, it does so by creating a deposit equal to the loan amount. Therefore, when our system creates $400 000 in loans, this is done through the creation of $400 000 in demand deposits.

Bank Balance Sheet (redesigned)			
Assets		**Liabilities**	
Reserves	$ 1 000 000	Demand deposits **Demand Deposits (new)**	$ 6 000 000 **4 000 000**
Loans **Loans (new)**	5 000 000 **4 000 000**		
Buildings	2 000 000	Capital	2 000 000
Total Assets	**$12 000 000**	**Total Liabilities and Capital**	**$12 000 000**

17. Suppose the simplified balance sheet shown below is for the entire banking system.

Bank Balance Sheet			
Assets		**Liabilities**	
Reserves	$ 500 000	Demand deposits	$2 000 000
Loans	1 600 000		
Buildings	1 200 000	Capital	1 300 000
Total Assets	**$3 300 000**	**Total Liabilities and Capital**	**$3 300 000**

If the desired reserve ratio is 10 percent, how much in excess reserves does the banking system have? If the banking system was to loan out those excess reserves, what is the potential expansion in demand deposits? Redesign the above balance sheet to show how it would look after this amount has been loaned.

18. Suppose the simplified balance sheet shown below is for the entire banking system.

Bank Balance Sheet			
Assets		**Liabilities**	
Reserves	$ 300 000	Demand deposits	$1 500 000
Loans	1 200 000		
Buildings	500 000	Capital	500 000
Total Assets	**$2 000 000**	**Total Liabilities and Capital**	**$2 000 000**

If the desired reserve ratio is 15 percent, how much in excess reserves does the banking system have? If the banking system was to loan out those excess reserves, what is the potential expansion in demand deposits? Redesign the above balance sheet to show how it would look after this amount has been loaned.

19. Suppose the simplified balance sheet shown below is for the entire banking system.

Bank Balance Sheet			
Assets		**Liabilities**	
Reserves	$ 750 000	Demand deposits	$3 500 000
Loans	2 500 000		
Buildings	1 250 000	Capital	1 000 000
Total Assets	**$4 500 000**	**Total Liabilities and Capital**	**$4 500 000**

If the desired reserve ratio is 20 percent, how much in excess reserves does the banking system have? If the banking system was to loan out those excess reserves, what is the potential expansion in demand deposits? Redesign the above balance sheet to show how it would look after this amount has been loaned.

section

20.1 The Bank of Canada

■ What is the Bank of Canada?

■ What are the main responsibilities of the Bank of Canada?

WHAT IS THE BANK OF CANADA?

In most countries of the world, the job of controlling the supply of money belongs to the central bank. The Bank of Canada is Canada's central bank. It was established in 1935, largely as a result of the economic problems of the Great Depression and the need for better control of the money supply. Chartered banks' goal, remember, is to maximize profits for their shareholders. However, the banks' behaviour can have adverse effects on the nation's money supply. For example, during a period of economic recession, banks may have increasing concerns about the ability of new borrowers to repay their loans, or they may find that their customers are withdrawing more cash due to fears that the banks may fail. As a result, the banks may choose to hold more excess reserves for safety and liquidity, rather than loaning those excess reserves out. Thus, during a period of economic recession, there is a tendency for the money supply to decrease, which further destabilizes the economy. A central bank, however, can use certain tools to adjust the money supply in order to help stabilize the economy.

The Bank of Canada is owned by the federal government. It is controlled by a board of directors, which is appointed by the government. The governor of the Bank of Canada, who is the chief executive, is appointed for a seven-year term. The current governor, Stephen Poloz, was appointed in 2013. Although the government has final responsibility for the Bank of Canada's actions, the governor has considerable independence in the day-to-day operations of the Bank of Canada. This operational independence is important, as studies have shown that central banks with greater degrees of independence appear to have a lower annual inflation rate (see Exhibit 1). If there was a very significant disagreement between the governor and the government, the government could issue a written directive to the governor, forcing him or her to either comply with the directive or resign.

The objectives of the Bank of Canada are outlined in the Bank of Canada Act, which starts out:

Whereas it is desirable to establish a central bank in Canada to regulate credit and currency in the best interests of the economic life of the nation, to control and protect the external value of the national monetary unit and to mitigate by its influence fluctuations in the general level of production, trade, prices and employment, so far as may be possible within the scope of monetary action, and generally to promote the economic and financial welfare of Canada. ...

Inflation control is how the Bank of Canada contributes to improved economic performance. Low inflation allows the economy to function more efficiently, resulting in better economic growth over time and reduced short-run cyclical fluctuations in output and employment. In 1991, the Bank of Canada and the federal government jointly announced inflation targets. The current inflation target aims to keep the annual inflation rate within a target range of 1 to 3 percent.

The Federal Reserve System

In Canada, as in most countries, the central bank is a single bank. In the United States, however, the central bank is 12 institutions, closely tied together and collectively called the *Federal Reserve System*. The Federal Reserve System, or the Fed, as it is nicknamed, comprises separate banks in Boston, New York, Philadelphia, Richmond, Atlanta, Dallas, Cleveland, Chicago, St. Louis, Minneapolis–St. Paul, Kansas City, and San Francisco. As Exhibit 2 shows, while these banks and their branches are spread all over the country, they are most heavily concentrated in the eastern states.

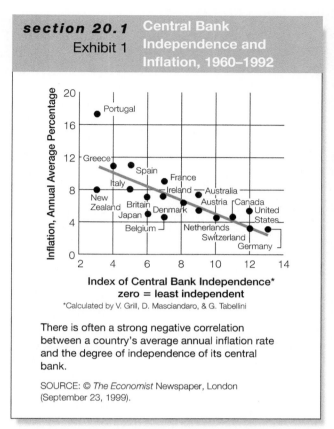

section 20.1
Exhibit 1
Central Bank Independence and Inflation, 1960–1992

Index of Central Bank Independence*
zero = least independent
*Calculated by V. Grill, D. Masciandaro, & G. Tabellini

There is often a strong negative correlation between a country's average annual inflation rate and the degree of independence of its central bank.

SOURCE: © *The Economist* Newspaper, London (September 23, 1999).

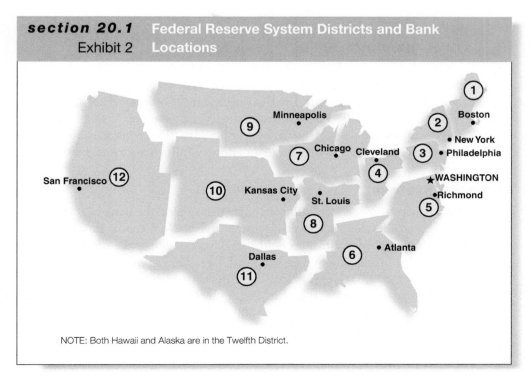

section 20.1
Exhibit 2
Federal Reserve System Districts and Bank Locations

NOTE: Both Hawaii and Alaska are in the Twelfth District.

Each Federal Reserve bank has its own board of directors and, to a limited extent, can set its own policies. Effectively, however, the 12 banks act in unison on major policy issues, with control of major policy decisions resting with the Board of Governors and the Federal Open Market Committee (FOMC). The chairman of the Federal Reserve Board of Governors, currently Janet L. Yellen, is generally regarded as one of the most important and powerful economic policymakers in the United States.

Created in 1913, the Federal Reserve System is privately owned by the banks that "belong" to it. This private ownership, however, is essentially meaningless, as the Federal Reserve Board of Governors, which controls major policy decisions, is appointed by the president of the United States, not by the shareholders.

WHAT ARE THE MAIN RESPONSIBILITIES OF THE BANK OF CANADA?

According to the Bank of Canada's website, in its role as Canada's central bank, the Bank of Canada has four main areas of responsibility:

- Currency
- Funds management
- Financial system
- Monetary policy

Currency

The Bank of Canada has monopoly power over issuing legal tender in the form of Bank of Canada banknotes. The Bank of Canada is responsible for note design, for overseeing the printing and distribution of banknotes, and for replacing worn-out currency. Included as part of this currency function is the role the Bank of Canada plays in counterfeit prevention. A considerable amount of Bank resources have been used to research and develop banknotes that are durable, easy to verify, and difficult to counterfeit. Directly related to this objective is the polymer series of banknotes first issued by the Bank of Canada in 2011.

Funds Management

The Bank of Canada acts as a fiscal agent to the federal government by providing debt-management services, such as policy advice on new debt offerings and the servicing of existing debt. In addition to this, the Bank also manages the government's foreign exchange reserves. Specifically, the Bank assists the federal government in managing its foreign reserves to maintain an adequate level of liquidity. The Bank may also engage directly in foreign exchange transactions in an effort to influence exchange rates.

Financial System

As a central participant in Canada's national payments system, the Bank of Canada acts as a bank to the various financial institutions that operate in Canada. In Chapter 19, we explained that financial institutions hold a small proportion of their reserves as currency in their vaults. In addition to this "vault cash" they hold a portion of their reserves as demand deposit at the Bank of Canada. These deposits at the Bank of Canada allow financial institution to make payments to each other. For example, let's say you pay your monthly rent by writing a cheque for $800 on your chequing account at the TD Bank. Your landlord deposits the cheque in her chequing account at the Royal Bank. The Royal Bank will credit your landlord's chequing account for $800. But the Royal Bank will want payment of $800 from the TD Bank. Therefore, as the cheque clears,

$800 will be deducted from the TD Bank's reserve account at the Bank of Canada and transferred to the Royal Bank's reserve account at the Bank of Canada. Of course, once the cheque clears, the TD Bank will deduct $800 from your chequing account.

DEBATE

SHOULD CANADA, THE UNITED STATES, AND MEXICO SHARE A COMMON CURRENCY?

For:

Money is central to a national government's economy, but it's also a medium of exchange. In recent years, some governments have gone beyond just thinking about sharing a currency with their neighbours—the euro is an example of this. As a common currency, the euro provides a number of benefits in trading goods and services between countries, while getting rid of the risks and transaction costs involved with currency exchanges. Because the North American economy is so entwined, it seems natural for Canada, the United States, and Mexico to move closer to a common currency too. Many of the barriers to trade exist not because of a lack of markets or customers, but because there are major barriers to getting products to market at competitive prices. Transaction costs are significant for companies—not only the straight exchange costs, but also the cost of converting, paying, and hedging funds just to pay for the goods and services. Having a common currency means that many of those transaction costs disappear and the savings can be reinvested back into firms' productivity and innovation. Basically, useless costs turn into productive costs—with longer-term benefits to the whole economy. By unifying some of the currencies, whole economies benefit and grow more than they would as independents. So a common currency provides for a strong economic foundation that all can benefit from. It's argued that Canada and the United States are so strikingly similar that the differences in our currencies are minor. While the two nations' people live in different regions, they still maintain their cultural differences. This is true at present in the United States, where the folks in the Midwest are regarded as different from those in New England or California. And it's true in Canada: People living in Quebec have retained their culture even as they share one currency and one federal government with the other provinces. The strength of culture is what will endure—it's not based on the independent currencies. So, what a country loses in autonomy of monetary policy when it switches to a common currency, it gains in added trade, wealth, and employment. Surely it's clear that Canada, the United States, and Mexico should adopt a common currency. What are other points could you make that would justify and strengthen the arguments presented above? What other arguments could you make to further justify the unification of a common North American currency?

Against:

Economic freedom is not the same as political freedom, and moving toward a common currency usually ends up with one country dominating the others, both politically and economically. This is evident in the current European Union, where Germany's policies end up holding more weight than the policies of the other nations. The way those policies are carried out and received by the other nations is not always harmonious. In the EU, how Germany wants to move is how the rest of the union moves. This would be similar in North America, because the United States is the dominant nation and whatever policies it favoured would likely be imposed on the other two countries. Having different monetary policies can also be an advantage that countries are unwilling to lose. For example, during the lead-up to the Great Recession of 2008–09, Canada and the United States had significantly different monetary policies: While the United States was more liberal in regulating the economy, Canada was more conservative. At the end of the day, it was the conservative nature of our policies that best helped us through the recession—the same can't be said for U.S. citizens. Keeping independent currencies allows for a nation to have its own monetary policy, which is one of the main reasons why Britain didn't rush to join the EU—it valued its own ability to regulate the economy through currency adjustments and monetary policy. Trade benefits from freeing up access, and there is no question that the allure of a common currency is attractive to the business community. But there are significant losses to a country, and not all of those losses have to do with its currency. As countries break down barriers, they become culturally more integrated. Money as well as monetary policy allows countries to keep their character and uniqueness. Surely these are strong reasons to avoid a common currency in North America. What are some of the other reasons countries would argue against a common currency?

The Bank of Canada also serves as a "lender of last resort." When a deposit-taking financial institution finds itself in financial distress because it is short of reserves and cannot meet the withdrawal demands of its customers, the Bank of Canada may act as a lender of last resort and lend reserves to the bank in order to help maintain stability in the financial system.

Finally, the Bank of Canada acts as a banker to the federal government. The federal government has a demand deposit account at the Bank of Canada and at the chartered banks as well. The Bank of Canada manages the government's bank accounts in these different financial institutions.

Monetary Policy

monetary policy
the policy decisions that the Bank of Canada makes in managing the money supply and interest rates, consistent with its inflation-control objective

The Bank of Canada's most important responsibility is **monetary policy,** that is, the policy decisions that the Bank of Canada makes in managing the money supply and interest rates, consistent with its inflation-control objective. Currently, the Bank of Canada inflation-control target range is between 1 and 3 percent, with a policy aim of keeping inflation at a midpoint amount of 2 percent.

SECTION CHECK

■ The Bank of Canada is Canada's central bank. It is owned by the federal government, which has the final responsibility for the Bank of Canada's policies. Despite this goal dependence, the governor of the Bank of Canada has considerable independence in formulating the Bank of Canada's monetary policy.
■ The Bank has four main responsibilities: currency, funds management, the financial system, and monetary policy. Of the four main responsibilities of a central bank, the most important is its role in monetary policy.

section
20.2   Tools of the Bank of Canada

■ What are the tools of the Bank of Canada?
■ What is the Bank of Canada's approach to monetary policy?

WHAT ARE THE TOOLS OF THE BANK OF CANADA?

As noted previously, the most important responsibility of the Bank of Canada is monetary policy. The Bank of Canada decides whether to lower interest rates (expand the money supply) or to raise interest rates (contract the money supply), based on how the economy is performing relative to its inflation-control objective. The Bank of Canada has two primary methods that it can use to enact monetary policy: It can alter its target for the overnight interest rate or it can engage in open market operations.

The Target for the Overnight Interest Rate

overnight interest rate
the interest rate that major financial institutions charge each other for one-day loans

The Bank of Canada's main tool for executing monetary policy is raising and lowering the target for the **overnight interest rate,** the interest rate that major financial institutions charge each other for one-day loans. Under normal economic circumstances, the Bank of Canada operates a system that has the overnight interest rate fluctuating within a one-half of a percentage point (50 basis points) operating band.

The top of the band is the **bank rate,** the interest rate that the Bank of Canada charges major financial institutions on the loans it extends to them. The bottom of the band is the **bankers' deposit rate,** the interest rate that Bank of Canada pays major financial institutions on surplus funds deposited at the Bank of Canada.

For example, say the Bank of Canada sets a target of 3 percent for the overnight interest rate. That means that major financial institutions can borrow funds from each other at an interest rate of 3 percent. To achieve this, the Bank of Canada establishes an operating band around the target overnight interest rate. The operating band is the target overnight interest rate plus or minus one-quarter of a percentage point. The upper limit of the band (one-quarter of a percentage point above the target overnight interest rate) is the bank rate and the lower limit (one-quarter of a percentage point below the target overnight interest rate) is the bankers' deposit rate. In this case, the bank rate would be 3.25 percent and the banker's deposit rate would be 2.75 percent. We can now see that if one financial institution needed to borrow reserves overnight (because its actual reserves were less than its desired reserves), it would first try to borrow those reserves from a second bank that had some excess reserves. What overnight interest rate might those two banks find it beneficial to agree to?

The actual overnight interest rate will fall somewhere between 2.75 percent and 3.25 percent. The first bank will not borrow reserves from the second bank for more than 3.25 percent, since it can borrow reserves from the Bank of Canada at that interest rate. Likewise, the second bank will not lend reserves to the first bank for less than 2.75 percent, since it can earn that rate of interest by holding its excess reserves at the Bank of Canada. Thus, an overnight interest rate of, say, 3 percent would benefit the chartered bank trying to borrow reserves overnight as well as the chartered bank trying to lend excess reserves overnight. In practice, the actual overnight rate does in fact remain very close to the middle of the operating band established by the bank rate and bankers' deposit rate.

If the Bank of Canada raises the target for the overnight interest rate, it makes it more costly for banks to borrow funds to increase their reserves. The higher the interest rate that banks have to pay on the borrowed funds, the lower the potential profit from any new loans made from borrowed reserves, so fewer new loans will be made and less money created. Conversely, if the Bank of Canada lowers the target for the overnight interest rate, it makes it less costly for banks to borrow funds to increase their reserves. This lower interest rate will raise the potential profit from any new loans made from these borrowed reserves, so more new loans will be made and more money created.

Open Market Operations

Open market operations involve the purchase and sale of Government of Canada securities (bonds and Treasury bills) by the Bank of Canada. When the Bank of Canada purchases Government of Canada bonds from the nonbank public, an investment dealer, for example, the Bank of Canada pays for the bonds with a cheque drawn on itself. The investment dealer receiving the payment will likely deposit the cheque in its chequing account at its chartered bank, thereby increasing the money supply in the form of a demand deposit. More important, the chartered bank will collect payment of this cheque from the Bank of Canada. The Bank of Canada will credit the chartered bank's reserve account at the Bank of Canada. Therefore, the chartered bank, in return for crediting the chequing account of the investment dealer with a new deposit, gets a credit in its reserve account at the Bank of Canada.

For example, suppose the Loans R Us National Bank has no excess reserves and that one of its customers, an investment dealer, sells a bond for $10 000 to the Bank

bank rate
the interest rate that the Bank of Canada charges major financial institutions on the loans it extends to them

bankers' deposit rate
the interest rate that Bank of Canada pays major financial institutions on surplus funds deposited at the Bank of Canada

open market operations
purchase and sale of government securities by the Bank of Canada

of Canada. The customer deposits the cheque from the Bank of Canada for $10 000 into its account, and the Bank of Canada credits the Loans R Us National Bank with $10 000 in reserves. Suppose the desired reserve ratio is 10 percent. The Loans R Us National Bank, then, needs new reserves of only $1000 ($10 000 × 0.10) to support the $10 000 demand deposit, meaning that it has acquired $9000 in new excess reserves ($10 000 new actual reserves minus $1000 in new desired reserves). Loans R Us National Bank can, and probably will, lend out its excess reserves of $9000, creating $9000 in new deposits in the process. The recipients of the loans, in turn, will likely spend the money, leading to still more new deposits and excess reserves in other banks, as discussed in Chapter 19. This series of transactions is illustrated in Exhibit 1.

In other words, the Bank of Canada's purchase of the bond directly creates $10 000 in money in the form of demand deposits, and indirectly permits up to $90 000 in additional money to be created through the multiple expansion in bank deposits. (The money multiplier is 1/0.10, or 10; 10 × $9000 = $90 000.) Thus, if the desired reserve

---

section 20.2
Exhibit 1
Open Market Operations: Bank of Canada Buys Securities from Investment Dealer

a. Investment Dealer (nonbank public)

Assets		Liabilities
Securities	−$10 000	
Demand deposits	+$10 000	

b. Loans R Us Bank

Assets		Liabilities	
Reserves	+$10 000	Demand deposits	+$10 000

10 percent desired reserve ratio

c. Bank of Canada

Assets		Liabilities	
Securities	+$10 000	Reserves of Loans R Us Bank	+$10 000

d. Loans R Us Bank

Assets		Liabilities	
Reserves	$1000	Demand deposits	$10 000
Loans	$9000		

When the Bank of Canada buys securities from the nonbank public in the open market, it creates reserves. The nonbank public exchanges its securities for deposits, as seen in Exhibit 1(a). These additional deposits increase bank reserves, as seen in Exhibit 1(b). The additional bank reserves, along with the original purchase of securities, increase both assets and liabilities at the Bank of Canada, as seen in Exhibit 1(c). The increase in bank reserves will likely trigger additional lending and therefore money creation, as seen in Exhibit 1(d).

ratio is 10 percent, a potential total of up to $100 000 in new money is created by the purchase of one $10 000 bond by the Bank of Canada.

The process works in reverse when the Bank of Canada sells a bond. The investment dealer purchasing the bond will pay the Bank of Canada by cheque, lowering demand deposits in the banking system. Reserves of the bank where the investment dealer has a bank account will likewise fall. If the bank had zero excess reserves at the beginning of the process, it will now be short of reserves. The bank will likely reduce its volume of loans, which will lead to a further reduction of demand deposits. A multiple contraction of deposits, and money, will begin.

WHAT IS THE BANK OF CANADA'S APPROACH TO MONETARY POLICY?

The process that the Bank of Canada follows in implementing monetary policy is directly linked to its objective of inflation-rate control. As we identified earlier, the joint Bank of Canada/Government of Canada inflation-control agreement targets a

Business *CONNECTION*

WHEN THE BANK RATE INCREASES, BEWARE!

One of the Bank of Canada's most important responsibilities is monetary policy. Generally speaking, there are two ways in which the central bank can put its monetary policy into effect: (1) by raising or lowering its target for the overnight interest rate via changes to the bank rate, which increases or decreases the money supply, respectively, or (2) by buying or selling bonds, which again has the effect of increasing or decreasing the money supply, respectively.

The Bank of Canada changes the bank rate mainly to adjust the money supply. A change in the money supply may not readily affect a business, but a change in the bank rate will often directly and immediately start having a negative effect on the profitability of most businesses—particularly those that have either outstanding short-term bank loans or funds deposited in short-term bank securities. This occurs because the rate that the Canadian chartered banks charge their business customers is tied to the *prime rate,* an index rate that in turn is tied to the Bank of Canada bank rate.

An increase in a company's bank loan rate is just one of several concerns. When a company experiences an increase in its bank loan rate, the interest expense charges it must pay to the bank will also rise. Without any other changes, increases in loan interest expenses will reduce the company's profits. Faced with the reality of higher interest rates, many consumers and businesses that use credit to finance their purchases will refrain from taking out loans and will accordingly reduce their expenditures. The net effect is that for most businesses, revenue growth will be constrained. Also, when the Bank of Canada causes an increase in loan interest rates, there is usually concern that the economy is overheating and should be restrained. As the Bank of

Canada tries to restrain the economy, the Government of Canada may simultaneously be taking fiscal policy steps to cool the economy. If governments put into effect fiscal policies that lead to higher tax rates on profit, business will also find that after-tax profits are reduced.

So when the Bank of Canada causes an increase in interest rates, companies must be aware of three developments:

1. Those with debt will in the first instance see profits eroded due to higher interest expense.
2. Revenue growth will come under pressure.
3. Fiscal policies such as higher tax rates will reduce after-tax profits.

These three developments can have a major negative impact on a company's overall profitability. As a result, the typical business with some debt can't afford to be unaware of the actions of the Bank of Canada with respect to immediate and long-term plans for the overnight interest rate target.

1. What are some of the tactics that a business can use to hedge its bets when interest rates increase? Are your suggestions practical in the short term or over the long term?
2. What strategies can a business use when interest rates decrease? Are your suggestions practical in the short term or over the long term?
3. As a business owner, if you had to choose between deflation or hyperinflation, which would be your choice and why?

range of inflation between 1 and 3 percent, with a policy aim of keeping inflation at the midpoint amount of 2 percent. The Bank of Canada accomplishes monetary policy by changing the target for the overnight rate, which in turn causes changes to other commercial interest rates, the exchange rate, and ultimately the overall level of economic activity.

Suppose the Bank of Canada expects the rate of inflation to rise and persist above the 2 percent control target (caused by overall demand in the economy exceeding overall supply in the economy—a positive output gap). To address this issue, the Bank of Canada would typically raise the target for the overnight interest rate, which would raise other commercial interest rates as well as the exchange rate of the Canadian dollar. The higher cost of borrowing will have the effect of lowering consumption and investment, while the higher exchange rate of the Canadian dollar will lower Canadian exports. The ultimate impact of these changes will be a reduction in the overall demand for goods and services in the economy. As overall demand begins to align with overall supply, the rate of inflation will begin to fall back toward the desired 2 percent target rate.

Conversely, if the Bank of Canada expects the rate on inflation to fall and persist below the 2 percent control target, it lowers the target for the overnight interest rate. The resulting lower commercial interest rates and lower exchange rate of the Canadian dollar will have the effect of raising overall demand. As overall demand and overall supply begin to align, the rate of inflation will begin to increase back up to the target 2 percent level.

SECTION CHECK

- The two major tools of the Bank of Canada are open market operations and changing the target for the overnight interest rate.
- The Bank of Canada will raise the target for the overnight interest rate in response to an expectation of inflation above the 2 percent control target. A higher target for the overnight interest rate will raise other commercial interest rates and the exchange rate for the Canadian dollar, thus lowering overall economic demand. This reduction in overall demand will have the effect of returning the rate of inflation back to its 2 percent target. If the Bank of Canada expects the rate of inflation to fall below its 2 percent control target, it will lower the target for the overnight interest rate. The resulting lower commercial interest rates and exchange rate for the Canadian dollar will lead to greater overall demand in the economy, thus increasing the inflation rate back toward the 2 percent target.

section 20.3 Money and Inflation

- What is the equation of exchange?
- What is the quantity theory of money and prices?

For many centuries, scholars have known that there is a positive relationship among the money supply, the price level, the growth in the money supply, and the inflation rate. In the 1500s, a huge influx of gold and silver into Europe followed the Spanish conquest in the New World. The influx of precious metals almost tripled the money supply of Europe—too many coins were chasing what goods were available and prices rose steadily.

One of the major reasons that the control of the money supply is so important is that, in the long run, the amount of money in circulation and the overall price level are closely linked. It is virtually impossible for a country to have sustained inflation without a rapid growth in the money supply. The inflation rate tends to be greater in periods of rapid monetary expansion than in periods of slower growth in the money supply. In Exhibit 1, we see that international data support the relationship between higher money growth and a higher inflation rate.

WHAT IS THE EQUATION OF EXCHANGE?

The role that money plays in determining equilibrium GDP, the level of prices, and real output of goods and services has attracted the attention of economists for generations. The equation of exchange is a useful relationship that can help us to understand the role of money in the national economy. The equation of exchange (or quantity equation) can be presented as follows:

$$M \times V = P \times Q$$

where M is the money supply, however defined (usually M2 or M2+); V is the velocity of money; P is the average level of prices of final goods and services; and Q is the physical quantity of final goods and services produced in a given period (usually one year).

The expression $P \times Q$ represents the dollar value of all final goods and services sold in a country in a given year. Does that sound familiar? It should, because that is the definition of nominal gross domestic product (GDP). Thus, for our purposes, we may

---

section 20.3 Money Supply Growth and Inflation Rates in
Exhibit 1 Selected Countries, 1980–2002

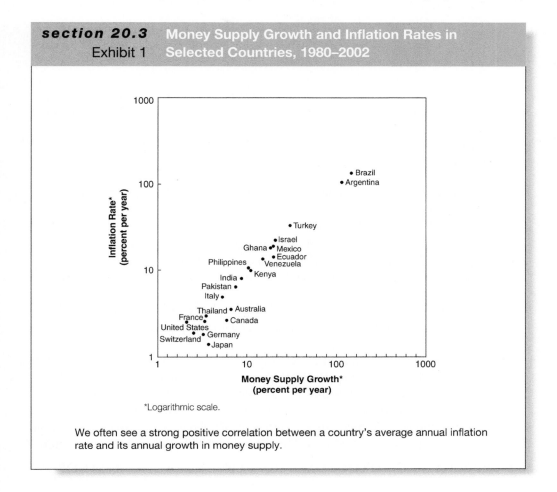

*Logarithmic scale.

We often see a strong positive correlation between a country's average annual inflation rate and its annual growth in money supply.

---

consider the average level of prices (*P*) times the physical quantity of final goods and services in a given time period (*Q*) to be equal to nominal GDP.

velocity of money (V)
the average number of times that a dollar is used in purchasing final goods or services in a one-year period

The **velocity of money, V,** represents the average number of times that a dollar is used in purchasing final goods or services in a one-year period. So if individuals are hoarding their money, velocity will be low; if individuals are writing lots of cheques on their chequing accounts and spending currency as fast as they receive it, *velocity* will tend to be high. Velocity is defined as the nominal or current dollar value of output divided by the money supply, or

$$V = \frac{P \times Q}{M}$$

Suppose we have a simple economy that produces only frozen yogurt. The economy produces 200 litres of frozen yogurt per year. The frozen yogurt sells for $5 a litre and the quantity of money in the economy is $100. Plugging the number into our equation for velocity, we get

$$V = \frac{P \times Q}{M} = \frac{\$5 \times 200}{\$100} = 10$$

That is, the people in the economy spend $1000 per year on frozen yogurt. If there is only $100 of money in the economy, each dollar must change hands on average 10 times per year. Thus, the velocity is 10.

WHAT IS THE QUANTITY THEORY OF MONEY AND PRICES?

quantity theory of money and prices
a theory of the connection between the money supply and the price level when the velocity of money is constant

If we make certain assumptions about the variables in the equation of exchange, we can clearly see the relationship between the money supply and the price level. The **quantity theory of money and prices** is a theory of the connection between the money supply and the price level when the velocity of money is constant. If velocity (*V*) and real GDP (*Q*) both remain constant, then a 10 percent increase in the money supply will lead to a 10 percent increase in the price level—that is, the money supply and the price level change in the same proportion. We can extend this equation to link the growth rates of these four variables. Using the *growth version of the quantity equation,* we can transform $M \times V = P = Q$ into

Growth rate of the money supply + Growth rate of velocity =
Growth rate of the price level (inflation rate) + Growth rate of real output

This makes it easier to see the effects of the money supply on the inflation rate. Suppose money growth is 5 percent per year, the growth of real output is 3 percent per year, and velocity has not changed at all—its growth rate is 0 percent. What is the inflation rate?

The growth rate of *M* (5 percent) + The growth rate of *V* (0 percent) =
The growth rate of *P* (_____ percent) + The growth rate of *Q* (3 percent)

In this situation, the growth rate of prices (*P*), the inflation rate, is equal to 2 percent. We can also extend the analysis to predict the inflation rate when real GDP and velocity also vary. For example, if velocity grew at 1 percent annually rather than zero as in our example, the inflation rate would be 3 percent rather than 2 percent.

If velocity remains constant, the growth rate of velocity (the percentage change from one year to the next) will be zero. Then we can simplify our equation once more:

Inflation rate = Growth rate of the money supply − Growth rate of real GDP

If this is the case, there are three possible scenarios:

1. If the money supply grows at a faster rate than real GDP, there will be inflation.
2. If the money supply grows at a slower rate than real GDP, there will be deflation.
3. If the money supply grows at the same rate as real GDP, the price level will be stable.

Economists once expected that they could treat the velocity of money as a given because the determinants of velocity they focused on would change very slowly. We now know that velocity is not constant but often moves in a fairly predictable pattern. Historically, the velocity of money has been quite stable over a long period of time, particularly when using the M2 definition of money. Thus, the connection between money supply and the price level is still fairly predictable, especially during periods of high inflation.

If an increase in the money supply leads to inflation in the long run, why do countries allow the growth rate of their money supply to increase so rapidly? There are several possible reasons. For instance, due to war or political instability, countries' spending may exceed what they can raise through borrowing from the public or by taxation, so they create more money to pay their bills. The more money these countries create, the larger amount of inflation they will experience.

Hyperinflation

The relationship between the growth rate of the money supply and the inflation rate is particularly strong when there is very rapid inflation, called *hyperinflation*. One of the most famous cases of hyperinflation was in Germany in the 1920s—inflation rose to roughly 300 percent *per month* for over a year. The German government had incurred large amounts of debt as a result of the World War I and could not raise enough money to pay its expenses, so it printed huge amounts of money. The inflation rate became so rapid that store owners would change their prices in the middle of the day, firms had to pay workers several times a week, and many resorted to barter. Brazil and Argentina in the early 1990s and, more recently, Zimbabwe have experienced hyperinflation. The cause of hyperinflation is simply excessive money growth.

AP Photo/Tsvangirayi Mukwazhi

A man carries an armful of cash in Zimbabwe in order to make his daily purchases. During the 2004–09 hyperinflation in Zimbabwe, the *monthly* rate of inflation reached an estimated 79 600 000 000 percent, ultimately leading to an abandonment of the domestic currency.

SECTION CHECK

- The equation of exchange is expressed as $M \times V = P \times Q$, where M is the money supply, V is the velocity of money, P is the average level of prices of final goods and services, and Q is real GDP in a given year.
- The theory that draws a connection between the money supply and the price level when the velocity of money is constant is referred to as the *quantity theory of money and prices*.

For Your Review

Section 20.1

1. Which of the following are functions of the Bank of Canada?
   a. provide loans to developing economies
   b. supervise banks
   c. back the Canadian dollar with gold
   d. issue currency
   e. regulate the money supply
   f. loan reserves to banks
   g. act as the bank for the Canadian government
   h. set interest rates on mortgages

2. How independent is the Bank of Canada?

Section 20.2

3. If the Bank of Canada purchases from the nonbank public $10 million worth of government bonds in the open market when the desired reserve ratio is 5 percent, what is the potential change in the money supply? If the desired reserve ratio is 25 percent? Using T-accounts, show the impact of this transaction on the nonbank public, the banking system, and the Bank of Canada.

4. Answer question 3 again but this time have the Bank of Canada purchase the bonds directly from a bank within the banking system (as opposed to the nonbank public). Using T-accounts, show the impact of this transaction on the banking system and the Bank of Canada.

5. If the Bank of Canada sells a $10 000 bond to an investor, what is the potential change in the money supply if the desired reserve ratio is 10 percent?

6. The following table shows the balance sheet for the Loans R Us National Bank. If the desired reserve ratio decreases from 10 to 5 percent, what happens to the "reserves" and "excess reserves" on the bank's balance sheet? What is the potential change in the money supply?

Loans R Us National Bank			
Assets		**Liabilities**	
Reserves	$100 000	Demand Deposits	$1 000 000
Excess Reserves	0	Equity Capital	50 000
Loans	700 000		
Securities	250 000		

7. Answer question 6 again for the situation in which the bank increases the desired reserve ratio from 10 to 12.5 percent. Where can the bank acquire the additional funds necessary to cover the desired reserves?

8. In which direction would the money supply change if the Bank of Canada
   a. raised the target on the overnight interest rate?
   b. conducted an open market sale of government bonds?
   c. lowered the target on the overnight interest rate?
   d. conducted an open market sale of government bonds and raised the target on the overnight interest rate?
   e. conducted an open market purchase of government bonds and raised the target on the overnight interest rate?

9. How does an open market purchase by the Bank of Canada increase bank reserves? How does it increase the money supply?

10. Why would the Bank of Canada seldom do an open market purchase of government securities at the same time that it raises the target on the overnight interest rate?

Section 20.3

11. Answer the following questions.
    a. What is the equation of exchange?
    b. In the equation of exchange, if V doubled, what would happen to nominal GDP as a result?
    c. In the equation of exchange, if V doubled and Q remained unchanged, what would happen to the price level as a result?
    d. In the equation of exchange, if M doubled and V remained unchanged, what would happen to nominal GDP as a result?
    e. In the equation of exchange, if M doubled and V fell by half, what would happen to nominal GDP as a result?

12. Suppose that velocity and the money supply remain constant. If real GDP grows at an annual rate of 5 percent, what can you predict will happen to the price level using the equation of exchange? If real GDP falls by 2 percent?

13. If the money supply (for example, M2) is $10 billion and velocity is 4, what is the product of the price level and real output (nominal GDP)? If the price level is 2, what does the dollar value of output (nominal GDP) equal?

14. If nominal GDP is $200 billion and the money supply is $50 billion, what must velocity be?

Monetary Policy

Money, Interest Rates, and Aggregate Demand

■ What determines the money market?

■ How does the Bank of Canada affect RGDP in the short run?

■ Does the Bank of Canada target the money supply or the interest rate?

■ Which interest rate does the Bank of Canada target?

■ Does the Bank of Canada influence the real interest rate in the short run?

WHAT DETERMINES THE MONEY MARKET?

money market
market in which money demand and money supply determine the equilibrium nominal interest rate

The Bank of Canada's policies with respect to the money supply have a direct impact on short-run real interest rates and accordingly, on the components of aggregate demand. The **money market** is the market in which money demand and money supply determine the equilibrium *nominal* interest rate. When the Bank of Canada acts to change the money supply, it alters the money market equilibrium.

The Demand for Money

Money has several functions, but why would people hold money instead of other financial assets? That is, what is responsible for the demand for money? Transaction purposes, precautionary reasons, and asset purposes are at least three determinants of the demand for money.

Transaction Purposes First, the primary reason that money is demanded is for transaction purposes—to facilitate exchange. The higher one's income, the more transactions a person will make (because consumption is income-related), the greater GDP will be, and the greater the demand for money for transaction purposes will be, other things being equal.

Precautionary Reasons   Second, people like to have money on hand for precautionary reasons. If unexpected expenses require an unusual outlay of cash, people like to be prepared. The extent to which people demand cash for precautionary reasons depends partly on an individual's income and partly on the opportunity cost of holding money, which is determined by market rates of interest. The higher market interest rates, the higher the opportunity cost of holding money, and people will hold less of their financial wealth as money.

Asset Purposes   Third, money has a trait (liquidity) that makes it a desirable asset. Other things equal, people prefer more-liquid assets to less-liquid assets. That is, they would like to easily convert some of their assets into goods and services. For this reason, most people choose to have some of their portfolio in money form. At higher interest rates on other assets, the amount of money desired for this purpose will be smaller because the opportunity cost of holding money will have risen.

The Demand for Money and the Nominal Interest Rate

The quantity of money demanded varies inversely with the nominal interest rate. When interest rates are higher, the opportunity cost—in terms of the interest income on alternative assets—of holding monetary assets is higher, and people will want to hold less money. At the same time, the demand for money, particularly for transaction purposes, is highly dependent on income levels, because the transaction volume varies directly with income. And lastly, the demand for money depends on the price level. If the price level increases, buyers will need more money to purchase goods and services. Or if the price level falls, buyers will need less money to purchase goods and services.

The demand curve for money is presented in Exhibit 1. At lower interest rates, the quantity of money demanded is greater, a movement from A to B in Exhibit 1. An increase in income will lead to an increase in the demand for money, depicted by a rightward shift in the money demand curve, a movement from A to C in Exhibit 1.

section 21.1
Exhibit 1   Money Demand, Interest Rates, and Income

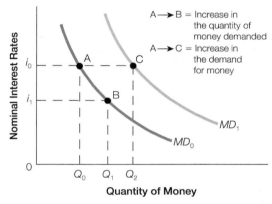

An increase in the level of income will increase the amount of money that people want to hold for transaction purposes at any given interest rate; therefore it shifts the demand for money to the right, from MD_0 to MD_1. The demand for money curve is downward sloping because at the lower nominal interest rate, the opportunity cost of holding money is lower.

The Supply of Money

The supply of money is largely governed by the monetary policies of the central bank. Whether interest rates are 4 percent or 14 percent, banks seeking to maximize profits will increase lending as long as they have reserves above their desired level. Even a 4 percent return on loans provides more profit than maintaining those excess reserves in noninterest-bearing cash. Given this fact, the money supply is effectively almost perfectly inelastic with respect to interest rates over their plausible range. Therefore, in Exhibit 2, we draw the money supply curve as vertical, other things equal, with changes in Bank of Canada policies acting to shift the money supply curve.

section 21.1   Changes in the Money
Exhibit 2   Market Equilibrium

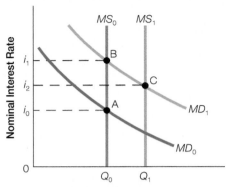

Combining the money demand and money supply curves, money market equilibrium occurs at that nominal interest rate where the quantity of money demanded equals the quantity of money supplied, initially at point A and interest rate i_0. An increase in income will shift the money demand curve to the right, from MD_0 to MD_1, raising the interest rate from i_0 to i_1 and resulting in a new equilibrium at point B. If the economy is presently at point B, an increase in the money supply resulting from expansionary monetary policies (e.g., the Bank of Canada buying bonds or lowering its target for the overnight interest rate) will shift the money supply curve to the right (from MS_0 to MS_1), lowering the nominal interest rate (from i_1 to i_2) and shifting the equilibrium to point C.

Changes in Money Demand and Money Supply and the Nominal Interest Rate

Equilibrium in the money market is found by combining the money demand and money supply curves in Exhibit 2. Money market equilibrium occurs at that *nominal* interest rate, where the quantity of money demanded equals the quantity of money supplied. Initially, the money market is in equilibrium, at point A in Exhibit 2.

For example, rising national income increases the demand for money, shifting the money demand curve to the right from MD_0 to MD_1, and leading to a new higher equilibrium interest rate. If the economy is now at point B, an increase in the money supply (e.g., the Bank of Canada buys bonds) will shift the money supply curve to the right from MS_0 to MS_1, lowering the nominal rate of interest from i_1 to i_2, and shifting the equilibrium to point C.

HOW DOES THE BANK OF CANADA AFFECT RGDP IN THE SHORT RUN?

The Bank of Canada Increases the Money Supply

Suppose the economy is headed for a recession and the Bank of Canada wants to pursue an expansionary monetary policy to increase aggregate demand. It will buy bonds on the open market or it will lower its target for the overnight interest rate. When the Bank of Canada uses either of these tools, the money supply increases. The immediate impact of expansionary monetary policy is to decrease the interest rates, as seen in Exhibit 3(a). The lower interest rate, or the fall in the cost of borrowing money, then leads to an increase in aggregate demand for goods and services at the current price level. The lower interest rate will increase home sales, car sales, business investments, and so on. The increase in the money supply will lead to lower interest rates and an increase in aggregate demand, as seen in Exhibit 3(b).

The Bank of Canada Lowers the Money Supply

Now suppose the Bank of Canada wants to contain an overheated economy—that is, pursue a contractionary monetary policy to reduce aggregate demand. It will sell bonds on the open market or it will raise its target for the overnight interest rate. The use of either of these tools leads to a reduction in the money supply or a leftward shift, as seen in the money market in Exhibit 4(a). The reduction of the money supply leads to an increase in the interest rate in the money market. The higher interest rate, or the rise in the cost of borrowing money, then leads to a reduction in aggregate demand for goods and services, as seen in Exhibit 4(b). That is, the higher interest rate will lead to a decrease in home sales, car sales, business investments, and so on. In sum, lowering of the money supply by the Bank of Canada leads to a higher interest rate and a reduction in aggregate demand, at least in the short run.

section 21.1
Exhibit 3   The Bank of Canada Increases the Money Supply

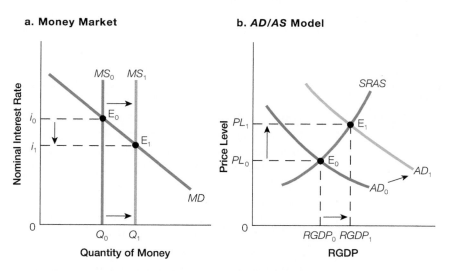

a. Money Market   **b. *AD/AS* Model**

If the Bank of Canada is pursuing an expansionary monetary policy (increasing the money supply), this will lower the interest rates, as seen in Exhibit 3(a). At lower interest rates, households and businesses will invest more and buy more goods and services, shifting the aggregate demand curve to the right, as seen in Exhibit 3(b).

section 21.1
Exhibit 4   The Bank of Canada Decreases the Money Supply

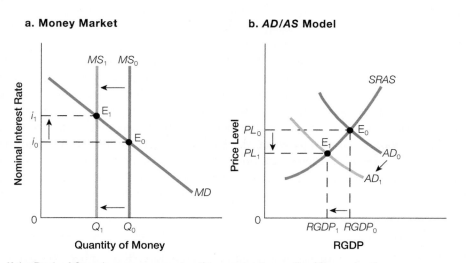

a. Money Market   **b. *AD/AS* Model**

If the Bank of Canada pursues a contractionary monetary policy (decreasing the money supply), this will lead to a reduction in the money supply or a leftward shift, as seen in the money market in Exhibit 4(a). The reduction of the money supply leads to an increase in the interest rate in the money market. The higher interest rate, or the rise in the cost of borrowing money, then leads to a reduction in aggregate demand for goods and services, as seen in Exhibit 4(b).

DOES THE BANK OF CANADA TARGET THE MONEY SUPPLY OR THE INTEREST RATE?

Some economists believe the Bank of Canada should try to control the money supply. Other economists believe the Bank of Canada should try to control the interest rate. Unfortunately, the Bank of Canada cannot do both—it must pick one or the other.

The economy is initially at point A in Exhibit 5, where the interest rate is i_0 and the quantity of money is at Q_0. Now suppose the demand for money was to increase because of an increase in national income, or an increase in the price level, or overall, people want to hold more money. As a result, the demand curve for money would shift to the right from MD_0 to MD_1. If the Bank of Canada decides it does not want the money supply to increase, it can pursue a no-monetary-growth policy; this will lead to an increase in the interest rate to i_1 at point C in Exhibit 5. The Bank of Canada could also try to keep the interest rate stable at i_0, but it can do so only by increasing the growth in the money supply through expansionary monetary policy. Since the Bank of Canada cannot simultaneously pursue a no-monetary-growth policy and an expansionary monetary policy, it must choose a higher interest rate or a greater money supply or some combination. The Bank of Canada cannot completely control both the growth in the money supply and the interest rate. If it attempts to keep the interest rate steady in the face of increased money demand, it must increase the growth in the money supply. And if it tries to keep the growth of the money supply in check in the face of increased money demand, the interest rate will rise.

section 21.1
Exhibit 5

Bank of Canada Targeting: Money Supply versus the Interest Rate

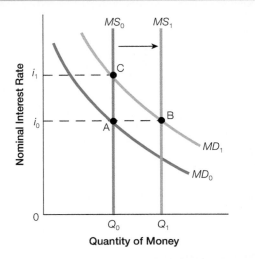

When the demand curve for money shifts out, the Bank of Canada must either settle for a higher interest rate, a greater money supply, or both. The Bank of Canada cannot completely control the growth in the money supply and the interest rate. If it attempts to keep the interest rate steady, it must increase the growth in the money supply. And if it tries to keep the growth of the money supply in check, the interest rate will rise.

The Problem

The problem with targeting the money supply is that the demand for money fluctuates considerably in the short run. Focusing on the growth in the money supply when the demand for money is changing unpredictably will lead to large fluctuations in the interest rate. These erratic changes in the interest rate could seriously disrupt the investment climate.

Keeping interest rates in check would also create problems. For example, when the economy grows, the demand for money also grows, so the Bank of Canada would have to increase the money supply to keep interest rates from rising. And if the economy was in a recession, the Bank of Canada would have to contract the money supply to keep the interest rate from falling. This would lead to the wrong policy prescription—expanding the money supply during a boom would eventually lead to inflation and contracting the money supply during a recession would make the recession even worse.

WHICH INTEREST RATE DOES THE BANK OF CANADA TARGET?

The Bank of Canada targets the overnight interest rate. Remember, the overnight interest rate is the interest rate that chartered banks charge each other for one-day loans. A bank that may be short of reserves might borrow from another bank that has excess reserves. The Bank of Canada has been targeting the overnight interest rate since about 1996. Announcements regarding the overnight interest rate—whether it will be increased, decreased, or made to stay the same—are made by the Bank of Canada on eight prespecified dates during the year.

Monetary policy actions can be conveyed through either the money supply or the interest rate. That is, if the Bank of Canada wants to pursue a contractionary monetary policy, this can be thought of as a reduction in the money supply or a higher interest rate. And, if the Bank of Canada wants to pursue an expansionary monetary policy, this can be thought of as an increase in the money supply or a lower interest rate. So why is the interest rate used? First, as we mentioned earlier, changes in the demand for money can significantly affect money supply targets. Second, many economists believe that the primary effects of monetary policy are felt through the interest rate. Finally, people are more familiar with changes in interest rates than changes in the money supply.

DOES THE BANK OF CANADA INFLUENCE THE REAL INTEREST RATE IN THE SHORT RUN?

In Chapter 16, we saw how the equilibrium real interest rate was found at the intersection of the investment demand curve and the saving supply curve in the saving and investment market. In this chapter, we have seen how the equilibrium nominal interest rate is found at the intersection of the demand for money and the supply of money in the money market. Both are important and the saving and investment market and money markets are interconnected.

Most economists believe that in the short run the Bank of Canada can control the nominal interest rate and the real interest rate. Recall that the *real interest rate is equal to the nominal interest rate minus the expected inflation rate*. So a change in the nominal interest rate tends to change the real interest rate by the same amount because the expected inflation rate is slow to change in the short run. That is, if the expected inflation rate does not change, there is a direct relationship between the nominal and real interest rates; a 1 percent reduction in the nominal interest rate will generally lead to a 1 percent reduction in the real interest rate in the short run. However, in the long run, over several years after the inflation rate has adjusted, the equilibrium real interest rate is found by the intersection of the saving supply curve and investment demand curve.

SECTION CHECK

- ■ The money market is the market where money demand and money supply determine the equilibrium interest rate. Money demand has three possible motives: transaction purposes, precautionary reasons, and asset purposes. The quantity of money demanded varies inversely with interest rates and directly with income. The supply of money is effectively almost perfectly inelastic with respect to interest rates over their plausible range, as controlled by Bank of Canada policies.
- ■ When the Bank of Canada sells bonds to the private sector or raises its target for the overnight interest rate, this leads to a reduction in the money supply, which in turn leads to a higher interest rate and a reduction in aggregate demand, at least in the short run. When the Bank of Canada buys bonds or lowers its target for the overnight interest rate, the money supply increases. The increase in the money supply will lead to lower interest rates and an increase in aggregate demand.
- ■ Since the Bank of Canada cannot completely control both the growth of the money supply and the interest rate, it must choose which target to manage.
- ■ The Bank of Canada signals its intended monetary policy through the overnight interest rate target it sets.
- ■ Since a change in the nominal interest rate tends to change the real interest rate by the same amount in the short run, most economists believe the Bank of Canada can control both the nominal and real interest rates in the short run.

section
21.2
Expansionary and Contractionary Monetary Policy

■ How does expansionary monetary policy work in a recessionary gap?
■ How does contractionary monetary policy work in an inflationary gap?
■ How does monetary policy work in the open economy?

HOW DOES EXPANSIONARY MONETARY POLICY WORK IN A RECESSIONARY GAP?

Suppose the initial equilibrium is E_0, the point at which AD_0 intersects the short-run aggregate supply curve in Exhibit 1(c). At this point, output is equal to $RGDP_0$ and the price level is PL_0. If the Bank of Canada engages in expansionary monetary policy to combat a recessionary gap, the increase in the money supply will lower the interest rate, as seen in Exhibit 1(a). The lower interest rate leads to an increase in investment demanded, as seen in Exhibit 1(b). For example, business executives invest in new plant and equipment whereas individuals increase their investment in housing at the lower interest rate. In short, lower interest rates lead to greater investment spending. Since investment spending is one of the components of aggregate demand $[C + I + G + (X - M)]$, when interest rates fall, total expenditures rise. That is, as investment expenditures increase, the aggregate demand curve shifts from AD_0 to AD_1, as seen in Exhibit 1(c). The increase in aggregate expenditures then triggers the multiplier effect, which shifts aggregate demand even further, from AD_1 to AD_2. The result is greater RGDP and a higher price level, at E_2. In this case, the Bank of Canada has eliminated the recession and RGDP is equal to the potential level of output at $RGDP_{NR}$.

section 21.2
Exhibit 1   **Expansionary Monetary Policy in a Recessionary Gap**

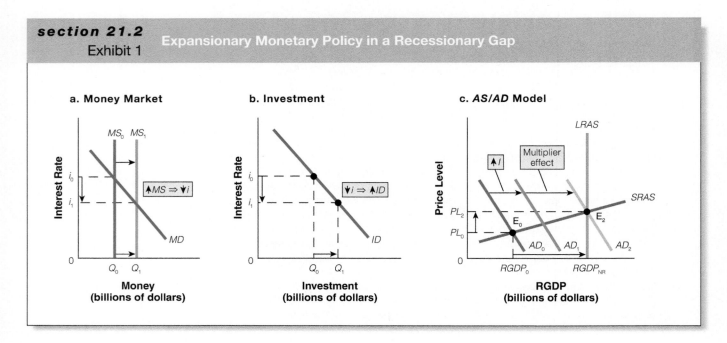

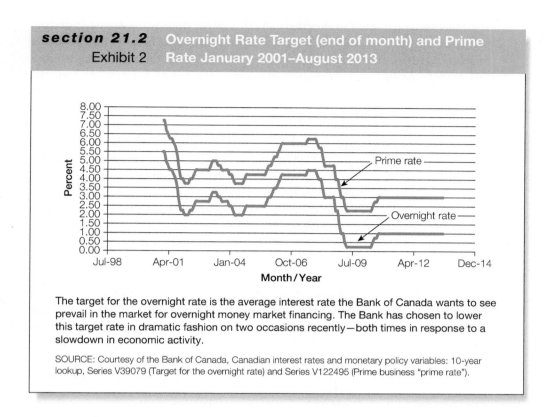

section 21.2   **Overnight Rate Target (end of month) and Prime**
Exhibit 2   **Rate January 2001–August 2013**

The target for the overnight rate is the average interest rate the Bank of Canada wants to see prevail in the market for overnight money market financing. The Bank has chosen to lower this target rate in dramatic fashion on two occasions recently—both times in response to a slowdown in economic activity.

SOURCE: Courtesy of the Bank of Canada, Canadian interest rates and monetary policy variables: 10-year lookup, Series V39079 (Target for the overnight rate) and Series V122495 (Prime business "prime rate").

As seen in Exhibit 2, during 2001, the Bank of Canada aggressively lowered its target for the overnight interest rate to stimulate aggregate demand when faced with a slowing economy. Between January 2001 and January 2002, the Bank of Canada cut its overnight target rate by 3.5 percentage points, from 5.50 percent to 2.00 percent, clearly demonstrating that it was concerned that the economy was dangerously close to falling into a recession.

The 2008–09 Recession

Historically low interest rates in the United States in the early 2000s, along with relaxed lending standards and the introduction of innovative adjustable-rate mortgages, led to a massive U.S. housing bubble between 2000 and 2006. By 2005, however, the Federal Reserve had become concerned with rising housing prices and began to raise short-term interest rates. Higher interest rates and falling housing prices, however, were a recipe for disaster and, consequently, many U.S. homes went into default and foreclosure. The collapse of the U.S housing market was a huge hit for the U.S. economy and by December of 2007, the United States was officially in a recession. The Canadian economy would soon follow by the fourth quarter of 2008.

When housing prices fell and mortgage delinquencies soared in the United States, securities that had been backed by these subprime mortgages lost most of their value. When subprime borrowers defaulted, the result was a large decline in the capital of many banks and financial institutions in the United States, which in turn tightened credit around the world. Financial markets depend on lenders making funds available to borrowers, but when lenders become reluctant to make loans, it becomes difficult to assess credit risk. This is exactly what happened in 2008, which led central banks from around the world (including the Bank of Canada) to pour hundreds of billions of dollars (euros, pounds, etc.) into credit markets to ease the pain of the financial crisis.

Several factors contributed to the financial crisis. First, there was a dramatic decline in the U.S. housing market. Second, many financial institutions became insolvent as a result of investments in the U.S. real estate market. Third, the financial crisis led to a decline in confidence and a credit crunch. Because a number of large global financial institutions were in trouble, many borrowers had a difficult time securing a loan, even for promising investment projects. This led to a reduction in overall demand for goods and services in the global economy.

As was first detailed in Chapter 18, the 2008–09 recession resulted in an unprecedented fiscal policy response by the Canadian government. Did the government also introduce monetary policy to combat this severe economic downturn? The answer to this question is a resounding *yes*! Accompanying the Canadian government's fiscal policy response, the Bank of Canada, in unison with central banks around the world, undertook dramatic steps to lower interest rates by increasing liquidity in the financial system.

As seen in Exhibit 2, the Bank of Canada reduced its target overnight interest rate from a high of 4.5 percent in November of 2007 to just 0.25 percent by August 2009. One significant impact of this dramatic reduction in the target overnight interest rate was the decline in the prime interest rate—the benchmark rate that chartered banks use when setting both residential and commercial interest rates (see Exhibit 2). The Bank of Canada maintained this historically low level for the target overnight interest rate for over a year before beginning to slowly moving it upward. Currently the target overnight interest rate sits at 1 percent, a rate that historically is still considered very low.

HOW DOES CONTRACTIONARY MONETARY POLICY WORK IN AN INFLATIONARY GAP?

The Bank of Canada may engage in contractionary monetary policy if the economy faces an inflationary gap. Suppose the economy is at initial short-run equilibrium, E_0, in Exhibit 3(c). In order to combat inflation, suppose the Bank of Canada

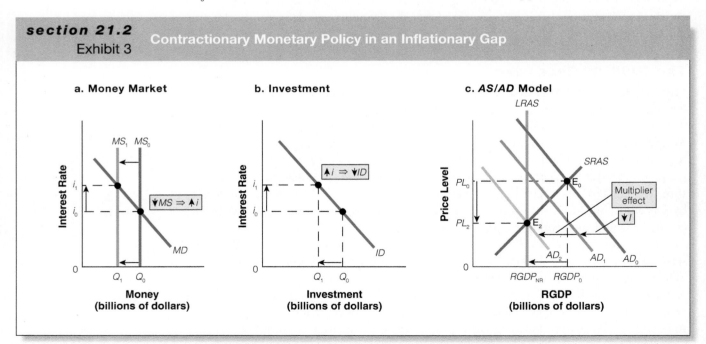

section 21.2
Exhibit 3   Contractionary Monetary Policy in an Inflationary Gap

engages in either an open market sale of bonds or an increase in its target for the overnight interest rate. This would lead to a decrease in the money supply, shifting the MS_0 leftward to MS_1, causing the interest rate to rise from i_0 to i_1, as seen in Exhibit 3(a). The higher interest rate leads to a decrease in the quantity of investment demanded, from Q_0 to Q_1, as seen in Exhibit 3(b). Investment expenditures fall as firms find it more costly to invest in plant and equipment and households find it more costly to finance new homes. Since the decrease in investment spending causes a reduction in aggregate expenditures, the aggregate demand curve shifts leftward from AD_0 to AD_1 in Exhibit 3(c). The decrease in aggregate expenditures triggers the multiplier effect that reduces aggregate demand even further, shifting the aggregate demand curve from AD_1 to AD_2. The result is a lower RGDP and a lower price level, at E_2. The economy is now at $RGDP_{NR}$, where RGDP equals the potential level of output.

HOW DOES MONETARY POLICY WORK IN THE OPEN ECONOMY?

For simplicity we have assumed that the global economy does not impact Canadian monetary policy. This is incorrect. Suppose the Bank of Canada decides to pursue an expansionary policy by buying bonds on the open market. As we have seen, if the Bank of Canada buys bonds on the open market or lowers its target for the overnight interest rate, the immediate effect is that the money supply will increase and the interest rate in Canada will fall. As some Canadian investors now seek to invest funds in foreign markets, they will exchange Canadian dollars for foreign currency, leading to a depreciation of the dollar (a decrease in the value of the dollar). The depreciation of the dollar makes Canadian goods and services more attractive to foreign buyers, and foreign goods and services relatively less attractive to Canadian buyers. That is, there is an increase in net exports—fewer imports and more exports—and an increase in RGDP in the short run.

Similarly, if the Bank of Canada reduces the money supply and causes Canadian interest rates to rise, foreign investors will convert their currencies into Canadian dollars to take advantage of the relatively higher interest rates in Canada. This will lead to an appreciation of the dollar (an increase in the value of the dollar). The appreciation of the dollar will make Canadian goods and services relatively more expensive to foreign buyers, and foreign goods and services relatively cheaper to Canadian buyers. This leads to a decrease in net exports and a reduction in RGDP in the short run.

Thus, you can see that in an open economy, like Canada's, monetary policy operates on aggregate demand through two channels: the interest rate and the exchange rate. An expansionary monetary policy causes interest rates to fall and the exchange rate to depreciate, both of which, in turn, cause aggregate demand to increase. Similarly, a contractionary monetary policy causes interest rates to rise and the exchange rate to appreciate, both of which, in turn, cause aggregate demand to decrease.

DEBATE

SHOULD BANK OF CANADA APPOINTMENTS REMAIN OUT OF VOTERS' HANDS?

For:

Both fiscal policy and monetary policy are best served by keeping the two apart. The Bank of Canada is Canada's central bank and its main responsibility is monetary policy. It carries out this responsibility by using a variety of tools, the most important of which is its ability to target the overnight interest rate. The combination of these tools helps the Bank, in conjunction with the government's fiscal policy, to meet the economic goals of the nation. Fiscal policy uses the political process of the government to adjust spending and taxes. It has been a tradition to separate the political decisions of fiscal policy from those of the more staid decisions of the Bank, ensuring that the conservative nature of monetary policy is not marginalized by self-serving politicians setting unreasonable fiscal policy. But since 2008, there have been political rumblings that the central bank should be more accountable to the citizens. Politicians, though, are self-serving because their goal is to get re-elected—they will prefer to lower taxes and use spending to entice the electorate to vote for them. While the central bank can use monetary policy to counter questionable policies by politicians, especially around election time, the need for independence is even more critical in times when the economy is under pressure. Also, should the membership to the bank become an elected position, the best banker will not necessarily get elected, but certainly the most popular one will. The economy is already represented by elected individuals who do their best to ensure that economic goals are met. If the best banker is appointed through a vetting process made up of elected and appointed officials, the qualifications of the banker are of great importance in getting appointed. There is also the argument that those who feel well qualified may not want to put their name forward in a political process. Further, in making economic decisions, banks employ knowledgeable professionals versed in economics and monetary policy. On the other hand, with politicians there are no guarantees that they understand the complexities of the issues. Surely it's clear that central bankers need to be free from the political process. Without this independence, what types of situations might be harmful to the economy?

Against:

Fiscal policy has to mesh with monetary policy, and without some integration, the two policies can work against one another. So individuals who have similar views should have the opportunity to work with each other, and that opportunity is best done through the political process, where in the end the electorate makes the decision about who serves. At the moment, the Bank of Canada makes decisions that affect all of society, yet answers only to a few politically nonaccountable individuals. Canadians should expect that those who make such public decisions be answerable to the public. There is no guarantee that the best individual is appointed—appointments actually may have less accountability to the public than would be preferred. It can also be argued that these appointments may not include methods for removal if the appointed banker makes grievous errors and actually harms the economy. On the one hand this independence may be preferred, but when there are errors in appointments, it may be virtually impossible to relieve individuals from their positions. The best process for this may be the political process. What are some other reasons to justify some political influence in central bank policy?

SECTION CHECK

■ An expansionary monetary policy can combat a recessionary gap. By increasing the money supply, the Bank of Canada can lower interest rates, thereby causing an increase in real GDP and the price level.

■ A contractionary monetary policy can close an inflationary gap. By reducing the money supply, the Bank of Canada can raise interest rates, thereby causing a decline in real GDP and the price level.

■ In the open economy, interest rate changes can impact exchange rates. Higher interest rates produced by contractionary monetary policy lead to an appreciation of the Canadian dollar. This appreciation can cause net exports to decline and RGDP to be reduced in the short run. Expansionary monetary policy, having the opposite effect, can increase net exports and expand RGDP in the short run.

Problems in Implementing Monetary and Fiscal Policy

■ What problems exist in implementing monetary and fiscal policy?

WHAT PROBLEMS EXIST IN IMPLEMENTING MONETARY AND FISCAL POLICY?

The lag problem inherent in adopting fiscal policy changes is much less acute for monetary policy, largely because the decisions are not slowed by the same budgetary process. The Bank of Canada, because of its independence, can act very quickly in undertaking open market operations. However, the length and variability of the impact lag before its effects on output and employment are felt are still significant, and the time before the full price level effects are felt is even longer and more variable. The major effects of a change in monetary policy on growth in the overall production of goods and services and on inflation are usually spread over six to eight quarters (18 to 24 months).

Chartered Banks and Monetary Policy

One limitation of monetary policy is that it ultimately must be carried out through the banking system. The central bank can change the environment in which banks act, but the banks themselves must take the steps necessary to increase or decrease the money supply. Usually, when the Bank of Canada is trying to constrain monetary expansion, there is no difficulty in getting chartered banks to make appropriate responses. If the Bank of Canada sells bonds and/or raises the bank rate, banks will call in loans that are due for collection, and in the process of collecting loans, they lower the money supply.

When the Bank of Canada wants to induce monetary expansion, however, it can provide banks with excess reserves (by buying government bonds), but it cannot force the banks to make loans, thereby creating new money. Ordinarily, of course, banks want to convert their excess reserves to interest-earning income by making loans. But in a deep recession or depression, banks might be hesitant to make enough loans to put all those reserves to work, fearing that they will not be repaid. Their pessimism might lead them to perceive that the risks of making loans to many normally creditworthy borrowers outweigh any potential interest earnings (particularly at the low real interest rates that are characteristic of depressed times).

Fiscal and Monetary Coordination Problems

Another possible problem that arises out of existing institutional policymaking arrangements is the coordination of fiscal and monetary policy. The Canadian government makes fiscal policy decisions, whereas monetary policy decision making is in the hands of the Bank of Canada. A macroeconomic problem arises if the federal government's fiscal decision makers differ with the Bank of Canada's monetary decision makers on policy objectives or targets. For example, the Bank of Canada may be more concerned about keeping inflation low, whereas fiscal policymakers may be more concerned about keeping unemployment low.

Some people believe that monetary policy should be more directly controlled by the federal government so that all macroeconomic policy will be determined more directly

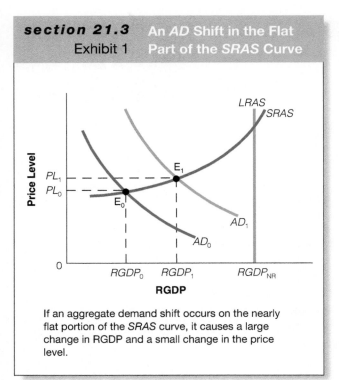

section 21.3   An *AD* Shift in the Flat
Exhibit 1   Part of the *SRAS* Curve

If an aggregate demand shift occurs on the nearly flat portion of the *SRAS* curve, it causes a large change in RGDP and a small change in the price level.

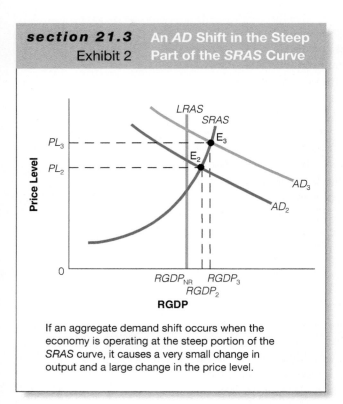

section 21.3   An *AD* Shift in the Steep
Exhibit 2   Part of the *SRAS* Curve

If an aggregate demand shift occurs when the economy is operating at the steep portion of the *SRAS* curve, it causes a very small change in output and a large change in the price level.

by the political process. Others, however, argue that it is dangerous to turn over control of the nation's money supply to politicians, rather than allowing decisions to be made by an independent central bank that is more focused on price stability and more insulated from political pressures.

The Shape of the Aggregate Supply Curve and Policy Implications

Many economists argue that the short-run aggregate supply curve is relatively flat at very low levels of real GDP, when the economy has substantial excess capacity, and very steep when the economy is near maximum capacity, as shown in Exhibits 1 and 2.

Why is the *SRAS* curve in Exhibit 1 flat over the range where there is considerable excess capacity? Firms are operating well below their potential output at $RGDP_{NR}$, so the marginal cost of producing more rises little as output expands. Firms can also hire more labour without increasing the wage rate. With many idle resources, producers are willing to sell additional output at current prices because there are few shortages to push prices upward. In addition, many unemployed workers are willing to work at the going wage rate, which diminishes the power of workers to increase wages. In short, when the economy is operating at levels significantly lower than full-employment output, input prices are sticky (relatively inflexible). Empirical evidence for the period 1983–1987, when the Canadian economy was experiencing significant unemployment, appears to confirm that the short-run aggregate supply curve was very flat when the economy was operating with significant excess capacity.

Near the top of the *SRAS* curve, however, the economy is operating close to maximum capacity (and beyond the output level that could be sustained over time). That is, at this level of output, it will be very difficult or impossible for firms to expand output any further—firms may already be running double shifts and paying overtime. At this point, an increase in aggregate demand will be met almost exclusively with a higher price level in the short run.

In short, if the government is using fiscal and/or monetary policy to stimulate aggregate demand, it must carefully assess where it is operating on the *SRAS* curve. As we have seen in Exhibit 1, if the economy is operating on the flat portion of the *SRAS* curve, far from full capacity, an increase in the money supply, a tax cut, or an increase in government spending will result in an increase in output but little change in the price level—a movement from E_0 to E_1 in Exhibit 1. In this case, the expansionary policy works well: higher RGDP and employment with little change in the price level. However, if the shift in aggregate demand occurs when the economy is operating near maximum capacity, the result will be a substantial increase in the price level with very little change in the output level—a movement from E$_2$ to E$_3$ in Exhibit 2. That is, if the economy is operating on the steep portion of the *SRAS* curve, expansionary policy does not work well.

Furthermore, what if the expansionary policy involves an increase in government spending, with no change in the money supply? If the economy is operating in the steep portion of the *SRAS* curve, the increase in *AD* largely causes the price level to rise. The increase in the price level leads to an increase in the demand for money and higher interest rates, which act to crowd out consumer and business investment. This also undermines the effectiveness of the government policy.

It is also easy to see in Exhibits 1 and 2 that contractionary monetary or fiscal policy (a tax increase, a decrease in government spending, and/or a decrease in the money supply) to combat inflation is more effective in the steep region of the *SRAS* curve than in the flat region. In the steep region, contractionary monetary and/or fiscal policy results in a large fall in the price level and a small change in real GDP; in the flat region of the *SRAS* curve, the contractionary policy would result in a large decrease in output and a small change in the price level.

Some economists believe that fine-tuning the economy is like driving a car with an unpredictable steering lag on a winding road.

Overall Problems with Monetary and Fiscal Policy

Much of macroeconomic policy in this country is driven by the idea that the federal government can counteract economic fluctuations: stimulating the economy (with increased government purchases, tax cuts, transfer payment increases, and easy money) when it is weak, and restraining it when it is overheating. But policymakers must adopt the right policies in the right amounts at the right time for such "stabilization" to do more good than harm. And for this, government policymakers need far more accurate and timely information than experts can give them.

First, economists must know not only which way the economy is heading, but also how rapidly. And the unvarnished truth is that in our incredibly complicated world, no one knows exactly what the economy will do, no matter how sophisticated the econometric models used. It has often been said, and not completely in jest, that the purpose of economic forecasting is to make astrology look respectable.

But let's assume that economists can outperform astrologers at forecasting. Indeed, let's be completely unrealistic and assume that economists can provide completely accurate economic forecasts of what will happen if macroeconomic policies are unchanged. Even then, they could not be certain of how best to promote stable economic growth.

If economists knew, for example, that the economy was going to dip into another recession in six months, they would then need to know exactly how much each possible policy would spur activity in order to keep the economy stable. But such precision is unattainable, given the complex forecasting problems faced. Furthermore, despite assurances to the contrary, economists aren't always sure what effect a policy will have on the economy. Will an increase in government purchases quicken economic growth? It is widely assumed so. But how much? And increasing government purchases increases the budget deficit, which could send a frightening signal to the bond markets. The result can be to drive up interest rates and choke off economic activity. So even when policymakers know which direction to nudge the economy, they can't be sure which policy levers to pull, or how hard to pull them, to fine-tune the economy to stable economic growth.

But let's further assume that policymakers know when the economy will need a boost, and also which policy will provide the right boost. A third crucial consideration is how long it will take for a policy to have an effect on the economy. The trouble is that, even when increased government purchases or expansionary monetary policy does give the economy a boost, no one knows precisely how long it will take to do so. The boost may come very quickly, or many months (or even years) in the future, when it may add inflationary pressures to an economy that is already overheating, rather than helping the economy recover from a recession.

In this way, macroeconomic policymaking is like driving down a twisting road in a car with an unpredictable lag and degree of response in the steering mechanism. If you turn the wheel to the right, the car will eventually veer to the right, but you don't know exactly when or how much. In short, there are severe practical difficulties in trying to fine-tune the economy. Even the best forecasting models and methods are far from perfect. Economists are not exactly sure where the economy is or where or how fast it is going, making it very difficult to prescribe an effective policy. Even if we do know where the economy is headed, we cannot be sure how large a policy's effect will be or when it will take effect.

Unexpected Global and Technological Events   The Bank of Canada must take into account the influences of many different factors that can either offset or reinforce monetary policy. This isn't easy because sometimes these developments occur unexpectedly, and because the size and timing of their effects are difficult to estimate.

For example, during the 1997–1998 currency crisis in East Asia, economic activity in several countries in that region either slowed or declined. This led to a reduction in the aggregate demand for Canadian goods and services. In addition, the foreign exchange value of most of their currencies depreciated, and this made Asian-produced goods less expensive for us to buy and Canadian-produced goods more expensive in Asian countries. Both of these factors would reduce aggregate demand in Canada and lower output and employment. So the Bank of Canada must consider these global events in formulating its monetary policy.

During the late 1990s, the Canadian economy experienced a productivity increase through high-tech and other developments. This "new" economy increased productivity growth, allowing for greater economic growth without creating inflationary pressures. The Bank of Canada was then faced with estimating how fast productivity was increasing and whether those increases were temporary or permanent. Not an easy task.

By 2007, the Canadian economy was facing a new set of global challenges—the Canadian dollar was trading around par with its American counterpart (a reality that had last occurred during the mid-1970s), the U.S. economy was experiencing an economic slowdown, and oil prices had risen to near-record levels. An added complication for the Bank of Canada was the fact that, unlike the 1970s, the high oil prices had not produced strong inflationary expectations for consumers. To successfully navigate this set of challenges, the Bank of Canada would have to carefully consider a wide range of policy options.

By the end of 2007 and into 2008, the Canadian economy had begun to experience the effects of the global economic crisis. The U.S. economy, by this time, was already in the grip of a major recession and global financial markets were experiencing a severe financial crisis. The coordinated response of expansionary fiscal policy and expansionary monetary policy from the Government of Canada and the Bank of Canada is widely believed to have greatly minimized the recessionary effects of the global economic crisis for Canada.

SECTION CHECK

■ Monetary policy faces somewhat different implementation problems than fiscal policy. Both face difficult forecasting and lag problems, but the Bank of Canada can take action much more quickly. However, the effectiveness of monetary policy depends largely on the reaction of the private banking system to its policy changes. In Canada, monetary and fiscal policy are carried out by different decision makers, thus requiring cooperation and coordination for effective policy implementation.

The Phillips Curve

section 21.4

■ What is the Phillips curve?
■ How does the Phillips curve relate to the aggregate supply and demand model?

We usually think of inflation as an evil—higher prices mean lower real incomes for people on fixed incomes, whereas those with the power to raise the prices charged for goods or services they provide may actually benefit. Nevertheless, some economists believe that in the short run, inflation could actually help eliminate unemployment. For example, if output prices rise but money wages do not go up as quickly or as much, real wages fall. At the lower real wage, unemployment is less because the lower wage makes it profitable to hire more, now cheaper, employees than before. The result is real wages that are closer to the full-employment equilibrium wage that clears the labour market. Hence, with increased inflation, one might expect lower unemployment in the short run. In the long run, there is no trade-off between unemployment and inflation. In the long run, output is determined by the *LRAS* curve, and unemployment is at its natural rate.

WHAT IS THE PHILLIPS CURVE?

An inverse short-run relationship between the rate of unemployment and the changing level of prices has been observed in many periods and places in history. Credit for identifying this relationship generally goes to British economist A. H. Phillips, who in the late 1950s published a paper setting forth what has since been called the *Phillips curve*. Phillips and many others since have suggested that at higher rates of inflation, the rate of unemployment is lower, whereas during periods of relatively stable or falling prices, unemployment is substantial. In summary, the cost of lower unemployment appears to be greater inflation, and the cost of greater price stability appears to be higher unemployment, at least in the short run.

Exhibit 1 shows the actual inflation–unemployment relationship for Canada for the 1960s. The points in this graph represent the combination of the inflation rate and the rate of unemployment for the period 1960–1969. The curved line—the Phillips curve—is the smooth line that best fits the data points.

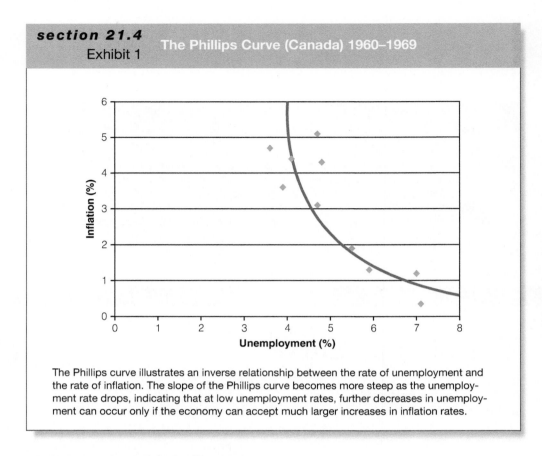

section 21.4
Exhibit 1   The Phillips Curve (Canada) 1960–1969

The Phillips curve illustrates an inverse relationship between the rate of unemployment and the rate of inflation. The slope of the Phillips curve becomes more steep as the unemployment rate drops, indicating that at low unemployment rates, further decreases in unemployment can occur only if the economy can accept much larger increases in inflation rates.

The Slope of the Phillips Curve

In examining Exhibit 1, it is evident that the slope of the Phillips curve is not the same throughout its length. The curve is steeper at higher rates of inflation and lower levels of unemployment. This relationship suggests that once the economy has relatively low unemployment rates, further reductions in the unemployment rate can occur only if the economy can accept larger increases in the inflation rate. Once the unemployment rate is low, it takes larger and larger doses of inflation to eliminate a given quantity of unemployment. Presumably, at lower unemployment rates, an increased part of the economy is already operating at or near full capacity. Further fiscal or monetary stimulus primarily triggers inflationary pressures in sectors already at capacity, while eliminating decreasing amounts of unemployment in those sectors where some excess capacity and unemployment still exist.

HOW DOES THE PHILLIPS CURVE RELATE TO THE AGGREGATE SUPPLY AND DEMAND MODEL?

In Exhibit 2, we see the relationship between aggregate supply and demand analysis and the Phillips curve. Suppose the economy moved from a 2 percent annual inflation rate to a 4 percent inflation rate, and the unemployment rate simultaneously fell from 5 percent to 4 percent. In the Phillips curve, we see this change as a move up the curve from point A to point B in Exhibit 2(a). We can see a similar relationship in the *AD/AS* model in Exhibit 2(b). Imagine that an increase in aggregate demand occurs. Consequently, the price level increases from PL_0 to PL_1 (the inflation rate rises) and output increases from $RGDP_0$ to $RGDP_1$ (the unemployment rate falls). To increase output, firms employ more workers, so employment increases and unemployment falls—the movement from point A to point B in Exhibit 2(b).

section 21.4
Exhibit 2 · The Phillips Curve and the *AD/AS* Curves

a. Phillips Curve

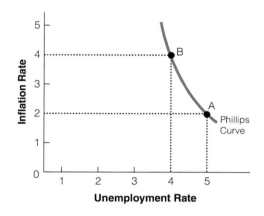

b. Aggregate Supply and Demand

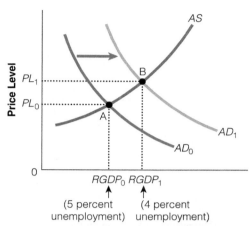

As shown in Exhibit 2(b), if the aggregate supply curve is positively sloped, an increase in aggregate demand will cause higher prices and higher output (lower unemployment); a decrease in aggregate demand will cause lower prices and lower output (higher unemployment). This same trade-off is illustrated in the Phillips curve in Exhibit 2(a), in the shift from point A to point B.

Business*CONNECTION*

GETTING A JUMP ON INFLATION IN MODERN TIMES

Monetary policies are policies that the government uses to control the nation's money supply. In Canada, this control is delegated to the Bank of Canada. The central bank's policies in regard to the money supply have a direct impact on short-run real interest rates and, accordingly, on at least two of the components of aggregate demand (the total demand for all of the final goods and services in the economy): consumer expenditure and business investment. A business with an eye on revenues will always be concerned about the demand for its goods or services. Many businesses producing big-ticket items—such as housing, cars, and appliances—find revenues extremely sensitive to interest rates, because purchasers often need to finance purchases with borrowed funds.

Sales are also extremely sensitive to the overall demand resulting from the government's fiscal policies. How can business read the road ahead regarding fiscal and monetary policies? The fact is that this area of macroeconomics is fraught with complexity for business. Unfortunately, independent businesses can't change macroeconomic policy—they can only consider the economic climate and hope to

make wise decisions. Policymakers have great difficulty predicting the impact that various policy approaches will have on the economy and in forecasting when the expected outcomes will come about. Businesses find it almost impossible to gauge the collective impact that government and central bank policy decisions will have on costs of operations, revenue levels, and profitability. There are some pockets of reliable economic theory, such as the *Phillips curve* (the inverse relationship between the rate of unemployment and the rate of inflation), but such theories may have to be updated.

The work of economist A. H. Phillips suggested that there is a trade-off between inflation and unemployment in the short term. Basically, the cost of lower unemployment appears to be greater inflation, and the cost of greater price stability appears to be higher unemployment. Firms recognize that, when faced with a recessionary gap, governments use expansionary monetary policy to reduce unemployment—resulting in a gradual increase in the inflation rate. As attempts are made to further reduce unemployment, the rate of inflation is likely to increase more sharply.

(continued)

But what happens when expansionary policies don't produce the stimulation in the economy as predicted? This might be the case currently, in the wake of unprecedented levels of monetary injections that were made to stimulate economies that had been under strain since the 2008 start of the Great Recession. The anemic growth rates, coupled with higher rates of unemployment (where some economists predict the natural rate of unemployment has increased) have kept inflation rates at, or near, record lows. Consumers might welcome such lows levels on the consumption side (because of lower or more stable prices), but they certainly won't appreciate the impact on real wages (because the low inflation rates will dampen wage growth). Couple that with increases in productivity through automation and mechanization, and there is notable downward pressure on employment rates. If this situation carries on, although firms may enjoy stable input prices, they will find it difficult to raise their own selling prices and will surely find fewer consumers willing or able to purchase. What's more, without modest increases in inflation, firms won't be able to afford the significant costs of R&D that could propel their product lines.

While many have doubted the likelihood of longer-term stagnation, we only have to look at Japan's past generation of anemic growth and see the damage inflicted on that economy. A further investigation is warranted with the current situation in the European Union. Inflation had plummeted to 0.5 percent in May 2014.* Reza Moghadam, director of the European Department at the International Monetary Fund, coined the term "lowflation" to describe the EU's dilemma—a period of stagnation caused by low inflation and high debt that burdens economic growth. Given the choice, firms would much prefer the perils of high inflation over lowflation or deflation, which are harder to control.

1. It is suggested that fiscal policy has a more immediate and dramatic effect on the economy than does monetary policy. Do you think business owners prefer one over the other? Why?

2. One of the most contentious issues facing manufacturing businesses in Canada is the preference of the Bank of Canada to raise the value of the Canadian dollar through its intervention in the market. What is your opinion of this strategy?

3. Do you think that innovation reaches a point where most consumers would have marginal benefit? If this is the case, what do you think the appropriate monetary policy response would be?

*Eurostat Press Office. *Eurostat News Release*, June 3, 2014, "Euro area annual inflation down to 0.5%—May 2014."

SECTION CHECK

- The inverse relationship between the rate of unemployment and the rate of inflation is called the *Phillips curve*.
- The Phillips curve relationship can also be seen indirectly from the *AD/AS* model.

For Your Review

Section 21.1

1. Why would both the transaction motive and the precautionary motive for holding money tend to vary directly with the price level? Why would the quantity of money people want to hold for both motives tend to vary inversely with interest rates?

2. How does a higher price level affect the money market? How does it affect aggregate demand?

3. Why can't the Bank of Canada target both the money supply and the interest rate at the same time?

4. What is the motive for holding money in each of the following cases (precautionary, transaction, or asset)?

   a. Concerned about the fluctuations of the stock market, you sell stock and keep cash in your brokerage account.

b. You keep ten $20 bills in your earthquake-preparedness kit.

c. You go to Vancouver with a large sum of money in order to complete your holiday shopping.

d. You keep $20 in your glove compartment just in case you run out of gas.

5. Using the following diagrams, answer the following questions.

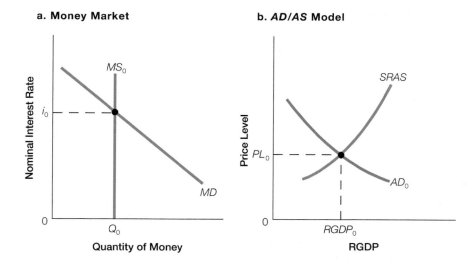

a. Money Market

b. *AD/AS* Model

a. Show the effects in each of the indicated markets of an open market purchase of government bonds by the Bank of Canada.

b. Show the effects in each of the indicated markets of an open market sale of government bonds by the Bank of Canada.

Section 21.2

6. During the Great Depression in Canada, the price level fell, real GDP fell, and unemployment reached almost 20 percent. Investment fell and the money supply fell. Show the effect of these changes from a vibrant 1929 economy to a battered 1933 economy using the *AD/AS* model? What would have been the appropriate monetary policy response in 1933?

7. Using the following diagram, answer the following questions.

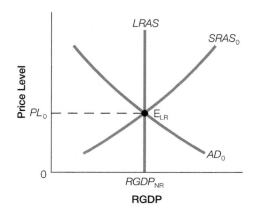

a. On the diagram, illustrate the short-run effects of an increase in aggregate demand caused by expanding the money supply.

b. On the diagram, illustrate the long-run effects of an increase in aggregate demand caused by expanding the money supply.

8. Predict the impact of a decrease in the money supply on the following variables in the short run and in the long run.

a. the inflation rate

b. the unemployment rate

c. real output

d. real wages

9. How will an expansionary monetary policy affect RGDP and the price level at less than full employment?

10. How will a contractionary monetary policy affect RGDP and the price level at a point beyond full employment?

Section 21.3

11. Why does the effect of a given increase in aggregate demand have a larger effect on real output in the short run, the more excess capacity exists in the economy?

12. How does the slope of the short-run aggregate supply curve depend on the degree of excess capacity in the economy?

13. How is the coordination or, more correctly, the lack of coordination, between fiscal and monetary policy a potential problem of effective policy implementation?

14. Why is the lag time for adopting policy changes shorter for monetary policy than for fiscal policy?

15. Why would a banking system that wanted to keep some excess reserves rather than lending out all of them hinder the Bank of Canada's ability to increase the money supply?

Section 21.4

16. Suppose the following data represent points along a short-run Phillips curve. Are the data consistent with what you would expect? Why or why not?

	Inflation Rate (%)	Unemployment Rate (%)
A	0	5.0
B	1	4.5
C	2	3.75
D	3	2.75
E	4	1.5

17. Why does a movement up and to the left along a Phillips curve correspond to a movement up and to the right along a short-run aggregate supply curve?

18. Why does a movement down and to the right along a Phillips curve correspond to a movement down and to the left along a short-run aggregate supply curve?

19. What is the argument for why the Phillips curve is relatively steeper at lower rates of unemployment and higher rates of inflation?

22

International Trade

Canada's Merchandise Trade

■ Who are Canada's trading partners?
■ What does Canada import and export?

WHO ARE CANADA'S TRADING PARTNERS?

In its early history, Canadian international trade was largely directed toward Europe and to Great Britain, in particular. Now Canada trades with a vast number of countries. Exhibit 1 shows the country's most important trading partners. The United States is Canada's most important trading partner, accounting for an enormous 73 percent of our exports of goods and 63 percent of our imports of goods. Trade with countries of the European Union (EU) and Japan is also particularly important.

The extent to which the overall health of the Canadian economy is dependent on both exports and imports cannot be understated. However, as Exhibit 2 illustrates, Canada is not alone in its significant involvement in global trade. Several economies (most notably the United States, the European Union, China, Germany, and the United Kingdom) trade on a magnitude that is several times greater than that of the Canadian economy.

WHAT DOES CANADA IMPORT AND EXPORT?

Throughout its history, Canada has been a large exporter of natural resource-based products to the rest of the world. Today, as Exhibit 3 shows, Canada's exports of natural resource-based products (including farm, fishing, and intermediate food products; energy products; mineral products; basic and industrial chemical, plastic, and rubber products; and forestry products) total over $260 billion, or nearly 60 percent of our

section 22.1
Exhibit 1 Major Canadian Trading Partners

Top Trading Partners—Exports of Goods in 2012

Rank	Country	% of Total
1	United States	73.2%
2	European Union	8.9
3	Japan	2.3
4	Other countries	15.6

Top Trading Partners—Imports of Goods in 2012

Rank	Country	% of Total
1	United States	62.5%
2	European Union	9.4
3	Japan	2.3
4	Other countries	25.8

SOURCE: Statistics Canada, CANSIM Table 228-0058 and author calculations.

section 22.1
Exhibit 2 Amounts of Merchandise Exports and Imports: Selected Developed Countries, 2012/2013 (est.)

Exports

Rank	Country	Amount (billions of US$)	Year
1	China	$2210	2013 est.
2	European Union	2173	2012 est.
3	United States	1575	2013 est.
4	Germany	1493	2013 est.
5	United Kingdom	813	2013 est.
6	Japan	697	2013 est.
7	France	579	2013 est.
8	Netherlands	577	2013 est.
9	South Korea	557	2013 est.
10	Russia	515	2013 est.
11	Italy	474	2013 est.
12	**Canada**	**459**	**2013 est.**

Imports

Rank	Country	Amount (billions of US$)	Year
1	European Union	$2312	2012 est.
2	United States	2273	2013 est.
3	China	1950	2013 est.
4	Germany	1233	2013 est.
5	United Kingdom	783	2013 est.
6	Japan	767	2013 est.
7	France	660	2013 est.
8	Hong Kong	521	2013 est.
9	South Korea	517	2013 est.
10	Netherlands	511	2013 est.
11	**Canada**	**471**	**2013 est.**

SOURCE: Central Intelligence Agency, *The World Factbook 2013*.

exports of goods. However, Canada's exports of industrial machinery, electrical equipment, motor vehicles, aircraft and other transportation equipment, and consumer goods total $184 billion, or about 40 percent of our exports of goods.

On the import side, Canada's imports are much more concentrated on finished goods. Imports of electronic and electrical equipment, motor vehicles, and consumer goods total $56 billion, $83 billion, and $93 billion, respectively, and account for nearly half of all imports of goods.

	Exports (billions of $)	% of Total	Imports (billions of $)	% of Total	Trade Balance (billions of $)
Farm, fishing, and intermediate food products	$ 27.2	5.9%	$12.3	2.6%	$14.9
Energy product	105.1	22.7	45.8	9.6	59.3
Metal ores and non-metallic mineral	18.5	4.0	10.0	2.1	8.5
Metal and non-metallic mineral product	54.4	11.8	43.5	9.2	10.9
Basic and industrial chemical, plastic, and rubber products	33.0	7.1	38.1	8.0	−5.1
Forestry products and building and packaging materials	30.6	6.6	20.5	4.3	10.1
Industrial machinery, equipment, and parts	26.8	5.8	45.2	9.5	−18.4
Electronic and electrical equipment and parts	22.9	5.0	55.5	11.7	−32.6
Motor vehicles and parts	68.5	14.8	82.8	17.5	−14.3
Aircraft and other transportation equipment and parts	17.3	3.7	12.7	2.7	4.6
Consumer goods	48.5	10.5	93.0	19.6	−44.5
Other transactions and adjustments	9.6	2.1	5.3	1.1	4.3

SOURCE: Statistics Canada, CANSIM Table 228-0059, Merchandise imports and exports, customs and balance of payments basis for all countries, by seasonal adjustment and North American Product Classification System (NAPCS) monthly.

When we compare the trade balance (exports of goods minus imports of goods) for the major categories of goods, we can see that the largest trade surpluses exist for energy products ($59.3 billion) and farm, fishing, and intermediate food products ($14.9 billion). By far, the largest trade deficit is in the consumer goods category ($44.5 billion).

Business *CONNECTION*

FACING THE LURE OF INTERNATIONAL MARKETS

Domestic businesses often find that sales for their products have peaked, the domestic market is saturated with their offerings, or the domestic market has simply matured. Faced with this type of challenge, how does a firm increase sales? The obvious answer is to go international. If this move is successful, revenues will increase and, hopefully, so will profits. But the decision to go international needs to be properly structured to reduce risk.

When a company is thinking of entering an international market, one important factor it needs to consider is the business climate of the host country. Many experienced businesses have encountered cultural, legal, and economic

roadblocks as they tried to penetrate foreign markets. Many key questions also need to be answered before making this big leap. For instance:

1. First and foremost, is there indeed a demand for the firm's product in the host country's target market? Until a business is satisfied that there is foreign demand or that it can cultivate such demand, it should avoid venturing into a foreign market.

2. Can the firm customize its products to suit the demands of the foreign customers while achieving attractive profit margins?

(continued)

3. Is the business climate of the foreign market favourable for the firm? (Is gross domestic product growing? What is the withholding tax rate? Can the firm obtain the necessary skills and knowledge to actually conduct business in the host country?)

4. Can the firm protect its intellectual property rights in the foreign lands? Intellectual property rights are the foundational assets for most firms and, despite the lure of access to larger markets, the revenues (and hoped-for profits) may be put in danger by the loss of the company's competitive advantage. The protection of intellectual property is fast becoming one of the key hurdles governments have to overcome to protect their domestic firms.

If the answers to all of the above questions are yes, there is every indication that the attempt to enter foreign markets will be operationally feasible.

The next step is to evaluate the likelihood of earning profits. In this area, the firm needs to assess the political and the financial risks. The traditional factors in evaluating broad political risks include the attitude of the local consumers toward the purchasing of foreign-produced or foreign-branded goods, the host government's position toward multinational corporations, wars or threat of wars, and bureaucratic problems and corruption. In considering the broad financial risk involved in conducting business, the host country's growth in gross domestic product, prevailing interest rates, rates of unemployment, and rate of inflation (or deflation) need to be taken into account.

The firm then needs to evaluate the operational feasibility and potential profitability of its product. Only after making such assessments is a business reasonably informed and able to make a decision about whether to stay domestic or to go international. Even if the opportunity looks promising from a product perspective, firms have to assess the risks and rewards of one other market before heading into international trade—the currency market—with which most domestically based small and medium-sized enterprises (SMEs) have little experience. (See Chapter 23.)

1. Given the choice between competing in international markets, or in domestic markets knowing the growth opportunities would not be as great, what do you think the majority of North American businesses would choose?

2. To protect domestic markets, the government is contemplating either adding import quotas or subsidizing domestic producers. What would your firm prefer and why? (Think in broad terms rather than a product-specific, narrow focus.)

3. One barrier to Canada obtaining a free trade agreement with the European Union is the government's quotas that protect some industries (dairy, poultry, etc.). Other than the businesses that benefit from the quotas, how do you think the other firms might feel about the quotas? What would be these firms' rationales?

SECTION CHECK

- Our most important trading partner, the United States, accounts for 73 percent of our exports and 64 percent of our imports. Trade with Japan and the countries of the European Union is also particularly important to Canada.
- Exports of natural resource-based products make up over one-half of our export of goods. Our imports are concentrated in finished goods, like electronic and electrical equipment, motor vehicles, and consumer goods.

section 22.2 International Trade Agreements

- What has been the impact of international trade on Canada?
- What international trade agreements is Canada involved in?

WHAT HAS BEEN THE IMPACT OF INTERNATIONAL TRADE ON CANADA?

In a typical year, about 15 percent of the world's output is traded in international markets. Of course, the importance of the international sector varies enormously from country to country. Some nations are almost closed economies (no interaction with other economies), with foreign trade equalling only a very small portion

section 22.2
Exhibit 1

Canada's Exports and Imports as a Percentage of GDP

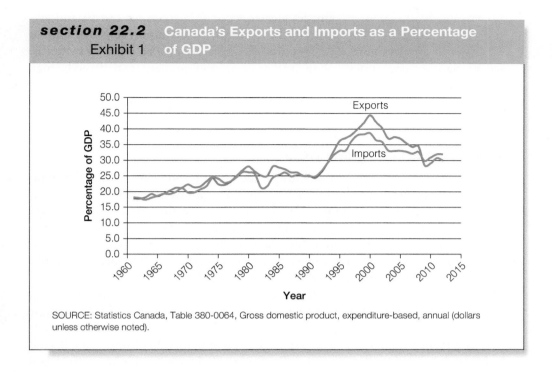

SOURCE: Statistics Canada, Table 380-0064, Gross domestic product, expenditure-based, annual (dollars unless otherwise noted).

(perhaps 5 percent) of total output. The impact of international trade on the Canadian economy is illustrated in Exhibit 1, which shows the current dollar value of Canadian exports and imports of goods and services as a percentage of GDP. As Exhibit 1 shows, the value of both exports and imports has grown from around 20 percent in the 1960s to 30 percent of GDP for exports and 32 percent of GDP for imports in 2012. In the United States, by contrast, exports were only 14 percent of GDP, whereas imports were 17 percent of GDP, in 2012.

WHAT INTERNATIONAL TRADE AGREEMENTS IS CANADA INVOLVED IN?

International trade agreements have been a positive force in expanding global trade, thereby contributing to economic growth and prosperity in countries covered by such agreements. Government trade policies have contributed to the remarkable rise in international trade for Canada. Listed below are the major trade agreements to which Canada is a participant.

The General Agreement on Tariffs and Trade

Canada and 22 other nations in 1947 signed the General Agreement on Tariffs and Trade (GATT). The objective of GATT was to reduce barriers to international trade, such as tariffs (taxes on imported goods) and quotas (government-imposed restrictions on the quantity of imports allowed). GATT was based on a few key principles. First, each member nation was to apply any tariffs equally to all countries—that is, in a non-discriminatory manner. Second, reductions in tariffs were to be the result of multilateral negotiations. And third, quotas were to be eliminated and replaced by tariffs. (We will examine the economic impact of tariffs and quotas later in this chapter.)

Eight rounds of multilateral negotiations took place under GATT, with the last round of negotiations, called the Uruguay Round, taking effect in 1995. That agreement eliminated or reduced trade barriers on a wide range of goods and services.

It also gave the world's poorer countries greater access to markets for textiles and garments in developed (richer) nations. On the agricultural side, export subsidies were to be reduced and import quotas on agricultural products were to be replaced by tariffs. Canadian egg and dairy farmers had their trade protection from quotas replaced by high tariffs. Although this has protected Canadian farmers in the short run, as these tariffs are reduced over time, we would expect a higher level of Canadian imports of these products.

The World Trade Organization

In 1995, GATT was replaced by the World Trade Organization (WTO), another multilateral trade organization. The WTO has over 140 nations as members, who negotiate on areas such as liberalizing trade in services, protecting intellectual property rights, and giving fair treatment to foreign investment. Member countries have their international trade disputes resolved by a WTO arbitration board. When the board makes its ruling, the losing country must comply with the ruling. If it does not comply, the winning country can impose trade sanctions on the losing country.

The Doha Development Round, which began in November 2001, is the current negotiation round for the WTO members. The aim of this latest round is "to achieve major reform to the international trade system through the introduction of lower trade barriers and revised trade rules." Unfortunately, as of summer 2012, the Doha Round had not yet been delivered. The most significant differences are between developed nations led by the European Union and the United States and the major developing nations led primarily by China and India. Issues of access to domestic markets for manufactured goods and agricultural subsidies are proving the most difficult for WTO members to resolve.

Despite positive words from outgoing Director-General Pascal Lamy describing the Doha Round as having "strengthened the WTO as a global trade body, as a major pillar of global economic governance," many see the WTO as an organization in crisis.

The European Union

In addition to multilateral trade agreements, a large number of regional trade agreements are in effect around the world. The largest such trading bloc is the European Union (EU), consisting of 28 European nations, including France, Germany, Italy, and the United Kingdom. An important aspect of the EU is that it allows for the free movement of labour and capital between member nations. As well, nearly all products are traded freely among member nations, and there is a common system of tariffs for goods from outside the EU.

North American Free Trade Agreement

Canada's first major bilateral trade agreement was the Canada–U.S. Free Trade Agreement (FTA), which came into effect in 1989. It called for the reduction or elimination of tariffs and other barriers to trade, free trade in energy products, freer trade in services, and a reduction in subsidies. As well, it set up a dispute-settlement mechanism to resolve trade disputes between the two countries. This free trade agreement, in particular, has had a significant impact on the volume of exports and imports for Canada. Since 1989, Canadian exports and imports have increased sharply, as shown in Exhibit 1, with virtually all of this rise the result of increased trade with the United States.

In 1994, the Canada–U.S. Free Trade Agreement was replaced by the North American Free Trade Agreement (NAFTA), creating a trading bloc for Canada, the

United States, and Mexico. NAFTA's objectives have been to eliminate trade barriers among the three countries, promote fair competition, increase investment opportunities, protect intellectual property rights, and resolve trade disputes.

Since 1994, as expected, Canada's exports and imports with the United States and Mexico have increased substantially. There have been concerns, however, about the impact of free trade with Mexico on Canadian industries and workers. Mexico's lower

DEBATE

SHOULD CANADA CUT BACK ON TRADE WITH CHINA?

For:

China has become the manufacturing locale for the world, and a vast amount of consumer goods that Canadians buy come from there. The goods are of good quality and provide Canadians with relatively lower costs than if they were manufactured in North America, but because they aren't made in North America, the jobs that were once involved in making those products have left for China and elsewhere. The paradox is that the more jobs we lose, the more those jobless individuals rely on the lower-cost goods. By 2012, annual Canada/China trade was totalling $70 billion, of which $50 billion was Canadian imports—which left only $20 billion worth of goods going to China. Of that $20 billion, over 90 percent was from basic resources (ore, wood/wood pulp, grains/seeds, and petroleum energy products), which account for very little employment for the dollar amount traded. On the other hand, of the $50 billion imported, those goods were primarily manufactured goods with just electronics and machinery valued at over $23 billion. There were virtually no goods entering Canada that were not "value-added" products, so virtually all of the $50 billion meant jobs going to China, and very few jobs in return. Canada can't sustain trade deficits at this level in the medium and long term—trade has to account for jobs, not just revenue for corporations. Corporations and owners of capital argue that trade is good for Canada—that a nation with 1.3 billion people offers great opportunities for Canadian goods. But the questions are: Do Canadian companies actually get access to those markets? Do they do so on a level playing field, or do they have to pay for access through tariffs and quotas? Who are the companies that get access—are they small to medium-sized companies, or is it multinationals who themselves are not owned by Canadians and take profits out of Canada? There is some concern too that the tremendous trade imbalance between Canada and China allows the Chinese to take their Canadian dollars and purchase valuable land and resources within Canada. The lure of short-term benefits of lower-cost products will be an immense cost to future Canadian generations. Surely it's clear that Canada should cut back on trade with China. What would be the costs if Canada continued on the present path? Are there other key arguments to support the resolution?

Against:

Canada is part of the global economy, and being internally focused would eventually cost Canada jobs. The Canadian population is just 2.5 percent of China's. If Canadians hope to increase their wealth, they will have to have access to a market much larger than their own. It's not just the size of the market that's appealing to Canadian companies, but who the market is made up of. The per capita income in China is only $7000 a year, and as the economy in China grows, so will the wealth of the citizens who will then be able to buy more consumer goods. It's this emerging market that is so attractive to North American companies. Others may argue that it's vital for Canada to continue to trade with China because our own markets are becoming saturated, and that firms that can't find new markets to make up for the loss of sales from domestic markets are doomed to fail. If Canada chooses not to trade with China, what other alternative do these producers have? Another argument for continuing trade with China is rather perverse: It is that China has so much foreign credit that any decision by North American governments to regulate or reduce trade with China may have a major impact on political relations with China, and given the economic power of China, no country would feel confident in risking regulations to find out what those consequences would actually be. The impact on the North American economy could be big enough to cause a significant recession. What are other strong arguments for not cutting back on trade with China? Arguing to cease trading may be unreasonable, so how could you use tariffs or quotas to even the trade between the countries?

labour and environmental standards, as well as fears that Canadian businesses would relocate to Mexico to take advantage of the lower wages there, are often discussed. Economists, however, have tried to emphasize the benefits to Canada of freer trade that result from increased specialization and exchange (a topic we look at in the next section). There certainly have been labour market adjustments in Canada since NAFTA, as some Canadian industries have become smaller, resulting in reduced employment in those sectors. At the same time, however, the United States and Mexico represent a combined market of more than 400 million people, providing many Canadian businesses with the opportunity to expand their sales and create additional jobs in Canada.

In addition to NAFTA, Canada has also entered into the following bilateral agreements: Canada–Israel Free Trade Agreement, 1997; Canada–Chile Free Trade Agreement, 1997; Canada–Costa Rica Free Trade Agreement, 2002; Canada–European Free Trade Association, 2009; Canada–Peru Free Trade Agreement, 2009; Canada–Colombia Free Trade Agreement, 2011; Canada–Jordan Free Trade Agreement, 2012; and the Canada–Panama Free Trade Agreement, 2013.

SECTION CHECK

■ The volume of international trade has increased substantially in Canada over the past 50 years. During that time, exports and imports have grown from about 20 percent of GDP to over 30 percent.

■ The numerous trade agreements in which Canada is an active participant range from multilateral global trade agreements (such as membership in the WTO) to regional agreements (such as the Canada–Costa Rica Free Trade Agreement). This substantial involvement is a major reason why Canada has experienced a rise in international trade.

section 22.3
Comparative Advantage and Gains from Trade

■ Why do economies trade?
■ What is the principle of comparative advantage?

WHY DO ECONOMIES TRADE?

Using simple logic, we conclude that the very existence of trade suggests that trade is economically beneficial. This is true if one assumes that people are utility maximizers, are rational and intelligent, and engage in trade on a voluntary basis. Because almost all trade is voluntary, it would seem that trade occurs because the participants feel that they are better off because of the trade. Both participants of an exchange of goods and services anticipate an improvement in their economic welfare. Sometimes, of course, anticipations are not realized (because the world is uncertain), but the motive behind trade remains an expectation of some enhancement in utility or satisfaction by both parties.

Granted, "trade must be good because people do it" is a rather simplistic explanation. The classical economist David Ricardo is usually given most of the credit for developing the economic theory that more precisely explains how trade can be mutually beneficial to both parties, raising output and income levels in the entire trading area.

WHAT IS THE PRINCIPLE OF COMPARATIVE ADVANTAGE?

Ricardo's theory of international trade centres on the concept of comparative advantage. A person, a region, or a country can gain by specializing in the production of the good in which they have a comparative advantage. A comparative advantage occurs when a person or a country can produce a good or service at a lower opportunity cost than others can. In other words, a country or a region should specialize in producing and selling those items that it can produce at a lower opportunity cost than other regions or countries.

Absolute Advantage versus Comparative Advantage

A common point of confusion regarding specialization and trade involves the concepts of absolute advantage and comparative advantage. **Absolute advantage** refers to the ability of a party (nation, region, or individual) to produce more of a good or service while using the same amount of inputs. That is, having an absolute advantage means a nation can produce a good or service more cheaply than other nations. The danger in using the concept of absolute advantage in determining what a nation should specialize in and trade is that a nation could actually lack an absolute advantage in anything. In this case, according to the theory of absolute advantage, the nation would not be involved in trade at all and the case for free trade collapses. By contrast, comparative advantage is never absent; even if a nation is bad at everything, it will still possess a comparative advantage at something.

absolute advantage
the ability of a party (nation, region, or individual) to produce more of a good or service while using the same amount of inputs

To help distinguish between these two important concepts, consider the following example. Canada may be able to produce more clothing per worker than India, but that does not mean Canada should necessarily sell clothing to India. Indeed, Canada has an absolute advantage or productive superiority over India in nearly every good, given the higher levels of output per person in Canada. Yet India's inferiority in producing some goods is much less than for others. In goods where India's productivity is only slightly less than that of Canada, such as perhaps in clothing, it probably has a comparative advantage over Canada. How? For a highly productive nation to produce goods in which it is only marginally more productive than other nations, the nation must take resources from the production of other goods in which its productive abilities are markedly superior. As a result, the opportunity costs in India of making clothing may be less than in Canada. With that, both can gain from trade, despite potential absolute advantages for every good in Canada.

Comparative Advantage and the Production Possibilities Curve

To help illustrate the concepts involved, the principle of comparative advantage can be applied to trading areas. In fact, trade has evolved in large part because different geographic areas have different resources and therefore different production possibilities. In Exhibit 1, we show the production possibilities curves (PPCs) for two trading areas. A "trading area" may be a locality, a region, or (as in this example) a nation. We see that if Canada devotes all of its resources to producing food, it can produce 40 kilograms of food per day; if it devotes all of its resources to producing cloth, it can produce 100 metres of cloth per day. We also see that when India uses all of its resources to

section 22.3
Exhibit 1 — Production Possibilities, Canada and India

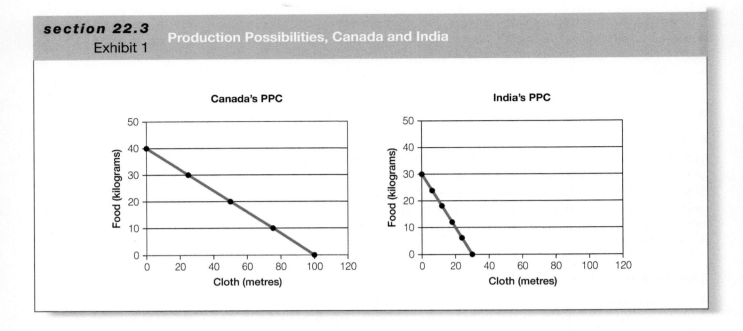

section 22.3
Exhibit 2 — Specialization and Trade

Region	Food	Cloth
Canada	(kilograms per day)	(metres per day)
	0	100
	10	75
	20	50
	30	25
	40	0
India	0	30
	6	24
	12	18
	18	12
	24	6
	30	0
Before Specialization		
Canada	10	75
India	18	12
Total	28	87
After Specialization		
Canada	0	100
India	30	0
Total	30	100

produce food, it can produce only 30 kilograms per day, and when it uses all of its resources to produce cloth, it can produce 30 metres per day.

Canada and India have various potential combinations of food and cloth that they can produce. For each region, the cost of producing more food is the output of cloth that must be forgone, and vice versa. We see in Exhibit 1 that Canada can produce more food (40 kilograms per day) and more cloth (100 metres per day) than India can (30 kilograms and 30 metres per day, respectively), perhaps reflecting superior resources (more or better labour, more land, and so on). This means that Canada has an absolute advantage in both products.

Suppose that, before specialization, Canada chooses to produce 75 metres of cloth and 10 kilograms of food per day. Similarly, suppose India decides to produce 12 metres of cloth and 18 kilograms of food per day. Collectively, then, the two areas are producing 87 metres of cloth (75 + 12) and 28 kilograms of food (10 + 18) per day before specialization.

Looking at Exhibit 2, now suppose the two nations specialize. Canada decides to specialize in cloth and devotes all its resources to making that product. As a result, cloth output in Canada rises to 100 metres per day, some of which is sold to India. India, in turn, devotes all its resources to food, producing 30 kilograms of food per day and selling some of it to Canada. Together, the two nations are producing more of both cloth and food than before—100 metres instead of 87 metres of cloth and 30 kilograms instead of 28 kilograms of food per day. Both areas could, as a result, have more of both products than before they began specializing and trading.

How can this happen? In Canada, the opportunity cost of producing food is very high—25 metres of cloth must be forgone to get 10 more kilograms of food. The cost of

1 kilogram of food is 2.5 metres of cloth (25 divided by 10). In India, by contrast, the opportunity cost of producing 6 more kilograms of food is 6 metres of cloth that must be forgone; so the cost of 1 kilogram of food is 1 metre of cloth. In Canada, a kilogram of food costs 2.5 metres of cloth, whereas in India the same amount of food costs only 1 metre of cloth. Food is more costly in Canada in terms of cloth forgone than in India, so India has a comparative advantage in food even though Canada has an absolute advantage in food.

With respect to cloth production, an increase in output by 25 metres, say, from 25 to 50 metres, costs 10 kilograms of food forgone in Canada. The cost of 1 more metre of cloth is 0.4 kilograms of food (10 divided by 25). In India, the cost of 1 metre of cloth is 1 kilogram of food. Cloth is more costly (in terms of opportunity cost) in India and cheaper in Canada, so Canada has a comparative advantage in the production of cloth.

Thus, by specializing in products in which it has a comparative advantage, an area has the potential of consuming more goods and services, assuming it trades the additional output for other desirable goods and services that others can produce at a lower opportunity cost. In the scenario presented here, the people in Canada would specialize in cloth, and the people in India would specialize in food. If Canada exports 20 metres of cloth and imports 11 kilograms of food, it can consume 80 metres of cloth and 11 kilograms of food after trade. Likewise, if India exports 11 kilograms of food and imports 20 metres of cloth, it can consume 20 metres of cloth and 19 kilograms of food after trade. We can see from this example that specialization increases both the division of labour and the interdependence among nations.

SECTION CHECK

- Voluntary trade occurs because the participants feel that they are better off because of the trade.
- A nation, a geographic area, or even a person can gain from trade if the good or service is produced relatively cheaper than anyone else can produce it. That is, an area should specialize in producing and selling those items that it can produce at a lower opportunity cost than others. Through trade and specialization in products in which it has a comparative advantage, a country can enjoy a greater array of goods and services at a lower cost.

Supply and Demand in International Trade

- What are consumer surplus and producer surplus?
- Who benefits and who loses when a country becomes an exporter?
- Who benefits and who loses when a country becomes an importer?

WHAT ARE CONSUMER SURPLUS AND PRODUCER SURPLUS?

The difference between what the consumer is willing and able to pay and what the consumer actually pays for a quantity of a good or service is called **consumer surplus.** The difference between the lowest price at which a supplier is willing and able to supply a good or service and the actual price received for a given quantity of a good or

consumer surplus
the difference between what the consumer is willing and able to pay and what the consumer actually pays for a quantity of a good or service

producer surplus

the difference between the lowest price at which a supplier is willing and able to supply a good or service and the actual price received for a given quantity of a good or service

service is called **producer surplus.** With the tools of consumer and producer surplus, we can better analyze the impact of trade. Who gains? Who loses? What happens to net welfare?

The demand curve represents maximum prices that consumers are willing and able to pay for different quantities of a good or service; the supply curve represents minimum prices that suppliers require to be willing to supply different quantities of that good or service. In Exhibit 1, for example, for the first unit of output, the consumer is willing to pay up to $7 and the producer would demand at least $1 for producing that unit. However, the equilibrium price is $4, as indicated by the intersection of the supply and demand curves. It is clear that the two would gain from getting together and trading that unit because the consumer would receive $3 of consumer surplus ($7 − $4) and the producer would receive $3 of producer surplus ($4 − $1). Both would also benefit from trading the second and third units of output—in fact, from every unit up to the equilibrium output. Once the equilibrium output is reached at the equilibrium price, all of the mutually beneficial opportunities from trade between suppliers and demanders will have taken place; the sum of consumer surplus and producer surplus is maximized.

It is important to recognize that the total gains to the economy from trade are the sum of consumer and producer surplus. That is, consumers benefit from additional amounts of consumer surplus and producers benefit from additional amounts of producer surplus.

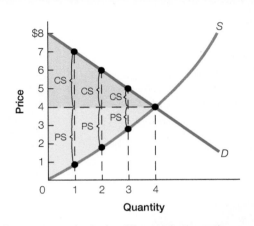

section 22.4
Exhibit 1
Consumer and Producer Surplus

Consumer surplus is the difference between the price a consumer has to pay ($4) and the price the consumer is willing to pay. For unit 1, consumer surplus is $3 ($7 − $4). Producer surplus is the difference between the price a seller receives for selling a good or service ($4) and the price at which he is willing to supply that good or service. For unit 1, producer surplus is $3 ($4 − $1).

WHO BENEFITS AND WHO LOSES WHEN A COUNTRY BECOMES AN EXPORTER?

Using the concepts of consumer and producer surplus, we can graphically show the net benefits of free trade. Imagine an economy with no trade, where the equilibrium price, P_{BT}, and the equilibrium quantity, Q_{BT}, of wheat are determined exclusively in the domestic economy, as seen in Exhibit 2. Say that this imaginary economy decides to engage in free trade. You can see that the world price (established in the world market for wheat), P_{WORLD}, is higher than the domestic price before trade, P_{BT}. In other words, the domestic economy has a comparative advantage in wheat because it can produce wheat at a lower relative price than the rest of the world. So this wheat-producing country sells some wheat to the domestic market and some wheat to the world market, all at the going world price.

The price after trade (P_{AT}) is higher than the price before trade (P_{BT}). Because the world market is huge, the demand from the rest of the world at the world price (P_{WORLD}) is assumed to be perfectly elastic. That is, domestic wheat farmers can sell all the wheat they want at the world price. If you were a wheat farmer in Saskatchewan, would you rather sell all of your bushels of wheat at the higher world price or the lower domestic price? As a wheat farmer, you would surely prefer the higher world price. But this is not good news for domestic cereal and bread eaters, who now have to pay more for products made with wheat, because P_{AT} is greater than P_{BT}.

Graphically, we can see how free trade and exports affect both domestic consumers and domestic producers. At the higher world price, P_{AT}, domestic producers supply Q_{AT}^S, whereas domestic consumers demand Q_{AT}^D. The difference between these two quantities

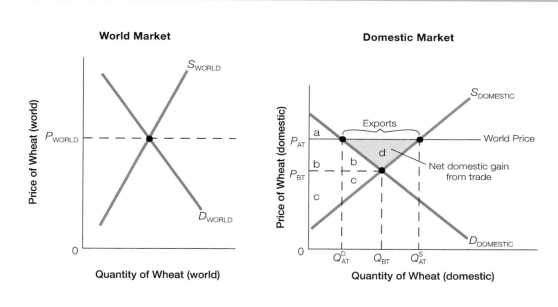

section 22.4
Exhibit 2   Free Trade and Exports

World Market

Domestic Market

Domestic Gains and Losses from Free Trade (exports)

Area	Before Trade	After Trade	Change
Consumer Surplus (*CS*)	a + b	a	– b
Producer Surplus (*PS*)	c	b + c + d	+ (b + d)
Total Welfare from Trade (*CS* + *PS*)	a + b + c	a + b + c + d	+ d

Domestic producers gain more than domestic consumers lose from exports when there is free trade. On net, domestic welfare rises by area d.

is the amount of wheat exported to the world market. At the higher world price, P_{AT}, domestic wheat producers are receiving larger amounts of producer surplus. Before trade, they received a surplus equal to area c; after trade, they received surplus b + c + d, for a net gain of area b + d. However, part of the domestic producers' gain comes at

In 1993, the North American Free Trade Agreement (NAFTA) was passed. This lowered the trade barriers among Mexico, Canada, and the United States. Proponents of freer trade, especially economists, viewed the agreement as a way to gain greater wealth through specialization and trade for all three countries. Opponents thought the agreement would take away Canadian and U.S. jobs and lower living standards.

domestic consumers' expense. Specifically, consumers had a consumer surplus equal to area a + b before the trade (at P_{BT}), but they now have only area a (at P_{AT})—a loss of area b.

Area b reflects a redistribution of income because producers are gaining exactly what consumers are losing. Is that good or bad? We can't say objectively whether consumers or producers are more deserving. However, the net benefits from allowing free trade and exports are clearly visible in area d. Without free trade, no one gets area d. That is, on net, members of the domestic society gain when domestic wheat producers are able to sell their wheat at the higher world price. Although domestic wheat consumers lose from the free trade, those negative effects are more than offset by the positive gains captured by producers. Area d is the net increase in domestic welfare (the welfare gain) from free trade and exports.

WHO BENEFITS AND WHO LOSES WHEN A COUNTRY BECOMES AN IMPORTER?

Now suppose that our economy does not produce shirts as well as other countries of the world. In other words, other countries have a comparative advantage in producing shirts. This means that the domestic price for shirts is above the world price. This scenario is illustrated in Exhibit 3. At the new, lower world price, the domestic producer will supply quantity Q_{AT}^S. However, at the lower world price, the domestic

---

section 22.4
Exhibit 3   Free Trade and Imports

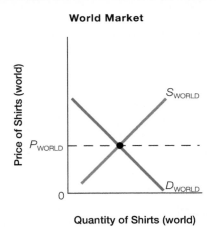

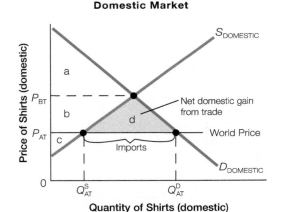

Domestic Gains and Losses from Free Trade (imports)

Area	Before Trade	After Trade	Change
Consumer Surplus (*CS*)	a	a + b + d	+ (b + d)
Producer Surplus (*PS*)	b + c	c	− b
Total Welfare from Trade (*CS* + *PS*)	a + b + c	a + b + c + d	+ d

Domestic consumers gain more than domestic producers lose from imports when there is free trade. On net, domestic welfare rises by area d.

producers will not produce the entire amount demanded by domestic consumers, Q_{AT}^D. At the world price, reflecting the world supply and demand for shirts, the difference between what is domestically supplied and what is domestically demanded is supplied by imports.

At the world price (established in the world market for shirts), we assume the world supply curve to the domestic market is perfectly elastic—that the producers of the world can supply all that domestic consumers are willing to buy at the going price. At the world price, Q_{AT}^S is supplied by domestic producers and the difference between Q_{AT}^D and Q_{AT}^S is imported from other countries.

Who wins and who loses from free trade and imports? Domestic consumers benefit from paying a lower price for shirts. In Exhibit 3, before trade, consumers received only area a in consumer surplus. After trade, the price fell and quantity purchased increased, causing the area of consumer surplus to increase from area a to area a + b + d, a gain of b + d. Domestic producers lose because they are now selling their shirts at the lower world price, P_{AT}. The producer surplus before trade was b + c. After trade, the producer surplus falls to area c, reducing producer surplus by area b. Area b, then, represents a redistribution from producers to consumers, but area d is the net increase in domestic welfare (the welfare gain) from free trade and imports.

SECTION CHECK

- The difference between what a consumer is willing and able to pay and what a consumer actually has to pay is called *consumer surplus*. The difference between what a supplier is willing and able to receive and the price a supplier actually receives for selling a good or service is called *producer surplus*.
- With free trade and exports, domestic producers gain more than domestic consumers lose.
- With free trade and imports, domestic consumers gain more than domestic producers lose.

Tariffs, Import Quotas, and Subsidies

- What is a tariff?
- What is the impact of tariffs on the domestic economy?
- What are some arguments in favour of tariffs?
- What are import quotas?
- What is the impact of import quotas on the domestic economy?
- What is the economic impact of subsidies?

WHAT IS A TARIFF?

A **tariff** is a tax on imported goods. Tariffs are usually relatively small revenue producers that retard the expansion of trade. They bring about higher prices and revenues to domestic producers, and lower sales and revenues to foreign producers. Moreover, tariffs lead to higher prices for domestic consumers. In fact, the gains to producers are more than offset by the loss to consumers. Let us see how this works graphically.

tariff
a tax on imported goods

WHAT IS THE IMPACT OF TARIFFS ON THE DOMESTIC ECONOMY?

The domestic economic impact of tariffs is presented in Exhibit 1, which illustrates the supply and demand curves for domestic consumers and producers of shoes. In a typical international supply and demand illustration, the intersection of the world supply and demand curves would determine the domestic market price. However, with import tariffs, the domestic price of shoes is greater than the world price, as in Exhibit 1. We consider the world supply curve (S_{WORLD}) to domestic consumers to be perfectly elastic; that is, we can buy all we want at the world price (P_{WORLD}). At the world price, domestic producers are willing to provide only quantity Q_S, but domestic consumers are willing to buy quantity Q_D—more than domestic producers are willing to supply. Imports make up the difference.

As you can see in Exhibit 1, the imposition of the tariff shifts up the perfectly elastic supply curve from foreigners to domestic consumers from S_{WORLD} to $S_{WORLD + TARIFF}$, but it does not alter the domestic supply or demand curve. At the resulting higher domestic price (P_{W+T}), domestic suppliers are willing to supply more, Q'_S, but domestic consumers

section 22.5
Exhibit 1   Free Trade and Tariffs

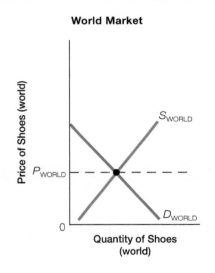

World Market

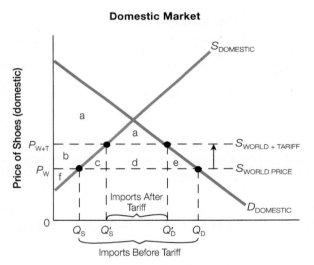

Domestic Market

Gains and Losses from Tariffs

Area	Before Tariff	After Tariff	Change
Consumer Surplus (*CS*)	a + b + c + d + e	a	– (b + c + d + e)
Producer Surplus (*PS*)	f	b + f	+ b
Government Revenues (Tariff)	—	d	+ d
Total Welfare from Tariff (*CS* + *PS* + Tariff Revenues)	a + b + c + d + e + f	a + b + d + f	– (c + e)

In the case of a tariff, we see that consumers lose more than producers and government gain. On net, the deadweight loss associated with the new tariff is represented by area c + e.

are willing to buy less, Q'_D, reducing the quantity of imported shoes. Overall, then, tariffs lead to (1) a smaller total quantity sold; (2) a higher price for shoes for domestic consumers; (3) greater sales of shoes at higher prices for domestic producers; and (4) lower sales of foreign shoes.

Although domestic producers do gain more sales and higher earnings, consumers lose much more. The increase in price from the tariff results in a loss in consumer surplus, as shown in Exhibit 1. After the tariff, shoe prices rise to P_{W+T} and, consequently, consumer surplus falls by area b + c + d + e, representing the welfare loss to consumers from the tariff. Area b in Exhibit 1 shows the gain to domestic producers as a result of the tariff. That is, at the higher price, domestic producers are willing to supply more shoes, representing a welfare gain to producers resulting from the tariff. As a result of the tariff revenues, government gains area d. This is the import tariff—the revenue government collects on imports. However, we see from Exhibit 1 that consumers lose more than producers and government gain from the tariff. That is, on net, the deadweight loss associated with the tariff is represented by area c + e.

WHAT ARE SOME ARGUMENTS IN FAVOUR OF TARIFFS?

Despite the preceding arguments against trade restrictions, they continue to be levied. Some rationale for their existence is necessary. Four common arguments for the use of trade restrictions deserve our critical examination.

Temporary Trade Restrictions Help Infant Industries Grow

A country might argue that a protective tariff will allow a new industry to more quickly reach a scale of operation at which economies of scale and production efficiencies can be realized. That is, temporarily shielding the young industry from competition from foreign firms will allow the infant industry a chance to grow. With the early protection, these firms will eventually be able to compete effectively in the global market. It is presumed that without this protection, the industry could never get on its feet. At first hearing, the argument sounds valid, but there are many problems with it. How do you identify "infant industries" that genuinely have potential economies of scale and will quickly become efficient with protection? We do not know the long-run average total cost curves of industries, a necessary piece of information. Moreover, if firms and governments are truly convinced of the advantages of allowing an industry to reach a large scale, would it not be wise to make massive loans to the industry, allowing it to instantly begin large-scale production rather than slowly and at the expense of consumers? In other words, the goal of allowing the industry to reach its efficient size can be reached without protection. Finally, the history of infant industry tariffs suggests that the tariffs often linger long after the industry is mature and no longer in need of protection.

Tariffs Can Reduce Domestic Unemployment

Exhibit 1 showed how tariffs increase output by domestic producers, thus leading to increased employment and reduced unemployment in industries where tariffs were imposed. Yet the overall employment effects of a tariff imposition are not likely to be positive; the argument is incorrect. Why? First, the imposition of a tariff by Canada on, say, foreign steel is going to be noticed in the countries adversely affected by the tariff. If a new tariff on steel lowers Japanese steel sales to Canada, the Japanese likely will retaliate by imposing tariffs on Canadian exports to Japan, for example, on beef exports. The retaliatory tariff will lower Canadian sales of beef and thus decrease employment in the Canadian beef industry. As a result, the gain in employment in the steel industry will be offset by a loss of employment elsewhere.

Even if the other countries did not retaliate, Canadian employment would likely suffer outside the industry being protected. The way that other countries pay for Canadian goods is by getting Canadian dollars from sales to Canada—imports to us. If new tariffs lead to restrictions on imports, fewer Canadian dollars will be flowing overseas in payment for imports, which means that foreigners will have fewer Canadian dollars available to buy our exports. Other things being equal, this will tend to reduce our exports, thus creating unemployment in the export industries.

Tariffs Are Necessary for National Security Reasons

Sometimes it is argued that tariffs are a means of preventing a nation from becoming too dependent on foreign suppliers of goods vital to national security. That is, by making foreign goods more expensive, we can protect domestic suppliers. For example, if oil is vital to running planes and tanks, a cutoff of foreign supplies of oil during wartime could cripple a nation's defences.

The national security argument is usually not valid. If a nation's own resources are depletable, tariff-imposed reliance on domestic supplies will hasten depletion of domestic reserves, making the country even *more* dependent on imports in the future. If we impose a high tariff on foreign oil to protect domestic producers, we will increase domestic output of oil in the short run, but in the process, we will deplete the stockpile of available reserves. Thus, the defence argument is often of questionable validity. From a defence standpoint, it makes more sense to use foreign oil in peacetime and perhaps stockpile "insurance" supplies so that larger domestic supplies would be available during wars.

Tariffs Are Necessary to Protect against Dumping

Dumping occurs when a foreign country sells its products at prices below the country's costs or below the prices for which the products are sold on the domestic market. For example, the Japanese government has been accused for years of subsidizing Japanese steel producers while they attempt to gain a greater share of the world steel market and greater market power. That is, using this strategy, the short-term losses from selling below cost may be offset by the long-term economic profits. Some have argued that tariffs are needed to protect domestic producers against low-cost dumpers because the tariffs will raise the cost to foreign producers and offset the producers' cost advantage.

Canada has anti-dumping laws; if a Canadian producer suspects that imported goods are being dumped or subsidized, they can file a written complaint with the Canadian Border Services Agency (CBSA). It is then up to the Canadian International Trade Tribunal to establish if the dumping or subsidizing is causing injury to Canadian industry. If the Tribunal finds such evidence, the CBSA is then given the authority to impose anti-dumping or countervailing duties on the dumped or subsidized imports. The duties are designed to raise the price of the foreign goods that are being dumped or subsidized and give Canadian industry an opportunity to compete fairly with the imported goods.

WHAT ARE IMPORT QUOTAS?

import quota
a legal limit on the imported quantity of a good that is produced abroad and can be sold in domestic markets

An **import quota** is a legal limit on the imported quantity of a good that is produced abroad and can be sold in domestic markets. Like tariffs, import quotas directly restrict imports, leading to reductions in trade and thus preventing nations from fully realizing their comparative advantage. The case for quotas is probably even weaker than the case for tariffs. Suppose that the Japanese have been sending 50 000 cars annually to Canada but now are told that, because of quota restrictions, they can send only 30 000 cars. If the Japanese manufacturers are allowed to determine how the quantity reduction is to occur, they will likely collude, leading to higher prices. Suppose that each producer is simply told to reduce sales by 40 percent. They will substantially raise the price of the cars to Canadians above what the 50 000 original buyers would have paid for them.

The Government Does Not Collect Revenues from Import Quotas

Unlike what occurs with a tariff, the Canadian government does not collect any revenue as a result of the import quota. Despite the higher prices, the loss in consumer surplus, and the loss in government revenue, quotas come about because people often view them as being less "protectionist" than tariffs—the traditional, most maligned form of protection.

Besides the rather blunt means of curtailing imports by using tariffs and quotas, nations have devised still other, more subtle means to restrict international trade. For example, nations sometimes impose product standards, ostensibly to protect consumers against inferior merchandise. Effectively, however, sometimes those standards are simply a means to restrict foreign competition. For example, France might keep certain kinds of wine out of the country on the grounds that the wines were made with allegedly inferior grapes or had an inappropriate alcoholic content. Likewise, Canada might prohibit automobile imports that do not meet certain standards in terms of pollutants, safety, and fuel efficiency. Even if these standards are not intended to restrict foreign competition, the regulations may nonetheless have that impact, restricting consumer choice.

WHAT IS THE IMPACT OF IMPORT QUOTAS ON THE DOMESTIC ECONOMY?

The domestic economic impact of an import quota on autos is presented in Exhibit 2. The introduction of an import quota increases the price from the world price, P_W (established in the world market for autos) to P_{W+Q}. The quota causes the price to rise above the world price. The domestic quantity demanded falls and the domestic quantity supplied rises. Consequently, the number of imports is much smaller than it would be without the import quota. Compared to free trade, domestic producers are better off but domestic consumers are worse off. Specifically, the import quota results in a gain in producer surplus of area b and a loss in consumer surplus of area b + c + d + e. However, unlike the tariff case, where the government gains area d in revenues, the government does not gain any revenues with a quota. Consequently, the deadweight loss is even greater with quotas than with tariffs. That is, on net, the deadweight loss associated with the quota is represented by area c + d + e. Recall that the deadweight loss was only c + e for tariffs.

If tariffs and import quotas hurt importing countries, why do they exist? The reason they exist is that producers can make large profits or "rents" from tariffs and import quotas. Economists call producer efforts to gain profits from government protection **rent seeking.** Because this is money, time, and effort that could have been spent producing something else rather than spent on lobbying efforts, the deadweight loss from tariffs and quotas that we just illustrated will likely understate the true deadweight loss to society.

rent seeking
producer efforts to gain profits from government protections such as tariffs and import quotas

WHAT IS THE ECONOMIC IMPACT OF SUBSIDIES?

subsidy

a program of financial assistance paid out to producers

Working in the opposite direction to a tariff or import quota, a **subsidy** is a program of financial assistance paid out to producers in a particular industry. As a form of protectionism or trade barrier, subsidies artificially make domestic goods and services competitive against imports. Specifically, an export subsidy involves giving revenue to producers for each exported unit of output, therefore encouraging producers to export. Although not a barrier to trade like tariffs and quotas, objections can be raised that subsidies distort trade patterns and lead to inefficiencies. How does this happen? With subsidies, producers will export goods not because their costs are lower than that of a foreign competitor, but because their costs have been artificially reduced by government action, transferring income from taxpayers to the exporter. The subsidy does not reduce the actual labour, raw material, and capital costs of production—society has the same opportunity costs as before. A nation's taxpayers end up subsidizing the output of producers who, relative to producers in other countries, are inefficient. The nation, then, exports products in which it does not have a comparative advantage. Gains from trade in terms of world output are reduced by such subsidies. Thus, subsidies, usually

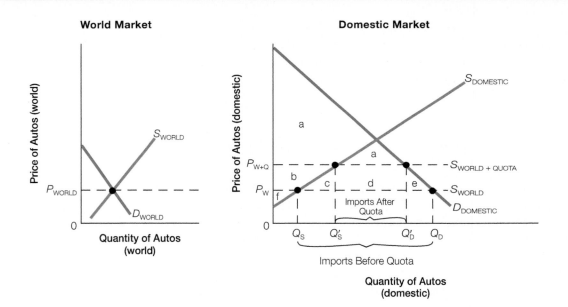

section 22.5
Exhibit 2   Free Trade and Import Quotas

World Market

Domestic Market

Gains and Losses from Import Quotas

Area	Before Quota	After Quota	Change
Consumer Surplus (*CS*)	a + b + c + d + e	a	− (b + c + d + e)
Producer Surplus (*PS*)	f	b + f	+ b
Total Welfare (*CS* + *PS*) from Quota	a + b + c + d + e + f	a + b + f	− (c + d + e)

With an import quota, the price rises from P_w to P_{w+Q}. Compared to free trade, consumers lose area b + c + d + e and producers gain area b. The deadweight loss from the quota is area c + d + e. Under quotas, consumers lose and producers gain. The difference in deadweight loss between quotas and tariffs is area d that the government is not able to pick up with import quotas.

defended as a means of increasing exports and improving a nation's international financial position, are usually of dubious worth to the world economy and even to the economy doing the subsidizing.

Several Canadian subsidy programs have drawn the criticism of other economies. The most controversial of these are the ones provided to our agricultural, forest products, and mining and steel industries.

According to the World Bank and the International Monetary Fund, world trade has benefited enormously from greater trade openness since 1950. Tariffs on goods have fallen from a worldwide average of 26 percent to less than 9 percent today. On average, trade has grown more than twice as fast as output. While tariff use has declined, the incidence of nontariff barriers such as import quotas and export subsidies has risen sharply, indicating that there is still work to be done.

SECTION CHECK

- A tariff is a tax on imported goods.
- Tariffs bring about higher prices and revenues to domestic producers, and lower sales and revenues to foreign producers. Tariffs lead to higher prices and reduce consumer surplus for domestic consumers. Tariffs result in a net loss in welfare because the loss in consumer surplus is greater than the gain to producers and the government.
- Arguments in favour of the use of tariffs include: tariffs help infant industries grow; tariffs can reduce domestic unemployment; tariffs are necessary for national security reasons; and tariffs protect against dumping.
- Import quotas are legal limits on the quantity of an imported good that can be produced abroad and sold in domestic markets.
- Like tariffs, import quotas restrict imports, lowering consumer surplus and preventing countries from fully realizing their comparative advantage. There is a net loss in welfare from quotas, but it is proportionately larger than for a tariff because there are no government revenues.
- Sometimes government tries to encourage production of a certain good by subsidizing its production with taxpayer dollars. Because subsidies stimulate exports, they are not a barrier to trade like tariffs and import quotas. However, they do distort trade patterns and cause overall inefficiencies.

For Your Review

Section 22.1

1. What is the major difference between the nature of Canadian exports and imports?

2. Why would Canadian producers and consumers be more concerned about American trade restrictions than Swedish trade restrictions?

Section 22.2

3. Why is it important to understand the effects of international trade?

4. The North American Free Trade Agreement (NAFTA) is an agreement among Canada, the United States, and Mexico to reduce trade barriers and promote the free flow of goods and services across borders. Some Canadian labour groups were opposed to NAFTA. Can you explain why? Can you predict how NAFTA might affect the nature and production methods of goods and services produced in the participating countries?

Section 22.3

5. Bud and Larry have been shipwrecked on a deserted island. Their economic activity consists of either gathering berries or fishing. We know that Bud can catch four fish in one hour or harvest two buckets of berries. In the same time, Larry can catch two fish or harvest two buckets of berries.

   a. Fill in the following table assuming that they *each* spend four hours a day fishing and four hours a day harvesting berries.

	Fish per Day	Buckets of Berries per Day
Bud	_____	_____
Larry	_____	_____
Total	_____	_____

   b. If Bud and Larry don't trade with each other, who is better off? Why?

   c. Assume that Larry and Bud operate on straight-line production possibilities curves. Fill in the following table:

	Opportunity Cost of a Bucket of Berries	Opportunity Cost of a Fish
Bud	_____	_____
Larry	_____	_____

   d. If they trade, who has the comparative advantage in fish? In berries?

   e. If Larry and Bud specialize in and trade the good in which they have a comparative advantage, how much of each good will be produced in an eight-hour day? What are the gains from trade?

6. Suppose Canada can produce cars at an opportunity cost of 2 computers for each car it produces. Suppose Mexico can produce cars at an opportunity cost of 8 computers for each car it produces. Indicate how both countries can gain from free trade.

7. The following represents the production possibilities in two countries.

Country A		Country B	
Good X	Good Y	Good X	Good Y
0	32	0	24
4	24	4	18
8	16	8	12
12	8	12	6
16	0	16	0

Which country has a comparative advantage at producing Good X? How can you tell? Which country has a comparative advantage at producing Good Y?

8. Evaluate the following statement: "Canada has an absolute advantage in growing wheat. Therefore, it must have a comparative advantage in growing wheat."

9. Assume that Freeland could produce 8 units of X and no Y, 16 units of Y and no X, or any linear combination in between, and Braveburg could produce 32 units of X and no Y, 48 units of Y and no X, or any linear combination in between.

   a. What is the opportunity cost of producing X in Freeland? In Braveburg?

   b. If Freeland and Braveburg specialize according to comparative advantage, in which directions will traded goods flow?

   c. If trade occurs, what will be the terms of trade between X and Y?

   d. How large would transaction costs, transportation costs, or tariffs have to be to eliminate trade between Freeland and Braveburg?

10. If country A is the lower opportunity cost producer of X and country B is the lowest opportunity cost producer of Y, what happens to their absolute and comparative advantages if country A suddenly becomes three times more productive at producing both X and Y than it was before?

Section 22.4

11. How does voluntary trade generate both consumer and producer surplus?

12. To protect its domestic apple industry, Botswana has for many years prevented international trade in apples. The following graph represents the Botswana domestic market for apples. P_{BT} is the current price, and P_{AT} is the world price.

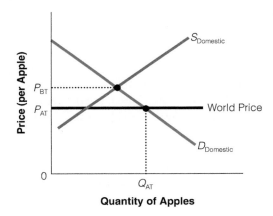

   a. If the government allows world trade in apples, what will happen to the price of apples in Botswana? Why?

   b. Indicate the amount of apples domestic producers produce after there is trade in apples as Q_{DT}. How many apples are imported?

   c. Trade in imports causes producer surplus to be reduced by the amount b. Show b on the graph.

   d. The gains from trade equal the amount that increased consumer surplus exceeds the loss in producer surplus. Show this gain, g, on the graph.

   e. Explain why consumers in Botswana would still be better off if they were required to compensate producers for their lost producer surplus.

13. Using the following graph, illustrate the domestic effects of opening up the domestic market to international trade on the domestic price, the domestic quantity

purchased, the domestic quantity produced, imports or exports, consumer surplus, producer surplus, and the total welfare gain from trade.

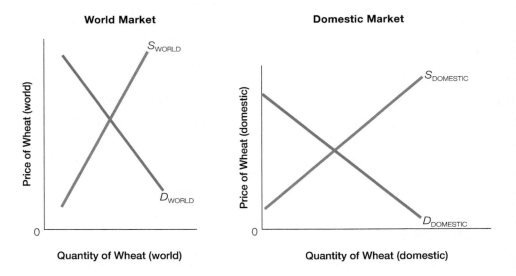

14. When a country has a comparative advantage in the production of a good, why do domestic producers gain more than domestic consumers lose from free international trade?

15. When a country has a comparative disadvantage in the production of a good, why do domestic consumers gain more than domestic producers lose from free international trade?

Section 22.5

16. Use the following graph to illustrate the domestic effects of imposing a tariff on imports on the domestic price, the domestic quantity purchased, the domestic quantity produced, the level of imports, consumer surplus, producer surplus, the tariff revenue generated, and the total welfare effect from the tariff.

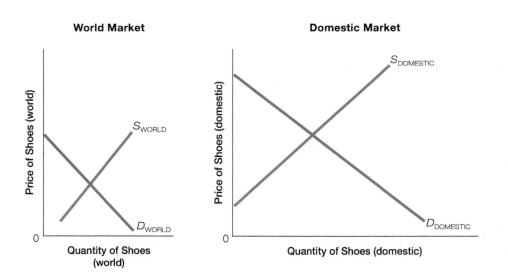

17. Explain why imposing a tariff causes a net welfare loss to the domestic economy.

18. If imposing tariffs and quotas harms consumers, why don't consumers vigorously oppose the implementation of these protectionist policies?

19. Why does rent seeking imply that the traditional measure of deadweight loss from tariffs and quotas will likely understate the true deadweight loss to society?

20. Would you be in favour of freer trade or against it in the following circumstances?

    a. The move to freer trade is in another country and you are an exporter to that country.

    b. The move to freer trade is in your country and you compete with imports from other countries.

    c. The move to freer trade is in your country and you import parts for products you sell domestically.

21. Go through your local newspaper and locate four news items regarding the global economy. Identify the significance of each of these news items to the Canadian economy and whether they are likely to affect international trade.

section

23.1 The Balance of Payments

- What is the balance of payments?
- What is the current account?
- What is the capital account?
- What is the statistical discrepancy?

WHAT IS THE BALANCE OF PAYMENTS?

balance of payments
the record of international transactions of a nation over a year

The record of the international transactions of a nation over a year is called the **balance of payments.** The balance of payments is a statement that records all the exchanges requiring an outflow of funds to foreign nations or an inflow of funds from other nations. Just as an examination of gross domestic product accounts gives us some idea of the economic health and vitality of a nation, the balance of payments provides information about a nation's world trade position. The balance of payments is divided into three main sections: the current account, the capital account, and an "error term" called the *statistical discrepancy*. These are highlighted in Exhibit 1. Let us look at each of these components beginning with the current account, which is largely made up of imports and exports of goods and services.

WHAT IS THE CURRENT ACCOUNT?

Export Goods and the Current Account

current account
a record of a country's imports and exports of goods and services, net primary income, and net secondary income

The **current account** is a record of a country's imports and exports of goods and services, net primary income, and net secondary income. Anytime a foreign buyer purchases a good from a Canadian producer, the foreign buyer must pay the Canadian producer for the good. Usually, the foreigner must pay for the good in Canadian dollars because the seller wants to pay his workers and for other inputs with dollars. This requires the foreign buyer to exchange units of his currency with a foreign exchange dealer for Canadian dollars. Because Canada obtains foreign currency, exports of Canadian goods abroad are considered a credit or plus (+) item in the Canadian balance of payments.

section 23.1
Exhibit 1   **Canadian Balance of Payments, 2012 (billions of dollars)**

Type of Transaction					
Current Account			**Capital Account**		
1. Exports of goods	$463		10. Net acquisition of financial assets	$−121	
2. Imports of goods	−475		11. Net incurrence of liabilities	185	
3. Merchandise trade balance (lines 1 + 2)		−12	12. Financial account balance (lines 10 + 11)		64
4. Exports of services	84		13. Statistical discrepancy		−2
5. Imports of services	−108		14. Net balance (lines 9 + 12 + 13)		$0
6. Services trade balance (lines 4 + 5)		−24			
7. Net primary income		−22			
8. Net secondary income		−4			
9. Current account balance (lines 3 + 6 + 7 + 8)		−62			

SOURCE: Statistics Canada. CANSIM Table 376-0101, Balance of international payments, current account and capital account.

Import Goods and the Current Account

When a Canadian consumer buys an imported good, however, the reverse is true: The Canadian importer usually must pay the foreign producer in the foreign nation's currency. Typically, the Canadian buyer will go to a foreign exchange dealer and exchange Canadian dollars for units of that foreign currency. Imports are thus a debit (−) item in the balance of payments, because Canada loses foreign currency in order to buy imports.

Services and the Current Account

Although imports and exports of goods are the largest components of the balance of payments, they are not the only ones. Nations import and export services as well. A particularly important service is tourism. When Canadian tourists go abroad, they are buying foreign-produced services. Those services include the use of hotels, sightseeing tours, restaurants, and so forth. In the current account, these services are included in imports. On the other hand, foreign tourism in Canada provides us with foreign currencies, so they are included in exports.

Net Primary and Net Secondary Income

Another item that affects the current account is net primary income—Canadian investors hold foreign assets

When a foreign tourist visits the CN Tower in Toronto, how does that affect the current account? Tourism provides Canada with foreign currency, which is included in exports.

© ROYALTY-FREE/CORBIS

and foreign investors hold Canadian assets. When Canadian investors hold foreign assets, they earn investment income in the form of interest and dividends, which is a credit item. When foreign investors hold Canadian assets, they earn investment income in the form of interest and dividends, which is a debit item. In Exhibit 1, investment income paid to foreigners on their Canadian assets exceeded the investment income received by Canadians on their foreign assets by $22 billion.

There is also net secondary income in the current account, which is largely private and government grants and gifts to and from other countries. When the Canadian government gives foreign aid to another country, this creates a debit in the Canadian balance of payments. Private gifts, such as Canadian individuals receiving money from relatives or friends in foreign countries, show up in the current account as a credit item.

Current Account Balance

The balance on the current account is the net amount of credits or debits after adding up all transactions of goods (merchandise imports and exports), services, net primary income, and net secondary income. If the sum of credits exceeds the sum of debits, the nation is said to be running a surplus on the current account. If debits exceed credits, however, the nation is running a deficit on the current account.

The current account balance for 2012 is presented in Exhibit 1. Note that exports and imports of goods were by far the largest credits and debits. Note also that Canadian imports of goods were $12 billion more than Canadian exports of goods. Canada, therefore, experienced a $12 billion deficit in the merchandise trade balance. In addition to this $12 billion merchandise trade deficit was a $23 billion deficit in the services trade balance. When the $22 billion net primary income payment and the $4 billion net secondary income are also included, the overall current account deficit was $62 billion.

WHAT IS THE CAPITAL ACCOUNT?

How was this deficit on the current account financed? We borrowed from the rest of the world. The current account deficit is reflected by movements of financial, or capital, assets. These transactions are recorded in the *capital account,* so a current account deficit is financed by a capital account surplus. In short, the **capital account** is a record of the foreign purchases or assets in the domestic economy (a monetary inflow) and domestic purchases of assets abroad (a monetary outflow).

capital account
a record of the foreign purchases or assets in the domestic economy (a monetary inflow) and domestic purchases of assets abroad (a monetary outflow)

Capital Account Transactions

Capital account transactions include items such as international bank loans, purchases of corporate stocks and bonds, government bond purchases, and direct investments in foreign subsidiary companies. In Exhibit 1, we see that Canadians purchased an additional $121 billion of foreign assets in 2012, which was a debit because Canada lost foreign currency. On the other hand, foreigners purchased an additional $185 billion of Canadian assets in 2012 which was a credit because it provided Canadians with foreign currency. On balance, then, there was a surplus in the capital account from capital movements of $64 billion, offsetting the $62 billion deficit in the current account.

It is important to highlight one particular capital account transaction: purchases and sales of foreign currencies by the Bank of Canada in the foreign exchange market. The Bank of Canada can intervene in the foreign exchange market to counter disruptive short-term movements in the external value of the Canadian dollar. For example, to moderate a decline in the value of the Canadian dollar, the Bank of Canada can sell foreign currency (usually U.S. dollars) and buy Canadian dollars on the foreign exchange market, thereby putting upward pressure on the Canadian dollar. Similarly, if the Canadian dollar is appreciating too rapidly, the Bank of Canada can buy foreign currency (usually U.S. dollars) and sell Canadian dollars on the foreign exchange market, thereby putting downward pressure on the Canadian dollar. These purchases and sales of foreign currencies by the Bank of Canada affect the level of Canada's official international reserves (the Government of Canada's holdings of foreign currencies), and these transactions are recorded in the capital account of the balance of payments.

WHAT IS THE STATISTICAL DISCREPANCY?

In the final analysis, it is true that the overall balance of payments account must balance so that credits and debits are equal. Why is this so? Because every unit of foreign currency used (debit) must have a source (credit). We can see that the current account deficit ($62 billion debit) does not exactly equal the capital account surplus ($64 billion credit). That is because there are considerable international flows of goods and capital that government authorities are unable to measure and record (e.g., smuggling of goods, or undeclared financial investments). These "errors" are entered into the balance of payments as the statistical discrepancy. In Exhibit 1, the statistical discrepancy was $2 billion (debit). By including the statistical discrepancy with the current account balance and the capital account balance, the overall balance of payments does balance.

Balance of Payments: A Useful Analogy

In concept, the international balance of payments is similar to the personal financial transactions of individuals. Each individual has his or her own "balance of payments," reflecting that person's trading with other economic units: other individuals, corporations, or governments. People earn income or credits by "exporting" their labour service to other economic units, or by receiving investment income (a return on capital services). Against that, they "import" goods from other economic units; we call these imports *consumption*. This debit item is sometimes augmented by payments made to outsiders (e.g., banks) on loans, and so forth. Fund transfers, such as gifts to children or charities, are other debit items (or credit items for recipients of the assistance).

As individuals, if our spending on our consumption ("imports") exceeds our income from our "exports" of our labour and capital services, we have a "deficit" that must be financed by borrowing or selling assets. On the other hand, if we "export" more than we "import," we can make new investments and/or increase our "reserves" (savings and investment holdings). Like nations, individuals who run a deficit in daily transactions must make up for it through accommodating transactions (e.g., borrowing or reducing their savings or investment holdings) to bring about an ultimate balance of credits and debits to their personal account. Likewise, individuals who run a surplus in daily transactions must make new investments and/or increase their savings and investment holdings to bring about a balance of credits and debits.

In summary, the international balance of payments works like this: A country that runs a current account surplus lends that surplus to the rest of the world, creating a capital account deficit; a country that runs a current account deficit finances that deficit by borrowing from the rest of the world, thus creating a capital account surplus.

SECTION CHECK

■ The balance of payments is the record of all the international financial transactions of a nation for any given year.

■ The current account is a record of a country's imports and exports of goods and services, net primary income, and net secondary income. If the sum of credits exceeds the sum of debits for all transactions of goods, services, primary income, and secondary income, the current account is in surplus. If the opposite is true, the account is in deficit.

■ The capital account is a record of the foreign purchases or assets in Canada and Canadian purchases of assets abroad. Capital account surpluses finance current deficits.

■ To ensure the balance of payments account does in fact balance, an "error" category—the statistical discrepancy—is included.

section 23.2 Exchange Rates

■ What are exchange rates?
■ How are exchange rates determined?

When Canadian consumers buy goods from people in other countries, the sellers of those goods want to be paid in their own domestic currencies. Canadian consumers, then, must first exchange Canadian dollars for the seller's currency in order to pay for those goods. Canadian importers must, therefore, constantly buy U.S. dollars, yen, euros, pesos, and other currencies in order to finance their purchases. Similarly, people in other countries buying Canadian goods must sell their currencies to obtain Canadian dollars in order to pay for those goods.

WHAT ARE EXCHANGE RATES?

exchange rate
the price of one unit of a country's currency in terms of another country's currency

The price of one unit of a country's currency in terms of another country's currency is called the **exchange rate.** If a Canadian importer has agreed to pay euros (the currency of the European Union) to buy a BMW M6 made in southern Bavaria, Germany, she would then have to exchange Canadian dollars for euros. If it takes $2 to buy 1 euro, then the exchange rate is $2 per euro. From the German perspective, the exchange rate is 0.50 euros per Canadian dollar.

Exhibit 1 shows the exchange rate for the Canadian dollar against the currencies of some of our major trading partners. The exchange rates listed were the average exchange rates for the year 2012. It took 1.0004 U.S. dollars to buy one Canadian dollar (i.e., the exchange rate of the Canadian dollar in terms of the U.S. dollar). Conversely, it took 0.9996 Canadian dollars to buy one U.S. dollar (i.e., the exchange rate of the U.S. dollar in terms of the Canadian dollar). Note carefully that 0.9996 equals 1 divided by 1.0004. Similarly, it took 80 Japanese yen to buy one Canadian dollar, and it took 0.0125 Canadian dollars (1 divided by 80) to buy one Japanese yen.

currency appreciation
an increase in the value of a currency

A review of exchange rates over time will reveal that they are not constant: They can increase and decrease. An increase in the value of a currency is referred to as a **currency appreciation.** For example, suppose the exchange rate rises from 25 to 30 Russian rubles

section 23.2
Exhibit 1   Exchange Rates for the Canadian Dollar in 2012

Country	Currency	Units of Foreign Currency per Canadian Dollar	Canadian Dollars per Unit of Foreign Currency
Australia	Dollar	0.9659	1.0353
China	Renminbi	6.3131	0.1584
European Monetary Union	Euro	0.7782	1.2850
Hong Kong	Dollar	7.7580	0.1289
India	Rupee	53.1915	0.0188
Japan	Yen	80.0000	0.0125
Mexico	Peso	13.1579	0.0760
New Zealand	Dollar	1.2349	0.8098
Norway	Krone	5.8207	0.1718
Russia	Rouble	31.0559	0.0322
South Korea	Won	1111.1111	0.0009
Sweden	Krona	6.7751	0.1476
Switzerland	Franc	0.9379	1.0662
United Kingdom	Pound	0.6313	1.5840
United States	Dollar	1.0004	0.9996

SOURCE: Bank of Canada Financial Markets Department, *Year Average of Exchange Rates, 2012.*

per Canadian dollar. Since you can now get more Russian rubles for each Canadian dollar, the dollar is said to have appreciated. A decrease in the value of a currency is referred to as **currency depreciation.** If the exchange rate falls from 15 to 10 Mexican pesos per Canadian dollar, the dollar is said to have depreciated.

currency depreciation
a decrease in the value of a currency

The euro makes it easy to compare prices for the same goods in different European countries using this currency. For example, if you use mail order or shop on the Internet, it is easier to spot the bargains between countries.

Changes in Exchange Rates Affect the Domestic Demand for Foreign Goods

Prices of goods in their currencies combine with exchange rates to determine the domestic price of foreign goods. Suppose the BMW M6 sells for 128 000 euros in Germany. What is the price to Canadian consumers? Let us assume that tariffs and other transaction costs are zero. If the exchange rate is $2 = 1 euro, then the equivalent Canadian dollar price of the BMW M6 is 128 000 euros times $2 per euro, or $256 000. If the exchange rate was to change to $3 = 1 euro, fewer cars would be demanded in Canada, because the effective Canadian dollar price of the cars would rise to $384 000 (128 000 euros times $3 per euro). The new higher relative value of a euro compared to the dollar (or equivalently, the lower relative value of a dollar compared to the euro) would lead to a reduction in Canadian demand for German-made cars.

© Fingerhut/Shutterstock

DEBATE

IS A LOW LOONIE GOOD FOR CANADA'S ECONOMY?

For:

Canada has long enjoyed a "discounted dollar," which gives Canadian exporters an artificial competitive advantage by making their goods seem to have more value simply because of the lower cost. It's as if Canadian products are "on sale" to the rest of the world. Over the course of the last decade, Canadians have seen their dollar fluctuate between 69 cents and US$1.03. This is a wild swing that has major effects on our economy. According to *The Globe and Mail*, experts tend to agree that a 90-cent dollar is close to fair value.* Those who trade with Canada desire a low Canadian dollar—it keeps the prices of Canadian products down and is more of a value to those who buy our goods. Trade unions and Canadian manufacturing firms enjoy the benefits of a low dollar because it provides the illusion of value. Surely it's clear that a low loonie is good for Canada's economy. Is it good for the long-term viability of a firm? Why or why not? Who are the other stakeholders that would benefit from a low dollar and what would be some other reasons to justify their views?

----

*B. McKenna. "Why a lower loonie is (mostly) good for Canada." *The Globe and Mail* (January 11, 2014).

Against:

A rising Canadian dollar sends a message to the world—that the Canadian economy and Canadian products are strong and desirable. A high dollar value is also much better for a resource-based economy. Canada has many resource-based firms that rely on the "value-added" (the difference between the sale price and the production cost of a product), and they would like to sell their products at the highest Canadian dollar price they can. It simply brings them the most revenues possible when they sell to foreign entities. When the dollar is low, it's as if the product is discounted to the world. A low dollar may be seen as a negative to Canadian manufacturing firms (although many firms would argue against that). This is because when the dollar is low, those firms sell more products internationally, but it's the value of the dollar that sells the product, not necessarily the value of the product itself. When the dollar appreciates, those firms find it difficult to compete. They should take the opportunity to improve their firms' productivity when they are selling more in preparation for when the value of the Canadian dollar eventually appreciates. A low Canadian dollar is bad for the migrating seniors who head south each year and it's bad for cross-border shoppers—they have to spend more Canadian dollars to pay for the goods they buy in the United States. All in all, surely a high loonie is preferable. What is the impact on the goals of growth, employment, and inflation when the dollar value is higher? What are other reasons why Canada should embrace the rising dollar? Are the arguments that are made in *The Globe and Mail* article detailed in the footnote sound, or could you argue against some aspects of it?

The Demand for a Foreign Currency

derived demand
the demand for an input derived from consumers' demand for the good or service produced with that input

The demand for foreign currencies is an example of what economists call a **derived demand**—a demand for an input derived from consumers' demand for the good or service produced with that input. Specifically, the demand for foreign currency is derived from the demand for foreign goods and services or for foreign assets. The more foreign goods are demanded, the more of that foreign currency will be needed to pay for those goods. Such an increased demand for the currency will push up the exchange rate of that currency relative to other currencies.

The Supply of a Foreign Currency

Similarly, the supply of foreign currency is provided by foreigners who want to buy the exports of another nation. For example, the more that foreigners demand Canadian products, the more of their currencies they will supply in exchange for Canadian dollars, which they use to buy our products.

HOW ARE EXCHANGE RATES DETERMINED?

We know that the demand for foreign currencies is derived in part from the demand for foreign goods, but how does that affect the exchange rate? Just as in the product market, the answer lies with the forces of supply and demand. In this case, it is the supply of and demand for a foreign currency that determine the equilibrium price (exchange rate) of that currency.

The Demand Curve for a Foreign Currency

As Exhibit 2 shows, the demand curve for a foreign currency—the euro, for example—is downward sloping, just as a demand curve is in product markets. In this case, however, the demand curve has a negative slope because as the price of the euro falls relative to the Canadian dollar (i.e., the euro depreciates in value), European products become relatively cheaper for Canadian consumers, who therefore buy more European goods. To do so, the quantity of euros demanded by Canadian consumers will increase to buy more European goods as the price of the euro falls. This is why the demand for foreign currencies is considered to be a derived demand.

The Supply Curve for a Foreign Currency

The supply curve for a foreign currency is upward sloping, just as a supply curve is in product markets. In this case, as the price of the euro increases relative to the Canadian dollar (i.e., the euro appreciates in value), Canadian products will become relatively cheaper for European buyers and they will increase the quantity of dollars they demand. Europeans will, therefore, increase the quantity of euros supplied to the foreign exchange market by buying more Canadian products. Hence, the supply curve is upward sloping.

Equilibrium in the Foreign Exchange Market

Equilibrium is reached where the demand and supply curves for a given currency intersect. In Exhibit 2, the equilibrium price of a euro is $1.20. As in the product market, if the Canadian dollar price of euros is higher than the equilibrium price, an excess

section 23.2
Exhibit 2   Equilibrium in the Foreign Exchange Market

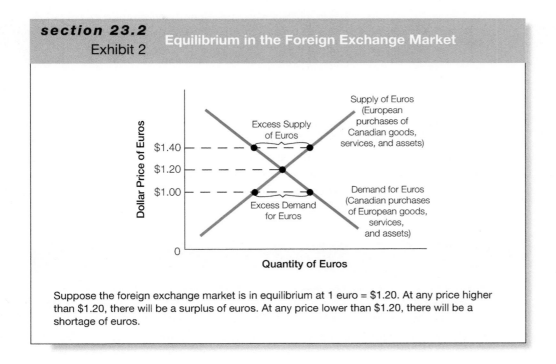

Suppose the foreign exchange market is in equilibrium at 1 euro = $1.20. At any price higher than $1.20, there will be a surplus of euros. At any price lower than $1.20, there will be a shortage of euros.

Business *CONNECTION*

MANAGING TRANSACTION RISKS

Companies that trade internationally incur transaction fees, amounts payable, and amounts receivable that expose the firm's cash flow to fluctuations in exchange rates. The risk is that the amount payable might increase if the foreign currency actually appreciates in value relative to the domestic currency between the time the payable was incurred and the date of payment. Similarly, if the international transaction results in an amount receivable, the foreign exchange risk is the risk that the amount to be received might drop in value if the foreign currency actually depreciates in value relative to the domestic currency between the time the receivable was incurred and the actual date of receipt.

What can businesses do to manage transaction exposure to fluctuations in foreign currencies? First, on an ongoing basis, the business should try to measure the net exposure it has to each foreign currency. The net exposure for each currency in a period is the amounts receivable less the amounts payable. Once this net amount is determined for each currency, the firm can manage the exposure using a variety of methods. For example, if the net amount is payable, the firm can buy a *futures* or *forward contract* to obtain the currency at a predetermined exchange rate in the future. Alternatively, the firm can arrange a *currency swap* (involving the exchange of principal and/or interest on a loan in one currency for that in another currency) through a financial intermediary such as a bank, or it can buy a *call option* on the foreign currency (giving the firm the right to buy the currency at a specified exchange rate at any time during a specified period). At times, the firm might want to borrow its home currency and convert the proceeds into the foreign currency that will be needed in the future to pay the net amount payable.

Hedging reduces the risk of loss. To hedge a net receivable, the firm could sell a futures or forward contract in order to sell the currency at a predetermined exchange rate in the future. (Futures contracts and forward contracts normally yield similar results, but forward contracts are private agreements and so are more flexible than standardized futures contracts.) As in the case of payables, the firm could arrange a currency swap through a financial intermediary such as a bank, or sell a *put optio*n (which gives the holder the right to sell at a specified price within a fixed period) on the foreign currency. The firm could also consider borrowing the foreign currency and converting the proceeds into its domestic currency, repaying the loan with the net receivable in due course.

With some forward planning, the transaction risk associated with fluctuations in exchange rates can be softened. This is especially true for companies that operate within nations that have significant amounts of foreign trade, and unfortunately even for small and medium-sized businesses that don't have any appreciative direct foreign trade, with the state of the world's global economy, no country and certainly no firm is immune to currency fluctuations. These days, all firms must understand the way that world currencies can affect their own operations.

1. As a business owner interested in doing business with China, how do you feel about the Chinese government holding its currency at low rates to have competitive advantages over North American firms? Would your opinion change if your firm purchases their products for operating your business?

2. What are the benefits and costs to businesses that undertake the various methods detailed in this feature?

3. Do you think a common North American currency would be an advantage for Canadian business? Why or why not?

quantity of euros will be supplied at that price, or a surplus of euros. Competition among euro sellers will push the price of euros down toward equilibrium. Likewise, if the dollar price of euros is lower than the equilibrium price, an excess quantity of euros will be demanded at that price, or a shortage of euros. Competition among euro buyers will push the price of euros up toward equilibrium.

SECTION CHECK

■ The price of a unit of one foreign currency in terms of another currency is called the *exchange rate.*
■ The exchange rate for a currency is determined by the supply of and demand for that currency in the foreign exchange market.

Equilibrium Changes in the Foreign Exchange Market

■ What are the major determinants in the foreign exchange market?

WHAT ARE THE MAJOR DETERMINANTS IN THE FOREIGN EXCHANGE MARKET?

The equilibrium exchange rate of a currency changes many times daily. Sometimes, these changes can be quite significant. Any force that shifts either the demand for or supply of a currency will shift the equilibrium in the foreign exchange market, leading to a new exchange rate. These factors include changes in consumer tastes for goods, changes in income, changes in tariffs, changes in relative interest rates, changes in relative inflation rates, and speculation.

Increased Tastes for Foreign Goods

Because the demand for foreign currencies is derived from the demand for foreign goods, any change in the demand for foreign goods will shift the demand schedule for foreign currency in the same direction. For example, if a cuckoo clock revolution sweeps through Canada, German producers would have reason to celebrate, knowing that many Canadian buyers will turn to Germany for their cuckoo clocks. The Germans, however, will accept payment only in the form of euros, so Canadian consumers and retailers must convert their dollars into euros before they can purchase their clocks. The increased taste for European goods in Canada would, therefore, lead to an increased demand for euros. As shown in Exhibit 1, this increased demand for

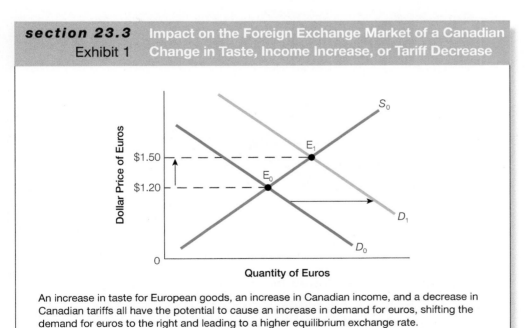

| section 23.3 | Impact on the Foreign Exchange Market of a Canadian |
| Exhibit 1 | Change in Taste, Income Increase, or Tariff Decrease |

An increase in taste for European goods, an increase in Canadian income, and a decrease in Canadian tariffs all have the potential to cause an increase in demand for euros, shifting the demand for euros to the right and leading to a higher equilibrium exchange rate.

What impact will an increase in travel to Paris by Canadian consumers have on the Canadian dollar price of euros? In order for a consumer to buy souvenirs at the Eiffel Tower, she will need to exchange dollars for euros. This would increase the demand for euros and result in a new higher dollar price of euros.

euros shifts the demand curve to the right, resulting in a new, higher equilibrium dollar price of euros.

Canadian Income Increases or Reductions in Canadian Tariffs

Any change in the average income of Canadian consumers will also change the equilibrium exchange rate, *ceteris paribus*. If, on the whole, incomes increased in Canada, Canadians would buy more goods, including imported goods, so more European goods would be bought. This increased demand for European goods would lead to an increased demand for euros, resulting in a higher exchange rate for the euro. A decrease in Canadian tariffs on European goods would tend to have the same effect as an increase in incomes by making European goods more affordable. As Exhibit 1 shows, this would again lead to an increased demand for European goods and a higher equilibrium exchange rate for the euro.

Changes in European Income, Tariffs, or Tastes

If European incomes rose, European tariffs on Canadian goods fell, or European tastes for Canadian goods increased, the supply of euros in the foreign exchange market would increase. Any of these changes would cause Europeans to demand more Canadian goods, and therefore more Canadian dollars in order to purchase those goods. To obtain those added dollars, Europeans must exchange more of their euros, increasing the supply of euros on the foreign exchange market. As Exhibit 2 demonstrates, the

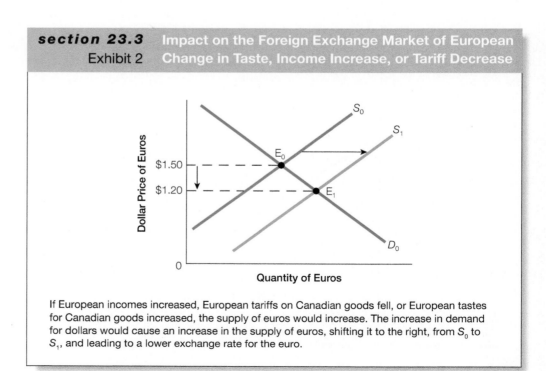

section 23.3   **Impact on the Foreign Exchange Market of European**
Exhibit 2   **Change in Taste, Income Increase, or Tariff Decrease**

If European incomes increased, European tariffs on Canadian goods fell, or European tastes for Canadian goods increased, the supply of euros would increase. The increase in demand for dollars would cause an increase in the supply of euros, shifting it to the right, from S_0 to S_1, and leading to a lower exchange rate for the euro.

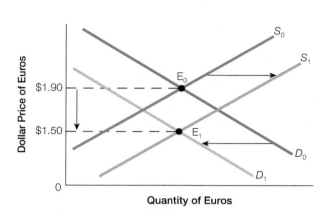

When Canadian interest rates increase, European investors will increase their supply of euros to buy dollars—the supply curve of euros increases from S_0 to S_1. In addition, Canadian investors will also shift their investments away from Europe, decreasing their demand for euros and shifting the demand curve from D_0 to D_1. This will lead to a depreciation of the euro and an appreciation of the dollar.

effect of this would be a rightward shift in the euro supply curve, leading to a new equilibrium at a lower exchange rate for the euro.

Changes in Relative Interest Rates

If interest rates in Canada were to increase relative to, say, European interest rates, other things equal, the rate of return on Canadian bonds would increase relative to that on European bonds. European investors would thus increase their demand for Canadian bonds, and therefore offer euros for sale to buy dollars to buy Canadian bonds, shifting the supply curve for euros to the right, from S_0 to S_1 in Exhibit 3.

In this scenario, Canadian investors would also shift their investments away from Europe by decreasing their demand for euros, from D_0 to D_1 in Exhibit 3. A subsequent lower equilibrium exchange rate ($1.50) would result for the euro due to an increase in the Canadian interest rate. That is, the euro would depreciate. In short, the higher Canadian interest rate attracted more investment to Canada and led to a relative appreciation of the dollar and a relative depreciation of the euro.

You may remember this analysis from our discussion of monetary policy in the open economy in Chapter 21. When the Bank of Canada runs a contractionary monetary policy and causes Canadian interest rates to rise, the Canadian dollar appreciates, which leads to a decrease in net exports and a reduction in real GDP in the short run.

Changes in Relative Inflation Rates

If Europe experienced an inflation rate greater than that experienced in Canada, other things being equal, what would happen to the exchange rate? In this case, European products would become relatively more expensive for Canadian consumers. Canadians would decrease the quantity of European goods demanded and, therefore, decrease their demand for euros. The result would be a leftward shift of the demand curve for euros.

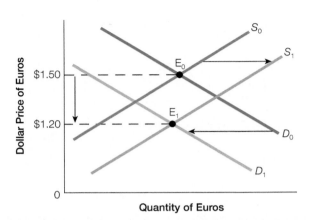

If Europe experienced a higher inflation rate than Canada, European products would become relatively more expensive to Canadian consumers. As a result, those consumers would demand fewer euros, shifting the demand for euros to the left, from D_0 to D_1. At the same time, Canadian goods would become relatively cheaper to Europeans, who would then buy more dollars by supplying euros, shifting the euro supply curve to the right, from S_0 to S_1. The result: a new lower equilibrium exchange rate for the euro.

On the other side of the Atlantic, Canadian goods would become relatively cheaper for Europeans, leading Europeans to increase the quantity of Canadian goods demanded and, therefore, to demand more Canadian dollars. This increased demand for dollars translates into an increased supply of euros, shifting the supply curve for euros rightward. Exhibit 4 shows the shifts of the supply and demand curves and the new lower equilibrium exchange rate for the euro resulting from the higher European inflation rate.

Expectations and Speculation

Every trading day, billions of Canadian dollars trade hands in the foreign exchange markets. Suppose currency traders believed Canada was going to experience more rapid inflation in the future than Japan. If currency speculators believe that the value of the dollar will soon be falling because of the anticipated rise in the Canadian inflation rate, those traders that are holding dollars will convert them to yen. This leads to an increase in the demand for yen—the yen appreciates and the dollar depreciates relative to the yen, *ceteris paribus*. In short, if speculators believe that the price of a country's currency is going to rise, they will buy more of that currency, pushing up the price and causing the country's currency to appreciate.

SECTION CHECK

■ Any force that shifts either the demand or supply curves for a foreign currency will shift the equilibrium in the foreign exchange market and lead to a new exchange rate. Changes in tastes, tariffs, income levels, relative interest rates, relative inflation rates, or speculation will cause the demand for and supply of a currency to shift.

Flexible Exchange Rates

■ How are exchange rates determined today?

■ What are the advantages of a flexible exchange rate system?

■ What are the disadvantages of a flexible exchange rate system?

HOW ARE EXCHANGE RATES DETERMINED TODAY?

Since 1973, the world has essentially operated on a system of flexible exchange rates. With flexible exchange rates, currency prices are allowed to fluctuate with changes in supply and demand, without governments stepping in to prevent those changes. Prior to 1973, governments operated under what was called the *Bretton Woods fixed exchange rate system*, in which they would maintain a stable exchange rate by buying or selling currencies or reserves to bring demand and supply for their currencies together at the fixed exchange rate. The present system of flexible exchange rates evolved out of the Bretton Woods fixed-rate system and occurred by accident, not design. Governments were unable to agree on an alternative fixed-rate approach when the Bretton Woods system collapsed, so nations simply let market forces determine currency values.

Government Intervention in the Exchange Rate System

To be sure, governments sensitive to sharp changes in the exchange value of their currencies do still intervene from time to time to prop up their currency's exchange rate if it is considered to be too low or falling too rapidly, or to depress its exchange rate if it is considered to be too high or rising too rapidly. However, present-day fluctuations in exchange rates are not determined solely by market forces. Economists sometimes say that the current exchange rate system is a **dirty float system,** meaning that fluctuations in currency values are partly determined by market forces and partly influenced by government intervention. Over the years, however, such governmental support attempts have been insufficient to dramatically alter exchange rates for long, and currency exchange rates have changed dramatically.

When exchange rates change, they affect not only the currency market but the product markets as well. For example, if Canadian consumers were to receive fewer and fewer British pounds and Japanese yen per Canadian dollar, the effect would be an increasing price for foreign imports, *ceteris paribus*. It would now take a greater number of dollars to buy a given number of yen or pounds, which Canadian consumers use to purchase those foreign products. It would, however, lower the cost of Canadian exports to foreigners. If, however, the dollar increased in value relative to other currencies, then the relative price of foreign goods would decrease, *ceteris paribus*. But foreigners would find that Canadian goods were more expensive in terms of their own currency prices, and, as a result, would import fewer Canadian products.

dirty float system
a description of the exchange rate system that means that fluctuations in currency values are partly determined by market forces and partly influenced by government intervention

The exchange rate is the rate at which one country's currency can be traded for another country's currency. Under a flexible-rate system, the government allows the forces of supply and demand to determine the exchange rate. Changes in exchange rates occur daily or even hourly.

pablographix/iStock/Thinkstock

WHAT ARE THE ADVANTAGES OF A FLEXIBLE EXCHANGE RATE SYSTEM?

As mentioned earlier, the present system of flexible exchange rates was not planned. Indeed, most central bankers thought that a system where rates were not fixed would lead to chaos. What in fact has happened? Since the advent of flexible exchange rates, world trade has not only continued but expanded. Over a one-year period, the world economy adjusted to the shock of a fourfold increase in the price of its most important internationally traded commodity, oil. Although the OPEC oil cartel's price increase certainly had adverse economic effects, it did so without paralyzing the economy of any one nation.

The most important advantage of the flexible-rate system is that the recurrent crises that led to speculative rampages and major currency revaluations under the fixed Bretton Woods system have significantly diminished. Under the fixed-rate system, price changes in currencies came infrequently, but when they came, they were large: 20 percent or 30 percent changes overnight were fairly common. Today, price changes occur daily or even hourly, but each change is much smaller, with major changes in exchange rates typically occurring only over periods of months or years.

Fixed Exchange Rates Can Result in Currency Shortages

Perhaps the most significant problem with a fixed-rate system is that it can result in currency shortages, just as domestic price and wage controls lead to shortages. Suppose we had a fixed-rate system with the price of one euro set at $1, as shown in Exhibit 1. In this example, the original quantity of euros demanded and supplied is indicated by curves D_0 and S, so $1 is the equilibrium price. That is, at a price of $1, the quantity of euros demanded (by Canadian importers of European products and others wanting euros) equals the quantity supplied (by European importers of Canadian products and others).

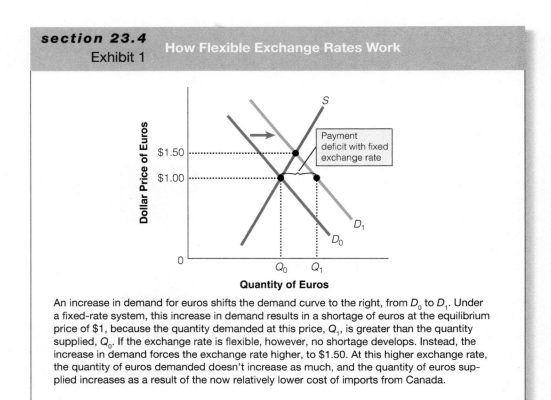

section 23.4
Exhibit 1   **How Flexible Exchange Rates Work**

An increase in demand for euros shifts the demand curve to the right, from D_0 to D_1. Under a fixed-rate system, this increase in demand results in a shortage of euros at the equilibrium price of $1, because the quantity demanded at this price, Q_1, is greater than the quantity supplied, Q_0. If the exchange rate is flexible, however, no shortage develops. Instead, the increase in demand forces the exchange rate higher, to $1.50. At this higher exchange rate, the quantity of euros demanded doesn't increase as much, and the quantity of euros supplied increases as a result of the now relatively lower cost of imports from Canada.

Suppose that some event happens to increase Canadian demand for Dutch goods. For this example, let us assume that Royal Dutch Shell discovers new oil reserves in the North Sea and thus has a new product to export. As Canadian consumers begin to demand Royal Dutch Shell oil, the demand for euros increases. That is, at any given dollar price of euros, Canadian consumers want more euros, shifting the demand curve to the right, to D_1. Under a fixed exchange rate system, the dollar price of euros must remain at \$1, where the quantity of euros demanded, Q_1, now exceeds the quantity supplied, Q_0. The result is a shortage of euros—a shortage that must be corrected in some way. As a solution to the shortage, Canada may borrow euros from the Netherlands, or perhaps ship the Netherlands some of its reserves of gold. The ability to continually make up the shortage (deficit) in this manner, however, is limited, particularly if the deficit persists for a substantial period of time.

Flexible Rates Solve the Currency Shortage Problem

Under flexible exchange rates, a change in the supply or demand for euros does not pose a problem. Because rates are allowed to change, the rising Canadian demand for European goods (and thus for euros) would lead to a new equilibrium price for euros, say, at \$1.50. At this higher price, European goods are more costly to Canadian buyers. Some of the increase in demand for European imports, then, is offset by a decrease in quantity demanded resulting from higher import prices. Similarly, the change in the exchange rate will make Canadian goods cheaper to Europeans, thus increasing Canadian exports and, with that, the quantity of euros supplied. For example, a \$40 software program that cost Europeans 40 euros when the exchange rate was \$1 per euro costs less than 27 euros when the exchange rate increases to \$1.50 per euro (\$40 divided by \$1.50).

Flexible Rates Affect Macroeconomic Policies

With flexible exchange rates, the imbalance between debits and credits arising from shifts in currency demand and/or supply is accommodated by changes in currency prices, rather than through the special financial borrowings or reserve movements necessary with fixed rates. In a pure flexible exchange rate system, deficits and surpluses in the balance of payments tend to disappear automatically. The market mechanism itself is able to address world trade imbalances, dispensing with the need for bureaucrats attempting to achieve some administratively determined price. Moreover, the need to use restrictive monetary and/or fiscal policy to end such an imbalance while maintaining a fixed exchange rate is alleviated. Nations are thus able to feel less constraint in carrying out internal macroeconomic policies under flexible exchange rates. For these reasons, many economists welcomed the collapse of the Bretton Woods system and the failure to arrive at a new system of fixed or quasi-fixed exchange rates.

WHAT ARE THE DISADVANTAGES OF A FLEXIBLE EXCHANGE RATE SYSTEM?

Despite the fact that world trade has grown and dealing with balance-of-payments problems has become less difficult, flexible exchange rates have not been universally endorsed by everyone. Several disadvantages of this system have been cited.

Flexible Rates and World Trade

Traditionally, the major objection to flexible rates was that they introduce considerable uncertainty into international trade. For example, if you order some perfume from France with a commitment to pay 1000 euros in three months, you are not certain what the dollar price of euros, and therefore of the perfume, will be three months from now because the exchange rate is constantly fluctuating. Because people prefer certainty to uncertainty and are generally risk-averse, this uncertainty raises the costs of international transactions. As a result, flexible exchange rates can reduce the volume of trade, thus reducing the potential gains from international specialization.

Proponents of flexible rates have three answers to this argument. First, the empirical evidence shows that international trade has, in fact, grown in volume faster since the introduction of flexible rates. The exchange rate risk of trade has not had any major adverse effect. Second, it is possible to, in effect, buy insurance against the proposed adverse effect of currency fluctuations. Rather than buying currencies for immediate use in what is called the *spot market* for foreign currencies, one can contract today to buy foreign currencies in the future at a set exchange rate in the forward or future market. By using this market, a perfume importer can buy euros now for delivery to her in three months; in doing so, she can be certain of the dollar price she is paying for the perfume. Since floating exchange rates began, booming futures markets in foreign currencies have opened in Toronto, Chicago, New York, and other foreign financial centres. The third argument is that the alleged certainty of currency prices under the old Bretton Woods system was fictitious because the possibility existed that nations might, at their whim, drastically revalue their currencies to deal with their own fundamental balance-of-payments problems. Proponents of flexible rates, then, argue that they are therefore no less disruptive to trade than fixed rates.

Flexible Rates and Inflation

A second, more valid criticism of flexible exchange rates is that they can contribute to inflationary pressures. Under fixed rates, domestic monetary and fiscal authorities have an incentive to constrain their domestic prices because lower domestic prices increase the attractiveness of exported goods. This discipline is not present to the same extent with flexible rates. The consequence of a sharp monetary or fiscal expansion under flexible rates would be a decline in the value of one's currency relative to those of other countries.

Advocates of flexible rates would argue that inflation need not occur under flexible rates. Flexible rates do not cause inflation; rather, it is caused by the expansionary macroeconomic policies of governments and central banks. Actually, flexible rates give government decision makers greater freedom of action than do fixed rates; whether decision makers act responsibly is determined not by exchange rates but by domestic policies.

SECTION CHECK

- Today, rates are free to fluctuate based on market transactions, but governments occasionally intervene to increase or depress the price of their currencies.
- Changes in exchange rates occur more often under a flexible-rate system, but the changes are much smaller than the large overnight revaluations of currencies that occurred under the fixed-rate system. Under a fixed-rate system, the supply and demand for currencies shift, but currency prices are not allowed to shift to the new equilibrium leading to surpluses and shortages of currencies.
- The main arguments presented against flexible exchange rates are that international trade levels will be diminished due to uncertainty of future currency prices and that the flexible rates would lead to inflation. Proponents of flexible exchange rates have strong counterarguments to those views.

Section 23.1

1. Indicate whether each of the following represents a credit or debit in the Canadian current account.

   a. A Canadian imports a BMW from Germany.

   b. A Japanese company purchases software from a Canadian company.

   c. Canada gives $100 million in financial aid to Afghanistan.

   d. A Canadian company sells lumber to the United Kingdom.

2. Indicate whether each of the following represents a credit or debit in the Canadian capital account.

   a. A French bank purchases $100 000 worth of Canadian government bonds.

   b. BlackBerry purchases U.S. telecommunications company.

   c. A Canadian resident buys company shares in the Japanese stock market.

   d. A Japanese company purchases a shopping mall in Vancouver.

3. How is each of the following events likely to affect the Canadian merchandise trade balance?

   a. The European price level increases relative to the Canadian price level.

   b. The Canadian dollar appreciates in value relative to the currencies of its trading partners.

   c. The Canadian government offers subsidies to firms that export goods.

   d. The Canadian government imposes tariffs on imported goods.

   e. The United States experiences a severe recession.

4. How is each of the following classified, as a debit or as a credit, in the Canadian balance-of-payments accounts?

	Credit	**Debit**
a. Canadians buy autos from Japan.	_____	_____
b. Canadian tourists travel to Japan.	_____	_____
c. Japanese consumers buy rice grown in Canada.	_____	_____
d. Canada gives foreign aid to Rwanda.	_____	_____
e. BlackBerry, a Canadian company, earns profits in France.	_____	_____
f. Royal Dutch Shell earns profits from its Canadian operations.	_____	_____
g. BlackBerry builds a new plant in Vietnam.	_____	_____
h. Japanese investors purchase Canadian government bonds.	_____	_____

5. Following is a list of balance of payments figures for the economy of Bravo. All figures are in millions. Using this data, construct Bravo's balance of payments.

Exports of goods	$50
Merchandise trade balance	10
Net acquisition of financial assets	−45
Imports of services	20
Net primary income	5
Exports of services	10
Financial account balance	15
Net secondary income	−15

6. Following is a list of balance of payments figures for the economy of Delta. All figures are in millions. Using this data, construct Delta's balance of payments.

Exports of services	$320
Imports of goods	470
Net secondary income	30
Net incurrence of liabilities	160
Imports of services	410
Exports of goods	530
Statistical discrepancy	10
Current account balance	60

Section 23.2

7. Assume that a product sells for $100 in Canada.
   a. If the exchange rate between British pounds and Canadian dollars is $2 per pound, what would be the price of the product in the United Kingdom?
   b. If the exchange rate between Mexican pesos and Canadian dollars is 8 pesos per dollar, what would be the price of the product in Mexico?
   c. In which direction would the price of the $100 Canadian product change in a foreign country if Canadians' tastes for foreign products increased?
   d. In which direction would the price of the $100 Canadian product change in a foreign country if incomes in the foreign country fell?
   e. In which direction would the price of the $100 Canadian product change in a foreign country if interest rates in Canada fell relative to interest rates in other countries?

8. Why is a strong Canadian dollar a mixed blessing?

9. When a Canadian dollar buys relatively more British pounds, why does the cost of imports from England fall in Canada?

10. When a Canadian dollar buys relatively fewer yen, why does the cost of Canadian exports fall in Japan?

11. As euros become cheaper relative to the Canadian dollar, why does the quantity of euros demanded by Canadians increase? Why doesn't the demand for euros increase as a result?

Section 23.3

12. How is each of the following events likely to affect the value of the Canadian dollar relative to the euro?

    a. Interest rates in the European Union increase relative to those in Canada.

    b. The European Union price level rises relative to the Canadian price level.

    c. The Bank of Canada intervenes by buying Canadian dollars on the foreign exchange market.

    d. The price level in Canada rises relative to the price level in Europe.

13. What happens to the supply curve for Canadian dollars in the foreign exchange market under the following conditions?

    a. Canadians want to buy more Japanese consumer electronics.

    b. A Canadian mutual fund wants to buy shares of Microsoft.

14. How would each of the following affect the supply of euros, the demand for euros, and the dollar price of euros?

Change	Supply of Euros	Demand for Euros	Dollar Price of Euros
Reduced Canadian tastes for European goods			
Increased incomes in Canada			
Increased Canadian interest rates			
Decreased inflation in Europe			
Reduced Canadian tariffs on imports			
Increased European tastes for Canadian goods			

15. How would each of the following events impact the foreign exchange market?

    a. Canadian travel to Europe increases.

    b. Japanese investors purchase Canadian company shares.

    c. Canadian interest rates abruptly increase relative to world interest rates.

    d. Other countries become less politically and economically stable relative to Canada.

Section 23.4

16. What happens to the supply curve for dollars in the currency market under the following conditions?

    a. Canadians want to buy more Japanese consumer electronics.

    b. Canada wants to prop up the value of the yen.

17. If the demand for a domestic currency decreases in a country using a fixed exchange rate system, what must the central bank do to keep the currency value steady?

18. What is the uncertainty argument against flexible exchange rates? What evidence do proponents of flexible exchange rates cite in response?

Answers to Odd-Numbered Problems

CHAPTER 1

1. The definition of *economics* must recognize the central parts of the economist's point of view: Resources are scarce, scarcity forces us to make choices, and the cost of any choice is the cost of the lost opportunity with the highest value.

3. a. Both normative and positive statements. This first statement (positive statement) expresses a fact or a testable theory that a higher income tax rate would generate increased tax revenues. The second statement (normative statement) expresses an opinion regarding how any additional tax revenues should be used.

    b. Normative statements. Both statements are expressions of opinion, the first regarding the relative value of studying physics as opposed to sociology, and the second regarding the value of studying either physics or sociology.

    c. Positive statements. Both statements are expressions of facts or testable theories regarding the relationship between the price of wheat and how much wheat will be purchased and produced.

    d. Both normative and positive statements. The first statement (positive statement) expresses a fact or testable theory regarding the relationship between the price of butter and how much will be purchased. The second statement (normative statement) is an expression of opinion about the social value of buying butter.

    e. Positive statements. Both statements are expressions of fact or testable theory regarding demographic change.

5. The statement illustrates the fallacy of composition—it assumes that what is true for one person must be true for all others.

7. Being poor means that you have access to few resources, which limits the goods and services you consume. Scarcity means you don't have enough resources to do everything you want to do, so you have to make choices. Everyone experiences scarcity, because we can always think of more things that we want than we can produce with our resources.

9. Scarce goods are those that people pay for in either time or money or, in other words, have an opportunity cost. Garbage and dirty air in the city are not scarce goods since we either pay to get rid of them or pay with the consequences of their presence. Similarly, salt water is not a scarce good—although it is in limited supply, there is no price you need to pay to obtain some (assuming you are on the shore). Clothes, clean air, and public libraries are scarce goods because their production requires the use of scarce resources that could be used for the production of other goods.

11. The opportunity cost of this decision valued in dollars would be $33.50 ($30 forgone pay for not tutoring for two hours + $3.50 for the cup of coffee).

13. a. The opportunity cost of going to college or university includes the income you could have earned by working instead; it also includes the money spent on school-specific expenses like tuition and textbooks. Room and board and transportation would not necessarily be included since you would need those services even if you were not going to school.

    b. The opportunity cost of missing a lecture includes the potential damage to one's grade in a course from not being present while important subject material is covered, as well as the knowledge's forgone value in the "real world." The magnitude of the opportunity cost depends partly on how much essential information the instructor provides during the missed class session.

    c. The opportunity cost of spending $100 today is the $105 you could have spent next year. If you are withdrawing the money just to have cash in your pocket, the opportunity cost of holding money is the 5 percent interest you could have been earning.

    d. The opportunity cost of snowboarding the weekend before final examinations is the expected reduction in grades that will result, in addition to the cost of a lift ticket.

15. a. $57; $88

    b. 43; 44; He would produce as long as the price (marginal benefit) exceeded the marginal cost.

17. Positive incentives are those that either increase benefits or reduce costs and thus tend to increase the level of an activity. Both of the following are examples of positive incentives: (b) a trip to Hawaii paid for by your parents or significant other for earning an "A" in your economics course; (d) a subsidy for installing solar panels on your house. Negative incentives either reduce benefits or increase costs, and thus tend to decrease the level of the related activity or behaviour. Both of the following are examples of negative incentives: (a) a fine for not cleaning up after your dog defecates in the park; (c) a higher tax on cigarettes and alcohol.

19. The Chinese government is attempting to promote population control. As the world's most populated country (2013), China has historically struggled with controlling population growth in it attempts to manage economic growth and national standards of living. The sanctions and penalties associated with not following the one-child policy would be considered negative incentives designed to discourage couples from having more than one child. The rewards and honours associated with following the policy would be considered positive incentives designed to promote adherence to the policy.

21. The opportunity cost of growing soybeans is the lost value because Fran can't grow corn worth $1800 (3000 kg × $0.60). The opportunity cost of growing corn on her land is the lost opportunity to grow and sell soybeans, which equals $2250 (1500 kg × $1.50). Fran should specialize in soybeans, which is the crop with the lowest opportunity cost. For each hectare of corn Fran converts to soybeans, she will gain $450.

23. If the country or region with the lower opportunity cost produces the good, the opportunity cost of consuming that good is minimized. Trade allows people, countries, and regions to specialize in producing those goods in which they have the lowest opportunity cost, so reducing trade restrictions will encourage specialization, thereby increasing efficiency.

25. Hollywood will probably make more movies like *Titanic* because of consumer sovereignty. Consumers, "voting" with their dollars, have shown they want movies like *Titanic*. Since movie studios are in the business to make money, not simply movies, they will produce what the consumers want, not what the critics like.

APPENDIX: WORKING WITH GRAPHS

1. A $(-2, 2)$
    B $(2, 1)$
    C $(3, 2)$
    D $(-1, -2)$
    E $(2, -1)$
    F $(-2, -1)$

3. a. Semester 1
    b. Semesters 3 and 4
    c. Semester 2
    d. Total number of boys: 372; total number of girls: 366

5. a. 2
    b. -3
    c. -0.5
    d. Undefined
    e. 0

CHAPTER 2

1. a.

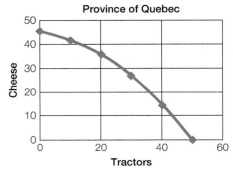

b. 1 side of beef; 6 kegs of beer; 9 kegs of beer

c. 35 kegs of beer

d. No; that combination is inside the production possibilities curve, which means more of one good could be produced without giving up any production of the other good.

e. No; that combination is beyond the production possibilities curve and therefore unattainable.

3. This is the law of increasing opportunity cost in action. As you planted more and more of your land in wheat, you would move into some of the less fertile land and, consequently, wheat yields on this additional land would fall. If you were to go so far as to plant the entire island with wheat, you would find that some of the less fertile land would yield virtually no extra wheat. It would, however, have been great for cattle grazing—a large loss. So the opportunity cost of using that marginal land for wheat rather than cattle grazing would be very high.

5. a.

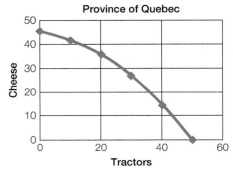

b.

	A	B	C	D	E	F
	−3	−6	−9	−12	−15	
Cheese	45	42	36	27	15	0
Tractors	0	10	20	30	40	50
	+10	+10	+10	+10	+10	

As indicated in the table above, if the province of Quebec is to continually increase tractor production by 10 tractors it must give up increasing amounts of cheese—thus illustrating the law of increasing opportunity cost.

c.

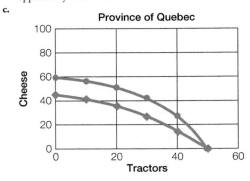

d. The alteration in production from production alternative B to alternative E represents an increase in capital goods and a decrease in consumption goods. As a result, the prediction would be that the province of Quebec would experience greater economic growth in the future.

7. Investment in capital goods increases the future productive potential of an economy. Economy A will grow more rapidly, shifting the production possibilities curve outward to a greater extent over time, if it invests in a higher proportion of capital goods than does Economy B.

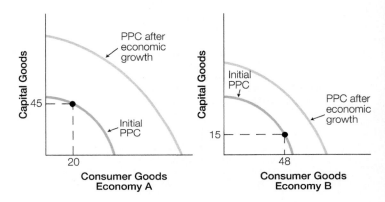

9. The politician would be able to keep her promise if the economy was operating inside the production possibilities curve. It would then be possible to have more of both schools and prisons by better utilizing available resources. Alternatively, an advance in technology or an increase in available resources (perhaps due to immigration) would also make it possible to have more of both goods by shifting the production possibilities curve in an outward direction.

11. The definition of a market focuses on the process of exchange not on the physical location where the exchange takes place. Therefore, even though online buyers and sellers are never actually in the same place, their behaviour still constitutes a market transaction due to the fact that goods and services are being exchanged.

13. Options (a), (b), and (c) would cause increases in the relative value and price of potatoes. In option (d), the reduction in the prices of potato substitutes would make alternatives more attractive and reduce the relative value and price of potatoes.

15.

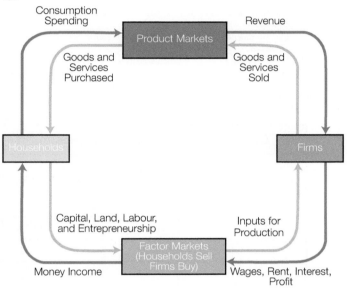

17. a. Claire getting paid $800 as a rental agent and Markus getting paid $70 to teach a fitness class both occur in the factor market.
   b. Clair spending $40 a week on her gym membership and Markus spending $200 on a rental car both occur in the product market.

CHAPTER 3

1. a.

P	Q_D
$5	4
4	8
3	12
2	16
1	20

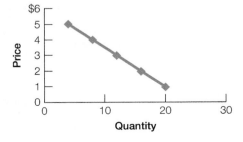

b.

P	Q_D
$5	6
4	12
3	18
2	24
1	30

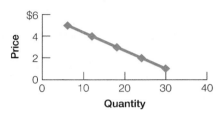

c.

P	Q_D
$5	5
4	10
3	15
2	20
1	25

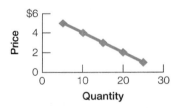

3.

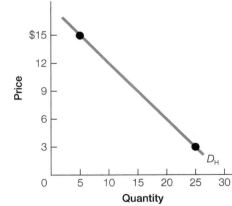

5. a. Demand decreases (Determinant: Price of substitute falls)
   b. Demand decreases (Determinant: Price of complement rises)
   c. Demand increases (Determinant variable: Taste increase)
   d. Demand increases (Determinant: Number of consumers increases)
7. a. Point B represents an increase in quantity demanded.
   b. Point E represents an increase in demand.
   c. Point F represents a decrease in demand.
   d. Point C represents a decrease in quantity demanded.

9. a. Hamburger and ketchup are complements. An increase in the price of hamburger will decrease the demand for ketchup.

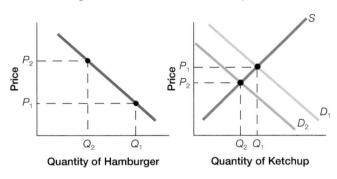

Quantity of Hamburger   **Quantity of Ketchup**

b. Coca-Cola and Pepsi are substitutes. An increase in the price of Coca-Cola will increase the demand for Pepsi.

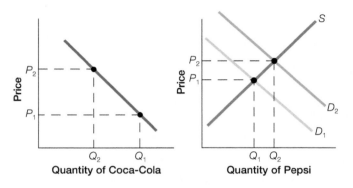

Quantity of Coca-Cola   **Quantity of Pepsi**

c. iPhones and iPhone cases are complements. An increase in the price of an iPhone will decrease the demand for iPhone cases.

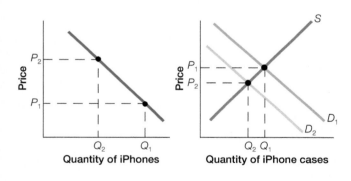

Quantity of iPhones   **Quantity of iPhone cases**

d. Golf clubs and golf balls are complements. An increase in the price of golf clubs will decrease the demand for golf balls, *ceteris paribus*.

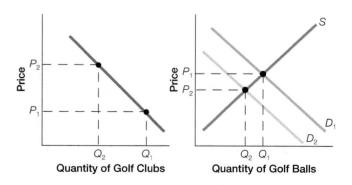

Quantity of Golf Clubs   **Quantity of Golf Balls**

e. Assuming that skateboards and razor scooters are substitutes, an increase in the price of skateboards will increase the demand for razor scooters.

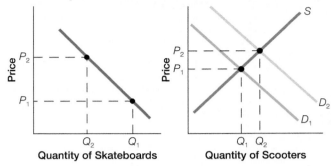

Quantity of Skateboards   **Quantity of Scooters**

11. a. The shift from D_0 to D_1 is called an *increase in demand*.
   b. The movement from B to A is called a *decrease in the quantity demanded*.
   c. The movement from A to B is called an *increase in the quantity demanded*.
   d. The shift from D_1 to D_0 is called a *decrease in demand*.

13. The market price of wheat would have to rise for Felix to have the incentive to produce from the second field. Because costs are higher in the second field, Felix must receive a higher price to compensate him for his higher costs.

15.

Quantity Supplied (barrels per month)				
Price ($ per barrel)	Rolling Rock	Armadillo Oil	Pecos Petroleum	Market
5	10 000	8 000	2 000	20 000
10	15 000	10 000	5 000	30 000
15	20 000	12 000	8 000	40 000
20	25 000	14 000	11 000	50 000
25	30 000	16 000	14 000	60 000

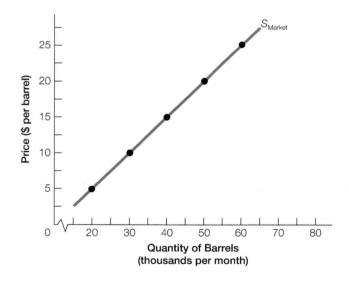

17. a. The shift from S_0 to S_1 is called an *increase in supply*.
   b. The movement from A to B is called an *increase in the quantity supplied*.
   c. The movement from B to A is called a *decrease in the quantity supplied*.
   d. The shift from S_1 to S_0 is called a *decrease in supply*.

19. **a.** It would increase the quantity of corn supplied, but not the supply of corn. This is because a change in the price of corn causes the market for corn to experience a movement in supply (as opposed to a shift in supply).
    b. It would decrease the supply of wheat, which is a substitute in production to corn. This is because a change in the price of corn—a substitute in production with wheat—causes the market for wheat to experience a shift in supply (as opposed to a movement).
21. **a.** Supply decreases (Determinant: Bad weather)
    b. Supply decreases (Determinant: Input prices rise)
    c. Supply increases (Determinant: Subsidies)
    d. Supply increases (Determinant: Technology advance)
    e. Supply decreases today (Determinant: Expected future price increases)
23. **a.** Point B represents an increase in quantity supplied
    b. Point C represents an increase in supply
    c. Point D represents a decrease in quantity supplied
    d. Point E represents a decrease in supply
25. **a.** The supply of oil decreases, reducing the quantity exchanged and pushing up the price of oil.
    b. The supply of oil increases, increasing the quantity exchanged and decreasing the market price of oil.
    c. The demand for heating oil increases. The price and quantity of oil exchanged will increase as a result.
    d. The market supply of oil increases. The quantity exchanged will increase and the equilibrium price of oil will decrease as a result.
    e. Fewer people will drive gasoline-powered automobiles, decreasing the demand for oil. The equilibrium price and quantity of oil exchanged will decrease as a result.

CHAPTER 4

1. When a price is above the equilibrium price, the quantity of a good or service willingly supplied by sellers exceeds the quantity willingly demanded by buyers. If sellers want to sell a greater quantity of goods or services, it is necessary to reduce the price (or otherwise improve the terms of sale, such as with free delivery or lower interest rate financing) in order to induce buyers to make additional purchases. Market forces thus exert a downward pressure on price in the direction of equilibrium price. A surplus is eliminated once price falls to the equilibrium price.

   If a price is below the equilibrium price, then the quantity of a good or service willingly demanded by buyers exceeds the quantity willingly supplied by sellers. In order to induce sellers to provide a greater quantity to the marketplace, it is necessary for buyers to offer a higher price for the good or service. Market forces exert upward pressure on price in the direction of the equilibrium. A shortage is eliminated once price increases to the equilibrium price.
3. **a.** Equilibrium price = $400; Equilibrium quantity = 6.3 million units
   b. A shortage exists at any price below $400; market forces would raise the price of a tablet computer up to $400 to self-regulate a solution to this shortage situation.
   c. A surplus exists at any price above $400; market forces would lower the price of a tablet computer down to $400 to self-regulate a solution to this surplus situation.
5. **a.**

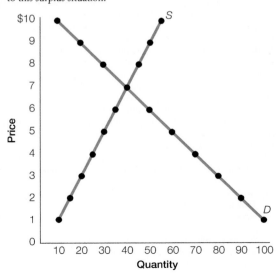

b. $7; 40 units traded.
c. Surplus. At $9, above the equilibrium price, there will be a surplus of 30 units of Z [the quantity supplied at $9 (50) minus the quantity demanded at $9 (20)].
d. Shortage. At $3, below the equilibrium price, there will be a shortage of 60 units of Z [the quantity demanded at $3 (80) minus the quantity supplied at $3 (20)].
e. $8, with 45 units traded (at the new supply and demand intersection).
f. $6, with 50 units traded (at the new supply and demand intersection).
7. The deputy parks commissioner may be correct. Fewer young people may want to be lifeguards now than in the past. An economist, however, knows that shortages are caused by prices that are below equilibrium. Since the number of lifeguards demanded in Vancouver exceeds the supply, it would seem that wages are too low. An economist would advise the city to raise lifeguards' wages in order to eliminate the shortage.

9. **a.**

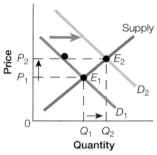

Hamburger Market

b.

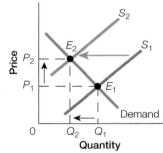

Toronto Cab Trips

c.

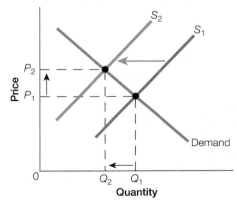

Supply of Strawberry Crops

11. Even though the tuition "price" is the same in both cases, student demand for 10 A.M. classes is typically greater than for 8 A.M. classes. Students often prefer to sleep in later than punctual attendance at an 8 A.M. class would allow. A shortage of 10 A.M. class spaces relative to demand is the likely result. There may be a surplus of class spaces in 8 A.M. courses if the demand for early morning classes is sufficiently low.

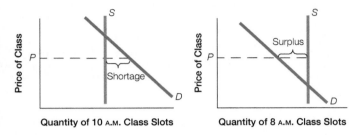

Quantity of 10 A.M. Class Slots   Quantity of 8 A.M. Class Slots

13. Fresh fruit is less expensive in the summer because the supply curve for fresh fruit shifts rightward in the summer, thus lowering equilibrium price and increasing equilibrium quantity.
    - This event is supply-side, since it deals with how growers are making product available for sale.
    - The event is a shift since the price of fresh fruit is not independently changing in the question.
    - The event is expansionary, since Canadian producers are seen as being able to make more fresh fruit available in the summer, when it is in season, as opposed to in the winter.

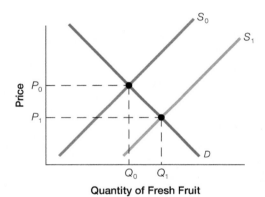

Quantity of Fresh Fruit

15.

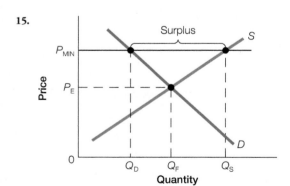

Quantity

    a. If the price floor is raised, the quantity supplied increases, the quantity demanded decreases, and the surplus increases; if the price floor is lowered, the quantity supplied decreases, the quantity demanded increases, and the surplus decreases.
    b. The quantity supplied does not change, the quantity demanded increases, and the surplus decreases.
    c. The quantity supplied increases, the quantity demanded does not change, and the surplus increases.

17. A price ceiling set above the equilibrium rental price would have no impact on a rental market. (A price ceiling is a maximum allowed price, not a mandated market price.) If a price ceiling is set below the equilibrium rental price, a shortage will result.

19. The $2 price ceiling will likely result in a shortage of movie tickets. At the new, lower price, quantity demanded will rise. People will want more tickets at $2 than they did at $10. Assuming that the equilibrium price is somewhere around $10, the ceiling will cause the quantity of tickets sold to decline. Some theatres may reduce their hours of operation and some may even go out of business. Some theatres may stop showing first-run movies. Theatre owners will certainly suffer. While some movie-goers may benefit from lower prices, they may also have to stand in long lines to buy tickets. They may also see a reduction in the quality of movies offered by theatres.

CHAPTER 5

1. a. Chevrolets (more substitutes). Chevrolets have more substitutes than cars in general since any other brand is a good substitute.
   b. Housing (greater share of budget). The price elasticity of demand for housing will be greater than for salt because of the large role housing plays in the household budget.
   c. Natural gas over the course of a year. Natural gas has a more price-elastic demand in the long run since this gives consumers time to adjust their habits and complementary capital to any change. Also, the price elasticity of demand for a product will increase as more and better substitutes are available.

3. a. Demand for Paul Mitchell Shampoo is likely more elastic than is demand for shampoo in general. There are more substitutes available for a particular brand of shampoo than there are substitutes for shampoo generally.
   b. The urgent need to travel quickly and on short notice to visit an ill family member makes demand relatively more inelastic than that for vacation air travel.
   c. Elasticity of demand is likely much greater for apartment rentals. The rent on an apartment comprises a much larger portion of one's annual budget than do paper clips.
   d. More substitutes are generally available for a generic headache remedy than for prescription heart medication. Therefore, the elasticity of demand for generic headache remedy will be greater than that for heart medicine.

5. The average of prices and quantities demanded does not change when the direction of movement is reversed, so the percentage changes in price and quantity demanded do not change. However, when the initial price and quantity demanded are used for calculating the percentage changes, a movement down along a demand curve starts with a higher initial price and lower initial quantity demanded than the same movement up along it, changing the percentage changes.

7. If the price increases by 10 percent, quantity demanded will fall by 15 percent when the elasticity of demand for hamburgers equals -1.5. Hamburger sales will decline by approximately 6000 (15 percent of 40 000). If the price of hamburgers decreases by 5 percent, then quantity demanded will increase by approximately 3000 hamburgers (7.5 percent of 40 000).

9. If the price rises from $3 to $5, the change in price is $2. Using the midpoint technique, the midpoint price ($4) is used to calculate the percentage change in price. It will be (2/4 × 100 percent) = 50 percent. Similarly, the percentage change in quantity is based on the change in quantity (−600) divided by the midpoint (1200) or −50 percent. The elasticity of demand is 1.

11. If the elasticity of demand is estimated to equal -1.6, then demand is relatively elastic. A decrease in ticket prices would increase the quantity of tickets demanded sufficiently to increase the overall revenue from ticket sales. If the elasticity of demand is estimated to equal -0.4, then demand is relatively inelastic. In this case, an increase in ticket prices would boost the revenue from ticket sales.

13. The demand is relatively elastic at prices above the midpoint of a straight-line demand curve and relatively inelastic below the midpoint, so it is relatively elastic for a price change from $12 to $10 but relatively inelastic for a price change from $6 to $4.

15. a. Total revenue increases from $200 ($4 × 50) to $300 ($3 × 100).
    b. Since total revenue increased with a decrease in price, demand must be relatively elastic.
    c. Since total revenue goes down from $300 ($2 × 150) to $200 ($1 × 200) as price falls from $2 to $1, demand must be relatively inelastic in that range of the demand curve.

17. 20 percent ÷ −10 percent = −2

19. If the income elasticity of demand for a good is positive, it is a normal good. If it is negative, it is an inferior good.

21. **a.** The income elasticity of demand equals (Percentage change in the quantity demanded)/(Percentage change in incomes). The percentage change in quantity demanded over the period equals (19.5 − 20)/ ([20 + 19.5]/2) = −0.025. The income elasticity of demand for rail travel equals (−0.025)/(0.13) = −0.19.

b. The cross-price elasticity equals (Percentage change in quantity demanded)/(Percentage change in the price of air travel). The percentage change in quantity demanded equals (19 − 17.5)/([19 + 17.5]/2) = 0.082. The cross-price elasticity of demand for rail travel equals (0.082)/(0.075) = 1.09.

c. The positive cross-price elasticity shows us that air travel and rail travel are substitute goods. The negative income elasticity shows us that rail travel is an inferior good.

23. **a.** The elasticity of supply would equal 1.

b. The elasticity of supply would equal 0.5.

c. The elasticity of supply would equal 2.

25. If the price of tablet computers increases by 5 percent, quantity supplied will increase by 3 percent when price elasticity of supply is 0.6. Production volumes will increase by 1.5 million units (3 percent of 50 million). If the price of tablet computers decreases by 8 percent, then quantity supplied will decrease by 4.8 percent, or 2.4 million units (4.8 percent of 50 million).

27. Relative inelasticities of supply and demand determine the incidence of a tax. If the difference between the short-run and long-run elasticity was greater on one side of the market than the other, the long-run incidence could be dramatically different from the short-run incidence. For example, if supply was very inelastic in the short run but very elastic in the long run, suppliers could bear most of the short-run burden of a tax, but very little of the burden in the long run. Since the greater long-run elasticities of supply and demand lead to larger reductions in the quantity exchanged, the revenue from a given tax would tend to decrease over time, other things being equal.

CHAPTER 6

1. We know that the person's marginal utility for the next bite is negative—that the person's total utility will be reduced if she or he eats one more bite. However, while we know that the person's marginal utility is negative, that tells us nothing beyond the fact that each previous bite had a positive marginal utility—that it raised the person's total utility.

3. The ski resort knows that the utility you derive from an additional 4 hours of skiing will be less than the first 4 hours of skiing (law of diminishing marginal utility). As a result, in order to make the second 4 hours of skiing economically justifiable, the resort must sell the second 4 hours of skiing at a lower price ($23 as opposed to $10).

5. The highlighted numbers in the table below are the ones that were missing.

Number of Smartphone Apps.	Total Utility	Marginal Utility
0	0	—
1	12	12
2	22	10
3	29	7
4	33	4
5	33	0
6	31	−2

7. The marginal utility per dollar derived from soft drinks equals 6 utils per dollar, while the marginal utility derived from pizza consumption equals 2 utils per dollar (4 utils/$2). Since the satisfaction per dollar derived from the last soft drink consumed exceeds the satisfaction per dollar derived from the last slice of pizza, Brandy should purchase more soft drinks and less pizza. As Brandy consumes more soft drinks, the marginal utility per dollar spent on soft drinks will fall (since marginal utility will diminish). As less pizza is consumed, the marginal utility per dollar spent on pizza will increase (since the marginal utility derived from pizza will increase).

9. In consumer equilibrium, the typical student will purchase 4 cups of coffee (49 utils) and 1 muffin (6 utils), for a total of 55 utils of satisfaction.

Cups of Coffee					Muffins			
Number of Cups	TU	MU	MU/P		Number of Muffins	TU	MU	MU/P
0	0	—	—		0	0	—	—
1	16	16	8		1	6	6	6
2	29	13	6.5		2	10	4	4
3	40	11	5.5		3	11	1	1
4	49	9	4.5		4	11	0	0
5	54	5	2.5		5	9	−2	−2

11. The highlighted numbers in the table below are the ones that were missing.

Hockey Games					Football Games			
Number	TU	MU	MU/P		Number	TU	MU	MU/P
0	0	—	—		0	0	—	—
1	20	20	1.250		1	18	18	1.50
2	36	16	1.000		2	30	12	1.00
3	48	12	0.750		3	36	6	0.50
4	58	10	0.625		4	42	6	0.50
5	66	8	0.500		5	45	3	0.25
6	72	6	0.375		6	45	0	0.00

The sports fan will attend 2 football games (30 utils) and 4 hockey games (58 utils), generating a total of 88 utils of satisfaction.

13. **a.** Steve is willing to pay $4.50 for one bag of potato chips.
   b. Steve is willing to pay $4.00 for a second bag of potato chips.
   c. Steve's consumer surplus is $5.00 when he buys five bags. He gets a $2.00 surplus on the first bag, $1.50 on the second, $1.00 on the third, and $0.50 on the fourth. At $2.50 per bag, he gets no consumer surplus on the fifth bag.
   d. Steve's total willingness to pay for 5 bags is $17.50. He is willing to pay $4.50 for the first bag, $4.00 for the second, $3.50 for the third, $3.00 for the fourth, and $2.50 for the fifth bag.

15. If the demand for apples increased from D_1 to D_2 in the diagram below as a result of a news story that highlighted the health benefits of two apples a day, producer surplus would increase as indicated.

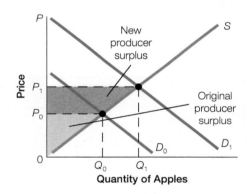

17. **a.** $30; he will produce 3 units.
   b. Producer surplus will increase from $30 to $60; he will now produce 4 units.

CHAPTER 7

1. As urban development continues, placing increasing pressures on key scarce resources such as the Greenbelt, the opportunity cost (forgone alternative) of using the Greenbelt for farming and environmental protection will continue to increase. As the opportunity cost increases, so will the economic cost of using this land for farming and environmental protection.

3. Anglers may not have to pay their relatives to work as crew but that does not mean this strategy has no cost. Employing relatives reduces the anglers' explicit cost because crew salaries are reduced. However, there are still opportunity costs. Implicit costs will increase as long as the relatives have alternative uses of their time. Employing relatives might increase accounting profits but it can decrease economic profits at the same time.

5. **a.**

Labour (workers)	Total Product (visits per hour)	Marginal Product
0	0	—
1	10	10
2	22	12
3	31	9
4	39	8
5	43	4
6	41	−2

   b. Beginning with the third worker.
   c. Beginning with the sixth worker.

7.

Labour (workers)	Total Product (kilograms)	Marginal Product (kilograms)
0	0	—
1	20	20
2	44	24
3	62	18
4	74	12
5	80	6
6	78	−2

   a. Candy's Candies begins to experience diminishing marginal product with the third worker, the first one for which marginal product begins to fall.
   b. Candy's Candies experiences a negative marginal product beginning with the sixth worker.

9. **a.** The marginal product of the seventh worker equals 6 units of output.
   b. The law of diminishing product begins with the fifth worker hired.
   c. A firm would never choose to hire nine workers under these conditions, since the marginal product of the ninth worker is negative.

11. See the table below.

Output	Total Fixed Costs	Total Variable Costs	Total Costs	Average Fixed Costs	Average Variable Costs	Average Total Costs	Marginal Costs
1	$100	$30	$130	$100.00	$30.00	$130.00	$30
2	100	50	150	50.00	25.00	75.00	20
3	100	60	160	33.33	20.00	53.33	10
4	100	64	164	25.00	16.00	41.00	4
5	100	90	190	20.00	18.00	38.00	26
6	100	126	226	16.67	21.00	37.67	36
7	100	168	268	14.29	24.00	38.29	42
8	100	218	318	12.50	27.25	39.75	50

13. Your choice will affect your fixed and variable costs. If you choose to pay the flat fee, your fixed costs for the film will equal $5000 for the week. Your variable costs associated with the leasing of the film would then equal zero. If you choose to pay $2 per customer, then the costs associated with leasing the film will all be variable.

15. Not necessarily. It is marginal cost that is critical. The next barrel of oil might cost $30 to produce because the well may be drying up or the company might have to drill deeper to get additional oil, making it even more costly to retrieve. It is possible that the *marginal cost* of the additional barrels of oil may be greater than the market price and, thus, no longer profitable.

17. The note-taker's wage is a fixed cost, which does not vary with the number of subscriptions sold.

19. a. Average fixed cost (*AFC*)
b. Average variable cost (*AVC*)
c. Average total cost (*ATC*)
d. Marginal cost (*MC*)
e. Where *MC* is less than *AVC*, *AVC* is falling; when *MC* equals *AVC*, *AVC* does not change; and when *MC* exceeds *AVC*, *AVC* is rising, so the intersection of *MC* and *AVC* is at the minimum point of *AVC*; when *MC* is less than *ATC*, *ATC* is falling, when MC equals *ATC*, *ATC* does not change, and when *MC* exceeds *ATC*, *ATC* is rising, so the intersection of *MC* and *ATC* is at the minimum point of *ATC*.
f. The point where *MC* equals *AFC* has no economic significance.

21. a. *AVC* is at its minimum at the Q_1 level of output, where the *AVC* and *MC* curves intersect. This point marks the minimum of *AVC* because at levels of output below this (such as Q_0) *MC* is less than *AVC*, forcing *AVC* downward. For levels of output above this (such as Q_2) *MC* is greater than *AVC*, pulling *AVC* upward.
b. *ATC* is at its minimum at the Q_2 level of output, where the *ATC* and *MC* curves intersect. This point marks the minimum of *ATC* because at levels of output below this (such as Q_1), *MC* is less than *ATC*, forcing *ATC* downward. For levels of output above this (such as Q_3), *MC* is greater than *ATC*, pulling *ATC* upward.
c. *MC* is at its minimum at the Q_0 level of output. This level of output marks the minimum of *MC* since it coincides with the point where diminishing marginal productivity sets in.

23. a. C
b. B
c. Diseconomies of scale

25.

Change	AVC	MC	ATC
a. The government imposes a tax that is applied to every unit produced	↑	↑	↑
b. The price of rent increases*	R/u	R/u	↑
c. New technology that improves productivity is introduced	↓	↓	↓
d. The cost of labour increases	↑	↑	↑
e. The cost of materials used in manufacturing decrease	↓	↓	↓
f. Property taxes increase*	R/u	R/u	↑

*These changes impact only *ATC* (and have no effect on *AVC* and MC) because they cause only *FC* to change.
Note: "R/u" stands for "Remains unchanged."

CHAPTER 8

1. A perfectly competitive market is approximated most closely by competitive sellers selling a homogenous product. Of the markets listed, the fishing industry and the Toronto Stock Exchange most closely resemble perfectly competitive markets.

3. Farms can be thought of as perfectly competitive businesses, which produce products that are very close to perfect substitutes. For example, one farmer's eggs are very good substitutes for any other farmer's eggs. Any advertising for eggs will increase the market demand for all farmers' eggs. All farms will benefit since the market price will rise. In this situation, no single farm has an incentive to invest in advertising since the price it can charge will increase and it will benefit from the advertising of others.

5. a.

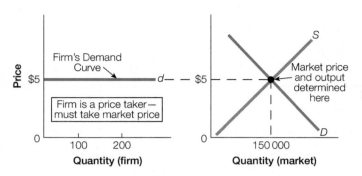

b.

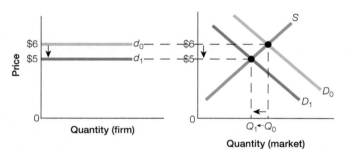

7. Average revenue equals total revenue divided by output, or $25 at all output levels. Marginal revenue is the addition to total revenue from selling one more unit of output, also equal to $25 at all levels of output. If marginal revenue is constant and equal to $25 at all levels of output, $25 must be the market price. The short-run profit-maximizing (loss-minimizing) level of output is found where marginal revenue equals marginal cost (provided that price exceeds average variable cost). Marginal revenue equals marginal cost for the third unit.

9. When average total cost is $3, profit will be total revenue (1000 × $5 = $5000) minus total costs (1000 × $3 = $3000) or $2000. When average total cost is $6, profit will be total revenue (1000 × $5 = $5000) minus total costs (1000 × $6 = $6000) or −$1000. A firm will make a profit if price exceeds average total cost for the quantity produced and sold, and a loss if price is less than average total cost for the quantity produced and sold.

11. a.

Quantity	Price	Total Revenue	Marginal Revenue	Marginal Cost	Total Profit
10	$12	$120	$12	$8	$25
11	12	132	12	9	28
12	12	144	12	11	29
13	12	156	12	12	29
14	12	168	12	14	27

b. Marginal revenue equals marginal costs at 13 units of output, so 13 units is the profit-maximizing output level (to be precise, the entrepreneur could produce either 12 or 13 and earn the same profit, since *MR* and *MC* are equal on the 13th unit). Even though the firm does not increase profits on the 13th unit, it will still produce since it is covering its costs, so the entrepreneur is earning an amount equal to his opportunity costs.

c. At a price of $9, the profit-maximizing output would be 11 units, where price equals marginal cost. If the firm produced 12 units, profits would fall by $2 (marginal cost minus marginal revenue).

13. a. $35 per unit, 85 units

b. *TR* = $35 × 85 = $2975, *TC* = $31 × 85 = $2635, Economic profits = $2975 − $2635 = $340

c. *TR* = $25 × 65 = $1625, *TC* = $31 × 65 = $2015, Economic profits = $1625 − $2015 = −$390 (loss)
The firm should continue to produce in the *SR* since price (*MR*) is greater than its *AVC*.

d. The firm should choose to shut down in the *SR* since price (*MR*) is now less than its *AVC*.

15. a. False. When economic profits are zero, firms are earning normal profits. Total revenue is sufficient to cover all costs of production, including a normal rate of return for business owners.

b. False. In the long run, a perfectly competitive firm maximizes profit at a level of output where average total cost is minimized. In the short run, however, if a profit-maximizing firm is earning economic profits, it will not produce at an output level where average total cost (or any other cost) is minimized. Rather, the firm chooses output where marginal revenue equals marginal cost.

c. False. The statement is ambiguous. For example, a firm could minimize overall costs by not producing any output at all. Such a strategy would certainly not result in positive economic profits. In the long run, if a firm is producing at the output level where average total cost is minimized, it is also maximizing its profits. However, in the short run, choosing an output level at which average total cost is minimized is unlikely to yield maximum profits for the firm. Instead, to maximize profits, the firm should choose to produce a quantity of output where marginal revenue equals marginal cost.

17. If firms are currently earning economic profits, that will attract entry into the industry, shifting the industry supply to the right. That will lower the price and reduce economic profits. If firms are currently earning economic losses, firms will exit the industry. That will raise the price and reduce economic losses.

19.

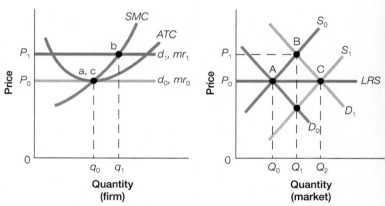

a. The short-run effect of an increase in demand on the perfectly competitive firm is illustrated by the movement from point a to b in the firm diagram and from point A to point B in the market diagram.

b. The long-run effect of an increase in demand for a constant-cost industry is illustrated by the movement from point b to point c (same as point a) in the firm diagram and from point A to point C in the market diagram.

21. a. Increasing-cost, since more teams will bid up the price of good pitchers and reduce the quality of the average pitcher.

b. Constant-cost, since expansion of output will not significantly increase the price of these unspecialized inputs.

c. Increasing-cost, since industry expansion will put upward pressure on the wages offered to these trained workers.

CHAPTER 9

1. a. Although many actresses compete for acting roles, in some sense, an actress like Kate Hudson has a monopoly over her own special talents.

b. While not the only means, electricity is the predominant way in which we power the various items we use on a daily basis. Electricity is therefore largely a product without alternative. Since BC Hydro is the sole provider of electricity for most if not all of the province of British Columbia, we could consider BC Hydro to be a monopoly.

c. The only doctor in a small town has a local monopoly over physician services. Such a doctor's monopoly power is likely to be limited, however, if physicians are available in nearby towns.

d. Ford Motor Company would not be considered to be a monopoly.

3. Being a *price maker* does give the monopolist the ability to set price at a desired level. However, in doing so, the monopolist must accept whatever quantity consumers are willing to buy at that price. A monopolist can determine either price or quantity sold, but not both.

5.

Quantity	Price	Total Revenue	Marginal Revenue	Demand Elastic or Inelastic?
1	$11	$11	$11	Elastic
2	10	20	9	Elastic
3	9	27	7	Elastic
4	8	32	5	Elastic
5	7	35	3	Elastic
6	6	36	1	Elastic
7	5	35	−1	Inelastic
8	4	32	−3	Inelastic
9	3	27	−5	Inelastic
10	2	20	−7	Inelastic
11	1	11	−9	Inelastic

7. a.

Quantity	Price	Total Revenue	Marginal Revenue	Elastic or Inelastic?
30	$3.65	$109.50		
31	3.58	110.98	$1.48	Elastic
32	3.51	112.32	1.34	Elastic
33	3.44	113.52	1.20	Elastic
34	3.37	114.58	1.06	Elastic
35	3.30	115.50	0.92	Elastic
36	3.22	115.92	0.42	Elastic
37	3.14	116.18	0.26	Elastic
38	3.06	116.28	0.10	Elastic
39	2.98	116.22	(0.06)	Inelastic
40	2.90	116.00	(0.22)	Inelastic
41	2.82	115.62	(0.38)	Inelastic
42	2.74	115.08	(0.54)	Inelastic
43	2.66	114.38	(0.70)	Inelastic
44	2.58	113.52	(0.86)	Inelastic
45	2.50	112.50	(1.02)	Inelastic
46	2.42	111.32	(1.18)	Inelastic
47	2.34	109.98	(1.34)	Inelastic
48	2.25	108.00	(1.98)	Inelastic
49	2.15	105.35	(2.65)	Inelastic
50	2.04	102.00	(3.35)	Inelastic

b. At first marginal revenue is positive as the price declines. After the price falls below $3.06, marginal revenue becomes negative as the price declines. Marginal revenue is always less than price beyond the first unit of output.

c. Marginal revenue is negative as the price declines when the demand curve is inelastic, so the demand becomes inelastic below a price of $3.06.

d. NorOnt Phones will increase the number of substitutes for northern Ontario phone long-distance service. An increase in the number of substitutes will increase the elasticity of the demand facing Star Phone.

9. To sell two units we have to lower the price on both units to $8. That is, the seller doesn't receive $10 from unit one and $8 for unit two, but rather, receives $8 for each of the units. So what happens to marginal revenue? There are two parts to this answer. One, there is a loss in revenue, $2, from selling the first unit at $8 instead of $10. Two, there is a gain in revenue from selling the additional output—the second unit—at $8. So the marginal revenue is $6 ($8 − $2), which is less than the price of the good, $8.

11. If economic profits are zero, the firm is earning a normal profit, so there is no incentive to leave the industry. It is possible for a monopolist earning positive economic profits to maintain them in the long run, because barriers prevent new firms from entering and competing away economic profits.

13. The short-run profit-maximizing level of output is found where marginal revenue equals marginal cost at five units of output ($MR = \$10 = MC$). Price equals $30 at that level of output and the firm earns a normal profit, because total revenue exceeds total cost.

15. a. At profit maximization: $P^* = \$18$, $Q^* = 60$ units, $ATC_{Q^*} = \$13$ $TR = \$18 \times 60 = \$1080$, $TC = \$13 \times 60 = \$780$, therefore, Total profit = $300

b. No, the monopolist is not achieving productive efficiency at Q^*. This is because the monopolist is not producing at the minimum of ATC when operating at Q^* (minimum of ATC is $12).

c. No, the monopolist is not achieving allocative efficiency at Q^*. This is because, at Q^*, the monopolist experiences $P > MC$ (allocative efficiency is achieved where $P = MC$).

17. a. The efficient result is determined by the marginal cost pricing alternative—point C.

b. Since price is below average total cost at point C, the monopolist is incurring a loss (indicated by the shaded area).

c. The average cost-pricing alternative is detailed on the graph at point B. A normal rate of return is earned.

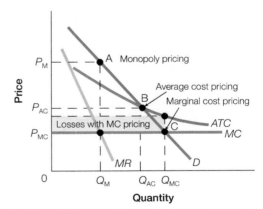

19. a. Students' demand for movie tickets tends to be more elastic than for the average individual. To entice students to the movie theatre more frequently, theatres offer discounts to students who can show a student ID.

b. The long-distance service is practising price discrimination by offering lower rates to those who make longer calls than to those who make very short calls. This type of quantity discount is a form of price discrimination.

c. Seniors, who often live on fixed incomes and perhaps have more time to search for good deals, tend to have more elastic demands for many goods and services. Local restaurants offer discounts to seniors to attract them to their restaurants (but often restrict them to "early bird" times, so seniors don't crowd out regular-price dinner customers at the peak demand period).

d. Coupon discounts are offered only to those individuals who are willing to take the time and effort to locate, clip, and bring the laundry detergent coupon to the store. People whose demand for laundry detergent is relatively elastic are more likely to clip and organize coupons than are those with relatively inelastic demand. The use of coupons separates customers into groups with different elasticities of demand, charging different groups different effective prices.

21. If the differences in prices of haircuts for people with different hair lengths reflect differences in the costs of providing a haircut, then it is not price discrimination.

23. The airline industry has found that business travellers have a more inelastic demand for air travel than vacationers do. The airlines know that business travellers are generally unwilling to stay over for the weekend (away from home, family, or their favourite golf course), spend only a day or two at their destination, and often do not make their reservations far in advance. All of which means the business traveller has a more inelastic demand curve for flights (fewer substitutes). If the airlines cut prices for business travellers, airline revenues would fall. Personal travellers (perhaps vacationers) are operating on a much more elastic demand curve—they are much more flexible. For these travellers, many substitutes are available, such as other modes of transportation, different times (non–peak times), and so on. Clearly the airlines can make more money by separating the market according to each group's elasticity of demand rather than by charging all users the same price.

CHAPTER 10

1. The market for soybeans is perfectly competitive, as large numbers of buyers and sellers trade standardized products on a world market. Retail clothing stores and restaurants offer differentiated products and services, and are therefore monopolistically competitive.

3. Answers will vary. One's choice of gas stations may be based on the price of gasoline; gas station location and services and amenities offered; the quality of gas; brand identity; etc.

5. Some restaurants are more successful at differentiating their establishments and appealing to customers than are others. Restaurants that are particularly successful in promoting customer goodwill may continue to earn economic profits even while other restaurants in the area fail.

7. Starbucks differentiates its product by location, hours of operation, service, and product quality. Starbucks is generally open late at night when many people want to drink coffee because of its caffeine stimulant. People who generally opt for doughnuts and bagels in the morning often drink coffee throughout the day.

9.

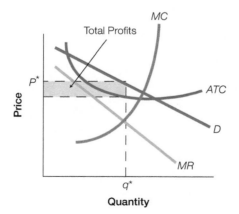

In the above diagram, the firm is making economic profits because the price the firm is able to charge (P^*) at output q^* is greater than the firm's average total costs at output q^*. These positive economic profits will attract the entry of new firms into the industry, cutting into the market demand of existing firms. The demand curves for each of these existing firms will therefore shift downward. This decline will continue until the average total cost (ATC) curve becomes tangent to the demand curve and economic profits are reduced to zero.

11. a. When price is greater than average total cost at q^* (the intersection of marginal revenue and marginal cost), the firm will earn positive economic profits.

b. When price is less than average total cost at q^* (the intersection of marginal revenue and marginal cost), the firm will earn economic losses.

c. and d. When price is equal to average total cost at q^* (the intersection of marginal revenue and marginal cost), the firm will earn zero economic profits. This is also the long-run condition as a result of entry and exit.

13. a. In reading the brief opening description of this firm, we would consider it to be monopolistically competitive because (1) it is one of several firms in the industry, (2) it has differentiated its service from its competition, and (3) firms have been able to enter the industry with relative ease.

b.

Quantity (number of oil changes)	Price ($)	TR ($)	MR($)	MC ($)	ATC ($)
0	50.00	0.00			
1	45.00	45.00	45.00	13.00	30.50
2	40.00	80.00	35.00	18.00	26.75
3	35.00	105.00	25.00	23.00	24.75
4	30.00	120.00	15.00	28.00	26.25
5	25.00	125.00	5.00	33.00	28.75
6	20.00	120.00	−5.00	38.00	32.50

According to the above table, $MR = MC$ at a quantity of 3 oil changes ($q^* = 3$). If we assume that the firm cannot provide a partial oil change, the profit-maximizing number of oil changes is 3, since the 4th oil change delivers more marginal cost than marginal revenue. Our monopolistically competitive business will change a price of $35 per oil change as a result.

c. At the q^* of 3 oil changes, P^* is greater than ATC_{q^*}; as a result, this firm is generating positive economic profits at profit maximization. TR (at q^*) = $105; TC (at q^*) = $74.25 ($24.75 × 3). Therefore, total profits = $30.75.

15. Both types of firms operate in industries with many other sellers and with no real barriers to entry or exit. They follow similar rules when choosing the level of output. Both types of firms also will experience zero economic profits in the long run. In the short run, monopolistic competitors and perfectly competitive firms follow similar rules for choosing the profit-maximizing output. They produce where marginal revenue equals marginal cost. Monopolistic competitors will produce less than perfectly competitive firms because the relationship between price and marginal revenue differs between those types of firms. Since firms that are monopolistic competitors face a negatively sloped demand curve, they output less than the output where price equals marginal cost since they are price takers. In the long run, entry will force both types of firms to the output where economic profits are equal to zero, which occurs where the demand curves are tangent to the average total cost curve. Because the monopolistic competitor faces a negatively sloped demand curve, this point will be at a level of output less than the perfect competitor.

17.

Perfect Competition	Monopolistic Competition
Standardized product	Differentiated product
Allocative efficiency	Downward-sloping demand curve
Productive efficiency	Excess capacity
Horizontal demand curve	
No control over price	

19. Answers will vary. Certainly not all individuals will respond to each and every advertisement. By advertising, a firm hopes it can both increase demand and make it more inelastic, thereby enhancing profits. Critics of advertising argue that advertisers attempt to manipulate preferences and engender brand loyalty to reduce competition. Defenders of advertising argue that production costs can be reduced if substantial economies of scale exist. Also, by raising consumer awareness of substitute products, advertising can help increase the competitiveness within markets and lead to lower prices. Advertising may be considered a "waste" by someone who always knows which good he wants, but advertising would not be used by sellers who do not think it would increase demand sufficiently to make it profitable.

21. By advertising, firms hope to increase the demand and create a less elastic demand curve for their products, thus enhancing revenues and profits.

23. The following markets are oligopolistic: (b) funeral services, (c) airline travel, (e) oil, and (f) breakfast cereals.

25. Unlike perfectly competitive firms, oligopolists can earn economic profits in the long run if barriers to entry are sufficiently high to deter new firms from entering the market.

27. Since the market for wheat is highly competitive, it is unlikely that the Smith–Jones cartel will be at all successful or have any impact on the price of wheat. There are too many good substitutes available for the wheat produced by Farmers Smith and Jones. If Smith and Jones choose to restrict their combined output, their profits will in all likelihood fall, with virtually no effect on the market price.

29. a. If the Canadian and Russian mines provide a significant share of the world's supply, increasing the supply will result in the price of diamonds falling. This will be the result of the breakdown of the cartel.

b. CSO will no longer be willing to advertise to increase the demand for all diamonds in general. This type of advertising might instead sell more Canadian or Russian diamonds and generate no profit for CSO. If CSO continues to advertise diamonds, it will try to distinguish the diamonds it is selling. CSO might try to establish a brand to differentiate its product from the others.

31. If both firms employ small advertising budgets, then they both earn modest profits of $50 million. If one firm opts for a large ad budget, but the other does not, then the firm with the large ad budget enjoys significantly greater profits than the firm that does not. If both firms spend large sums of money on advertising, then each earns the greatest amount of profit possible, equal to $150 million. This is a Nash equilibrium.

33. a. There is a dominant strategy, which is for both prisoners to confess. Whichever strategy the other prisoner adopts, the prisoner in question gets less time by confessing.

b. Since each does as well as possible given the actions of the other, this same strategy (both prisoners confessing) is a Nash equilibrium.

35. Shirking at school may be a one-shot game with no future consequences. At work, however, it is a repeated game with adverse future consequences.

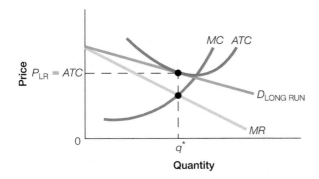

CHAPTER 11

1. The demand for unskilled labour used to produce hamburgers and fries would increase as well.

3.

Quantity of Labour	Total Output/Week	Marginal Product of Labour	Marginal Revenue Product of Labour
0	—		
1	250	250	$1000
2	600	350	1400
3	900	300	1200
4	1125	225	900
5	1300	175	700
6	1450	150	600
7	1560	110	440

5.

Workers	Total Corn Output	Marginal Product of Labour
1	4 000	4 000
2	10 000	6 000
3	15 000	5 000
4	18 000	3 000
5	19 000	1 000
6	18 000	−1 000

7.

Workers	Total Output	Marginal Product	Price	Marginal Revenue Product
1	200	200	20	4000
2	380	180	20	3600
3	540	160	20	3200
4	680	140	20	2800
5	800	120	20	2400
6	900	100	20	2000
7	980	80	20	1600
8	1040	60	20	1200

9. The equilibrium wage would tend to decrease if a company provided on-the-job training and dental benefits to its workers (since part of the compensation to employees would come in the form of these benefits). If the government mandated a minimum wage of $9 per hour, employers would likely respond by reducing benefits such as dental insurance and on-the-job training.

11. An influx of immigrants into a country will increase the supply of labour and decrease real wages. On the other hand, the home countries of the departing immigrants will experience a decrease in the supply of available labour, which puts upward pressure on real wages.

13. a. E; b. C; c. G; d. I; e. A; f. B; g. D; h. F; i. H

15. a., b.

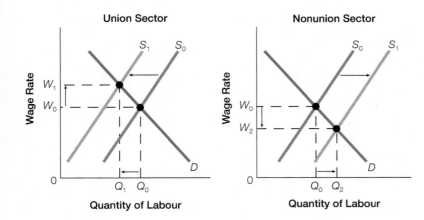

Union Sector

Nonunion Sector

c. Union wages go up and the number of union workers hired goes down; nonunion wages go down, and the number of nonunion workers hired goes up.

17. The official data may overstate the actual degree of income inequality because it fails to take into consideration differences in age, demographic factors such as the increasing number of both divorced couples and double-income families, and government redistributive activities (by ignoring the effects of taxes and in-kind subsidies).

19. a. A massive influx of low-skilled immigrants would increase the proportion of the overall population earning low incomes.

    b. In the event of a baby boom, some individuals would opt to become full-time parents, transforming two-income families into single-income families. This would tend to reduce the proportion of the population in high-income quintiles and increase the proportion in the low-income quintiles.

    c. When the babies in (b) enter their twenties and begin working, the proportion of the population in low-income quintiles will likely increase (since young workers earn lower incomes on average then middle-aged workers).

    d. When the babies in (b) reach age 65 or older, again the proportion of the population in low-income quintiles will increase (as retirees earn lower incomes on average than middle-aged workers do).

21. Even with the same lifetime incomes, some would be in their peak earning years and others would be in low earning years (e.g., young or retired people) at a given point in time, resulting in current income inequality.

23. Economic growth could potentially reduce absolute measures of poverty by increasing real incomes. However, economic growth by itself cannot eliminate relative measures of poverty because there will always be some with lower real incomes than others.

25. From the text, the reader should be able to identify the following determinants of poverty.

Household type: Households with two parents are unlikely to be poor, whereas single-parent families (particularly, female single-parent families) have a much higher incidence of poverty.

Age of major income earner: The age of the major income earner has a dramatic impact on the incidence of poverty. Families in which the major income earner was younger than 24 were over four times more likely to be poor when compared to families where the major income earner was between the ages of 45 and 54.

Education: Education has a significant impact on household income and the risk of poverty. An individual with less than a high school education usually earns a fraction of what someone with a university degree can earn. Therefore, a household headed by someone with less than a high school education has a much higher incidence of low income when compared to households headed by individuals with a university degree.

CHAPTER 12

1. Positive externalities:

    b. You are given a flu shot.

    d. A local youth group cleans up trash along a two-kilometre stretch of highway.

Negative externalities:

    a. During a live-theatre performance, an audience member's cellphone rings loudly.

    e. A firm dumps chemical waste into a local stream.

    f. The person down the hall in your residence plays a Britney Spears CD loudly while you are trying to sleep.

No externalities:

    c. You purchase and drink a soft drink during a break from class.

3. If the steel company is not held liable for dumping crud into the air, it will consider only the $25 labour costs and the $10 equipment costs.

5. If diesel engines were banned, there would be fewer future incidences of the sorts of cancer it causes. However, the advantages of transportation and other production processes using diesel engines would be lost. The cost of shipping freight would likely increase, raising the prices of many goods.

7. a. When taxes are imposed to address external costs, the costs of production to producers will rise, shifting supply curves up (left). The market result of such decreases in supply is higher prices for the goods whose production imposes external costs. When subsidies are given to address external benefits, the net of subsidy costs of production to producers will fall, shifting supply curves down (right). The market result of such increases in supply is lower prices for the goods whose production creates external benefits.

    b. Workers would benefit from subsidies to an industry that address external benefits—more output will increase the demand for workers and other inputs—but they would be hurt by taxes that address external costs.

9. a. A higher tax on gasoline encourages people to drive less and therefore reduces air pollution.

    b. An annual tax on automobiles based on average emissions might discourage some people from buying a car, but is unlikely to alter the driving habits of individual car owners in any significant way.

    c. An annual tax on total emissions from a particular model of car in a year would encourage both less driving and more switching to more environmentally friendly cars.

11. A pollution reduction program that relies on emissions standards would force firms to limit pollution levels, regardless of the cost of doing so. With an emissions permit program, firms that can reduce pollution levels at relatively low marginal cost can sell their permits to firms that can reduce pollution levels only at higher marginal costs. The same level of pollution reduction can be achieved with either program. However, the latter program would achieve the reduction in pollution at lower cost to society.

13. The demand for lumber is a derived demand that depends on the demand for wood and paper products. If the price of paper decreased due to less paper consumption or more recycling, then the demand for lumber would decrease. The quantity supplied of lumber, and very likely the number of trees planted on private land, would decrease as a result.

15. A change in the law is not necessary to achieve an efficient outcome in this situation. If the resort owner and chemical factory could reach an agreement whereby the resort owner compensates the chemical factory for hauling the pollution to the toxic waste dump, the socially efficient outcome could be achieved. Since the damage to the resort owner exceeds the cost of hauling the pollution to the toxic waste dump site, this is a possibility, as long as the property rights are clearly defined and the cost of negotiating and transacting is low enough.

17. **a.** Hot dogs: Private good
    b. Cable TV: Nonrival; private good
    c. Broadcast TV: Nonrival; nonexclusive; public good
    d. Automobiles: Private good
    e. National defence: Nonrival; nonexclusive; public good
    f. Pollution-control device: Nonrival; nonexclusive; public good
    g. Parking spot in a parking structure: Private good
    h. A sunset: Nonrival; nonexclusive; public good
    i. Admission to a theme park: Private good

19. Buffalo almost became extinct because people did not have clear property rights for buffalo, unlike cattle. You can buy a buffalo burger today because people now have clear property rights to buffalo.

CHAPTER 13

1. Answers will vary based on information obtained at the time.
3. **a.** 80 percent (160 million/200 million)
   b. 70 percent (140 million/200 million)
   c. The labour force participation rate would become 65 percent (130 million/200 million).
   d. Nothing; neither the adult population nor the size of the labour force would change.
5. **a.** Sam is a discouraged worker who is not actively seeking work and is therefore not considered to be unemployed.
   b. The 12-year-old is under 15 years of age and therefore is not considered to be part of the labour force.
   c. The factory worker is unemployed as long as she is looking for work.
   d. The receptionist is considered to be employed, even though she would like to work more hours each week.
   e. The high-school graduate is not actively seeking work and therefore is not considered to be unemployed.
7. **a.** Re-entrant
   b. Job loser
   c. New entrant
   d. Job leaver
9. **a.** Frictional; increase
   b. Seasonal; increase
   c. Frictional; decrease
   d. Structural; increase
   e. Structural; decrease
   f. Cyclical; increase
11. **a.** A natural rate of 6 percent would account for the sum of structural and frictional unemployment. The additional 2 percent of unemployment above the natural rate would be attributed to cyclical unemployment.
    b. Since cyclical unemployment cannot be negative, the only way actual unemployment can fall below the natural rate is if either structural or frictional levels of unemployment fall below their maximums (that is, below-average levels of either structural or frictional unemployment).
13. If union bargaining raises the union wage above the equilibrium level, the quantity of unionized labour demanded will decrease and the quantity of unionized labour supplied will increase. Some union workers will be unemployed as a result and will either seek nonunion work or wait to be rehired in the union sector. Union workers who are still employed are better off due to their higher earnings.
15. **a.** Retirees on fixed incomes: Hurt
    Workers: Hurt (unless wages kept up with inflation)
    Debtors: Helped

Creditors: Hurt
Shoe-leather costs: Increased
Menu costs: Increased
    b. Workers, debtors, and creditors would be unaffected. If retirees stayed on their fixed incomes, they would be hurt. Shoe-leather costs would be unaffected but menu costs would rise.

17. Price index 2011 = $16/$16 × 100 = 100
    Price index 2012 = $17.28/$16 × 100 = 108
    Price index 2013 = $20/$16 × 100 = 125

    Inflation rate 2011–12 = (108 − 100)/100 = 8 percent
    Inflation rate 2011–13 = (125 − 100)/100 = 25 percent
    Inflation rate 2012–13 = (125 − 108)/108 = 15.7 percent

19. A variable rate mortgage protects lenders against inflation by guaranteeing lenders a particular real rate of interest. An adjustable rate mortgage shifts the risk of inflation from the lenders to the borrowers. If the rate of inflation increases (decreases), the interest paid by borrowers will increase (decrease) accordingly.

21. Expansion phase
23. **a.** Year 3
    b. Years 4, 5, and 6
    c. Year 7
    d. Years 1, 2, 8, 9, and 10

CHAPTER 14

1. The following are included in Canadian GDP calculations:
   a. cleaning services performed by a cleaning company
   d. prescription drugs manufactured in Canada and sold at a local pharmacy
   g. toxic waste cleanup performed by a local company
   h. car parts manufactured in Canada for assembly of a car in Mexico
3. Gross domestic product measures the total value of production, which can be determined by either the expenditure or the income approach. Both approaches will deliver an equivalent result since every buyer must have a seller. The use of the expenditure approach to measure total production is based on the understanding that the total value of what is bought (the expenditure of the buyer) will be equal to the total value of what has been produced (considering only final goods and services). Therefore, since everything that is bought must be purchased (thereby creating income for the seller), the income approach is based on the understanding that the total value of factor payments generated from production will be equal to the total value of what has been produced.
5. **a.** Ministry of Transportation snow-clearing services: Government spending
   b. Automobiles exported to Europe: Exports
   c. Refrigerator: Consumption (consumer durables)
   d. Newly constructed four-bedroom house: Investment
   e. Restaurant meal: Consumption
   f. Additions to inventory at a furniture store: Investment
   g. Purchases of new computers by Statistics Canada: Government spending
   h. New steel mill: Investment
7.

Consumption	$6500
Consumption of durable goods	$1200
Consumption of semi-durable goods	$1100
Consumption of nondurable goods	$1800
Consumption of services	$2400
Investment	$1400
Fixed investment	$ 800
Inventory investment	$ 600
Government expenditures on goods and services	$1600
Government transfer payments	$ 500
Exports	$ 500
Imports	$ 650
Net exports	−$150
GDP	$9350

9. Economic forecasters focus so much on consumption purchases and their determinants because consumption purchases are by far the largest component of GDP (in Canada, nearly 60 percent); what happens to consumption purchases is therefore crucial to what happens to GDP.

11.

Personal consumption expenditures	$210
Gross investment	100
Government current purchases of goods and services	60
Exports	10
Imports	(20)
GDP – Expenditure Approach	360
Compensation of employees	$210
Corporation profits before taxes	62
Net mixed income	21
Indirect taxes (less subsidies)	35
Capital consumption allowances (depreciation)	32
GDP – Income Approach	360

13.

Year	Nominal GDP	Real GDP
2009	($720 billion/100) × 100 = $720 billion	
2010	($750 billion/102) × 100 = approximately $735 billion	
2011	($800 billion/110) × 100 = approximately $727 billion	
2012	($900 billion/114) × 100 = approximately $789 billion	
2013	($960 billion/120) × 100 = $800 billion	

The real economic growth rate for 2013 was 1.4 percent:

$$\left(\frac{\$800 - \$789}{\$789} \right) \times 100 = 1.4\%$$

15. **a.**

Year	Nominal GDP (in millions of $)	GDP Deflator	Real GDP (in millions of $)
2008	3237.0	93.3	3469.5
2009	3156.4	97.2	3247.3
2010	2995.3	100	2995.3
2011	3376.2	103.2	3271.5
2012	3517.6	101.4	3469.0
2013	3797.3	102.6	3701.1

b. The base year is 2010 (identified by the GDP deflator value of 100). The significance of the year 2010 is that the conversion of nominal GDP values into real GDP involves the conversion of current dollar output (nominal GDP) to constant dollar output (real GDP). The constant dollars that real GDP is measured in is 2010 dollars.

c. Looking at the behaviour of real GDP between 2008 and 2013, the following trends are apparent; 2008–10, real GDP (production) is falling; 2010–13, real GDP (production) is rising.

17. **a.** Next year's real GDP can exceed next year's nominal GDP, but only if the price level falls. If the price level rises, next year's nominal GDP will exceed next year's real GDP.

b. Yes. It will happen when the population growth rate exceeds the growth rate of real GDP.

c. Since only what is produced can be consumed, if we measured all sources of output accurately, real per capita consumption possibilities could expand only when real per capita GDP grows. However, if, say, the underground (therefore, unmeasured) economy grew fast enough, real per capita consumption possibilities could increase despite measured decreases in real per capita GDP.

d. Leisure is valuable but its value is not counted in GDP. So changing amounts of leisure over time will not be accurately incorporated into GDP measures. Further, while a decrease in leisure (an increase in labour market work) would increase measured GDP, people would be better off only if their real after-tax wages were higher than the value of the leisure they gave up, which is not always the case (especially when workers are fooled by inflation).

19. Since nonmarket activities are not included in GDP, GDP would understate the true value of total output more for a country with a relatively high level of nonmarket activities than for a country with a smaller proportion of nonmarket activities, making countries with smaller shares of nonmarket activities look more productive relative to countries with larger shares of nonmarket activities.

CHAPTER 15

1. **a.**

0.5 percent	140	years
1.0 percent	70	years
1.4 percent	50	years
2.0 percent	35	years
2.8 percent	25	years
3.5 percent	20	years
7.0 percent	10	years

b.

1.4 percent	$200 billion
2.8 percent	$400 billion
7.0 percent	$3200 billion

3. **a.** Using the Rule of 70, Country A's real per capita GDP would double every 50 years (70/1.4) and Country B's real per capita GDP would double every 25 years (70/2.8). In the course of 100 years, Country B's real per capita GDP would double four times, while Country A's would double only two times. If they started at the same size, Country B's real per capita GDP would be four times that of Country A after that period of time, but since Country B started out one-fourth as large as Country A, their real per capita GDP would end up the same size in 100 years.

b. At 2.8 percent annual growth, Country A's real per capita GDP would double every 25 years, or four times in a century. At 3.5 percent annual growth, Country B's real per capita GDP would double every 20 years, or five times in a century. As a result, Country B's real per capita GDP would be twice that of Country A after a century.

5. **d.** The annual percentage change in real GDP per capita best measures economic growth.

7. It depends. Both capital investment and human capital investment increase productivity, so the answer depends on which is more productive in a given case. If education (human capital investment) is more productive, shifting from capital investment to human capital investment would increase the growth rate of real per capita GDP. If education (human capital investment) is less productive, shifting from capital investment to human capital investment would decrease the growth rate of real per capita GDP.

9. Each of the following will likely improve the productivity of labour:

a. On-the-job experience

b. College education

d. Improvements in management of resources

11.

	Real GDP Growth	Real GDP Growth per Capita
An increase in population	Increase	Indeterminate
An increase in labour force participation	Increase	Increase
An increase in population and labour force participation	Increase	Increase
An increase in current consumption	Decrease	Decrease
An increase in technology	Increase	Decrease
An increase in illiteracy	Decrease	Decrease
An increase in tax rates	Decrease	Decrease
An increase in productivity	Increase	Increase
An increase in tariffs on imported goods	Decrease	Decrease
An earlier retirement age in the country	Decrease	Decrease
An increase in technology and a decrease in labour force participation	Indeterminant	Indeterminant
An earlier retirement age and an increase in the capital stock	Indeterminant	Indeterminant

13. Permanently lower marginal tax rates would increase the after-tax rate of return to each of these productive activities, which, over time, would increase the levels of the capital stock, education, and technology, and the amount of developed natural resources.

15. **a.** Real GDP will grow while real GDP per capita falls whenever the population growth rate exceeds the growth rate of real GDP.

b. Country A has a higher real per capita GDP growth rate of 2 percent (4 percent real GDP growth minus 2 percent population growth). Country B's real per capita GDP growth rate is 1 percent (6 percent real GDP growth minus 5 percent population growth).

17. Malthus's prediction that population growth results in a subsistence level of wages was based on the assumption of an agricultural society with land and labour as the only factors of production. Assuming that the amount of land was fixed, population and the labour force would grow to where production exhibited the law of diminishing returns, with output growing more slowly than increases in the variable input, labour, which would reduce per capita incomes, eventually to the point of subsistence.

CHAPTER 16

1. **a.** 0.90
b. 0.80
c. 0.60
d. $300 000; 0.75
e. $120 000; 1.2

3. **a.** The quantity of investment demanded increases but the investment demand curve does not shift.
b. The investment demand curve shifts to the left.
c. The investment demand curve shifts to the right.
d. The quantity of saving supplied increases but the saving supply curve does not shift.
e. The saving supply curve shifts to the right.

5. An increase in current disposable income would increase the saving supply curve, shifting it to the right. A decrease in new technologies creating investment opportunities would shift the investment demand curve to the left, moving the equilibrium down along the saving supply curve but not shifting it.

7. In a closed economy, exports (*X*) and imports (*M*) are both zero. Therefore, GDP − *C* − *G* is what is left over from income (GDP) after spending on consumption (*C*) and government purchases (*G*), which is what is available for investment (*I*). But in equilibrium, investment must equal saving.

9. **a.** Decrease; decrease; decrease
b. Decrease; decrease; increase; increase
c. Decrease; decrease

11. A reduced price level increases the real value of people's currency holdings; as their wealth increases, so does the quantity of real goods and services demanded, particularly consumption goods. Therefore, the aggregate demand curve, which represents the relationship between the price level and the quantity of real goods and services demanded, slopes downward as a result.

13. The open economy effect occurs when a higher domestic price level raises the prices of domestically produced goods relative to the prices of imported goods. This reduces the quantity of domestically produced goods demanded (by both citizens and foreigners) as relatively cheaper foreign-made goods are substituted for them. The result is a downward-sloping aggregate demand curve, as a higher price level results in a lower quantity of domestic real GDP demanded.

15. A rapid depletion of inventories is consistent with a rightward shift of the aggregate demand curve. As a result of an increase in aggregate demand, both output and investment are likely to increase.

17. **a.** Investment expenditures will increase.
b. Investment expenditures will decrease.
c. Investment expenditures will decrease.
d. Investment expenditures will decrease.

19. Any recession in the United States reduces the incomes of Americans. As a result, Americans probably buy fewer Canadian goods and services, decreasing Canadian exports and aggregate demand.

CHAPTER 17

1. This is an example of the misperception effect. The misperception effect implies an upward-sloping short-run aggregate supply curve.

3. Profit incentives are the key to understanding what happens to real output as the price level changes in the short run (before input prices completely adjust to the price level). When the prices of outputs rise relative to the prices of inputs (costs), as when aggregate demand increases in the short run, profit margins increase, which increases the incentives to produce, which leads to increased real output. When the prices of outputs fall relative to the prices of inputs (costs), as when aggregate demand decreases in the short run, profit margins decrease, which decreases the incentives to produce, which leads to decreased real output.

5. **a.** Shift *SRAS* to the right
b. Shift *SRAS* to the left
c. Shift *SRAS* to the right
d. No shift of the *SRAS* occurs (aggregate demand increases and there is a movement up along the *SRAS*)
e. Shift *SRAS* to the left

7. **a.** A decrease in *SRAS*
b. A decrease in both *SRAS* and *LRAS*
c. A decrease in *SRAS*
d. An increase in both *SRAS* and *LRAS*

9. **a.**

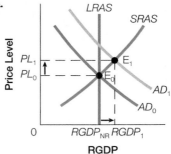

With greater confidence in the economy, consumers would undertake more consumption. This increase in consumption would cause aggregate demand to increase.

The price level increases, real output increases, employment increases, and unemployment decreases.

b.

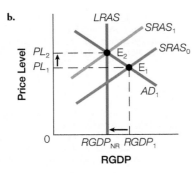

The price level ends up higher, real output ends up back where it began at potential output, employment ends up back where it began at full employment, and unemployment ends up back where it began at the natural rate of unemployment.

11. a.

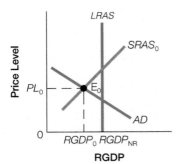

b.

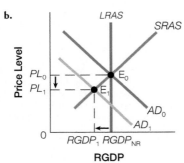

In the long run, the price level will end up lower than before, but real output and unemployment will return to their long-run equilibrium levels.

13. Cost-push inflation occurs when the short-run aggregate supply curve shifts to the left, pushing up prices. Demand-pull inflation occurs when the aggregate demand curve shifts to the right, pulling up prices. Examples will vary. Cost-push inflation may be caused by an increase in input prices, such as the price of crude oil or wages. Demand-pull inflation may be caused by an increase in consumer confidence or a decrease in taxes.

15. An increase in aggregate demand will have the following impact: output increases; unemployment decreases; the price level increases. A decrease in short-run aggregate supply will have the following impact: output decreases; unemployment increases; the price level increases.

17. a.

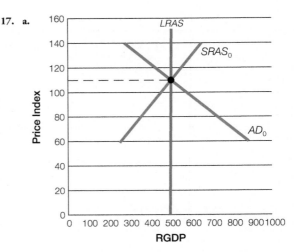

b. The equilibrium price level is 110 and the equilibrium level of real GDP is $500 billion.

c. As the initial equilibrium (a short-run equilibrium) occurs at potential output, the economy is experiencing neither a recessionary nor an inflationary gap, initially.

d.

Price Index	AD_0 (billions)	AS_0 (billions)	AD_1 (billions)
60	$875	$250	$750
70	800	300	675
80	725	350	600
90	650	400	525
100	575	450	450
110	500	500	375
120	425	550	300
130	350	600	225
140	275	650	150

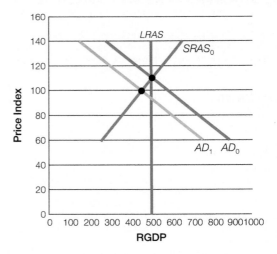

New equilibrium price level is 100; equilibrium level of real GDP is $450 billion.

e. At this short-run equilibrium, the economy of Adanac is experiencing a $50 billion recessionary gap.

APPENDIX: THE KEYNESIAN AGGREGATE EXPENDITURE MODEL

1. **a.** An increase in interest rates
   c. A decrease in disposable income
   d. An increase in income taxes
3. **a.** An increase in consumer optimism
   c. An increase in the sale of exports
   e. An increase in government spending due to the outbreak of war
5. Both an increase in real wealth and more optimistic expectations would increase autonomous consumption, so together they must also increase autonomous consumption.
7. As MPS increases, MPC decreases, so the consumption function rotates to become flatter.
9. If MPC was greater than one, the aggregate expenditure line would never intersect the 45-degree expenditure equals output line, so there would not be any stable equilibrium.
11. An increase in planned investment shifts up the aggregate expenditure line, increasing the equilibrium level of real GDP. An unplanned increase in investment, however, indicates that real GDP is greater than its equilibrium level, which will lead to a decrease in real GDP toward that equilibrium level.
13. An increase in unplanned investment would indicate real GDP was greater than its equilibrium level, leading to a decrease in real GDP produced. In contrast, an increase in planned investment would increase planned expenditures, tending to increase real GDP produced.
15. This is confused. The Keynesian assumption of wage and price rigidity best corresponds to the *flattest* (not steepest) portion of the aggregate supply curve where factories are operating well below capacity.

CHAPTER 18

1. **a.** An increase in government spending would decrease a budget surplus.
   b. An increase in government spending would increase aggregate demand.
   c. When the threat of a recession is developing
3. **a.** An increase in taxes would decrease a budget deficit.
   b. An increase in taxes would decrease aggregate demand.
   c. When the threat of an unsustainable, inflationary boom is likely
5. Suppose the government places an additional $1 per package tax on cigarettes. For individuals who have an income of $50, this amounts to 2 percent of their income; however, for individuals who have an income of $100, the tax amounts to only 1 percent. Uniform taxes, such as excise taxes on cigarettes, have a greater impact on lower-income individuals.
7. **a.** $MPC = 0.25$, multiplier value is 1.33, the tax multiplier value is 0.33
   b. $MPC = 0.5$, multiplier value is 2, the tax multiplier value is 1
   c. $MPC = 0.75$, multiplier value is 4, the tax multiplier value is 3
9. The multiplier, which is 1 divided by 1 minus the *MPC*, could also be written as 1 divided by the *MPS*, because the *MPS* is equal to 1 minus the *MPC*.
11. **a.** GDP will increase.
    b. GDP will decrease.
    c. GDP will increase.
    d. GDP will decrease.
13. A reduction in taxes of $10 billion; a reduction in taxes of $15.5 billion.
15.

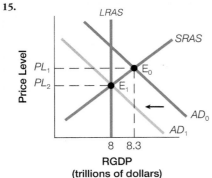

An economy can operate above the full employment level of output temporarily by using resources intensively. For example, factories can run three shifts per day, instead of two. Employees can be asked to work more hours each week. Firms can attempt to lure workers away from other firms by offering higher wages. As firms compete for scarce resources to maintain high levels of production, there will be upward pressure on input prices. When that occurs, the short-run aggregate supply curve will shift to the left, moving the economy back toward full employment and the economy will experience inflation. The government may be able to prevent inflation from occurring by decreasing government spending. To determine the correct magnitude, the government would need to know the size of the multiplier and then use this value to determine the appropriate reduction in government spending to eliminate the $25 billion inflationary gap.

17. **a.** At point E_3
    b. The economy would end up at a long-run equilibrium at point E_2.
    c. The economy would end up at a long-run equilibrium at point E_0.
    d. At point E_1
    e. The economy would end up in long-run equilibrium at E_0.
    f. The economy would end up in long-run equilibrium at E_2.
19. Discretionary fiscal policy requires new policies to be made, so it is subject to time lags in deciding what the problem is and what to do about it, and in implementing a solution. Since automatic stabilizers do not require new policy to be adopted, those lags do not handicap it in the same way.
21. Some taxes, such as progressive income taxes and corporate profits taxes, automatically increase as the economy grows, and this increase in taxes restrains disposable income and the growth of aggregate demand below what it would have been otherwise. Similarly, these taxes automatically decrease in recessions, and this decrease in taxes increases disposable income and acts as a partial offset to the fall in aggregate demand. The result is reduced business cycle instability.
23. **a.** An increase in government purchases increases the government budget deficit. The increased government borrowing increases the demand for loanable funds, which increases real interest rates, other things equal, which reduces, or crowds out, some of the investment that would otherwise have taken place.
    b. The crowding out of investment increases the more that interest rates are bid up by the government borrowing and the more that investment falls as a result of increased interest rates.
    c. The greater the crowding out effect, the smaller the net effect of a given increase in government purchases on aggregate demand.
25. In the short run, deficit reduction is contradictory fiscal policy; either tax increases and/or a reduction in government purchases will shift the aggregate demand curve to the left, and a lower price level and lower RGDP will result.

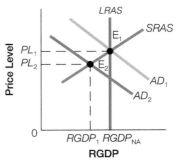

27. Arguments can be made that the generation of the taxpayers living at the time that the debt is issued shoulders the true cost of the debt, because the debt permits the government to take command of resources that would be available for other, private uses. However, the issuance of debt does involve some intergenerational transfer of incomes. Long after federal debt is issued, new generations of taxpayers are making interest payments to people of the generation that bought the bonds issued to finance that debt. If public debt is created intelligently, however, the "burden" of the debt should be less than the benefits derived from the resources acquired as a result; this is particularly true when the debt allows for an expansion in real economic activity or for the development of vital infrastructure for the future.

CHAPTER 19

1. An economics professor might find it difficult to locate a trading partner willing to listen to economics lectures or receive economic advice in exchange for a new car. There may be significant search costs involved in locating such a trading partner. The professor might have to provide lectures in exchange for goods that are not desired, hoping that ultimately, after perhaps a series of trades, to be able to obtain a new car.

3. As the economy becomes more complex, the number of exchanges between people in the economy grows very rapidly. This means that the transaction cost advantages of using money instead of barter for those exchanges also grow very rapidly as the economy becomes more complex.

5. ATMs and online banking have made it far easier to convert savings accounts into chequing accounts, so savings accounts have become more liquid as a result.

7. Interest-earning chequing accounts provide the same ability to make transactions as noninterest-earning demand deposit accounts but are more attractive to many consumers because they earn interest. Overdraft protection means that consumers do not have to keep as much money in demand deposit accounts "just in case" in order to protect against overdrawing their accounts.

9. Money is both an asset and a liability. It is an asset to those who possess it, but it is a liability of the banking system.

11. A new $10 000 deposit adds that amount to both your demand deposit account and to the reserves of your bank. But only a fraction of the added reserves are required by the addition to your demand deposit account. The rest are excess reserves, which the bank will look to convert to interest-earning loans or other assets.

13. **a.**
10 percent	$10 000
15 percent	Zero (it has zero excess reserves)
20 percent	Zero (it has insufficient reserves)

   b.
10 percent	$46 000
15 percent	$34 000
20 percent	$22 000

15. **a.** $50,000 ($5,000 × 1/0.10)
   b. −$500 (−$50 × 1/0.10)
   c. While the balance sheets of the individual banks are affected, there is no change in the level of demand deposits in the overall banking system.

17. Excess reserves equal $300 000. The potential expansion in demand deposits from loaning out these excess reserves equals $3 000 000 ($300 000 × 1/0.10).

10 percent desired reserve ratio

Bank Balance Sheet (revised)			
Assets		**Liabilities**	
Reserves	$ 500 000	Demand deposits	$2 000 000
Loans	1 600 000	Demand deposits (new)	3 000 000
Loans (new)	3 000 000	Total Liabilities	$5 000 000
Buildings	1 200 000	Capital	1 300 000
Total Assets	**$6 300 000**	**Total Liabilities and Capital**	**$6 300 000**

19. Excess reserves equal $50 000. The potential expansion in demand deposits from loaning out these excess reserves equals $250 000 ($50 000 × 1/0.20).

20 percent desired reserve ratio

Bank Balance Sheet (revised)			
Assets		**Liabilities**	
Reserves	$ 750 000	Demand deposits	$3 500 000
Loans	2 500 000	Demand deposits (new)	250 000
Loans (new)	250 000	Total Liabilities	$3 750 000
Buildings	1 250 000	Capital	1 000 000
Total Assets	**$4 750 000**	**Total Liabilities and Capital**	**$4 750 000**

CHAPTER 20

1. The following are functions of the Bank of Canada:
   b. Supervise banks
   d. Issue currency
   e. Regulate the money supply
   f. Loan reserves to banks
   g. Act as the bank for the Canadian government

3.

Nonbank Public			
Assets		**Liabilities**	
Securities	−$10 million		
Demand deposits	+$10 million		

Banking System				Bank of Canada			
Assets		**Liabilities**		**Assets**		**Liabilities**	
Reserves	+$10 million	Demand deposits	+$10 million	Securities	+$10 million	Reserves of banking system	+$10 million

25 percent desired reserve ratio

Banking System			
Assets		**Liabilities**	
Reserves	$2 500 000	Demand deposits	$10 million
Excess reserves	$7 500 000		

Potential money creation   = $30 million $7.5 million × 1/0.25
(Bank system lending)
Initial demand deposit   = $10 million

Total increase in money supply = $40 million

5. The potential change in the money supply is −$100 000 (−$10 000 × 1/0.10).
7. If the bank increases the desired reserve ratio to 12.5 percent, there would be insufficient reserves for the $1 000 000 in deposits by an amount of $25 000. The $100 000 in reserves would support only $800 000 in deposits, so this would decrease the money supply by $200 000.
9. When the Bank of Canada pays for an open market purchase and its cheque (electronic payment) clears, it will add that amount of new reserves to the bank where the payment is deposited by the seller. The excess reserves created by that process lead to an expansion of bank loans of those reserves, creating additional demand deposits and therefore additional money.
11. **a.** $M \times V = P \times Q$
    b. Nominal GDP would double.
    c. The price level would double.
    d. Nominal GDP would double.
    e. Nominal GDP would remain unchanged.
13. If the money supply is $10 billion and velocity is 4 (so that $M \times V = $40 billion), the product of the price level and real output ($P \times Q$, or nominal output), must also be $40 billion. If the price level is 2, real output would equal the $40 billion nominal output divided by the price level of 2, or $20 billion.

CHAPTER 21

1. The higher the price level, the more money will be needed to conduct a given real value of transactions or for "just in case" precautionary purposes, so the demand for money for such purposes will be roughly proportionate to the price level. People will want to hold less money for either purpose when the opportunity cost of holding money—the interest rate—is higher.
3. When the demand for money increases, if there is no change in the money supply, interest rates will rise. Alternatively, to keep interest rates from rising will require an increase in the money supply.
5. **a.**

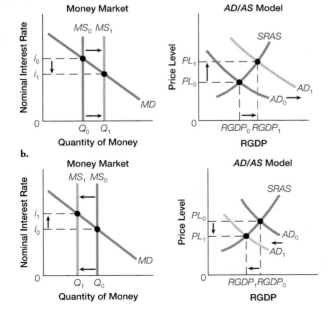

b.

7. **a.**

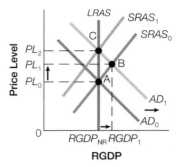

The short-run result is indicated by the movement from point A to point B in the diagram above.

b.

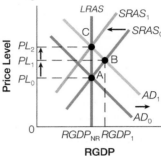

The long-run result is indicated by the movement from point B to point C in the diagram above.

9. An expansionary monetary policy shifts aggregate demand to the right. Starting from less than full employment, the result will be an increase in the price level, an increase in real output, and a decrease in unemployment as the economy moves up along the short-run aggregate supply curve. This increased output will be sustainable if it does not exceed the natural level of real output.
11. The more excess capacity there is in the economy, the flatter the short-run aggregate supply curve over that range of output. Therefore, the more excess capacity there is in the economy, a given shift in aggregate demand will result in a larger effect on real output and a smaller effect on the price level.
13. In Canada, fiscal policy is implemented by the Government of Canada while monetary policy is delivered by the Bank of Canada. The separation between these two economic decision-making bodies introduces the possibility of conflicting policy initiatives being introduced simultaneously.
15. A desire on the part of the banking system to keep some excess reserves would reduce the money supply, other things being equal. The retention of some excess reserves essentially equates to a higher desired reserve ratio (R), which would have a negative effect on the size of the money multiplier. Such a change would thus at least partly offset the effects of the Bank of Canada's expansionary policy changes, which would hinder the Bank of Canada's ability to successfully use expansionary monetary policy to increase the money supply.
17. A movement up and to the left along a Phillips curve indicates an increase in inflation and a reduction in unemployment. A movement up and to the right along a short-run aggregate supply curve (achieved by a rightward shift in aggregate demand) indicates a price level increase (higher inflation) and an increase in RGDP (lower unemployment).
19. The argument is that once capacity utilization is high and unemployment is low, an increased part of the economy is already operating at or near full capacity; further fiscal or monetary policy stimulus primarily triggers inflationary pressures in sectors already at capacity, while eliminating decreasing amounts of unemployment in those fewer sectors where excess capacity and high unemployment still exist.

CHAPTER 22

1. The nature of Canadian exports has been, and continues to be, predominantly natural resource-based products (farm, fishing, and intermediate food products; energy products; mineral products; basic and

industrial chemical, plastic, and rubber products; and forestry products).
As for imports, the Canadian economy imports predominantly finished
goods (electronic and electrical equipment, motor vehicles, and consumer
goods).

3. All countries are importantly affected by international trade, although
the magnitude of the international trade sector varies substantially by
country. International connections mean that any of a large number of
disturbances that originate elsewhere may have important consequences
for the domestic economy.

5. a.

	Fish per Day	Buckets of Berries per Day
Bud	16	8
Larry	8	8
Total	24	16

b. Bud is better off because he can produce and consume more fish
while producing the same quantity of berries.

c.

	Opportunity Cost of a Bucket of Berries	Opportunity Cost of a Fish
Bud	2 fish	1/2 bucket of berries
Larry	1 fish	1 bucket of berries

d. Bud has a comparative advantage in fishing and Larry has a comparative advantage in picking berries.

e. A total of 32 fish and 16 buckets of berries will be produced. There
will be 8 more fish and no fewer berries produced if they both completely specialize according to their comparative advantage.

7. Country B has a comparative advantage over the production of Good X
because its opportunity cost of producing 1 unit of Good X is only 1.5
units of Good Y versus 2 units of Good Y in country A. Country A has a
comparative advantage in the production of Good Y.

9. a. The opportunity cost of producing X in Freeland is 2Y. The opportunity cost of producing X in Braveburg is 1.5Y.

b. Since Braveburg has a comparative advantage in producing X, it will
ship X to Freeland in exchange for Y produced in Freeland.

c. The terms of trade will have to be between 1.5Y per X and 2Y per X
(the opportunity costs of producing X in the two countries).

d. Transaction costs, transportation costs, or tariffs greater than the net
gains from trade (0.5 units of Y per X traded) would eliminate trade
between Freeland and Braveburg.

11. Voluntary trade generates consumer surplus because a rational consumer
would not purchase if he did not value the benefits of the purchase at
greater than its cost, and consumer surplus is the difference between that
value and the cost he is forced to pay. Voluntary trade generates producer
surplus because a rational producer would not sell additional units unless
the price he received was greater than his marginal cost, and producer
surplus is the difference between the revenues received and the costs producers must bear to produce the goods that generate those revenues.

13.

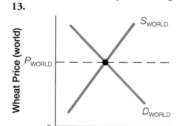
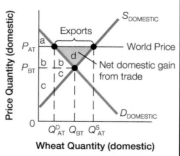

Domestic Gains and Losses from Free Trade (exports)

Area	Before Trade	After Trade	Change
Consumer surplus (*CS*)	a + b	a	−b
Producer surplus (*PS*)	c	b + c + d	+(b + d)
Total welfare from trade (*CS* + *PS*)	a + b + c	a + b + c + d	+d

15. When a country has a comparative disadvantage in producing a good, the
marginal cost of importing is the world price, which is less than the additional
value (along the domestic demand curve) for those units of expanded domestic
consumption and less than the marginal cost of the domestic production
"crowded out." Therefore, there are net domestic gains to international trade
(the gains to domestic consumers exceed the losses to domestic producers).

17. The imposition of a tariff results in a loss of consumer surplus that is
greater than the gain to domestic producers (in the form of producer surplus) and to the government (in the form of tariff revenue).

19. The resources used in lobbying government in favour of zero-sum or
negative-sum protectionism produce nothing of value, and so are losses
from society's point of view. Those resources used up must be added to
the traditional welfare cost measures.

21. Answers will vary.

CHAPTER 23

1. a. Debit
b. Credit
c. Debit
d. Credit

3. a. Canadian exports will increase, imports decrease, and the trade deficit
(surplus) will decrease (increase).

b. Canadian exports will decrease, imports increase, and the trade deficit
(surplus) will increase (decrease).

c. Canadian exports will increase and the trade deficit (surplus) will
decrease (increase).

d. Canadian imports will decrease and the trade deficit (surplus) will
decrease (increase).

e. Canadian exports will decrease, imports increase, and the trade deficit
(surplus) will increase (decrease).

5.

Current Account		Capital Account	
Exports of goods	$50	Net acquisition of financial assets	−$45
Imports of goods	40	Net incurrence of liabilities	60
Merchandise trade balance	10		
Exports of services	10	Financial account balance	15
Import of services	20	Statistical discrepancy	−5
Services trade balance	−10		
Net primary income	5	Net balance	$0
Net secondary income	−15		
Current account balance	−10		

7. **a.** 50 pounds
   b. 800 pesos
   c. The Canadian dollar would depreciate, making the Canadian product cheaper in the other country.
   d. The Canadian dollar would depreciate, making the Canadian product cheaper in the other country.
   e. The Canadian dollar would depreciate, making the Canadian product cheaper in the other country.

9. When a Canadian dollar buys relatively more British pounds, the cost of imports from England falls in Canada because it takes fewer Canadian dollars to buy a given number of British pounds to pay English producers. In other words, the price in Canadian dollars of English goods and services has fallen.

11. As euros become cheaper relative to the Canadian dollar, European products become relatively more inexpensive to Canadians, who therefore buy more European goods and services. To do so, the quantity of euros demanded by Canadian consumers will rise to buy them, as the price (exchange rate) for euros falls. The demand (as opposed to quantity demanded) of euros doesn't increase because this represents a movement along the demand curve for euros caused by a change in exchange rates, rather than a change in demand for euros caused by some other factor.

13. **a.** The supply curve for Canadian dollars shifts to the right.
    b. The supply curve for Canadian dollars shifts to the right.

15. **a.** Demand for euros increases (demand shifts right in the euro market), the Canadian dollar will depreciate, and the euro will appreciate, *ceteris paribus*.
    b. Demand for dollars increases (demand shifts right in the dollar market), the dollar will appreciate, and the yen will depreciate, *ceteris paribus*. Alternatively, you could think of this as an increase in supply in the yen market.
    c. International investors will increase their demand for dollars in the dollar market to take advantage of the higher interest rate. The dollar will appreciate relative to other foreign currencies, *ceteris paribus*.
    d. More foreign investors will want to buy Canadian assets, causing an increase in demand for dollars. The dollar will appreciate relative to other foreign currencies.

17. The central bank must purchase the currency using foreign reserve assets to prevent its currency from falling in value relative to foreign currencies.

Glossary

absolute advantage the ability of a party (nation, region, or individual) to produce more of a good or service while using the same amount of inputs p. 541

accounting profits total revenues minus total explicit costs p. 160

aggregate the total amount—such as the aggregate level of output p. 3

aggregate demand (*AD*) the total demand for all final goods and services in the economy p. 399

aggregate demand curve a graphical representation that shows the inverse relationship between the price level and RGDP demanded p. 408

aggregate supply (*AS*) curve a graphical representation that shows the positive relationship between the price level and real gross domestic product supplied p. 417

allocative efficiency where *P* = *MC* and production is allocated to reflect consumer preferences p. 206

automatic stabilizers changes in government spending or tax collections that automatically help counter business cycle fluctuations p. 461

autonomous determinants of consumption expenditures expenditures not dependent on the level of current disposable income p. 438

average cost pricing production where the price of a good equals average total cost p. 233

average fixed cost (*AFC*) a per-unit measure of fixed costs; fixed costs divided by output p. 166

average propensity to consume (*APC*) the fraction of total disposable income that households spend on consumption p. 400

average revenue (*AR*) total revenue divided by the number of units sold p. 191

average total cost (*ATC*) a per-unit cost of operation; total cost divided by output p. 166

average variable cost (*AVC*) a per-unit measure of variable costs; variable costs divided by output p. 166

backward-bending labour supply curve above a certain wage rate, a worker might prefer to work less and enjoy more leisure (the income effect dominates the substitution effect) p. 281

bads items that we do not desire or want p. 10

balance of payments the record of international transactions of a nation over a year p. 558

balance sheet a financial record that indicates the balance between a bank's assets and its liabilities plus capital p. 485

bandwagon effect a positive network externality where a consumer's demand for a product increases because other consumers own it p. 269

bank rate the interest rate that the Bank of Canada charges major financial institutions on the loans it extends to them p. 503

bankers' deposit rate the interest rate that Bank of Canada pays major financial institutions on surplus funds deposited at the Bank of Canada p. 503

bar graph represents data using vertical bars rising from the horizontal axis between price and quantity demanded p. 30

barter direct exchange of goods and services without the use of money p. 475

boom prolonged expansion in economic activity p. 348

budget deficit government spending exceeds tax revenues for a given fiscal year p. 449

budget surplus tax revenues are greater than government expenditures for a given fiscal year p. 449

business cycles short-term fluctuations in the economy relative to the long-term trend in output p. 346

capital the equipment and structures used to produce goods and services p. 10

capital account a record of the foreign purchases or assets in the domestic economy (a monetary inflow) and domestic purchases of assets abroad (a monetary outflow) p. 560

capital-intensive production that uses a large amount of capital p. 23

cartel a collection of firms that agree on sales, pricing, and other decisions p. 261

cash transfer direct cash payment such as public pensions, social assistance, and Employment Insurance benefits p. 298

causation when one event causes another event to occur p. 6

ceteris paribus holding everything else constant p. 5

change in demand a change in a determinant of demand leads to a change in demand, a shift of the entire demand curve p. 67

change in quantity demanded a change in a good's price leads to a change in quantity demanded, a move along a given demand curve p. 67

chartered banks financial institutions that accept deposits and make loans p. 483

circular flow model of income and output an illustration of the continuous flow of goods, services, inputs, and payments between firms and households p. 55

Coase theorem states that where property rights are defined in a clear-cut fashion, externalities are internalized p. 321

collective bargaining negotiations between representatives of employers and unions p. 287

collude when firms act together to restrict competition p. 261

command economy the government uses central planning to coordinate most economic activities p. 22

common resource a rival good that is not excludable p. 324

comparative advantage occurs when a person or a country can produce a good or service at a lower opportunity cost than others can p. 19

complement an increase (a decrease) in the price of one good causes a decrease (an increase) in the demand of another good p. 68

constant-cost industry an industry where input prices (and cost curves) do not change as industry output changes p. 202

constant returns to scale occur in an output range where *LRATC* does not change as output varies p. 174

consumer equilibrium allocation of consumer income that balances the ratio of marginal utility to the price of the goods purchased p. 144

Consumer Price Index (CPI) a measure of the prices of a basket of consumable goods and services that serves to gauge inflation p. 340

consumer sovereignty consumers vote on economic affairs with their dollars in a market economy p. 22

consumer surplus the monetary difference between the price a consumer is willing and able to pay for an additional unit of a good and the price the consumer actually pays; for the entire market, it is the sum of all of the individual consumer surpluses for those consumers who have purchased the good pp. 145, 543

consumption (*C*) purchases of consumer goods and services by households p. 360

contraction when the economy's output is falling—measured from the peak to the trough p. 347

contractionary fiscal policy use of fiscal policy tools to reduce output by decreasing government spending and/or increasing taxes p. 449

cooperative game collusion by two firms in order to improve their profit maximizations p. 264

correlation two events that usually occur together p. 6

cost-push inflation a price level increase due to a negative supply shock or increase in input prices p. 425

cross-price elasticity of demand a measure of the impact that a price change of one good will have on the quantity demanded of another good at a given price p. 125

crowding-out effect theory that government borrowing drives up the interest rate, lowering consumption by households and investment spending by firms p. 462

currency consists of coins and banknotes that an institution or government has created to be used in the trading of goods and services and the payment of debts p. 477

currency appreciation an increase in the value of a currency p. 562

currency depreciation a decrease in the value of a currency p. 563

current account a record of a country's imports and exports of goods and services, net primary income, and net secondary income p. 558

cyclical unemployment unemployment due to short-term cyclical fluctuations in the economy p. 336

deadweight loss net loss of total surplus that results from the misallocation of resources p. 150

decreasing-cost industry an industry where input prices fall (and cost curves fall) as industry output rises p. 205

deflation a decrease in the overall price level p. 339

demand deposits balances in bank accounts that depositors can access on demand p. 478

demand-pull inflation a price level increase due to an increase in aggregate demand p. 425

depression a severe recession p. 348

derived demand the demand for an input is derived from the consumers' demands for a good or service produced with that input pp. 276, 564

desired reserve ratio the percentage of deposits that a bank chooses to hold as cash reserves p. 486

diminishing marginal product as a variable input increases, with other inputs fixed, a point will be reached where the additions to output will eventually decline p. 165

diminishing marginal utility the concept that, as an individual consumes more and more of a good, each successive unit generates less and less utility (or satisfaction) p. 142

dirty float system a description of the exchange rate system that means that fluctuations in currency values are partly determined by market forces and partly influenced by government intervention p. 571

discouraged workers people who have left the labour force because they could not find work p. 332

diseconomies of scale occur in an output range where *LRATC* rises as output expands p. 174

disposable income the personal income available after taxes p. 366

dissaving consuming more than total available income p. 407

dominant strategy will be optimal regardless of the opponents' actions p. 265

double counting adding the value of a good or service twice by mistakenly counting intermediate goods and services in GDP p. 358

durable goods consumer goods that can be used repeatedly for more than one year, such as automobiles p. 361

economic growth an upward trend in the real per capita output of goods and services p. 381

economic profits total revenues minus explicit and implicit costs p. 160

economics the study of the allocation of our limited resources to satisfy our unlimited wants p. 1

economies of scale occur in an output range where *LRATC* falls as output increases p. 174

efficiency getting the most from society's scarce resources p. 52

elastic demand segment a portion of the demand curve where the percentage change of quantity demanded is greater than the percentage change in price ($E_D > 1$) p. 114

empirical analysis the examination of data to see if the hypothesis fits well with the facts p. 5

entrepreneurship the process of combining labour, land, and capital together to produce goods and services p. 10

equilibrium price the price at the intersection of the market supply and demand curves; at this price, the quantity demanded equals the quantity supplied p. 92

equilibrium quantity the quantity at the intersection of the market supply and demand curves; at this quantity, the quantity demanded equals the quantity supplied p. 92

excess capacity occurs when the firm produces below the level where average total cost is minimized p. 252

excess reserves cash reserves that are in excess of desired reserves p. 486

exchange rate the price of one unit of a country's currency in terms of another country's currency p. 562

excise tax a sales tax on individual products such as alcohol, tobacco, and gasoline p. 452

expansion when output (real GDP) is rising significantly—the period between the trough of a recession and the next peak p. 347

expansionary fiscal policy use of fiscal policy tools to foster increased output by increasing government spending and/or lowering taxes p. 449

expenditure approach calculation of GDP by adding up how much market participants spend on final goods and services over a period of time p. 360

expenditure multiplier the multiplier that considers only the impact of consumption changes on aggregate expenditures p. 444

explicit costs the opportunity costs of production that require a monetary payment p. 158

externality a benefit or cost from consumption or production that spills over onto those that are not consuming or producing the good p. 307

factor (input) markets the market where households sell the use of their inputs (capital, land, labour, and entrepreneurship) to firms p. 55

factor payments wages (salaries), rent, interest payments, and profits paid to the owners of productive resources p. 365

fallacy of composition even if something is true for an individual, it is not necessarily true for a group p. 7

fiat money a means of exchange established by government declaration p. 478

fiscal policy use of government spending and/or taxes to alter RGDP and the price level p. 448

fixed costs costs that do not vary with the level of output for an economy, given the inputs and technology available p. 166

fixed investments all new spending on capital goods by producers p. 361

fractional reserve system a system in which banks hold reserves equal to some fraction of their demand deposits p. 484

free rider a party that derives benefits from something without paying for it p. 323

frictional unemployment the temporary unemployment that results from workers searching for suitable jobs and firms looking for suitable workers p. 335

game theory firms attempt to maximize profits by acting in ways that minimize damage from competitors p. 264

GDP deflator a price index that helps to measure the average price level of all final goods and services produced in the economy p. 367

gold standard a monetary system that defines the value of the dollar as equivalent in value to a certain amount of gold, thereby allowing direct convertibility from currency to gold p. 481

goods items we value or desire p. 10

goods and services flow the continuous flow of inputs and outputs in an economy p. 55

gross domestic product (GDP) the measure of economic performance based on the value of all final goods and services produced in a country during a given period of time p. 358

human capital the productive knowledge and skill people receive from education and on-the-job training p. 10

hyperinflation extremely high rates of inflation for a sustained period of time p. 343

hypothesis a testable proposition p. 4

implicit costs the opportunity costs of production that do not require a monetary payment p. 159

import quota a legal limit on the imported quantity of a good that is produced abroad and can be sold in domestic markets p. 550

income approach calculation of GDP based on the summation of incomes received by the owners of resources used in the production of goods and services p. 364

income effect at higher prices, buyers feel poorer, causing a lowering of quantity demanded p. 64

income elasticity of demand a measure of the responsiveness of the quantity demanded of a good to a change in income p. 126

income flow the continuous flow of income and expenditure in an economy p. 55

increasing-cost industry an industry where input prices rise (and cost curves rise) as industry output rises p. 204

individual demand curve a graphical representation that shows the inverse relationship between price and quantity demanded p. 64

individual demand schedule a table that shows the relationship between price and quantity demanded p. 64

individual supply curve a graphical representation that shows the positive relationship between the price and the quantity supplied p. 74

inelastic demand segment a portion of the demand curve where the percentage change in quantity demanded is less than the percentage change in price ($E_D < 1$) p. 115

inferior good if income increases, the demand for a good decreases; if income decreases, the demand for a good increases p. 69

inflation a continuous rise in the overall price level p. 339

inflationary gap an output gap that occurs when the actual output is greater than the potential output p. 425

in-kind transfers transfers of goods and services rather than cash p. 293

innovation applications of new knowledge that create new products or improve existing products p. 387

internalized externalities when an industry is forced to compensate those enduring some negative externality caused by its production p. 313

inventory investment all purchases by businesses that add to the stocks of goods kept by the firm to meet consumer demand p. 362

investment (*I*) the creation of capital goods to augment future production p. 361

job leaver a person who quits his or her job p. 332

job loser an individual who has been laid off or fired p. 332

joint profit maximization determination of price based on the marginal revenue derived from the market demand schedule and marginal cost schedule of the firms in the industry p. 261

labour the physical and mental effort used by people in the production of goods and services p. 10

labour force persons 15 years of age and over who are employed or are unemployed and seeking work p. 329

labour force participation rate the percentage of the population (aged 15 years and over) in the labour force p. 333

labour-intensive production that uses a large amount of labour p. 23

land the natural resources used in the production of goods and services p. 10

law of demand the quantity of a good or service demanded varies inversely (negatively) with its price, *ceteris paribus* p. 63

law of increasing opportunity cost as more of one item is produced by an economy, the opportunity cost of additional units of that product rises p. 44

law of supply the higher (lower) the price of the good, the greater (smaller) the quantity supplied, *ceteris paribus* p. 74

leading economic indicators factors that typically change before changes in economic activity p. 349

legal tender refers to coins and banknotes officially declared to be acceptable for the settlement of debts incurred in financial transactions p. 477

leverage the use of borrowed money for the purpose of investing p. 487

leverage ratio the ratio of total assets to bank capital p. 487

liquidity the ease with which one asset can be converted into another asset or into goods and services p. 480

long run a period over which all production inputs are variable p. 163

long-run aggregate supply (*LRAS*) curve the graphical relationship between RGDP and the price level when output prices and input prices can fully adjust to economic changes p. 417

low-income cut-off (LICO) income level at which a family may be in straitened circumstance because it has to spend a greater proportion of its income on the basics (food, clothing, and shelter) than the average family of similar size p. 296

M2 currency outside chartered banks plus demand and savings deposits at chartered banks p. 480

M2+ M2 plus demand and savings deposits at trust companies, mortgage loan companies, credit unions, caisses populaires, and other financial institutions p. 480

macroeconomics the study of the aggregate economy, including the topics of inflation, unemployment, and economic growth p. 3

marginal cost (*MC*) the change in total costs resulting from a one-unit change in output p. 167

marginal cost pricing the decision to set production where the price of a good equals marginal cost p. 232

marginal product (*MP*) the change in total product *resulting from a unit change in input* p. 164

marginal propensity to consume (*MPC*) the additional consumption resulting from an additional dollar of disposable income pp. 401, 439

marginal propensity to save (*MPS*) the additional saving that results from an additional dollar of income p. 439

marginal resource cost (*MRC*) the amount that an extra input adds to the firm's total costs p. 277

marginal revenue (*MR*) the increase in total revenue that results from the sale of one more unit p. 191

marginal revenue product (*MRP*) the additional revenue that a firm obtains from one more unit of input p. 277

marginal thinking focusing on the additional, or incremental, choices p. 14

marginal utility (*MU*) extra satisfaction generated by an additional unit of a good that is consumed in a particular time period p. 140

market the process of buyers and sellers exchanging goods and services p. 51

market demand curve the horizontal summation of individual demand curves p. 65

market economy goods and services are allocated based on the private decisions of consumers, input suppliers, and firms p. 22

market equilibrium the point at which the market supply and the market demand curves intersect p. 92

market failure when the economy fails to allocate resources efficiently on its own p. 53

market supply curve the horizontal summation of individual supply curves p. 75

means of deferred payment the attribute of money that makes it easier to borrow and to repay loans p. 477

measure of value money as a common "ruler" of worth allowing for the comparison of diverse goods and services p. 476

medium of exchange the primary function of money, which is to facilitate transactions and lower transactions costs p. 475

menu costs the costs incurred by a firm as a result of changing its listed prices p. 344

microeconomics the study of the smaller units within the economy, including the topics of household and firm behaviour and how they interact in the marketplace p. 3

minimum efficient scale the output level where economies of scale are exhausted and constant returns to scale begin p. 175

mixed economy government and the private sector together determine the allocation of resources p. 22

monetary policy the policy decisions that the Bank of Canada makes in managing the money supply and interest rates, consistent with its inflation-control objective p. 502

money anything generally accepted in exchange for goods or services p. 475

money market the market in which money demand and money supply determine the equilibrium nominal interest rate p. 512

money multiplier measures the potential amount of demand deposit money that the banking system generates with each dollar of reserves p. 490

monopolistic competition a market structure with many firms selling differentiated products p. 246

monopoly a market with only one seller of a product that has no close substitute and there are natural and legal barriers to entry that prevent competition p. 216

monopsony a market with a single buyer p. 285

multiplier effect a chain reaction of additional income and purchases that results in total purchases that are greater than the initial increase in purchases p. 454

mutual interdependence when a firm shapes its policy with an eye to the policies of competing firms p. 259

Nash equilibrium firms that are interacting with one another each chooses its best strategy given the strategies of the other firms p. 266

national income accounting a uniform means of measuring economic performance p. 357

national saving the sum of both private and public saving p. 405

natural monopoly a firm that can produce at a lower cost than a number of smaller firms could p. 218

natural rate of unemployment the amount of unemployment that is unavoidable, equal to the sum of frictional and structural unemployment when they are at a maximum p. 337

negative externality when costs spill over to an outside party that is not involved in producing or consuming the good p. 307

negative incentives incentives that either increase costs or reduce benefits, resulting in a decrease in the activity or behaviour p. 18

negative network externality when a consumer's quantity demanded for a good increases because fewer consumers are purchasing the same good p. 268

negative relationship when two variables change in opposite directions p. 32

net benefits the difference between the expected marginal benefits and expected marginal costs p. 15

net domestic income at factor cost a measure of income earned by the owners of factors of production p. 365

net exports the difference between the value of exports and the value of imports p. 402

network externality when the number of other people purchasing the good influences quantity demanded p. 268

new entrant an individual who has not held a job before but is now seeking employment p. 332

nominal interest rate the reported interest rate that is not adjusted for inflation p. 344

noncooperative game each firm sets its own price without consulting other firms p. 264

nondurable goods tangible consumer items that are typically consumed or used only once, such as food p. 361

normal good if income increases, the demand for a good increases; if income decreases, the demand for a good decreases p. 69

normative analysis a subjective, biased approach p. 8

oligopoly a market structure with only a few sellers offering similar or identical products p. 258

open economy a type of model that includes international trade effects p. 401

open market operations purchase and sale of government securities by the Bank of Canada p. 503

opportunity cost the highest or best forgone opportunity resulting from a decision p. 12

overnight interest rate the interest rate that major financial institutions charge each other for one-day loans p. 502

payoff matrix a summary of the possible outcomes from the various strategies p. 265

peak the point in time when the expansion comes to an end, when output is at the highest point in the cycle p. 347

perfect competition a market with many buyers and sellers, all selling a homogeneous product; market entry and exit is easy, and no firm can affect the market price p. 186

personal income the amount of income received by households before taxes p. 366

pie chart a circle subdivided into proportionate slices that represent various quantities that add up to 100 percent p. 30

pollution tax tax levied by government on a firm for environmental pollution p. 318

positive analysis an objective, value-free approach, utilizing the scientific method p. 7

positive externality when benefits spill over to an outside party that is not involved in producing or consuming the good p. 308

positive incentives incentives that either reduce costs or increase benefits, resulting in an increase in the activity or behaviour p. 18

positive network externality when a consumer's quantity demanded for a good increases because a greater number of consumers purchase the same good p. 268

positive relationship when two variables change in the same direction p. 32

potential output the amount of real output the economy would produce if its labour and other resources were fully employed—that is, at the natural rate of unemployment p. 337

poverty a state in which a family's income is too low to be able to buy the quantities of food, shelter, and clothing that are deemed necessary p. 296

price ceiling a legally established maximum price p. 102

price controls government-mandated minimum and maximum prices p. 102

price discrimination the practice of charging different consumers different prices for the same good or service when the cost of providing that good or service is not different for different consumers p. 234

price elasticity of demand a measure of the responsiveness of quantity demanded to a change in price p. 113

price elasticity of supply the measure of the sensitivity of the quantity supplied to changes in the price of a good p. 127

price floor a legally established minimum price p. 102

price index a measure of the trend in prices for a certain bundle of goods and services over a given time period p. 339

price level the average level of prices in the economy p. 339

price maker a monopolistic firm that sets the price of its product so as to maximize profits p. 216

price taker a perfectly competitive firm takes the price that it is given by the intersection of the market demand and market supply curves p. 186

private good a good with rivalrous consumption and excludability p. 322

private saving the amount of income that households have left over after consumption and taxes p. 405

producer goods capital goods that increase future production capabilities p. 361

producer surplus the difference between what a producer is paid for a good and the cost of producing that unit of the good; for the market, it is the sum of all the individual sellers' producer surpluses—the area above the market supply curve and below the market price pp. 147, 544

product differentiation the accentuation of unique product qualities, real or perceived, to develop a specific product identity p. 247

product markets the markets for consumer goods and services p. 55

production function the relationship between the quantity of inputs and the quantity of outputs produced p. 163

production possibilities curve the potential total output combinations of any two goods p. 41

productive efficiency where a good or service is produced at the lowest possible cost p. 206

productivity the amount of goods and services a worker can produce per hour p. 384

profit-maximizing output rule a firm should always produce at the level of output where $MR = MC$ p. 192

profits the difference between total revenue and total cost p. 160

progressive tax the amount of an individual's tax rises as a proportion of income, as the person's income rises p. 452

progressive tax system as a person's income rises, the amount of his or her tax as a proportion of income rises p. 298

proportional tax designed so that all taxpayers are subject to the tax rate, regardless of earnings p. 452

public good a good that is nonrivalrous in consumption and nonexcludable p. 322

public saving the amount of income that the government has left over after paying for its spending p. 405

quantity theory of money and prices a theory of the connection between the money supply and the price level when the velocity of money is constant p. 508

real gross domestic product (RGDP) the total value of all final goods and services produced in a given time period, such as a year or a quarter, adjusted for inflation p. 328

real gross domestic product per capita real output of goods and services per person p. 369

real interest rate the nominal interest rate minus the inflation rate p. 344

recession a period of significant decline in output and employment p. 347

recessionary gap an output gap that occurs when the actual output is less than the potential output p. 425

re-entrant an individual who worked before and is now re-entering the labour force p. 332

regressive tax the amount of an individual's tax falls as a proportion of income, as the person's income rises p. 452

relative price the price of a specific good compared to the prices of other goods p. 339

rent seeking producer efforts to gain profits from government protections such as tariffs and import quotas p. 551

research and development (R&D) activities undertaken to create new products and processes that will lead to technological progress p. 389

resources inputs used to produce goods and services p. 1

rule of rational choice individuals will pursue an activity if the expected marginal benefits are greater than the expected marginal costs p. 15

savings deposits financial institution accounts containing funds that cannot be used directly for payment p. 480

scarcity the situation that exists when human wants exceed available resources p. 10

semi-durable goods consumer items that can be used more than once and have an expected lifetime of around one year, such as clothing p. 361

service an intangible act that people want p. 10

shocks unexpected aggregate supply or aggregate demand changes p. 424

shoe-leather cost the time and inconvenience cost incurred when individuals reduce their money holdings because of inflation p. 344

shortage where quantity demanded exceeds quantity supplied p. 93

short run a period too brief for some production inputs to be varied p. 163

short-run aggregate supply (SRAS) curve the graphical relationship between RGDP and the price level when output prices can change but input prices are unable to adjust p. 417

short-run market supply curve the horizontal summation of the individual firms' supply curves in the market p. 196

short-run supply curve as a cost relationship, this curve shows the marginal cost of producing any given output; as a supply curve, it shows the equilibrium output that the firm will supply at various prices in the short run p. 196

slope the ratio of rise (change in the Y variable) over the run (change in the X variable) p. 36

specializing concentrating on the production of one, or a few, goods p. 19

stagflation a situation in which lower growth and higher prices occur together p. 425

store of value how money provides a means of saving or accumulating purchasing power from the present and transferring it to the future p. 476

structural unemployment unemployment that occurs due to a lack of skills necessary for available jobs p. 335

subsidy a program of financial assistance paid out to producers p. 552

substitute an increase (a decrease) in the price of one good causes an increase (a decrease) in the demand for another good p. 68

substitution effect at higher prices, buyers increasingly substitute other goods for the good that now has a higher relative price p. 64

sunk costs costs that have been incurred and cannot be recovered p. 161

surplus where quantity supplied exceeds quantity demanded p. 93

switching costs the costs involved in changing from one product to another brand or in changing suppliers p. 269

tariff a tax on imported goods p. 547

tax incidence the analysis of the effect of a particular tax on the distribution of economic welfare p. 130

the economic problem scarcity forces us to choose, and choices are costly because we must give up other opportunities that we value p. 1

theory an established explanation that accounts for known facts or phenomena p. 4

time-series graph shows changes in the value of a variable over time p. 30

tit-for-tat strategy used in repeated games, where one player follows the other player's move in the previous round; leads to greater cooperation p. 268

total cost (TC) the sum of the firm's total fixed costs and total variable costs p. 166

total fixed cost (TFC) the sum of the firm's fixed costs p. 166

total product (*TP*) the total output of a good produced by the firm p. 163

total revenue (*TR*) the product price times the quantity sold p. 190

total utility (*TU*) total amount of satisfaction derived from the consumption of a certain number of units of a good or service p. 140

total variable cost (*TVC*) the sum of the firm's variable costs p. 166

total welfare gains the sum of consumer and producer surplus p. 150

transferable pollution rights a right given to a firm to discharge a specified amount of pollution; its transferable nature creates incentive to lower pollution levels p. 318

trough the point in time when output stops declining; it is the moment when business activity is at its lowest point in the cycle p. 347

underemployment a situation in which workers have skills higher than necessary for a job p. 333

unemployment rate the percentage of the people in the labour force who are unemployed p. 330

unintended consequences the secondary effects of an action that may occur after the initial effects p. 106

unit elastic demand demand with a price elasticity of 1; the percentage change in quantity demanded is equal to the percentage change in price p. 116

unplanned inventory investment collection of inventory that results when people do not buy the products firms are producing p. 440

util one unit of satisfaction p. 139

utility a measure of the relative levels of satisfaction consumers get from consumption of goods and services p. 139

variable something that is measured by a number, such as your height p. 31

variable costs costs that vary with the level of output p. 166

velocity of money (*V*) the average number of times that a dollar is used in purchasing final goods or services in a one-year period p. 508

wage and price inflexibility the tendency for prices and wages to only adjust slowly downward to changes in the economy p. 427

X-axis the horizontal axis on a graph p. 30

Y-axis the vertical axis on a graph p. 30

Index

Chapter in Review

The Role and Method of Economics

Section 1.1 Economics: A Brief Introduction

- *What is economics?*

  Economics is the study of the allocation of our limited resources to satisfy our unlimited wants.

- *Why study economics?*

  Economics is a problem-solving science that teaches you to ask intelligent questions.

- *What distinguishes macroeconomics from microeconomics?*

  Macroeconomics deals with the aggregate, or total, economy, while microeconomics focuses on smaller units within the economy.

Section 1.2 Economic Theory

- *What are economic theories?*

  Economic theories are statements used to explain and predict patterns of human behaviour.

- *Why do we need to abstract?*

  Economic theories, through abstractions, provide a broad view of human economic behaviour.

- *What is a hypothesis?*

  A hypothesis makes a prediction about human behaviour and is then tested.

- *What is the* ceteris paribus *assumption?*

  In order to isolate the effects of one variable on another, we use the *ceteris paribus* assumption.

- *Why are observations and predictions harder in the social sciences?*

  With its focus on human behaviour, which is more variable and less predictable, observation and prediction are more difficult in the social sciences.

- *What distinguishes between correlation and causation?*

  The fact that two events are related does not mean that one caused the other to occur.

- *What are positive analysis and normative analysis?*

  Positive analysis is objective and value-free, while normative analysis involves value judgments and opinions about the desirability of various actions.

Section 1.3 Scarcity

- *What is scarcity?*

  Scarcity exists when our wants exceed the available resources of land, labour, capital, and entrepreneurship.

- *What are goods and services?*

  Goods and services are things that we value.

Section 1.4 Opportunity Cost

- *Why do we have to make choices?*

  Scarcity means we all have to make choices.

- *What do we give up when we have to choose?*

  When we are forced to choose, we give up the next highest-valued alternative.

Key Terms

economics *the study of the allocation of our limited resources to satisfy our unlimited wants p. 1*

resources *inputs used to produce goods and services p. 1*

the economic problem *scarcity forces us to choose, and choices are costly because we must give up other opportunities that we value p. 1*

macroeconomics *the study of the aggregate economy, including the topics of inflation, unemployment, and economic growth p. 3*

aggregate *the total amount— such as the aggregate level of output p. 3*

microeconomics *the study of the smaller units within the economy, including the topics of household and firm behaviour and how they interact in the marketplace p. 3*

theory *an established explanation that accounts for known facts or phenomena p. 4*

hypothesis *a testable proposition p. 4*

empirical analysis *the examination of data to see if the hypothesis fits well with the facts p. 5*

ceteris paribus *holding everything else constant p. 5*

correlation *two events that usually occur together p. 6*

causation *when one event causes another event to occur p. 6*

fallacy of composition *even if something is true for an individual, it is not necessarily true for a group p. 7*

positive analysis *an objective, value-free approach, utilizing the scientific method p. 7*

normative analysis *a subjective, biased approach p. 8*

scarcity *the situation that exists when human wants exceed available resources p. 10*

labour *the physical and mental effort used by people in the production of goods and services p. 10*

- *Why are "free" lunches not free?*

Because the production of any good uses up some of society's resources, there is no such thing as a free lunch.

Section 1.5 Marginal Thinking

- *What do we mean by marginal thinking?*

Economists are usually interested in the effects of additional, or incremental, changes in a given situation.

- *What is the rule of rational choice?*

The rule of rational choice states that individuals will pursue an activity if they expect the marginal benefits to be greater than the marginal costs, or $E(MB) > E(MC)$.

Section 1.6 Incentives Matter

- *Can we predict how people will respond to changes in incentives?*

Incentives change the expected marginal benefits and expected marginal costs of certain behaviour. Therefore, when people are acting rationally, they respond to incentives in predictable ways.

- *What are positive and negative incentives?*

A negative incentive increases costs or reduces benefits, thus discouraging consumption or production, while a positive incentive decreases costs or increases benefits, thus encouraging consumption or production.

Section 1.7 Specialization and Trade

- *Why do people specialize?*

Specialization is important for individuals, businesses, regions, and nations. It allows them to make the best use of their limited resources.

- *How does specialization and trade lead to greater wealth and prosperity?*

Specialization and trade increase wealth by allowing a person, a region, or a nation to specialize in those products that it produces at a lower opportunity cost and to trade for those products that others produce at a lower opportunity cost.

Section 1.8 The Three Questions Every Society Faces

- *What is to be produced?*

Every economy has to decide what to produce. In a decentralized market economy, millions of buyers and sellers determine what and how much to produce. In a mixed economy, the government and the private sector determine the allocation of resources.

- *How are the goods and services to be produced?*

The best form of production is the one that conserves the relatively scarce (more costly) resources and uses more of the abundant (less costly) resources. When capital is relatively scarce and labour is plentiful, production tends to be labour-intensive. When capital is relatively abundant and labour is relatively scarce, production tends to be capital-intensive.

- *Who will get the goods and services?*

In a market economy, the amount of goods and services one is able to obtain depends on one's income. The amount of one's income depends on the quantity and the quality of the scarce resources that the individual controls.

Scarcity, Trade-Offs, and Production Possibilities

Section 2.1 The Production Possibilities Curve

- *What is a production possibilities curve?*

  A production possibilities curve represents the potential total output combinations of any two goods available to a society, given its resources and existing technology.

- *What is efficiency?*

  Efficiency requires society to use its resources to the fullest extent—no wasted resources. If the economy is operating within the production possibilities curve, the economy is operating inefficiently.

- *How is opportunity cost measured?*

  The cost of altering production within the production possibilities curve framework, at efficiency, is measured in forgone units of the sole alternative.

- *What is the law of increasing opportunity costs?*

  A bowed production possibilities curve means that the opportunity costs of producing additional units of a good rise as society produces more of that good (the law of increasing opportunity costs).

Section 2.2 Economic Growth and the Production Possibilities Curve

- *How do we show economic growth on the production possibilities curve?*

  Economic growth is represented by an outward shift of the production possibilities curve, indicating the possibility of producing more of all goods. Despite this, scarcity inevitably remains a fact of life.

- *How can we summarize the production possibilities curve?*

  The production possibilities model is an effective way of illustrating the economic concepts of scarcity, choice, opportunity costs, efficiency, and economic growth.

Section 2.3 Market Prices Coordinate Economic Activity

- *What is a market?*

  Markets consist of buyers and sellers exchanging goods and services with one another.

- *What are the roles of buyers and sellers in a market?*

  Buyers determine the demand side of the market and sellers determine the supply side of the market.

- *How does a market system allocate scarce resources?*

  Through voluntary exchange and the price system, the market system provides a way for producers and consumers to allocate scarce resources.

- *What is a market failure?*

  A market failure occurs when an economy fails to allocate resources efficiently on its own.

Key Terms

production possibilities curve *the potential total output combinations of any two goods for an economy, given the inputs and technology available* p. 41

law of increasing opportunity cost *as more of one item is produced by an economy, the opportunity cost of additional units of that product rises* p. 44

market *the process of buyers and sellers exchanging goods and services* p. 51

efficiency *getting the most from society's scarce resources* p. 52

market failure *when the economy fails to allocate resources efficiently on its own* p. 53

product markets *the markets for consumer goods and services* p. 55

factor (input) markets *the market where households sell the use of their inputs (capital, land, labour, and entrepreneurship) to firms* p. 55

goods and services flow *the continuous flow of inputs and outputs in an economy* p. 55

income flow *the continuous flow of income and expenditure in an economy* p. 55

circular flow model of income and output *an illustration of the continuous flow of goods, services, inputs, and payments between firms and households* p. 55

Key Exhibits/ Graphs

Section 2.1, Exhibit 2
Section 2.2, Exhibit 1
Section 2.2, Exhibit 2
Section 2.2, Exhibit 3
Section 2.2, Exhibit 4
Section 2.4, Exhibit 1

Section 2.4 The Circular Flow Model

- *What are product markets?*

  In the product market, households are buyers and firms are sellers.

- *What are factor markets?*

  In the factor markets, households are the sellers and firms are the buyers.

- *What is the goods and services flow?*

  The goods and services flow represents the continuous flow of inputs and outputs in an economy.

- *What is the income flow?*

  The income flow represents the continuous flow of income and expenditure in an economy.

- *What is the circular flow model?*

  The circular flow model illustrates the flow of goods, services, and payments among firms and households.

Chapter in Review

Supply and Demand

Section 3.1 Demand

- *What is the law of demand?*

  The law of demand states that when the price of a good falls (rises), the quantity demanded rises (falls), *ceteris paribus*.

- *What is an individual demand schedule and curve?*

  An individual demand schedule is a table that shows the relationship between the price of a good and the quantity demanded.

- *What is a market demand curve?*

  A market demand curve shows the amount of a good that all the buyers in the market would be willing and able to buy at various prices.

Section 3.2 Shifts in the Demand Curve

- *What is the difference between a change in demand and a change in quantity demanded?*

  A change in the quantity demanded describes a movement along a given demand curve in response to a change in the price of the good. A change in demand shifts the entire demand curve in response to a change in some determinant of demand.

- *What are the determinants of demand?*

  Some possible determinants of demand (demand shifters) are the prices of related goods, income, number of buyers, tastes, and expectations.

- *Can we review the distinction between changes in demand and changes in quantity demanded?*

Change in Variable and Change in Demand

Variable	Change in Variable	Change in Demand
1. Price of a complement good	↑	↓
2. Price of a substitute good	↑	↑
3. Income (normal good)	↑	↑
4. Income (inferior good)	↑	↓
5. Number of buyers	↑	↑
6. Tastes and preferences	↑	↑
7. Expected future price	↑	↑

Key Terms

law of demand *the quantity of a good or service demanded varies inversely (negatively) with its price, ceteris paribus* p. 63

substitution effect *at higher prices, buyers increasingly substitute other goods for the good that now has a higher relative price* p. 64

income effect *at higher prices, buyers feel poorer, causing a lowering of quantity demanded* p. 64

individual demand schedule *a table that shows the relationship between price and quantity demanded* p. 64

individual demand curve *a graphical representation that shows the inverse relationship between price and quantity demanded* p. 64

market demand curve *the horizontal summation of individual demand curves* p. 65

change in quantity demanded *a change in a good's price leads to a change in quantity demanded, a move along a given demand curve* p. 67

change in demand *a change in a determinant of demand leads to a change in demand, a shift of the entire demand curve* p. 67

substitute *an increase (a decrease) in the price of one good causes an increase (a decrease) in the demand for another good* p. 68

complement *an increase (a decrease) in the price of one good causes a decrease (an increase) in the demand of another good* p. 68

normal good *if income increases, the demand for a good increases; if income decreases, the demand for a good decreases* p. 69

inferior good *if income increases, the demand for a good decreases; if income decreases, the demand for a good increases* p. 69

Section 3.3 Supply

- *What is the law of supply?*

  The law of supply states that the higher (lower) the price of the good, the greater (smaller) the quantity supplied.

- *What is an individual supply curve?*

  The individual supply curve shows the positive relationship between the price and quantity supplied of a given good or service.

- *What is a market supply curve?*

  The market supply curve is a graphical representation of the amount of goods and services that suppliers are willing and able to supply at various prices.

Section 3.4 Shifts in the Supply Curve

- *What is the difference between a change in supply and a change in quantity supplied?*

  A movement along a given supply curve is caused by a change in the price of the good in question. A shift of the entire supply curve is called a *change in supply*.

- *What are the determinants of supply?*

  Input prices, the prices of related products, expectations, the number of suppliers, technology, regulation, taxes and subsidies, and weather can all lead to changes in supply (shifts in supply).

- *Can we review the distinction between a change in supply and a change in quantity supplied?*

Change in Variable and Change in Supply

Variable	Change in Variable	Change in Supply
1. Input prices	↑	↓
2. Price of substitute in production	↑	↓
3. Price of complement in production	↑	↑
4. Expected future price	↑	↓
5. Number of suppliers	↑	↑
6. Government regulation	↑	↓
7. Taxes	↑	↓
8. Subsidies	↑	↑
9. Technology	↑	↑

Bringing Supply and Demand Together

Section 4.1 Market Equilibrium Price and Quantity

- *What is the equilibrium price and the equilibrium quantity?*

  The intersection of the supply and demand curve shows the equilibrium price and equilibrium quantity in a market.

- *What is a shortage and what is a surplus?*

  A surplus is where quantity supplied exceeds quantity demanded. A shortage is where quantity demanded exceeds quantity supplied.

Section 4.2 Changes in Equilibrium Price and Quantity

- *What happens to equilibrium price and equilibrium quantity when the demand curve shifts?*

  Changes in demand will cause a change in the equilibrium price and quantity, *ceteris paribus*. An increase (decrease) in demand will cause an increase (decrease) in both equilibrium price and equilibrium quantity.

- *What happens to equilibrium price and equilibrium quantity when the supply curve shifts?*

  Changes in supply will cause a change in the equilibrium price and quantity, *ceteris paribus*. An increase (decrease) in supply will cause a decrease (increase) in equilibrium price and an increase (decrease) in equilibrium quantity.

- *What happens when both supply and demand shift in the same time period?*

  When there are simultaneous shifts in both supply and demand curves, either the equilibrium price or the equilibrium quantity will be indeterminate without more information.

Section 4.3 Price Controls

- *What are price controls?*

  Price controls involve government mandates to keep prices above or below the market-determined equilibrium price.

- *What are price ceilings?*

  Price ceilings are government-imposed maximum prices. When price ceilings are set below the equilibrium price, shortages will result.

- *What are price floors?*

  Price floors are government-imposed minimum prices. When price floors are set above the equilibrium price, surpluses will result.

Key Terms

market equilibrium *the point at which the market supply and the market demand curves intersect* p. 92

equilibrium price *the price at the intersection of the market supply and demand curves; at this price the quantity demanded equals the quantity supplied* p. 92

equilibrium quantity *the quantity at the intersection of the market supply and demand curves; at this quantity, the quantity demanded equals the quantity supplied* p. 92

surplus *where quantity supplied exceeds quantity demanded* p. 93

shortage *where quantity demanded exceeds quantity supplied* p. 93

price controls *government-mandated minimum and maximum prices* p. 102

price ceiling *a legally established maximum price* p. 102

price floor *a legally established minimum price* p. 102

unintended consequences *the secondary effects of an action that may occur after the initial effects* p. 106

Key Exhibits/ Graphs

Notes

Chapter in Review

Elasticity

Section 5.1 Price Elasticity of Demand

- *What is price elasticity of demand?*

  Price elasticity of demand measures the percentage change in quantity demanded divided by the percentage change in price.

- *How do we measure consumers' responses to price changes?*

  If the demand for a good is price elastic in the relevant range, quantity demanded is very responsive to a price change. If the demand for a good is relatively price inelastic, quantity demanded is not very responsive to a price change.

- *How do we use the "midpoint method" in calculating price elasticities of demand?*

  The midpoint method for calculating percentage change involves using the average of the changing values, thereby eliminating the direction bias found in the traditional approach.

- *What determines the price elasticity of demand?*

  The price elasticity of demand depends on (1) the availability of close substitutes, (2) the proportion of income spent on the good, and (3) the amount of time that buyers have to respond to a price change.

Section 5.2 Total Revenue and Price Elasticity of Demand

- *How does the price elasticity of demand impact total revenue?*

  If demand is price elastic ($E_D > 1$), total revenue will vary inversely with a change in price. If demand is price inelastic ($E_D < 1$), total revenue will vary in the same direction as a change in price.

- *How does the price elasticity of demand change along a linear demand curve?*

  A linear demand curve is more price elastic at higher price ranges and more price inelastic at lower price ranges, and it is unit elastic at the midpoint: $E_D = 1$.

Section 5.3 Other Demand Elasticities

- *What is the cross-price elasticity of demand?*

  The cross-price elasticity of demand is the percentage change in the quantity demanded of one good divided by the percentage change in the price of another related good (complements and substitutes).

- *What is the income elasticity of demand?*

  The income elasticity of demand is the percentage change in quantity demanded divided by the percentage change in income (normal and inferior goods).

Section 5.4 Price Elasticity of Supply

- *What is the price elasticity of supply?*

  The price elasticity of supply measures the relative change in the quantity supplied that results from a change in price.

- *What determines the price elasticity of supply?*

  Supply tends to be more elastic in the long run than in the short run.

Section 5.5 Elasticity and Taxes

- *What is tax incidence?*

Key Terms

price elasticity of demand *a measure of the responsiveness of quantity demanded to a change in price p. 113*

elastic demand segment *a portion of the demand curve where the percentage change of quantity demanded is greater than the percentage change in price ($E_D > 1$) p. 114*

inelastic demand segment *a portion of the demand curve where the percentage change in quantity demanded is less than the percentage change in price ($E_D < 1$) p. 115*

unit elastic demand *demand with a price elasticity of 1; the percentage change in quantity demanded is equal to the percentage change in price p. 116*

cross-price elasticity of demand *a measure of the impact that a price change of one good will have on the quantity demanded of another good at a given price p. 125*

income elasticity of demand *a measure of the responsiveness of the quantity demanded of a good to a change in income p. 126*

price elasticity of supply *the measure of the sensitivity of the quantity supplied to changes in the price of a good p. 127*

tax incidence *the analysis of the effect of a particular tax on the distribution of economic welfare p. 130*

Key Exhibits/ Graphs

Tax incidence refers to the analysis of the effect of particular taxes on the distribution of economic welfare.

- *How does the relative elasticity of supply and demand determine the tax burden?*

  If demand is more elastic than supply, producers bear the greater burden of the tax; however, if supply is more elastic than demand, consumers bear the greater burden of the tax.

Key Equations

$$E_D = \frac{\text{Percentage change in quantity demanded}}{\text{Percentage change in price}}$$

$$E_{AB} = \frac{\text{Percentage change in quantity demanded of A}}{\text{Percentage change in price of B}}$$

$$E_I = \frac{\text{Percentage change in quantity demanded}}{\text{Percentage change in income}}$$

$$E_s = \frac{\text{Percentage change in quantity supplied}}{\text{Percentage change in price}}$$

Midpoint Method

$$E_D = \frac{\left[\dfrac{Q_A - Q_B}{\left(\dfrac{Q_A + Q_B}{2}\right)}\right]}{\left[\dfrac{P_A - P_B}{\left(\dfrac{P_A + P_B}{2}\right)}\right]}$$

Chapter in Review

Consumer Choice and Market Efficiency

Section 6.1 Consumer Behaviour

- *What is utility?*

  Utility is the level of satisfaction an individual receives from consumption of a good or service. Total utility measures the amount of satisfaction derived from all units consumed, while marginal utility measures the change in utility from consuming one additional unit of a good or service.

- *What is diminishing marginal utility?*

  The less and less satisfaction an individual enjoys as he or she consumes more and more of a good or service describes the concept of diminishing marginal utility.

Section 6.2 Consumer Choice

- *What is the "best" decision for consumers?*

  To maximize consumer satisfaction, income must be allocated so that the ratio of the marginal utility to the price is the same for all goods purchased.

- *What is the connection between the law of demand and the law of diminishing marginal utility?*

  A fall in a good's price will raise its marginal utility–price (*MU/P*) ratio above that of other goods purchased. This relatively greater *MU/P* ratio will lead a rational consumer to purchase more of this good at the expense of other goods.

Section 6.3 Consumer and Producer Surplus

- *What is consumer surplus?*

  The difference between how much a consumer is willing and able to pay and how much a consumer has to pay for a unit of the good is called *consumer surplus*. An increase (decrease) in supply will lead to an increase (decrease) in consumer surplus.

- *What is producer surplus?*

  Producer surplus is the difference between what a producer is paid for a good and the cost of producing that good. An increase (decrease) in demand will lead to an increase (decrease) in producer surplus.

- *How do we measure the total gains from exchange?*

  The economy's total welfare gains from exchange can be measured by the sum of consumer and producer surplus.

Key Equations

$$MU = \frac{\Delta TU}{\Delta Q}$$

Key Terms

utility *a measure of the relative levels of satisfaction consumers get from consumption of goods and services* p. 139

util *one unit of satisfaction* p. 139

total utility *(TU) total amount of satisfaction derived from the consumption of a certain number of units of a good or service* p. 140

marginal utility *(MU) extra satisfaction generated by an additional unit of a good that is consumed in a particular time period* p. 140

diminishing marginal utility *the concept that, as an individual consumes more and more of a good, each successive unit generates less and less utility (or satisfaction)* p. 142

consumer equilibrium *allocation of consumer income that balances the ratio of marginal utility to the price of the goods purchased* p. 144

consumer surplus *the monetary difference between the price a consumer is willing and able to pay for an additional unit of a good and the price the consumer actually pays; for the entire market it is the sum of all the individual consumer surpluses for those consumers who have purchased the good* p. 145

producer surplus *the difference between what a producer is paid for a good and the cost of producing that unit of the good; for the market, it is the sum of all the individual sellers' producer surpluses—the area above the market supply curve and below the market price* p. 147

total welfare gains *the sum of consumer and producer surplus* p. 150

deadweight loss *net loss of total surplus that results from the misallocation of resources* p. 150

Key Exhibits/ Graphs

Chapter in Review

Production and Costs

Section 7.1 Profits: Total Revenues Minus Total Costs

- *What are explicit and implicit costs?*

  Total cost consists of both explicit costs and implicit costs. Explicit costs are the opportunity costs of production that require a monetary payment, while implicit costs are the opportunity costs that do not represent an outlay of money or a contractual obligation.

- *What are profits?*

  Profits are the difference between the total revenues of a firm and its total costs. Accounting profits are revenues minus explicit costs, while economic profits are revenues minus total opportunity costs—both explicit and implicit.

- *What are sunk costs?*

  Sunk costs are irretrievable and irrelevant to the firm.

Section 7.2 Production in the Short Run

- *What is the difference between the short run and the long run?*

  The short run is defined as a period too brief for some inputs to be varied, whereas the long run is a period of time long enough to allow the firm to adjust all inputs. Inputs like buildings and equipment that do not change with output are called *fixed inputs*.

- *How does production in the short run behave?*

  Total output increases as variable inputs are increased. Marginal product initially rises but eventually declines as variable inputs are added. Finally, negative marginal product can occur, indicating a fall in total output.

Section 7.3 Costs in the Short Run

- *What are fixed costs, variable costs, and total costs?*

  Total fixed costs do not change with the level of output, total variable costs change as the level of output changes, and total costs are the sum of total variable costs and total fixed costs.

- *What are average costs?*

  Average total cost (ATC) is total cost divided by output; average fixed cost (AFC) is fixed cost divided by output; and average variable cost (AVC) is variable cost divided by output.

- *What is marginal cost?*

  Marginal cost (MC) is the added cost of producing one more unit of output; it is the change in total cost associated with one more unit of output. It is this cost that is relevant to decisions to produce more or less.

Section 7.4 The Shape of the Short-Run Cost Curves

- *What is the relationship between marginal costs and marginal product?*

  An inverse relationship exists between marginal product and marginal cost—when marginal product increases, marginal cost must fall, and when marginal product falls, marginal cost must rise.

- *What is the relationship between marginal and average amounts?*

  Adding a marginal amount affects the value of the average amount—the average will rise (fall) when the marginal amount is larger (smaller) than the initial average.

Key Terms

explicit costs *the opportunity costs of production that require a monetary payment* p. 158

implicit costs *the opportunity costs of production that do not require a monetary payment* p. 159

profits *the difference between total revenue and total cost* p. 160

accounting profits *total revenues minus total explicit costs* p. 160

economic profits *total revenues minus explicit and implicit costs* p. 160

sunk costs *costs that have been incurred and cannot be recovered* p. 161

short run *a period too brief for some production inputs to be varied* p. 163

long run *a period over which all production inputs are variable* p. 163

production function *the relationship between the quantity of inputs and the quantity of outputs produced* p. 163

total product (TP) *the total output of a good produced by the firm* p. 163

marginal product (MP) *the change in total product resulting from a unit change in input* p. 164

diminishing marginal product *as a variable input increases, with other inputs fixed, a point will be reached where the additions to output will eventually decline* p. 165

fixed costs *costs that do not vary with the level of output* p. 166

total fixed cost (TFC) *the sum of the firm's fixed costs* p. 166

variable costs *costs that vary with the level of output* p. 166

total variable cost (TVC) *the sum of the firm's variable costs* p. 166

Key Exhibits/ Graphs

- *Why is the average total cost curve U-shaped?*

  Average total cost declines with expanding output as average fixed costs decline, but then increases as output expands due to increasing marginal cost.

- *What is the relationship between marginal cost and average variable and average total cost?*

  When marginal cost is less than (greater than) an average cost, the average cost must be falling (rising); when marginal cost is greater than (less than) an average cost, the average cost must be rising (falling).

Section 7.5 Cost Curves: Short Run and Long Run

- *How is the long-run average total cost curve created?*

  In the long run, firms can vary inputs that are fixed in the short run, such as plant size and equipment, in some cases, lowering average costs per unit. The long-run average total cost curve shows the lowest average total cost for producing each output in the long run.

- *What are economies of scale?*

  At low output levels, when all inputs can be varied, some firms will experience economies of scale, where their per-unit costs are decreasing as output increases. In intermediate output ranges, firms may exhibit roughly constant returns to scale; in this range, their per-unit costs remain stable as output increases. Firms that expand all inputs beyond a certain point will encounter diseconomies of scale, incurring rising per-unit costs as output grows in the long run.

- *Why would cost curves shift?*

  Input prices, taxes, technology, and regulation can shift the cost curves.

Key Equations

$$MP = \frac{\Delta \text{Total product}}{\Delta \text{Variable input}}$$

Total cost (TC) = Total variable cost (TVC) + Total fixed cost (TFC)

$$\text{Average fixed cost } (AFC) = \frac{TFC}{Q}$$

$$\text{Average variable cost } (AVC) = \frac{TVC}{Q}$$

$$\text{Average total cost } (ATC) = \frac{TC}{Q} = AVC + AFC$$

$$\text{Marginal cost } (MC) = \frac{\Delta TC}{\Delta Q}$$

Chapter in Review

Perfect Competition

Section 8.1 The Four Major Market Structures

- *What are the four major market structures?*

  There are four major market structures: perfect competition, monopoly, monopolistic competition, and oligopoly.

- *What are the characteristics of a perfectly competitive market?*

  A perfectly competitive market has the following characteristics: many buyers and sellers, so that neither buyers nor sellers have control over price; a homogeneous product—consumers believe that all firms sell virtually identical products; no significant barriers to entry or exit.

- *Why is it useful to study the perfectly competitive market structure?*

  Studying the perfectly competitive market structure provides us with important information about how markets operate (entry, exit, costs) that can be applied to imperfect market structures. In addition, the perfectly competitive structure can give us a point of comparison to evaluate real-world markets.

Section 8.2 An Individual Price Taker's Demand Curve

- *What does the individual price taker's demand curve look like?*

  Individual sellers won't sell at a higher price than the going price because buyers can purchase the same good from someone else at the going price. Individual sellers won't sell for less than the going price, either, because they are so small relative to the market that they can sell all they want at the going price. Therefore, the individual price taker's demand curve is horizontal over its entire range of output.

- *What effect will a change in market price have on an individual price taker's demand curves?*

  The position of the individual firm's demand curve varies directly with the market price.

Section 8.3 Profit Maximization

- *What is total revenue?*

  Total revenue is price times the quantity sold ($TR = P \times q$).

- *What is average revenue and marginal revenue?*

  Average revenue is total revenue divided by the quantity sold ($AR = TR/q$). Marginal revenue is the change in total revenue from the sale of an additional unit of output ($MR = \Delta TR/\Delta q$). In a competitive industry, $P = AR = MR$.

- *How do firms maximize profits?*

  The profit-maximizing output rule says a firm should always produce where $MR = MC$. When $MR > MC$, the seller should expand production because producing and selling those units adds more to revenues than to costs, or increases profits. However, if $MR < MC$, the seller should decrease production.

Section 8.4 Short-Run Profits and Losses

- *How do we determine if a firm is generating an economic profit or loss?*

  The profit-maximizing output level is found by equating $MR = MC$ at q^*. If at q^* the firm's price is greater than its ATC, it is making an economic profit. If at q^* the price is less than ATC, the firm is incurring an economic loss. If at q^* the price is equal to ATC, the firm is making zero economic profits; that is, it is making a normal rate of return.

Key Terms

perfect competition *a market with many buyers and sellers, all selling a homogeneous product; market entry and exit is easy, and no firm can affect the market price* p. 186

price taker *a perfectly competitive firm takes the price that it is given by the intersection of the market demand and market supply curves* p. 186

total revenue (TR) *the product price times the quantity sold* p. 190

average revenue (AR) *total revenue divided by the number of units sold* p. 191

marginal revenue (MR) *the increase in total revenue that results from the sale of one more unit* p. 191

profit-maximizing output rule *a firm should always produce at the level of output where $MR = MC$* p. 192

short-run supply curve *as a cost relationship, this curve shows the marginal cost of producing any given output; as a supply curve, it shows the equilibrium output that the firm will supply at various prices in the short run* p. 196

short-run market supply curve *the horizontal summation of the individual firms' supply curves in the market* p. 196

constant-cost industry *an industry where input prices (and cost curves) do not change as industry output changes* p. 202

increasing-cost industry *an industry where input prices rise (and cost curves rise) as industry output rises* p. 204

decreasing-cost industry *an industry where input prices fall (and cost curves fall) as industry output rises* p. 205

productive efficiency *where a good or service is produced at the lowest possible cost* p. 206

allocative efficiency *where $P = MC$ and production is allocated to reflect consumer preferences* p. 206

- *What is the individual firm's short-run supply curve?*

  The portion of the *MC* curve that lies above the minimum of the *AVC* curve is the short-run supply curve for the individual competitive seller.

- *Can we review the short-run production decisions of an individual competitive firm?*

  As market price rises, the output decisions of a competitive firm evolve from not producing at all (shutting down) to operating at an economic loss, to economically breaking even, to generating an economic profit.

Section 8.5 Long-Run Equilibrium

- *What happens to economic profits and losses in the long run?*

  Economic profits will encourage the entry of new firms, which will shift the market supply curve to the right, driving down the firm's prices and therefore its revenues. Any economic losses signal resources to leave the industry, leading to supply reduction, higher prices, and increased revenues.

- *What is the long-run equilibrium for the competitive firm?*

  Only at zero economic profits is there no tendency for firms to either enter or exit the industry. This is the long-run equilibrium for the competitive firm.

Section 8.6 Long-Run Supply

- *What are constant-cost industries?*

  In constant-cost industries, the cost curves of the firm are not affected by changes in the output of the entire industry. Such industries must be very small demanders of resources in the market.

- *What are increasing-cost and decreasing-cost industries?*

  In an increasing-cost industry, the cost curves of the individual firms rise as total output increases. In a decreasing-cost industry, the cost curves decline as total output increases. The increasing-cost case is the most typical.

- *How is perfect competition economically efficient?*

  Perfect competition long-run equilibrium achieves productive efficiency (production at least possible cost), allocative efficiency ($P = MC$), and production allocated to reflect consumers' wants, thereby making perfect competition economically efficient.

Key Equations

$TR = P \times q$

Total profit $= TR - TC$

$AR = \dfrac{TR}{q}$ or $\dfrac{P \times q}{q} = P$

$MR = \dfrac{\Delta TR}{\Delta q}$

Chapter in Review

Monopoly

Section 9.1 Monopoly: The Price Maker

- *What is a monopoly?*

  A pure monopoly exists where there is only one seller of a product for which no close substitute is available.

- *What are the sources of monopoly power?*

  Sources of monopoly power include legal barriers, economies of scale, and control over important inputs.

Section 9.2 Demand and Marginal Revenue in Monopoly

- *How does the demand curve for a monopolist differ from that of a perfectly competitive firm?*

  The monopolist's demand curve is downward sloping because it is the market demand curve. To produce and sell another unit of output, the firm must lower its price on all units. As a result, the marginal revenue curve lies below the demand curve.

- *Why is marginal revenue less than price in a monopoly?*

  The monopolist's marginal revenue will always be less than price because there is a downward-sloping demand curve. In order to sell more output, the monopolist must accept a lower price on all units sold. This means that the monopolist receives additional revenue from the new unit sold but receives less revenue on all of the units it was previously selling.

- *What is the relationship between the elasticity of demand and total and marginal revenue?*

  Along the elastic portion of the demand curve, a fall in price leads to an increase in total revenue, making marginal revenue positive. Along the inelastic portion of the demand curve, a fall in price leads to a fall in total revenue, making marginal revenue negative. Therefore, the monopolist will operate in the elastic portion of its demand curve.

Section 9.3 The Monopolist's Equilibrium

- *How does the monopolist determine the profit-maximizing output?*

  The monopolist, like the perfect competitor, maximizes profits at that output where marginal revenue equals marginal cost. Price is set according to the demand for the product at the profit-maximizing output.

- *How do we know if the monopolist is making a profit or a loss?*

  Monopoly profits can be found by comparing price per unit and average total cost at Q^*. If $P > ATC$, there are economic profits. If $P < ATC$, there are economic losses.

Section 9.4 Monopoly and Welfare Loss

- *Does monopoly promote inefficiency?*

  Monopoly results in smaller output and a higher price than would be the case under perfect competition. Since the monopolist produces at an output where $P > MC$, this means the value to society of the last unit produced is greater than its cost. In other words, the monopoly is not producing enough output from society's standpoint.

- *Does monopoly hinder innovation?*

  Monopoly may lead to greater concentration of economic power and could hinder innovation.

Key Terms

monopoly *a market with only one seller of a product that has no close substitute and there are natural and legal barriers to entry that prevent competition p. 216*

price maker *a monopolistic firm that sets the price of its product so as to maximize profits p. 216*

natural monopoly *a firm that can produce at a lower cost than a number of smaller firms could p. 218*

marginal cost pricing *the decision to set production where the price of a good equals marginal cost p. 232*

average cost pricing *production where the price of a good equals average total cost p. 233*

price discrimination *the practice of charging different consumers different prices for the same good or service when the cost of providing that good or service is not different for different consumers p. 234*

Key Exhibits/ Graphs

Section 9.2, Exhibit 1
Section 9.2, Exhibit 3
Section 9.2, Exhibit 5
Section 9.3, Exhibit 1
Section 9.3, Exhibit 2
Section 9.3, Exhibit 3
Section 9.4, Exhibit 1

Section 9.5 Monopoly Policy

- *What is the objective of anti-combine laws?*

  Anti-combine laws are designed to reduce the abuses of monopoly power and push production closer to the social optimum.

- *What is government regulation?*

  Privately owned monopolies may be allowed to operate, but under the regulation of a government agency.

- *What is marginal cost pricing?*

  Marginal cost pricing sets price equal to marginal cost, where demand intersects marginal cost. This regulation achieves allocative efficiency.

- *What is average cost pricing?*

  Average cost pricing sets price equal to average total cost, where the demand curve intersects average total costs.

Section 9.6 Price Discrimination

- *What is price discrimination?*

  When producers charge different prices for the same good or service when no cost differences exist, it is called *price discrimination*.

- *Why does price discrimination exist?*

  Price discrimination is a result of the profit-maximization motive. If different groups have different demand curves for a good or service, a seller can make more money by charging these different buyers different prices.

Monopolistic Competition and Oligopoly

Section 10.1 Monopolistic Competition

- *What is monopolistic competition?*

  Monopolistic competition describes a market structure where many producers of somewhat different products compete with one another.

- *What are the three basic characteristics of monopolistic competition?*

  The theory of monopolistic competition is based on three primary characteristics: many sellers, product differentiation, and free entry.

Section 10.2 Price and Output Determination in Monopolistic Competition

- *How is short-run equilibrium determined?*

  In the short run, a monopolistically competitive firm achieves profit maximization at the intersection of the marginal revenue and marginal cost curves. A monopolistically competitive firm is making short-run economic profits when the equilibrium price is greater than average total costs at the equilibrium output. When equilibrium price is below average total cost at the equilibrium output, the firm is minimizing its economic losses.

- *How is long-run equilibrium determined?*

  In the long run, equilibrium price equals average total costs. With that, economic profits are zero, so there are no incentives for firms to either enter or exit the industry.

Section 10.3 Monopolistic Competition versus Perfect Competition

- *What are the differences and similarities between monopolistic competition and perfect competition?*

  While both the competitive firm and the monopolistically competitive firm may earn short-run economic profits, these profits will be eliminated in the long run. Because monopolistically competitive firms face a downward-sloping demand curve, average total cost is not minimized in the long run, after entry and exit have eliminated profits. Monopolistically competitive firms fail to reach productive efficiency, producing at output levels less than the efficient output. The monopolistically competitive firm does not achieve allocative efficiency because it does not operate where the price is equal to marginal costs.

- *What are the real costs of monopolistic competition?*

  The inefficiencies of monopolistic competition are a by-product of product differentiation and must be weighed against the social benefits of increased product variety.

- *Are the differences between monopolistic competition and perfect competition exaggerated?*

  The difference between the long-run price level and the price that would prevail under perfect competition varies directly with the strength of product differentiation.

Section 10.4 Advertising

- *Why do firms advertise?*

  With advertising, a firm hopes it can alter the elasticity of the demand for its product, making it more inelastic and causing an increase in demand that will enhance profits.

- *Is advertising good or bad from society's perspective?*

  To some, advertising manipulates consumer tastes and creates "needs" for trivial products. Where substantial economies of scale exist, it is possible that average production costs will

Key Terms

monopolistic competition *a market structure with many firms selling differentiated products* p. 246

product differentiation *the accentuation of unique product qualities, real or perceived, to develop a specific product identity* p. 247

excess capacity *occurs when the firm produces below the level where average total cost is minimized* p. 252

oligopoly *a market structure with only a few sellers offering similar or identical products* p. 258

mutual interdependence *when a firm shapes its policy with an eye to the policies of competing firms* p. 259

collude *when firms act together to restrict competition* p. 261

cartel *a collection of firms that agree on sales, pricing, and other decisions* p. 261

joint profit maximization *determination of price based on the marginal revenue derived from the market demand schedule and marginal cost schedule of the firms in the industry* p. 261

game theory *firms attempt to maximize profits by acting in ways that minimize damage from competitors* p. 264

cooperative game *collusion by two firms in order to improve their profit maximizations* p. 264

noncooperative game *each firm sets its own price without consulting other firms* p. 264

dominant strategy *will be optimal regardless of the opponents' actions* p. 265

payoff matrix *a summary of the possible outcomes from the various strategies* p. 265

Nash equilibrium *firms interacting with one another each chooses its best strategy given the strategies of the other firms* p. 266

Key Exhibits/ Graphs

decline more than the amount of per-unit costs of advertising in the long run. By making consumers aware of different "substitute" products, advertising may lead to more competitive markets and lower consumer prices.

Section 10.5 Oligopoly

- *What is oligopoly?*

Oligopolies exist where relatively few firms control all or most of the production and sale of a product. The products may be homogeneous or differentiated, but the barriers to entry are often very high and, consequently, there may be long-run economic profits.

- *Why do oligopolies exist?*

In oligopoly markets, economies of large-scale production make operation on a small scale extremely unprofitable. Recognition of this fact discourages new firms from entering the market and is the primary reason why oligopolies exist.

- *Why is it so difficult for the oligopolist to determine its profit-maximizing price and output?*

Because in oligopoly the pricing decision of one firm influences the demand curve of competing firms, the oligopolist faces considerable uncertainty as to the location and shape of its demand and marginal revenue curves. Thus, it is difficult for an oligopolist to determine its profit-maximizing price and output.

Section 10.6 Collusion and Cartels

- *Why do firms collude?*

The mutual interdependence of oligopolists tempts them to collude in order to reduce uncertainty and increase potential for monopoly profits.

- *What is joint profit maximization?*

Joint profit maximization requires the determination of price based on the market demand for the product and the marginal costs of the various firms.

- *Why are most collusive oligopolies short-lived?*

Most strong collusive oligopolies are rather short-lived for two reasons: (1) Collusive oligopolies are strictly illegal under Canadian anti-combine laws, and (2) there is a great temptation for firms to cheat on the agreement of the collusive oligopoly.

Section 10.7 Game Theory and Strategic Behaviour

- *What is game theory?*

Game theory stresses the tendency of various parties to minimize damage from opponents. A firm may try to figure out its competitors' most likely countermoves to its own policies and then formulate alternative defence measures.

- *What are cooperative and noncooperative games?*

Players in cooperative games can talk and set binding contracts, while those in noncooperative games are assumed to act independently, with no communication and no binding contracts. The prisoners' dilemma is an example of a noncooperative game.

- *What about repeated games?*

In one-shot games, the participants' self-interest tends to prevent cooperative behaviour, but in repeated games, cooperation occurs as long as others continue to cooperate (a tit-for-tat strategy).

- *What are network externalities?*

Positive (negative) network externality occurs when a consumer's quantity demanded increases (decreases) because a greater (smaller) number of consumers purchase the same good.

Chapter in Review

Labour Markets and the Distribution of Income

Section 11.1 Labour Markets

- *What determines the price paid to workers?*

  Supply and demand determine the prices paid to workers.

- *What is derived demand?*

  In factor or input markets, demand is derived from consumers' demand for the final good or service that the input produces.

Section 11.2 Supply and Demand in the Labour Market

- *Will hiring that extra worker add more to revenue than costs?*

  Whether or not an additional worker is hired depends on the worker's marginal revenue product (*MRP*) and marginal resource cost (*MRC*).

- *Why is the labour demand curve downward sloping?*

  The demand curve for labour is downward sloping because of diminishing marginal product. That is, if additional labour is added to a fixed quantity of land or capital equipment, output will increase, but at some point it will increase by diminishing amounts.

- *How many workers will an employer hire?*

  Profits are maximized if the firm hires only up to the point where the wage equals the expected marginal revenue product.

- *What is the shape of the labour supply curve?*

  Along a market supply curve, a higher wage rate will increase the quantity supplied of labour supplied and a lower wage rate will decrease the quantity of labour supplied.

Section 11.3 Labour Market Equilibrium

- *How is equilibrium determined in a competitive labour market?*

  The intersection of the labour demand curve and the labour supply curve determines the equilibrium wage and employment in competitive labour markets.

- *What shifts the labour demand curve?*

  The labour demand curve can shift if there is a change in productivity or a change in the demand for the final product.

- *What shifts the labour supply curve?*

  The labour supply curve can shift if there are changes in immigration or population growth, workers' preferences, nonwage income, or amenities.

- *What is a monopsony?*

  Any market with a single buyer is a monopsony; the labour market represents the most relevant situation.

Section 11.4 Labour Unions

- *Why do labour unions exist?*

  Workers realize that acting together gives them collective bargaining power; this is the primary reason why unions exist. Labour unions try to increase their members' wages and improve working conditions.

Key Terms

derived demand *the demand for an input is derived from the consumer's demands for a good or service* p. 276

marginal revenue product (*MRP*) *the additional revenue that a firm obtains from one more unit of labour* p. 277

marginal resource cost (*MRC*) *the amount that an extra input adds to the firm's total costs* p. 277

backward-bending labour supply curve *above a certain wage rate, a worker might prefer to work less and enjoy more leisure to meet personal preferences (the income effect dominates the substitution effect)* p. 281

monopsony *a market with a single buyer* p. 285

collective bargaining *negotiations between representatives of employers and unions* p. 287

in-kind transfers *transfers of goods and services rather than cash* p. 293

poverty *a state in which a family's income is too low to be able to buy the quantities of food, shelter, and clothing that are deemed necessary* p. 296

low-income cut-off (*LICO*) *income level at which a family may be in straitened circumstances because it has to spend a greater proportion of its income on the basics (food, clothing, and shelter) than the average family of similar size* p. 296

progressive tax system *as a person's income rises, the amount of his or her tax as a proportion of income rises* p. 298

cash transfer *direct cash payment such as public pensions, social assistance, and Employment Insurance benefits* p. 298

- *What is the impact of unions on wages?*

  Through restrictive membership, a union can reduce the labour supply in the market for union workers, thus reducing employment and raising wages. This increases the supply of workers in the nonunion sector, shifting supply to the right and lowering wages for nonunion workers.

- *Can unions increase worker productivity?*

  By reducing discontent and increasing worker retention, some economists argue that unions can actually increase worker productivity.

Section 11.5 Income Distribution

- *What has happened to income distribution since 1951?*

  Since 1951, the distribution of income in Canada has been relatively stable.

- *How much income inequality exists in other countries?*

  Income inequality among nations is substantial.

- *Are we overstating the disparity in the distribution of income?*

  Demographics and government programs affect the disparity in income inequality. Not taking these issues into consideration when evaluating income distribution could result in the inequality being overstated.

- *Why do some earn more than others?*

  Differences in ages, skill, education and training, preferences related to risk and leisure, and discrimination are all possible reasons why some people make more money than others.

- *How can we remedy discrimination?*

  In Canada, the problem of employment discrimination is addressed primarily through the Employment Equity Act (2005).

Section 11.6 Poverty

- *How do we define poverty?*

  In Canada, poverty is defined on a relative income basis. If a household's income is too low to buy the necessary quantities of food, shelter, and clothing, it is classified as poor.

- *How many people live in poverty?*

  The incidence of low income varies depending on the characteristics of the household, such as family type, age, and education.

- *What government programs help to reduce poverty?*

  A variety of programs are designed to reduce poverty: progressive income tax, cash transfer, in-kind transfers, social assistance, and minimum wages.

Key Equations

$$MRP = MP \times P$$

chapter 12
Chapter in Review

Market Failure and the Environment

Section 12.1 Externalities

- *What are externalities?*

  Externalities are the costs or benefits from either production or consumption that spill over onto those that are not producing or consuming the good.

- *What are negative externalities?*

  If a market activity has a negative physical impact on an outside party, that side effect is called a negative externality.

- *What are positive externalities?*

  If a market activity has a positive physical impact on an outside party, that side effect is called a positive externality.

- *What can the government do to correct for positive externalities?*

  The government can provide subsidies or other forms of regulation to correct the underallocation problem associated with positive externalities.

- *Are there nongovernmental solutions to externalities?*

  Nongovernment solutions to externalities are possible if people self-regulate personal behaviour to either prevent negative externalities or to promote positive externalities.

Section 12.2 Negative Externalities and Pollution

- *What are social costs?*

  Social costs are those costs that accrue to the total population; private costs are incurred only by the producer of a good or service.

- *Can externalities be accurately measured?*

  Given the difficulties in establishing real-world social and private costs and benefits, externalities are often difficult to measure.

Section 12.3 Public Policy and the Environment

- *Why is a clean environment not free?*

  In a world of scarcity, we can increase our consumption of a clean environment only by giving up something else—the opportunity cost of environmental policy.

- *What can be done to reduce pollution?*

  Environmental regulations force companies to find less pollution-intensive ways of producing goods and services. Pollution taxes can be used to force firms to internalize externalities and allow the relatively efficient private sector to operate according to market forces in a manner that takes socially important spillover costs into account. The transferable pollution rights policy encourages polluters to come up with cheaper ways of reducing pollution because the firm that reduces pollution is able to sell its remaining pollution credits to others.

- *What is an ideal pollution-control policy?*

  The objectives of pollution-control policies are to achieve the efficient level of pollution, achieve pollution reduction at the lowest cost, and motivate advances in abatement technology.

Section 12.4 Property Rights

- *What is the relationship between externalities and property rights?*

Key Terms

externality *a benefit or cost from consumption or production that spills over onto those that are not consuming or producing the good p. 307*

negative externality *when costs spill over to an outside party that is not involved in producing or consuming the good p. 307*

positive externality *when benefits spill over to an outside party that is not involved in producing or consuming the good p. 308*

internalized externalities *when an industry is forced to compensate those enduring some negative externality caused by its production p. 313*

pollution tax *tax levied by a government on a firm for environmental pollution p. 318*

transferable pollution rights *a right given to a firm to discharge a specified amount of pollution; its transferable nature creates incentive to lower pollution levels p. 318*

Coase theorem *states that where property rights are defined in a clear-cut fashion, externalities are internalized p. 321*

public good *a good that is nonrivalrous in consumption and nonexcludable p. 322*

private good *a good with rivalrous consumption and excludability p. 322*

free rider *a party that derives benefits from something without paying for it p. 323*

common resource *a rival good that is not excludable p. 324*

Key Exhibits/ Graphs

Section 12.2, Exhibit 1
Section 12.3, Exhibit 1

In a world with no externalities, property owners (with only a few exceptions) could use their property in any manner they desired. Ultimately, then, externalities involve an evaluation of the legal arrangements in which we operate our economy.

- *What is the Coase theorem?*

The Coase theorem states that where property rights are defined in a clear-cut fashion, externalities are internalized. This condition holds where information and transaction costs are close to zero.

Section 12.5 Public Goods

- *What are private goods versus public goods?*

A public good is both nonrivalrous in consumption (one person's usage of it does not diminish another's ability to use it) and nonexclusive (no one can be excluded from using it), whereas a private good is both rivalrous and excludable.

- *What is the free-rider problem with public goods?*

Despite their demand, because public goods are not rival and not excludable, there is little incentive for private individuals to produce them.

- *Why does the government provide public goods?*

The free-rider problem prevents the private market from supplying the efficient quantity of public goods, whereas a private good is both rivalrous and excludable.

- *What is a common resource?*

A common resource is rival in consumption but is not excludable.

Key Equations

$MSC = MPC +$ External costs

Chapter in Review

Introduction to the Macroeconomy

Section 13.1 Macroeconomic Goals

- *What are the three major macroeconomic goals in Canada?*

  The three major macroeconomic goals in Canada are employment, price-level stability, and economic growth.

- *Are these macroeconomic goals universal?*

  Individuals have their own reasons for valuing certain goals more than others. As a result, there is debate as to what is most important for an economy.

Section 13.2 Employment and Unemployment

- *What is the unemployment rate?*

  The unemployment rate is found by taking the number of people officially unemployed and dividing by the number in the labour force. Unemployment rates are higher for teenagers, men, and those living in eastern Canada.

- *Are unemployment statistics accurate reflections of the labour market?*

  No. The overall accuracy of the unemployment rate is impacted by factors such as discouraged workers, the treatment of part-time work, and the underground economy.

- *What are the categories of unemployment?*

  There are four main categories of unemployed workers: job losers, job leavers, re-entrants, and new entrants.

- *What is the labour force participation rate?*

  Labour force participation measures the percentage of the adult population that is participating in the labour force. In Canada, women's labour force participation has increased dramatically over the past 40 years.

Section 13.3 Different Types of Unemployment

- *What is frictional unemployment?*

  Frictional employment is the temporary unemployment that results from workers searching for suitable jobs and firms looking for suitable workers.

- *What is structural unemployment?*

  Structural unemployment results when people who are looking for jobs lack the required skills for the jobs that are available, or a long-term change in demand occurs.

- *What is cyclical unemployment?*

  Cyclical unemployment is caused by short-term cyclical fluctuations in the economy, such as recessions.

- *What is the natural rate of unemployment?*

  When cyclical unemployment is eliminated, our economy is said to be operating at full employment, or at a natural rate of unemployment.

Section 13.4 Inflation

- *Why is the overall price level important?*

  Price-level stability is a desirable goal because it limits inflationary costs. A continuous rise in the price level defines the case of inflation, whereas a fall in the overall price level defines the case for deflation.

Key Terms

real gross domestic product (RGDP) *the total value of all final goods and services produced in a given time period, such as a year or a quarter, adjusted for inflation p. 328*

labour force *persons 15 years of age and over who are employed or are unemployed and seeking work p. 329*

unemployment rate *the percentage of the people in the labour force who are unemployed p. 330*

discouraged workers *people who have left the labour force because they could not find work p. 332*

job loser *an individual who has been laid off or fired p. 332*

job leaver *a person who quits his or her job p. 332*

re-entrant *an individual who worked before and is now re-entering the labour force p. 332*

new entrant *an individual who has not held a job before but is now seeking employment p. 333*

underemployment *a situation in which workers have skills higher than necessary for a job p. 333*

labour force participation rate *the percentage of the population (aged 15 years and over) in the labour force p. 333*

frictional unemployment *the temporary unemployment that results from workers searching for suitable jobs and firms looking for suitable workers p. 335*

structural unemployment *unemployment that occurs due to a lack of skills necessary for available jobs p. 335*

cyclical unemployment *unemployment due to short-term cyclical fluctuations in the economy p. 336*

natural rate of unemployment *the amount of unemployment that is unavoidable, equal to the sum of frictional and structural unemployment when they are at a maximum p. 337*

- *How is inflation measured using the Consumer Price Index (CPI)?*

A price index allows us to compare prices paid for goods and services over time. The Consumer Price Index (CPI) is the best-known price index.

- *Who are the winners and losers during inflation?*

Inflation generally hurts creditors and those on fixed incomes and pensions; debtors generally benefit from inflation.

- *What are the costs of inflation?*

Unanticipated inflation causes unpredictable transfers of wealth and reduces the efficiency of the market system by distorting price signals.

- *What is the relationship between inflation and interest rates?*

The nominal interest rate is the actual amount of interest you pay. The real interest rate is the nominal rate minus the inflation rate. Inflationary expectations tend to increase nominal interest rates.

Section 13.5 Economic Fluctuations

- *What are short-term economic fluctuations?*

Business cycles (or economic fluctuations) are short-term fluctuations in the amount of economic activity, relative to the long-term growth trend in output.

- *What are the four phases of a business cycle?*

The four phases of a business cycle are expansion, peak, contraction, and trough.

- *How long does a business cycle last?*

Recessions occur during the contraction phase of a business cycle. Severe, long-term recessions are called *depressions*, while prolonged expansions are referred to as *booms*. The economy often goes through short-term contractions even during a long-term growth trend. Overall, the duration of any one business is uncertain.

Key Equations

$$\text{Unemployment rate} = \frac{\text{Number of unemployed}}{\text{Total civilian labour force}} \times 100$$

$$\text{Price index} = \frac{\text{Cost of market basket in current year}}{\text{Cost of market basket in base year}} \times 100$$

$$\text{Real interest rate} = \text{Nominal interest rate} - \text{Inflation rate}$$

Key Exhibits/Graphs

Section 13.5, Exhibit 2

Chapter in Review

Measuring Economic Performance

Section 14.1 National Income Accounting: Measuring Economic Performance

- *Why do we measure our economy's performance?*

  We measure our economy's status in order to see how its performance has changed over time. These economic measurements are important to government officials, private businesses, and investors.

- *What is gross domestic product (GDP)?*

  Gross domestic product (GDP) is the value of all final goods and services produced within a country during a given time period. The two different ways to measure GDP are the expenditure approach and the income approach.

Section 14.2 The Expenditure Approach to Measuring GDP

- *What is the expenditure approach to measuring GDP?*

  The expenditure approach to measuring GDP involves adding up the purchases of final goods and services by market participants. Four categories of spending are used in the GDP calculation: consumption (C), investment (I), government purchases (G), and net exports (X – M).

- *What is consumption (C)?*

  Consumption includes spending on nondurable consumer goods—tangible items that are usually consumed or used only once; semi-durable goods—items that can be used more than once and have an expected lifetime of around one year; durable consumer goods—items that can be used repeatedly for more than one year; and services—intangible items of value.

- *What is investment (I)?*

  Fixed investment includes all spending on capital goods, such as machinery, tools, and buildings. Inventory investment includes the net expenditures by businesses to increase their inventories.

- *What are government purchases (G)?*

  Purchases of goods and services are the only part of government spending included in GDP. Transfer payments are not included in these calculations because that spending is not payment for a newly produced good or service.

- *What are net exports (X – M)?*

  Net exports are calculated by subtracting total imports from total exports.

Section 14.3 The Income Approach to Measuring GDP

- *What is the income approach to measuring GDP?*

  The income approach to measuring GDP involves summing the incomes received by the producers of goods and services. These payments to the owners of productive resources are also known as *factor payments*. The income approach to GDP adds together wages and salaries, corporate profits, interest income, and net income of farm and unincorporated businesses to obtain net domestic income at factor cost. Adding indirect taxes less subsidies and depreciation to net domestic income gives GDP.

- *What do personal income and disposable income measure?*

  Personal income measures the amount of income received by households (including transfer payments) before taxes. Disposable income is the personal income available after taxes.

Key Terms

national income accounting *a uniform means of measuring economic performance p. 357*

gross domestic product (GDP) *the measure of economic performance based on the value of all final goods and services produced in a country in a given period of time p. 358*

double counting *adding the value of a good or service twice by mistakenly counting intermediate goods and services in GDP p. 358*

expenditure approach *calculation of GDP by adding up how much market participants spend on final goods and services over a period of time p. 360*

consumption (*C*) *purchases of consumer goods and services by households p. 360*

nondurable goods *tangible consumer items that are typically consumed or used only once, such as food p. 361*

semi-durable goods *consumer items that can be **semi-durable goods** consumer items that can be used more than once and have an expected lifetime of around one year, such as clothing, p. 361*

durable goods *consumer goods that can be used repeatedly for more than one year, such as automobiles p. 361*

investment (*I*) *the creation of capital goods to augment future production p. 361*

fixed investments *all new spending on capital goods by producers p. 361*

producer goods *capital goods that increase future production capabilities p. 361*

inventory investment *all purchases by businesses that add to the stocks of goods kept by the firm to meet consumer demand p. 362*

Key Exhibits/ Graphs

Section 14.1, Exhibit 1

Section 14.4 Issues with Calculating an Accurate GDP

- *What are the problems with GDP in measuring output?*

  It is difficult to compare nominal GDP over time because of the changing value of money over time.

- *How is real GDP calculated?*

  The GDP deflator is a price index that measures the average level of prices of all final goods and services produced in the economy. It is used to convert nominal measures of GDP into equivalent real measures of GDP.

- *What is real GDP per capita?*

  Real GDP per capita is real output of goods and services per person. In some cases, real GDP may increase, but real GDP per capita may actually drop as a result of population growth.

Section 14.5 Problems with GDP as a Measure of Economic Welfare

- *What are some of the deficiencies of GDP as a measure of economic welfare?*

  Several factors make it difficult to use GDP as a welfare indicator, including nonmarket transactions, the underground economy, leisure, and externalities. Nonmarket transactions are the exchanges of goods and services that do not occur in traditional markets, so no money is exchanged. The underground economy is the unreported production and income that come from certain legal and illegal activities. The presence of positive and negative externalities also make it difficult to measure GDP accurately.

Key Equations

$$GDP = C + I + G + (X - M)$$

$$\text{Net investment} = \text{Gross investment} - \text{Depreciation}$$

$$\text{Real GDP} = \frac{\text{Nominal GDP}}{\text{GDP deflator}} \times 100$$

Chapter in Review

Economic Growth in the Global Economy

Section 15.1 Economic Growth

- *How does economic growth differ from the business cycle?*

  Economic growth refers to the long-run trend rate of growth for an economy. Business cycles refer to the short-run fluctuations in economic activity around this trend rate of growth.

- *What is economic growth?*

  Economic growth is usually measured by the annual percentage change in real output of goods and services per capita. Improvements in and greater stocks of land, labour, capital, and entrepreneurial activity will lead to greater economic growth and shift the production possibilities curve outward.

- *What is the Rule of 70?*

  According to the Rule of 70, if you take a nation's growth rate and divide it into 70, you have the approximate time it will take to double the income level.

Section 15.2 Determinants of Economic Growth

- *What factors contribute to economic growth?*

  The factors that contribute to economic growth are the same factors that determine growth in productivity. They include physical capital, quantity and quality of labour resources, natural resources, and technology.

Section 15.3 Public Policy and Economic Growth

- *What policies can a nation pursue to increase economic growth?*

  Generally speaking, those policies and institutional structures that promote higher levels of saving, more research and development, better protection of private property rights, freer trade, and more education will lead to greater economic growth.

- *Can rates of economic growth between different economies converge?*

  While certain factors such as the ability to adopt existing technology would seem to allow developing nations to grow faster than developed nations, population growth and low literacy rates tend to have the opposite effect. Therefore, there seems to be no clear indication that rates of economic growth between economies will converge

Section 15.4 Population and Economic Growth

- *What is the effect of population growth on per capita economic growth?*

  Population growth may increase per capita output in resource-rich countries such as Canada, the United States, Australia, and Saudi Arabia, because they have more resources for each labourer to produce with. They are more likely to be able to exploit economies of large-scale production, and they are more likely to have rapidly expanding technology.

- *What is the Malthusian prediction?*

  The Malthusian prediction was that, due to limited productive resources and rapid population growth, eventually per capita economic growth would become negative.

Key Terms

economic growth *an upward trend in the real per capita output of goods and services p. 381*

productivity *the amount of goods and services a worker can produce per hour p. 384*

innovation *applications of new knowledge that create new products or improve existing products p. 387*

research and development (R&D) *activities undertaken to create new products and processes that will lead to technological progress p. 389*

Key Exhibits/ Graphs

Section 15.1, Exhibit 1
Section 15.1, Exhibit 2
Section 15.2, Exhibit 1

Notes

Chapter in Review

Aggregate Demand

Section 16.1 The Determinants of Aggregate Demand

- *What is aggregate demand?*

  Aggregate demand is the sum of the demand for all final goods and services in the economy. It can also be seen as the quantity of real GDP demanded at different price levels.

- *What is consumption?*

  Consumption—the purchases of consumer goods and services by households—is the largest component of aggregate demand. Empirical evidence suggests that consumption increases directly with any increase in income.

- *What is investment?*

  Investment spending refers to the purchases of investment goods such as machinery and equipment. Changes in investment spending are often responsible for changes in the level of economic activity.

- *What are government purchases?*

  Government purchases are made up of federal, provincial and territorial, and local purchases of goods and services.

- *What are net exports?*

  Net exports are the difference between the value of exports and the value of imports.

Section 16.2 The Investment and Saving Market

- *What is the investment demand curve?*

  The investment demand curve is downward sloping, reflecting the fact that the quantity of investment demanded varies inversely with the real interest rate. Technology, inventories, expectations, and business taxes can shift the investment demand curve at a given real interest rate.

- *What is the saving supply curve?*

  The supply of national saving is composed of both private saving and public saving. The saving supply curve is upward sloping, reflecting the fact that the quantity of savings is positively related to the real interest rate. Two noninterest determinants of the saving supply curve are disposable (after-tax) income and expected future earnings.

- *How is equilibrium determined in the investment and saving market?*

  In equilibrium, desired investment equals desired national saving at the intersection of the investment demand curve and the saving supply curve. A surplus of saving will occur at real interest rates above equilibrium and shortages of saving will occur at real interest rates below equilibrium.

- *What effect do budget surpluses and budget deficits have on the investment and saving market?*

  Budget surpluses lead to an increase in national saving, a lowering of the real interest rate and an increase in the quantity of saving and investment. Budget deficits reduce national saving, increase the real interest rate, and lower the quantity of saving and investment.

Section 16.3 The Aggregate Demand Curve

- *How is the quantity of real GDP demanded affected by the price level?*

  An increase in the price level causes RGDP demanded to fall. Conversely, if there is a reduction in the price level, quantity demanded of RGDP increases.

Key Terms

aggregate demand (AD) *the total demand for all final goods and services in the economy* p. 399

average propensity to consume (APC) *the fraction of total disposable income that households spend on consumption* p. 400

marginal propensity to consume (MPC) *the additional consumption resulting from an additional dollar of disposable income* p. 401

open economy *a type of model that includes international trade effects* p. 401

net exports *the difference between the value of exports and the value of imports* p. 402

private saving *the amount of income that households have left over after consumption and taxes* p. 405

public saving *the amount of income that the government has left over after paying for its spending* p. 405

national saving *the sum of both private and public saving* p. 405

dissaving *consuming more than total available income* p. 407

aggregate demand curve *a graphical representation that shows the inverse relationship between the price level and RGDP demanded* p. 408

Key Exhibits/ Graphs

Section 16.2, Exhibit 6
Section 16.3, Exhibit 1
Section 16.4, Exhibit 2

- *Why is the aggregate demand curve negatively sloped?*

  The aggregate demand curve is downward sloping because of the real wealth effect, the interest rate effect, and the open economy effect.

Section 16.4 Shifts in the Aggregate Demand Curve

- *What variables cause the aggregate demand curve to shift?*

  A change in the price level causes a movement along the aggregate demand curve, not a shift in the aggregate demand curve. Aggregate demand is made up of total spending, or $C + I + G + (X - M)$. Any change in these factors will cause the aggregate demand curve to shift. A change in the price level causes a movement along the aggregate demand curve, but not a shift in the aggregate demand curve.

- *Can we review the determinants that change aggregate demand?*

Variable	Change in Variable	Change in Aggregate Demand
1. Consumption (C)	↑	↑
2. Investment (I)	↑	↑
3. Government purchases (G)	↑	↑
4. Exports (X)	↑	↑
5. Imports (M)	↑	↓
6. Net exports (X – M)	↑	↑

Key Equations

$$MPC = \frac{\text{Change in consumption}}{\text{Change in disposable income}}$$

$$APC = \frac{\text{Consumption}}{\text{Disposable income}}$$

$$S = (GDP - C - T) + (T - G)$$

chapter 17

Chapter in Review

Aggregate Supply and Macroeconomic Equilibrium

Section 17.1 The Aggregate Supply Curve

- *What is the aggregate supply curve?*

  The aggregate supply curve is the relationship between the overall price level and the total quantity of final goods and services that suppliers are *willing and able* to produce.

- *Why is the short-run aggregate supply curve positively sloped?*

  The short-run aggregate supply curve measures how much RGDP suppliers are willing to produce at different price levels when input prices are unable to adjust. For this reason, producers can make a profit by expanding production when the price level rises. Producers also may be fooled into thinking that the relative price of the item they are producing is rising, so they increase production.

- *Why is the long-run aggregate supply curve vertical at the natural rate of output?*

  In the long run, the aggregate supply curve is vertical. In the long run, input prices change proportionally with output prices. The position of the *LRAS* curve is determined by the level of capital, land, labour, entrepreneurship, and technology at the natural rate of output, $RGDP_{NR}$.

Section 17.2 Shifts in the Aggregate Supply Curve

- *What factors of production affect the short-run and the long-run aggregate supply curves?*

  Any increase in the quantity of any of the factors of production—capital, land, labour, entrepreneurship, or technology—available will cause both the long-run and short-run aggregate supply curves to shift to the right. A decrease in any of these factors will shift both of the aggregate supply curves to the left.

- *What factors exclusively shift the short-run aggregate supply curve?*

  Changes in wages and other input price, productivity, and temporary supply shocks shift the short-run aggregate supply curve but do not affect the long-run aggregate supply curve.

- *Can we review the determinants that change aggregate supply?*

Variable	Change in Variable	Change in SRAS	Change in LRAS
1. Costs			
• Wages	↑	↓	n/c*
• Other input prices	↑	↓	n/c*
2. Government policy			
• Taxes	↑	↓	↓
• Regulatory framework	↑	↓	↓
• Trade barriers	↑	↓	↓
• Waste and inefficiency	↑	↓	↓
3. Economic growth			
• Quantity of human capital	↑	↑	↑
• Quantity of physical capital	↑	↑	↑
• Technology and entrepreneurship	↑	↑	↑
• Labour productivity	↑	↑	↑
4. Other			
• Unfavourable weather	↑	↓	n/c*
• Natural disasters, war	↑	↓	n/c*
n/c* — The curve does not shift unless the variable change is permanent.			

Key Terms

aggregate supply (*AS*) curve *a graphical representation that shows the positive relationship between the price level and real gross domestic product supplied* p. 417

short-run aggregate supply (*SRAS*) curve *the graphical relationship between RGDP and the price level when output prices can change but input prices are unable to adjust* p. 417

long-run aggregate supply (*LRAS*) curve *the graphical relationship between RGDP and the price level when output prices and input prices can fully adjust to economic changes* p. 417

shocks *unexpected aggregate supply or aggregate demand changes* p. 424

recessionary gap *an output gap that occurs when the actual output is less than the potential output* p. 425

inflationary gap *an output gap that occurs when the actual output is greater than the potential output* p. 425

demand-pull inflation *a price level increase due to an increase in aggregate demand* p. 425

stagflation *a situation in which lower growth and higher prices occur together* p. 425

cost-push inflation *a price level increase due to a negative supply shock or increases in input prices* p. 425

wage and price inflexibility *the tendency for prices and wages to only adjust slowly downward to changes in the economy* p. 427

autonomous determinants of consumption expenditures *expenditures not dependent on the level of current disposable income* p. 438

marginal propensity to consume (MPC) *the additional consumption resulting from an additional dollar of disposable income* p. 439

Section 17.3 Macroeconomic Equilibrium

- *How is macroeconomic equilibrium determined?*

  Short-run macroeconomic equilibrium is shown by the intersection of the aggregate demand curve and the short-run aggregate supply curve. A short-run equilibrium is also a long-run equilibrium only if it is at potential output on the long-run aggregate supply curve.

- *What are recessionary and inflationary gaps?*

  If short-run equilibrium occurs at less than the potential output of the economy, $RGDP_{NR}$, there is a recessionary gap. If short-run equilibrium temporarily occurs beyond $RGDP_{NR}$, there is an inflationary gap.

- *How can the economy self-correct to a recessionary gap?*

  It is possible for the economy to self-correct from a recessionary gap through declining wages and prices. The short-run aggregate supply curve eventually increases, returning the economy to the long-run equilibrium, at $RGDP_{NR}$, at a lower price level.

- *How can the economy self-correct to an inflationary gap?*

  It is possible for the economy to self-correct from an inflationary gap through increasing wages and prices. The short-run aggregate supply curve ultimately decreases, returning the economy to the long-run equilibrium, at $RGDP_{NR}$, at a higher price level.

Chapter in Review

Fiscal Policy

Section 18.1 Fiscal Policy

- *What is fiscal policy?*

  Fiscal policy is the use of government spending on goods and services and/or taxes to affect aggregate demand and to alter RGDP and the price level.

- *How does fiscal policy affect the government's budget?*

  Expansionary fiscal policies will increase the budget deficit (or reduce a budget surplus) through greater government spending, lower taxes, or both. Contractionary fiscal policies will increase a budget surplus (or reduce a budget deficit) through reduced government spending, higher taxes, or both.

Section 18.2 Government: Spending and Taxation

- *What are the major categories of government spending?*

  Twenty-five percent of federal government spending is in the form of major transfers to persons, such as Employment Insurance and Old Age Security programs. Other major expenditures are transfers to other levels of government (21 percent) and expenditures associated with the operation of other departments and agencies (18 percent).

- *What are the major sources of government revenue?*

  The largest source of federal revenue is income taxes on individuals and corporations (49 percent and 13 percent, respectively). Other taxes and duties collected by the federal government account for 10 percent of revenue.

Section 18.3 The Multiplier Effect

- *What is the multiplier effect?*

  The multiplier effect is a chain reaction of additional income and purchases that results in total purchases that are greater than the initial increase in purchases.

- *What impact does the multiplier effect have on the aggregate demand curve?*

  Initially, the *AD* curve shifts rightward by the amount of the original increase in expenditure. The multiplier effect has the effect of shifting the *AD* curve farther rightward.

- *What impact does the multiplier effect have on tax cuts?*

  Because taxes have only an indirect impact on aggregate demand, the tax multiplier is smaller than the government spending multiplier.

- *What factors can potentially reduce the size of the multiplier?*

  Because of a time lag, the full impact of the multiplier effect on GDP may not be felt until a year or more after the initial purchase. Also, the ultimate size of the multiplier may be reduced by increases in savings rates, taxes, and money spent on imported goods.

Section 18.4 Fiscal Policy and the AD/AS Model

- *How can fiscal policy alleviate a recessionary gap?*

  A government decision to spend more and/or cut taxes would increase total purchases and shift out the aggregate demand curve. If the correct magnitude of expansionary fiscal policy is used in a recession, it could potentially bring the economy to full employment at a higher price level.

Key Terms

fiscal policy *use of government spending and/or taxes to alter RGDP and the price level p. 448*

budget deficit *government spending exceeds tax revenues for a given fiscal year p. 449*

budget surplus *tax revenues are greater than government expenditures for a given fiscal year p. 449*

expansionary fiscal policy *use of fiscal policy tools to foster increased output by increasing government spending and/or lowering taxes p. 449*

contractionary fiscal policy *use of fiscal policy tools to reduce output by decreasing government spending and/or increasing taxes p. 449*

progressive tax *the amount of an individual's tax rises as a proportion of income, as the person's income rises p. 452*

excise tax *a sales tax on individual products such as alcohol, tobacco, and gasoline p. 452*

regressive tax *the amount of an individual's tax falls as a proportion of income, as the person's income rises p. 452*

proportional tax *designed so that all taxpayers are subject to the tax rate, regardless of earnings p. 452*

multiplier effect *a chain reaction of additional income and purchases that results in total purchases that are greater than the initial increase in purchases p. 454*

automatic stabilizers *changes in government spending or tax collection that automatically help counter business cycle fluctuations p. 461*

crowding-out effect *theory that government borrowing drives up the interest rate, lowering consumption by households and investment spending by firms p. 462*

Key Exhibits/ Graphs

Section 18.4, Exhibit 1
Section 18.4, Exhibit 2

- *How can fiscal policy alleviate an inflationary gap?*

Use of the correct magnitude of contractionary fiscal policy in an inflationary boom could potentially bring the economy back to full employment at a lower price level.

Section 18.5 Automatic Stabilizers

- *What are automatic stabilizers?*

Automatic stabilizers are changes in government transfer payments or tax collections that happen automatically and have effects that vary inversely with business cycles.

- *How does the tax system stabilize the economy?*

The tax system is the most important automatic stabilizer; it has the greatest ability to smooth out swings in GDP during business cycles. Other automatic stabilizers are Employment Insurance and social assistance payments.

Section 18.6 Possible Obstacles to Effective Fiscal Policy

- *How does the crowding-out effect limit the economic impact of expansionary fiscal policy?*

The crowding-out effect states that as the government borrows to finance the budget deficit, it drives up the interest rates and crowds out private investment spending. If crowding-out causes a higher Canadian interest rate, it will attract foreign funds. In order to invest in the Canadian economy, foreigners will have to first convert their currencies into Canadian dollars. The increase in the demand for dollars relative to other currencies will cause the dollar to appreciate in value, making imports relatively cheaper in Canada and Canadian exports relatively more expensive in other countries. This will cause net exports ($X - M$) to fall. This is the crowding-out effect in the open economy.

- *How do time lags in policy implementation affect policy effectiveness?*

The time lag between when a fiscal policy may be needed and when it eventually affects the economy is considerable. Time lags are generally grouped in three classifications: recognition lags, implementation lags, and impact lags.

Section 18.7 The Federal Government Debt

- *How is the budget deficit financed?*

The budget deficit is financed by issuing debt.

- *What has happened to the federal budget balance?*

Improvement in the federal budget balance since the mid-1990s resulted from economic growth, increased tax revenues, and the efforts of the federal government to control the growth of government spending.

- *What is the impact of reducing a budget deficit?*

In the short run, reducing a budget deficit can lead to a recession (if not offset by expansionary monetary policy). In the long run, however, deficit reduction increases economic growth and lowers the price level.

- *How much is the burden of government debt in Canada?*

With greater fiscal responsibility and increased economic growth, Canada has managed to lower its debt–GDP ratio (the international measure of debt burden).

Key Equations

$$\text{Multiplier} = \frac{1}{1 - MPC}$$

$$\text{Tax multiplier} = \frac{MPC}{1 - MPC}$$

Chapter in Review

Money and the Banking System

Section 19.1 What Is Money?

- *What is money?*

  Money is anything that is generally accepted in exchange for goods or services.

- *What are the four functions of money?*

  The four important functions of money are money as a medium of exchange, money as a store of value, money as a unit of account, and money as a means of deferred payment.

Section 19.2 Measuring Money

- *What is currency?*

  Currency refers to the coins and banknotes that are issued by institutions and governments to facilitate the trading of goods and services and the payment of debts. Canadian currency consists of Government of Canada-issued banknotes and coins, and demand and savings deposits held in various financial institutions.

- *What are demand and savings deposits?*

  Demand and savings deposits are two types of bank accounts. Demand deposits are balances in financial institution accounts that depositors can access on demand, while savings deposits are deposited funds that cannot be used directly for payment.

- *What is liquidity?*

  The ease with which one asset can be converted into another asset or into goods and services is called *liquidity*.

- *How is the money supply measured?*

  M2 is made up of currency outside chartered banks plus demand and savings deposits at chartered banks. M2+ includes M2 plus demand and savings deposits at trust companies, mortgage loan companies, credit unions, caisses populaires, and other financial institutions.

- *What backs the money supply?*

  Money is backed by our faith that others will accept it from us in exchange for goods and services.

Section 19.3 How Banks Create Money

- *What types of financial institutions exist in Canada?*

  While a variety of financial intermediaries exist in the Canadian financial system, the financial sector is dominated by deposit-accepting institutions—banks. The Canadian banking industry itself is dominated by six large chartered banks. The "Big Six" hold the majority of the financial assets in the banking industry.

- *How do banks create money?*

  Money is created when banks make loans. Borrowers receive newly created demand deposits.

- *What does a bank balance sheet look like?*

  A bank balance sheet is a financial record that indicates the balance between a bank's assets and its liabilities plus capital. A bank's largest asset is loans and its largest liability is deposits.

- *What is a desired reserve ratio?*

  A desired reserve ratio is the percentage of deposits a bank chooses to keep on hand in the form of cash reserves.

Key Terms

money *anything generally accepted in exchange for goods or services p. 475*

medium of exchange *the primary function of money, which is to facilitate transactions and lower transaction costs p. 475*

barter *direct exchange of goods and services without the use of money p. 475*

measure of value *money as a common "ruler" of worth allowing for the comparison of diverse goods and services p. 476*

store of value *how money provides a means of saving or accumulating purchasing power from the present and transferring it to the future p. 476*

means of deferred payment *the attribute of money that makes it easier to borrow and to repay loans p. 477*

currency *consists of coins and banknotes that an institution or government has created to be used in the trading of goods and services and the payment of debts p. 477*

legal tender *refers to coins and banknotes officially declared to be acceptable for the settlement of debts incurred in financial transactions p. 477*

fiat money *a means of exchange established by government declaration p. 478*

demand deposits *balances in bank accounts that depositors can access on demand p. 478*

savings deposits *financial institution accounts containing funds that cannot be used directly for payment p. 480*

liquidity *the ease with which one asset can be converted into another asset or into goods and services p. 480*

M2 *currency outside chartered banks plus demand and savings deposits at chartered banks p. 480*

Key Exhibits/ Graphs

Section 19.4 The Money Multiplier

- *How does the multiple expansion of the money supply process work?*

  New loans mean new money (demand deposits), which can increase spending as well as the money supply. New loans also create excess reserves in other banks, which leads to still further increases in both loans and the money supply.

- *What is the money multiplier?*

  The money multiplier is equal to 1 divided by the desired reserve ratio.

- *Why is it only "potential" money creation?*

  The banking system as a whole can potentially create new money equal to several times the amount of new reserves—as determined by the money multiplier. However, due to various leakages and time lags, the actual monetary impact of an initial deposit created out of excess reserves within a short period of time will be less than that calculated by the money multiplier.

Key Equations

$$\text{Money multiplier} = \frac{1}{\text{Desired reserve ratio}}$$

$$\text{Potential money creation} = \text{Initial deposit} \times \text{Money multiplier}$$

Chapter in Review

The Bank of Canada

Section 20.1 The Bank of Canada

- *What is the Bank of Canada?*

  The Bank of Canada is Canada's central bank. It is owned by the federal government, which has final responsibility for the Bank of Canada's policies. Despite this goal dependence, the governor of the Bank of Canada has considerable independence in formulating the Bank of Canada's monetary policy.

- *What are the main responsibilities of the Bank of Canada?*

  The Bank of Canada has four main areas of responsibility: currency, funds management, the financial system, and monetary policy.

Section 20.2 Tools of the Bank of Canada

- *What are the tools of the Bank of Canada?*

  The two major tools of the Bank of Canada are open market operations and changing the target for the overnight interest rate.

- *What is the Bank of Canada's approach to monetary policy?*

  The Bank of Canada will raise the target for the overnight interest rate in response to an expectation of inflation above the 2 percent control target. A higher target for the overnight interest rate will raise other commercial interest rates and the exchange rate for the Canadian dollar, thus lowering overall economic demand. This reduction in overall demand will have the effect of returning the rate of inflation back to its 2 percent target. If the Bank of Canada expects the rate of inflation to fall below its 2 percent control target, it will lower the target for the overnight interest rate. The resulting lower commercial interest rates and exchange rate for the Canadian dollar will lead to greater overall demand in the economy, thus increasing the inflation rate back toward the 2 percent target.

Section 20.3 Money and Inflation

- *What is the equation of exchange?*

  The equation of exchange is expressed as $M \times V = P \times Q$, where M is the money supply, V is the velocity of money, P is the average level of prices of final goods and services, and Q is real GDP in a given year.

- *What is the quantity theory of money and prices?*

  The theory that draws a connection between the money supply and the price level when the velocity of money is constant is referred to as the *quantity theory of money and prices*.

Key Equations

$$M \times V = P \times Q$$

$$V = \frac{P \times Q}{M}$$

Key Terms

monetary policy *the policy decisions that the Bank of Canada makes in managing the money supply and interest rates, consistent with its inflation-control objective p. 502*

overnight interest rate *interest rate that major financial institutions charge each other for one-day loans p. 502*

bank rate *the interest rate that the Bank of Canada charges major financial institutions on the loans it extends to them p. 503*

bankers' deposit rate *the interest rate Bank of Canada pays major financial institutions on surplus funds deposited at the Bank of Canada p. 503*

open market operations *purchase and sale of government securities by the Bank of Canada p. 503*

velocity of money (V) *the average number of times that a dollar is used in purchasing final goods or services in a one-year period p. 508*

quantity theory of money and prices *a theory of the connection between the money supply and the price level when the velocity of money is constant p. 508*

Key Exhibits/ Graphs

Section 20.2, Exhibit 1

Notes

Chapter in Review

Monetary Policy

Section 21.1 Money, Interest Rates, and Aggregate Demand

- *What determines the money market?*

  The money market is the market in which money demand and money supply determine the equilibrium interest rate. Money demand has three possible motives: transaction purposes, precautionary reasons, and asset purposes. The quantity of money demanded varies inversely with interest rates and directly with income. The supply of money is effectively almost perfectly inelastic with respect to interest rates over their plausible range, as controlled by Bank of Canada policies.

- *How does the Bank of Canada affect RGDP in the short run?*

  When the Bank of Canada sells bonds to the private sector or raises its target for the overnight interest rate, there is a reduction in the money supply, which in turn leads to a higher interest rate and a reduction in aggregate demand, at least in the short run. When the Bank of Canada buys bonds or lowers its target for the overnight interest rate, the money supply increases. The increase in the money supply will lead to lower interest rates and an increase in aggregate demand.

- *Does the Bank of Canada target the money supply or the interest rate?*

  Since the Bank of Canada cannot completely control both the growth of the money supply and the interest rate, it must choose which target to manage.

- *Which interest rate does the Bank of Canada target?*

  The Bank of Canada signals its intended monetary policy through the overnight interest rate target that it sets.

- *Does the Bank of Canada influence the real interest rate in the short run?*

  Since a change in the nominal interest rate tends to change the real interest rate by the same amount in the short run, most economists believe the Bank of Canada can control both the nominal and real interest rates (in the short run).

Section 21.2 Expansionary and Contractionary Monetary Policy

- *How does expansionary monetary policy work in a recessionary gap?*

  An expansionary monetary policy can combat a recessionary gap. By increasing the money supply, the Bank of Canada can lower interest rates, thereby causing an increase in real GDP and the price level.

- *How does contractionary monetary policy work in an inflationary gap?*

  A contractionary monetary policy can close an inflationary gap. By reducing the money supply, the Bank of Canada can raise interest rates, thereby causing a decline in real GDP and the price level.

- *How does monetary policy work in the open economy?*

  In the open economy, interest rate changes can impact exchange rates. Higher interest rates produced by contractionary monetary policy lead to an appreciation of the Canadian dollar. This appreciation can cause net exports to decline and RGDP to be reduced in the short run. Expansionary monetary policy, having the opposite effect, can increase net exports and expand RGDP in the short run.

Key Terms

money market *market in which money demand and money supply determine the equilibrium interest rate p. 512*

Key Exhibits/ Graphs

Section 21.1, Exhibit 2
Section 21.1, Exhibit 3
Section 21.1, Exhibit 4
Section 21.2, Exhibit 1
Section 21.2, Exhibit 2
Section 21.2, Exhibit 3

Section 21.3 Problems in Implementing Monetary and Fiscal Policy

- *What problems exist in implementing monetary and fiscal policy?*

  Monetary policy faces somewhat different implementation problems than fiscal policy. Both face difficult forecasting and lag problems, but the Bank of Canada can take action much more quickly. However, its effectiveness depends largely on the reaction of the private banking system to its policy changes. In Canada, monetary and fiscal policy are carried out by different decision makers, thus requiring cooperation and coordination for effective policy implementation.

Section 21.4 The Phillips Curve

- *What is the Phillips curve?*

  The inverse relationship between the rate of unemployment and the rate of inflation is called the *Phillips curve*.

- *How does the Phillips curve relate to the aggregate supply and demand model?*

  When the aggregate supply curve is positively sloped, an increase in aggregate demand will cause higher prices and higher output (lower unemployment). A decrease in aggregate demand will cause lower prices and lower output (higher unemployment).

International Trade

Section 22.1 Canada's Merchandise Trade

- *Who are Canada's trading partners?*

  Our most important trading partner, the United States, accounts for 73 percent of our exports and 63 percent of our imports. Trade with Japan and the countries of the European Union is also particularly important to Canada.

- *What does Canada import and export?*

  Exports of natural resource-based products make up nearly 60 percent of our exports of goods. Our imports are concentrated in finished goods, like electronic and electrical equipment, motor vehicles, and consumer goods.

Section 22.2 International Trade Agreements

- *What has been the impact of international trade on Canada?*

  The volume of international trade has increased substantially in Canada over the past 50 years. During that time, exports and imports have grown from about 20 percent of GDP to over 30 percent.

- *What international trade agreements is Canada involved in?*

  The numerous trade agreements in which Canada is an active participant range from multilateral global trade agreements (such as GATT/WTO) to regional agreements (such as the Canada–Costa Rica Free Trade Agreement). This substantial involvement is a major reason why Canada has experienced a rise in international trade.

Section 22.3 Comparative Advantage and Gains from Trade

- *Why do economies trade?*

  Voluntary trade occurs because the participants feel that they are better off because of the trade.

- *What is the principle of comparative advantage?*

  A nation, a geographic area, or even a person can gain from trade if the good or service is produced relatively cheaper than anyone else can produce it. So an area should specialize in producing and selling those items that it can produce at a lower opportunity cost than others can. Through trade and specialization in products in which it has a comparative advantage, a country can enjoy a greater array of goods and services at a lower cost.

Section 22.4 Supply and Demand in International Trade

- *What is consumer surplus and producer surplus?*

  The difference between what a consumer is willing and able to pay and what a consumer actually has to pay is called *consumer surplus*. The difference between what a supplier is willing and able to receive and the price a supplier actually receives for selling a good or service is called *producer surplus*.

- *Who benefits and who loses when a country becomes an exporter?*

  With free trade and exports, domestic producers gain more than domestic consumers lose.

- *Who benefits and who loses when a country becomes an importer?*

  With free trade and imports, domestic consumers gain more than domestic producers lose.

Key Terms

absolute advantage *the ability of a party (nation, region, or individual) to produce more of a good or service while using the same amount of inputs p. 541*

consumer surplus *the difference between what the consumer is willing and able to pay and what the consumer actually pays for a quantity of a good or service p. 543*

producer surplus *the difference between the lowest price at which a supplier is willing and able to supply a good or service and the actual price received for a given quantity of a good or service p. 544*

tariff *a tax on imported goods p. 547*

import quota *a legal limit on the imported quantity of a good that is produced abroad and can be sold in domestic markets p. 550*

rent seeking *producer efforts to gain profits from government protections such as tariffs and import quotas p. 551*

subsidy *a program of financial assistance paid out to producers p. 552*

Key Exhibits/ Graphs

Section 22.4, Exhibit 2
Section 22.4, Exhibit 3
Section 22.5, Exhibit 1
Section 22.5, Exhibit 2

Section 22.5 Tariffs, Import Quotas, and Subsidies

- *What is a tariff?*

  A tariff is a tax on imported goods.

- *What is the impact of tariffs on the domestic economy?*

  Tariffs bring about higher prices and revenues to domestic producers, and lower sales and revenues to foreign producers. Tariffs lead to higher prices and reduce consumer surplus for domestic consumers. Tariffs result in a net loss in welfare because the loss in consumer surplus is greater than the gain to producers and the government.

- *What are some arguments in favour of tariffs?*

  Arguments for the use of tariffs include: Tariffs help infant industries grow, they can reduce domestic unemployment, they are necessary for national security reasons, and they protect against dumping.

- *What are import quotas?*

  Import quotas are legal limits on the quantity of an imported good that can be produced abroad and sold in domestic markets.

- *What is the impact of import quotas on the domestic economy?*

  Like tariffs, import quotas restrict imports, lowering consumer surplus and preventing countries from fully realizing their comparative advantage. There is a net loss in welfare from quotas, but it is proportionately larger than for tariffs because there are no government revenues.

- *What is the economic impact of subsidies?*

  Sometimes a government tries to encourage production of a certain good by subsidizing its production with taxpayer dollars. Because subsidies stimulate exports, they are not a barrier to trade like tariffs and import quotas are. However, they do distort trade patterns and cause overall inefficiencies.

Chapter in Review

International Finance

Section 23.1 The Balance of Payments

- *What is the balance of payments?*

  The balance of payments is the record of all of the international financial transactions of a nation for any given year.

- *What is the current account?*

  The current account is a record of a country's imports and exports of goods and services, net primary income, and net secondary income. If the sum of credits exceeds the sum of debits for all transactions of goods, services, primary income, and secondary income, the current account is in surplus. If the opposite is true, the account is in deficit.

- *What is the capital account?*

  The capital account records the foreign purchases or assets in Canada and Canadian purchases of assets abroad. Capital account surpluses finance current deficits.

- *What is the statistical discrepancy?*

  To ensure that the balance of payments account does in fact balance, an "error" category—the statistical discrepancy—is included.

Section 23.2 Exchange Rates

- *What are exchange rates?*

  The price of a unit of one foreign currency in terms of another currency is called the *exchange rate*.

- *How are exchange rates determined?*

  The exchange rate for a currency is determined by the supply of and demand for that currency in the foreign exchange market.

Section 23.3 Equilibrium Changes in the Foreign Exchange Market

- *What are the major determinants in the foreign exchange market?*

  Any force that shifts either the demand or supply curves for a foreign currency will shift the equilibrium in the foreign exchange market and lead to a new exchange rate. Changes in tastes, tariffs, income levels, relative interest rates, relative inflation rates, or speculation will cause the demand for and supply of a currency to shift.

Section 23.4 Flexible Exchange Rates

- *How are exchange rates determined today?*

  Today, rates are free to fluctuate based on market transactions, but governments occasionally intervene to increase or depress the price of their currencies.

- *What are the advantages of a flexible exchange rate system?*

  Changes in exchange rates occur more often under a flexible-rate system but the changes are much smaller than the large overnight revaluations of currencies that occurred under the fixed-rate system. Under a fixed-rate system, the supply and demand for currencies shift, but currency prices are not allowed to shift to the new equilibrium, leading to surpluses and shortages of currencies.

- *What are the disadvantages of a flexible exchange rate system?*

  The main arguments presented against flexible exchange rates are that international trade levels could be diminished due to uncertainty of future currency prices and that the flexible rates would lead to inflation. Proponents of flexible exchange rates have strong counterarguments to those views.

Key Terms

balance of payments *the record of international transactions of a nation over a year p. 558*

current account *a record of a country's imports and exports of goods and services, net investment income, and net income p. 558*

capital account *a record of the foreign purchases or assets in the domestic economy (a monetary inflow) and domestic purchases of assets abroad (a monetary outflow) p. 560*

exchange rate *the price of one unit of a country's currency in terms of another country's currency p. 562*

currency appreciation *an increase in the value of a currency p. 562*

currency depreciation *a decrease in the value of a currency p. 563*

derived demand *the demand for an input derived from consumers' demand for the good or service produced with that input p. 564*

dirty float *system a description of the exchange rate system that means that fluctuations in currency values are partly determined by market forces and partly influenced by government intervention p. 571*

Key Exhibits/ Graphs

Notes